DOS 6
Principles
with Practice

Carolyn Z. Gillay

Saddleback College

FRANKLIN, BEEDLE & ASSOCIATES INCORPORATED
8536 SW St. Helens Drive, Suite D
Wilsonville, Oregon 97070
(503) 682-7668

Dedication:

To Bette Peat, who began as my network guru and became my friend.

C.Z.G

Publisher	Jim Leisy
Manuscript Editor	Elizabeth Sutherland
	Tom Sumner
Production Manager	Bill DeRouchey
Production	Tom Sumner
Additional Production	Steve Klinetobe
	Jeff Tade
	Lisa Cannon
Proofreader	FBA
Cover Design	Hampton Graphics
Manufacturing	RR Donnelley Norwest, WCP Division

Rights and Permissions
FRANKLIN, BEEDLE & ASSOCIATES INCORPORATED
8536 SW St. Helens Drive, Suite D
Wilsonville, Oregon 97070

Library of Congress Cataloging-in-Publication Data

Gillay, Carolyn Z.
    DOS 6 principles with practice / Carolyn Z. Gillay.
        p.   cm.
    Includes index.
    ISBN 0-928661-66-3
      1. Operating systems (computer)   2. PC-DOS (Computer file)   3. PC
-DOS (Computer file) I. Title.
QA76.76.O63G5434 1995
005.4'469--dc20
                                       94-29627
                                          CIP

Preface

For Beginners to Advanced Computer Users

This book assumes no prior experience with computers, software, or PC/MS DOS. It is intended to be used as the core textbook for a course which focuses exclusively on PC/MS DOS. It is appropriate for use in a beginning through advanced sequence of DOS courses. It may also be used for the PC/MS-DOS portion of an operating system course for students studying programming. It leads the student from a basic to a sophisticated use of DOS. Each chapter has questions for both novice and advanced students so that the advanced student can be challenged without sacrificing the concerns of the beginning student. Furthermore, while this text does teach the various DOS commands, it also stresses the concepts, purpose, theory, and understanding of operating systems in general.

DOS 6.22 Focus, but Compatible with Earlier Versions of DOS

This textbook was written to focus specifically on DOS 6.22. Thus, it is not a retread of old versions of DOS. However, earlier versions of DOS are not eliminated. All versions of DOS 2.0 through 6.22 are included. The core commands common to all versions of DOS are covered and can be used in any DOS environment. The new features of DOS 6.22 commands are so indicated. DOS 6.22 is not required to master DOS concepts, particularly in the beginning chapters.

Covers Hard-Disk Management Concepts

Today, most students and schools use system configurations that include hard disks. Students are anxious to learn hard disk management. Although the student uses the hard disk, all activities are written to floppy disk, not the laboratory hard disks. The text is designed so that the student may also work at home or at the office without compromising the integrity of the assignments.

The primary tool for understanding hard disks is subdirectories. Subdirectories are introduced early and included with commands and exercises so that students are comfortable using paths and directories prior to covering them in depth in Chapter 5. Furthermore, Chapter 9 goes beyond the use and understanding of subdirectory commands with a practical approach to principles and practices of organizing a hard disk. Students use the DATA disk to accomplish real-life examples of disk organization. Thus, the instructor and laboratory environment need not be concerned with students writing to hard disks or network disks.

Included with the book is an ACTIVITIES disk that provides files the student can manipulate. The files on the ACTIVITIES disk are easily installed to a subdirectory on a hard disk (via an accompanying batch file) on a stand-alone computer or a network server. This subdirectory is used exclusively with this book. The exercises do not direct the student to save files to the hard disk or network server. Early on, the student creates a DATA disk so that all files are written to the DATA disk. This approach provides the real-life experience of working with the hard disk or server without harming other files on the hard disk or network server.

Intermediate and Advanced DOS Concepts

At Saddleback College, I teach the DOS course as a beginning eight- or nine-week class and as an intermediate eight- or nine-week class. The first eight chapters are used for the beginning DOS class, and the second eight chapters are used for the intermediate class. The value of pipes, filters, and redirection used with batch files is covered in a thorough step-by-step methodology. Advanced batch files are covered in detail, building on programming logic in an easily understood way. The students cover all batch file commands and are introduced to DEBUG.

Many computer students need to customize their installation, so special atten-tion has been paid to CONFIG.SYS. Chapter 13 introduces the critical configuration commands the students need to know. Again, care is taken so that the students boot off a floppy disk with the CONFIG.SYS file to avoid harming any computer laboratory environment. Chapter 14 introduces useful utilities with a complete discussion of DOSKEY. Students are introduced to the power of ANSI.SYS and learn to write batch files for ANSI.SYS. Essential components of MODE are introduced. Since students are concerned about viruses, MSAVE is discussed. Chapter 15 is an advanced chapter that deals with optimizing computer systems. The ability to manipulate CONFIG.SYS with HIMEM.SYS and EMM386.EXE is covered, as well as caching and using SMARTDRV. Again, care is taken to have the students boot off a floppy disk to avoid harming networked environments. Using MemMaker, disk compression, and MSBACKUP are covered as reading exercises so that the student can understand these critical areas without having to implement these commands.

EDIT, DOS Shell, installing and upgrading DOS, and partitioning the hard disk have been treated outside the main body of the text in the appendices. Their presentation is left to the discretion of the instructor.

Network Aware

I am well aware that many lab or work environments are on networks, which can create special problems for students. This textbook addresses those concerns. Again, students never write to the server, only to the DATA disk, so the integrity of the network is never compromised. The network administrator, after installing the subdirectory, can provide the usual network security (scan and read-only privi-leges), and it will not impact the student exercises. Furthermore, any activities students perform that could interfere with the operation of a network can be performed outside the network system without sacrificing the necessary operating system concepts. With this approach, students becomes comfortable working on any computer in any environment. There are numerous warnings and cautions alerting a student when a possible network conflict could arise. I have conscientiously written this textbook to be user-friendly in a network environment.

Step-through Approach that Demystifies DOS

Each DOS command is presented in a careful student-oriented step-by-step approach. Interspersed within the steps are the reasons for and results of each action. At the end of each chapter are discussion questions which allow the student to apply his knowledge independently and prove mastery of the subject area through critical thinking skills. In addition, each command is presented in a syntactically correct manner so that, when students have completed the course, they will be able to use software documentation because they will be able to read syntax diagrams as well as know how to solve problems independently using the documentation at hand. Thus, no matter what changes are made to future versions of DOS, they will be able to use the new commands. This skill also transfers to the use of application packages and other operating system environments like Windows.

ACTIVITIES Disk with Shareware Programs and Data Files

The most difficult part of teaching DOS to students is the esoteric nature of operating systems. Although students find the material interesting, the question that I repeatedly get is, "What good is DOS? It doesn't do anything." If instructors attempt to use a complex application program, such as WordPerfect, they spend their time teaching the application, not DOS. Thus, there are two simple shareware applications: a simple database (The Home-Phone-Book Program) and a simple spreadsheet (The Thinker) that students work with. They have the opportunity to load an application program and prewritten data files as well as create simple data files. The student then can understand the differences between data files and program files and use DOS commands to manipulate both types. In addition, included are several educationally sound shareware games that reinforce certain DOS concepts in an enjoyable manner.

Self-Mastery

Each chapter includes a chapter summary, key terms, and discussion questions that can be assigned as homework. In addition, shrinkwrapped with the text is a student workbook that includes application assignments performed at the computer. These assignments help to reinforce the material learned in the chapter as well as develop problem-solving abilities. Also in the workbook are complete paper-and-pencil exercises including true/false, fill-in, matching, multiple choice, responding to commands, and writing commands questions for every chapter. A complete set of questions has the answers in the workbook. Another set has the answers in the Instructor's Manual.

Special Note to Instructors

One of the hardest aspects of teaching a DOS course is developing assignments that provide consistent grading standards, and, in addition, require critical thinking skills on the part of the student. It is also useful to develop assignments that do not overload the instructor. Where I teach, enrollments typically have been over one hundred students per semester. It is impossible to look at every student's screen to know what has been mastered. Printing screens is problematic due to the time and the amount paper needed, as well as wear and tear on the printer. Furthermore, if answers to problems are free-form, the student will not only be unsure what is required, but also will create answers that vary from other students. To remedy this situation, a two-prong approach was developed. There are two sets of Application Assignments. Both require the student to work with DOS on a computer. The first problem set requires that student manipulate DOS and write the resulting answers on a Scantron form. The second problem set also requires students to manipulate DOS, but place the answers on a printout. The results that the student achieves are sent to a batch file provided with the ACTIVITIES disk. The batch file is an easily followed program. The student supplies his solution to the problems. Then, the resulting printout includes not only the answers in a format that is consistent, but also the student's name and other instructor-directed identifying information, such as chapter number and other classroom-related data. The output typically prints on fewer than two pages.

Reference Tools

The book is useful as a reference to DOS commands. The first appendix provides instructions to install the subdirectory to the hard disk. This feature is particularly useful for those students who work at home or in an office. The rest of the appendices include a tutorial on EDIT, DOSKEY, DOSSHELL, installing/upgrading DOS to the hard disk, as well as an introduction to partitioning hard disks, MSBACKUP, MSAV, and an introduction to CONFIG.SYS. There is also a complete command reference as well as a glossary.

Supplementary Material

This book comes with an Instructor's Manual. It includes:

❑ A syllabus for both an eight/nine-week course and a sixteen/seventeen-week course.

❑ Teaching suggestions for each chapter.

❑ Answers to all the questions and application assignments.

❑ Tests and transparencies for each chapter.

❑ Midterms and final exams.

Acknowledgments

A project of this scope is difficult to complete successfully without the contributions of many individuals. Thank you to all who contributed. A special thanks to:

Bette Peat, who has an incredible eye for detail and found nearly every problem in working through the chapters so they are no longer problems.

Kathryn Maurdeff for once again knowing all the latest educational theories and putting them to good use in all the questions.

Sonia Maurdeff for the original glossary.

Steven Tuttle and Mary Brown for working through each activity and exercise in the book.

Nick Markiw for writing a utility program.

Pat Sullivan who is always there for me in more ways than I can count.

Darrin Fowler for his technical help.

To all the wonderful authors of the shareware included in the book that help make learning DOS a real-life experience.

To the students at Saddleback College—and at the different workshops I have given—who have taken the DOS courses and provided me with many insights and who, in many ways, make all of this worthwhile.

To my colleagues in the Computer Information Management Department at Saddleback College with a special thanks to Nancy Reynolds who assisted in answering network questions.

California Business Education Association and National Business Education Association for providing a forum for professional growth as well as inviting me to make presentations sharing my teaching experiences.

Jim Leisy, my publisher, for once again being the sage and wise publisher, keeping me out of trouble, and best of all, my friend through it all.

A special thanks to all the sung and unsung heroes at FBA—Tom, Bill, Steve, Jeff, Samantha, Ann, Lisa, Christina, Sandra, Sean, Victor, Daniel, and J.D.

To the following reviewers, whose insight and suggestions were indispensable:

Norma Irwin	*Belleville Area College*
David Valdez	*Dona Ana Branch Community College*
Janet Gerth	*Essex Community College*
Jane Workman	*Harford Community College*
David Campbell	*Rowan Cabarrus Community College*
Barbara Hoyle	*Wake Technical Community College*

And, of course, to the person who suffers the most and works the most with me through this long and arduous process, my beloved husband, Frank Panezich. You had no idea what I was getting you into! Yes, we will go to Italy next summer. I promise.

Anyone who wishes to offer suggestions, improvements, or just share ideas can contact me via CompuServe, 71756,0675.

Table of Contents

Preface   iii

Chapter 1
Microcomputer Systems: Hardware, Software, and the Operating System 1

1.1	An Introduction to Computers	2
1.2	Categories of Computers	2
1.3	Computer Components	3
1.4	Microcomputer Hardware Components	4
1.5	The System Unit	5
1.6	Central Processing Unit	6
1.7	Random Access Memory	6
1.8	Cache Memory	7
1.9	Read-only Memory	7
1.10	Adapter Cards	7
1.11	Peripherals: Input Devices	7
1.12	Peripherals: Output Devices	8
1.13	Output Devices: Monitors	8
1.14	Output Devices: Printers	9
1.15	Modems	9
1.16	Disks and Disk Drives	10
1.17	Capacity Measurement: Bits and Bytes	10
1.18	Minifloppy Disks	11
1.19	Microfloppy Disks	12
1.20	CD-ROM	13
1.21	Hard Disks	13
1.22	Dividing the Disk	14
1.23	Disk Drives	15
1.24	Device Names	16
1.25	Software	17
1.26	Operating System Fundamentals	19
1.27	Networks	22
	Chapter Summary	22

Chapter 2
Getting Started with DOS: Booting the System, Using the Keyboard, Using DIR, VER, CLS, MSD, Date/Time, and DISKCOPY 27

2.1	What Is DOS?	28
2.2	Versions of DOS	29
2.3	Overview of Files and Disks	29

2.4	File Names, File Types, and Directories	30
2.5	Identifying Your System Configuration	32
2.6	Booting the System	32
2.7	*Activity:* Booting the System	33
2.8	Computer Configuration Guide	35
2.9	What is a Command?	37
2.10	*Activity:* Using the DIR Command	37
2.11	The Keyboard	40
2.12	The Backspace Key	41
2.13	*Activity:* Correcting Errors Using the Backspace Key	42
2.14	The Escape Key	42
2.15	*Activity:* Using the Escape Key	42
2.16	The Shift Key	42
2.17	*Activity:* Using the Shift Key	43
2.18	The Print Screen Keys	43
2.19	The Control Key and Print Screen Key	43
2.20	Freezing the Display	44
2.21	*Activity:* Using the Pause, Control, and the S Key	44
2.22	Canceling a Command	45
2.23	*Activity:* Using DIR and Canceling a Command	45
2.24	The VER Command	45
2.25	*Activity:* Using the VER Command	46
2.26	The CLS Command	46
2.27	*Activity:* Using the CLS Command	46
2.28	The DATE and TIME Commands	46
2.29	*Activity:* Using the DATE and TIME Commands	47
2.30	Media Types and MSD	49
2.31	*Activity:* Using MSD (If You Have DOS 6.0 or Above)	50
2.32	Ethical Considerations in Copying Disks	51
2.33	Making a Copy of the ACTIVITIES Disk: DISKCOPY	51
2.34	*Activity:* Using DISKCOPY	52
2.35	How to End the Work Session	55
2.36	*Activity:* Ending the Work Session	55
	Chapter Summary	55

Chapter 3
Command Syntax Using the DIR Command
with Parameters and Wildcards 59

3.1	Command Syntax	60
3.2	What Are Parameters?	60
3.3	Reading a Syntax Diagram	61
3.4	Using Fixed Parameters with the DIR Command	61
3.5	*Activity:* Using Fixed Parameters with the DIR Command	62
3.6	Using File Names as Variable Parameters	66
3.7	*Activity:* Using File Names as Variable Parameters	68

3.8	Drives as Device Names	70
3.9	Defaults	71
3.10	*Activity:* Working with Defaults	71
3.11	A Brief Introduction to Subdirectories—the Path	75
3.12	*Activity:* Using Path with the DIR Command	76
3.13	Changing Defaults	78
3.14	*Activity:* Changing the Default Drive	78
3.15	Changing Directories	81
3.16	*Activity:* Changing Directories	81
3.17	Global File Specifications: Wildcards, the ? and the *	84
3.18	*Activity:* DIR and Wildcards	84
3.19	Redirection	91
3.20	*Activity:* Redirecting Output to a File	91
3.21	Redirecting Output to the Printer	93
3.22	*Activity:* Redirecting the Output to the Printer	94
3.23	Getting Help	96
3.24	*Activity:* Using HELP	97
	Chapter Summary	103

Chapter 4
Disks and Formatting **107**

4.1	Why Format a Disk?	108
4.2	Structure of a Disk	108
4.3	Formatting a Disk	113
4.4	Clarifying Procedures	114
4.5	*Activity:* Formatting a Floppy Disk	114
4.6	Formatting a Disk with a Volume Label	118
4.7	*Activity:* Using the VOL Command	120
4.8	The LABEL Command	123
4.9	*Activity:* Using the LABEL Command	123
4.10	Unformatting a Disk	124
4.11	*Activity:* Using Unformat on the Data Disk	125
4.12	Formatting a Disk Using the /Q and /U Parameters	128
4.13	*Activity:* Using the /Q and /U Parameters	128
4.14	Bootable and Nonbootable Disks	130
4.15	High-Density Disks and Disk Drives	132
	Chapter Summary	134

Chapter 5
Program Files, Data Files, and Subdirectories **137**

5.1	Why DOS?	138
5.2	Program Files, Data Files, and DOS	139
5.3	Shareware	140
5.4	*Activity:* Using DIR to Locate the HPB Program	141

5.5	Using Application Programs and Data Files	143
5.6	*Activity:* Using Application Programs and Data Files	143
5.7	Using DOS To Manage Program and Data Files	149
5.8	Hierarchical Filing System or Tree-structured Directories	150
5.9	Creating Subdirectories	155
5.10	*Activity:* How to Create Subdirectories	156
5.11	The Current Directory	161
5.12	*Activity:* Using the CD Command	161
5.13	Relative and Absolute Paths	163
5.14	*Activity:* Creating More Subdirectories	165
5.15	Knowing the Default Directory	170
5.16	The PROMPT Command	170
5.17	*Activity:* Changing the Prompt	171
5.18	Subdirectory Markers	174
5.19	*Activity:* Using Subdirectory Markers	174
5.20	Changing the Names of Directories DOS 6.0 and Above	178
5.21	*Activity:* Using MOVE To Rename a Directory	179
5.22	The TREE Command	180
5.23	*Activity:* Using the TREE Command	180
5.24	Removing Directories	183
5.25	*Activity:* Using the RD Command	184
5.26	The DELTREE Command—DOS 6.0 and Above	186
5.27	*Activity:* Using DELTREE	186
5.28	Understanding the PATH Command	188
5.29	*Activity:* Using the PATH Command	189
	Chapter Summary	193

Chapter 6
Internal Commands: COPY and TYPE 197

6.1	Why Learn DOS Commands?	198
6.2	The COPY Command	199
6.3	Review of File-Naming Rules	200
6.4	*Activity:* Making Copies of Files	201
6.5	Using Wildcards with the COPY Command	205
6.6	*Activity:* Using Wildcards with the COPY Command	205
6.7	The TYPE Command	206
6.8	*Activity:* Displaying Files Using the TYPE Command	207
6.9	Dummy Files	210
6.10	*Activity:* Using the COPY and TYPE Commands	211
6.11	Making Additional Files on the Same Disk	214
6.12	*Activity:* Using the COPY Command	214
6.13	Using Wildcards with the COPY Command	218
6.14	*Activity:* Using Wildcards with the COPY Command	218
6.15	Using COPY and DIR with Subdirectories	220

6.16   *Activity:* Using COPY with Subdirectories   220
6.17   Using Subdirectory Markers with the COPY Command   227
6.18   *Activity:* Using Shortcuts: The Subdirectory Markers   228
6.19   Overwriting Files with the COPY Command   229
6.20   *Activity:* Overwriting Files Using the COPY Command   231
6.21   Combining Text Files with the COPY Command   233
6.22   *Activity:* Combining Files Using the COPY Command   234
6.23   Printing Files   241
6.24   *Activity:* Printing Files   242
        Chapter Summary   244

Chapter 7
Using ERASE, DEL, UNDELETE,
DELTREE, RENAME, and MOVE...............................247

7.1   Eliminating Files with the ERASE and DEL Commands   248
7.2   *Activity:* Using the ERASE and DEL Commands   249
7.3   Deleting Files on Other Drives and Directories   253
7.4   *Activity:* Using the DEL Commands with Individual Files   254
7.5   Using Wildcards with the DEL Command   259
7.6   *Activity:* Using the ERASE and DEL Commands   259
7.7   The /P Parameter with the DEL Command   262
7.8   *Activity:* Using /P with the DEL Command   262
7.9   Recovering Deleted Files   265
7.10   *Activity:* Using UNDELETE   266
7.11   Changing the Names of Files   271
7.12   *Activity:* Using the REN Command   272
7.13   Using RENAME with Wildcards   276
7.14   *Activity:* Using RENAME with Wildcards   276
7.15   Using RENAME on Different Drives and Directories   279
7.16   *Activity:* Using RENAME on Different Drives   279
7.17   Moving Files and Renaming Directories   284
7.18   *Activity:* Moving Files and Renaming Directories   285
7.19   DELTREE Revisited   292
7.20   *Activity:* Using RD and Deltree   292
7.21   Backing Up Your DATA Disk   294
7.22   *Activity:* Backing Up with the DISKCOPY Command   295
7.23   Backing Up Files with the COPY Command   298
        Chapter Summary   300

Chapter 8
Informational Commands: CHKDSK, ATTRIB,
SCANDISK, DEFRAG, FC, and More DIR...............................303

8.1   File Attributes and the ATTRIB Command   304
8.2   *Activity:* Using ATTRIB to Make Files Read-only   305

8.3	Using the Hidden and Archive Attributes with ATTRIB	311
8.4	*Activity:* Using the H and the A Attributes	312
8.5	Comparing Files	318
8.6	*Activity:* Using the FC Command	319
8.7	Checking a Disk and Memory	323
8.8	*Activity:* Using the CHKDSK Command	324
8.9	The Verbose Parameter with the CHKDSK Command	329
8.10	*Activity:* Using the /V Parameter; Using DIR Parameters	329
8.11	Contiguous and Noncontiguous Files	333
8.12	*Activity:* Using CHKDSK to See If Files Are Contiguous	337
8.13	Using the /F Parameter with CHKDSK	341
8.14	SCANDISK	344
8.15	*Activity:* Using SCANDISK on the DATA Disk	348
8.16	Optimizing Performance on Disks	351
8.17	*Activity:* Using DEFRAG on the Data Disk	353
	Chapter Summary	361

Chapter 9
Organizing the Hard Disk 363

9.1	Why Organize a Hard Disk?	364
9.2	Methods of Organizing a Hard Disk	369
9.3	Organizing a Disk	374
9.4	*Activity:* Making a Copy of the DATA Disk	374
9.5	Organizing the DATA Disk	376
9.6	*Activity:* Setting up the PROG Subdirectory	377
9.7	The XCOPY Command	379
9.8	*Activity:* Using the XCOPY Command	380
9.9	The REPLACE Command	386
9.10	*Activity:* Using the REPLACE Command	387
9.11	The MOVE Command Revisited	393
9.12	*Activity:* Using MOVE to Organize Your Disk	394
9.13	A Utility Program—RNS.EXE	398
9.14	*Activity:* Using RNS, a Rename Subdirectory Utility	398
9.15	The Pretender Commands—SUBST, ASSIGN, and JOIN	401
9.16	The SUBST Command	403
9.17	*Activity:* Using SUBST	404
9.18	The ASSIGN Command	406
9.19	The JOIN Command	408
9.20	The APPEND Command	409
	Chapter Summary	414

Chapter 10
Introduction to Batch Files 417

10.1	Concepts of Batch and Interactive Processing	418
10.2	How DOS Batch Files Work	419
10.3	Using EDIT to Write Batch Files	420
10.4	*Activity:* Writing and Executing a Batch File	421
10.5	Writing and Executing a Batch File to Save Keystrokes	424
10.6	*Activity:* Writing and Executing a One-letter Batch File	425
10.7	Using Batch Files to Load Application Software	428
10.8	*Activity:* Using the HPB Application Package	428
10.9	Writing a Batch File to Load an Application Program	434
10.10	*Activity:* Writing a Batch File to Execute HPB	434
10.11	Special Batch File Commands	436
10.12	The REM Command	437
10.13	*Activity:* Using REM	437
10.14	The ECHO Command	439
10.15	*Activity:* Using ECHO	440
10.16	The PAUSE Command	443
10.17	*Activity:* Using PAUSE	443
10.18	Stopping a Batch File from Executing	445
10.19	*Activity:* Quitting a Batch File	445
10.20	Replaceable Parameters in Batch Files	447
10.21	*Activity:* Using Replaceable Parameters	448
10.22	Multiple Replaceable Parameters in Batch Files	454
10.23	*Activity:* Using Multiple Replaceable Parameters	454
10.24	Creating Menus with Batch Files	460
10.25	*Activity:* Writing Menus	461
10.26	Completing the Menu	470
10.27	*Activity:* Completing the Menu	470
10.28	Understanding AUTOEXEC.BAT	475
10.29	*Activity:* Writing and Using an AUTOEXEC.BAT File	476
10.30	Controlling the Boot Process	481
10.31	*Activity:* Bypassing AUTOEXEC.BAT	482
10.32	Running a Program When You Boot	484
10.33	*Activity:* Loading a Program Automatically	485
	Chapter Summary	488

Chapter 11
Pipes, Filters, and Redirection 491

11.1	Redirection of Standard I/O (Input/Output	492
11.2	*Activity:* Using the > to Redirect Standard Output	494
11.3	*Activity:* Using the < to Redirect Standard Input	495
11.4	*Activity:* Using the >> to Add Redirected Output to a File	497

11.5	Filters	498
11.6	The SORT Command	499
11.7	*Activity:* Using SORT	499
11.8	Filters and Redirection	502
11.9	*Activity:* Using the SORT Command with Redirection	502
11.10	The FIND Filter	505
11.11	*Activity:* Using the FIND Filter	505
11.12	Pipes	507
11.13	The MORE Filter	509
11.14	*Activity:* Using the MORE Filter	509
11.15	Combining Commands with Pipes and Filters	514
11.16	*Activity:* Combining Commands	515
11.17	Batch Files with Pipes and Filters	518
11.18	*Activity:* Writing a Batch File with Pipes and Filters	518
	Chapter Summary	523

Chapter 12
Advanced Batch Files 525

12.1	Batch File Commands	526
12.2	A Review of the REM, PAUSE, and ECHO Commands	527
12.3	Advanced Features of ECHO and REM	528
12.4	*Activity:* Using ::, ECHO, CTTY, and NUL	529
12.5	The GOTO Command	531
12.6	*Activity:* Using the GOTO Command	532
12.7	The SHIFT Command	533
12.8	*Activity:* Using the SHIFT Command	534
12.9	The IF Command	540
12.10	IF Command Using Strings	541
12.11	*Activity:* Using the IF Command with Strings	542
12.12	Testing for Null Values	544
12.13	*Activity:* Using Null Values	545
12.14	The IF EXIST/IF NOT EXIST Command	548
12.15	*Activity:* Using IF EXIST to Test for a File	548
12.16	The IF ERRORLEVEL Command Testing	552
12.17	*Activity:* Using IF ERRORLEVEL with XCOPY	552
12.18	Writing Programs to Test for Key Codes	554
12.19	*Activity:* Writing a Script File	556
12.20	The CHOICE Command	559
12.21	*Activity:* Using CHOICE	559
12.22	The Environment	562
12.23	*Activity:* Using SET and the Environment in Batch Files	563
12.24	The DIRCMD Environmental Variable	568
12.25	*Activity:* Using DIRCMD	568
12.26	The FOR..IN..DO Command	571

12.27	*Activity:* Using the FOR..IN..DO Command	571
12.28	The CALL Command	578
12.29	*Activity:* Using CALL	579
	Chapter Summary	586

Chapter 13
Configuring the System *589*

13.1	Customizing DOS	590
13.2	The CONFIG.SYS File	591
13.3	Files	594
13.4	Buffers	595
13.5	Working with CONFIG.SYS and AUTOEXEC.BAT Files	598
13.6	The Bootable DOS System Disk—Introducing SYS	598
13.7	*Activity:* Preparing the Bootable DOS System Disk	599
13.8	*Activity:* Writing a CONFIG.SYS with Files and Buffers	602
13.9	Turning NumLock Off	605
13.10	*Activity:* Turning Off NumLock	606
13.11	Device Drivers	607
13.12	Virtual Disks	610
13.13	*Activity:* Writing a CONFIG.SYS Using RAMDRIVE.SYS	611
13.14	Memory	615
13.15	Extended Memory	616
13.16	Expanded Memory	617
13.17	Upper Memory Area	619
13.18	High Memory Area	619
13.19	Using Extended and Expanded Memory	620
13.20	The MEM Command	620
13.21	*Activity:* Using the MEM Command	621
13.22	MS-DOS Provided Memory Manager—HIMEM.SYS	622
13.23	Understanding LASTDRIVE	623
13.24	*Activity:* Installing HIMEM.SYS and LASTDRIVE	624
13.25	The DOS Command	627
13.26	*Activity:* Loading DOS High	628
13.27	The Shell	629
13.28	*Activity:* Using SET and SHELL	631
13.29	The SWITCHES Command	633
	Chapter Summary	634

Chapter 14
Utility Programs *639*

14.1	DOSKEY	640
14.2	*Activity:* Loading and Using DOSKEY	642
14.3	DOSKEY Macros	647
14.4	*Activity:* Creating Macros	647

14.5	Replaceable Parameters in Macros	650
14.6	*Activity:* Using Replaceable Parameters	650
14.7	Saving Macros	653
14.8	*Activity:* Saving Macros in Batch Files	653
14.9	Introducing ANSI.SYS	656
14.10	*Activity:* Using ANSI.SYS To Change Colors	658
14.11	Remapping Keys	663
14.12	*Activity:* Using ANSI.SYS To Remap Keys	663
14.13	Controlling Devices	668
14.14	The MODE Command	670
14.15	Setting Printer Characteristics with MODE Command	671
14.16	Using MODE with the Monitor	672
14.17	*Activity:* Using MODE to Change the Display	673
14.18	Using MODE to Change Keyboard Response Rate	673
14.19	*Activity:* Setting the Quickest Typematic Rate	673
14.20	Checking the Status of Devices	674
14.21	*Activity:* Checking the Status of Devices With MODE	675
14.22	Checking for Computer Viruses	676
14.23	*Activity:* Using MSAV	676
14.24	VSAFE	679
14.25	Backing Up Data Using MSBACKUP	679
14.26	Configuring MSBACKUP	680
14.27	After Configuring MSBACKUP	683
14.28	Using MSBACKUP	683
	Chapter Summary	690

Chapter 15
Optimizing the System 693

15.1	Controlling the Boot Process	694
15.2	*Activity:* Bypassing CONFIG.SYS and AUTOEXEC.BAT	694
15.3	Using EMM386.EXE to Emulate Expanded Memory	697
15.4	Using EMM386.EXE to Prepare Upper Memory	698
15.5	*Activity:* Using EMM386.EXE	700
15.6	STACKS and FCBS	704
15.7	Multiple Configurations	705
15.8	*Activity:* Creating Multiple Configuations	707
15.9	Caching with SMARTDRIVE	716
15.10	*Activity:* Using SMARTDRV	721
15.11	Optimizing System Performance with FASTOPEN	725
15.12	MemMaker	727
15.13	Optimizing Disk Space with DriveSpace	736
	Chapter Summary	743

Chapter 16
Windows *747*

16.1	What Is Windows?	748
16.2	Hardware Requirements for Windows	750
16.3	Elements of Windows	751
16.4	Pointing Devices	754
16.5	*Activity:* Loading Windows and Working with Windows	757
16.6	Using Windows	761
16.7	*Activity:* Foreground and Background Programs	761
16.8	Working with Help	772
16.9	*Activity:* Using Help	772
16.10	File Manager	777
16.11	*Activity:* Using File Manager	777
16.12	DOS Commands in File Manager	789
16.13	*Activity:* Using DOS Commands in File Manager	790
16.14	Selecting Multiple Files	797
16.15	*Activity:* Selecting Multiple Files	797
	Chapter Summary	806

Appendices

A	Installing the DOS6BK Directory and Shareware Registration	809
B	EDIT—The Text Editor	822
C	DOS Shell	832
D	Installing or Upgrading DOS	851
E	ANSI.SYS Keyboard Scancode Values	874
F	Command Summary	877
	Glossary	889
	Index	903

Chapter 1

Microcomputer Systems

Hardware, Software, and the Operating System

Learning Objectives

After completing this chapter you will be able to:

1. Categorize the latest types of computers in use today.
2. Identify and explain the functions of basic hardware components.
3. Explain how a CPU functions.
4. Compare and contrast RAM, CACHE, and ROM.
5. Explain how the use of adapter boards increases the capabilities of the computer.
6. List and explain the functions of the various peripheral input and output devices of a computer.
7. Explain what external storage devices are.
8. Explain how the capacity of a disk is measured.
9. Explain how disk drives write information to and read information from a disk.
10. Explain the purpose and function of the hard disk.
11. Compare the purpose and function of hard and floppy disks.
12. Explain how and why a disk is divided.
13. Explain how disk drives derive their names.
14. Compare and contrast system software and application software.
15. Explain the functions of an operating system.
16. Explain the advantages of using a network.

Chapter Overview

It is impossible to live in today's society without being affected by the widespread use of computers. Computers are used in public and private industry and found in every sector of the business world. Computer software is what makes computers useful for all types of applications: sophisticated scientific applications such as nuclear and atomic physics, general business applications such as payroll and banking functions, specialized applications in engineering and industrial research, teaching basic skills to children, record keeping and accounting in small businesses, and word processing, entertainment, and record keeping in the home. Computer usage only continues to grow.

While application software is what makes the computer useful to you, you must first understand how the operating system of a computer works. The operating system of a computer takes care of the mandatory functions for computer operations and allows the computer to run application programs. Operating systems must keep pace with the growth of hardware and software, so new versions appear regularly. This text is devoted to the most recent version of the most widely used computer operating system in use today—Microsoft's DOS 6.22 or MS-DOS 6.22.

1.1   An Introduction to Computers

At the most basic level, computers are calculators, but this definition is very narrow. Now, we use these machines to handle accounting chores (spreadsheets), to write books (word processing), and to organize and retrieve information (databases). In the visual arts computers have revolutionized the way films are made, games are played, and reality is perceived (virtual reality).

1.2   Categories of Computers

Computers are divided into categories based on a variety of factors such as size, processing speed, information storage capacity, and cost. In the ever-changing technical world, these classifications are not absolute. Technical advancements blur the categories. For instance, some microcomputers today exceed the capabilities of mainframes manufactured five years ago. Table 1.1 shows the major categories of computers.

Computer	Applications
Supercomputer: Very large computer	Used most often in sophisticated scientific applications such as nuclear physics, atomic physics, and seismology.
Mainframe: Large computer	General-purpose business machines. Typical applications include accounting, payroll, banking, and airline reservations.
Minicomputer: Small mainframe	Specialized applications such as engineering and industrial research.
Microcomputer: Small, general-purpose computers	Applications include word processing, accounting for a small business, time and record keeping for attorneys, and medical accounting.

Table 1.1   ***Computer Types***

1.3 Computer Components

Although the types of computers continue to grow, computers operate the same way, regardless of their category. Information is input, processed, and stored, and the resulting information is output. Figure 1.1 is a graphic representation of this process.

Figure 1.1   ***Components of a Computer System***

The figure shows the physical components of a computer system, referred to as **hardware**. All computer systems, from mainframes to notebooks, have the same basic hardware. Hardware by itself can do nothing. A computer system needs **software**. Software is a set of detailed instructions, called a program, that tell the hardware what operations to perform.

Data, in its simplest form, is related or unrelated numbers, words, or facts that, when arranged in a particular way, provide information. For example, if you want to add 2 plus 3 using a computer, the hardware does the work, the software instructions tell the computer how to add, you input the data (the numbers 2 and 3) so the program knows what to process, and you enter the appropriate software instructions so the addition takes place.

1.4 Microcomputer Hardware Components

This text is devoted to **microcomputers** (also called micros, personal computers, home computers, laptops, notebooks, PCs, or desktop computers), which are comprised of hardware components. Much like a stereo system, the basic components of a complete system, also called the **system configuration**, include an input device (typically a keyboard) for entering data and programs, a system unit that houses the electronic circuitry for storing and processing data and programs (CPU, adapter cards, ROM, and RAM), a visual display unit (a monitor), an external storage unit that stores data and programs on disks (disk drives), and a printer for producing a printed version of the results. Figure 1.2 represents a typical microcomputer system.

Figure 1.2   **A Typical Microcomputer System**

1.5   The System Unit

The system unit, as shown in Figure 1.3, is the "black box" that houses the electronic and mechanical parts of the computer. With the outer case removed, the unit looks like the diagram in Figure 1.4.

Figure 1.3   **The System Unit**

Figure 1.4   **Inside the System Unit**

The system unit has a power supply (to get power to the computer) and disk drives. In addition, it contains many printed electronic circuit boards, also called cards or **adapter cards**. One of these is a special printed circuit board called the **system board** or the "motherboard." Attached to the system board is the microprocessor chip that is the **central processing unit** or **CPU**, the RAM (random access memory), and the ROM (read-only memory).

1.6   Central Processing Unit

The central processing unit, most commonly referred to as the CPU, is the brain of the computer and is composed of transistors on a silicon chip. It comprehends and carries out instructions sent to it by a program and directs the activity of the computer. The CPU consists of two parts: the control unit and the arithmetic/logic unit (ALU). The **control unit** directs and coordinates program (software) instructions. It does not actually execute the instructions but directs the other parts of the system to carry them out. The **ALU** performs the arithmetic functions: addition, subtraction, multiplication and division, and the logical functions which, in most cases, are comparisons. Programs are designed to take action based on these comparisons.

The CPU is described in terms of its central processing chip and the model designation. Intel manufactures almost all the CPU chips in DOS-based PCs. The Intel 80386 processing chip is the most common one in use today. It has been in use since 1986 in its SX and DX versions. The next in popularity is the Intel 80486 chip introduced in 1989. It also has SX and DX versions. It is easiest to remember SX as the standard model and DX as the deluxe model. The most recent development is the 80586 or Pentium chip that appeared in 1993. Presently it has only one version.

All hardware **devices** must be connected in some way so that the CPU can deliver data. In computer terminology, signals travel back and forth by a common system **bus**. Bus refers to the electrical connections between the CPU and all the other devices. The bus travels at a speed that is measured in megahertz. The early PCs had a speed of 4.77 MHz. Today, bus architecture is available up to a speed of 100 MHz. The newest standard is the local bus which bypasses the system bus to allow devices to be directly connected to the CPU. As with all aspects of computing, bus performance will continue to improve.

1.7   Random Access Memory

RAM (random access memory) is the workspace of the computer. It is often referred to as **memory**. The growth in the size of RAM in the last few years has been phenomenal. Where 1 MB of memory was more than satisfactory just a few short years ago, the demand based on software needs has made 8 MB of RAM commonplace, and 16 MB of RAM desirable. Physically, RAM is contained in many electrical circuits. However, a computer's memory is not like a person's memory. RAM is not a permanent record of anything. RAM is the place where the programs and data are placed while the computer is working. Computer memory is temporary (volatile) and useful only while the computer is on. When the computer is turned off, what is in memory is lost.

1.8 Cache Memory

Cache memory is the latest method to improve processing speed. Basically cache memory stores frequently used RAM data, thereby speeding up the process of data access. Whenever the CPU needs data from RAM, it visits the cache first to see if the data is available. If it is, then rapid action occurs. If not, the CPU goes to RAM proper. Caches can be found in video and printer memory systems.

1.9 Read-only Memory

ROM (read-only memory) was designed to hold permanently stored programs installed by the computer manufacturer. ROM is made from electronic circuits. Read-only means exactly what it says. The CPU can only read the instructions from ROM; it cannot write, erase, or alter the contents of ROM in any way. ROM is nonvolatile, which means that when you turn off the computer, none of the information stored on ROM is lost. Actually, ROM has programs etched on it; it is a program-on-a-chip. Here, however, is where the terms hardware and software get somewhat blurred. ROM is hardware because it is a chip. However, it is also software because it contains instructions. Hence, ROM is sometimes called **firmware**, halfway between hardware and software. Nearly all computers use ROM to hold start-up programs, including the instructions for loading the operating system into RAM. Most ROM is located on the system board, but some ROM is located on adapter boards.

1.10 Adapter Cards

Adapter cards are printed circuit boards. They are installed in the system unit either when purchased or later as an addition. Adapter cards allow the user to add more RAM, use a special video display, or utilize a mouse, a modem, or a fax-modem. These items are considered **peripheral devices** and are installed within the CPU in **expansion slots**. The number of adapter card options you can install depends on how many slots your CPU has. Inexpensive CPUs usually have only one or two expansion slots, but a costly CPU, especially one designed to be a network server, can have seven or eight or more.

1.11 Peripherals: Input Devices

How do software programs and data get into RAM? This process is done with input devices. The most common input device is the keyboard, which is attached to the system unit with a cable. By keying in instructions and data, you communicate with the computer, which places the information into RAM.

You can also use a mouse or track ball to get to the place to enter data. A **mouse** is a hand-operated pointing device with two or three lever-like buttons on top. On the bottom is a ball that is moved around on a flat surface and in turn moves an arrow-shaped cursor around the screen. Data manipulation is as easy as moving the cursor where you want it on the screen and pressing one of the mouse buttons to enter it. The **trackball** is another device that is also hand operated, but the ball is on top and is rotated by either the hand or the fingers. When the cursor is moved to the proper place, data manipulation occurs by pressing one of the levers on the trackball.

Other input devices include the **light pen**, which has a light-sensitive cell. When the tip of the pen comes in contact with the monitor, it identifies a point on the screen. You can use the light pen to draw or enter data. **Scanners**, such as those in grocery stores, read the price code on an item as it is waved across an electrosensitive plate. This same technology has made text and graphics scanners readily available and will soon be common to most computer users.

1.12 Peripherals: Output Devices

In addition to getting information into the CPU, you also want to get it out. You may want to see what you keyed in on the monitor, or you might want to have a "hard" copy of the data printed. These processes are known as output. Output refers to where information is written. Thus, you "read" information in and "write" information out, commonly known as I/O for input and output.

1.13 Output Devices: Monitors

A **monitor**, also called a terminal, display screen, screen, cathode ray tube (CRT), or video display tube (VDT), looks like a television. The CPU writes information to the screen where it is displayed.

The monitors themselves come in two basic types, monochrome and color. Monochrome monitors display in one color. The user can choose the color: green characters on a black screen, amber characters on a black screen, and so on. Color monitors, obviously, display in color. Most monitors display character data, 80 characters across the screen and 25 lines down the screen. However, other types of monitors display an entire page. The clarity or resolution of what is displayed is measured in picture elements or **pixels**, which are dots that are adjusted by color or light intensity. The more pixels, the sharper the image.

Information written to the screen by the CPU needs a special kind of circuit board—a video display adapter card, commonly called a video card, which controls the monitor. In the early days of computing, the most popular adapters were the monochrome adapter and the color graphics adapter (CGA), which can display up to 16 colors. However, there was a trade-off. If you used the monochrome adapter, you got good resolution of characters. If, however, you wanted color, you lost the sharp resolution of characters. The enhanced graphics adapter (EGA) can paint up to 64 colors. The video graphics array (VGA) can paint up to 256 colors. Today, most people prefer the Super VGA format, which generates even sharper resolution within the 256 color spectrum.

1.14 Output Devices: Printers

A **printer** is attached to the system unit with a cable. The printer allows the user to have a **hard copy** (unchangeable because it is on paper) of information.

The two major types of printers are impact and nonimpact. An **impact printer** works like a typewriter. The element strikes some kind of ribbon, which in turn strikes the paper and leaves a mark. A **dot-matrix printer**, the most common type, forms characters by selecting dots from a grid pattern on a movable print head and permits printing in any style of letters and graphics (pictures). A dot-matrix printer operates from 80 characters per second (cps) to over 200. There are also impact printers that have elements on which the letters are already formed. The most well-known element printer is a **daisy-wheel printer**, which is considered a letter-quality impact printer. It operates from 12 cps to 55 cps. A dot-matrix impact printer tends to be faster, less expensive, and more versatile than a daisy-wheel printer, but its output does not have the same finished quality as the daisy-wheel printer.

Once again technology has done some wonderful things. You can now purchase a dot-matrix printer that has NLQ, or near letter quality. It gives a better output, usually because of the number of pins in the print head. For example, a nine-pin printer creates acceptable copy by going over the characters twice. A 24-pin printer, since it has more pins, gives an even sharper resolution and also prints twice. A dot-matrix printer in NLQ prints more slowly in NLQ mode. However, NLQ does give you nearly the quality of a daisy-wheel printer.

Nonimpact printers include **thermal printers** that burn images into paper using a dot-matrix grid. Some thermal printers heat the ribbon and melt ink onto the paper. **Ink-jet printers** spray drops of ink to shape characters. The **laser printer** has become by far the most popular nonimpact printer. This printer uses a laser beam instructed by the computer to form characters with powdered toner fused to the page by heat, like a photocopying machine. This printer produces high-quality character and graphic images. Laser printers operate noiselessly at speeds up to 900 cps (twenty-four pages per minute).

Color printers have finally become cost efficient even for the home user. Now dot-matrix, ink jet and thermal printers have color availability. At the PC level four-color printers are the most common. Basically, each color is printed separately by either the spot color separation (each color printed as a separate layer) or process color separation (each color separated into its primary color components first, then printed). Both methods produce high quality output.

1.15 Modems

A **modem** (**mo**dulator/**dem**odulator) translates the digital signals of the computer to the analog signals that travel over telephone lines. The speed at which the signal travels is called the baud rate—the unit of time for a signal to travel over a telephone line. The rate of transmission has increased to 14,000 baud, but for this transmission to occur, the party on the other end must also have a modem that translates the analog signals back into digital signals. In addition, the computer needs special instructions in the form of a software communication program for this activity to occur.

The growth of on-line services has made a modem a necessity. CompuServe, Prodigy, Internet, Bulletin Board Services (BBS), and the information highway make all kinds of information available. These services will be the libraries of the future.

1.16 Disks and Disk Drives

Since RAM is volatile and disappears when the power is turned off, a **secondary storage media** or **external storage media** is necessary to save information permanently.

Disks and disk drives are magnetic media that store data and programs in the form of magnetic impulses. Such media include floppy disks, hard disks, compact discs (**CD-ROM**), tape, magnetic cards, and tape cartridges. In the microcomputer world, the most common secondary storage media are **floppy disks** and **hard disks**.

Floppy disks serve a dual purpose. First, disks provide a permanent way to hold data. When power is turned off, the disk retains what has been recorded on it. Second, floppy disks are transportable. Programs or data developed on one computer can be used by another merely by inserting the disk. If it were not for this capability, programs such as the operating system or other application packages could not be used. Each time you wanted to do some work, you would have to write your own instructions.

Storing information on a disk is equivalent to storing information in a file cabinet. As in a file cabinet, disks store information in files. When the computer needs the information, it goes to the disk, opens a file, "reads" the information from the disk file into RAM, and works on it. When the computer is finished working on that file, it closes the file and returns ("writes") it back to the disk. In most cases, this process does not occur automatically. The application program in use will have instructions that enable the user to "save" or "write" to the disk.

1.17 Capacity Measurement: Bits and Bytes

A computer is made primarily of switches. All it can do is turn a switch on or off: 0 represents an off state and 1 represents an on state. A **bit** (from **b**inary dig**it**) is the smallest unit a computer can recognize. Bits are combined in meaningful groups, much as letters of the alphabet are combined to make words. The most common grouping is eight bits, called a **byte**. Thus, a byte can be thought of as one character.

Computer capacities like RAM and ROM are measured in bytes, originally in thousands of bytes or kilobytes but now in millions of bites or **megabytes** (MB or M). A computer is binary, so it works in powers of 2. A **kilobyte** is 2 to the 10th power (2^{10} or 1024) and K or KB is the symbol for 1024 bytes. If your computer has 64 KB of memory, its actual memory size is 64 times 1024 or 65,536 bytes. For simplification, KB is rounded off to 1000, so that 64 KB of memory means 64,000 bytes. Rapid technology growth has made megabytes the measuring factor. For example, a satisfactory RAM system was 1 MB, 1,024,000 bytes, just a few years ago. Now RAM expansion to 64 MB is not uncommon, because so many software programs rely on RAM to work effectively.

You should know the capacity of your computer's memory because it determines how big a program and/or data the computer can hold. For instance, if you have 640 KB of RAM on your computer and you buy a program that requires 1 MB of RAM, your computer will not have the memory capacity to use that program. Furthermore, if your computer has a hard disk capacity of 20 MB and the application program you buy requires at least 25 MB of space on the hard disk, you won't be able to install the program.

Disk capacity is also measured in bytes. A double-sided 5¼-inch disk holds 360 KB (360,000 bytes); a 3½-inch double-density disk holds 720 KB. Because high-density and hard disks hold so much more information, they are also measured megabytes (M or MB). A 5¼-inch high-density disk holds 1.2 MB; a 3½-inch high-density disk holds 1.44 MB. The new 3½-inch floppy holds 2.88 MB of information. Hard disks vary in size ranging from 20 MB to over 500 MB. Today, most people consider a 100 MB hard disk typical; it has a capacity of approximately 100 million bytes. Most computer users, when referring to megabytes, use the term **meg**. A hard disk with 100 million bytes is referred to as a 100 meg hard disk.

1.18 Minifloppy Disks

Floppy disks come in two sizes: 3½-inch and 5¼-inch. The standard size was the 5¼-inch floppy, but now the 3½-inch floppy is the standard. The 5¼-inch floppy disk, technically known as a **minifloppy** diskette, is a circular piece of plastic, polyurethane, or Mylar covered with magnetic oxide (see Figure 1.5). It is always inside a relatively rigid nonremovable protective jacket with a lined inner surface. Like a phonograph record, the disk has a hole (called a hub) in the center so that it can fit on the disk drive spindle. The disk drive spins the disk under the heads so that information can be read from or written to the disk. Once the disk is locked into the disk drive, it spins at about 300 revolutions per minute. The disk has an exposed opening called the **head slot** where data is written to and read from. A cutout on the side of the disk, known as a **write-protect notch**, can be covered with a write-protect tab. If a disk is write-protected, with the notch covered, the programs and data on the disk cannot be written over, so the original data and programs can never be lost. If the write-protect notch is not covered, data can be written to it as well as read from it. Some disks, like the original DOS System Disk, have no notch and therefore can never be written on. These disks are write-protected and can only be read.

Figure 1.5   A Minifloppy 5¼-Inch Disk

There is a small hole in the jacket near the center of the disk called the index or timing hole. If you rotated the plastic disk, you could find a small hole in the actual disk itself. The disk drive uses this hole to indicate where a circle has begun and ended, to help determine where information is stored on the disk. A disk with only one hole is considered **soft-sectored**; if it has many holes, it is considered **hard-sectored**. Most personal computers use a soft-sectored disk that indicates the first sector and track.

A 5¼-inch disk comes in two formats: double-density and high-density. The type of format you use depends on what kind of disk drive you have. A 5¼-inch double-sided, double-density disk can store approximately 360 KB, whereas a 5¼-inch double-sided, high-density disk can store 1.2 MB worth of information. A **high-density disk** is referred to most often as an HD disk, but sometimes the term **high-capacity disk** is used.

1.19 Microfloppy Disks

In principle, the 3½-inch microfloppy disks work the same way as the 5¼-inch disks, except that they are smaller and are enclosed in a rigid plastic shell. Instead of a write-protect notch like the 5¼-inch disk, each 3½-inch disk has a shutter that covers the read/write head. The computer's disk drive opens the shutter only when it needs access. When the disk is not in the drive, the shutter is closed. This disk does not use an index or timing hole; this function is performed by the sector notch next to the disk drive's spindle. The write-protect notch can be either a built-in slider or a breakaway tab. The 3½-inch disk also comes in two formats. A 3 ½-inch double-sided, double-density disk can store approximately 720 KB, whereas a 3½-inch double-sided, high-density disk can store 1.44 MB worth of information. There is also a newer size, the 3½-inch high-density disk that handles 2.88 MB of information. Figure 1.6 shows the 3½-inch disk.

Write-protect tab

Spindle

Indexing hole

Centering hole

Access hole

Shutter

Figure 1.6 *A Microfloppy 3½-Inch Disk*

1.20 CD-ROM

The latest transport device for software is the compact disc (CD). Borrowed from the music recording business, this disk can hold up to 600 MB of data and retrieves information by laser. Although presently only a read-only device, the write capabilities are well-known. CD-ROM drives are now becoming commonplace, and more and more software companies are using compact discs to ship software, simply because it is cost effective.

1.21 Hard Disks

A hard disk, also known as a fixed disk, a Winchester disk, or a hard drive, is a nonremovable disk that is usually permanently installed in the system unit (see Figure 1.7). A hard disk holds much more information than a removable floppy disk. If a floppy disk can be compared to a file cabinet that holds data and programs, a hard disk can be compared to a room full of file cabinets.

Figure 1.7   A Hard Disk

A hard disk is composed of two or more rigid platters, usually made of aluminum and coated with oxide, which allow data to be encoded magnetically. Both the platters and the read/write heads are permanently sealed inside a box; the user cannot touch or see the drive or disks. These platters are affixed to a spindle that rotates at about 3600 RPM, although this speed can vary, depending on the type of hard disk. The hard disk is much faster than a standard floppy disk drive. The rapidly spinning disks in the sealed box create air pressure that lifts the recording heads above the surface of the platters. As the platters spin, the read/write heads float on a cushion of air.

Because the hard disk rotates faster than a floppy disk and because the head floats above the surface, the hard disk can store much more data and access it much more quickly than a floppy disk. Today, a common hard disk storage capacity is 100 megabytes, with 500 MB not uncommon.

1.22 Dividing the Disk

A disk's structure is essentially the same whether it is a hard disk or a floppy disk. Data is recorded on the surface of a disk in a series of numbered concentric circles known as **tracks**, similar to the grooves in a phonograph record. Each track on the disk is a separate circle divided into numbered **sectors**. The amount of data that can be stored on a disk depends on the density of the disk—the number of tracks and the size of the sectors. Since a hard disk is comprised of several platters, it has an additional measurement, a **cylinder**. Two or more platters are stacked on top of one another with the tracks aligned. If you connect any one track through all the platters, you have a cylinder (see Figure 1.8).

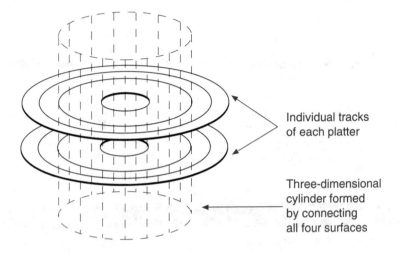

Individual tracks
of each platter

Three-dimensional
cylinder formed
by connecting
all four surfaces

Figure 1.8   ***Hard Disk Cylinders***

A **cluster** is the basic unit of disk storage. Whenever a computer reads or writes to a disk, it always reads and writes a full cluster, regardless of the space the data needs. Clusters are always made from adjacent sectors, from one sector to eight sectors or more. The location and number of sectors per cluster are determined by the software in a process known as **formatting**.

A disk is a random access medium, which does not mean that the data and/or programs are randomly arranged on the disk. It means that the head of the disk drive, which reads the disk, does not have to read all the information on the disk to get a specific item. The CPU can instruct the head of the disk drive to go directly to the track and sector that holds the specific item of information.

1.23 Disk Drives

A **disk drive** writes information to and from a disk. All disk drives have read/write heads, which read and write information back and forth between RAM and the disk, much like the ones on tape or video recorders.

A floppy disk drive is the device that holds a floppy disk. The user inserts the floppy disk into the disk drive (see Figure 1.9). The hub of the disk fits onto the hub mechanism, which grabs the disk. When the disk drive door is shut, the disk is secured to the hub mechanism. The jacket remains stationary while the floppy disk rotates. The disk drive head reads and writes information back and forth between RAM and the disk through the exposed head slot. Older disk drives are double-sided and can read and write to both sides of a disk but cannot read or write to a high-density floppy disk. The new generation of high-density disk drives read and write to both the old style floppy disk and new style high-density disk.

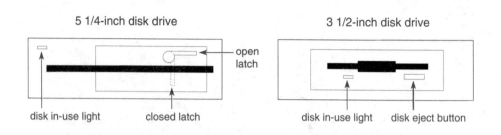

Figure 1.9   ***A Floppy Disk Drive***

1.24 Device Names

A device is a place for a computer to send information (write) or a place from which to receive information (read). In order for the system to know which device it is supposed to be communicating with at any given time, each device is given a specific and unique name. Device names, which are also known as reserved names, cannot be used for any other purpose. Disk drives are devices. A disk drive name is a letter followed by a colon.

Drive A: is the first floppy disk drive. Drive C: is the first hard disk drive. All other drives are lettered alphabetically from B: to Z:. You must be able to identify which disk drive you are using. There are certain rules that are followed. If you have two floppy drives that are stacked, the top one is always Drive A. If you have two floppy drives side-by-side, the one on the left is always Drive A. Some common examples are illustrated in Figure 1.10.

Figure 1.10   ***Disk Drive Configurations***

1.25 Software

Software is the step-by-step instructions that tell the computer what to do. These instructions are called **programs**. Programs need to be installed or **loaded** into RAM, where the CPU executes them. Programs usually come stored on disks. The program is read into memory from the floppy disk or hard disk. Software can also be divided into categories. The most common division is application software and system software.

Application software, as its name suggests, is a set of instructions, a complete program, that directs the computer to solve a particular problem. Application software solves problems and handles information. Application software may also be called packages, off-the-shelf software, canned software, or just software. You may have heard of application software by brand names such as WordPerfect or Lotus 1-2-3. There are thousands of commercially available application packages. The reason most people purchase a computer is the availability of application software.

System software is also a set of instructions or programs. These programs coordinate the operations of all the various hardware components. System software is usually supplied by the computer manufacturer because it is necessary to run application software. System software is always computer-oriented rather than user-oriented; that is, it takes care of what the computer needs so the computer can run application software (see Table 1.2).

Application Software	System Software
Solves problems.	Coordinates operation of hardware.
Handles information.	Necessary to run application software.
User-oriented.	Computer-oriented.

Table 1.2   Application and System Software

System software is also divided into three categories: operating systems, system utilities, and programming language processors (see Table 1.3).

Operating System	System Utility	Programming Language Processor
Handles input/output of the computer.	Enhances the usefulness of the computer.	Supports the use of programming languages.
Manages computer resources.	Adds capabilities.	
Enables the running of application software.		

Table 1.3   System Software

The **operating system** supervises the processing of application programs and all the input/output of the computer. Running a computer is somewhat analogous to producing a concert. The hardware is like the musicians and their instruments. They do not change. The application software is like the score the musicians play, anything from Ludwig van Beethoven to Paul McCartney. The computer hardware can "play" any application software from accounting to a game. Like the conductor who tells the violins or trumpets when to play and how loudly, the operating system makes the computer work. It is the first and most important program on the computer and *must* be loaded into memory (RAM) before any other program. Working with the operating system is known as being at the **system level**.

The operating system includes a **command processor**. The command processor has some built-in commands known as internal or **resident commands**, which are available as long as the power is on. **Internal commands** allow the user to manage disk files at the system level and to perform such activities as looking into the **directory** of a specific disk. In addition, the command processor allows the user to instruct the computer to load a system utility or an application program into RAM.

System utilities are special programs stored on an operating system disk. However, system utilities are not necessary to run the computer. They are only loaded and executed when the user needs them. Also known as **external** or **transient commands**, system utilities do useful tasks such as formatting a disk or giving statistical information about a disk. A system utility program formats a disk with the proper tracks and sectors so that it is a readable disk.

Programming language processors are programs that support the use of a programming language on a computer system. They are tools for the development of application packages. Only programmers who wish to write step-by-step instructions that tell the computer what to do use these programming language processors.

The term *operating system* is generic. Brand names for microcomputer operating systems include CP/M, Unix, Xenix, Apple-DOS, TRS-DOS, and UCSD-P. However, the standard operating system for microcomputers today is **DOS**, pronounced *dahs*. DOS, which stands for disk operating system, was developed and is owned by the Microsoft Corporation. Their version is known as **MS-DOS**. It is licensed to computer manufacturers who tailor it to their specific hardware. MS-DOS runs on the majority of personal computers in use today.

If you are going to use a computer and run application packages, first you are going to need to know how to use the operating system. No application program can be used without an operating system. Since DOS is the major microcomputer operating system in use today, this text is devoted to teaching the concepts of the operating system in general and DOS operations in particular.

1.26 Operating System Fundamentals

DOS is a program that is always working. No computer hardware can work unless it has an operating system in RAM. When you boot the system, you are loading the operating system software into RAM.

Some of the operating system software is built into the hardware. When you turn on the power to the computer, or "power up," the computer would not know what to do if there were no program to tell it what to do. A read-only memory chip called **ROM-BIOS** (read-only memory—basic input/output system), abbreviated to RIOS, pronounced *RYE-ose*, is built into the hardware of the microcomputer system. ROM-BIOS programs provide the interface between the hardware and DOS.

Thus, when you turn on the computer, the power goes first to ROM-BIOS. The first set of instructions is to run a self-test to check the hardware. The program checks the RAM and equipment attached to the computer. Thus, before getting started, the user knows whether or not there is a hardware failure. Once the self-test is completed successfully, the next job or program to execute is loading the operating system.

Loading the operating system entails ROM-BIOS checking to see if a disk drive is installed. The program then checks to see if there is a disk in Drive A. If there is no disk in Drive A, and, if there is a hard disk, the program will check Drive C. It is looking for a special program called the **boot record**. If ROM-BIOS does not find the boot record or if there is something wrong with the boot record, you will get an error message. If the ROM-BIOS program does find the proper boot record, it reads the record from the DOS disk into RAM and turns control over to this program. The boot record is also a program that executes; its job is to read into RAM the rest of the operating system, in essence, pulling the system up by its **bootstraps**. Thus, one "**boots**" the computer instead of merely turning it on.

The purpose of the operating system files that are loaded into RAM is to manage the resources and primary functions of the computer to free application programs from worrying about how the document gets from the keyboard to RAM and from RAM to the screen. This whole process can be considered analogous to driving an automobile. Most of us use our cars to get from point A to point B. We would not like it if every time we wanted to drive, we first had to open the hood and attach the proper cables to the battery and to all the other parts that are necessary to start the engine. The operating system is the engine of the computer that lets the user run the application in the same manner as a person drives a car.

The first program loaded into RAM is stored on the booting disk as a file called **IO.SYS**. IO.SYS handles input and output as well as the addition of new peripheral devices, such as a hard disk, a new printer, or a display screen. It tells the computer that these devices exist and how to handle the I/O without making major hardware changes.

The next program loaded into RAM is stored on the booting disk in a file called **MSDOS.SYS**. It handles most of the disk routines, known as high-level interface. Disk routines include reading and writing to a disk, opening and closing files on a disk, searching the table of contents or directory of a disk, deleting files, reading and writing data, or placing and retrieving information on the disks. Both IO.SYS and MSDOS.SYS are hidden files; that is, you do not directly use these files, nor will you see them listed in any ordinary directory display.

The last program loaded into RAM is stored on the bootable disk in a file called **COMMAND.COM**. This program is known as the command processor. It is here that you actually communicate and interact. When you key in something on the keyboard, COMMAND.COM reads what you key in and decides what to do with it; this is why it is called the command processor or **command interpreter**. It processes or interprets what you have keyed in. However, you cannot just key in anything. COMMAND.COM is looking for specific predefined instructions to execute. What COMMAND.COM does is look for a match between what you key in and what it has. It first checks what you key in against an internal table. If it finds a match, it turns control over to that program. These are the internal commands.

If it does not find a match, it goes to the disk to look for a match on the disk. When it finds a match on the appropriate disk, it loads that program into RAM and executes it. They are called external commands because they are external to memory and must be loaded into memory from disk each time you wish to use them.

COMMAND.COM can recognize a program because the program will have a file name with the file extension .COM, .EXE, or .BAT.

Remember the operating system files are read from the disk when you boot the system. These programs remain in RAM until you turn off the computer.

In general, using the operating system, particularly the two hidden files, is transparent to you. The work is being done, but you do not see the operating activities, just the results. In other words, the first two system files take care of the tedious but vital routines such as moving information to and from disks. However, you actually interface with COMMAND.COM, the third system file.

Figure 1.11 illustrates the operation of the command processor. To let you know that it is ready to do some work, DOS displays a signal on the screen. The signal is called the **prompt**. When the prompt is displayed on the screen, the command processor has finished running one program or command and is waiting for the next. When you key in something on the keyboard, the command processor tries to follow the instructions. COMMAND.COM is always looking for a program to execute.

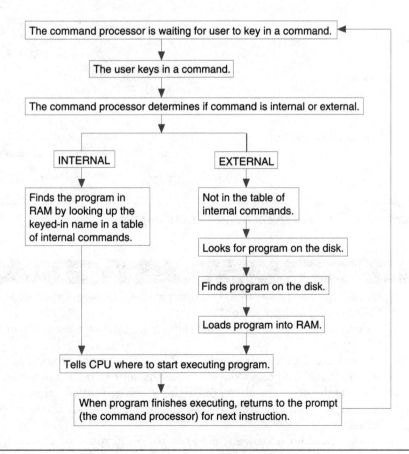

Figure 1.11 **Operation of the Command Processor**

1.27 Networks

Today, it is likely that you will be using a network in a work or lab environment. A **network** is two or more computers connected together. In addition, networks usually have various peripheral devices such as printers. A network lets users communicate and share information and devices. A network requires special hardware and software. Networks permit the use of electronic mail (E-mail). With E-mail users can send and receive messages within the network system.

There are two kinds of networks. A local area network (LAN) encompasses a small area such as one office. The hardware components such as the server, the terminals, and printers are directly connected by cables. (See Figure 1.12). A wide area network or WAN connects computers over a much larger area such as from building to building, state to state, or even worldwide. Hardware components of the WAN communicate over telephone lines, fiber optic cables or satellites. INTERNET is an example of a worldwide network.

Figure 1.12   A Typical Network Configuration

Chapter Summary

1.   All computers function in the same way. Data is input, processed, and stored. The results are the output.
2.   Hardware components include the system unit, the monitor, the keyboard, and the printer.
3.   The central processing unit (CPU) is the brain of the computer and can comprehend and carry out instructions sent to it by a program.
4.   Intel is the major producer of CPUs, which are called chips. They are differentiated by numbers, with the 80386 and 80486 being the most popular at this time.
5.   RAM (random access memory) is the workspace of the computer. RAM is volatile and is there only when the computer has power.

6. Cache memory is high-speed memory that stores the most recently used data.

7. ROM (read-only memory) is a chip with programs written on it. ROM is not volatile. It usually holds the start-up routines of the computer. CD-ROM drives are used to import data and install software from compact discs.

8. Adapter cards are printed circuit boards that allow the user to add various peripheral devices.

9. Peripherals are different devices that are attached to the system unit. The most common input device is a keyboard. The common output devices are the monitor and the printer.

10. Modems allow the transportation of data over telephone lines and allow computers to communicate.

11. Floppy disks, hard disks, and compact discs are a means of permanent storage for data and programs. A floppy disk is a piece of plastic inside a jacket. Floppy disks come in two popular sizes: 5¼-inch (minifloppy) and 3½-inch (microfloppy). Both sizes can be either double-sided, double-density or high-density. A hard disk is made of rigid platters that are permanently sealed inside a box. A compact disc is read-only but can handle up to 600 MB of data, which makes it a great device for transporting information.

12. All disks are divided into numbered tracks and sectors so that the computer can locate information.

13. A floppy disk drive is the device into which a floppy disk is inserted so that the computer can read from or write to it.

14. Disk drives have reserved names that consist of a letter of the alphabet followed by a colon. The left-hand or top disk drive is known as Drive A or A:. The first hard disk drive is known as Drive C or C:.

15. A byte represents a single character. The capacity of some floppy disks is measured in bytes, usually thousands of bytes or kilobytes (KB). The capacity of RAM, ROM, hard disks, or high-density floppy disks is measured in millions of bytes or megabytes (MB), often referred to as meg.

16. Software is the step-by-step instructions that tell the computer what to do. These instructions are called programs. Programs are loaded into RAM where the CPU executes each instruction. When programs are working in RAM, it is referred to as "running" or "executing" the program.

17. Programs are stored on disks and loaded into RAM from disk.

18. Software is divided into application software and system software.

19. Application software solves problems, handles information, and is user-oriented.

20. System software coordinates the operation of the hardware, is mandatory for running application software and is computer-oriented.

21. An operating system is comprised of programs called system software that perform the functions necessary to control the operations of the computer. The operating system tells the computer what to do and interfaces with the user.

22. ROM-BIOS (read-only memory—basic input/output system) is a chip that is built into the hardware of the system unit. It runs self-diagnostics and loads the boot record.

23. On an MS-DOS system disk, the system files have specific names. The program that deals with input/output devices is stored as a hidden file called IO.SYS. The program that deals with reading from and writing to disks is stored as a hidden file called MSDOS.SYS. The command interpreter is stored as a file called COMMAND.COM and is not hidden from the user.

24. Internal commands are programs loaded with the operating system in COMMAND.COM. They remain in memory until the power is turned off.

25. **External** commands are stored on a disk and must be loaded into memory each **time they are** used. External commands are transient and do not remain in **memory after** they are executed.

26. **The external commands** that come with DOS are known as system utilities or system utility **files.**

27. **Booting the system is** more than powering up the system; it means loading the operating **system.**

28. Application **packages are** external to the computer and must be loaded in order to be **executed.**

29. Networks are two or **more** computers connected together and usually share peripheral devices such as printers.

30. There are two basic types of networks, LANs and WANs. A LAN (local area network) is usually connected by cables and encompass a small area. A WAN (wide area network) connects computers over a much larger area such as building to building or every worldwide.

Key Terms

Adapter cards	Control unit	Hard copy
ALU	CPU	Hard disk
Application software	Cylinder	Hard-sectored
Bit	Daisy-wheel printer	Hardware
Boot	Data	Head slot
Boot record	Device	High-capacity disk
Bootstrap	Directory	High-density disk
Bus	Disk drive	Impact printer
Byte	DOS	Ink-jet printer
Cache memory	Dot-matrix printer	Internal commands
CD-ROM	Expansion slots	IO.SYS
Central processing	External commands	Kilobyte (KB)
unit	External storage	Laser printer
Cluster	media	Light pen
COMMAND.COM	Firmware	Loaded
Command interpreter	Floppy disks	Meg
Command processor	Formatting	Megabyte (MB)

Memory
Microcomputer
Microfloppy disk
Minifloppy disk
Modem
Monitor
Mouse
MS-DOS
MSDOS.SYS
Networks
Nonimpact printer
Operating system
Peripheral device
Pixels

Printer
Programming
   language
   processors
Programs
Prompt
RAM
Resident commands
ROM
ROM-BIOS
Scanners
Sectors
Secondary storage
   media

Soft-sectored
Software
System board
   configuration
System level
System software
System utilities
Trackball
Tracks
Transient
   commands
Write-protect notch

Discussion Questions

1. Define hardware.
2. Define software.
3. What is data?
4. What is meant by the system configuration?
5. Describe a typical microcomputer configuration.
6. Compare and contrast the SX and DX models of the microprocessor.
7. What is the purpose and function of the bus?
8. Compare and contrast RAM, cache, and ROM.
9. Explain firmware.
10. What is an adapter board?
11. List two input and two output devices and briefly explain how these devices work.
12. What are pixels?
13. Compare and contrast impact and nonimpact printers.
14. What purpose do disks serve?
15. What is the difference between disk storage and memory capacity?
16. What is a CD-ROM? What is its purpose?
17. How many types of disks are there? Describe them.
18. What is the difference between a hard disk and a floppy disk?
19. What are tracks and sectors? Where are they found?
20. What is a cluster? What are is it comprised of?
21. What is a device?
22. Compare and contrast application software with system software.
23. Can application packages run without an operating system? Why or why not?
24. Define DOS.
25. Where is DOS stored by the computer?

26. Define BIOS.
27. What is the function of an operating system?
28. Compare and contrast internal and external commands.
29. What files comprise DOS? What is the purpose of each file?
30. What is the purpose and function of a network?

Getting Started with DOS

Booting the System, Using the Keyboard, Using DIR, VER, CLS, MSD, Date/Time, and DISKCOPY

Learning Objectives

After completing this chapter, you will be able to:

1. Define DOS.
2. Define enhancements.
3. Explain the function and purpose of DOS version numbers.
4. List three types of system configurations.
5. Explain the need and procedure for booting the system.
6. Explain the function of disk files.
7. Explain the function of and rules used with file specifications.
8. List and explain the importance of the two types of computer files.
9. Describe the function and purpose of commands.
10. Compare and contrast internal and external commands.
11. Describe four keyboard groups and explain the purpose of each group of keys.
12. Identify and explain the functions performed by the **Backspace**, **Esc**, **Shift**, **PrtSc**, **Ctrl**, and **Pause** keys.
13. Explain the function and purpose of the DIR, VER, and CLS commands.
14. Explain the purpose of and the procedure for utilizing the DATE and TIME commands.
15. Explain the legal and ethical ramifications of copying disks that were not purchased.
16. Explain the purpose and function of the MSD command.
17. Explain the purpose and function of DISKCOPY command.
18. Explain the necessary steps to end a work session.

Student Outcomes

1. Identify your system configuration.
2. Boot the system.
3. Use the DIR command to display the files on the screen.
4. Use the [Backspace], [Esc], [Shift], [PrtSc], [Ctrl], and [Pause] keys where and when needed.
5. Cancel a command.
6. Use the VER command to determine which version of DOS is being used.
7. Use the CLS command to clear the screen.
8. Use the DATE and TIME commands to set or change the date and time on the computer.
9. Use MSD to identify system configuration and drive types.
10. Make a copy of a disk.
11. End a computer work session.

Chapter Overview

Most people who use computers are really interested in application software. They want programs that are easy to use and can help them solve specific problems. However, before you can utilize application software you must first know how to use the operating system. No computer can work unless it has an operating system in RAM. DOS, which is the major microcomputer operating system in use today on IBM and IBM-compatible microcomputers, takes care of the mandatory functions for computer operations such as handling the input and output of the computer, managing the computer resources, and running the application software. It enables the user to communicate with the computer.

In this chapter you will learn how to load the operating system into the computer, familiarize yourself with the keyboard, learn some basic commands, make a copy of the ACTIVITIES disk to use in future activities, learn your system configuration, and identify the version of DOS you are using.

2.1 What Is DOS?

The operating system is a software program. Although there are many different operating system "brand names," the major operating system in use today on IBM and IBM-compatible microcomputers is DOS, either PC-DOS or MS-DOS. MS-DOS was developed by Microsoft and licensed to IBM, which called it IBM PC-DOS. Other computer manufacturers also licensed DOS from Microsoft but call their versions MS-DOS. IBM, as of DOS 6.1, has decided to generate its own version of DOS. If you have an IBM microcomputer you are probably using PC-DOS, and, if you have a compatible that operates like an IBM, you are probably using MS-DOS. However, PC-DOS and MS-DOS are generally identical and function in the same way.

You need to load DOS into memory (RAM) before you can use other software programs. Furthermore, DOS is in charge of the hardware components of the computer. You, the user, communicate what you want the computer to do through

DOS **commands**, which are instructions that DOS understands. These commands are usually English words such as COPY or PRINT.

2.2   Versions of DOS

Microsoft and IBM periodically release new **versions** of DOS to take advantage of new technology. These new upgrades also contain **enhancements**. Enhancements simply mean more commands. In addition, new versions of DOS fix problems in older versions. This is known as fixing bugs. To keep track of these versions, they are assigned version numbers. DOS 1.0 was the first version, released in 1981, and DOS 6.22 is the most recent version.

This text is generally applicable to any version of DOS 2.0 or above. It is assumed in this textbook that DOS is installed on the hard disk or the network server. If you are working on your own computer, and have not yet installed DOS 6.2 or upgraded to it, refer to the appendices so that you can install DOS or upgrade to the latest version of DOS. If you are in a laboratory environment, check with your instructor to see what version of DOS you are working with.

2.3   Overview of Files and Disks

You need a way to store this information permanently. In the microcomputer world, the primary way to save data and programs permanently is to store them on a disk. After you have booted your computer, DOS reads the programs or data it needs from the disk back into its memory. However, in order for DOS to find this information, it has to have a way of organizing it, which it does by keeping programs and data in files on the disk. Just as you organize your written work in files, DOS organizes computer information in **disk files**.

A disk file is much like a file folder stored in a file cabinet. The file cabinet is the floppy disk or the hard disk. A file consists of related information stored on the disk in a "file folder" with a unique name. All information with which a computer works is contained and stored in files on the disk. (See Figure 2.1.)

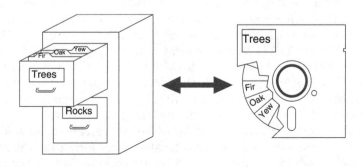

Figure 2.1   Disks and Files

2.4 File Names, File Types, and Directories

Because computers must follow very specific rules, there is a specific format for file names. Technically, a **file name** is called the **file specification**. The first rule is that the file specification must be unique. Second, the file specification is broken into two parts, a file name and a **file extension**. The file name typically describes or identifies the file, and the file extension typically identifies the kind of data in the file. Since the term file specification is rather awkward, most people simply refer to the file name, meaning both the file name and its extension.

There are two major types of computer files: data files and program (application) files. **Data files** contain information generated usually from an application program. Most often, only an application program can use the data file directly. **Program files** are application programs that allow the user to perform specific tasks; for example, a payroll program that lets you create and maintain a payroll system for a company.

You do not purchase a computer to run DOS. You purchase a computer so that you may do useful tasks such as writing letters, managing your checkbook, doing your taxes or creating a budget. If you needed to employ someone to do these tasks for you, you might go to a temporary employment agency and hire a secretary to write your letters or an accountant to manage your checkbook and taxes. You would employ a temporary secretary or accountant because you do not need the employee on a full-time basis.

In the computer world, you instead purchase application packages. These application packages fall into generic categories such as word processing or spreadsheet programs much like you refer generically to secretaries or accountants. In addition, you may be specific and wish to use a specific secretary such as Mr. Woo or a specific accountant such as Ms. Brown. In the computer world, application packages also have names and are brand names such as WordPerfect (the secretary) or Quicken (the accountant) or Lotus 1-2-3 (the budget manager). You can choose among a variety of employees—instead of choosing WordPerfect, you may prefer Word, or instead of Quicken, you may prefer Managing Your Money. These application packages are the "employees" who know how to do the job.

In order for these application programs to do work, they must be placed in RAM, the workspace of the computer. They are "temporary" employees because you only call on them when you need to do a specific task that only they can accomplish. When they are not working, they are kept on the disk in files. DOS is like the office manager. You tell DOS what work you want to do, and DOS goes to the disk to get the correct file and places it in RAM. This process is known as loading the program from disk into memory. DOS then lets the program do its job. This is known as executing the program. Program files are step-by-step instructions that direct the computer to "do" something—the task that you required.

Even though the secretary, WordPerfect, can create letters for anyone, you are interested only in the letters you create—the information that you want. Once you create your data, you also want to keep it permanently. Remember, all the work is occurring in RAM and RAM is volatile (temporary). In order to keep the information permanently, you direct WordPerfect to write (save) the information to disk as a data file. WordPerfect actually does not save the data; instead, it turns to DOS, which does the actual work of writing the file to disk. When you need to retrieve the information to alter it, WordPerfect again turns to DOS to retrieve the file. DOS then reads the disk to retrieve the appropriate data file and gives it to WordPerfect.

In order to be able to identify each file, a unique name must be assigned file. Program files have predetermined names such as WP.EXE for WordPerfect or Q.EXE for Quicken or 123.EXE for Lotus 1-2-3. Keying in the file name informs DOS to retrieve the program from the disk and place it in memory so you may work. Data files, on the other hand, are named by you, the user. You may call the file anything that you want. For instance, a good file name for a letter to your sister might be SISTER.LET or a name for your budget file might be BUDGET94.WK1.

The reason the file names look so peculiar is that DOS has rules for file names. Technically called a file specification, a unique name is assigned to every file. The file specification consists of two parts, the file name and a file extension. A file name can be from one to eight characters, but no longer than eight characters, and a file extension can be from one to three characters, but no longer than three characters. A file name is mandatory, but a file extension is not. A file name typically identifies the file such as WP for word processing or SISTER for your letter. The file name tells you about the file. The file extension identifies the kind of data in a file. For instance, .EXE is reserved for programs so that DOS knows it is a worker such as WP.EXE. .EXE stands for executable code.

Whether or not a data file has an extension depends on the rules of the application program. For instance, WordPerfect does not assign a file extension so that, when you called your letter SISTER.LET, you assigned the .LET to inform you that the file was a letter. On the other hand, the budget file that you created with Lotus (123.EXE), you named BUDGET94. That told you the data in the file was your 1994 budget. The file extension, however, is .WK1 (BUDGET94.WK1). Lotus assigned that .WK1 file extension (worksheet 1). That extension told Lotus that the data file was created with the Lotus program and helps you identify which data file belongs to which program.

Data files are generated by specific application programs, and the information or data in them can only be altered or viewed with the application package. It is the same idea that you would not give your tax information to the secretary and have the secretary make changes to it. You would only give that data to the accountant.

Data files do not stand alone. They only can be used in conjunction with an application program. Again, the job of DOS is to fetch and carry both program files and data files in and out of memory and to and from the disk (reading and writing). In addition, since DOS is the "office manager," you may also use DOS to do office related tasks such as copying a file or deleting a file. DOS does not know what is in the file folder nor can it make changes to the information in the file folder. It can manipulate the file folder by accomplishing such tasks as copying the information in it or by throwing it away.

To assist you in organizing your information further, DOS can divide or structure your disks into what are called directories. Technically they are subdirectories, but the terms directories and subdirectories are used interchangeably. Directories allows you to group related program or data files so they will be easy to locate at a later date. For instance, all the files related to the spreadsheet program such as LOTUS 1-2-3 could be stored in a directory named LOTUS. You might then group any data files you created with LOTUS, such as BUDGET93.WK1 and APRIL94.WK1, in another directory you called BUDGETS. This would allow you to know that when you wanted to locate the budget file called APRIL94.WK1, it would be in the directory called BUDGETS.

A primary directory (root) is automatically created when you prepare a disk to store information. It is named the root, but its symbol is the \ (backslash). You can create additional directories (subdirectories) for storing related files. Directories, including the root, will be discussed in full detail in Chapter 5.

2.5   Identifying Your System Configuration

All microcomputers come with disk drives of two basic types: the floppy disk drive and the hard or fixed disk drive. In the past, microcomputers had only one floppy drive. Today, however, most computer systems are configured in one of the three following ways:

❑ Two floppy disk drives with no hard drive.

❑ One hard disk drive and one floppy disk drive.

❑ One hard disk drive and two floppy disk drives.

The floppy disk drives can be any combination of the 5¼ 360 KB, the 5¼ 1.2 MB high-density, the 3½ 720 KB, and the 3½ 1.44 MB high-density disk drives. Most computers today have only high-density floppy disk drives. In order to follow the text, you must know which system configuration you have.

2.6   Booting the System

You must know how to get the operating system files from the bootable disk into memory (RAM) so that you can use the computer. This process is known as **booting the system**. These files can be on a floppy disk. However, today, usually, these files have been copied to the hard disk so that the user can boot from it and not have to use a floppy disk. The following activity allows you to have your first hands-on experience with the microcomputer. You are going to load DOS or "boot the system" using the hard disk. It is assumed that DOS is already installed on the hard disk or on a network server. If it is not, see the Appendices.

Materials Needed:

1. A microcomputer.
2. DOS installed on the hard drive.

Note: Since laboratory procedures will vary, check with your instructor before proceeding with these activities. A special process may be needed to boot the system if you are on a network.

2.7 Activity: Booting the System

Step 1   Check to see if the monitor has a separate on/off switch. If it does, turn on the monitor.

Step 2   Be sure there is no disk in Drive A. If your Drive A has a door that shuts or latches, be sure it is open. (Remember that your instructions may be different if you are booting to a network.) Power on the computer by locating the power switch and lifting it. The power switch location can vary. Sometimes it is on the front of the computer, other times on the side or back.

WHAT'S HAPPENING? The system checks itself in the diagnostic routine. You may see information about your computer appearing on the screen. After the system check is complete, the computer reads DOS into RAM from the hard disk (or network server). It reads the two hidden files, IO.SYS and MSDOS.SYS (IBMBIO.COM and IBMDOS.COM in PC-DOS), and the other system file, COMMAND.COM. When this happens, the disk drive makes a brief buzzing noise and a light on the drive flashes on, letting you know that the system is reading the disk. If the boot is successful, the screen displays the following message prompt. On some systems, you may see the version number and Microsoft's copyright date.

```
Microsoft(R) MS-DOS(R) Version 6.22
    (C)Copyright Microsoft Corp 1981-1994.

C:\>_
```

WHAT'S HAPPENING? You have successfully booted the system. The C:\> appeared on the screen. The C:\>, known as the C **prompt**, is the drive that the system reads from to get the operating system into memory. This process is sometimes also known as a "cold start." There is another process called a "warm start" or **rebooting** the system where you do not have to use the power switch. The power is already on. To reboot the system, you simultaneously hold down three separate keys: **Ctrl** + **Alt** + **Delete**. When you see keys with a + sign between them, it means to press all of the keys. The process is made intentionally awkward so you do not press the keys accidentally because this process erases everything in RAM and reloads the operating system from the disk. You use this process only in an emergency such as if your keyboard "freezes." Some systems have a reset button that performs the function of **Ctrl** + **Alt** + **Delete**. (Note: If you are on a network, your prompt may look different, such as P:\> or [J:\].) If you have booted and the C:\> is on the screen, you may proceed to Section 2.8.

What To Do If You Do Not See the C:\> Prompt

If you did not see the above screen, you probably booted into either Windows or DOSSHELL. Look at the following steps to return to the DOS system level. If you see any of the following screens, you will have to take additional steps to get to the C:\> prompt. Figure 2.2 shows a Windows screen, and Figure 2.3 shows an MS-DOS Shell Screen.

Figure 2.2 **Windows Screen**

WHAT'S HAPPENING? Your computer is set up to load Windows automatically. You must exit Windows.

Step 1   Press the $\boxed{\text{Alt}}$ + $\boxed{\text{F4}}$ keys. A message will then appear to confirm that you want to leave Windows.

Step 2   Press $\boxed{\text{Enter}}$

```
C:\>
```

WHAT'S HAPPENING? You have returned to DOS. If your prompt looks like C:\WINDOWS> or C:\DOS>, you must take another step.

Step 3   Key in the following: C:\WINDOWS>**CD ** **Enter**

C:\>_

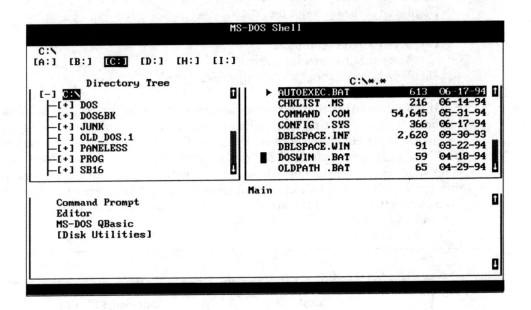

Figure 2.3   *MS-DOS Shell Screen*

WHAT'S HAPPENING? Your computer is set up to load DOSSHELL automatically. You must exit DOSSHELL.

Step 1:   Press the **Alt** + **F4** keys.

WHAT'S HAPPENING? The screen should now display C:\>. If your prompt looks like C:\DOS>, you must take another step.

Step 2:   Key in the following: C:\DOS>**CD ** **Enter**

C:\>_

2.8   *Computer Configuration Guide*

This textbook is based on a specific computer configuration, the one that is most common to DOS users. Therefore, the displayed prompts and directions will appear as follows:

Hard disk	C:
Floppy disk drive to be used	A:
Location of the DOS system utility files	C:\DOS
Path set to	C:\DOS
Displayed screen prompt for Drive C:	C:\>
Displayed screen prompt for DOS subdirectory on Drive C	C:\DOS>
Displayed screen prompt for DOS6BK subdirectory on Drive C	C:\DOS6BK>
Displayed screen prompt for floppy disk drive	A:\>

If your computer configuration conforms to the above, you can follow the textbook without making any adjustments. However, computer configuration setups vary particularly on network systems. Thus, your system configuration may be different. It is no problem to follow the textbook, but you must substitute what is on your system for the ones shown in the textbook. To help you remember the differences, if any, the following configuration table will be your reference guide. Your instructor will provide you with the information you will need for your personal configuration table.

Textbook	Your Substitution
C:\>	
C:\DOS>	
C:\DOS6BK>	
A:\>	
C:	
A:	
CD DOS	
CD DOS6BK	
DIR C:\DOS	
DIR DOS	
Drive A is a 5.25 inch high-density disk drive.	
Drive B is a 3.5 inch high-density disk drive.	

Table 2.1   **Configuration Table**

2.9   What is a Command?

DOS commands are programs and, like application programs, they perform specific tasks. DOS commands are of two types: internal or external. Internal commands are automatically loaded into memory (RAM) with COMMAND.COM when you boot the system. They are stored in memory. To use an internal command, you key in the command name. For an internal command, DOS checks memory, finds the program, loads it into RAM and executes it. They are called internal or resident commands because they are *residing* in memory or inside the computer (*internal*). Internal commands are limited in number because they take up valuable space in memory.

The external commands (system utility files) are stored as files on a disk. When you wish to use an external command, you call upon DOS to load the program into RAM by keying in the program's name. Since it is an external command, DOS cannot find the program internally, so it must go to the disk, locate the file, load it into RAM and execute it. If DOS cannot find the file, the program cannot be run. These commands are called external or transient commands because they reside in a file on a disk and must be read into RAM each time you key in the command.

Even though all programs are external, including application programs, the term external command is reserved for the group of programs that perform operating system functions. These programs are files that come with DOS and are usually copied to the hard disk to a subdirectory called \DOS. This group of files is generically referred to as the system utility files or the DOS system utility files.

In order to use commands, you must know their names. The DIR command, an internal command, is provided so that you may look for files on a disk. DIR stands for directory. When you key in DIR and press the **Enter** key, you are asking DOS to run the directory program. The purpose or task of DIR is to display on the screen the names of all the files on the disk, in other words, the table of contents of the disk. The DIR command is the first DOS internal command you will use.

2.10 Activity: Using the DIR Command

Step 1   Get the disk labeled ACTIVITIES that came with the textbook. The ACTIVITIES disk must be placed in Drive A. Look at Figure 2.4 to identify Drive A.

Note: You will need to refer to your Configuration Table in Chapter 2.8 from time to time to ensure that your operating procedures for this, and all other activities, are correct.

Figure 2.4   **Identifying Drive A**

Step 2   To insert a 5¼-inch disk properly into the disk drive, place your thumb on the label with the head slot facing away from you and toward the floppy disk drive. The write-protect notch should be facing left. If you have a 3½-inch disk, place your thumb on the label with the metal shutter facing away from you and toward the floppy disk drive (see Figure 2.5).

Figure 2.5   **Inserting the Disk**

Step 3   Gently lift the latch or door of Drive A on the system unit. Usually with 3½-inch disk drives you do not have a door to open. Instead, there is a slot into which you slip the disk until it clicks. Insert the master ACTIVITIES disk, label up, into Drive A. Shut or latch the drive door for a 5¼-inch disk drive. Some computers have a button that you push in after you place a disk in Drive A. For the 3½-inch disk drive, gently push the disk in the drive until you hear a click.

Note 1:   Remember, when you see the notation **Enter**, it means to press the **Enter** key located towards the right side and labeled Enter and/or ⊠.

Note 2:   Remember to refer to your Configuration Table if C:\> is not displayed.

Step 4   Key in the following: C:\>**CD** \ **Enter**

Step 5   Key in the following: C:\>**A:** **Enter**

```
C:\>CD \
C:\>A:
A:\>
```

WHAT'S HAPPENING? You confirmed that you were in the root directory of C and then changed the drive to A.

Step 6   Key in the following: A:\>**DIR** **Enter**

```
FILE2      SWT              18 12-06-94   10:46a
FILE3      CZG              18 12-06-94   10:46a
FILE3      FP               18 12-06-94   10:46a
FILE3      SWT              18 12-06-94   10:47a
FILE4      FP               18 12-06-94   10:47a
GETYN      COM              26 05-02-94   12:57a
DATA             <DIR>         05-07-94    1:51p
JAN        TMP              72 11-23-95   10:41a
FEB        TMP              74 11-23-95   10:41a
MAR        TMP              70 11-23-95   10:42a
APR        TMP              71 11-23-95   10:42a
LEFT       RED              53 05-07-94   11:05a
MIDDLE     RED              66 05-07-94   11:05a
RIGHT      RED              63 05-07-94   11:05a
DRESS      UP               25 05-07-94   11:06a
MIDDLE     UP               28 05-07-94   11:06a
RIGHT      UP               25 05-07-94   11:06a
TEST       TXT              64 03-14-93   11:07a
EMPLOYEE   ONE              52 05-07-94    9:00a
EMPLOYEE   THR              53 05-07-94    9:00a
```

```
EMPLOYEE TWO              53 05-07-94   9:00a
      106 file(s)            47,038 bytes
                             20,992 bytes free

A:\>_
```

WHAT'S HAPPENING? You see text moving vertically on the screen. This movement is known as **scrolling**, the result of executing the DIR command. DOS is displaying, or listing, all the files on the disk in Drive A and stops scrolling when the list ends. Locate the line on the screen that is the last file listed. You see the following:

```
EMPLOYEE  TWO    53    05-07-94     9:00a
```

EMPLOYEE is the name of the file. TWO is the file extension. (EMPLOYEE.TWO is the file specification. When you key in a file name, you *must* use a period between the name and its extension, but when the file name is displayed in the directory listing on the screen, the period is omitted.) Next is the number 53, the size of the file in bytes; the date, 05-07-94; and the time, 9:00a. The date and time indicate either when this file was created or when it was last modified. Now look at the bottom two lines of the screen. The line states: 106 file(s) 47,038 bytes and 20,992 bytes free. This line indicates the total number of files on the disk—106. The next number—47,038 bytes—indicates how much room the files take up on the disk. The commas are new to DOS 6.2. The next number—20,992—indicates how much room is left in bytes, so you will know if you have room on this disk for more files. On this disk, with only 20,992 bytes free, there is not much room left for more files.

All the files listed on the disk are practice files so that you may practice using DOS commands without harming any of your own files.

2.11 The Keyboard

The keyboard on a microcomputer is similar to a typewriter keyboard but has at least 40 additional keys, many with symbols rather than alphabetic characters. Generally, the keyboard can be broken down into four categories:

❑ **Alphanumeric keys**. These keys, located in the center of the keyboard, are the standard typewriter keys. They consist of the letters of the alphabet and Arabic numerals.

❑ **Function keys**. Keys labeled F1, F2, etc., located on the left side or across the top of the keyboard, are known as function keys. These keys are program-dependent which means that their functions are dependent on the software used. Often a notebook computer will have the function keys located in different spots on the keyboard due to space limitations.

❑ **Directional keys**. These keys, located between the alphanumeric keys and the number pad, are the cursor keys. These keys are also program-dependent and when used allow you to move the **cursor** in the direction of the arrows. Directly next to the directional keys are keys that are labeled `Insert`, `Home`, `PgUp`, `PgDn`, `Delete`, `End`, and `Delete`. These keys are also program-dependent. Older PC keyboards do not have separate directional keys or labeled keys. Instead, these keys are located on the numeric key pad. Notebook computers often have separate directional keys but `Home`, `PgUp` and other such keys share locations in the interest of saving space.

❑ **Numeric keys**. These keys, located to the right of the directional keys, are known as the number or numeric keypad. Numeric keys can be used in two ways: like a calculator keypad or with the directional arrows and other commands. The directional arrows in combination with other commands are program-dependent. The user must activate the mode desired (numeric keypad or directional arrows) with the `NumLock` key which acts as a **toggle switch**. A toggle switch acts like an on/off switch. Press the `NumLock` key once and the numbers are turned on. Press the `NumLock` key again and the numbers are turned off. Other toggle keys will be discussed later. On a notebook computer, the key labeled FN or Function toggles between the options.

The following activity will familiarize you with some of the special keys and features of a computer keyboard. Figure 2.6 shows one of the major types of keyboards used today.

Figure 2.6   *Sample Keyboard Layout*

2.12 The Backspace Key

The `Backspace` key, labeled Backspace or just with the symbol ← on it, allows you to erase characters you have keyed in prior to pressing `Enter`.

2.13 Activity: Correcting Errors Using the Backspace Key

Step 1   Key in the following: A\>The quick brown fox

Step 2   Press the **Backspace** key until you reach the A prompt (A:\>). As you see, each time you press this key, you delete a character.

2.14 The Escape Key

Esc is an abbreviation for Escape. Look for the key labeled Esc. When you press this key, it cancels a line you have keyed in, provided you have not yet pressed **Enter**. After you press the **Esc** key and DOS has eliminated the line of text, the line still appears on the screen, but DOS waits for you to key in something else.

2.15 Activity: Using the Escape Key

Step 1   Key in the following: A:\>The quick brown fox

Step 2   To erase this line, you could repeatedly press the **Backspace** key. However, you can use the **Esc** key to cancel the line instead. Press the **Esc** key.

```
A:\>The quick brown fox\
_
```

WHAT'S HAPPENING? DOS displayed a backslash (\) to show you that the line you keyed in was canceled. DOS then moved the cursor to the beginning of the next line. The A:\> is not shown where the cursor is blinking. The blinking indicates that DOS is ready for you to key in another command. DOS is ignoring the line you had keyed in. (If DOSKEY is installed, you will get only a blank line, and not the \ symbol.)

Step 3   Press **Enter**. DOS again displays the A:\> on the next line.

```
A:\>The quick brown fox\

A:\>_
```

2.16 The Shift Key

The **Shift** key is labeled Shift with an up arrow symbol 🠕 or just the up arrow symbol. This key allows the user to shift to uppercase letters and special characters such as the * above the number 8 key. There are usually two **Shift** keys, one on either side of the alphabet keys. To activate, you need only press one **Shift** key.

2.17 Activity: Using the Shift Key

Step 1   Press the letter **m**

```
A:\>m_
```

Step 2   Hold down the **Shift** key and press the letter **m**

```
A:\>mM_
```

Step 3   Press either **Backspace** or **Esc** to delete the letters.

2.18 The Print Screen Keys

Look for the key labeled **PrtSc** or **Print Screen**, which means print the screen. If you were going to print the screen, you would press the **PrtSc** key. This procedure would give you a hard copy or printed version of what the screen displays, like a "snapshot" of the screen at a specific moment in time. This procedure could be very useful if you had a problem and you wanted an expert to review it.

Printing the screen can present different problems, which is why you are not doing this as an activity. However, the steps will be illustrated.

1.   Be sure the printer is on before you press the **PrtSc** key.
2.   Older computers require that you press the **Shift** key while pressing the **PrtSc** keys.
3.   Ink-jet printers use a reset or clear button to eject a page.
4.   Laser printers require additional steps so that the paper is ejected after you press the **Print Screen** key.
     a. Press the Online button to turn it off.
     b. Press the Form Feed button to eject the page.
     c. Press the Online button to turn it back on.
5.   Network printers line up print jobs. You can hold up an entire print queue when you press the **PrtSc** key. Thus, if you ever want to try this procedure on a network, you will need instructions from the network administrator on printing procedures.

2.19 The Control Key and Print Screen Key

Look for the key labeled Ctrl, the control key. It has many functions depending on what combinations of keys are used. Pressing the Control key has no meaning by itself. However, when used with another key, it "triggers" a meaning for that key. When you see the notation **Ctrl**, ^, or Control key, it means to hold down the Control key with another key. For example, **Ctrl** + C is computer notation for pressing the control key and another key, the letter C. Do not type or key in the word *Control*, *Ctrl*, or ^.

When you print a screen, you can get only what was displayed on the screen. Any files or commands that scroll by are not printed. If, however, you hold down the **Ctrl** key and the **Print Screen** key, you toggle on the printer. DOS will then print everything as it is displayed. To toggle off the printer, press **Ctrl** + **Print Screen** again. This procedure can be used only on a dot-matrix printer that is not a network printer. On some networks, you can jam the network printer using the **Ctrl** + **Print Screen** keys.

2.20 Freezing the Display

You have already seen that when you use the DIR command, the display scrolls by so quickly on the screen that it is very difficult to read. There is a way to stop displays from rapidly scrolling on the screen. DOS allows you to read a long display by temporarily halting the scrolling procedure. How you do it depends on what kind of computer you have. Most new computers have a key labeled **Pause**; all you need to do is press **Pause**. Nearly every kind of computer, old or new, will let you use **Ctrl** + S for freezing the display. Older computers allow you to use the **Ctrl** key, but now you use it in conjunction with a key labeled **NumLock**. Locate the key with **NumLock** on it. If you have a fast computer, chances are it will process data faster than you can press the **Pause** key.

2.21 Activity: Using the Pause, Control, and the S Key

Step 1   Key in the following: A:\>**DIR** **Enter**

Step 2   Press the **Pause** key.

WHAT'S HAPPENING? Pressing this key halts or "freezes" the display on the screen. If you do not have a **Pause** key, repeat Step 1, but press the **Ctrl** + **NumLock** keys for Step 2. The display stops and the cursor remains blinking when you press these two keys. To continue scrolling, press any key.

Step 3   Press any key.

Step 4   Key in the following: A:\>**DIR** **Enter**

Step 5   Press the **Ctrl** key. While pressing the **Ctrl** key, press the S key.

WHAT'S HAPPENING? Pressing these keys halts or "freezes" the display on the screen. To continue scrolling, press any key.

Step 6   Press any key.

2.22 Canceling a Command

If you keyed in a command and pressed [Enter], but you either made an error or changed your mind about executing the command, you can cancel the command or cause it to stop executing. To cancel a command after you have pressed [Enter], press the [Ctrl] key in conjunction with the [Break] key or the letter C. Look for the key labeled [Break]. It is often paired with the [ScrollLock] key or the [Pause] key. This command is not the same as [Esc], which is used prior to pressing [Enter]. If you have a fast computer, by the time you press the keys, what you want to halt will no longer be on the screen.

2.23 Activity: Using DIR and Canceling a Command

Step 1   Key in the following: A:\>**DIR** [Enter]

Step 2   As soon as the directory starts displaying on the screen, hold the [Ctrl] key down. While holding down the [Ctrl] key, press the [Break] key.

WHAT'S HAPPENING? DOS stops running or executing the DIR command. You are returned to the A:\> prompt. You interrupted or stopped the program or the command from running, and, therefore, you see only a partial directory display. At the point where you pressed the [Ctrl] key and the [Break] key, you see ^C displayed on your screen. [Ctrl] + C has the same function and meaning as [Ctrl] + [Break].

Step 3   Key in the following: A:\>**DIR** [Enter]

Step 4   As soon as the directory information starts displaying on the screen, hold the [Ctrl] key down and then simultaneously press the letter C.

WHAT'S HAPPENING? This worked exactly like [Ctrl] + [Break]. DOS ceased executing the program or the DIR command and returned you to the A:\> prompt, ready for another command.

2.24 The VER Command

The VER command displays the version number of the operating system you are working with. Version 1.0 was the first version of DOS. When the number to the left of the decimal increases (for example, 2.0), it indicates a major change in the software. When the number to the right of the decimal increases (such as 2.1), it is a minor revision to the software. To know what version you are using, you can key in the internal command VER. Knowing the DOS version means knowing the features available to you. The VER command will also display the manufacturer of the software, in this case either IBM (International Business Machines) or MS (Microsoft). There are slight variations within each manufacturer but in essence, DOS is DOS. What you learn in this text will usually apply to either IBM-PC DOS or MS-DOS. The biggest variance will be what version you are working with in terms of what features and commands are available to you.

2.25 Activity: Using the VER Command

Step 1   Key in the following: A:\>**VER** [Enter]

```
A:\>VER

MS-DOS Version 6.22


A:\>
```

WHAT'S HAPPENING? In this particular case, this computer is running Microsoft DOS, Version 6.22 (MS-DOS 6.22). This text assumes version 6.22 of MS-DOS, but if you are working with an earlier version or with IBM-PC DOS, most commands will work the same.

2.26 The CLS Command

Your screen is filled with the display of the directory and other commands that you have keyed in. You may want to have a "fresh" screen, with nothing displayed except the A:\> prompt and the cursor in its "home" position (the upper left-hand corner of the screen). The internal command CLS clears or "refreshes" the screen. Whatever is displayed on the screen will go away, as if you erased a chalkboard. The command erases the screen, not your files.

2.27 Activity: Using the CLS Command

Step 1   Key in the following: A:\>**CLS** [Enter]

```
A:\>_
```

WHAT'S HAPPENING? The screen is now cleared, and the A:\> is back in the upper left-hand corner.

2.28 The DATE and TIME Commands

The computer, via a battery keeps track of the current date and time. This date and time are known as the **system date** and the **system time**. The system date and time are the date and time the computer uses when it opens and closes files (last date/time accessed) or when another program asks for the date and time. Newer computers have a built-in clock. Older computer systems may have an "add-on" built-in clock. You add it after you purchase the computer system. It is simply a built-in 24-hour battery-operated clock that sets the date and time automatically when you boot the system. You can change or check the system date and system time whenever you wish by using the internal DATE and TIME commands.

2.29 Activity: Using the DATE and TIME Commands

Step 1   Key in the following: A:\>**DATE** **[Enter]**

```
A:\>DATE
Current date is Mon 03-07-1994
Enter new date (mm-dd-yy):
```

WHAT'S HAPPENING? The date displayed on your screen is the current date, not the above example. If you did not wish to change the date, you would just press **[Enter]**, retaining the date displayed and returning you to the A:\>. However, if you do want to change the date, you respond to the prompt. You must key in the date in the above format such as 3-7-94. You may not key in character data such as March 4, 1994. Furthermore, you are allowed to use some other separators that, although not stated, can be used. You may key in 3/7/94 using the forward slash, or you may use periods such as 3.7.94. No other characters can be used.

Step 2   Key in the following: **12-31-99** **[Enter]**

```
A:\>_
```

WHAT'S HAPPENING? You did change the date, and we will examine this change in a moment. You can also change the time in the same fashion with the TIME command.

Step 3   Key in the following: A:\>**TIME** **[Enter]**

```
A:\>TIME
Current time is 12:14:36.22a
Enter new time:
```

WHAT'S HAPPENING? The time displayed on your screen is the current time, not the above example. If you did not wish to change the time, you would just press **[Enter]**, retaining the time displayed and returning you to the A:\>. However, if you do want to change the time, you respond to the prompt. You may use *only* the colon (:) to separate the numbers. Although, in this case, you are going to key in the seconds, usually most people key in only the hour and minutes. With DOS 4.0 and above, if you wish the time to be in the P.M., you add a "p" after the time. You may also use a 24 hour clock.

Step 4   Key in the following: **23:59:59** **[Enter]**

WHAT'S HAPPENING? You have just reset the computer clock with the DATE and TIME commands. These are internal commands. How do you know the system date and time have been changed? You can check by keying in the commands.

Step 5   Key in the following: A:\>**DATE** Enter

```
Current date is Sat 01-01-2000
Enter new date (mm-dd-yy):_
```

Step 6   Press Enter

Step 7   Key in the following: A:\>**TIME** Enter

```
Current time is 12:01:16.25a
Enter new time:_
```

Step 8   Press Enter

WHAT'S HAPPENING? Your time display numbers may be slightly different. What have you done? You have changed the system date and time. You entered the date of December 31, 1999 (12-31-99), prior to changing the time. The date now displayed is Sunday, January 1, 2000. How did that happen? Why is the displayed date different from the keyed-in date? After you entered the date of 12/31/99, you entered the time of 11:59 p.m. (23:59:59). When you set the time or clock, it runs until you turn off the power. Seconds went by; the time rolled over past midnight, and, when you are past midnight, you are into a new day. Hence, the day "rolled over" from December 31, 1999 to January 1, 2000. In other words, DOS keeps the date and time current based on the information you give.

The day of the week is displayed in the date. You can play around with DATE and TIME commands. For instance, you can find the day of your birthday in any future year by using the DATE command.

Step 9   Key in the following: A:\>**DATE** Enter

```
Current date is Sat 1-01-2000
Enter new date (mm-dd-yy):_
```

Step 10   At the prompt on the screen—date (mm-dd-yy)—key in your birthday for 1995. In the example below, I will use my birthday, 5-7-95. Key in the following: **5-07-95** Enter

Step 11   Key in the following: A:\>**DATE** Enter

```
Current date is Sun 5-07-1995
Enter new date (mm-dd-yy):_
```

WHAT'S HAPPENING? The screen display shows you the exact day of your birthday in 1995. In this case, my birthday will fall on a Sunday in 1995. If you wish to see or change the system date or time, use the DATE command and the TIME command.

Step 12   Use the DATE and TIME commands to enter the current date and time.

2.30 Media Types and MSD

When copying disks, it is very important that you know what type of media it is (see Table 2.2). Furthermore, it is important to know what type of floppy disk drive or drive you have on your system. This tells you the "native" format of the disk drive, whether or not you have a high-density disk drive, and which drive is Drive A. It is also extremely useful to know the DOS version and what type of computer you have. In DOS 6.0 and above, a new command was introduced (which actually was first available in Windows 3.1). It is called MSD for Microsoft Diagnostics. When you execute this program, it tells you the above information and more. MSD is an example of a DOS system utility program. In order to locate it, you must be in the directory where the DOS system utility files are located. Refer to the configuration table in Chapter 2.8 to locate your directory that holds the DOS system utility files and use your substitutions if they are not the same as the text.

Media Type	Source Disk (What you want to copy)	Destination/Target Disk (Where you want to copy it to)
5¼ inch	360 KB	New 360 KB disk or disk you no longer want the information on.
5¼ inch	1.2 MB	New 1.2 MB disk or disk you no longer want the information on.
3½ inch	720 KB	New 720 KB disk or disk you no longer want the information on.
3½ inch	1.44 MB	New 1.44 MB disk or disk you no longer want the information on.
3½ inch	2.88 MB	New 2.88 MB disk or disk you no longer want the information on.

Table 2.2   *Matching Disk Types When Using DISKCOPY*

2.31 *Activity: Using MSD (If You Have DOS 6.0 or Above)*

Step 1   Key in the following: A:\>**C:** [Enter]

Step 2   Key in the following: C:\>**CD \DOS** [Enter]

Step 3   Key in the following: C:\DOS>**MSD** [Enter]

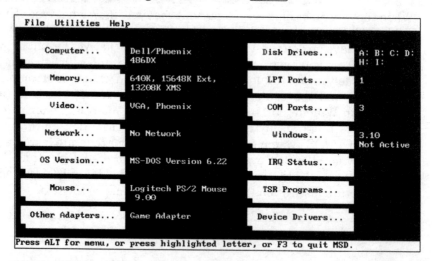

WHAT'S HAPPENING? You now see a display of information about your computer system. In this case, it is a DELL 486 computer running MS-DOS 6.22. If you want further information on each portion of the computer, you press the highlighted letter. In this case, you want to see what disk drive you have.

Step 4   Key in the following: **D**

```
 File  Utilities  Help
                        ═══════ Disk Drives ═══════
   Drive  Type                          Free Space  Total Size ↑
                                                                   D:
    A:   Floppy Drive, 5.25" 1.2M
           80 Cylinders, 2 Heads
           512 Bytes/Sector, 15 Sectors/Track
    B:   Floppy Drive, 3.5" 1.44M
           80 Cylinders, 2 Heads
           512 Bytes/Sector, 18 Sectors/Track
    C:   Fixed Disk, CMOS Type 55            78M        502M
           1022 Cylinders, 16 Heads
           512 Bytes/Sector, 63 Sectors/Track
    D:   CD-ROM Drive
    H:   DriveSpace Drive                   225M        346M      ve
           Actual Free Space               124M
           CVF Filename Is C:\DRVSPACE.002
    I:   DriveSpace Drive                   398M        511M
           Actual Free Space               100M
           CVF Filename Is C:\DRVSPACE.001                ↓

                            ▄▄▄▄
                            ▀OK ▀▄

 Disk Drives: Displays disk drive types and sizes.
```

WHAT'S HAPPENING? You can now see what disk drives you have. In this example, Drive A is a 5¼-inch 1.2 MB floppy drive which makes it a high-density drive. Drive B is a 3½-inch 1.44 MB floppy drive which makes it a high-density drive also. Now you can add this information to your Configuration Table in Chapter 2.8.

Step 5   Press Enter

Step 6   Press the F3 key.

```
C:\DOS>_
```

WHAT'S HAPPENING? You have exited the MSD program and returned to the DOS System level.

2.32 Ethical Considerations in Copying Disks

It is illegal to make a copy of a program or a disk that you did not purchase and do not own. Not only is it illegal, it is not ethical to do so. Making a copy of a program or receiving a copy of a program is stealing someone else's work. If you did not personally purchase the program, even if you are using it at work, it is still illegal to copy it and use it. However, most software manufacturers allow you and encourage you to make backup copies of program disks for your own personal use in case something happens to the original. Remember, however, you must have purchased the program or have permission to copy the disk in order to be both legal and ethical. This includes DOS and Windows. Both DOS and Windows are programs. They also may not be copied unless you purchased the programs.

In the following activity, you are going to copy the ACTIVITIES disk that comes with this book so that you have a working copy of the ACTIVITIES disk. You will work from a copy of the ACTIVITIES disk so that if anything happens, you can go back to the original ACTIVITIES disk to make another copy. Whenever possible, always work from a copy, never an original. This copy of the ACTIVITIES disk will be used in all future exercises. It is legal to make a copy for your personal use only. If you are in a computer lab, check with your instructor for the procedures in your specific lab.

2.33 Making a Copy of the ACTIVITIES Disk: DISKCOPY

You are now going to make a working copy of the ACTIVITIES disk. You are going to use another external program called DISKCOPY. It is stored as a file called DISKCOPY.COM in the DOS subdirectory. It does exactly what it says; it copies all the information from one floppy disk to another. However, the floppy disks must be compatible. DISKCOPY is not to be used with hard disks. It is for floppy disks only. Since DISKCOPY makes an identical copy, you must use the same type of disk. You can *never* use the DISKCOPY command to copy from a hard disk to a floppy disk or from a floppy disk to a hard disk. Please follow the instructions precisely. Be sure your screen looks like the sample, especially the prompt. The ACTIVITIES disk is a high-density 3½-inch floppy disk. Your blank disk must be the same media type in order to do the next activity.

2.34 *Activity: Using DISKCOPY*

Note 1:   If you are in a lab environment, check with your instructor to see if there are any special procedures in your lab.

Note 2:   Be sure your prompt displays C:\DOS>. If it does not, key in the following: **CD \DOS** [Enter].

Step 1   Get a new label. On the label write ACTIVITIES DISK—WORKING COPY and your name. Get a new disk or one that you no longer want the information on. Affix the label to the disk. See Figure 2.7 for the correct location of the label.

Label

Label

5¼-inch disk

3½-inch disk

Figure 2.7   ***Floppy Disk Label Placement***

Note: Check your Configuration Table in Chapter 2.8 if your system configuration varies.

Step 2   Place the ACTIVITIES disk that came with the textbook in Drive A.

Step 3   Key in the following: C:\DOS>**DISKCOPY A: A:** [Enter]

```
Insert SOURCE diskette in drive A:

Press any key to continue. . . . . _
```

WHAT'S HAPPENING? By keying in DISKCOPY, you are asking the command processor to find a program called DISKCOPY. It first looked in the internal table of commands. When it could not find a match, it went to the disk in Drive C and the subdirectory called DOS and found the program, loaded it into memory, and started executing it. This program has some prompts, which are simply instructions to follow. The program asks you to put the SOURCE disk that you wish to copy in Drive A. In this case, the ACTIVITIES disk, which you want to copy, already is in Drive A. Since you are going to use only one floppy disk drive, if you have a version of DOS lower than DOS 6.2, you will have to swap disks when prompted. If you have DOS 6.2 or above, you will not have to swap disks. Not swapping disks is an enhancement.

You are telling DOS to make a copy from the disk in Drive A to the disk in Drive A. To make the copy or begin executing the command DISKCOPY, press any key. This instruction literally means any key on the keyboard. Typically, you use **Enter**.

Step 4   Press **Enter**

```
C:\DOS>DISKCOPY A: A:

Insert SOURCE diskette in drive A:

Press any key to continue . . .

Copying 80 tracks, 15 sectors per track, 2 side(s)

Reading from source diskette . . .
```

WHAT'S HAPPENING? Track and sector numbers will vary depending on the type of disk used. The DISKCOPY command tells DOS to copy everything on the disk in Drive A (the SOURCE) to RAM. While this program is doing the copying, the cursor is flashing on the screen. When the command is completed or the program is finished copying, you will need to take another step. You see the following prompt:

```
Insert TARGET diskette in drive A:
Press any key to continue . . . . . _
```

WHAT'S HAPPENING? This prompt tells you to remove the SOURCE disk from Drive A and insert the blank or TARGET disk in Drive A so DOS has a place to copy the information.

Step 5   Remove the master ACTIVITIES disk from Drive A. Insert the blank disk labeled ACTIVITIES DISK—WORKING COPY into Drive A. Close or latch the drive door. Press **Enter**

WHAT'S HAPPENING? Again, you see the flashing cursor. Now, whatever was copied into RAM is being copied or written to the blank disk in Drive A.

For Versions Prior to DOS 6.22

If you have a version of DOS previous to 6.2, you will receive the following prompt:

```
Insert SOURCE diskette in drive A:
Press any key to continue. . . . . _
```

Because you do not have enough memory (RAM) to capture all of the ACTIVI-TIES disk in one transfer, you will have to swap disks back and forth in Drive A until the transfer is completed. The instructions will tell you to remove the TARGET diskette from Drive A and insert the SOURCE diskette (ACTIVITIES disk) into Drive A. Therefore, you remove the target disk from Drive A, insert the ACTIVI-TIES disk back into Drive A, and press **Enter** until you see the message Insert TARGET diskette in drive A. You continue to swap disks until you get the following screen display. With DOS 6.2, you do not need to do this because DOS uses the hard disk as a temporary storage area.

```
Writing to target diskette . . .

Do you wish to write another duplicate of this disk (Y/N)?
```

WHAT'S HAPPENING? In DOS 6.2, the enhancement to DISKCOPY feels that you might wish to make many copies of a floppy. It is giving you that opportunity.

Step 6   Press N

```
Volume Serial Number is 12CA-1D58

Copy another diskette (Y/N)?
```

WHAT'S HAPPENING? The prompt tells you that the program has finished executing and asks you a question. Do you want to execute this program again to make another copy of another disk? In this case, you do not wish to make another copy so you key in the letter N for no. The Volume Serial Number changes with each DISKCOPY command and is only seen in DOS 4.0 or above.

Step 7   Press N

```
C:\DOS>_
```

WHAT'S HAPPENING? You are returned to the C:\DOS> prompt. DOS is ready for a new command.

Step 8   Key in the following: C:\DOS>**CD** **Enter**

WHAT'S HAPPENING? You always want to return to the root directory, your starting point. You always want to start and end in the same place. By keying in CD\, you were telling DOS to change the directory. The \ always means the root, so you were saying change directory to the root.

2.35 How to End the Work Session

You can stop working with the computer any time you wish. Since your programs are stored on disks, you will not lose them. However, you should always exit your application program properly and return to the DOS system level. Whatever is in RAM (memory) will disappear, but that does not affect what is on your disk. The only thing you need to be cautious about is the disk drive light. When the disk drive light is on, it indicates that the head is reading or writing to the disk. Removing the disk at this time is the equivalent of taking a record off the turntable without first removing the needle. It is advisable to return to the root directory after you finish your work section.

2.36 Activity: Ending the Work Session

Note: Check with your lab instructor to see what special procedures you might need to follow in your lab environment.

Step 1   Key in the following: C:\>**CD** \ **Enter**

WHAT'S HAPPENING? You are confirming that you are at the root directory of C.

Step 2   Be sure no disk drive lights are on.

Step 3   Remove any disks that are in the disk drives. Place the floppy disks in their envelopes.

Note: Network users: If you are logged onto the network, be sure to perform your logout procedures correctly.

Step 4   Turn off the printer, the monitor, and the system unit.

Chapter Summary

1. An operating system is a software program that is required in order to run application software and to oversee the hardware components of the computer system.
2. DOS is the major operating system in use today on IBM and IBM-compatible microcomputers.
3. PC-DOS and MS-DOS are functionally the same.
4. DOS is released in different version numbers. New versions of DOS allow it to take advantage of new technology, to add new commands, and to fix bugs.

5. All microcomputers come with disk drives. There are two basic types of disk drives—the floppy disk drive and the hard disk drive.

6. Most computer systems are configured in one of three ways; two floppy disk drives and no hard drive, one floppy disk drive and one hard disk drive, or one hard disk drive and two floppy disk drives.

7. Booting the system, also known as a cold start, means more than powering on the system. Booting loads the operating system into memory and executes the self-diagnostic test routine.

8. Rebooting, also known as a warm start, involves pressing the **Ctrl**, **Alt**, and **Delete** keys, which erases everything from memory and reloads the operating system from the disk. Some systems have a Reset button, which will also reboot the system.

9. Internal commands are programs loaded in COMMAND.COM with the operating system. They remain in memory until the power is turned off.

10. External commands are stored on a disk and must be loaded into memory each time they are used. They are transient and do not remain in memory after being executed.

11. Programs and data are stored on disks as files. The formal name is file specification, which includes the file name and file extension.

12. A command is a program. A program is the set of instructions telling the computer what to do.

13. Programs (commands) must be loaded into memory in order to be executed.

14. To load a program into memory, the user keys in the command name at the system prompt.

15. The DIR command is an internal command that displays the directory (table of contents) of a disk.

16. The **Backspace** key deletes characters to the left.

17. The **Esc** key ignores what was previously keyed in before **Enter** is pressed.

18. The **Shift** key shifts letters to uppercase.

19. Pressing the **PrtSc** key prints the screen. Older computers require you to hold down the **PrtSc** and **Shift** keys to print the screen.

20. The **Ctrl** key and the **PrtSc** key when held down together toggle the printer on or off, but only for using a dot-matrix printer.

21. A toggle switch is like a light switch. In one position, the function is turned on. By pressing the same toggle switch again the function is turned off.

22. The **NumLock** key and the **Ctrl** key when held down together freeze the screen display on older computers. Newer computers use the **Pause** key. Both older and newer computers can use **Ctrl** + S.

23. The **Ctrl** key and the **Break** key or the **Ctrl** key and the letter C when held down together cancel a command that was entered.

24. Minor internal commands include CLS, DATE, and TIME.

25. VER displays the current version of DOS that is in memory.

26. CLS clears the screen.

27. DATE and TIME allow you to look at and/or change the system date and system time.

28. MSD is an external command that helps you identify the components of your computer system.
29. DISKCOPY is an external command that makes an identical copy of any disk, track for track, sector for sector. It was used to make a working copy of the ACTIVITIES disk but can be used to make exact copies of any two floppy disks that are the same media type.
30. To end a work session with the computer, remove any disks and turn off the monitor, printer, and system unit.

Key Terms

Alphanumeric keys	Enhancements	Program files
Booting the system	File extension	Prompt
Commands	File name	Rebooting
Cursor	File specification	Scrolling
Data files	Function keys	System date
Directional keys	Numeric keys	System time
Disk files	Operating system	Toggle switch

Discussion Questions

1. What is an operating system?
2. What are enhancements?
3. Define system configuration.
4. List three common ways that computer systems are configured.
5. Why is it necessary to boot the system?
6. How would you boot the system?
7. How do you reboot the system?
8. What is a file?
9. Identify and explain the purpose of the two major types of computer files.
10. Identify and explain the function and purpose of the two parts of a file specification.
11. What is the difference between a command and a program?
12. Compare and contrast internal and external commands.
13. What is the purpose of the DIR command?
14. Name and describe the functions of the four parts of a keyboard.
15. What is the purpose and function of a toggle switch?
16. What is the function of the **Backspace** key?
17. How may you correct typographical errors?
18. What is the function of the **Esc** key?
19. What is the function of the **Shift** key?
20. What is a hard copy?
21. Identify one way to print what is on the screen.
22. What is the function of the **Ctrl** key?
23. How can you stop the display from rapidly scrolling on the screen?
24. How can you cancel a command after you have pressed **Enter**?

25. What is the function of the VER command?
26. How can you determine if there has been a major or minor change in new releases of software?
27. What is the function of the CLS command?
28. What is the function of the system date and the system time?
29. How do you set the date when using the DATE command?
30. How do you set the time when using the TIME command?
31. What is the purpose of making a backup copy of a program?
32. Why should you work with a copy of a program rather than with the original?
33. Why is it important to know what type of media your are using when copying disks?
34. What is the purpose of the DISKCOPY command?
35. What steps should be taken when ending a work session?

Command Syntax Using the DIR Command with Parameters and Wildcards

Learning Objectives

After completing this chapter you will be able to:

1. Define command syntax.
2. Explain what parameters are and how they are used.
3. Explain the purpose and use of the DIR command.
4. Define prompts and explain how they are used.
5. Explain the purpose and function of a device.
6. Explain the purpose and function of device names.
7. Explain the purpose and function of defaults.
8. Explain the function and purpose of subdirectories (paths).
9. Define global specifications and identify their symbols.
10. Explain the purpose and function of redirection.

Student Outcomes

1. Read a syntax diagram and be able to name and explain what each part signifies.
2. Use both fixed and variable parameters with the DIR command.
3. Give the names of the disk drives on your computer.
4. Change the default drive and the directory.

5. Use subdirectories (paths) with the DIR command.
6. Use global specifications with the DIR command.
7. Redirect the output of the DIR command to either a file or a printer.
8. Use online help.

Chapter Overview

To communicate with any computer, you need to learn the computer's language, to follow its syntax, and to use punctuation marks the computer understands. As in mastering a new language, new vocabulary words must be learned, the word order (syntax) must be determined, and the method of separating statements into syntactic units must be understood. The computer has a very limited use of language so it is exceedingly important to be precise when you are speaking to it.

In this chapter you will learn some basic computer commands, the syntax or order of these commands, and where the commands begin and end. You will learn how to make your commands specific, how to use wildcards to affect a command, and how to determine which disk you want to write to or read from. You will also learn how to use the online help feature, which is significantly enhanced in DOS 6.0 and above.

3.1   Command Syntax

All languages have rules or conventions for speaking or writing. The **syntax** or order of a language is important. For example, in English the noun (person, place, or thing) is followed by the verb (the action). In another language, however, the syntax or order might be different: first the verb, followed by the noun. When you learn a language, you learn its syntax.

Anything you key into the computer must be a word the computer understands. The words you key in are actually commands to the computer to perform a specific task. These commands must also be in the correct order, that is, have the proper syntax. The computer cannot guess what you mean. For example, if I say, "Going I store," people will still understand. But if I key in an incorrect word or put correct words in the wrong order, the computer will respond with a message, `Bad command or file name`. This statement is the computer equivalent of "I do not understand."

In computer language, a command can be compared to a verb, the action you wish to take. In Chapter 2, you used the command DIR. In other words, when you keyed in DIR, you were asking DOS to take an action: run the program called DIR that lets you see the directory (table of contents) of a disk.

3.2   What Are Parameters?

A **parameter** is information you can use to modify or qualify a command. Some commands require parameters, while other commands let you add them when needed. Some parameters are variable. A **variable parameter** is one to which you supply the value. This process is similar to a math formula. For instance, $x + y = z$ is a simple formula. You can plug in whatever values you wish for x and y. If $x = 1$

and $y = 2$, you know the value of z, which is 3. These values can change or are variable so that x can equal 5 and y can equal 3, which makes z equal to 8. These variables can have any other numerical value you wish to use. You can also have $z = 10, x = 5$, and mathematically establish the value of y. No matter what numbers x, y, or z are, you will be able to establish the value of each.

Other parameters are fixed. For instance, if the formula now reads $x + 5 = z$, then the x is the variable parameter and the 5 is the fixed value. You can change the value of x but not the value of 5.

When you are working with some DOS commands, you are allowed to add one or more parameters to make the action of a command more specific. This process is the same in English. If I give my son my Visa card and tell him, "Go buy," I have given him an open-ended statement—he can buy anything (making him one happy guy). However, if I add a qualifier, "Go buy shoes," I have limited what he can do. This pattern is precisely what parameters do to a command.

3.3 Reading a Syntax Diagram

DOS is a language that has a vocabulary, grammar and syntax. To use the language of DOS, you must learn the vocabulary (commands) and understand the grammar (punctuation) and syntax (order). Prior to DOS 5.0, the *DOS Reference Manuals* provided **syntax diagrams** to explain the commands. Beginning with DOS 5.0 and above, DOS comes with a *User's Guide* with general information and a list of commands. The syntax information is now provided through online help. The **command syntax** diagrams tell you how to enter the command with its optional or mandatory parameters. However, you need to be able to interpret these syntax diagrams.

The following is a brief example of the formal command syntax diagram for the DIR command you used earlier:

```
DIR    [drive:][path][filename]  [/P]  [/W]
```

The first entry is the command name. You may only use this name. You cannot substitute another word such as DIRECTORY or INDEX. The parameters that follow the command are in brackets. Brackets indicate that the parameters are optional.

3.4 Using Fixed Parameters with the DIR Command

DIR is one of the commands with **optional parameters**. Prior to DOS 5.0, DIR had only two modifiers or **fixed parameters** that allowed you to control the way the operating system displayed the table of contents on the disk: /W for "wide display" and /P for "pause display." Most often in MS-DOS, a fixed parameter is referred to as a **switch** and typically begins with the /.

DOS 5.0 included many new parameters and DOS 6.2 added more, but the rules do not change even if the version numbers do. In the DIR command syntax diagram, the /W and the /P are in brackets. You never key in the brackets, only the / (forward slash or slash) and the W or P. You must be careful; there is only one slash—the forward slash /. The \ is a backslash and is always referred to as the backslash. When slash is referred to, it is always the forward slash.

When you key in DIR and the files scroll by, they move so quickly that you cannot read them. In the previous chapter, you learned that you could halt the display by pressing the **Pause** key or the **Ctrl** and S keys. However, there is a more efficient way to solve this problem by using the /P parameter. The /P parameter will display one screen of information at a time. It will also give you a prompt that you must respond to before it will display another screenful of information.

Note 1:   Be sure you know what your computer laboratory procedures are.
Note 2:   If your system varies from the textbook system in any way, refer to your Configuration Table in Chapter 2.8 for the appropriate values.

3.5 *Activity: Using Fixed Parameters with the DIR Command*

Note: Whenever the textbook refers to the ACTIVITIES disk, you will use the working copy you made in Chapter 2 that you labeled ACTIVITIES disk—Working Copy.

Step 1   Be sure there is no floppy disk in Drive A. Then, boot from the hard disk.

```
C:\>_
```

WHAT'S HAPPENING? You have successfully booted the system. You are the root directory of Drive C.

Step 2   Insert the ACTIVITIES disk in Drive A.

Step 3   Key in the following: C:\>**A:** **Enter**

WHAT'S HAPPENING? The default drive is now Drive A.

Step 4   Key in the following: A:\>**DIR /P** **Enter**

```
Volume in drive A is ACTIVITIES
Volume Serial Number is 12CA-1D58
Directory of A:\


JAN       NEW           71 01-23-93  11:48a
FEB       NEW           73 01-23-93  11:48a
MAR       NEW           69 01-23-93  11:49a
APR       NEW           70 01-23-93  11:49a
PERSONAL  FIL        2,305 12-06-93   4:45p
```

```
   MEDIA          <DIR>           12-06-93    4:45p
   Y         FIL            3  05-14-93   11:00a
   STEVEN    FIL           44  11-23-94    7:13a
   MARK      FIL           73  04-30-94    3:35p
   SPORTS         <DIR>           02-14-94   11:03a
   EXP94JAN  DAT          302  11-23-94    7:01a
   EXP94FEB  DAT          305  11-23-94    7:01a
   EXP94MAR  DAT          300  11-23-94    7:02a
   STATE     CAP          260  05-14-94    5:11p
   LEVEL-1        <DIR>           08-01-94    5:26p
   GOODBYE   TXT           32  11-23-94    7:07a
   GRAMMY    REC          419  02-26-94    5:50p
   DANCES    TXT           70  08-08-95    5:34p
   NAME      BAT        2,211  06-17-94   10:55p
   Press any key to continue . . .
   _
```

WHAT'S HAPPENING? You keyed in the command DIR followed by a slash / and the parameter P. The slash which must be included with a fixed parameter is commonly referred to in MS-DOS as a switch. However, the / is really a **delimiter**. A delimiter is a signal to DOS that one thing is ending and another is beginning. DOS uses different punctuation marks as delimiters, but the punctuation marks that it uses are very specific when they are used. The / is used only with fixed parameters.

In this example, the slash is the signal to the DIR command that additional instructions follow. The parameter P is the additional instruction. There can be no space between the slash and the P. The slash and the P stop the directory from scrolling. Thus, /P told the DIR command to fill the screen and then pause until the user takes some action. The message at the bottom of the screen tells you to press any key.

Step 5   Press **Enter**

```
   GO        BAT        3,766  06-17-94   10:55p
   FINANCE        <DIR>           08-01-94    5:45p
   FRANK     FIL           42  11-23-94    7:13a
   CAROLYN   FIL           45  11-23-94    7:13a
   STATES    USA        1,230  05-03-94   12:17a
   PHONE          <DIR>           01-14-95   12:32p
   GAMES          <DIR>           01-14-95   12:37p
   NEWAUTO   MAK          114  07-04-95    5:35p
   OLDAUTO   MAK          106  07-04-95    5:39p
   APRIL     TMP           70  01-23-93   11:49a
   BYE       TYP           43  10-12-94    7:07a
   CASES     FIL          315  11-23-94    7:04a
   SECOND    FIL           73  11-23-94    7:04a
   GOODBYE   TMP           32  11-23-94    7:07a
   BONJOUR   TMP           51  10-12-94    7:09a
```

```
JANUARY   TMP          71  01-23-93   11:48a
MARCH     TMP          69  01-23-93   11:49a
FEBRUARY  TMM          73  01-23-93   11:48a
OLIVE     OIL          96  10-12-94    7:10a
AWARD     MOV          41  11-23-93   12:57p
DATE1     NNN           9  01-24-93   10:57a
DATE2     NNN           9  08-07-92    5:50p
Press any key to continue . . .
```

WHAT'S HAPPENING? When you pressed **Enter** or any key, the display continued scrolling. Because there are still more files, the DIR command asks you to press any key again to continue the display. As you can see, the display stops each time the screen fills.

Step 6   Press **Enter**

Step 7   Press **Enter**

Step 8   Press **Enter**

Step 9   Press **Enter**

```
FILE3     SWT          18  12-06-94   10:47a
FILE4     FP           18  12-06-94  10:47a
GETYN     COM          26  05-02-94   12:57a
DATA         <DIR>         05-07-94    1:51p
JAN       TMP          72  11-23-95   10:41a
FEB       TMP          74  11-23-95   10:41a
MAR       TMP          70  11-23-95   10:42a
APR       TMP          71  11-23-95   10:42a
LEFT      RED          53  05-07-94   11:05a
MIDDLE    RED          66  05-07-94   11:05a
RIGHT     RED          63  05-07-94   11:05a
DRESS     UP           25  05-07-94   11:06a
MIDDLE    UP           28  05-07-94   11:06a
RIGHT     UP           25  05-07-94   11:06a
TEST      TXT          64  03-14-93   11:07a
EMPLOYEE  ONE          52  05-07-94    9:00a
EMPLOYEE  THR          53  05-07-94    9:00a
EMPLOYEE  TWO          53  05-07-94    9:00a
       106 file(s)         46,880 bytes
Press any key to continue . . .

(continuing A:\)
                           47,038 bytes free

A:\>_
```

WHAT'S HAPPENING? You kept pressing [Enter] until there were no more files
to display. The system prompt (A:\>) appears to signal that there are no more files
on this disk and that DOS is waiting for you to key in the next command. There is
another way to display the files on the screen. You may use the /W parameter to
display the directory in a wide format.

Step 10   Key in the following: A:\>**DIR /W** [Enter]

```
[MEDIA]           Y.FIL            STEVEN.FIL       MARK.FIL         [SPORTS]
EXP94JAN.DAT      EXP94FEB.DAT     EXP94MAR.DAT     STATE.CAP        [LEVEL-1]
GOODBYE.TXT       GRAMMY.REC       DANCES.TXT       NAME.BAT         GO.BAT
[FINANCE]         FRANK.FIL        CAROLYN.FIL      STATES.USA       [PHONE]
[GAMES]           NEWAUTO.MAK      OLDAUTO.MAK      APRIL.TMP        BYE.TYP
CASES.FIL         SECOND.FIL       GOODBYE.TMP      BONJOUR.TMP      JANUARY.TMP
MARCH.TMP         FEBRUARY.TMM     OLIVE.OIL        AWARD.MOV        DATE1.NNN
DATE2.NNN         DATE3.NNN        DATE4.NNN        DATE5.NNN        TEXT.NNN
README.NNN        CURRENT.BAT      OLDDATE.BAT      KEEPDATE.BAT     UNPUT.BAT
README.BAT        PUT.BAT          PUTFLOP.BAT      PUTX.BAT         PUTFLOPX.BAT
EXP93JAN.DAT      EXP93FEB.DAT     EXP93MAR.DAT     STATE2.CAP       [TEST]
WILD1.XXX         WILD2.YYY        WILD3.ZZZ        WILDONE          WILDONE.DOS
WILDTHR.DOS       WILDTWO.DOS      RNS.EXE          EXP95JAN.DAT     EXP95FEB.DAT
EXP95MAR.DAT      BLUE.JAZ         GREEN.JAZ        APR.99           FEB.99
JAN.99            MAR.99           JANUARY.TXT      FEBRUARY.TXT     MARCH.TXT
APRIL.TXT         HELLO.TXT        BYE.TXT          FILE2.CZG        FILE2.FP
FILE2.SWT         FILE3.CZG        FILE3.FP         FILE3.SWT        FILE4.FP
GETYN.COM         [DATA]           JAN.TMP          FEB.TMP          MAR.TMP
APR.TMP           LEFT.RED         MIDDLE.RED       RIGHT.RED        DRESS.UP
MIDDLE.UP         RIGHT.UP         TEST.TXT         EMPLOYEE.ONE     EMPLOYEE.THR
EMPLOYEE.TWO
       106 file(s)           47,038 bytes
                             20,992 bytes free

A:\>_
```

WHAT'S HAPPENING? The directory display is now spread across the screen,
five columns wide. In addition, the information about the files is not as comprehensive. All you see is the file specification—the file name and extension. You do not
see the file size, date, or time, but you still see the total number of files and the
number of bytes free. You can also identify the directories by the brackets around
them such as [MEDIA]. Thus, /W allows you to see the files side by side. You can
use more than one parameter at a time. Since there are so many files on this disk,
you did not see the entire directory.

Step 11   Key in the following: A:\>**DIR /P /W** [Enter]

```
Volume in drive A is ACTIVITIES
Volume Serial Number is 12CA-1D58
Directory of A:\

JAN.NEW           FEB.NEW          MAR.NEW          APR.NEW          PERSONAL.FIL
[MEDIA]           Y.FIL            STEVEN.FIL       MARK.FIL         [SPORTS]
EXP94JAN.DAT      EXP94FEB.DAT     EXP94MAR.DAT     STATE.CAP        [LEVEL-1]
```

```
GOODBYE.TXT     GRAMMY.REC      DANCES.TXT      NAME.BAT        GO.BAT
[FINANCE]       FRANK.FIL       CAROLYN.FIL     STATES.USA      [PHONE]
[GAMES]         NEWAUTO.MAK     OLDAUTO.MAK     APRIL.TMP       BYE.TYP
CASES.FIL       SECOND.FIL      GOODBYE.TMP     BONJOUR.TMP     JANUARY.TMP
MARCH.TMP       FEBRUARY.TMM    OLIVE.OIL       AWARD.MOV       DATE1.NNN
DATE2.NNN       DATE3.NNN       DATE4.NNN       DATE5.NNN       TEXT.NNN
README.NNN      CURRENT.BAT     OLDDATE.BAT     KEEPDATE.BAT    UNPUT.BAT
README.BAT      PUT.BAT         PUTFLOP.BAT     PUTX.BAT        PUTFLOPX.BAT
EXP93JAN.DAT    EXP93FEB.DAT    EXP93MAR.DAT    STATE2.CAP      [TEST]
WILD1.XXX       WILD2.YYY       WILD3.ZZZ       WILDONE         WILDONE.DOS
WILDTHR.DOS     WILDTWO.DOS     RNS.EXE         EXP95JAN.DAT    EXP95FEB.DAT
EXP95MAR.DAT    BLUE.JAZ        GREEN.JAZ       APR.99          FEB.99
JAN.99          MAR.99          JANUARY.TXT     FEBRUARY.TXT    MARCH.TXT
APRIL.TXT       HELLO.TXT       BYE.TXT         FILE2.CZG       FILE2.FP
FILE2.SWT       FILE3.CZG       FILE3.FP        FILE3.SWT       FILE4.FP
GETYN.COM       [DATA]          JAN.TMP         FEB.TMP         MAR.TMP
Press any key to continue . . .
```

WHAT'S HAPPENING? You can have no space between the / and the W or the / and the P. You can, however, have a space between /P and /W. By using both of these parameters together, you could see the files in a wide display, one screenful at a time.

Step 12: Press [Enter]

```
(continuing A:\)
APR.TMP         LEFT.RED        MIDDLE.RED      RIGHT.RED       DRESS.UP
MIDDLE.UP       RIGHT.UP        TEST.TXT        EMPLOYEE.ONE    EMPLOYEE.THR
EMPLOYEE.TWO
        106 file(s)             47,038 bytes
                                20,992 bytes free

A:\>_
```

WHAT'S HAPPENING? You have returned to the system prompt. DOS is ready for another command.

3.6 Using File Names as Variable Parameters

In the previous activities, you used the DIR command with two different optional fixed parameters, /P and /W. These optional fixed parameters have specific meanings. There is another parameter you can use with the DIR command: the name of the file.

File names are formally called file specifications. A file specification is broken into two parts, the file name and the file extension. When people refer to a **file** or file name, they really mean the file specification, the file name and file extension. For instance, when someone refers to John, he usually means someone specific such as John Smith. In the DOS world when you refer to a file name, you must give both its first name (file name) and its last name (file extension). When you create files in an application program, you are allowed to name the file. On this disk, the files already exist and thus, are already named. You cannot call them anything else. However, when you have the opportunity for naming files, you must follow the rules. DOS has rules or conventions for naming files. These are:

1. All files in a directory (subdirectory) must have unique names.

2. File names are mandatory. All files must have file names that may be less than but no more than eight characters. Typically, file names reflect the subject of the file, for example, EMPLOYEE, TAXES.

3. File extensions are optional. An extension may be less than but not more than three characters. Typically, file extensions refer to the type of data in the file, for example, .TXT (text), .DAT (data), .DBF (database), .WKS (spreadsheet).

4. Any alphanumeric character can be used in a file name or file extension, except the following:

   | Space Bar | . " / \ [ ] : ; | < > + = , * ?

When you key in the DIR command, you get the entire table of contents of the disk, known as the directory. Usually, you do not care about all the files. Most often, you are only interested in whether or not one specific file is located or stored on the disk. If you use one of the parameters, /P or /W, you still have to look through all the files. You can locate a specific file quickly by using the file name. Simply give the DIR command specific information about what file you seek. Look at the syntax diagram:

```
DIR [drive:][path][filename] [/P] [/W]
```

The *filename*, indicated above in brackets, is a variable optional parameter. You may include a file name, but DOS does not know what file you are looking for. You must plug in the value or the name of the file you are looking for [*filename*], much like the *x* in the formula discussed earlier. In some syntax diagrams, you will see [*filename*[.*ext*]]. The .*ext* is in brackets because it is part of the file name syntax. A file may not have an extension, but, if it does have an extension, you must include it. When you include it, there must be no spaces between the file name and the file extension. The delimiter that is used between a file name and file extension is a period, or what is called the **dot**. A dot, as a delimiter, is used only between a file name and the file extension. A file name is keyed in as MYFILE.TXT and, if verbalized, MY FILE dot TEXT. Remember, when you use the DIR command, you will not see the period or dot between the file name and the file extension on the screen. On the directory display, the dot is indicated by spaces.

3.7 Activity: Using File Names as Variable Parameters

Note: The ACTIVITIES disk should be in Drive A with the A:\> displayed.

Correcting Keystroke Errors

DOS provides a way to reuse the last command line. When you key in a command, it is stored in a memory buffer until it is replaced by the next command you key in. The command line can be recalled to the screen so you may edit it. To recall the command line, one letter at a time, press the ➡ or F1 key. To recall the entire command line, press the F3 key. You can move the cursor to the position on the command line you wish to edit using the ➡ or ⬅ (right or left arrow keys). Once in position, you can use the Insert key or the Delete keys to edit the line. To edit command lines fully, DOS 5.0 and above provides a tool called DOSKEY. For instructions on how to use DOSKEY, see Chapter 14, sections 14.1–14.2.

Step 1   Key in the following: A:\>**CLS** Enter

Step 2   Key in the following: A:\>**DIR** Enter

```
    FILE2      SWT              18 12-06-94   10:46a
    FILE3      CZG              18 12-06-94   10:46a
    FILE3      FP               18 12-06-94   10:46a
    FILE3      SWT              18 12-06-94   10:47a
    FILE4      FP               18 12-06-94   10:47a
    GETYN      COM              26 05-02-94   12:57a
    DATA            <DIR>          05-07-94    1:51p
    JAN        TMP              72 11-23-95   10:41a
    FEB        TMP              74 11-23-95   10:41a
    MAR        TMP              70 11-23-95   10:42a
    APR        TMP              71 11-23-95   10:42a
    LEFT       RED              53 05-07-94   11:05a
    MIDDLE     RED              66 05-07-94   11:05a
    RIGHT      RED              63 05-07-94   11:05a
    DRESS      UP               25 05-07-94   11:06a
    MIDDLE     UP               28 05-07-94   11:06a
    RIGHT      UP               25 05-07-94   11:06a
    TEST       TXT              64 03-14-93   11:07a
    EMPLOYEE   ONE              52 05-07-94    9:00a
    EMPLOYEE   THR              53 05-07-94    9:00a
    EMPLOYEE   TWO              53 05-07-94    9:00a
          106 file(s)        47,038 bytes
                             20,992 bytes free

    A:\>_
```

WHAT'S HAPPENING? First you cleared the screen by using the internal command CLS. Then, you keyed in DIR, and the entire table of contents of the disk in Drive A scrolled by on the screen. When there were no more files to display, DOS returned to the A:\> prompt. You are looking at the file specifications on the disk in Drive A. You see the file names and, separated by some spaces, the file extensions. The other information is the size in bytes and the date and time the files were last updated. Any name followed by <DIR>, such as DATA in the previous screen, is a directory.

Step 3   Key in the following: A:\>**CLS** `Enter`

Step 4   Key in the following: A:\>**DIR BYE.TYP** `Enter`

```
A:\>DIR BYE.TYP

 Volume in drive A is ACTIVITIES
 Volume Serial Number is 12CA-1D58
 Directory of A:\

BYE        TYP          43 10-12-94    7:07a
        1 file(s)              43 bytes
                       20,992 bytes free

A:\>_
```

WHAT'S HAPPENING? You asked the operating system a question. Does the table of contents on the disk in Drive A (DIR) have a specific file (BYE.TYP)? DIR is the command; BYE.TYP is the variable parameter. You substituted BYE.TYP for the [*filename*]. You did not key in the brackets, but, when you entered BYE and TYP, you separated the file name from the file extension with a period, called a dot. The dot must be entered between BYE and TYP because it separates the file name from the file extension. The DIR program will search the entire list of files on the disk in Drive A to find an exact match for BYE.TYP. DIR answered your question with the screen display. DIR is telling you that, yes, a file called BYE.TYP is on the disk in Drive A. The file name is BYE. The file extension is TYP. The file size is 43 bytes. The date and time the file was last modified is 10-12-94 and 7:07a. It also tells you that it found only one file with that name.

DOS is not case sensitive. You can key in commands and file names in either uppercase or lowercase letters. Most people use lowercase letters because it is easier. However, in this textbook for the sake of clarity, commands and file names will be in uppercase letters, and the file names will be in a different type style.

Step 5   Key in the following: A:\>**DIR STEVEN.FIL** `Enter`

```
A:\>DIR  STEVEN.FIL

 Volume in drive A is ACTIVITIES
 Volume Serial Number is 12CA-1D58
 Directory of A:\

STEVEN    FIL              44 11-23-94    7:13a
        1 file(s)                 44 bytes
                           20,992 bytes free

A:\>_
```

WHAT'S HAPPENING? This command tells you that it did find the file STEVEN.FIL on the disk in Drive A. Furthermore, STEVEN.FIL is the variable parameter. You substituted STEVEN.FIL for [*filename*]. If there were no file by that name, you would get the answer File not found.

Step 6   Key in the following: A:\>**DIR NOFILE.EXT** [Enter]

```
A:\>DIR  NOFILE.EXT

 Volume in drive A is ACTIVITIES
 Volume Serial Number is 12CA-1D58
 Directory of A:\

File not found

A:\>_
```

WHAT'S HAPPENING? File not found is a system message. Sometimes it is referred to as an error message. DIR is telling you that it looked through the entire list of files on the disk in Drive A and could not find a "match" or the file called NOFILE.EXT.

3.8 Drives as Device Names

A disk drive is an example of a device. A device is a place to send information (write) or a place from which to receive information (read). Disk drives have assigned **device names** which are letters of the alphabet followed by a colon so that DOS knows which disk drive to read from or write to. Thus, the prompt that is displayed on the screen is there so that you know what DOS is going to do and so that you know which device DOS is going to read or write to. If you are using a stand-alone computer, your drive names will typically be A: or B: or C: However, if you are on a network, disk drive letters can vary. They can include such drive letters as J or P or W. Again, the displayed prompt will tell you on what drive (device) DOS is going to take an action. Disk drives are not the only places where the system sends or receives information. Other common devices are the keyboard, the printer, and the monitor.

3.9 Defaults

In addition to understanding names of devices, it is also important to understand the concept of **defaults**. Computers must have very specific instructions for everything they do. However, there are implied instructions that the system "falls back to" or defaults to in the absence of other instructions. If you do not specify what you want, the system will make the assumption for you. For example, when A:\> is displayed on the screen, it is called the A prompt, but it is also the **default drive**. When you want any activity to occur but do not specify where you want it to happen, the system assumes the activity will occur on the default drive, the A:\> that is displayed on the screen.

When you key in DIR after A:\>, how does DOS know that you are asking for the system to give you a table of contents of the disk in Drive A? It knows for two reasons. First, when a specific direction is given, DOS must have a specific place to look. Second, A:\>, the default drive, is displayed on the screen. Since you did not specify which disk you wanted DIR to check, it made the assumption (programmed in by the programmer) that you want the table of contents or directory listing for the default drive or the disk in Drive A.

The prompt displayed on the screen is also known as the **designated drive** or the **logged drive**. All commands, if given no other instructions to the contrary, assume that all reads and writes to the disk drive must take place on the default drive. The default drive is indicated by the prompt displayed on the screen.

3.10 Activity: Working with Defaults

Note: Have the ACTIVITIES disk in Drive A and the A:\> displayed.

Step 1   Key in the following: A:\>**DIR** [Enter]

```
    FILE2    SWT              18  12-06-94   10:46a
    FILE3    CZG              18  12-06-94   10:46a
    FILE3    FP               18  12-06-94   10:46a
    FILE3    SWT              18  12-06-94   10:47a
    FILE4    FP               18  12-06-94   10:47a
    GETYN    COM              26  05-02-94   12:57a
    DATA            <DIR>         05-07-94    1:51p
    JAN      TMP              72  11-23-95   10:41a
    FEB      TMP              74  11-23-95   10:41a
    MAR      TMP              70  11-23-95   10:42a
    APR      TMP              71  11-23-95   10:42a
    LEFT     RED              53  05-07-94   11:05a
    MIDDLE   RED              66  05-07-94   11:05a
    RIGHT    RED              63  05-07-94   11:05a
    DRESS    UP               25  05-07-94   11:06a
    MIDDLE   UP               28  05-07-94   11:06a
    RIGHT    UP               25  05-07-94   11:06a
    TEST     TXT              64  03-14-93   11:07a
```

```
EMPLOYEE ONE                52  05-07-94     9:00a
EMPLOYEE THR                53  05-07-94     9:00a
EMPLOYEE TWO                53  05-07-94     9:00a
        106 file(s)             47,038 bytes
                                20,992 bytes free

A:\>_
```

WHAT'S HAPPENING? Displayed on the screen is the result of the DIR command you asked DOS to execute. Since you did not specify which disk drive DIR should look into, it assumed or defaulted to the disk in Drive A. Review the syntax diagram: DIR [*drive:*][*path*][*filename*] [/P] [/W]. The syntax diagram has [*drive:*], which is another optional variable parameter. You can substitute the letter of the drive you wish DIR to look into.

Step 2   Key in the following: A:\>**DIR A:** Enter

```
FILE2      SWT              18  12-06-94    10:46a
FILE3      CZG              18  12-06-94    10:46a
FILE3      FP               18  12-06-94    10:46a
FILE3      SWT              18  12-06-94    10:47a
FILE4      FP               18  12-06-94    10:47a
GETYN      COM              26  05-02-94    12:57a
DATA           <DIR>            05-07-94     1:51p
JAN        TMP              72  11-23-95    10:41a
FEB        TMP              74  11-23-95    10:41a
MAR        TMP              70  11-23-95    10:42a
APR        TMP              71  11-23-95    10:42a
LEFT       RED              53  05-07-94    11:05a
MIDDLE     RED              66  05-07-94    11:05a
RIGHT      RED              63  05-07-94    11:05a
DRESS      UP               25  05-07-94    11:06a
MIDDLE     UP               28  05-07-94    11:06a
RIGHT      UP               25  05-07-94    11:06a
TEST       TXT              64  03-14-93    11:07a
EMPLOYEE ONE                52  05-07-94     9:00a
EMPLOYEE THR                53  05-07-94     9:00a
EMPLOYEE TWO                53  05-07-94     9:00a
        106 file(s)             47,038 bytes
                                20,992 bytes free

A:\>_
```

WHAT'S HAPPENING? You substituted A: for the variable optional parameter, [*drive:*]. The display, however, is the same as DIR without specifying the A: because A:\> is the default drive. It is unnecessary to key in A: but not wrong to do so. If you want to see what files are on Drive C or Drive B, you must tell DIR to look on the drive you are interested in.

Note: Remember that if you are on a network, your drive letter may not be C:.
         Refer to your Configuration Table in Chapter 2.8 for the correct drive
         letter for your system.

Step 3   Key in the following: A:\>**C:** **Enter**

```
A:\>C:\

C:\>_
```

WHAT'S HAPPENING? You have changed the default drive to the hard disk,
Drive C.

Step 4   Key in the following: C:\>**DIR A:** **Enter**

```
        FILE2     SWT              18  12-06-94   10:46a
        FILE3     CZG              18  12-06-94   10:46a
        FILE3     FP               18  12-06-94   10:46a
        FILE3     SWT              18  12-06-94   10:47a
        FILE4     FP               18  12-06-94   10:47a
        GETYN     COM              26  05-02-94   12:57a
        DATA            <DIR>          05-07-94    1:51p
        JAN       TMP              72  11-23-95   10:41a
        FEB       TMP              74  11-23-95   10:41a
        MAR       TMP              70  11-23-95   10:42a
        APR       TMP              71  11-23-95   10:42a
        LEFT      RED              53  05-07-94   11:05a
        MIDDLE    RED              66  05-07-94   11:05a
        RIGHT     RED              63  05-07-94   11:05a
        DRESS     UP               25  05-07-94   11:06a
        MIDDLE    UP               28  05-07-94   11:06a
        RIGHT     UP               25  05-07-94   11:06a
        TEST      TXT              64  03-14-93   11:07a
        EMPLOYEE  ONE              52  05-07-94    9:00a
        EMPLOYEE  THR              53  05-07-94    9:00a
        EMPLOYEE  TWO              53  05-07-94    9:00a
            106 file(s)         47.038 bytes
                                20,992 bytes free

C:\>_
```

WHAT'S HAPPENING? The display of files, which scrolled by quickly, is still of
the files on Drive A, but you had to specify the drive. Because you keyed in DIR and
a drive letter, A:, you told DOS, "I want a display of the directory (DIR), but this
time I don't want you to display the files on the default drive. I want you to look only
on the ACTIVITIES disk in Drive A." As long as you tell DOS where to look, you
can work with any drive you wish. If you are not specific, DOS always defaults to
the disk drive shown by the prompt on the screen (A:\> or B:\> or C:\>).

Step 5   Key in the following: C:\>**DIR HELLO.TXT** [Enter]

```
C:\>DIR HELLO.TXT

 Volume in drive C has no label
 Volume Serial Number is 1CD1-5E42
 Directory of C:\

File not found

C:\>_
```

Step 6   Key in the following: C:\>**DIR A:HELLO.TXT** [Enter]

```
C:\>DIR A:HELLO.TXT

 Volume in drive A is ACTIVITIES
 Volume Serial Number is 12CA-1D58
 Directory of A:\

HELLO    TXT           52 11-23-95  10:44a
         1 file(s)           52 bytes
                        20,992 bytes free

C:\>_
```

WHAT'S HAPPENING? In Step 5, you asked DIR to look on the default drive for a file called HELLO.TXT. The default drive is Drive C. The prompt displayed on the screen, C:\>, is the default drive. Since you did not specify which drive to check for the file called HELLO.TXT, DIR assumed the default drive. DIR could not find the HELLO.TXT file on the default drive, so it responded with File not found. DOS is not smart enough to say, "Oh, this file is not on the default drive. Let me go check the ACTIVITIES disk in a different disk drive." DOS followed your instructions exactly.

In Step 6, you were specific. You made the same request: "Look for a file called HELLO.TXT." However, first of all, you told DIR what disk drive to look into—A:HELLO.TXT. The drive designator (A:) preceded the file name (HELLO.TXT) because you always tell DIR which "file cabinet" to look in (the disk drive) before you tell it which "folder" you want (HELLO.TXT). By looking at the syntax diagram, you can see that you can combine optional variable parameters. You gave DIR [*drive:*][*path*][*filename*] [/P] [/W] some specific values—DIR A:HELLO.TXT. The A: was substituted for the [*drive:*] and HELLO.TXT was substituted for [*filename*]. So far, you have used the optional variable parameters [*drive:*] and [*filename*] and the optional fixed parameters [/P] and [/W]. You have not used [*path*].

3.11 A Brief Introduction to Subdirectories—the Path

Subdirectories are used primarily but not exclusively with hard disks. Hard disks have a large capacity (from 10 MB to over 520 MB), and are therefore more difficult to manage than floppy disks. In general, users like to have similar files grouped together. Subdirectories allow a disk to be divided into smaller, more manageable portions.

Subdirectories can be used on floppy disks. If you think of a disk as a file cabinet, a subdirectory can be thought of as a drawer in the file cabinet. These file cabinet drawers (subdirectories) also hold disk files. Just as disk drives have a name, such as A: or B: or C:, subdirectories must also have names so DOS will know where to look. Since subdirectories are part of a disk, their names cannot be a single letter of the alphabet. Single letters of the alphabet are reserved for disk drives. Every disk comes with one directory that is named for you by DOS. This directory is called the root directory and is indicated by the backslash (\). The prompt displays the default directory as well as the default drive, as in A:\> or C:\>. Technically, there is only one directory on any disk—the root directory, referred to only as \. All others are subdirectories. All subdirectories on a disk have names. They are text names such as UTILITY or SAMPLE or any other name you choose (see Figure 3.1). However, people are sloppy with language and use the terms directories and subdirectories interchangeably. This textbook will also use the terms directory and subdirectory interchangeably.

When working with files on a disk, you need to perform certain tasks that can be summarized as finding a file, storing a file, and retrieving a file. Because there are subdirectories on a disk, simply telling DOS the drive that the file might be on is insufficient information. You must also tell DOS the **path** to the file. The path is the route followed by DOS to locate, save, and retrieve a file. Thus, in a syntax diagram, the path refers to the course leading from the root directory of a drive to a specific file. Simplistically, when you see path in a syntax diagram, you substitute the directory name or names. In essence, you are being very specific by telling DOS not to go just to the file cabinet (the disk) but to go to a drawer (subdirectory) in the file cabinet.

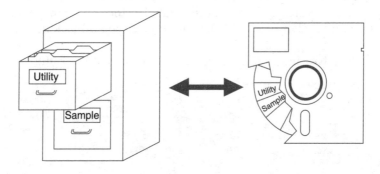

Figure 3.1   **File Cabinets and Subdirectories**

3.12 Activity: Using Path with the DIR Command

Note: The ACTIVITIES disk is in Drive A. The C:\> is displayed as the default drive and the default directory.

Step 1   Key in the following: C:\>**DIR A:** Enter

```
    FILE2      SWT             18 12-06-94   10:46a
    FILE3      CZG             18 12-06-94   10:46a
    FILE3      FP              18 12-06-94   10:46a
    FILE3      SWT             18 12-06-94   10:47a
    FILE4      FP              18 12-06-94   10:47a
    GETYN      COM             26 05-02-94   12:57a
    DATA            <DIR>         05-07-94    1:51p
    JAN        TMP             72 11-23-95   10:41a
    FEB        TMP             74 11-23-95   10:41a
    MAR        TMP             70 11-23-95   10:42a
    APR        TMP             71 11-23-95   10:42a
    LEFT       RED             53 05-07-94   11:05a
    MIDDLE     RED             66 05-07-94   11:05a
    RIGHT      RED             63 05-07-94   11:05a
    DRESS      UP              25 05-07-94   11:06a
    MIDDLE     UP              28 05-07-94   11:06a
    RIGHT      UP              25 05-07-94   11:06a
    TEST       TXT             64 03-14-93   11:07a
    EMPLOYEE   ONE             52 05-07-94    9:00a
    EMPLOYEE   THR             53 05-07-94    9:00a
    EMPLOYEE   TWO             53 05-07-94    9:00a
            106 file(s)         47,038 bytes
                                20,992 bytes free

    C:\>
```

WHAT'S HAPPENING? On the screen display there is one entry, DATA with <DIR> following its name. The <DIR> indicates that this is a subdirectory. How do you know what files are inside this subdirectory? Look at the syntax diagram: DIR [*drive:*][*path*][*filename*] [/P] [/W]. You will substitute the specific drive letter for [*drive:*] and substitute the specific subdirectory name for [*path*]. You include the \ to indicate that you want to begin at the top and look down.

Step 2   Key in the following: C:\>**DIR A:\DATA** Enter

```
C:\>DIR A:\DATA

   Volume in drive A is ACTIVITIES
   Volume Serial Number is 12CA-1D58
   Directory of A:\DATA
```

```
   .            <DIR>          05-07-94   1:51p
   ..           <DIR>          05-07-94   1:51p
BONJOUR   TXT             25 03-14-93   10:59a
GOOD      TXT             32 03-14-93   10:59a
HIGHEST   TXT             31 03-14-93   10:59a
MOTHER    LET            218 03-14-93   10:59a
TEA       TAX             51 03-14-93   10:59a
THANK     YOU            250 03-14-93   10:59a
THIN      EST             82 03-14-93   10:59a
        9 file(s)              689 bytes
                          20,992 bytes free

C:\>_
```

WHAT'S HAPPENING? You keyed in the command you wanted to execute, the drive letter you were interested in, the backslash to indicate that you wanted to start at the root directory, and finally the name of the subdirectory. The first backslash always indicates the root directory. The screen display shows you only what files are in the subdirectory (file drawer) called DATA. The third line of the display (Directory of A:\DATA) tells you the subdirectory you are looking in. What if you wanted to look for a specific file in a subdirectory? Once again, look at the syntax diagram: DIR [*drive:*][*path*][*filename*] [/P] [/W]. You will substitute the drive letter, the path name, and the file name you wish to see. You need a delimiter to separate the file name from the directory name. The delimiter that is reserved for path names is the backslash. It separates the path name from the file name so that DIR knows which is which. Remember that the first backslash always represents the root directory and any subsequent backslashes are delimiters separating file names from directory names.

Step 3   Key in the following: C:\>**DIR A:\DATA\THIN.EST** [Enter]

```
C:\>DIR A:\DATA\THIN.EST

 Volume in drive A is ACTIVITIES
 Volume Serial Number is 12CA-1D58
 Directory of A:\DATA

THIN      EST             82 03-14-93   10:59a
        1 file(s)               82 bytes
                          20,992 bytes free

C:\>_
```

WHAT'S HAPPENING? You keyed in the command you wanted to execute, the drive letter you were interested in, the first backslash indicating the root directory, the name of the subdirectory, then a backslash used as a delimiter, and finally the name of the file. The screen display shows you only the file called THIN.EST located on the ACTIVITIES disk in the subdirectory DATA.

3.13 Changing Defaults

Since you generally work on a specific drive, instead of keying in the drive letter every time, you can override or change the default drive so that DOS automatically uses the drive displayed on the screen as the default drive.

In addition, if your hard disk has been set up with subdirectories, which is usually the case, refer to your Configuration Table in Chapter 2.8, or consult your instructor to see where the DOS system utility files are located. If the DOS files are in a subdirectory other than the one called DOS, you will have to know the name of that subdirectory, and you will have to issue another command at this point to locate the DOS system utility files. With C:\> as the default drive, the command could be CD \BIN or CD \SYSTEM\DOS or CD \BIN\DOS. The actual name or subdirectory where the DOS system utility files are located is machine-specific, such as:

```
        DOS     <DIR>          11-23-94       1:03p
or
        BIN     <DIR>          11-23-94       1:03p
```

Once you have changed directories to the DOS subdirectory, the prompt displayed on your screen could look different from the textbook prompt. It could look like C:\BIN\DOS> or [P:\DOS] or [J:\DOS] depending on the setup of your hard disk or your network. In this text C:\DOS> will indicate the DOS subdirectory. The DOS subdirectory is another way of referring to the directory that holds the DOS system utility files. When you issue the command CD \DOS, you are changing the default directory so that you will be where the DOS system utility files are located. If your system is set up differently, you will need to substitute the proper path name for \DOS. If you have not filled out the information on your Configuration Table in Chapter 2.8, you may wish to do so at this time.

3.14 Activity: Changing the Default Drive

Note: The ACTIVITIES disk is in Drive A. The C:\> is displayed as the default drive and the default directory.

Step 1   Key in the following: C:\>**A:** **Enter**

```
A:\>_
```

WHAT'S HAPPENING? By keying in a letter followed by a colon, you are telling DOS that you want to change your work area to that designated drive. Thus, when you keyed in A:, you changed the work area from the hard disk, Drive C, to the floppy disk in Drive A. You have now made A: the default drive. The assumption DOS will make is that all files and work will come from the disk in Drive A. It will not look at the hard disk, Drive C, unless you specifically tell it to.

Step 2   Key in the following: A:\>**DIR** **Enter**

```
    FILE2      SWT              18 12-06-94   10:46a
    FILE3      CZG              18 12-06-94   10:46a
    FILE3      FP               18 12-06-94   10:46a
    FILE3      SWT              18 12-06-94   10:47a
    FILE4      FP               18 12-06-94   10:47a
    GETYN      COM              26 05-02-94   12:57a
    DATA           <DIR>           05-07-94    1:51p
    JAN        TMP              72 11-23-95   10:41a
    FEB        TMP              74 11-23-95   10:41a
    MAR        TMP              70 11-23-95   10:42a
    APR        TMP              71 11-23-95   10:42a
    LEFT       RED              53 05-07-94   11:05a
    MIDDLE     RED              66 05-07-94   11:05a
    RIGHT      RED              63 05-07-94   11:05a
    DRESS      UP               25 05-07-94   11:06a
    MIDDLE     UP               28 05-07-94   11:06a
    RIGHT      UP               25 05-07-94   11:06a
    TEST       TXT              64 03-14-93   11:07a
    EMPLOYEE ONE                52 05-07-94    9:00a
    EMPLOYEE THR                53 05-07-94    9:00a
    EMPLOYEE TWO                53 05-07-94    9:00a
           106 file(s)            47,038 bytes
                                  20,992 bytes free

A:\>_
```

WHAT'S HAPPENING? DIR does not display the directory of the hard disk. It displays the directory of the ACTIVITIES disk in Drive A. You have changed the assumption or default, and, since you did not specify which drive you wanted, DOS "defaulted" to the displayed prompt and showed the directory of the ACTIVITIES disk. Since the default is now A:\>, if you wish to locate any information on any other disk, you must specify the parameters and include the letter of the drive, and the subdirectory, if necessary, where the file is located.

Step 3   Key in the following: A:\>**DIR DISKCOPY.COM** Enter

```
A:\>DIR DISKCOPY.COM

  Volume in drive A is ACTIVITIES
  Volume Serial Number is 12CA-1D58
  Directory of A:\

File not found

A:\>_
```

WHAT'S HAPPENING? Because the default is the drive with the ACTIVITIES disk, DIR looked for this file only on the ACTIVITIES disk in Drive A. You must be aware of where you are (what the default drive and subdirectory are) and where your files are located.

Step 4   Key in the following: A:\>**DIR C:\DISKCOPY.COM** Enter

```
A:\>DIR C:\DISKCOPY.COM

 Volume in drive C has no label
 Volume Serial Number is 1CD1-5E42
 Directory of C:\

File not found

A:\>_
```

WHAT'S HAPPENING? Although you did tell DIR to look on Drive C, you were not specific enough. DIR looked only in the root directory of C and could not find the file of interest.

Step 5   Key in the following: A:\>**DIR C:\DOS\DISKCOPY.COM** Enter

Note: Substitute the drive and/or subdirectory that contains the DOS system utility files if it is different from this example. If the \DOS subdirectory was called \BIN and located on Drive P, the above command would be keyed in as:

A:\>**DIR P:\BIN\DISKCOPY.COM**

```
A:\>DIR C:\DOS\DISKCOPY.COM

 Volume in drive C has no label
 Volume Serial Number is 1CD1-5E42
 Directory of C:\DOS

DISKCOPY COM          13,335 05-31-94    6:22a
        1 file(s)            13,335 bytes
                        82,345,984 bytes free

A:\>_
```

WHAT'S HAPPENING? In this case, because you specified the drive and subdirectory as well as the file name, DIR knew where to look and located the file. You asked DIR not only to look on Drive C but more specifically to look on Drive C in the subdirectory called \DOS for the file called DISKCOPY.COM.

3.15 Changing Directories

In addition to changing drives, you can also change directories. When you work on a hard disk, it is usually divided into subdirectories. Thus, once you establish your default drive, you can also establish your default directory. Then, instead of keying in the path name every time, you can change the default directory so that DOS will use the directory displayed on the screen as the default directory. To change directories, you key in the command CD followed by the directory (path) name. The partial syntax is:

    CD [*path*]

If you key in CD with no parameters, it tells you the directory that is currently the default. If you wish to change the default, you follow CD with a path name such as CD \DOS.

3.16 Activity: Changing Directories

Note: The ACTIVITIES disk is in Drive A. The A:\> is displayed as the default drive and the default directory.

Step 1   Key in the following: A:\>**C:** **Enter**

Step 2   Key in the following: C:\>**CD** **Enter**

```
C:\>CD
C:\

C:\>_
```

WHAT'S HAPPENING? When you keyed in CD, the display showed you C:\ telling you that your current default drive is C and the current default directory is the root or \. In the last activity, when you wanted to locate the file called DISKCOPY.COM, you had to precede it with the path name \DOS\DISKCOPY.COM. If you change the directory to the DOS directory, the only place that DIR will look for that file is in the current default directory.

Step 3   Key in the following: C:\>**CD \DOS** **Enter**

```
C:\>CD \DOS

C:\DOS>_
```

WHAT'S HAPPENING? You have changed directories so that DOS is now the default directory. Notice how the prompt displays both the default drive and directory. Remember, in this case, DOS is the name of the directory where the DOS system utility files are kept. Whenever you execute any command, the command will look only in the current directory for the file of interest.

Step 4   Key in the following: C:\DOS>**DIR DISKCOPY.COM** [Enter]

```
C:\DOS>DIR DISKCOPY.COM

 Volume in drive C has no label
 Volume Serial Number is 1CD1-5E42
 Directory of C:\DOS

DISKCOPY COM          13,335 05-31-94    6:22a
        1 file(s)            13,335 bytes
                        82,345,984 bytes free

C:\DOS>_
```

WHAT'S HAPPENING? The command DIR looked only in the DOS directory and located the file called DISKCOPY.COM. Look at the line that states Directory of C:\DOS. DIR always tells you where it is looking. This works with any directory.

Step 5   Key in the following: C:\DOS>**CD ** [Enter]

```
C:\DOS>CD \

C:\>_
```

WHAT'S HAPPENING? Whenever you key in CD \, it always takes you to the root directory of the drive you are on.

Step 6   Key in the following: C:\>**A:** [Enter]

Step 7   Key in the following: A:\>**DIR DATA\THIN.EST** [Enter]

```
C:\>A:

A:\>DIR DATA\THIN.EST

 Volume in drive A is ACTIVITIES
 Volume Serial Number is 12CA-1D58
 Directory of A:\DATA

THIN     EST             82 03-14-93  10:59a
        1 file(s)              82 bytes
                        20,992 bytes free

A:\>_
```

WHAT'S HAPPENING? You used two steps. First, you changed the default drive to A. Then, you looked for the file called THIN.EST. Since it is located in the DATA directory, you had to precede the file name with the path name (DATA). You did not need to include the first backslash because your default directory was already the root of A. If you are going to use files in this directory only, you would tire of always keying in the path name DATA. In addition, you must remember to include the delimiter after DATA and before THIN.EST to separate the path name from the file name. Remember the rule of thumb—the first backslash always means the root directory and any other backslash is a delimiter. To eliminate this concern, you can change the default directory to DATA.

Step 8   Key in the following: A:\>**CD DATA** [Enter]

Step 9   Key in the following: A:\DATA>**DIR THIN.EST** [Enter]

```
A:\>CD DATA

A:\DATA>DIR THIN.EST

 Volume in drive A is ACTIVITIES
 Volume Serial Number is 12CA-1D58
 Directory of A:\DATA

THIN     EST          82 03-14-93  10:59a
         1 file(s)             82 bytes
                          40,448 bytes free

A:\DATA>_
```

WHAT'S HAPPENING? This time, since you changed the directory to DATA, you did not have to precede the file name with the path name of DATA. The DIR command looked only in the DATA subdirectory for the file called THIN.EST. The prompt, A:\DATA> showed you where DIR would look unless you specified otherwise. The line in the display, Directory of A:\DATA, confirmed where you were looking.

Step 10   Key in the following: A:\DATA>**CD ** [Enter]

```
A:\DATA>CD \

A:\>_
```

WHAT'S HAPPENING? You have now returned to the root directory of Drive A.

3.17 Global File Specifications: Wildcards, the ? and the *

Using the DIR command and a file specification, you can find one specific file that matches what you keyed in. Every time you wish to locate a file, you can key in the entire file specification. Often, however, you wish to work with a group of files that have similar names or a group of files whose names you do not know. DOS has a "shorthand" system that allows you to operate on a group of files rather than a single file. This system is formally called **global file specifications**; informally, it is called using **wildcards**. Conceptually, they are similar to playing cards, where the joker can stand for another card of your choice. In DOS the question mark (?) and the asterisk (*) are the wildcards. These symbols stand for unknowns. The * represents or substitutes for a group of characters; the ? represents or substitutes for a single character. Many commands allow you to use global file specifications. You will use the DIR command to demonstrate the use of wildcards.

3.18 Activity: DIR and Wildcards

Note: The ACTIVITIES disk is in Drive A. The A:\> is displayed as the default drive and the default directory.

Step 1   Key in the following: A:\>**C:** ⌷**Enter**⌷

Step 2   Key in the following: C:\>**CD \DOS** ⌷**Enter**⌷

Note: Remember that, if the DOS system utility files are in a subdirectory with a different name, you will have to substitute your subdirectory name for \DOS, i.e., CD \BIN.

WHAT'S HAPPENING? You have changed the default directory to where the DOS system utility files are located. If you wanted to locate a file and all you remembered about the file name was that it began with the letter F and that it was located on the default drive and subdirectory, you would not be able to find that file. You have insufficient information.

Step 3   Key in the following: C:\DOS>**DIR F** ⌷**Enter**⌷

```
C:\DOS>DIR F

 Volume in drive C has no label
 Volume Serial Number is 1CD1-5E42
 Directory of C:\DOS


File not found

C:\DOS>_
```

WHAT'S HAPPENING? First, note how the prompt reflects the subdirectory \DOS and shows C:\DOS>. When you keyed in DIR F, you were correct, but only somewhat. You first entered the work you wanted done or the command DIR. You did not need to enter the drive letter. DIR assumed both the default drive and default subdirectory. However, DIR specifically looked for a file called F. There was no file called F; that was simply the first letter of the file name. You could find out what files you have that begin with F by using the wildcard symbol * to represent all other characters—the file name and the file extension.

Step 4   Key in the following: C:\DOS>**DIR F*.*** [Enter]

```
C:\DOS>DIR F*.*

 Volume in drive C has no label
 Volume Serial Number is 1CD1-5E42
 Directory of C:\DOS

FDISK      EXE        29,336 05-31-94    6:22a
FORMAT     COM        22,974 05-31-94    6:22a
FASTHELP   EXE        11,481 05-31-94    6:22a
FASTOPEN   EXE        12,082 05-31-94    6:22a
FC         EXE        18,650 05-31-94    6:22a
FIND       EXE         6,770 05-31-94    6:22a
         6 file(s)         101,293 bytes
                       82,345,984 bytes free

C:\DOS>
```

WHAT'S HAPPENING? The files in the DOS subdirectory vary with the DOS version, so do not worry if your screen display is different.

In this example, you asked DIR what files that begin with the letter F were located on the disk in the default drive and default subdirectory. You did not know anything else about the file names or even how many files you might have that began with the letter F. You represented any and all characters following the letter F with the asterisk, separated the file name from the file extension with a period, and represented all the characters in the file extension with the second asterisk. Thus, F*.* (read as "F, star dot star") means all the files that start with the letter F can have any or no characters following the letter F, and can have any or no file extension. Now, DIR could look for a match. Although you might have keyed in a lowercase f, DIR returns uppercase F because all file names are stored in uppercase letters.

In this example, the first file DIR found that had the F you specified was FDISK.EXE. DOS could display this file because the * following the F matched DISK. Remember, the * represents any group of letters. The second * representing the file extension matched .EXE because, again, the * represents any group of characters. The second file DIR found that had the F you specified was FORMAT.COM. DIR could display this file because the * following the F matched ORMAT. Remember, the * represents any group of letters. The second * representing the file extension matched .COM because, again, the * represents any group of characters. The rest of the files match F*.* for the same reasons. You could have more or fewer files depending on how your system is set up.

There are other ways of requesting information using the *. Let us say that all you know about a group of files on the disk in the default drive is that the group has the common file extension .SYS. You could display these files on the screen using wildcards.

Step 5   Key in the following: C:\DOS>**DIR** *.**SYS** [Enter]

```
C:\DOS>DIR *.SYS

 Volume in drive C has no label
 Volume Serial Number is 1B93-9D8B
 Directory of C:\DOS

COUNTRY   SYS        26,936 05-31-94    6:22a
KEYBOARD  SYS        34,598 05-31-94    6:22a
EGA       SYS         4,885 03-10-93    6:00a
KEYBRD2   SYS        31,942 05-31-94    6:22a
ANSI      SYS         9,065 05-31-94    6:22a
CHKSTATE  SYS        41,600 05-31-94    6:22a
PRINTER   SYS        18,804 05-11-92    5:00a
DBLSPACE  SYS        22,502 09-30-93    6:20a
DISPLAY   SYS        15,789 05-31-94    6:22a
SMARTDRV  SYS         8,335 05-11-92    5:00a
DRVSPACE  SYS        22,996 05-31-94    6:22a
DRIVER    SYS         5,406 05-31-94    6:22a
HIMEM     SYS        29,136 05-31-94    6:22a
RAMDRIVE  SYS         5,873 05-31-94    6:22a
        14 file(s)         277,867 bytes
                        82,345,984 bytes free

C:\DOS>_
```

WHAT'S HAPPENING? The * represented any file name, but all the files must have .SYS as a file extension. Again, the number of files displayed may vary, depending on what is in the DOS subdirectory. The next activities will demonstrate the differences between the * and the ?.

Step 6   Key in the following: C:\DOS>**DIR** A:*.**TXT** [Enter]

```
C:\DOS>DIR A:\*.TXT

 Volume in drive A is ACTIVITIES
 Volume Serial Number is 12CA-1D58
 Directory of A:\
```

```
    GOODBYE    TXT           32 11-23-94    7:07a
    DANCES     TXT           70 08-08-95    5:34p
    JANUARY    TXT           72 11-23-95   10:41a
    FEBRUARY   TXT           74 11-23-95   10:41a
    MARCH      TXT           70 11-23-95   10:42a
    APRIL      TXT           71 11-23-95   10:42a
    HELLO      TXT           52 11-23-95   10:44a
    BYE        TXT           44 11-23-95   10:45a
    TEST       TXT           64 03-14-93   11:07a
           9 file(s)             549 bytes
                            20,992 bytes free


C:\DOS>_
```

WHAT'S HAPPENING? You asked DIR what files had an extension of .TXT and
were located on the ACTIVITIES disk. You did not know anything about the file
names, only the file extension. DIR searched the table of contents in Drive A since
you placed an A: prior to the *.TXT. It looked only in the root directory of the disk
since you preceded the *.TXT with the \. The command found nine files that
matched *.TXT. Now, how does the question mark differ from the asterisk?

Step 7   Key in the following: C:\DOS>**DIR A:\?????.TXT** ⎣Enter⎦

```
C:\DOS>DIR  A:\?????.TXT

   Volume in drive A is ACTIVITIES
   Volume Serial Number is 12CA-1D58
   Directory of A:\

    MARCH      TXT           70 11-23-95   10:42a
    APRIL      TXT           71 11-23-95   10:42a
    HELLO      TXT           52 11-23-95   10:44a
    BYE        TXT           44 11-23-95   10:45a
    TEST       TXT           64 03-14-93   11:07a
           5 file(s)             301 bytes
                            20,992 bytes free


C:\DOS>_
```

WHAT'S HAPPENING? This time you asked your question differently. You still
asked for any file that had the file extension of .TXT in the root directory of the
ACTIVITIES disk . However, instead of "any number of characters," you used the ?
five times. For DIR, this means look for any file name that starts with any letter
and that has a file name no longer than five characters. It can be fewer than five
characters but no more than five. Thus, the ????? represented five characters. You
then separated the file name from the file extension with a period saying any file
extension that had .TXT was fine. This time only five files matched your request.
Note how the above screen display differs from the screen display in Step 6. This

time you do not see the files called GOODBYE.TXT, DANCES.TXT., JANUARY.TXT, or FEBRUARY.TXT displayed on the screen. Those file names were longer than five characters. However, files such as TEST.TXT and BYE.TXT were displayed even though they did not have five-character file names, because their names had less than five. Remember, ????? means five characters *or fewer*. Try this.

Step 8   Key in the following: C:\DOS>**DIR A:\????.TXT** [Enter]

```
C:\DOS>DIR A:\????.TXT

 Volume in drive A is ACTIVITIES
 Volume Serial Number is 12CA-1D58
 Directory of A:\

BYE        TXT            44 11-23-95  10:45a
TEST       TXT            64 03-14-93  11:07a
       2 file(s)            108 bytes
                        20,992 bytes free

C:\DOS>_
```

WHAT'S HAPPENING? This time you asked DIR for any file name that used four characters or fewer in length, that had a file extension .TXT, and that was located on the ACTIVITIES disk in Drive A in the root directory. You separated the file name and file extension with a period. Note the differences in the screen displays. Using ????.TXT displayed two files that met the specification. The * is most commonly used. In fact, ????????.??? is the same as *.*. However, there are occasions when the ? is extremely useful.

Step 9   Key in the following: C:\DOS>**DIR A:\EXP*.*** [Enter]

```
C:\DOS>DIR A:\EXP*.*

 Volume in drive A is ACTIVITIES
 Volume Serial Number is 12CA-1D58
 Directory of A:\

EXP94JAN DAT           302 11-23-94   7:01a
EXP94FEB DAT           305 11-23-94   7:01a
EXP94MAR DAT           300 11-23-94   7:02a
EXP93JAN DAT           292 11-23-93   7:00a
EXP93FEB DAT           293 11-23-93   7:01a
EXP93MAR DAT           292 11-23-93   7:02a
EXP95JAN DAT           302 11-23-94   7:03a
```

```
EXP95FEB DAT              305 11-23-94     7:03a
EXP95MAR DAT              300 11-23-94     7:05a
        9 file(s)            2,691 bytes
                           20,992 bytes free


C:\DOS>_
```

WHAT'S HAPPENING? This time you asked DOS to show you all the files (DIR) located on the ACTIVITIES disk (Drive A) in the root directory (\ ) that start with the letters EXP, and that's all you know (EXP*.*). The *.* following the EXP represents the rest of the file name and the file extension. Here are some budget files. EXP means expenses, followed by the year (93, 94, or 95), followed by the month (JANuary, FEBruary, or MARch). The file extension is .DAT, to indicate these are data files, not program files. However, often you are not interested in all the files. You want only some of them. For example, you might want to know what expense files you have on the ACTIVITIES disk for the year 1993.

Step 10   Key in the following: C:\DOS>**DIR A:\EXP93*.*** **[Enter]**

```
C:\DOS>DIR A:\EXP93*.*


 Volume in drive A is ACTIVITIES
 Volume Serial Number is 12CA-1D58
 Directory of A:\

 EXP93JAN DAT             292 11-23-93     7:00a
 EXP93FEB DAT             293 11-23-93     7:01a
 EXP93MAR DAT             292 11-23-93     7:02a
         3 file(s)             877 bytes
                           40,448 bytes free


C:\DOS>_
```

WHAT'S HAPPENING? Here you asked for all the files (DIR) on the ACTIVITIES disk in Drive A in the root directory that were expense files for 1993 (EXP93). The rest of the file names were represented by *.*. On your screen display you got only the 1993 files. However, suppose your interest is in all the files for all the months of January. You no longer care which year, only which month.

Step 11   Key in the following: C:\DOS>**DIR A:\EXP*JAN.*** **[Enter]**

```
C:\DOS>DIR A:\EXP*JAN.*


 Volume in drive A is ACTIVITIES
 Volume Serial Number is 12CA-1D58
 Directory of A:\
```

```
    EXP94JAN DAT              302 11-23-94    7:01a
    EXP94FEB DAT              305 11-23-94    7:01a
    EXP94MAR DAT              300 11-23-94    7:02a
    EXP93JAN DAT              292 11-23-93    7:00a
    EXP93FEB DAT              293 11-23-93    7:01a
    EXP93MAR DAT              292 11-23-93    7:02a
    EXP95JAN DAT              302 11-23-94    7:03a
    EXP95FEB DAT              305 11-23-94    7:03a
    EXP95MAR DAT              300 11-23-94    7:05a
            9 file(s)           2,691 bytes
                           20,992 bytes free

C:\DOS>_
```

WHAT'S HAPPENING? This display is not quite what you wanted. It looks exactly like the display following Step 9 when you asked for DIR A:\EXP*.*. Why did DIR display all the files? The reason is that when you state your request as DIR A:\EXP*JAN.*, everything in the file name segment after the first * is ignored. Hence, the DIR command picked up all the files with EXP and ignored your specific JAN. Now, the question mark becomes useful.

Step 12   Key in the following: C:\DOS>**DIR A:\EXP??JAN.*** Enter

```
C:\DOS>DIR A:\EXP??JAN.*

 Volume in drive A is ACTIVITIES
 Volume Serial Number is 12CA-1D58
 Directory of A:\

EXP94JAN DAT              302 11-23-94    7:01a
EXP93JAN DAT              292 11-23-93    7:00a
EXP95JAN DAT              302 11-23-94    7:03a
        3 file(s)            896 bytes
                       20,992 bytes free

C:\DOS>_
```

WHAT'S HAPPENING? This time the ? was critical. It acted as a place holder. You asked for a file name that specifically started with EXP and ended with JAN. The middle two characters, represented by ??, could be any two characters, but they must be alphanumeric. The 93, 94, and 95 matched ?? because any character could have been there as long as there was something in that place in the file name.

Step 13   Key in the following: C:\DOS>**CD ** Enter

```
C:\DOS>CD\

C:\>_
```

WHAT'S HAPPENING? You have returned to the root directory of C.

Step 14: Key in the following: C:\>A: **[Enter]**

```
A:\>_
```

WHAT'S HAPPENING? Your default drive is A and the default directory is the root of A.

3.19 Redirection

DOS knows what you want to do because you key in commands. DOS always looks to the keyboard for input. The keyboard is considered the standard input device. In addition, after DOS executes a command, it knows to write the output to the screen. The screen is considered the standard output device.

DOS has a feature called **redirection**. Redirection allows you to tell DOS, instead of writing the output to the standard output device (the screen), to write the information somewhere else. Typically, this is to a file or to a printer. Redirection does not work with all DOS commands, but it does work with the DIR command since DIR gets its input from the standard input device, the keyboard, and writes to the standard output device, the screen. The syntax is *command > destination*. The command is what you key in such as DIR *.TXT. Then, you use the greater than symbol > to tell DOS to write to where you specify, instead of to the screen. A space is required on both sides of the > sign. The command would be keyed in as DIR *.TXT > MY.FIL if you want the output to be sent to a file you name. The command would be keyed in as DIR *.TXT > LPT1 if you wanted the output to go the printer. You must use the DOS reserved name for the printer, PRN or LPT1.

3.20 Activity: Redirecting Output to a File

Note: The ACTIVITIES disk is in Drive A. The A:\> is displayed as the default drive and the default directory.

Step 1   Key in the following: A:\>**DIR** *.NEW **[Enter]**

```
A:\>DIR *.NEW

 Volume in drive A is ACTIVITIES
 Volume Serial Number is 12CA-1D58
 Directory of A:\

JAN       NEW           71 01-23-93  11:48a
FEB       NEW           73 01-23-93  11:48a
```

```
     MAR      NEW             69 01-23-93  11:49a
     APR      NEW             70 01-23-93  11:49a
              4 file(s)             283 bytes
                           20,992 bytes free


     A:\>_
```

WHAT'S HAPPENING? You asked for all the files on the ACTIVITIES disk that have the file extension of .NEW. You saw the output displayed on the screen. You have four files that meet the criteria. You keyed in a command and the results were sent to the screen. See Figure 3.2.

INPUT

OUTPUT from DIR command displays on screen

```
A:\> DIR *.NEW

Volume in drive A is ACTIVITIES
Volume Serial Number is 12CA-1D58
Directory of A:\

JAN      NEW         71 01-23-93   11:48a
FEB      NEW         73 01-23-93   11:48a
MAR      NEW         69 01-23-93   11:49a
APR      NEW         70 01-23-93   11:49a
         4 Files(s)         283 bytes
                         20,992 bytes free
```

Figure 3.2   *Standard Input/Output*

Step 2:   Key in the following: A:\>**DIR *.NEW > MY.HW** [Enter]

```
A:\>DIR *.NEW > MY.HW


A:\>_
```

WHAT'S HAPPENING? This time you instructed DOS to send the output to a file called MY.HW, instead of sending the output to the screen. Note that redirection is an "instead of" procedure. You either have the results of the DIR command displayed on the screen, *or* you send it to a file. See Figure 3.3.

STANDARD INPUT

STANDARD OUTPUT
from DIR expects to
display on the screen

A:\> DIR *.NEW > MY.HW

A:\>

STANDARD OUTPUT
from DIR is redirected
to disk

MY.HW

Figure 3.3   ***Redirecting Output to a File***

Step 3:   Key in the following: A:\>**DIR MY.HW** [Enter]

```
A:\>DIR MY.HW


 Volume in drive A is ACTIVITIES
 Volume Serial Number is 12CA-1D58
 Directory of A:\

MY        HW              359 06-19-94  11:43a
         1 file(s)               359 bytes
                          20,480 bytes free


A:\>_
```

WHAT'S HAPPENING? You now have a file that has the contents of the DIR command.

3.21 Redirecting Output to the Printer

You have seen that you can redirect output to a file. You can also redirect output to the printer. Since the DIR command normally writes to the screen, you can redirect the output of the DIR command to the printer to get a printout of what normally would be written to the screen. However, you cannot use any name, as you did with the file. DOS has very specific names for its devices. You already know that a letter of the alphabet followed by a colon (:) is always a disk drive. Printers have names also. The printer device names are PRN, LPT1, or LPT2. Usually PRN and LPT1 are synonymous.

Before doing the next activity, check with your lab instructor to see if there are any special printing procedures in your lab. Sometimes, for instance, a network environment will not let you use the device name PRN. You must use the alternate name LPT1. Be sure to use the number one, not the lowercase L. Often, in a network environment, there is a shared printer, and you *cannot* redirect the output to the printer in the manner described.

3.22 *Activity: Redirecting the Output to the Printer*

Note 1:   **DO NOT DO** this activity until you have checked with your lab instructor for any special instructions. In fact, you may be unable to do the activity. If you cannot do it, read the activity.

Note 2:   The ACTIVITIES disk is in Drive A. The A:\> is displayed as the default drive and the default directory.

Note 3:   Be sure the printer is turned on and online before beginning this activity.

Step 1   Key in the following: A:\>**DIR** *.TXT [Enter]

```
A:\>DIR *.TXT

  Volume in drive A is ACTIVITIES
  Volume Serial Number is 12CA-1D58
  Directory of A:\

  GOODBYE   TXT           32 11-23-94    7:07a
  DANCES    TXT           70 08-08-95    5:34p
  JANUARY   TXT           72 11-23-95   10:41a
  FEBRUARY  TXT           74 11-23-95   10:41a
  MARCH     TXT           70 11-23-95   10:42a
  APRIL     TXT           71 11-23-95   10:42a
  HELLO     TXT           52 11-23-95   10:44a
  BYE       TXT           44 11-23-95   10:45a
  TEST      TXT           64 03-14-93   11:07a
          9 file(s)            549 bytes
                          20,480 bytes free

A:\>_
```

WHAT'S HAPPENING? You asked for all the files on the ACTIVITIES disk that had the file extension of .TXT.

Step 2   Key in the following: A:\>**DIR** *.TXT > **PRN** [Enter]

WHAT'S HAPPENING? You instructed DOS to send the output to an output device, specifically the printer, instead of displaying the output on the screen. The printer should be printing, and nothing should be on the screen. Redirection is an "instead of" procedure. You either have the results of the DIR command displayed on the screen, *or* you send it to the printer. See Figure 3.4.

STANDARD INPUT

STANDARD OUTPUT
from DIR expects to
display on the screen

```
A:\> DIR *.TXT > PRN
A:\>
```

STANDARD OUTPUT
from DIR is redirected
to the printer

Volume in Drive A is ACTIVITIES
Volume Serial Number is 12CA-1D58
Directory of A:\

Figure 3.4   *Redirected Output*

WHAT'S HAPPENING? If you have a dot-matrix printer, it printed the lines in the file and then it stopped. The printer did not advance to the beginning of a new page. If you wanted this printout (hard copy), you would have to go to the printer and roll the platen until the perforated line appeared so that you could tear off the page. If you have an ink jet printer or a laser printer, the situation is even stranger. No paper appears at all. In order to feed the paper manually with an ink jet printer, you would have to press the Reset button. With a laser printer, you would have to go the printer, turn the Online button off and the press the form feed (FF) button and then turn the Online button back on. In all these cases, you are doing what is called a hardware solution to a problem. You are manipulating the hardware to get the desired results.

With computers, there is always an easier way. What you want is a software solution, making the computer do the work. The problem in printing a page is that a computer has no idea what a page is or when it is finished printing. Thus, you want to send a signal to the printer that the page is over. You want the printer to eject the page that is printed and have the paper advance to a clean, empty sheet. This signal is known as a form feed, a page eject, or top of form. Most printers universally use the Ctrl+L as the signal for a form feed. The problem is how to send this signal from the computer to the printer. Again, you will use redirection and a command called ECHO. ECHO is an internal command that you have not used before. ECHO has the capability of sending a signal to the printer if you tell it to. Remember, when you see the notation of [Ctrl] + L, it means to hold down the [Ctrl] key and press the letter L. Many networks automatically send a form feed to the shared printer after each print job. If this is so in your lab, do not do Step 3.

Step 3   Key in the following: A:\>**ECHO** [Ctrl] + **L** > **PRN** [Enter]

```
A:\>DIR *.TXT > PRN

A:\>ECHO ^L > PRN

A:\>
```

WHAT'S HAPPENING? The paper should eject. Look at the screen. What you keyed in—[Ctrl] + L—appeared on the screen as ^L. Thus, the signal to the printer meant one thing, but the signal to the screen was something else. If this procedure did not work for you, you will need to roll the paper manually on a dot-matrix printer. For an ink jet printer, press the Reset or Clear button. For a laser printer, take the following steps:

❑   Turn the Online button off.

❑   Press the form feed (FF) button.

❑   Turn the Online button back on.

3.23 Getting Help

As you begin to use DOS commands, their name, purpose, and proper syntax become familiar. Initially, however, these commands are new to users. Prior to DOS 5.0, the only way to become familiar with a command or to check the proper syntax was to locate the command in the manual. The reference manual that comes with DOS or with any software package is called **documentation**. The completeness of the documentation can vary from software package to software package. The documentation that comes with DOS consists of at least the installation instructions and a command reference manual, which is a list of commands with a brief description and syntax for each. In DOS 6.0 and above, the documentation has become a users' manual that has getting started instructions, but does not list all the commands. With DOS 5.0 and above, a new feature was introduced called **online help**. Rather than going to the documentation, you can request immediate help. In DOS 6.0 and above, there are four ways to get online help.

1.   Key in HELP. On the screen will appear an alphabetic list of commands from which you can choose more details about each. When you select a specific

command, you are taken to another help screen that defines the command, provides the command syntax, and supplies notes and examples.

2. Key in HELP *command*. You can use this if you already know the name of the command. For instance, if you wanted help with DIR, you would key in HELP DIR. You then would be taken directly to the screen that provides the definition, syntax, notes, and examples.

3. Key in FASTHELP. FASTHELP is a streamlined version of help that provides an alphabetic list of all the commands with a definition for each. In DOS 5.0 FASTHELP is HELP.

4. Key in *command* /?. You use this procedure when you know the name of the command. For instance, if you key in DIR /?, you would get only the definition and syntax for DIR. This process is identical in DOS 5.0.

3.24 *Activity: Using HELP*

Note 1: The ACTIVITIES disk is in Drive A. The A:\> is displayed as the default drive and the default directory.

Note 2: HELP is one of the few places in DOS where a mouse can be used to click on choices and scroll through information.

Step 1 Key in the following: A:\>**C:** [Enter]

Step 2 Key in the following: C:\>**CD \DOS** [Enter]

```
A:\>C:

C:\>CD \DOS

C:\DOS>_
```

WHAT'S HAPPENING? You have made the DOS directory on the hard disk the default drive and directory.

Step 3 Key in the following: C:\DOS>**HELP** [Enter]

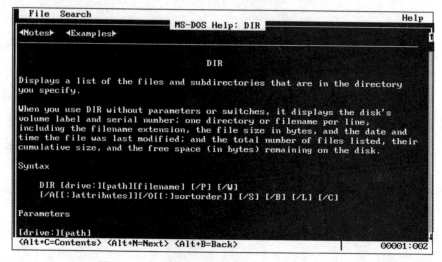

```
┌─────────────────────────────────────────────────────────────────────────┐
│  File   Search                                                      Help  │
│                   MS-DOS Help: Command Reference                          │
│ Use the scroll bars to see more commands. Or, press the PAGE DOWN key. For│
│ more information about using MS-DOS Help, choose How to Use MS-DOS Help    │
│ from the Help menu, or press F1. To exit MS-DOS Help, press ALT, F, X.    │
│                                                                           │
│ <What's New in MS-DOS 6.22?>                                              │
│                                                                           │
│ <ANSI.SYS>              <EMM386.EXE>              <Multi-config>          │
│ <Append>                <Erase>                   <Nlsfunc>               │
│ <Attrib>                <Exit>                    <Numlock>               │
│ <Batch commands>        <Expand>                  <Path>                  │
│ <Break>                 <Fasthelp>                <Pause>                 │
│ <Buffers>               <Fastopen>                <Power>                 │
│ <Call>                  <Fc>                      <POWER.EXE>             │
│ <Cd>                    <Fcbs>                    <Print>                 │
│ <Chcp>                  <Fdisk>                   <Prompt>                │
│ <Chdir>                 <Files>                   <Qbasic>               │
│ <Chkdsk>                <Find>                    <RAMDRIVE.SYS>         │
│ <CHKSTATE.SYS>          <For>                     <Rd>                    │
│ <Choice>                <Format>                  <Rem>                   │
│ <Cls>                   <Goto>                    <Ren>                   │
│ <Command>               <Graphics>                <Rename>               │
│ <Alt+C=Contents> <Alt+N=Next> <Alt+B=Back>              00006:002         │
└─────────────────────────────────────────────────────────────────────────┘
```

WHAT'S HAPPENING? An alphabetical list of DOS commands is displayed on
the screen.

Step 4   Locate <DIR> on the screen by pressing the ⬇ arrow key. When the
cursor is under the <DIR>, press **Enter**. If you have a mouse, you can
click on <DIR>.

```
┌─────────────────────────────────────────────────────────────────────────┐
│  File   Search                                                      Help  │
│ ◄Notes►  ◄Examples►        MS-DOS Help: DIR                               │
│                                                                           │
│                                                                           │
│                               DIR                                         │
│ Displays a list of the files and subdirectories that are in the directory │
│ you specify.                                                              │
│                                                                           │
│ When you use DIR without parameters or switches, it displays the disk's   │
│ volume label and serial number; one directory or filename per line,       │
│ including the filename extension, the file size in bytes, and the date and │
│ time the file was last modified; and the total number of files listed, their│
│ cumulative size, and the free space (in bytes) remaining on the disk.     │
│                                                                           │
│ Syntax                                                                    │
│                                                                           │
│     DIR [drive:][path][filename] [/P] [/W]                                │
│     [/A[[:]attributes]][/O[[:]sortorder]] [/S] [/B] [/L] [/C]             │
│                                                                           │
│ Parameters                                                                │
│                                                                           │
│ [drive:][path]                                                            │
│ <Alt+C=Contents> <Alt+N=Next> <Alt+B=Back>              00001:002         │
└─────────────────────────────────────────────────────────────────────────┘
```

Step 5   Press the ⬇ arrow key to scroll or move through the text of the syntax.

WHAT'S HAPPENING? This online display is quite elaborate. You are looking at
the purpose of the DIR command as well as the syntax. You can use the ⬇ arrow
key and ⬆ arrow key to move around in the text. If you have a mouse, you can use
it to scroll in the text. You have other choices on the menu bar. The <Notes> choice

gives you further information, and the <Examples> choice gives you different examples of how a command is used. You can use the **Tab** key to move among the three choices: <Syntax>, <Notes> or <Examples>. Only two choices are displayed on the menu bar at one time. If you are in the body of the text, you can press the **Ctrl** + **Home** keys to return to the menu bar to make another selection. If you have a mouse, you can click on any of the menu bar choices.

Step 6   Press the **Ctrl** + **Home** keys.

Step 7   Press the **Tab** key so that the cursor is under <Examples>. Press **Enter**

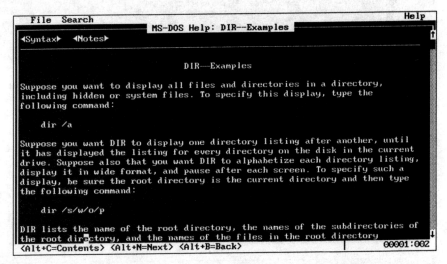

WHAT'S HAPPENING? Now you are looking at examples of how to use the DIR command. You want to exit Help. You tell the program that you want to exit by accessing the menu and choosing Exit.

Step 8   Press **Alt** + **F**

Step 9   Press **X**

```
C:\DOS>_
```

WHAT'S HAPPENING? Pressing **Alt** + F dropped down the File menu. Pressing X selected Exit, and you returned to the prompt. To make the exit process easy, Steps 8 and 9 can be combined into pressing **Alt** + F + X. You left Help and returned to the default prompt.

Step 10   Key in the following: C:\DOS>**HELP DIR** **Enter**

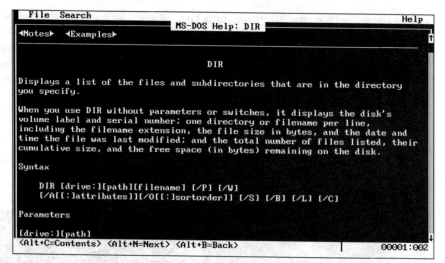

WHAT'S HAPPENING? You are taken directly to the help screen for the DIR command. You want to exit Help.

Step 11 Press **Alt** + **F**. Press **X**.

```
C:\DOS>_
```

WHAT'S HAPPENING? You have exited Help and returned to the default prompt. Sometimes, you would like a list of the commands and what they do.

Step 12 Key in the following: C:\DOS>**FASTHELP** **Enter**

```
          C:\DOS>FASTHELP

For more information on a specific command, type FASTHELP command-name.
APPEND    Allows programs to open data files in specified directories as if
          they were in the current directory.
ATTRIB    Displays or changes file attributes.
BREAK     Sets or clears extended CTRL + C checking.
CD        Displays the name of or changes the current directory.
CHCP      Displays or sets the active code page number.
CHDIR     Displays the name of or changes the current directory.
CHKDSK    Checks a disk and displays a status report.
CLS       Clears the screen.
COMMAND   Starts a new instance of the MS-DOS command interpreter.
COMP      Compares the contents of two files or sets of files.
COPY      Copies one or more files to another location.
CTTY      Changes the terminal device used to control your system.
DATE      Displays or sets the date.
DBLSPACE  Sets up or configures DoubleSpace compressed drives.
DEBUG     Starts Debug, a program testing and editing tool.
DEFRAG    Reorganizes the files on a disk to optimize the disk.
DEL       Deletes one or more files.
```

```
DELOLDOS Deletes the OLD_DOS.1 directory and the files it contains.
DELTREE  Deletes a directory and all the files and subdirectories in it.
DIR      Displays a list of files and subdirectories in a directory.
—More—
```

WHAT'S HAPPENING? Displayed on the screen is an alphabetical list of DOS commands. Locate DELTREE on the screen. You see that it defines the purpose of DELTREE.

Step 13 Press **Enter** until you return to the C:\DOS> prompt.

Step 14 Key in the following: C:\DOS>**DIR /?** **Enter**

```
Displays a list of files and subdirectories in a directory.

DIR [drive:][path][filename] [/P] [/W] [/A[[:]attribs]] [/O[[:]sortord]]
    [/S] [/B] [/L] [/C[H]]

  [drive:][path][filename]   Specifies drive, directory, and/or files to list.
  /P      Pauses after each screenful of information.
  /W      Uses wide list format.
  /A      Displays files with specified attributes.
  attribs  D  Directories   R  Read-only files        H  Hidden files
           S  System files  A  Files ready to archive  -  Prefix meaning "not"
  /O      List by files in sorted order.
  sortord  N  By name (alphabetic)      S  By size (smallest first)
           E  By extension (alphabetic) D  By date & time (earliest first)
           G  Group directories first   -  Prefix to reverse order
           C  By compression ratio (smallest first)
  /S      Displays files in specified directory and all subdirectories.
  /B      Uses bare format (no heading information or summary).
  /L      Uses lowercase.
  /C[H]   Displays file compression ratio; /CH uses host allocation unit size.

Switches may be preset in the DIRCMD environment variable.  Override
preset switches by prefixing any switch with - (hyphen)—for example, /-W.

C:\DOS>_
```

WHAT'S HAPPENING? Any command followed by a /? will also provide help. You can use Help to refresh your memory about a command and its syntax. You are going to try a new parameter, /O for sort order, followed by N for name sort order. You will sort the files in alphabetical order by file name on the ACTIVITIES disk.

Step 15 Key in the following: C:\DOS>**DIR A:/ON** **Enter**

```
    RIGHT    RED           63 05-07-94  11:05a
    RIGHT    UP            25 05-07-94  11:06a
```

```
RNS       EXE            7,269 11-22-89  10:35p
SECOND    FIL               73 11-23-94   7:04a
SPORTS          <DIR>          02-14-94  11:03a
STATE     CAP              260 05-14-94   5:11p
STATE2    CAP              265 04-16-94   5:36p
STATES    USA            1,230 05-03-94  12:17a
STEVEN    FIL               44 11-23-94   7:13a
TEST            <DIR>          05-07-94   1:48p
TEST      TXT               64 03-14-93  11:07a
TEXT      NNN            1,216 04-28-94   2:24p
UNPUT     BAT            1,848 04-24-94  12:07a
WILD1     XXX               63 05-07-93   9:03a
WILD2     YYY               63 05-07-93   9:03a
WILD3     ZZZ               63 05-07-93   9:03a
WILDONE                     92 05-07-93   9:04a
WILDONE   DOS              180 05-07-93   9:02a
WILDTHR   DOS              180 05-07-93   9:03a
WILDTWO   DOS              181 05-07-93   9:03a
Y         FIL                3 05-14-93  11:00a
       107 file(s)           47,397 bytes
                             20,400 bytes free

C:\DOS>_
```

WHAT'S HAPPENING? The files scrolled by quickly, but they were in alphabetical order, from A to Z. You used the / to indicate a parameter, the O for order, and the N for file name order. By using another parameter, you can sort the file names in reverse alphabetical order.

Step 16 Key in the following: C:\DOS>**DIR A:/O-N** [Enter]

```
DRESS     UP                25 05-07-94  11:06a
DATE5     NNN                8 01-24-93  10:58p
DATE4     NNN                9 08-07-92   6:01p
DATE3     NNN                8 02-27-94  12:11p
DATE2     NNN                9 08-07-92   5:50p
DATE1     NNN                9 01-24-93  10:57a
DATA            <DIR>          05-07-94   1:51p
DANCES    TXT               70 08-08-95   5:34p
CURRENT   BAT               17 08-07-92   6:32p
CASES     FIL              315 11-23-94   7:04a
CAROLYN   FIL               45 11-23-94   7:13a
BYE       TYP               43 10-12-94   7:07a
BYE       TXT               44 11-23-95  10:45a
BONJOUR   TMP               51 10-12-94   7:09a
BLUE      JAZ               18 10-12-94  10:40a
AWARD     MOV               41 11-23-93  12:57p
APRIL     TMP               70 01-23-93  11:49a
```

```
   APRIL    TXT           71 11-23-95  10:42a
   APR      NEW           70 01-23-93  11:49a
   APR      99            71 11-23-95  10:42a
   APR      TMP           71 11-23-95  10:42a
         107 file(s)          47,397 bytes
                             20,480 bytes free

C:\DOS>_
```

WHAT'S HAPPENING? Again, the file names scrolled by quickly, but they were in reverse alphabetical order, from Z to A. Thus, by using the parameters /O-N, O for order, the - for reverse, and N for file name, you accomplished your task.

Step 17   Key in the following: C:\DOS>**CD** \ **Enter**

WHAT'S HAPPENING? You have returned to the root directory of the hard disk.

Chapter Summary

1. Command syntax means using the correct command and the proper order for keying in commands.
2. A parameter is some piece of information that you want a command to have. It allows a command to be specific.
3. A delimiter indicates where parts of a command begin or end. It is similar to punctuation marks in English.
4. Some commands require parameters. They are called mandatory parameters. Other commands allow parameters, but these are called optional parameters.
5. A variable parameter is one that requires the user to supply a value. A fixed parameter switch has its value determined by DOS.
6. A syntax diagram is a graphic representation of a command and its syntax.
7. The DIR command is an internal command that displays the directory (table of contents) of a disk.
8. The basic syntax diagram for DIR is:

    ```
    DIR [drive:][path][filename] [/P] [/W]
    ```

9. DIR has five parameters in all versions of DOS: /P to stop the display from scrolling, /W to have a wide display of only file names and extensions, *drive* to specify which drive, *path* to search a specific subdirectory, and *filename* that allows you to search for specific files.
10. The syntax for DIR is:

    ```
    DIR [drive:][path][filename] [/P] [/W] [/A[[:]attributes]]
    [/O[[:]sortorder]] [/S] [/B] [/L]
    ```

11.   You have many more parameters to choose from. One of the newer parameters is O for sort order. You can sort files A to Z or Z to A. Any item you want sorted in reverse order must be preceded by a hyphen.

12.   A file specification has two parts, the file name and the file extension. The file name may be no longer than eight characters. The file extension may be no longer than three characters. A file name is mandatory; however, a file extension is optional. If you use a file extension, separate it from the file name by a period, called a dot.

13.   A valid file name contains legal characters, most often alphanumeric characters. It cannot contain illegal characters.

14.   Every device attached to the computer has a reserved, specific, and unique name so that the operating system knows what it is communicating with. Disk drives are designated by a letter followed by a colon, as in A:. The printer has the device name of PRN, LPT1, or LPT2.

15.   Defaults are implied instructions the operating system falls back to when no specific instructions are given.

16.   A subdirectory allows a disk to be divided into areas that can hold files. Subdirectories are named by the user, except the root directory whose name is \. The subdirectory name is the path name.

17.   The system prompt displayed on the screen is the default drive and directory.

18.   You can change the default drive and default subdirectory.

19.   To change the default drive, you key in the drive letter followed by a colon as in A: or B:.

20.   To change the default subdirectory, you key in CD followed by the subdirectory name such as CD \PROG or CD \DOS.

21.   The subdirectory that contains the DOS system utility files is often called \DOS. It may sometimes be called \BIN or \PROG.

22.   You can look for files on drives and subdirectories other than the default if you tell DOS where to look by prefacing the file names with a drive designator and/or path name.

23.   If the file is in a subdirectory, the file name must be prefaced by the drive designator and followed by the subdirectory name. A user must include the subdirectory name in the command, as in C:\DOS\FILENAME.

24.   Global file specifications (* or ?) or wildcards allow the user to substitute a wildcard for an unknown.

25.   The ? represents one character in a file name; the * matches a group of characters.

26.   The output for a command that normally is displayed on the screen may be redirected to a file. You key in the command and add the redirection symbol (>) and then the file name.

27.   The output for a command that is normally displayed on the screen may be redirected to a printer. You key in the command and add the redirection symbol (>) and then the device name of LPT1 or PRN.

28.   DOS includes a comprehensive online help feature.

29. To use the online help, the user keys in HELP *command-name* or *command-name* /?.
30. The DIR command allows you to sort the directory listing by use of the parameter /O followed by the sort order letter you are interested in. For instance, to sort by name, you would key in DIR /ON.

Key Terms

Command syntax	File	Path
Default	Fixed parameters	Redirection
Default drive	Global file	Subdirectories
Delimiter	specifications	Switch
Designated drive	Logged drive	Syntax
Device names	Online help	Syntax diagram
Documentation	Optional parameters	Variable parameter
Dot	Parameter	Wildcards

Discussion Questions

1. Define command syntax.
2. Why is syntax important when using a commands?
3. Define parameters.
4. What is the difference between a variable and a fixed parameter?
5. How would you use a syntax diagram? Why is the diagram important?
6. The syntax diagram for DIR is

```
DIR [drive:][path][filename] [/P] [/W]
```

Identify each item in this diagram and explain its purpose.

7. Name two parameters that can be used with DIR command. Explain why you would use the parameters.
8. Define delimiters. Give an example of a delimiter.
9. Define file specifications.
10. What is the difference between a file name and a file extension?
11. How do you separate a file name from a file specification?
12. What is the function and purpose of a device?
13. Explain the function and purpose of the default drive.
14. How can you tell which drive is the default drive?
15. Define default subdirectory.
16. How can you tell which directory is the default subdirectory?
17. What does A:\> mean?
18. What steps must be followed to change the default drive? Why would you change the default drive?
19. What steps must be followed to change a directory? Why would you change a directory?

20. What is the significance of the first backslash in a command?
21. Define global file specifications.
22. How are wildcards used?
23. If you see C:\DOS> on the screen, what does it mean?
24. What is the purpose and function of redirection?
25. How would you get online help if you forgot the parameters for the DIR command?

Chapter 4

Disks and Formatting

Learning Objectives

After completing this chapter you will be able to:

1. Explain the need for formatting a disk.
2. Describe the structure of a disk.
3. Name and explain the purpose of each section of a disk.
4. Define formatting.
5. Explain the difference between internal and external commands.
6. List and explain the steps in formatting a floppy disk.
7. Explain the purpose and function of the LABEL command.
8. Explain the purpose and function of the UNFORMAT command.
9. Explain the purpose and function of the /Q and /U parameters used with the FORMAT command.
10. Explain the difference between a bootable and a nonbootable disk.
11. Explain how to format a double-density floppy disk in a high-density floppy disk drive.

Student Outcomes

1. Format a floppy disk.
2. Format a floppy disk with a system and volume label.
3. Use the LABEL command to change the volume label on a disk.
4. View the current volume label using the VOL command.
5. Use the UNFORMAT command to rebuild a disk.
6. Use the /Q and /U parameters to format a disk.
7. Know how to format a double-density floppy disk in a high-density floppy disk drive.

Chapter Overview

Disks are the mainstay of the computer work station. They are used for storing data and programs, for data distribution from one computer to another computer, and for backup purposes, a necessity in these days of power outages and power surges. In order for disks to be used, they must be formatted. Formatting is the process by which an operating system sets up the guidelines so that it may read and write to a disk. In DOS, you use the FORMAT command.

In this chapter you will learn how a disk is structured, how DOS uses disks, and how to format and electronically label a disk. In addition, you will learn how to change the label. Formatting a disk is a dangerous operation because it removes all the data from a disk. Thus, you will learn the UNFORMAT command and when to use it.

4.1 Why Format a Disk?

Each operating system has a unique way of recording information on a disk. One of the factors that make a computer compatible with another is not the brand name such as Apple, IBM, or Compaq but the operating system that each computer uses. Thus, a computer should not be called IBM-compatible but a DOS-based computer. This concept is based almost entirely on which operating system the computer uses and how each operating system prepares its disk so that information can be read from and written to it. The disk manufacturers cannot prepare the disks in advance without knowing what kind of operating system you will use. The process of preparing a disk so that it will be compatible with an operating system is known as **formatting** or **initializing** the disk.

Since this is a DOS textbook, the only kind of formatting that you are interested in is DOS-based. So far, the disks that you have used with this text were already prepared for a DOS-based environment. When you want to prepare a disk for use, you will use a DOS system utility command called FORMAT.

Although you can purchase DOS based pre-formatted disks, the so-called IBM-compatible disks, they are typically more costly. Even if you purchase pre-formatted disks, it is inevitable that you will want to reuse them. Disks that have been used but have information that is no longer needed can be "erased" or reprepared with the FORMAT command. All disks, including hard disks, must be formatted. Hard disks are typically formatted at the time of purchase and are rarely reformatted because formatting eliminates what is on the disk. Although the FORMAT command works for both hard and floppy disks, this text deals only with formatting floppy disks.

4.2 Structure of a Disk

Formatting a disk consists of two parts; **low-level formatting** or **physical formatting** and **high-level formatting** or **logical formatting**. Low-level or physical formatting creates and sequentially numbers tracks and sectors for identification purposes. Tracks are concentric circles on a disk. Each track is then divided into smaller units called sectors. In the DOS-based world a sector which is the smallest unit on a disk is always 512 bytes. The number of tracks and sectors vary depending on the type of disk. When data needs to be written to or read from a disk, the identification number of the tracks and sector tells the read/write head where to position itself. This process accounts for every space on a disk. It is similar to assigning every house on a street a unique address so that it can be instantly identifiable. However, even after a disk is physically prepared to hold data, it still is not ready for use.

The second part of formatting is considered high-level or logical formatting. In logical formatting DOS builds the structure of a disk so it can keep track of where files are located. Formatting a hard disk involves only logical formatting. The low-level formatting of a hard disk is usually done as part of the manufacturing process. Low-level formatting can also be done by the computer system vendor, or you may purchase special software programs to low-level format your hard disk. Most commonly, when you purchase a computer system, the high-level and low-level formatting of the hard disk is done. However, when you format a floppy disk, both the physical and logical formatting processes occur.

Logical formatting determines how DOS uses disks, both hard and floppy. The logical format process builds a way for DOS to manage files on a disk so that files can be easily saved and retrieved. This process is accomplished by the use of the FORMAT command. When you execute the FORMAT command, it first checks for any bad spots on the disk which it marks as unusable; it then creates three critical elements, the boot record, the File Allocation Table, and the root directory. These elements occupy the first portion of the disk and take only about one to two percent of the disk space. The remainder of the disk is used for file storage. See Figure 4.1.

Boot Record

File Allocation Table (FAT)

File Allocation Table (FAT)

Root Directory

Files Area (data sectors)

Figure 4.1   ***Logical Structure of a Disk***

The order of the sections is always the same. The boot record, two copies of the FAT, and the root directory table are always located in the first sectors. These elements control how the files are stored on a disk and how DOS saves and retrieves files. The data sectors are where the data or files are actually stored.

Boot Record

The boot record is a very short program on the first part of a disk. This program begins the process of loading DOS from the disk into memory. Loading means that the necessary files are copied from the disk into memory. It does this by looking for a file called IO.SYS on the disk. If it finds it, it turns control over to that file, which continues to load itself and the other necessary files (MSDOS.SYS and COMMAND.COM). If you have certain versions of DOS 6, a file called DBLSPACE.BIN or DRVSPACE.BIN is also loaded.

Starting a computer is called booting the system because the system pulls itself up by its bootstraps. If the disk is not an operating system disk (**bootable disk**) with the appropriate files, the boot record cannot load the operating system into memory. This program is smart enough to tell you so by displaying the following message:

```
Non-system disk or disk error
Replace and press any key when ready
```

If it is a bootable disk only. Although every disk has a boot record, it must also have the operating system files on it (IO.SYS, MSDOS.SYS, and COMMAND.COM) to boot the system. Furthermore, the boot record contains information about the physical characteristics of a disk—the number of bytes per sector, sectors per track and so forth. The boot record also includes which version of DOS was used to format the disk, the size of the FAT, the size of the root directory, and the volume serial number. From the boot record DOS can identify disks by type, a hard disk, a 720 KB disk, etc.

File Allocation Table (FAT)

DOS needs a way to keep track of the status of all the data sectors on a disk so it can answer critical questions—does a sector already have information in it and thus cannot be used or is it a damaged sector and cannot be used, or is it empty and available for data storage? Since a disk, particularly a hard disk, can have so many sectors, managing them a sector at a time would be too time consuming and unwieldy. DOS, therefore, combines one or more sectors into logical units called clusters. When DOS writes a file to a disk, it copies the contents of the file to unused clusters. The smallest unit that DOS actually works with (reading or writing to disk) is a cluster, also called an **allocation unit** because it allocates space on a disk.

To be able to read and write files to a disk, DOS tracks the location in the **File Allocation Table** (FAT). The FAT is a map of the data section and is made up of entries that correspond to every cluster on a disk. The number of clusters varies from one type of disk to another. Table 4.1 indicates cluster size for common disk types.

Disk	Cluster Size
3½-inch 2.88 MB disk	2 sectors make a cluster (1024 bytes)
3½-inch 1.44 MB disk	1 sector makes a cluster (512 bytes)
3½-inch 720 KB disk	2 sectors make a cluster (1024 bytes)
5¼-inch 1.2 MB disk	1 sector makes a cluster (512 bytes)
5¼-inch 360 KB disk	2 sectors make a cluster (1024 bytes)
Hard disk (size varies)	4 sectors make a cluster (2048 bytes)
	8 sectors make a cluster (4096 bytes)
	16 sectors make a cluster (8192 bytes)

Table 4.1   ***Common Cluster Size***

Since the smallest unit DOS deals with is a cluster, if you want to save a file that is only 100 bytes long on a 3½-inch 1.44 MB disk, the file will actually occupy 512 bytes on the disk. Furthermore, as you can imagine, a data file is hardly ever exactly one cluster in size nor would it necessarily be an even number. Thus, to manage the data, each entry in the FAT is a number that indicates the status of the cluster. A 0 (zero) in the FAT means the cluster is empty and available for use. Other specific numbers indicate that a cluster is reserved (do not use) or bad (do not use). Any other number indicates that a cluster is in use.

In order for DOS to follow the trail of a data file that is longer than one cluster, the number in the FAT is a pointer to the next cluster that holds data in that file. That entry becomes a pointer to the next cluster that holds data in the same file. A special entry in the FAT indicates that no more data is in the file. Thus, the numbers in the FAT are used to link or chain clusters that belong to the same file. The FAT works in conjunction with the root directory table. Since the FAT is used to control the entire disk, two copies of the FAT are kept on the disk in case one is damaged. The FAT occupies as many sectors as it needs to map out the disk.

Root Directory

Next on the disk is the root directory. The root directory is a table that records information about each file on the disk. When you key in DIR, the information that is displayed on the screen comes from this root directory table. The root directory stores information in a table about every file on a disk and includes the file name, the file extension, the size of the file in bytes, the date and time the file was last modified, and the file attributes. A file can be flagged with the attributes: (1) read-only, which means the file normally cannot be erased; (2) hidden status, which means that a file will not be displayed when you issue the DIR command; (3) system status, which typically marks the file as the system files, such as IO.SYS; (4) volume label; (5) subdirectory name, if needed; (6) archive status, which indicates that the file was modified since it was last backed up. In addition to these attributes, the starting cluster number indicates which cluster holds the first portion of the file, or the first FAT address. The DOS root directory does not say where a specific file is located on a disk; instead, it points to an entry in the FAT. Thus, the root directory table keeps track of what the files are, and the FAT keeps track of where the files are located.

Data Portion or Files Area

The rest of the disk, and its largest part, is used for storing the files or data. As far as DOS is concerned, all files, programs, and data are just chains of bytes laid out in sequence. Space is allocated to files on an as-needed basis, one cluster at a time. When a file is written to a disk, DOS begins writing to the first available cluster. It writes in adjacent or **contiguous** clusters if possible, but, if adjacent sectors are already in use (allocated by the FAT), DOS skips to the next available space (unallocated). Thus, a file can be **noncontiguous**, that is, physically scattered over a disk.

How the FAT and the Root Directory Table Interact

To illustrate how the root directory table and the FAT work, imagine you want to create a file called MYFILE.TXT that will occupy three clusters on a disk. Let us say that clusters 3, 4 and 6 are free. DOS first creates an entry in the root directory table and fills in the file information (file name, file extension, date, time, etc.). DOS then places in the first free cluster the number 3 as the starting cluster number in the root directory table. DOS knows it will need three clusters and it must link or chain them. It does this by placing a 4 (a pointer) in the number 3 cluster pointing to the next available cluster. When it gets to cluster 4, it places a 6 (another pointer) pointing to the next available cluster. The FAT continues to cluster 6. When it gets to cluster 6, it places an end of file marker, a "note," indicating that the file ends here.

To make an analogy, imagine a self-storage facility comprised of storage bins that hold things (data). The front office that manages the self-storage facility does not care what is in the bins. The front office only has to know how many bins there are, where they are located, and if anything is in them. The front office has a map of all its numbered storage bins (FAT). The bins are numbered so that the front office knows where the bins are located. The front office also needs a list (directory) of all the people who have rented bins. Thus, I walk in and say I want the boxes stored for Gillay. The front office first looks up Gillay in the list to be sure they have stored my boxes. In this case, they find the name Gillay, so they know I have rented at least one bin. Besides my name, the directory list points to another list that says to go to the map (FAT), starting with bin 3. The front office goes to the map (FAT) and sees that storage bin 3 is linked to storage bin 4, which is linked to storage bin 6. Storage bin 6 has no links. Now the front office knows that Gillay has bins 3, 4, and 6 full of boxes. The front office can send someone (rotate the disk) to bins 3, 4, and 6 to retrieve the boxes. To look at this process graphically, see Figure 4.2.

| Directory | File Allocation Table | Data Sectors |

Figure 4.2   ***Storing Files***

This analogy gives you some of the basic information you need in order to understand the structure of a disk.

4.3 *Formatting a Disk*

When a disk has already been formatted, formatting that disk again simply erases the record of the files from the root directory and the FAT. The data in the files is still on the disk because the low-level format was not performed. This is called a safe format because, since the data is still on the disk, it can be unformatted and the data recovered. However, the data can be recovered only if you immediately discover you have formatted the wrong disk. The moment you begin to write data to the disk the old data is overwritten and irrevocably lost. Thus, when you format a previously used disk, you must know positively that you do not want the data on the disk. The data is still on the disk, but, when you format it, the root directory entries and FAT chains are gone, leaving no map to locate the data. You cannot count on **unformatting** a disk to recover data if you have a version of DOS less than 5.0 where there was no UNFORMAT command.

The rule is to be cautious when using the FORMAT command. Since FORMAT can be used on any disk, including hard disks, be especially careful because, when you format a disk, everything on the disk, even a hard disk, will be gone—programs and data. In this text, you will be formatting only floppy disks. If you are working in a computer laboratory, please familiarize yourself with the proper laboratory procedures so that a computer tragedy does not occur.

4.4 Clarifying Procedures

1. DOS subdirectory. You will boot off Drive C. You should then get the C:\>. If the prompt is C>, key in the following: PROMPT pg. You will also have to change your directory so that you are in the subdirectory that has the DOS system utility files. If your DOS system utility files are in the DOS subdirectories, key in CD \DOS, and your prompt should then read C:\DOS>. Remember to refer to your Configuration Table in Chapter 2.8 to ensure that all substitutions have been made before you begin this activity.
2. A blank or new disk. Whenever a new or blank disk is referred to, you may use a brand-new disk or an old disk with information on it. However, it is assumed that if there is information on the disk, you no longer want it, because it will be written over in the format process.
3. If you are in a lab environment, you need to check with your instructor to see what the procedures are in your lab. For instance, in some networked environments, you cannot format a floppy disk in Drive A.

4.5 Activity: Formatting a Floppy Disk

WARNING: Never format an application disk or a disk that has data you wish to keep. Also, if you have a hard disk, you must be *exceedingly* careful. *Never, never* key in C:\>FORMAT or C:\>FORMAT C:. If you do, you will *completely* erase, forever, all the information on the hard disk.

Step 1   Boot the system, if it is not already booted.

Step 2   Key in the following: C:\>**CD \DOS** [Enter]

```
C:\>CD \DOS

C:\DOS>_
```

WHAT'S HAPPENING? You have changed the default to directory to the \DOS subdirectory. The prompt should display C:\DOS>.

To format a disk, you use the FORMAT command. FORMAT is another example of a system utility program, also called an external command, stored as a file in the DOS subdirectory. The default drive and subdirectory in this situation become a very important. Whenever you key in a command, you are telling the operating system to look for a file that matches what you keyed in.

Remember that the prompt on the screen represents the default drive and subdirectory. When the operating system looks for an external command, it will only look on the default drive (in this case, drive C) and in the default subdirectory (in this case, \DOS) for the command or file name that you keyed in. You can tell DOS to look or do something on a different disk drive or different subdirectory, but you must specify that disk drive and/or subdirectory. In this case, you are looking for the command FORMAT. You can see whether or not this command, which is stored as a file called FORMAT.COM, is located on the disk in the default drive and in the default subdirectory.

Step 3   Key in the following: C:\DOS>**DIR FORMAT.COM** Enter

```
C:\DOS>DIR FORMAT.COM

 Volume in drive C has no label
 Volume Serial Number is 1CD1-5E42
 Directory of C:\DOS

FORMAT    COM         22,974 05-31-94    6:22a
        1 file(s)          22,974 bytes
                      82,345,984 bytes free

C:\DOS>_
```

WHAT'S HAPPENING? The screen display tells you that the FORMAT command, stored as the file named FORMAT.COM, is located on the default drive, Drive C. In addition, since your DOS system utility files are in a subdirectory, you will not only be on Drive C but also in a subdirectory called \DOS. To use, (execute, or run) the FORMAT program, you key in the name of the command.

Step 4   Key in the following (be sure to include the drive letter):

C:\DOS>**FORMAT A:** Enter

```
C:\DOS>FORMAT A:
Insert new diskette for drive A:
and press ENTER when ready...
```

WHAT'S HAPPENING? In Step 3 you used the DIR command to locate the file. You called the program by keying in the name of the file. When you do that, you are instructing DOS to find the file called FORMAT.COM and load it into memory. FORMAT is the command that tells the system what work you want it to do. The A: tells the system that the disk you want to format is in Drive A. If you did not specify a lettered drive, A:, B:, or C:, you would receive a message that you were missing a parameter—the drive letter. In earlier versions of DOS, the FORMAT command would not ask for a drive letter and would format the default drive. Since the default drive is C and C is the hard disk, FORMAT would have erased everything on the hard disk. You *never* want this to happen. Never!

   In addition, you are getting a message or prompt that tells you what to do. Before you get involved in the following activity, it is exceedingly important that you know what kind of disk drive you have so that you can choose the correct disk with the correct format. If you are not sure, refer to your Configuration Table in Chapter 2.8. Once you have identified the type of floppy disk drive that is on your system, the following table tells you what type of floppy disk to use. If you do not use the specified floppy disk, you will have problems.

Floppy Disk Drive Type	Blank Floppy Disk to Use
5¼-inch 360 KB double-density drive	5¼-inch 360 KB double-density disk
5¼-inch 1.2 MB high-density drive	5¼-inch 1.2 MB high-density disk
3½-inch 720 KB double-density drive	3½-inch 720 KB double-density disk
3½-inch 1.44 MB high-density drive	3½-inch 1.44 MB high-density disk

Table 4.2   *Matching Floppy Drives to Floppy Disks*

Get a blank disk out and prepare a label for it. Write your name and the words DATA DISK on the label. Place the label on the disk. Insert the disk into Drive A. Be sure that this disk is blank. Everything on it will be eliminated after you press **Enter**.

Step 5   Press **Enter**

```
C:\DOS>FORMAT A:
Insert new diskette for drive A:
and press ENTER when ready...

Checking existing disk format.
Formatting 1.2M
17 percent of disk formatted
```

WHAT'S HAPPENING? The light on the floppy disk drive is glowing, indicating that activity is taking place on the disk you are formatting. The FORMAT displays what media type it is formatting. The Formatting 1.2M that appears in the above screen display will vary depending on the type of floppy disk you are formatting. If you are formatting a previously used disk or a preformatted disk, you will get the following additional message:

```
Checking existing disk format.
Saving UNFORMAT information
Formatting 1.2M
17 percent of disk formatted
```

The message Saving UNFORMAT information protects you. If you want to unformat the disk, DOS will save a picture of the disk as it used to be. The message nn percent of disk being formatted tells you that DOS is formatting the disk. The nn represents a number that changes as the disk is formatted, until it reaches 100 percent. If you have an earlier version of DOS, the messages will vary. Do not do anything until you see the following message displayed on the screen.

```
C:\DOS>FORMAT A:
Insert new diskette for drive A:
and press ENTER when ready...

Checking existing disk format.
Formatting 1.2M
Format complete.

Volume label (11 characters, ENTER for none)?_
```

WHAT'S HAPPENING? DOS automatically ask for a volume label. However, you are not going to place a volume label on the disk at this time.

Step 6   Press `Enter`

```
Format complete.

Volume label (11 characters, ENTER for none)?

   1,213,952 bytes total disk space
   1,213,952 bytes available on disk

        512 bytes in each allocation unit.
      2,371 allocation units available on disk.

Volume Serial Number is 1024-11FA

Format another (Y/N)?
```

Step 7   Press N. Press `Enter`

```
C:\DOS>_
```

WHAT'S HAPPENING? You have completed formatting your disk. The command called FORMAT was executed. You formatted the disk in Drive A. The bytes available will vary depending on what your disk capacity is. You also receive a status report that tells you how many spots were bad on the disk (if any). In addition, it tells you the allocation units on the disk. In this case, the allocation unit—the cluster— is 512 bytes so that you know that one sector on a 5¼-inch high-density disk is a cluster. If you multiplied the size of the allocation unit by the number of allocations units available, you would come up with the number of available bytes (512 * 2,371 = 1,213,952 bytes). DOS can now read and write to this disk because it has set up the tracks and sectors, boot record, FAT, root directory, and data section as needed.

Step 8   Key in the following: C:\DOS>**CD** \ [Enter]

```
C:\DOS>CD \

C:\>_
```

WHAT'S HAPPENING? You have returned to the root directory. The root directory of any disk is always \. When you have completed a task or are ending a work session, it is always wise to return to the root directory. Then, when you want to begin your next task, you have a "clean slate" so to speak; you will begin at the beginning

4.6   Formatting a Disk with a Volume Label

You can use parameters other than the disk drive letter that with the FORMAT command. The FORMAT command has many parameters, some of which are used much more than others. The syntax for the FORMAT command is:

```
FORMAT drive: [/V[:label]] [/Q] [/U] [/F:size] [/B | /S] [/C]
FORMAT drive: [/V[:label]] [/Q] [/U] [/T:tracks /N:sectors] [/B | /S] [/C]
FORMAT drive: [/V[:label]] [/Q] [/U] [/1] [/4] [/B | /S] [/C]
FORMAT drive: [/Q] [/U] [/1] [/4] [/8] [/B | /S] [/C]
```

```
/V[:label]        Specifies the volume label.
/Q                Performs a quick format.
/U                Performs an unconditional format.
/F:size           Specifies the size of the floppy disk to format
                  such as 160, 180, 320, 360, 720, 1.2, 1.44, 2.88).
/B                Allocates space on the formatted disk for system files.
/S                Copies system files to the formatted disk.
/T:tracks         Specifies the number of tracks per disk side.
/N:sectors        Specifies the number of sectors per track.
/1                Formats a single side of a floppy disk.
/4                Formats a 5¼ 360K floppy disk in a high-density drive.
/8                Formats eight sectors per track.
/C                Tests clusters that are currently marked "bad."
```

Although this syntax diagram may look intimidating, it really is not. In this list of syntax possibilities, DOS begins with the most current version of the syntax.

```
FORMAT drive: [/V[:label]] [/Q] [/U] [/F:size] [/B | /S] [/C]
```

These are the ones that are important to remember. The other versions of the syntax show parameters that still work but have been superseded. Beginning with DOS version 3.3, the *drive:* or drive letter is mandatory. It *must* be included. This mandatory drive letter prohibits you from accidentally formatting the disk in the default drive.

The /V allows you to place a volume label on a disk but, as you have already seen, the FORMAT command asks you for a volume label whether or not you include the /V. The /Q performs a quick format, but a quick format can be used only on a disk that has been previously formatted. It is "quick" because it simply deletes the entries from the FAT and the root directory and essentially leaves the file area untouched.

The /U is an "unconditional" format that not only zeroes out the entries in the FAT and root directory, but also overwrites the entire file area with dummy data. When you use the /U parameter, the disk can *never* be unformatted.

The /F:*size* parameter is an easy way to format floppy disks that do not match the capacity of a floppy disk drive. For instance, if you have a high-density disk drive but wish to format a 360 KB disk, you would inform the FORMAT command using /F:360. However, /F:size does not solve all your mismatching problems. If you have a 360 KB disk drive, you cannot format a high-density 1.2 MB floppy disk in that drive. The 360 KB disk drive is older technology and does not recognize the new high-density media type. Do not format a floppy disk at a size higher than it was designed for. This means, for example, if you have a 360 KB disk, do not format it as a 1.2 MB disk. Table 4.3 shows the valid numbers that can be used.

Disk Capacity	Number to Use with /F:
160 KB	160
180 KB	180
320 KB	320
720 KB	720
1.2 MB	1.2
1.44 MB	1.44
2.88 MB	2.88

Table 4.3   *Valid Disk Sizes*

Notice the [/B | /S]. Both /B and /S are fixed parameters, but they are in one bracket separated by a vertical bar. Whenever you see a [|], it means you have an either/or choice. You can either choose to use /B, or you can choose to use /S but not both. The /B parameter allows room on a floppy disk for the operating system files, if you wish to add them at a later date. In the early days of DOS, these files could only be in the first tracks and sectors of a disk, but today that is no longer necessary.

The /S is a very important parameter because it makes a disk bootable. When you use the /S parameter, you are instructing the FORMAT command not only to prepare the disk for use but also to copy the operating system files to the disk. Including this parameter is the only way these files can be copied and the only way to make a disk bootable. The hard disk is bootable because it was originally formatted with the /S parameter. The /S parameter is the only way to make a floppy disk bootable.

The last parameter in the syntax diagram is the most recent addition to the FORMAT command. Prior to this version, FORMAT always retested the bad clusters. Now, you must include the /C parameter if you wish the bad clusters to be retested.

In the next activity, you are going to use the /V parameter to place a volume label on the disk you are formatting. A **volume label** is an electronic name. It is very much like labeling a file drawer so you know what it contains. The switch is /V, which tells the FORMAT command that it is to format a disk and place an electronic volume label on it. Whenever you format a disk, in recent versions of DOS, it automatically asks you for a volume label, even if you do not include /V.

4.7   Activity: Using the VOL Command

Note: Your default directory is the root of C and the C:\ > displayed. The disk just formatted is in Drive A.

Step 1   Key in the following: C:\>**CD \DOS** Enter

```
C:\>CD \DOS

C:\DOS>_
```

WHAT'S HAPPENING? You made \DOS the default subdirectory.

Step 2   Key in the following: C:\DOS>**FORMAT A:/V** Enter

```
C:\DOS>FORMAT A:/V
Insert new diskette for drive A:
and press ENTER when ready...
```

WHAT'S HAPPENING? The FORMAT command was loaded from disk into memory. Since this disk was previously formatted, the FORMAT command does a safe format. It does not delete the data in the files area but instead zeroes out the FAT and the root directory table. It also scans the disk for any bad surfaces that might have appeared since the last time you formatted the disk.

Step 3   You should have the DATA disk in Drive A. Press Enter

```
Checking existing disk format.
Saving UNFORMAT information.
Verifying 1.2M
```

WHAT'S HAPPENING? You have begun the process of formatting the DATA disk. As you can see, FORMAT saves information so that it can later unformat, if you so desire. Do not do anything until you see the following message:

```
Format complete.

Volume label (11 characters, ENTER for none)?_
```

WHAT'S HAPPENING? Even if you did not include the /V parameter, later versions of DOS will ask you for a volume label anyway. The first portion, Volume label, may not look like a question, but it is. The question is "Do you want to place a volume label on this disk?" If you answer yes, your volume label cannot exceed 11 characters (11 characters). If you do not want a volume label, you press **Enter** (Enter for none). In this case, you do want a volume label.

Step 4   Key in the following after the question mark: **SAMPLE DATA** **Enter**

```
Volume label (11 characters, ENTER for none)? SAMPLE DATA

    1,213,952 bytes total disk space
    1,213,952 bytes available on disk

        512 bytes in each allocation unit.
      2,371 allocation units available on disk.

Volume Serial Number is 3829-11FC

Format another (Y/N)?_
```

Step 5   Key in the following: **N** **Enter**

WHAT'S HAPPENING? Since you do not want to format another disk, you pressed N for no. A volume label is the only place in DOS where you are allowed to use spaces as characters as you did in SAMPLE<space>DATA. You named your disk SAMPLE DATA because on this disk you are going to store samples. Whenever you use a volume label, make it as meaningful as possible so that you do not have to look at all the files on the disk to know what is on the disk. Examples of meaningful names (volume labels) could include DOS6 System to indicate that the disk is a bootable floppy disk or INCOMETAXES for a disk that contains your income tax data. There are two ways to see your volume label.

Step 6   Key in the following: C:\DOS>**DIR A:** **Enter**

```
C:\DOS>DIR A:

 Volume in drive A is SAMPLE DATA
 Volume Serial Number is 3829-11FC
 Directory of A:\

File not found

C:\DOS>_
```

WHAT'S HAPPENING? You can see displayed the label you entered, SAMPLE DATA. The internal command, VOL, lets you look at the volume label on any disk or check to see if there is a label. By using this command, you can quickly see what is on a disk without having to execute the directory command. The syntax is:

```
VOL [d:]
```

Step 7   Key in the following: C:\DOS>**VOL** [Enter]

```
C:\DOS>VOL

 Volume in drive C has no label
 Volume Serial Number is 1CD1-5E42

C:\DOS>_
```

WHAT'S HAPPENING? The volume label on your hard disk may well be different depending on whether a volume label was entered when the hard disk was formatted. In this example, no volume label was placed on the hard disk so you see the message Volume in drive C has no label. When you used the VOL command, DOS looked only on Drive C, the default drive. To look at the volume label on Drive A, you must specifically request that DOS look on Drive A by giving VOL another parameter, the variable parameter [d:] where d: represents the drive letter.

Step 8   Key in the following: C:\DOS>**VOL A:** [Enter]

```
C:\DOS>VOL A:

 Volume in drive A is SAMPLE DATA
 Volume Serial Number is 3829-11FC

C:\DOS>_
```

WHAT'S HAPPENING? Since you placed a volume label on the DATA disk, you can see it with the VOL command. If a volume label is meaningful, it clearly identifies what files are on the disk.

4.8   The LABEL Command

It would be very inconvenient if every time you wanted to change the volume label on a disk, you had to reformat the disk. Not only is this fatal to your data, but it takes time to format disks. In version 3.3, the LABEL command was introduced. It is an external command that lets you ⚘ change the volume label without reformatting the disk. Remember, VOL, an internal command, lets you see the volume label, but LABEL lets you change the volume label. Bracketed items are always optional. The syntax is:

```
LABEL [drive:][label]
```

4.9   Activity: Using the LABEL Command

Note: Your default directory is the \DOS subdirectory on Drive C, and you have the C:\DOS> displayed. The disk just formatted is in Drive A.

Step 1   Key in the following: C:\DOS>**LABEL A:** **Enter**

```
C:\DOS>LABEL A:
Volume in drive A is SAMPLE DATA
Volume Serial Number is 3829-11FC
Volume label (11 characters, ENTER for none)?_
```

WHAT'S HAPPENING? This message looks exactly like the one you saw when you used the /V parameter with the FORMAT command. At this point, you can key in a new volume label.

Step 2   Press **Enter**

```
Delete current volume label (Y/N)?_
```

WHAT'S HAPPENING? The LABEL command knows that you already have a volume label so it is asking you if you want to remove it.

Step 3   Key in the following: **Y** **Enter**

```
Delete current volume label (Y/N)? Y

C:\DOS>_
```

WHAT'S HAPPENING? You deleted the current volume label.

Step 4   Key in the following: C:\DOS>**VOL A:** **Enter**

```
C:\DOS>VOL A:
```

```
    Volume in drive A has no label
    Volume Serial Number is 3829-11FC

  C:\DOS>_
```

WHAT'S HAPPENING? You no longer have a volume label on the disk. In the next step you are going to place a volume label on the DATA disk, but you are going to take a shortcut. You are going to use the volume label SAMPLE. Since you already know what you want to key in, you do not have to wait for the LABEL command to ask you what label you want.

Step 5   Key in the following: C:\DOS>**LABEL A:SAMPLE** [Enter]

```
  C:\DOS>LABEL A:SAMPLE

  C:\DOS>_
```

WHAT'S HAPPENING? You are returned to the system level prompt. Did your volume label change on the DATA disk?

Step 6   Key in the following: C:\DOS>**VOL A:** [Enter]

```
  C:\DOS>VOL A:

   Volume in drive A is SAMPLE
   Volume Serial Number is 3829-11FC

  C:\DOS>_
```

WHAT'S HAPPENING? You indeed quickly changed the label.

4.10 Unformatting a Disk

A disk can be unformatted in DOS 5.0 and above if you have not used the /U parameter. UNFORMAT may be able to recover files and directories on the disk. Unformat can be used on hard disks also, but as you can imagine, it is better not to have to use it because you may not recover all your data. Formatting initializes only the FAT and the root directory table and leaves the file area intact. This means the data is still on the disk. In addition, the FORMAT command told you that it was Saving UNFORMAT information, creating a hidden mirror file that is simply a mirror image of the FAT and the root directory before the disk was formatted. When you use UNFORMAT, it searches for the mirror file and uses it to rebuild the FAT and the root directory to what it was before the disk was formatted. The syntax of the command is

```
UNFORMAT drive: [/J]
UNFORMAT drive: [/U] [/L] [/TEST] [/P]
UNFORMAT /PARTN [/L]
```

drive: Specifies the drive to unformat.
/J   Verifies that the mirror files agree with the system
            information on the disk.
/U   Unformats without using MIRROR files.
/L   Lists all file and directory names found, or, when used
            with the /PARTN switch, displays current partition
            tables.
/TEST   Displays information but does not write changes to
            disk.
/P   Sends output messages to printer connected to LPT1.
/PARTN   Restores disk partition tables.

MIRROR, UNDELETE, and UNFORMAT Copyright (C) 1987-1993 Central
Point Software, Inc.

There are some very useful parameters. The /L parameter lists what it would find if it were to unformat a disk. In addition, you can use the /TEST parameter to show you what will happen if you use UNFORMAT, but it will take no action.

4.11 Activity: Using Unformat on the Data Disk

Note: Your default directory is the \DOS subdirectory on Drive C, and you have the C:\DOS> displayed. The disk just formatted is in Drive A.

Step 1   Key in the following: C:\DOS>**UNFORMAT A:/L** **Enter**

```
C:\DOS>UNFORMAT A:/L

Insert disk to rebuild in drive A:
and press ENTER when ready.
```

WHAT'S HAPPENING? It is telling you that it is getting ready to rebuild the disk.

Step 2   Press **Enter**

```
CAUTION !!
This attempts to recover all the files lost after a
format, assuming you've not been using the MIRROR command.
This method cannot guarantee complete recovery of your files.

The search-phase is safe: nothing is altered on the disk.
You will be prompted again before changes are written to the disk.

Using drive A:
```

```
Are you sure you want to do this?
If so, press Y; anything else cancels.
? N
```

WHAT'S HAPPENING? UNFORMAT is very cautious. It tells you that it can guarantee nothing. It is also telling you that this is safe because nothing is going to be altered on the disk. The N for No is the default. This next step will take some time (at least 15 minutes), so be patient.

Step 3   Key in the following: **Y** ⌨**Enter**

```
Searching disk...
100% searched, 0 subdirectories found.
No files or subdirectories found for the root.
No action taken.

C:\DOS>_
```

WHAT'S HAPPENING? Since this disk had nothing on it, there was no action to take. If you are unformatting a previously used disk, you will have recovered data information on your screen.

Step 4   Key in the following: C:\DOS> **UNFORMAT A:** ⌨**Enter**

```
C:\DOS>UNFORMAT A:

Insert disk to rebuild in drive A:
and press ENTER when ready.
```

WHAT'S HAPPENING? You are going to UNFORMAT this disk. It is ready for you to continue.

Step 5   Press ⌨**Enter**

```
Restores the system area of your disk by using the image file created
by the MIRROR command.

    WARNING !!          WARNING !!

This command should be used only to recover from the inadvertent use of
the FORMAT command or the RECOVER command.  Any other use of the UNFORMAT
command may cause you to lose data!  Files modified since the MIRROR image
file was created may be lost.

Searching disk for MIRROR image.

The last time the MIRROR or FORMAT command was used was at 10:50 on 06-20-94.

The MIRROR image file has been validated.
```

```
Are you sure you want to update the system area of your drive A (Y/N)?_
```

WHAT'S HAPPENING? Again, you can see how cautious the UNFORMAT command wants you to be. It gives you plenty of warning. In this case, it found the MIRROR image and also gives you the last time either MIRROR or FORMAT was used. (Note: The next step does not require pressing ⌷Enter⌷. When you press Y, UNFORMAT completes its job.)

Step 6   Press **Y**

```
The system area of drive A has been rebuilt.

You may need to restart the system.

C:\DOS>_
```

WHAT'S HAPPENING? Your system area (the FAT and root directory) has been rebuilt. Although there are no files on this disk, there was a change. You changed the volume label. It has been restored to its previous state of no volume label.

Error Message

If you get an error message that reads `Error reading logical sector`, press **A** for `Abort`. This message tells you that the disk you are using cannot be unformatted.

Step 7   Key in the following: C:\DOS>**VOL A:** ⌷Enter⌷

```
C:\DOS>VOL A:

 Volume in drive A has no label
 Volume Serial Number is 1024-11FA

C:\DOS>_
```

WHAT'S HAPPENING? The volume label is in the state it was before you formatted the disk. Remember, UNFORMAT is to be used as a last resort, when there is no other way to recover data.

4.12 Formatting a Disk Using the /Q and /U Parameters

When you format a disk with the FORMAT command, the data is not really gone from the disk until you begin to write new data to the disk. Often, you will want to clear the disk totally to ensure that there is really nothing on the disk, as earlier versions of FORMAT did. Now, you may do this with the /U parameter, which lets you format a disk unconditionally so no data can be recovered. The /U parameter not only initializes the root directory table and the FAT but also overwrites everything in the files area with special hexadecimal numbers so that there is no data on the disk. There are many reasons for using the /U parameter. For one thing, it saves time when you format a new disk. On a new disk why take the time to save the unformat information when there is nothing on the disk? Another reason is that sometimes, when a disk is reported as bad, using the /U parameter clears the so-called bad sectors.

Another feature that was added to the FORMAT command was the /Q parameter which stands for "quick" format. The /Q only works on a disk that has been previously formatted. It works like the usual FORMAT command by clearing the FAT and root directory as it prepares a disk for new files, but in order to clear the disk rapidly, /Q will not check for bad sectors on a disk. The /Q is a very fast way to erase a disk.

4.13 Activity: Using the /Q and /U Parameters

Note: Your default directory is the \DOS subdirectory on Drive C, and the C:\DOS> is displayed. The disk just formatted is in Drive A.

Step 1   Key in the following: C:\DOS>**FORMAT A:/Q** ⬛Enter⬛

```
C:\DOS>FORMAT A:/Q
Insert new diskette for drive A:
and press ENTER when ready...
```

WHAT'S HAPPENING? FORMAT is asking you for a disk to format. Since you already have a disk in the drive, you may proceed.

Step 2   Be sure the DATA disk is in Drive A. Then press ⬛Enter⬛

```
Checking existing disk format.
Saving UNFORMAT information.
QuickFormatting 1.2M
Format complete.

Volume label (11 characters, ENTER for none)?
```

WHAT'S HAPPENING? Notice how fast the formatting occurred. FORMAT is asking you for a volume label.

Step 3   Press **Enter**

```
1,213,952 bytes total disk space
1,213,952 bytes available on disk

        512 bytes in each allocation unit.
      2,371 allocation units available on disk.

Volume Serial Number is 3A46-13DC

QuickFormat another (Y/N)?
```

WHAT'S HAPPENING? The FORMAT command wants to know if you have any more disks to quick format.

Step 4   Press **N** **Enter**

```
QuickFormat another (Y/N)?N


C:\DOS>_
```

WHAT'S HAPPENING? You returned to the system prompt. When you use the next parameter, /U for unconditional formatting, you will format the disk in such a way that the information on it cannot be recovered.

Step 5   Be sure the DATA disk is in Drive A. Key in the following:

        C:\DOS>**FORMAT A:/U** **Enter**

```
C:\DOS>FORMAT A:/U
Insert new diskette for drive A:
and press ENTER when ready...
```

Step 6   Press **Enter**

```
Formatting 1.2M
Format complete.

Volume label (11 characters, ENTER for none)?
```

Step 7   Press **Enter**

```
1,213,952 bytes total disk space
1,213,952 bytes available on disk

        512 bytes in each allocation unit.
      2,371 allocation units available on disk.
```

```
Volume Serial Number is 1632-13DF

Format another (Y/N)?_
```

Step 8   Press **N** **Enter**

```
Format another (Y/N)?N


C:\DOS>_
```

WHAT'S HAPPENING? You unconditionally formatted the DATA disk, which is the most drastic form of formatting. This disk is no longer unformattable. As you saw, it began formatting immediately and did not give you the Saving UNFORMAT information message. Use the /U parameter to format new disks because they have nothing on them and will format rapidly.

Step 9   Key in the following: C:\DOS>**CD ** **Enter**

```
C:\DOS>CD \

C:\>_
```

WHAT'S HAPPENING? You returned to the root directory of the hard disk.

4.14 Bootable and Nonbootable Disks

Note: Although this section is not an activity to perform, if you are working on your own computer, it would be a good idea to create a bootable floppy disk. The steps are listed in this section.

There is another major parameter you can use with the FORMAT command. It is the /S parameter which allows you to place the operating system files on a disk, thereby making a **nonbootable disk** bootable. You have learned that, in order for a computer to work, an operating system must be resident in memory. The computer has the operating system in memory because you booted the system from the hard disk, where the system files are. It is from the hard disk that the operating system files were copied into memory. These critical files, the actual operating system, are comprised of two hidden system files IO.SYS and MSDOS.SYS and the nonhidden file COMMAND.COM.

If you did not personally format the hard disk and install DOS on it, someone else did. When he did this task, he used the FORMAT command with the /S parameter copying the operating system files to your hard disk. This was done so that when you wanted to use your computer, you could boot from the hard disk. The FORMAT /S was only necessary and only done when the hard disk was initially formatted. Even on a network server (the computer that you may be using), it was also initially formatted with a /S, making it bootable. Since the hard disk or server is already bootable, why would you want to make a floppy disk bootable?

If you have an older notebook computer, you may have no hard drive and will need to boot from a floppy disk. However, the most important reason to have a bootable floppy disk is in case of emergencies. When you power on the computer, it always looks to Drive A first for a disk with the operating system files. If it does not find them and if you have a hard disk, it next looks to Drive C. It always looks in this order and no other. You cannot boot from a disk in Drive B, nor can you boot from any other hard disk than C.

The reason for this scenario is that, should you have a problem with your hard disk, you will not be able to boot from it. Now, you need a way to boot the computer because you may be able to solve the problem on the hard disk. However, if you cannot access the hard disk, you cannot boot from it. Thus, by placing a bootable floppy disk in Drive A, the computer will look for the operating system first in Drive A. This time it will find the operating system files and boot the system. Once you have booted the system, you can then access the hard disk and perhaps solve your problem. A disk that does not have the operating system files on it is not a system disk. To create a bootable floppy disk, also called a system disk, is easy. The command would be:

C:\DOS>**FORMAT A:/S**

Remember, the disk must be the same media type as your Drive A. If you are using your own computer, this would be a good time to do this. You do not need to do this in a lab environment because the network administrator has already done this.

Get a new blank disk—not the DATA disk or the ACTIVITIES disk. Place a label on it—EMERGENCY BOOTABLE DOS SYSTEM DISK. Then place the disk in Drive A. Key in **FORMAT A:/S** Enter

When the task is completed, you will see the following screen display:

```
Checking existing disk format.
Saving UNFORMAT information.
Verifying 1.2M
Format complete.
System transferred

Volume label (11 characters, ENTER for none)?_

    1,213,952 bytes total disk space
      198,656 bytes used by system
    1,015,296 bytes available on disk

          512 bytes in each allocation unit.
        1,983 allocation units available on disk.
```

```
Volume Serial Number is 2C76-1DCE

Format another (Y/N)?N
```

WHAT'S HAPPENING? You can see the message `System Transferred`. This message means that the two hidden files `IO.SYS` and `MSDOS.SYS` and the unhidden `COMMAND.COM` have been copied to the disk in Drive A. You can see how much disk space they occupy. Now remove this disk and place it a safe location. If you ever have a problem with your hard disk, you can now boot from this floppy disk. However, should all floppy disks be bootable, particularly if it is a disk that is only going to be used for data? Usually, after you have made your emergency bootable floppy disk, you do not need to place the operating system on other disks. Operating system files take a fair amount of room. How much room they take depends on which version of DOS you are using.

4.15 High-Density Disks and Disk Drives

If you have a newer computer, you probably have what are called high-capacity or high-density disk drives. If your disk drive or drives, either 5¼ or 3½, are of this type, whenever you use the FORMAT command, it will format any disk placed in the drive in its "native" format; it assumes that the disk to be formatted is a blank high-density disk. Thus, if you placed a 5¼-inch 360 KB double-density disk in a 5¼-inch high-density drive, FORMAT will prepare it as a high-density disk. Because a DS/DD (double-sided/double-density) was not designed as DS/HD (double-sided/high-density disk), it does not have as many magnetic particles and should not be formatted as a high-density disk. In fact, you will get an error message that will show many bytes as bad sectors.

If you have high-density disk drives and use only high-density disks, you will have no problems. The problems begin to occur when you try to mix and match different density disks with different density drives. If you format a 3½-inch 720 DS/DD in a 3½-inch 1.44 high-density disk drive, it will format the disk as a 1.44 DS/HD disk and will make that disk unreadable in a 720 DS/DD drive.

Older computers have older disk drives, the DS/DD. These disk drives cannot read or write to the new DS/HD disk. The newer computers with the new technology have the DS/HD disk drives. These drives can both read and write to either the DS/DD or DS/HD disks. This is one of the ways that hardware and software maintain what is called **downward compatibility**—something that is developed on a new computer that can still be used on an old computer. The only problem you run into is in formatting disks. You can format a 360 KB disk in a DS/HD drive by using the FORMAT /F:360 parameter as described in Section 4.6. Table 4.4 shows you which disks you can use in what drives.

Disk Drive Type	Floppy Disks That May Be Used	Format Command
5¼-inch DS/DD 360 KB disk drive	360 KB DS/DD disks	FORMAT A: FORMAT B:
3½-inch DS/DD 720 KB disk drive	720 KB DS/DD disks	FORMAT A: FORMAT B:
5¼-inch DS/HD 1.2 MB disk drive	360 KB DS/DD disks	FORMAT A:/F:360 FORMAT B:/F:360
5¼-inch DS/HD 1.2 MB disk drive	1.2 MB DS/HD disks	FORMAT A: FORMAT B:
3½-inch DS/HD 1.44 MB disk drive	720 KB DS/DD disks	FORMAT A:/F:720 FORMAT B:/F:720
3½-inch DS/HD 1.44 MB disk drive	1.44 MB DS/HD disks	FORMAT A: FORMAT B:
3½-inch DS/HD 2.88 MB extra high-density disk drive	720 KB DS/DD disks	FORMAT A:/F:720 FORMAT B:/F:720
3½-inch DS/HD 2.88 MB extra high-density disk drive	1.44 MB DS/HD disks	FORMAT A:/F:1.44 FORMAT B:/F:1.44
3½-inch DS/HD 2.88 MB extra high-density disk drive	2.88 MB DS extra high-density disks	FORMAT A: FORMAT B:

Table 4.4 *Format Compatibility between Disks and Drives*

By using this table, you can quickly identify which disk can be used in which disk drive. In addition, you will know how to format a lower density disk in a high-density drive. If you do not know what type of disk drive you have and you do not have MSD, a quick way to identify the drive type is to format a blank disk in the drive in the native format. The FORMAT command report will tell you how many bytes it formatted. You can then place the information on your Configuration Table in Chapter 2.8. The important thing is to be aware of what type of floppy disk drive or drive you have and what media type floppy disks you are using.

Chapter Summary

1. Floppy disks that are purchased are usually not ready to use. They must first be prepared for use.
2. Each type of computer has its own specific way of recording information on a disk. This text is only concerned with DOS-based computers.
3. The command processor is stored as a file called `COMMAND.COM`. It processes what the user keys in. When you boot the system, this file is one of the operating system files placed in memory. `COMMAND.COM` has internal commands that are resident in memory until the computer is turned off.
4. Disks are the means to store data and programs permanently.
5. All disks must be formatted by a utility program stored as a file called `FORMAT.COM` so that DOS can read and write data and programs to them.
6. Disks that have information on them can be formatted again.
7. If a disk has files on it, formatting the disk will remove all of those files.
8. Since the FORMAT command removes all data, formatting a hard disk can be dangerous.
9. Formatting a disk means that the physical layout of the disk is defined to determine how the information is stored on the disk so that DOS can locate what is stored.
10. DOS uses sections of a disk, whether it is a hard disk or a floppy disk. A disk is divided into concentric circles called tracks. Each track is divided into sectors. The number of tracks, sectors, and sides of a disk determine the capacity of the disk.
11. The smallest unit that DOS will read from or write to is a cluster. A cluster is made up of one or more adjacent sectors depending on the kind of disk.
12. Each disk has a root directory and File Allocation Table (FAT).
13. When formatted, all disks have a boot record, a FAT, a directory, and data sectors.
14. A boot record has a routine to load DOS if it is a system disk or a message indicating that it is not a system disk.
15. The FAT (File Allocation Table) is a map of every track and sector on the disk and tells DOS where files are on the disk. The FAT links a file together by pointing to the next cluster that holds the file's data.
16. The root directory has information about the files including the file name and the file's starting cluster entry in the FAT.
17. The data sectors are where files are actually stored.
18. Files are chains of bytes laid out in sequence.
19. DOS writes files to a disk at the first available cluster, if possible in adjacent or contiguous clusters. If the adjacent clusters are already in use, DOS skips to the next available space or noncontiguous cluster.
20. A disk is formatted with the FORMAT command, an external utility program.
21. The syntax of the FORMAT command is:

```
FORMAT drive:[/V:label][/S][/4][/N:xx/T:yy]
```

22. Later versions of DOS have many more parameters with the FORMAT command. The syntax is:

```
FORMAT drive: [/V[:label]] [/Q] [/U] [/F:size] [/B | /S] [/C]
FORMAT drive: [/V[:label]] [/Q] [/U] [/T:tracks /N:sectors] [/B | /S] [/C]
FORMAT drive: [/V[:label]] [/Q] [/U] [/1] [/4] [/B | /S] [/C]
FORMAT drive: [/Q] [/U] [/1] [/4] [/8] [/B | /S] [/C]
```

23. In recent versions of DOS, the FORMAT command tracks information so that the disk can be unformatted.
24. The internal VOL command allows you to view the internal electronic label.
25. The external LABEL command allows you to change the internal electronic label.
26. The /U parameter performs an unconditional format so that a disk cannot be unformatted.
27. The /Q parameter performs a quick format that does not check for bad sectors on a disk. In addition, it can only be used on a disk that was previously formatted.
28. A bootable disk is one that has been formatted with the /S parameter. This parameter formats the disk and copies the system files (IO.SYS, MSDOS.SYS, and COMMAND.COM) to the disk.
29. A bootable disk is one that allows you to load the operating system files. Typically, the hard disk is a bootable disk. You may also create a bootable floppy disk so that you may boot from Drive A when the need arises.
30. Always use the correct media type when formatting disks.

Key Terms

Allocation Unit	Formatting	Physical formatting
Bad sectors	High-level formatting	Unformatting
Bootable disk	Initializing	Volume label
Contiguous	Logical formatting	
Downward	Low-level formatting	
compatibility	Nonbootable disk	
File Allocation	Noncontiguous	
Table (FAT)		

Discussion Questions

1. What purpose do disks serve?
2. Why must you format a disk?
3. Compare and contrast physical (low-level) formatting with logical (high-level) formatting of a disk.
4. Define tracks, sectors, and clusters.
5. What is the purpose and function of the boot record?
6. Define FAT. How is it used on a disk?
7. What is the function of the numbers in FAT?

8. What is the purpose and function of the root directory.
9. Define file attributes. List at least two types of attributes and explain their purpose and function.
10. How is space allocated to files?
11. FORMAT can be a dangerous command. Explain.
12. What does the prompt on the screen represent?
13. List the four types of floppy disks.
14. Compare and contrast internal and external commands.
15. What steps can you take when you see the message, `Bad command or file name`?
16. What is a volume label?
17. What happens when you use the command FORMAT /S?
18. In later versions of DOS, when formatting a disk, the drive letter is a mandatory parameter. Why?
19. Give the syntax for the FORMAT command and explain each item.
20. Explain the purpose and function of a quick format.
21. When using the FORMAT command what are the purposes and functions of the parameters /S and /V?
22. What is the purpose and function of the VOL command?
23. What is the purpose and function of the LABEL command?
24. When using the FORMAT command, what is the difference between the /Q and /U parameters?
25. When using the FORMAT command, when would you use the /Q parameter? The /U parameter?
26. What is a bootable disk?
27. How can you unformat a disk? Why would you unformat a disk?
28. How can you create a bootable floppy disk?
29. What is a high-density disk?
30. Can you use a 1.2MB 5¼-inch disk in a 360 KB drive? Why or why not?

Chapter 5

Program Files, Data Files, and Subdirectories

After completing this chapter you will be able to:

1. List and explain the three major reasons for learning DOS.
2. Explain the difference between program files and data files.
3. Explain the difference between freeware and shareware programs.
4. Explain the hierarchical filing system of a tree-structured directory.
5. Explain the purpose and function of a root directory and tell how and when it is created.
6. Explain what subdirectories are and tell how subdirectories are named, created, and used.
7. Explain the purpose and use of subdirectory markers.
8. Identify the commands that can be used with subdirectories.
9. Explain the purpose and function of the MOVE command.
10. Explain the purpose and function of the TREE command.
11. List the steps to remove a directory.
12. Explain the purpose and function of the DELTREE command.

1. Load and use an application program.
2. Create subdirectories using the MD command.
3. Display the default directory using the CD command.
4. Change directories using the CD command.

5. Use the PROMPT command with metastrings to change the prompt to reflect the default drive and subdirectory.
6. Use subdirectory markers with commands.
7. Rename a directory using the MOVE command.
8. Use the TREE command to see the structure of a disk.
9. Use the RD command to eliminate a directory.
10. Use the DELTREE command to remove an entire tree structure.

Chapter Overview

You do not purchase a computer to use DOS. You purchase a computer to help you be more efficient in doing what work you want. Work on a computer is comprised of two aspects—the programs that do the work and the information you create. When you work with a computer, you accumulate many programs and many data files. If you are going to be an efficient user, you must have a way to manage these files. Part of the power of DOS is the ability to manage files. One tool you have used is the DIR command, which lists the files stored on a disk. In previous chapters, the directories that were used contained a small number of files, and it was fairly easy to locate a specific file. When a directory contains hundreds of files it becomes much more difficult to locate a specific file.

The major tool that DOS provides that allows you to group files logically is subdirectories. The main directory that is used to store files is always automatically created when a disk is formatted. It is called the root directory, but it can contain only a limited number of files. Furthermore, there is no order to the way that files are added to the root directory. It is first come, first served. To solve these file management problems, subdirectories were developed as a means of further organizing files on a disk.

A subdirectory is a special file that contains lists of files that have been grouped together under one name. Subdirectories can be created and deleted as needed. Thus, creating, deleting, and using subdirectories makes it possible to manage large numbers of files efficiently.

In this chapter you will learn to use a program file and a data file. You will also learn the subdirectory commands to help you manage your files.

5.1 Why DOS?

So far, you have used DOS commands to prepare a disk for use (FORMAT), to copy a disk (DISKCOPY), and to see what files are on a disk (DIR). In addition, you are able to set the date and time (DATE and TIME) and clear the screen (CLS). Each of these commands is useful, but no one buys a computer to use DOS. A person purchases a computer to assist in doing work, and the way one does work on a computer is by the purchase and use of application programs. The four major categories of application programs include word processors to make writing easier, spreadsheets to manage budgets and do financial projections, databases to manage and manipulate a collection of data, and graphics to create artistic drawings and designs. The application programs that use graphics generically include CAD (computer aided design) and desktop publishing. Each program has its own instructions which must be learned. If this is true, why are you learning DOS, the disk operating system?

Here, again, are the reasons for learning DOS. First and foremost, you cannot run an application program without first loading DOS. DOS is the manager of the system, supervising the hardware and software components, allowing you to load and execute specific application packages. Application programs run under the supervision of DOS.

The second reason for learning DOS is that application programs are stored as files on disks and usually generate data files. DOS has a variety of commands that allow you to manage and manipulate program and data files. DOS manages files, but not the information you put into files.

The third reason for learning DOS is that it allows you to install and manage special hardware devices such as a mouse or a scanner. These devices make your work easier, but require special files that only DOS can manage.

5.2 Program Files, Data Files, and DOS

On the hard disk is a subdirectory called DOS6BK. This subdirectory was created by installing the files and directories from the ACTIVITIES disk to the hard disk. It was placed on the hard disk or network server by the instructor. If you are using your own computer, you will have to do this task yourself. Appendix A gives you the instructions on how do this. The subdirectory DOS6BK contains other subdirectories, among which are two called PHONE and FINANCE. These subdirectories have application programs, one called HPB and the other called THINKER, which will help you understand how DOS works in the "real world."

HPB is a simple application program that works much like a Rolodex. It is a database that allows you to keep track of names, addresses, and phone numbers. THINKER is a spreadsheet program that allows you to manipulate numbers in columns and rows. You are going to use DOS to load these programs, load data files, and list the files that are there.

The DOS commands help you understand how DOS works in conjunction with the various types of files. An application or program file is a file DOS loads from disk into memory. DOS then turns control over to the application program. When the application program needs to interface with the hardware, such as when it wants to write a character to the screen, the application program tells DOS what to write, and DOS does the actual labor of writing to the screen.

The application program is usually not enough. You also want to produce results, or data. Data is also stored in files that most often can be used only by the specific application program. That is the relationship between the application program and the data file. You may ask yourself how then does DOS fit into the picture? DOS is the means by which the application program gets loaded into memory. Remember, work takes place only in memory. DOS also assists in loading the data file into memory so that the application program can use the data. This cooperative effort among DOS, the application program, and the data files is the true work of DOS. An operating system takes care of all these tedious but necessary tasks. You, the user, do not directly interface with DOS at this level. There is another component: the commands that DOS provides. Commands are also programs. These DOS commands allow you to interface directly with DOS to manage your program and data files.

5.3 Shareware

Some of you may have already purchased commercial application packages such as WordPerfect, Word, or Lotus 123. There are hundreds of different programs to choose from that will meet almost any computer user's needs from managing your checkbook (Quicken) to playing a game (Flight Simulator).

The subdirectory DOS6BK contains data files, freeware, and shareware programs. Freeware and shareware programs are available from a wide variety of sources. You can receive these programs by logging into an electronic bulletin board, called a BBS, if you have a modem and the necessary software. Friends and acquaintances may pass programs to you; members of computer clubs share their programs, or you can receive them from a source such as this textbook.

Freeware is software that is in the public domain. The authors (programmers) of these programs have donated the programs to anyone who wants to use them with the understanding that people will use them but not alter them. The programmers do not expect to be paid in any way—although sometimes they will ask for a small donation for expenses.

Shareware is a trial version of a program. The program is not distributed through commercial channels, thus saving the programmer the costs of marketing and distribution. After you purchase commercial software, if you do not like it or it does not meet your needs, you usually cannot return it. On the other hand, shareware is something you can try out. If you like it, you then register it with the programmer for a nominal fee. If you do not like it, you simply delete the file or files from your disk. Trying these programs costs you nothing. If you decide to retain and use the program, the programmer does expect to be paid. The programmer or programmers who write shareware are professional programmers, students, and people who just enjoy programming.

Sometimes, to encourage people to register, the program will be a limited version without all the features of the shareware program or will have annoying screens that pop up to remind you to register it. When you do register it, you receive the full version or the latest version of the program, the documentation, notices of updates and technical support. Documentation is a manual of commands and instructions. The update notices will provide you with the latest version corrections to the programs. Technical support means you can call the programmer(s) for help if something is not going right.

This textbook includes both freeware and shareware. Appendix A lists all the shareware programs with the fees and addresses necessary to register them. If, after you complete the textbook, you wish to continue using the shareware programs, please pay the appropriate fees and register the programs. Otherwise, delete the files. Shareware provides some really great programs and by registering them, you are encouraging the programmer to write shareware. Who knows, you may be assisting the next Bill Gates or Steve Jobs.

5.4 Activity: Using DIR to Locate the HPB Program

Note 1: It is assumed that you have booted off the hard disk. The C:\> is displayed on the screen.

Note 2: It is also assumed that the subdirectory DOS6BK has been installed to the hard disk. If you are using your own computer, refer to Appendix A for instructions on how to complete this installation.

Correcting Keystroke Errors

When keying in commands, you may use the function keys to correct typographical errors. To edit command lines fully, you may use DOSKEY (see Appendix B).

Step 1   Key in the following: C:\>**DIR DO*.*** [Enter]

```
C:\>DIR DO*.*

   Volume in drive C has no label
   Volume Serial Number is 1B93-9D8B
   Directory of C:\

DOS           <DIR>         02-22-93    1:14p
DOS6BK        <DIR>         06-19-94   10:32a
        2 file(s)              0 bytes
                    66,396,160 bytes free

C:\>_
```

WHAT'S HAPPENING? You are verifying that you have a subdirectory called DOS6BK. In this example, only two entries match the criteria you requested. You asked DIR to find any file or any directory on the hard disk that begins with a DO and has any other characters in the file name and any file extension. Your display may vary depending on how many other files you have that begin with DO. In this example, there is the DOS subdirectory where the DOS system utility files are located and the DOS6BK directory. If the entry named DOS6BK is not displayed, refer to Appendix A and take the necessary steps before continuing.

Step 2   Key in the following: C:\>**CD \DOS6BK\PHONE** [Enter]

```
C:\>CD \DOS6BK\PHONE

C:\DOS6BK\PHONE>_
```

WHAT'S HAPPENING? You changed the default directory to the DOS6BK and then to the PHONE subdirectory where the HPB program is located.

Step 3   Key in the following: C:\DOS6BK\PHONE>**DIR HPB.EXE** ⌜Enter⌝

```
C:\DOS6BK\PHONE>DIR HPB.EXE

 Volume in drive C has no label
 Volume Serial Number is 1CD1-5E42
 Directory of C:\DOS6BK\PHONE

HPB       EXE        164,420 07-03-93   8:01a
        1 file(s)           164,420 bytes
                         66,387,968 bytes free

C:\DOS6BK\PHONE>_
```

WHAT'S HAPPENING? You used the DIR command to see if the file called HPB.EXE is on the hard disk in the subdirectory called DOS6BK\PHONE. DIR is the command; \DOS6BK\PHONE is the path, and HPB.EXE is the file name of the program. All the DIR command does is allow you to see if the file is on the disk. DIR does not let you use the program; it just lets you see if it is available. The name of the file is HPB. The HPB stands for Home Phone Book. The name of the extension is .EXE. The .EXE file extension has a special meaning: executable code. This extension lets DOS know the file is a program. The file extensions .EXE and .COM always indicate programs to DOS.

Step 4   Key in the following: C:\DOS6BK\PHONE>**DIR HPB.DAT** ⌜Enter⌝

```
C:\DOS6BK\PHONE>DIR HPB.DAT

 Volume in drive C has no label
 Volume Serial Number is 1CD1-5E42
 Directory of C:\DOS6BK\PHONE

HPB       DAT          4,368 12-12-96  10:46p
        1 file(s)             4,368 bytes
                         66,387,968 bytes free

C:\DOS6BK\PHONE>_
```

WHAT'S HAPPENING? You used the DIR command to see if the file called HPB.DAT is in this subdirectory. DIR is the command; HPB is the file name and DAT is the file extension. DIR does not let you use the data; it just lets you see if it is there.

want to load. Each of the following keys you press will execute a command in this program. Be sure you begin by pressing the forward slash (/), not the backslash(\).

Step 12 Press /

Step 13 Press **F**

Step 14 Press **R**

WHAT'S HAPPENING? You went through a series of steps to get to the retrieve command in this program. Every program has different commands to load a data file. But, in all cases, when you key in a data file name, the program will turn to DOS to locate the data file and load it into memory.

Step 15 Key in the following: **HOMEBUD** Enter

```
A1:
                                                    Status:ENTER
              A              B          C          D          E
1                         JANUARY   FEBRUARY    MARCH
2
3   RENT                  450.00     450.00     450.00
4   ELECTRICITY            35.00      39.00
5   GAS                    25.45      23.74
6   PHONE                  32.98      34.75
7   CABLE                  14.50      14.50      14.50
8   FOOD                  257.98     233.45
9   PERSONAL               37.50      41.25
10  ENTERTAINMENT          78.00      85.00
11  TRANSPORTATION        110.00     113.00
12
13  TOTAL                1041.41    1034.69     464.50
14
15
16
17
18
19
20
/-Command F1-Help F2-Edit F5-GOTO F9-Recalc          The Thinker(c)82,86
```

WHAT'S HAPPENING? You have loaded the data file called HOMEBUD.TKR. The numbers and text displayed on the screen are the data you want to see.

Step 16   Press **/**

Step 17   Press **F**

Step 18   Press **R**

```
A1:
Enter name of file to retrieve:(HOMEBUD.TKR):
                                                    Status:ENTER
              A              B          C          D          E
1                         JANUARY   FEBRUARY    MARCH
2
3   RENT                  450.00     450.00     450.00
4   ELECTRICITY            35.00      39.00
5   GAS                    25.45      23.74
6   PHONE                  32.98      34.75
7   CABLE                  14.50      14.50      14.50
8   FOOD                  257.98     233.45
9   PERSONAL               37.50      41.25
10  ENTERTAINMENT          78.00      85.00
11  TRANSPORTATION        110.00     113.00
12
13  TOTAL                1041.41    1034.69     464.50
14
15
16
17
18
19
20
/-Command F1-Help F2-Edit F5-GOTO F9-Recalc          The Thinker(c)82,86
```

WHAT'S HAPPENING? By using the correct commands in this program, you are given the opportunity to load another data file with different information. The data file that you are currently looking at is HOMEBUD.TKR.

Step 19   Key in the following: **BUDGET** |Enter|

```
C18:+C7-C16

                                                        Status:ENTER
        A       B       C       D       E       F       G       H
1                       BUDGET EXAMPLE IN $1000
2
3    Revenues                Q1      Q2      Q3      Q4      Total
4    --------------------------------------------------------------
5    Sales                   134     154     166     175     629
6    Interest                 12      14      16      18      60
7    Total                   146     168     182     193     689
8
9    Expenses
10   --------------------------------------------------------------
11   Rent                     44      44      46      46      180
12   Utilities                 5       5       5       5      20
13   Salaries                 88      90      92      94      364
14   Travel                    3       6       3       6      18
15   Misc                     12      14      16      17      59
16   Total                   152     159     162     168     641
17   --------------------------------------------------------------
18   Profit                   -6       9      20      25      48
19
20
/-Command F1-Help F2-Edit F5-GOTO F9-Recalc            The Thinker(c)82,86
```

WHAT'S HAPPENING? You have loaded a different data file with different information.

Step 20   Press /

Step 21   Press **Q**

Step 22   Press **Y**

```
C:\DOS6BK\FINANCE>_
```

Step 23   Key in the following: C:\DOSBK\FINANCE>**CD** \ **Enter**

```
C:\_
```

WHAT'S HAPPENING? You exited the program THINKER and returned to the system prompt. You are now at the DOS system level. Next you returned to the root directory. Thus, you used DOS to load the application program called HPB, which can work with only one data file that also was loaded. You used DOS to change to the directory where the THINKER program was located. You then used the commands of the THINKER program to load the data files, HOMEBUD.TKR and BUDGET.TKR. When you used the commands in THINKER, THINKER told DOS to get the data files you specified so that THINKER could place the data file in memory to let you work with the information in them. You followed the instructions of the programs HPB and THINKER. When you were finished with each program, you returned to the DOS system level.

5.7 Using DOS To Manage Program and Data Files

In the last few activities, you moved around the hard disk and loaded both program files and data files. Although you did not spend much time working with each program, the experience should give you some idea of how many different types of programs there are. With each new program, you generate new data files. You need to manage these programs and data files so that you can quickly locate what you need and get to work.

As an example of what you are faced with, imagine that you own ten books. By reading each title, you can quickly peruse the authors and titles and locate the book you wish to read. Suppose your library grows and you now have 100 books. You do not want to have to read each author and title looking for a specific book, so you classify the information. A common classification scheme is to arrange the books alphabetically by the author's last name. Now you have shortened your search time. If you want a book by Gillay, you quickly go to G. You may have more than one book by an author that begins with G but by going to the letter G, you have narrowed your search. Now imagine you have 10,000 books—alphabetically by author is still not enough. You may have 200 books by authors whose last names begin with G. So you further classify your books. You first divide them into categories like computer or fiction. Then, within the category, you arrange alphabetically by last name. So, if you wanted a computer book by Gillay, you would first go to the computer section, then to the letter G. If you wanted a novel by Greenleaf, you would first go to the fiction section and then the letter G. As you can see, you are classifying and categorizing information so that you can find it quickly.

This process is exactly what you want to do with files. Remember, you have many program and many data files. You want to be able to locate them quickly and group them logically. The way you do this in DOS is by the means of subdirectories.

5.8 Hierarchical Filing System or Tree-structured Directories

As you learned in the last chapter, every disk must be formatted before you can use it. When you format a disk, a directory known as the **root directory** is automatically created. Every disk must have a root directory so that files can be located on the disk. The root directory table is the area of the disk that contains information about what is stored there. It is like an index to the disk. However, there is a limit to the number of files or entries that can be placed in the root directory table. See Table 5.1.

Disk Size	Number of Root Directory Entries
5¼-inch and 3½-inch DS/DD Disks	112 root directory entries
5¼-inch and 3½-inch DS/HD Disks	224 root directory entries
hard disk	512 root directory entries

Table 5.1 **Root Directory File Limits**

location. You expect not only the stove to be there but also all the tools you need—the sink, the spices, the pots and pans. If you want to go to sleep, you will go to the bedroom because that is where you expect the bed. Subdirectories have names that you or a program chooses. The only exception is the root directory, which is created when you format the disk and is always known as \ (backslash). The root directory always has the same name on every disk.

Because computers are so rigid, they must follow certain rules when naming anything. Subdirectories follow the same rigid naming conventions as files: a maximum of eight characters for the file name, a period, and a maximum of three characters for a file extension. Usually, subdirectory names do not have extensions. Although DOS treats subdirectories as files, the subdirectories themselves cannot be manipulated with the standard file manipulation commands. Subdirectories have their own special commands. Table 5.2 lists the directory management commands.

Command	Function
CHDIR or **CD**	Changes the directory.
MKDIR or **MD**	Makes or creates a directory.
RMDIR or **RD**	Removes or erases a directory.
PATH	Defines the search paths.
PROMPT	Changes the look of the prompt to identify what subdirectory is the default.
DELTREE	Allows you to remove an entire tree with one command—new to 6.0.
MOVE	Allows you to rename a directory—new to 6.0.

Table 5.2   ***Directory Management Commands***

5.9 Creating Subdirectories

When you create a subdirectory, you are setting up an area where files can be stored. There is nothing in the subdirectory initially. The internal MD command creates a subdirectory. When you format a disk, you are preparing it to hold files. When you set up a subdirectory, you are also preparing it to hold files but in a logical group. The syntax of the command is:

```
        MD      [drive:]path
or
        MKDIR   [drive:]path
```

In the following activity, you will create two subdirectories under the root directory on the DATA disk. These subdirectories will be for two classes: one in political science and the other in physical education.

5.10 Activity: How to Create Subdirectories

Note: The C:\> is displayed as the default drive and directory.

Step 1   Place the DATA disk used in Chapter 4 into Drive A. Key in the following:

C:\>**FORMAT A:/Q/V:DATADISK** [Enter]

```
C:\>FORMAT A:/Q/V:DATADISK
Insert new diskette for drive A:
and press ENTER when ready...
```

WHAT'S HAPPENING? You are going to format the DATA disk again. In addition to using the /Q parameter to format the disk quickly, you also used a shortcut to place a volume label on the disk so that you did not have to wait for the volume label prompt. If you want to include a volume label on a disk, you can do it at the time of issuing the FORMAT command. However, when you use the /V (followed by a colon), you cannot have spaces in the volume label name.

Step 2   Press [Enter]

```
C:\>FORMAT A:/Q/V:DATADISK
Insert new diskette for drive A:
and press ENTER when ready...

Checking existing disk format.
Saving UNFORMAT information.
QuickFormatting 1.2M
Format complete.


    1,213,952 bytes total disk space
    1,213,952 bytes available on disk

        512 bytes in each allocation unit.
      2,371 allocation units available on disk.

Volume Serial Number is 2F26-1901

QuickFormat another (Y/N)?
```

WHAT'S HAPPENING? You formatted the disk and placed a volume label on it.

Step 3   Press **N** [Enter]

Step 4   Key in the following: C:\>**A:** [Enter]

```
C:\>A:

A:\>_
```

WHAT'S HAPPENING? You have changed the default drive to where the DATA disk is. However, you are in more than a default drive: you are in a default directory—the root of A. This is the only directory that is on this disk and was created when you formatted it. You can tell that you are in the root directory because when you look at the prompt, it displays not just A: but also the \ indicating the root.

Step 5   Key in the following: A:\>**MD POLYSCI** [Enter]

Step 6   Key in the following: A:\>**MD PHYSED** [Enter]

```
A:\>MD POLYSCI

A:\>MD PHYSED

A:\>_
```

WHAT'S HAPPENING? You created two subdirectories called POLYSCI and PHYSED under the root directory on the DATA disk. POLYSCI will hold all the files that involve classes in political science, and PHYSED will hold files that involve classes in physical education. Although you have created the subdirectories to hold the files, they are now "empty" file cabinets. When you used the MD command, all you saw on the screen was the system prompt. How do you know that you created subdirectories? You can see the subdirectories you just created by using the DIR command.

Step 7   Key in the following: A:\>**DIR** [Enter]

```
A:\>DIR

 Volume in drive A is DATADISK
 Volume Serial Number is 2F26-1901
 Directory of A:\

POLYSCI       <DIR>         06-20-94    5:59p
PHYSED        <DIR>         06-20-94    6:00p
        2 file(s)             0 bytes
                      1,212,928 bytes free

A:\>
```

WHAT'S HAPPENING? The DIR command displayed the contents of the disk. In this case, there are only the two subdirectory files you just created. It is the <DIR> after each file name that indicates a subdirectory. POLYSCI and PHYSED are subdirectories. It is also important to note that the \ following the `Directory of A:\` that appears on the screen indicates the root directory of the disk.

One of the new parameters for the DIR command is /A for attributes. The only attribute you are interested in is D for directories. If you look at the complete syntax diagram, it indicates the /A followed by a list of the attributes you can request. The D is for directories:

```
DIR   [drive:][path][filename]   [/P]   [/W]   [/A[[:]attributes]]
```

/A   Displays files with specified attributes

Attributes:

D   Directories   R   Read-only files

H   Hidden files   A   Files ready for archiving

S   System files   –   Prefix meaning "not"

Step 8   Key in the following: A:\>**DIR /AD** Enter

```
A:\>DIR /AD

 Volume in drive A is DATADISK
 Volume Serial Number is 2F26-1901
 Directory of A:\

POLYSCI        <DIR>          06-20-94    5:59p
PHYSED         <DIR>          06-20-94    6:00p
        2 file(s)                  0 bytes
                      1,212,928 bytes free

A:\>
```

WHAT'S HAPPENING? You see displayed only the directories on the DATA disk because that is all that the disk contains. What if you want to look at a disk that already has directories and files on it?

Step 9   Key in the following: A:\>**DIR C:\DOS6BK** Enter

```
    FILE2     SWT            18 12-06-94   10:46a
    FILE3     CZG            18 12-06-94   10:46a
    FILE3     FP             18 12-06-94   10:46a
    FILE3     SWT            18 12-06-94   10:47a
    FILE4     FP             18 12-06-94   10:47a
    GETYN     COM            26 05-02-94   12:57a
    DATA          <DIR>         05-07-94   10:33a
    JAN       TMP            72 11-23-95   10:41a
    FEB       TMP            74 11-23-95   10:41a
```

```
  MAR       TMP             70 11-23-95   10:42a
  APR       TMP             71 11-23-95   10:42a
  LEFT      RED             53 05-07-94   11:05a
  MIDDLE    RED             66 05-07-94   11:05a
  RIGHT     RED             63 05-07-94   11:05a
  DRESS     UP              25 05-07-94   11:06a
  MIDDLE    UP              28 05-07-94   11:06a
  RIGHT     UP              25 05-07-94   11:06a
  TEST      TXT             64 03-14-93   11:07a
  EMPLOYEE  ONE             52 05-07-94    9:00a
  EMPLOYEE  THR             53 05-07-94    9:00a
  EMPLOYEE  TWO             53 05-07-94    9:00a
          92 file(s)          24,669 bytes
                         82,313,216 bytes free

  A:\>
```

WHAT'S HAPPENING? As you can see, using DIR with no parameters shows you all files, not just directories.

Step 10 Key in the following: A:\>**DIR C:\DOS6BK /AD** Enter

```
  A:\>DIR C:\DOS6BK /AD

   Volume in drive C has no label
   Volume Serial Number is 1CD1-5E42
   Directory of C:\DOS6BK

   .              <DIR>          06-19-94   10:32a
   ..             <DIR>          06-19-94   10:32a
   MEDIA          <DIR>          12-06-93   10:32a
   SPORTS         <DIR>          02-14-94   10:32a
   LEVEL-1        <DIR>          08-01-94   10:32a
   FINANCE        <DIR>          08-01-94   10:32a
   PHONE          <DIR>          01-14-95   10:33a
   GAMES          <DIR>          01-14-95   10:33a
   TEST           <DIR>          05-07-94   10:33a
   DATA           <DIR>          05-07-94   10:33a
          10 file(s)                   0 bytes
                         82,313,216 bytes free

  A:\>
```

WHAT'S HAPPENING? The above command listed only the directories on the hard disk in the subdirectory called DOS6BK. But what if you wish to see the names of the files inside the directory? Since POLYSCI is a subdirectory, not just a file, you can display the contents of the directory with the DIR command. Remember, the terms directory and subdirectory are interchangeable. The truth, though, is that there is only one directory—the root directory. Although others may be called directories, they are really subdirectories. Again, the syntax of the DIR command is DIR *[drive:][path]*. You use the subdirectory name for *path*.

Step 11   Key in the following: A:\>**DIR POLYSCI** [Enter]

```
A:\>DIR POLYSCI

 Volume in drive A is DATADISK
 Volume Serial Number is 2F26-1901
 Directory of A:\POLYSCI

 .              <DIR>         06-20-94    5:59p
 ..             <DIR>         06-20-94    5:59p
       2 file(s)                  0 bytes
                        1,212,928 bytes free

A:\>_
```

WHAT'S HAPPENING? The directory line, Directory of A:\POLYSCI, tells you the path. You are looking from the root directory into the subdirectory called POLYSCI. Even though you just created the subdirectory POLYSCI, it seems to have two subdirectories in it already, . (one period, also called "the **dot**") and . . (two periods, also called "the **double dot**") followed by <DIR>. Every subdirectory, except the root directory, *always* has two named subdirectories. The subdirectory named . is another name or abbreviation for POLYSCI. The subdirectory name . . is an abbreviation for the parent directory, in this case the root directory \. The . (dot) and . . (double dot) are called **subdirectory markers**.

Step 12   Key in the following: A:\>**DIR PHYSED** [Enter]

```
A:\>DIR PHYSED

 Volume in drive A is DATADISK
 Volume Serial Number is 2F26-1901
 Directory of A:\PHYSED

 .              <DIR>         06-20-94    6:00p
 ..             <DIR>         06-20-94    6:00p
       2 file(s)                  0 bytes
                        1,212,928 bytes free

A:\>
```

WHAT'S HAPPENING? The line that reads Directory of A:\PHYSED tells you the path. You are looking from the root directory into the subdirectory called PHYSED, the same way you looked when you asked for a directory on another drive. If, for instance, you asked for a directory of the disk in Drive B, that line would read

Directory of B:\. If you had asked for a directory of Drive C, that line would have read Directory of C:\. It tells you not only what drive but also what subdirectory is displayed on the screen.

5.11 The Current Directory

Just as DOS keeps track of the default drive, it also keeps track of the **current directory**, or default directory. When you boot the system, the default drive is the drive where you loaded DOS, and the default directory is the root directory of the current drive. You can change the directory just as you can change the drive. Doing so makes a specific subdirectory the default. In previous chapters you used the CD command to change the default directory to the \DOS subdirectory on the hard disk. It was important to have that as the default subdirectory so that you could use the DOS external commands.

The change directory (CHDIR or CD) command has two purposes. If you key in CD with no parameters, DOS displays the name of the current default directory. If you include a parameter, the name of a directory after CD, it changes the default directory to the directory that you requested and makes that directory the default. This process is similar to changing drives by keying in the desired drive letter followed by a colon, i.e., A:, B:, C:. However, do not be fooled. If your default drive and directory is the root of A so that the displayed prompt is A:\> and you key in CD C:\DOS6BK, you will not change drives. What you will do is change directories on Drive C from where you were to \DOS6BK but your current default drive and directory will still be the root of A and your displayed prompt will still be A:\>. The syntax is:

    CD [drive:][path]

or

    CHDIR [drive:][path]

5.12 Activity: Using the CD Command

Note: The DATA disk is in Drive A. The default drive is Drive A, and the A:\> is displayed on the screen.

Step 1   Key in the following: A:\>**CD** **Enter**

    A:\>CD
    A:\

    A:\>_

WHAT'S HAPPENING? This display tells you that you are in the root directory of the DATA disk and that any command you enter will apply to this root directory, which is also the default directory. You can change the default subdirectory by using the CD command. You are going to change the default subdirectory from the root to the subdirectory called POLYSCI.

Step 2   Key in the following: A:\>**CD POLYSCI** [Enter]

Step 3   Key in the following: A:\POLYSCI>**CD** [Enter]

```
A:\>CD POLYSCI

A:\POLYSCI>CD
A:\POLYSCI

A:\POLYSCI>_
```

WHAT'S HAPPENING? In Step 2, CD followed by the name of the subdirectory changed the default from the root directory to the subdirectory, POLYSCI. Since you changed the default directory, the prompt now says A:\POLYSCI>. However, you can always confirm that you changed the default directory by keying in CD. CD with no parameters always displays the default drive and default subdirectory. When you keyed in CD, it displayed A:\POLYSCI. This display tells you that you are in the subdirectory \POLYSCI on the DATA disk in Drive A and indicates that any command you enter with no parameters will apply to this default subdirectory. You can think of the command this way: CD with no parameters shows you the current directory; CD followed by a subdirectory name changes the subdirectory. CD cannot be used to change drives.

Step 4   Key in the following: A:\POLYSCI>**DIR** [Enter]

```
A:\POLYSCI>DIR

 Volume in drive A is DATADISK
 Volume Serial Number is 2F26-1901
 Directory of A:\POLYSCI

.              <DIR>         06-20-94    5:59p
..             <DIR>         06-20-94    5:59p
        2 file(s)                 0 bytes
                        1,212,928 bytes free

A:\POLYSCI>_
```

WHAT'S HAPPENING? You are displaying the contents of the default directory, but the default is now the directory of \POLYSCI rather than the root directory. Thus, when you use a command, it always assumes the default drive and default subdirectory, unless you specify another drive and/or subdirectory.

Step 5   Key in the following: A:\POLYSCI>**CD ** [Enter]

```
A:\POLYSCI>CD \

A:\>_
```

WHAT'S HAPPENING? By keying in CD \, you were telling DOS to move you to the root directory of the DATA disk. The first backslash always means the root directory.

5.13 Relative and Absolute Paths

You are going to add additional subdirectories to the tree structure so that the levels will look like those in Figure 5.7. To create these additional subdirectories, you use the MD or make directory command (MKDIR or MD). The command syntax allows these parameters: MD [*drive:*]*path*.

Figure 5.7   *Directory with Subdirectories*

The *drive:* is the letter of the drive that contains the disk on which the subdirectory is to be created (such as A: or B: or C:). If you omit the drive designator, DOS creates the subdirectory on the default or current drive. The *path* is the path name of the directory in which the subdirectory is to be created. If you omit the path name, the subdirectory is created in the default or current subdirectory.

It is important to understand the **absolute path** and the **relative path**. The absolute path is the complete and total hierarchical structure. You start at the top and work your way down through every subdirectory without skipping a directory. The absolute path is always absolutely correct.

To give an example, imagine you are on holiday in Paris and staying at a secluded hotel, the *du Jeu de Paume* on the *l'Île Saint Louis*. There are many places you want to see: the Eiffel Tower, the *Palais Royal*, the *Musée du Louvre*, and *l'Opéra*. To get around Paris, you will use the Metro (the subway). The closest station to your hotel (and the only one you can find) is *Gare du Pont Marie*. You are unfamiliar with Paris, but the *Pont Marie* station is your root—you always start at this station.

You have purchased tickets to see the French ballet at *l'Opéra*. To get to *l'Opéra*, you are going to take the Metro. You begin at the *Pont Marie* station, which stops at the *Palais Royal*, and you arrive at *l'Opéra*. The path from *Pont Marie* to *l'Opéra* is absolute. You must stop at every station and always move in the same direction from the root (*Pont Marie*) to your destination (*l'Opéra*). The same principle applies to directories. When you give an absolute path, you are absolutely starting at the root (the top) and passing by every directory on the way to the file you are trying to find. You skip nothing.

The relative path is relative to where you are. You are at *l'Opéra* and now you want to go the *Louvre*. You are going to meet a friend. He knows how to get the *Palais Royal*. You both can meet there and go to the *Louvre*. Neither of you needs to go back to your original station—*Pont Marie* (the root). You can go to the *Palais Royal* station and catch another train to the *Louvre*. This is the relative path, relative to where you are. If you are already at the *Palais Royal* station, you can go either to the *Louvre* or to *l'Opéra*. The same principle holds true with subdirectories. If you are already in a subdirectory, you do not have to return to the root directory to move to a directory beneath you in the hierarchical structure. DOS will know where to go by your relative position in directory structure, the path going down the hierarchy.

However, a directory knows only about the directories immediately beneath it and the directory immediately above it. There can be many directories beneath it (many children directories) but only one directory above it (the parent directory). Each directory knows only its immediate children directories and its parent directory—no more. If you want to move to a different parent subdirectory, you must return to the root. The root is the only parent of all the directories.

Thus, returning to the holiday in Paris, if you want to go to the Eiffel Tower, you cannot get there from the *Louvre* or *l'Opéra*. Nor does it help to return to the *Palais Royal*. The Eiffel Tower is another subway line altogether. You must return to the *Pont Marie* station (the root) and take another subway line (path) to visit the Eiffel Tower. The same is true of subdirectories. If the subdirectory is not in your current hierarchical structure, you must return to the root. Once you get to the root, you can choose where you want to go. There are many places to go. It is like a subway—you must pass through all the stations to get to your destination. Furthermore, if you take a holiday in New York (different disk), it also has Grand Central Station (root) and entirely different places to visit (subdirectories) like the Empire State Building, the Lincoln Center for the Performing Arts, and the Metropolitan Museum of Art, but the principle is the same—you still need a path to follow. See Figure 5.8.

Figure 5.8   The Paris Metro

5.14 Activity: Creating More Subdirectories

Note: The DATA disk is in Drive A. The A:\> is displayed as the default drive and the default directory.

Step 1   Key in the following: A:\>**CD** **Enter**

```
A:\>CD
A:\

A:\>_
```

WHAT'S HAPPENING? You confirmed that the default directory is the root of the DATA disk. To create three subdirectories under POLYSCI, you will use the MD command along with the subdirectory names. The subdirectories will be called USA, JAPAN, and FRANCE. You will begin with an absolute path and then use a relative path.

Step 2   Key in the following: A:\>**MD A:\POLYSCI\USA** Enter

```
A:\>MD A:\POLYSCI\USA

A:\>_
```

WHAT'S HAPPENING? You have given absolute instructions to DOS as to where to create the directory. You issued the command—MD (make a directory)—followed by the location (Go to Drive A, under the root directory—the first backslash—under the directory called POLYSCI.) The next backslash is a delimiter to separate POLYSCI from the next entry. Then you can add your new subdirectory called USA. You could not create USA until you created POLYSCI because it is a hierarchy. Looking at the screen, however, nothing seems to have happened.

Step 3   Key in the following: A:\>**DIR POLYSCI** Enter

```
A:\>DIR POLYSCI

 Volume in drive A is DATADISK
 Volume Serial Number is 2F26-1901
 Directory of A:\POLYSCI

 .            <DIR>         06-20-94    5:59p
 ..           <DIR>         06-20-94    5:59p
 USA          <DIR>         06-20-94    6:08p
        3 file(s)                  0 bytes
                        1,212,416 bytes free

A:\>_
```

WHAT'S HAPPENING? You indeed have a subdirectory called USA under the root under POLYSCI. You are now going to create the subdirectory called JAPAN. Here you can use a relative path. The default prompt shows you that you are already in Drive A. If you are already in Drive A, you do not need to include the drive letter because DOS assumes the default drive, unless you tell it otherwise. The default directory is the root. The \ is shown in the prompt, which tells you that you are in the root directory and that it is your default. Since you are already in the root, you do not need to include it.

Step 4   Key in the following: A:\>**MD POLYSCI\JAPAN** Enter

Step 5   Key in the following: A:\>**DIR POLYSCI** Enter

```
A:\>MD POLYSCI\JAPAN

A:\>DIR POLYSCI
```

```
Volume in drive A is DATADISK
Volume Serial Number is 2F26-1901
Directory of A:\POLYSCI


.              <DIR>         06-20-94    5:59p
..             <DIR>         06-20-94    5:59p
USA            <DIR>         06-20-94    6:08p
JAPAN          <DIR>         06-20-94    6:09p
         4 file(s)               0 bytes
                       1,211,904 bytes free

A:\>_
```

WHAT'S HAPPENING? You created the subdirectory JAPAN under POLYSCI and then you used the DIR command to see that JAPAN was indeed created. As you can see, in Step 2, you used the absolute path to create the directory. In Step 4, you used the default values and created a subdirectory using the relative path.

Step 6   Key in the following: A:\>**CD POLYSCI** [Enter]

```
A:\>CD POLYSCI

A:\POLYSCI>_
```

WHAT'S HAPPENING? You have changed the default directory to POLYSCI, which is under the root directory. Using the relative path, you are going to create one more subdirectory, FRANCE, under the root that is under POLYSCI. Remember, you are in POLYSCI under the root on the DATA disk, so all you need to do is use a relative path name—relative to where you are.

Step 7   Key in the following: A:\POLYSCI>**MD FRANCE** [Enter]

Step 8   Key in the following: A:\POLYSCI>**DIR** [Enter]

```
A:\POLYSCI>MD FRANCE

A:\POLYSCI>DIR

 Volume in drive A is DATADISK
 Volume Serial Number is 2F26-1901
 Directory of A:\POLYSCI
```

```
         .           <DIR>         06-20-94    5:59p
         ..          <DIR>         06-20-94    5:59p
         USA         <DIR>         06-20-94    6:08p
         JAPAN       <DIR>         06-20-94    6:09p
         FRANCE      <DIR>         06-20-94    6:11p
                5 file(s)               0 bytes
                              1,211,392 bytes free


  A:\POLYSCI>_
```

WHAT'S HAPPENING? You needed only to key in FRANCE. The path was assumed from the position relative to where you were.

Step 9   Key in the following: A:\POLYSCI>**MD \MEXICO** [Enter]

Step 10   Key in the following: A:\POLYSCI>**DIR** [Enter]

```
  A:\POLYSCI>MD \MEXICO

  A:\POLYSCI>DIR

     Volume in drive A is DATADISK
     Volume Serial Number is 2F26-1901
     Directory of A:\POLYSCI

         .           <DIR>         06-20-94    5:59p
         ..          <DIR>         06-20-94    5:59p
         USA         <DIR>         06-20-94    6:08p
         JAPAN       <DIR>         06-20-94    6:09p
         FRANCE      <DIR>         06-20-94    6:11p
                5 file(s)               0 bytes
                              1,210,880 bytes free


  A:\POLYSCI>_
```

WHAT'S HAPPENING? You created the subdirectory MEXICO, but where is it? Here is a common mistake users make. When you keyed in \MEXICO, you were keying in an absolute path. Remember, the first backslash *always* means the root so now the directory called MEXICO is under the root, not under POLYSCI.

Step 11   Key in the following: A:\POLYSCI>**DIR ** [Enter]

```
  A:\POLYSCI>DIR \

     Volume in drive A is DATADISK
     Volume Serial Number is 2F26-1901
     Directory of A:\
```

```
POLYSCI        <DIR>          06-20-94    5:59p
PHYSED         <DIR>          06-20-94    6:00p
MEXICO         <DIR>          06-20-94    6:12p
        3 file(s)                  0 bytes
                         1,210,880 bytes free

A:\POLYSCI>_
```

WHAT'S HAPPENING? By keying in `DIR \`, you asked to look at the root directory. As you can see, looking at the screen display of the DATA disk, `MEXICO` is under the root directory. DOS simply followed your instructions. Remember, there are no files in the newly created subdirectories. You have made "rooms" for files. You can create subdirectories wherever you wish as long as the proper path is included. You must pay attention to where you are and whether you are keying in an absolute path or a relative path. If you key in an absolute path, you will always be correct. If you key in a relative path, you must remember that DOS will create the subdirectory relative to where you are.

Step 12   Key in the following: `A:\POLYSCI>`**MD \PHYSED\TENNIS** [Enter]

```
A:\POLYSCI>MD \PHYSED\TENNIS

A:\POLYSCI>_
```

WHAT'S HAPPENING? Since the default or "current" directory at this time is `POLYSCI`, you first had to tell DOS to return to the root (`\`) and then go to the subdirectory called `PHYSED`. Remember, the relative path only looks down or under `POLYSCI`. Thus, the path is `\PHYSED`. You told DOS that under `PHYSED` the name for the new subdirectory was `TENNIS`. The second backslash (`PHYSED\TENNIS`) is a delimiter separating the first subdirectory name from the second subdirectory name. The first backslash indicates the root. Any other backslash is a delimiter. This statement is always true. The MD command does not change the current or default directory. You can verify that you created the subdirectory `TENNIS` under the subdirectory `\PHYSED` by using the DIR command with the path name.

Step 13   Key in the following: `A:\POLYSCI>`**DIR \PHYSED** [Enter]

```
A:\POLYSCI>DIR \PHYSED

  Volume in drive A is DATADISK
  Volume Serial Number is 2F26-1901
  Directory of A:\PHYSED


  .              <DIR>          06-20-94    6:00p
  ..             <DIR>          06-20-94    6:00p
  TENNIS         <DIR>          06-20-94    6:13p
```

```
        3 file(s)                   0 bytes
                         1,210,368 bytes free

A:\POLYSCI>_
```

WHAT'S HAPPENING? The subdirectory PHYSED is displayed with the TENNIS subdirectory listed. It was very important to key in the backslash in \PHYSED in order to tell DIR to go up to the root and then down to the subdirectory PHYSED. If you had not included the \ and had keyed in DIR PHYSED only, DOS would have given you a File not found message because DIR would have looked below POLYSCI *only*. PHYSED is under the root directory, not under the subdirectory POLYSCI.

5.15 Knowing the Default Directory

Since DOS always uses default values unless you specify otherwise, knowing the current default is very important. Recognizing the default drive is easy because the screen displays the prompt or disk drive letter, A> or B>, or C>. Knowing the default subdirectory is not so easy. You can always key in the CD command, which will display the default or current drive and directory you are in, but it would be easier if you could display the default subdirectory as well as the default drive on the screen. For most systems today, when you boot the system, there is a special file called AUTOEXEC.BAT that sets the prompt so that it displays the current drive and directory. It does this by means of the internal command called PROMPT. The PROMPT command can be used at any time to alter the prompt. The prompt will stay the way you set it until you change it or turn off the computer. There are many options to the PROMPT command that will be explored.

5.16 The PROMPT Command

The system or command prompt is a letter of the alphabet designating the default or disk drive, followed by the greater than sign, such as A> or C>. This prompt is always displayed when you first boot the system. With the introduction of DOS 6.0, if you do not set the prompt to display the default directory as well as the default drive, DOS will do it for you. However, the prompt can be changed to reflect what you want displayed because all you are changing is the way the prompt looks. The new display does not limit the function of the prompt. The new display will function as always. You can do this because PROMPT is an internal command. The syntax is:

PROMPT   [*text*]

The PROMPT command also has some special characters that mean specific things. These are called **metastrings**. When you include one of these metastrings, it establishes a specific value for its meaning. Metastrings always have the syntax $c where c represents any of the following values:

```
PROMPT [text]
```

```
text      Specifies a new command prompt.
Prompt    Can be made up of normal characters and the following
          special codes:
  $Q      = (equal sign)
  $$      $ (dollar sign)
  $T      Current time
  $D      Current date
  $P      Current drive and path
  $V      MS-DOS version number
  $N      Current drive
  $G      > (greater-than sign)
  $L      < (less-than sign)
  $B      | (pipe)
  $H      Backspace (erases previous character)
  $E      Escape code (ASCII code 27)
  $_      Carriage return and linefeed
```

Type PROMPT without parameters to reset the prompt to the old default setting of
C>.

The following activity allows you to change the prompt and use text data as well as
metastrings. PROMPT when keyed in without any parameters returns the displayed prompt to the default value (A> or B> or C>).

5.17 Activity: Changing the Prompt

Note: The DATA disk is in Drive A. The default drive is Drive A. The default
          subdirectory is POLYSCI. The A:\POLYSCI> is displayed.

Step 1   Note it is the letter G, not the letter Q. Key in the following:
          A:\POLYSCI>**PROMPT HELLO $g** [Enter]

```
A:\POLYSCI>PROMPT HELLO $g

HELLO >_
```

WHAT'S HAPPENING? You changed the way the prompt looks. You no longer see
A:\POLYSCI>, but instead the text you supplied, HELLO. The greater than sign, >,
appeared because you keyed in $g. Every time DOS sees $g, it returns the
metastring value for g, which is the >. The function of the prompt has not changed,
only its appearance. The new prompt works just as if A > or B> or C> were displayed.
Any command keyed in works the same way. Remember to key in what appears after
the >.

Step 2   Key in the following: HELLO >**VOL** [Enter]

```
HELLO >VOL

 Volume in drive A is DATADISK
 Volume Serial Number is 2F26-1901

HELLO >_
```

WHAT'S HAPPENING? As you can see, the VOL command works the same way. What if you change drives?

Step 3   Key in the following: HELLO >**C:** [Enter]

```
HELLO >C:

HELLO >_
```

WHAT'S HAPPENING? You changed the default drive to C, but, by looking at the screen, there is no way to tell what the default drive is.

Step 4   Key in the following: HELLO >**VOL** [Enter]

```
HELLO >VOL

 Volume in drive C has no label
 Volume Serial Number is 1CD1-5E42

HELLO >_
```

WHAT'S HAPPENING? You changed the designated drive. You can see, however, that having the default drive letter displayed on the screen is very important. You can always return the prompt to the default value by keying in the command with no parameters.

Step 5   Key in the following: HELLO >**PROMPT** [Enter]

```
HELLO >PROMPT

C>_
```

WHAT'S HAPPENING? Now you know what drive you are in. You can see the default drive, which is Drive C, displayed in the prompt.

Step 6   Key in the following: C>**A:** [Enter]

```
C>A:

A>_
```

WHAT'S HAPPENING? You know what drive you are in, but what subdirectory are you in? Knowing the default subdirectory is as important as knowing the default drive.

Step 7   Key in the following: A>**CD** Enter

```
A>CD
A:\POLYSCI

A>_
```

WHAT'S HAPPENING? Keying in CD with no parameters showed that you are in the POLYSCI directory. However, rather than keying in CD every time you want to know the default drive and directory, you can change the prompt so it will display the default drive and directory automatically.

Step 8   Key in the following: A>**PROMPT pg** Enter

```
A>PROMPT $p$g

A:\POLYSCI>_
```

WHAT'S HAPPENING? You changed the prompt to display not only the default disk drive but also the default subdirectory (pg). The metastring $p returns the value of the path, and the metastring $g returns the value of the greater than sign. Notice how DOS returned you to the last subdirectory you were in on the DATA disk. DOS keeps track of which subdirectory you were in the last time you were on that drive. Most users get this **customized prompt**, because someone placed this command in the AUTOEXEC.BAT file. You will learn about this file later. Thus, if you do not see the customized prompt, you know how to change it. In addition, there are certain conventions that are used. If you are using a stand-alone computer, most often you will see the prompt you just keyed in. However, networked systems tend to like to use brackets.

Step 9   Key in the following: A:\POLYSCI>**PROMPT [$p]** Enter

```
A:\POLYSCI>PROMPT [$p]

[A:\POLYSCI]_
```

WHAT'S HAPPENING? As you can see, the prompt looks different, but it performs in the same way. It does not matter what your prompt looks like as long as you can see the default drive and directory. If your prompt contains brackets, you do not need to change to the > sign.

Step 10   Key in the following: A: \ **PROMPT pg** [Enter]

```
A:\PROMPT $p$g

A:\POLYSCI>_
```

WHAT'S HAPPENING? You changed the prompt to display the path followed by the greater than sign (>).

5.18 Subdirectory Markers

The single . (one period) in a subdirectory is the specific subdirectory name. The . . (two periods) is the parent directory of the current subdirectory. The parent directory is the one immediately above the current subdirectory. You can use the . . as a shorthand version of the parent directory name to move up the subdirectory tree structure. You can move up the hierarchy because a child always has one parent. However, you cannot use the . . to move down the hierarchy because a parent can have many children.

5.19 Activity: Using Subdirectory Markers

Note: The DATA disk is in Drive A. The default drive is Drive A. The default subdirectory is POLYSCI. The A: \ POLYSCI> is displayed.

Step 1   Key in the following: A: \ POLYSCI> **CD ..** [Enter]

```
A:\POLYSCI>CD ..

A:\>_
```

WHAT'S HAPPENING? You used the .. to move up to the root directory. The root directory is the parent of the subdirectory \ POLYSCI.

Step 2   Key in the following: A: \ > **MD PHYSED \ GOLF** [Enter]

```
A:\>MD PHYSED\GOLF

A:\>_
```

WHAT'S HAPPENING? You created a subdirectory called GOLF under the subdirectory called PHYSED. Since you were at the root directory of the DATA disk, you needed to include the relative path name, PHYSED\GOLF. Had you keyed in MD \GOLF, the GOLF subdirectory would have been created in the root directory because the root directory is the default directory. However, you do not need to include the path name of PHYSED if you change directories and make PHYSED the default directory.

Step 3   Key in the following: A:\> **CD PHYSED** [Enter]

```
A:\>CD PHYSED

A:\PHYSED>_
```

WHAT'S HAPPENING? PHYSED is now the default directory. Any activity that occurs will automatically default to this directory, unless otherwise specified. You may use a relative path name.

Step 4   Key in the following: A:\PHYSED> **MD DANCE** [Enter]

Step 5   Key in the following: A:\PHYSED> **DIR** [Enter]

```
A:\PHYSED>MD DANCE

A:\PHYSED>DIR

 Volume in drive A is DATADISK
 Volume Serial Number is 2F26-1901
 Directory of A:\PHYSED

.              <DIR>        06-20-94    6:00p
..             <DIR>        06-20-94    6:00p
TENNIS         <DIR>        06-20-94    6:13p
GOLF           <DIR>        06-20-94    6:18p
DANCE          <DIR>        06-20-94    6:18p
        5 file(s)              0 bytes
                      1,209,344 bytes free

A:\PHYSED>_
```

WHAT'S HAPPENING? You used the relative path name. You did not have to key in the drive letter or the first backslash (the root), only the name of the directory DANCE that now is under the subdirectory called PHYSED.

Step 6   Key in the following: A:\PHYSED> **CD DANCE** [Enter]

```
A:\PHYSED>CD DANCE

A:\PHYSED\DANCE>_
```

WHAT'S HAPPENING? You used the relative path to move to the subdirectory DANCE that is under PHYSED, which is under the root. You are going to create one more directory under PHYSED called CYCLING, but you are going to use the subdirectory markers.

Step 7   Key in the following: A:\PHYSED\DANCE>**MD ..\CYCLING** Enter

Step 8   Key in the following: A:\PHYSED\DANCE>**DIR** Enter

Step 9   Key in the following: A:\PHYSED\DANCE>**DIR ..** Enter

```
 Volume in drive A is DATADISK
 Volume Serial Number is 2F26-1901
 Directory of A:\PHYSED\DANCE

 .              <DIR>         06-20-94   6:18p
 ..             <DIR>         06-20-94   6:18p
        2 file(s)                  0 bytes
                         1,208,832 bytes free


A:\PHYSED\DANCE>DIR ..

 Volume in drive A is DATADISK
 Volume Serial Number is 2F26-1901
 Directory of A:\PHYSED

 .              <DIR>         06-20-94   6:00p
 ..             <DIR>         06-20-94   6:00p
 TENNIS         <DIR>         06-20-94   6:13p
 GOLF           <DIR>         06-20-94   6:18p
 DANCE          <DIR>         06-20-94   6:18p
 CYCLING        <DIR>         06-20-94   6:19p
        6 file(s)                  0 bytes
                         1,208,832 bytes free


A:\PHYSED\DANCE>_
```

WHAT'S HAPPENING? When you used the MD command, you first used . . (the subdirectory markers) to tell DOS to go to the parent of DANCE, which is PHYSED. You then used the delimiter to tell DOS that you wanted to go down from PHYSED and create CYCLING. When you keyed in the DIR command, you were looking at the default directory DANCE. CYCLING does not appear there because you did not put it there. When you keyed the DIR command followed by . . you told DOS to look at the directory that was the parent of DANCE, which was PHYSED. CYCLING indeed appeared there.

Step 10   Key in the following: A:\PHSYED\DANCE>**CD ..** Enter

```
A:\PHYSED\DANCE>CD ..

A:\PHYSED>_
```

WHAT'S HAPPENING? You used the subdirectory markers to move to the parent of DANCE, which is PHYSED.

Step 11   Key in the following: A:\PHYSED>**CD** \ [Enter]

```
A:\PHYSED>CD \

A:\>_
```

WHAT'S HAPPENING? You moved to the root directory of the DATA disk. Using the command CD \ will always take you to the root directory of any disk. The following figures demonstrate what the DATA disk now looks like.

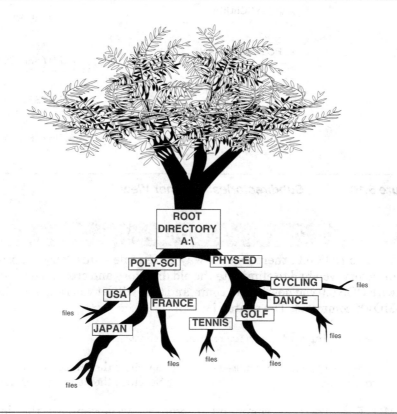

Figure 5.9   *Structure of the DATA Disk*

Another way to illustrate the subdirectory structure pictorially is:

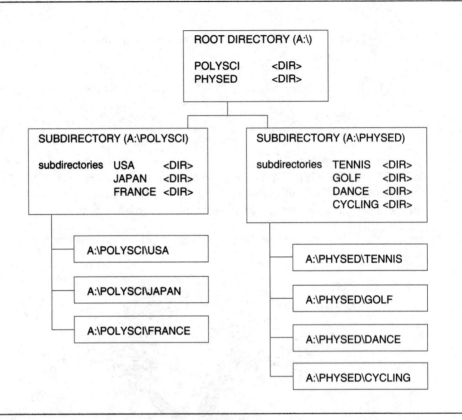

Figure 5.10   Subdirectories: Another View

5.20 Changing the Names of Directories DOS 6.0 and Above

Prior to DOS 6.0, there was no way to rename a directory. In order to rename a directory, you had to eliminate the old directory and create a new one. Fortunately, with DOS 6.0 you now have a command that will let you rename a directory. It is the MOVE command. The syntax is:

```
MOVE [drive:][path]dirname1 dirname2
```

```
[drive:][path]dirname1      Specifies the directory you want to rename.
dirname2                    Specifies the new name of the directory.
```

MOVE is an external command. It requires two parameters: the old directory name and the new directory name.

5.21 Activity: Using MOVE To Rename a Directory

Note: The DATA disk is in Drive A. The A:\> is displayed as the default drive
            and the default directory.

Step 1   Key in the following: A:\>**MOVE PHYSED GYM** [Enter]

Step 2   Key in the following: A:\>**DIR** [Enter]

```
A:\>MOVE PHYSED GYM
a:\physed => a:\gym [ok]


A:\>DIR

 Volume in drive A is DATADISK
 Volume Serial Number is 2F26-1901
 Directory of A:\

POLYSCI        <DIR>         06-20-94    5:59p
GYM            <DIR>         06-20-94    6:00p
MEXICO         <DIR>         06-20-94    6:12p
        3 file(s)                0 bytes
                    1,208,832 bytes free

A:\>_
```

WHAT'S HAPPENING? You used the MOVE command to change the name of the
PHYSED directory to GYM. You got a confirmation message on the screen that the
rename process was successful. You then used DIR to confirm the directory name
was changed. Indeed, PHYSED is no longer there, but GYM is.

Step 3   Key in the following: A:\>**MOVE GYM\CYCLING GYM\BIKING**
            [Enter]

Step 4   Key in the following: A:\>**DIR GYM** [Enter]

```
A:\>MOVE GYM\CYCLING GYM\BIKING
a:\gym\cycling => a:\gym\biking [ok]

A:\>DIR GYM

 Volume in drive A is DATADISK
 Volume Serial Number is 2F26-1901
 Directory of A:\GYM
```

```
    .               <DIR>           06-20-94    6:00p
    ..              <DIR>           06-20-94    6:00p
   TENNIS           <DIR>           06-20-94    6:13p
   GOLF             <DIR>           06-20-94    6:18p
   DANCE            <DIR>           06-20-94    6:18p
   BIKING           <DIR>           06-20-94    6:19p
         6 file(s)                      0 bytes
                            1,208,832 bytes free

   A:\>_
```

WHAT'S HAPPENING? You used the MOVE command to change the name of the CYCLING directory under GYM to BIKING. As long as you give the correct path name, either absolute or relative, you can be anywhere and rename a directory somewhere else. You got a confirmation message on the screen that the rename process was successful. You then used DIR to confirm the name change. Indeed, CYCLING is no longer there, but BIKING is.

5.22 The TREE Command

You have been creating subdirectories and changing their names. If you were working with many directories, how would you keep track of them? DOS has a solution to this problem: the TREE command. It shows you the structure of the tree-shaped directory on any disk. The syntax for this external command is:

```
TREE [drive:][path] [/F] [/A]

/F Displays the names of the files in each directory.
/A Uses ASCII instead of extended characters.
```

The /F parameter will show you all the files in the subdirectories. The /A allows you to use an alternate graphic character set. There are some other differences between the current TREE command and earlier DOS versions. First, the TREE command now displays its output in a graphical manner, whereas earlier DOS versions displayed the output in a text manner. Second, any version of the TREE command prior to 4.0 always shows the entire tree from the root level down. Newer versions allow you to select a subdirectory and look only at that subtree.

5.23 Activity: Using the TREE Command

Note: The DATA disk is in Drive A. The A:\> is displayed as the default drive and the default directory.

Step 1   Key in the following: A:\>**TREE** [Enter]

```
A:\>TREE
Directory PATH listing for Volume DATADISK
Volume Serial Number is 2F26-1901
A:.
```
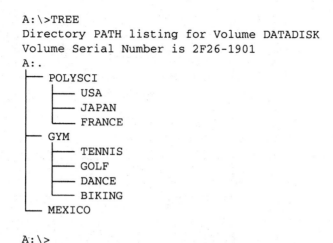
```
├── POLYSCI
│     ├── USA
│     ├── JAPAN
│     └── FRANCE
├── GYM
│     ├── TENNIS
│     ├── GOLF
│     ├── DANCE
│     └── BIKING
└── MEXICO
```

```
A:\>
```

WHAT'S HAPPENING? The TREE command displayed the directories in the shape of a hierarchical tree. The command started with the root directory and listed the subdirectories beneath the root, including any subdirectories that had subdirectories of their own. The only difference between the versions of DOS is the way the output is displayed.

Step 2   Key in the following: A:\>**TREE   C:\DOS6BK** [Enter]

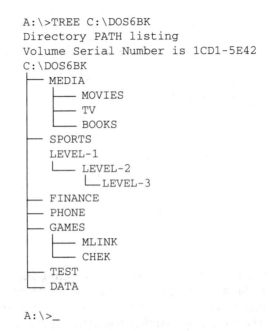

```
A:\>TREE C:\DOS6BK
Directory PATH listing
Volume Serial Number is 1CD1-5E42
C:\DOS6BK
├── MEDIA
│       ├── MOVIES
│       ├── TV
│       └── BOOKS
├── SPORTS
│   LEVEL-1
│       └── LEVEL-2
│               └──LEVEL-3
├── FINANCE
├── PHONE
├── GAMES
│       ├── MLINK
│       └── CHEK
├── TEST
└── DATA


A:\>_
```

WHAT'S HAPPENING? You used the TREE command to look at one branch on the hard disk, the DOS6BK directory. As you can see, it has many directories and subdirectories. So far, you have been dealing primarily with directories, However, as discussed in the beginning of the chapter, one of the concerns users have is locating files. You can use the TREE command and the /F parameter to locate files. You are going to look at the MEDIA branch, which is one of the DOS6BK branches. The MEDIA branch will be displayed with all its directories and files.

Step 3   Key in the following: A:\> **TREE C:\DOS6BK\MEDIA /F** Enter

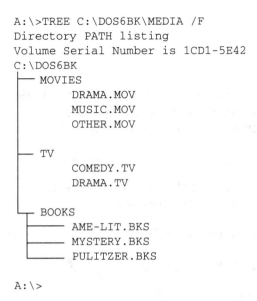

```
A:\>TREE C:\DOS6BK\MEDIA /F
Directory PATH listing
Volume Serial Number is 1CD1-5E42
C:\DOS6BK
├── MOVIES
│       DRAMA.MOV
│       MUSIC.MOV
│       OTHER.MOV
│
├── TV
│
│       COMEDY.TV
│       DRAMA.TV
│
└── BOOKS
    ├──────── AME-LIT.BKS
    ├──────── MYSTERY.BKS
    └──────── PULITZER.BKS

A:\>
```

WHAT'S HAPPENING? Now you can see that MEDIA is under the DOS6BK directory which is under the root of the hard disk. It has many subdirectories of its own—MOVIES, TV, and BOOKS. In addition, each of these directories has files in it. MOVIES has the files called DRAMA.MOV, MUSIC.MOV, and OTHER.MOV. The TV directory has the files called COMEDY.TV and DRAMA.TV. The BOOKS directory has the files AME-LIT.BKS, MYSTERY.BKS, and PULITZER.BKS. This time the /F parameter showed not only the subdirectories but also all the files inside each subdirectory. On a large hard disk the task of looking at all the files can seem endless. Most often, the user is interested only in a specific subdirectory and the files located there. The TREE command gives the user the ability to choose a specific subdirectory.

5.24 Removing Directories

In the same way a disk can be cluttered with files, so it can be even more cluttered with subdirectories. Removing subdirectories requires a special command, the remove directory command (RD or RMDIR). If a subdirectory has files in it, you cannot remove the subdirectory until the subdirectory is empty of files. This two-step process prevents you from accidentally wiping out not only a directory but also the files inside. Thus, if a subdirectory has files in it, you must delete (DEL) the file(s) first, then remove the subdirectory. You cannot delete a directory that has hidden or system files. In addition, you cannot remove the default directory. In order to remove a subdirectory, you must be in another directory. Furthermore, since you created the directories from the top down, to remove them, you must remove them from the bottom up. This means using RD on one directory at a time. You cannot use wildcards with RD. The command syntax is:

```
RMDIR       [drive:]path
```

or

```
RD [drive:]path
```

If you do not include the drive designator, DOS will use the default drive. The remove directory command will not remove the directory you are currently in (the current directory), nor will it ever remove the root directory.

5.25 Activity: Using the RD Command

Note: The DATA disk is in Drive A. The A:\> is displayed as the default drive and the default directory.

Step 1   Key in the following: A:\>**RD MEXICO** [Enter]

Step 2   Key in the following: A:\>**DIR** [Enter]

```
A:\>RD MEXICO

A:\>DIR

 Volume in drive A is DATADISK
 Volume Serial Number is 2F26-1901
 Directory of A:\

POLYSCI        <DIR>           06-20-94    5:59p
GYM            <DIR>           06-20-94    6:00p
        2 file(s)                   0 bytes
                        1,209,344 bytes free

A:\>_
```

WHAT'S HAPPENING? You indeed removed the directory called MEXICO in the root directory of the DATA disk.

Step 3   Key in the following: A:\>**CD POLYSCI\JAPAN** [Enter]

Step 4   Key in the following: A:\POLYSCI\JAPAN>**RD JAPAN** [Enter]

```
A:\>CD POLYSCI\JAPAN

A:\POLYSCI\JAPAN>RD JAPAN
Invalid path, not directory,
or directory not empty

A:\POLYSCI\JAPAN>_
```

WHAT'S HAPPENING? RD did not remove the directory, \POLYSCI\JAPAN. You got an error message. In this case, the path is valid. JAPAN is a directory and it is empty of files. The problem is that you cannot remove a directory you are in. RD will never remove the default directory. Thus, the root directory can never be removed.

Step 5   Key in the following: A:\POLYSCI\JAPAN>**CD** .. Enter

Step 6   Key in the following: A:\POLYSCI>**DIR** Enter

Step 7   Key in the following: A:\POLYSCI>**RD JAPAN** Enter

Step 8   Key in the following: A:\POLYSCI>**DIR** Enter

```
       .            <DIR>         06-20-94    5:59p
       ..           <DIR>         06-20-94    5:59p
 USA                <DIR>         06-20-94    6:08p
 JAPAN              <DIR>         06-20-94    6:09p
 FRANCE             <DIR>         06-20-94    6:11p
          5 file(s)                      0 bytes
                          1,209,344 bytes free

A:\POLYSCI>RD JAPAN

A:\POLYSCI>DIR

 Volume in drive A is DATADISK
 Volume Serial Number is 2F26-1901
 Directory of A:\POLYSCI

       .            <DIR>         06-20-94    5:59p
       ..           <DIR>         06-20-94    5:59p
 USA                <DIR>         06-20-94    6:08p
 FRANCE             <DIR>         06-20-94    6:11p
          4 file(s)                      0 bytes
                          1,209,856 bytes free

A:\POLYSCI>_
```

WHAT'S HAPPENING? You moved to the parent of JAPAN, which is POLYSCI. You used the DIR command to see that JAPAN was there. You then used the RD command and the DIR command again. The subdirectory entry JAPAN <DIR> is not displayed. You did indeed remove it. Remember, as you created the directories in a hierarchical fashion, top-down, you must remove directories bottom-up. So, if JAPAN had a subdirectory beneath it, such as \POLYSCI\JAPAN\INDUSTRY, you would have needed to remove the INDUSTRY subdirectory before you could remove the JAPAN subdirectory.

Step 9   Key in the following: A:\POLYSCI>**CD ** [Enter]

```
A:\POLYSCI>CD \

A:\>_
```

WHAT'S HAPPENING? You have moved to the root directory of the DATA disk.

5.26 The DELTREE Command—DOS 6.0 and Above

As you can see, to remove directories one at a time can be a very laborious process if you have a complex directory structure. Thus, in DOS 6.0, DELTREE was introduced. The DELTREE command, although very useful, can also be very dangerous. It is a command that deletes the directory structure and all the files in the directories from the top down. It is fast, but it is also fatal! It is a good idea to use the TREE command before using DELTREE to ensure you do not delete files or remove directories you wish to keep. The syntax is:

```
DELTREE [/Y] [drive:]path [[drive:]path[...]]
```

/Y   Suppresses prompting to confirm you want to
                delete the subdirectory.
[drive:]path   Specifies the name of the directory you want to
                delete.

Note 1:   Use DELTREE cautiously. Every file and subdirectory within the specified directory will be deleted.

Note 2:   **WARNING!** The version of DELTREE that was included in DOS 6.0 has a fatal flaw. It does not require any parameters. Thus, in DOS 6.0, if you issued the command DELTREE while in the root of C:\, it would completely eliminate *all* the files and *all* the directories on your hard disk. DOS 6.2 corrected this flaw, and now DELTREE requires you to include a subdirectory name. If you are using MS-DOS 6.0, be very, very careful when using DELTREE.

5.27 Activity: Using DELTREE

Note: The DATA disk is in Drive A. The A:\> is displayed as the default drive and the default directory.

Step 1   Key in the following: A:\>**TREE GYM /F** [Enter]

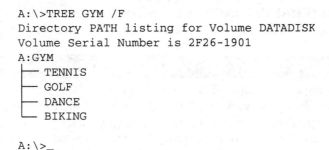

```
A:\>TREE GYM /F
Directory PATH listing for Volume DATADISK
Volume Serial Number is 2F26-1901
A:GYM
├── TENNIS
├── GOLF
├── DANCE
└── BIKING


A:\>_
```

WHAT'S HAPPENING? There are no files in GYM or any of its subdirectories. There is no directory you wish to keep.

Step 2   Key in the following: A:\>**DELTREE GYM** Enter

```
A:\>DELTREE GYM
Delete directory "gym" and all its subdirectories? [yn]_
```

WHAT'S HAPPENING? You get a chance to back out of the DELTREE command by pressing N for No. In this case, you do want to proceed.

Step 3   Press Y Enter

```
A:\>DELTREE GYM
Delete directory "gym" and all its subdirectories? [yn] y
Deleting gym...

A:\>_
```

WHAT'S HAPPENING? The DELTREE command informed you that it was deleting GYM. You can use the DIR command to confirm that GYM is gone.

Step 4   Key in the following: A:\>**DIR** Enter

```
A:\>DIR

  Volume in drive A is DATADISK
  Volume Serial Number is 2F26-1901
  Directory of A:\

POLYSCI      <DIR>          06-20-94   5:59p
       1 file(s)                 0 bytes
                     1,212,416 bytes free

A:\>_
```

WHAT'S HAPPENING? You removed GYM and all its subdirectories with one command. DELTREE is very useful, very fast, and very dangerous.

5.28 Understanding the PATH Command

You have so far changed the current or default subdirectory using the CD *path* command, which works well for locating various data files. In addition, in this chapter you executed two application programs, HPB and THINKER. You changed to the subdirectory where program files were located. You needed to do this in order to execute or run the programs.

The process of executing a program is simple and always the same. You key in the file name of the program, in this case THINK, and DOS looks for a file only in the current default drive and directory. DOS searches first for the file name THINK.COM. If it does not find a file by that name, it searches for THINK.EXE. If it finds no file by that name, its last last search is for THINK.BAT. If it finds no file by any one of those names, it returns to you a message, Bad file or command name. That is DOS's equivalent of telling you it could not find a file by one of those names in the current drive or directory. If it finds a file with the correct name, as it did with THINK.EXE, it takes a copy of the file, places it in memory, and turns control over to that application program. This is the procedure DOS uses to execute a program.

DOS's search for the correct file is limited to the file extensions .COM, .EXE, or .BAT. These are the only file extensions that indicate programs and are sometimes called executables. DOS, again, searched for the file only in the current drive and directory, which is why you had to key in CD \DOS6BK\FINANCE first. That is, where the file is located.

In addition, you have also used external commands such as FORMAT, DISK-COPY, MOVE and TREE which are also programs that are stored as files with either a .COM or .EXE file extension. These are examples of the DOS system utility files. They are just programs you want to execute (executables). When you use these programs, you did not have to key in C: and then CD \DOS in order to execute them. Why, then, when the root of the directory was the default drive and default directory, did those commands work? The files were not on the DATA disk. Based on this information, since those files were not in the default drive and subdirectory, DOS should have given you the message Bad command or file name.

The PATH command sets a search path to other drives and directories. This command tells DOS what other drives and directories you want it to look in for a program file that is not in the current drive or directory. The PATH command looks only for program files that can be executed — .COM, .EXE, or .BAT. All this means is that, when you key in a command and you have set the path, DOS will search for the program in the drives and subdirectories you have selected and, when it finds it, will load and execute it. DOS will not locate files with any other file extensions. You can set the path for command files to another subdirectory or disk drive. On most computer systems today, the default PATH includes the subdirectory where the DOS system utility files are located—C:\DOS. The command syntax is:

```
PATH  [[drive:]path[;...]]
```

To unset the path, the command syntax is:

```
PATH  ;
```

To see the current path, the command syntax is:

```
PATH
```

PATH is the command. PATH with no parameters displays the current path. *drive:* indicates which drive designator you want the path to follow. If you omit the drive designator, DOS will use the default drive. [*path*] is the path name of the subdirectory that contains the command files. You can have DOS search more than one subdirectory, by using the semicolon (;) to indicate another drive and subdirectory (with no spaces between the semicolon and the paths). The semicolon ; used without the drive or path cancels any paths you have set.

5.29 Activity: Using the PATH Command

WARNING! Do not do this activity if you are on a network unless instructed to by your instructor.

Note: The DATA disk is in Drive A. The A: \> is displayed as the default drive and the default directory.

Step 1   Key in the following: A: \>**PATH** **Enter**

```
A:\>PATH
PATH=C:\WINDOWS;C:\DOS;C:\PROG\MOUSE;C:\PROG\BATCH;H:\UTILS\ZIP

A:\>_
```

WHAT'S HAPPENING? You have displayed the current search path that is set. Your display will be different depending on what programs you have on your disk and their locations.

Step 2   Note that a semicolon follows the first PATH. Key in the following:
           A: \>**PATH ;** **Enter**

Step 3   Key in the following: A: \>**PATH** **Enter**

```
A:\>PATH ;

A:\>PATH
No Path


A:\>_
```

WHAT'S HAPPENING? By using ; following PATH, you undid all possible existing search paths. The second PATH command, with no parameters, indicates that there is No Path set.

Step 4   Key in the following: A:\>**TREE** [Enter]

```
A:\>TREE
Bad command or file name

A:\>_
```

WHAT'S HAPPENING? DOS could not execute the external command, TREE.COM, because TREE.COM is not stored as a file in the root directory of the DATA disk. Rather than having to key in C:, then CD \DOS where the file is stored, usually you will use the PATH command, which tells DOS that, if it does not find TREE in the current drive and directory, to continue the search. You tell it what drive and directories to search.

Step 5   Key in the following: A:\>**PATH C:\DOS** [Enter]

Note: Remember, if the DOS system utility programs are in a subdirectory on the hard disk other than \DOS, you must key in the appropriate path name. Refer to your Configuration Table in Chapter 2.8.

Step 6   Key in the following: A:\>**PATH** [Enter]

```
A:\>PATH C:\DOS

A:\>PATH
PATH=C:\DOS

A:\>_
```

WHAT'S HAPPENING? When you first keyed in the PATH C:\DOS command, it appeared that nothing happened. But it has. The second PATH command shows that you have set a path DOS will search. If it does not find the command (file) in the default drive and subdirectory, in this case A:\; it will go to the path set, the subdirectory called \DOS under the root directory of Drive C. There DOS will find the file called TREE.COM.

Step 7 Key in the following: A:\>TREE [Enter]

```
A:\>TREE
Directory PATH listing for Volume DATADISK
Volume Serial Number is 2F26-1901
A:GYM
└── POLYSCI
        ├── USA
        └── FRANCE

A:\>_
```

WHAT'S HAPPENING? You did not get Bad command or file name this time. When DOS could not find the file TREE.COM in the root directory of the DATA disk, it did not give up. Instead, it also searched the path that was set. It found the file on the hard disk in the subdirectory named \DOS, loaded it into memory, and executed it. You can set more than one location for DOS to search.

Step 8 Key in the following: A:\>THINK [Enter]

```
A:\>THINK
Bad command or file name

A:\>_
```

WHAT'S HAPPENING? The THINKER is an application program, but it is not located in the \DOS subdirectory. So, even though the search path is set, it is set only to one location, C:\DOS. In the beginning of this chapter, you found that this program was located in C:\DOS6BK\FINANCE and was called THINK.EXE. You had to change drive and directories in order to execute the program. You do not want to change the default drive and subdirectory to use this program. With the PATH command, you do not have to.

Step 9 Key in the following: A:\>PATH C:\DOS6BK\FINANCE [Enter]

Step 10 Key in the following: A:\>PATH [Enter]

```
A:\>PATH C:\DOS6BK\FINANCE

A:\>PATH
PATH=C:\DOS6BK\FINANCE

A:\>_
```

WHAT'S HAPPENING? You set the search path to the C:\DOS6BK\FINANCE subdirectory on the hard disk, but, by doing so, you canceled the path to the C:\DOS subdirectory. In this example, you wanted to keep both search paths. In other words, instead of just searching the default drive and directory for the necessary program, you want DOS to continue the search first in the C:\DOS subdirectory and then to look in the C:\DOS6BK\FINANCE directory. To instruct DOS to do this, you have to include *all* the directories you want searched in your PATH command. Each directory must be separated by a semicolon.

Step 11   Key in the following: A:\>**PATH   C:\DOS;C:\DOS6BK\FINANCE** [Enter]

Step 12   Key in the following: A:\>**PATH** [Enter]

```
A:\>PATH C:\DOS;C:\DOS6BK\FINANCE

A:\>PATH
PATH=C:\DOS;C:\DOS6BK\FINANCE

A:\>_
```

WHAT'S HAPPENING? You set the path so that, if DOS does not find the program you wish to execute in the default drive and subdirectory (A:\) it will next look in the \DOS directory on the hard disk. If DOS does not find the file there, it will look on the hard disk in the subdirectory C:\DOS6BK\FINANCE. Although it was not mandatory to include the drive letter preceding the subdirectory names, it is usually a good idea to do so. Thus, if you change drives, DOS will still know which drive to look on. In this example, the path was set to C:\DOS and C:\DOS6BK\FINANCE.

Step 13   Key in the following: A:\>**THINK** [Enter]

Step 14   Press [Enter]

WHAT'S HAPPENING? DOS still did not find the THINK.EXE file in the default directory of the DATA disk. However, since you set the search path to the C:\DOS subdirectory, DOS next looked there. The file THINK.EXE was not in that location. DOS then checked the search path and continued to the next location, C:\DOS6BK\FINANCE where The THINKER program is located. Once DOS found it, it could load it.

Step 15   Press **/**

Step 16   Press **Q**

Step 17   Press **Y**

```
A:\>_
```

WHAT'S HAPPENING? You are back at the system level. What if you want to cancel all the paths you set?

Step 18   Key in the following: A:\>**PATH ;** Enter

Step 19   Key in the following: A:\>**PATH** Enter

```
A:\>PATH ;

A:\>PATH
No Path


A:\>_
```

WHAT'S HAPPENING? The PATH command followed by a space and a semicolon cancels any currently set paths. You then executed the PATH command with no parameters. DOS responded with No Path, telling you that DOS will look only in the default drive and subdirectory for executable programs. The path that is set is set for the duration of the time the computer is on or until the user changes it. Most users, as mentioned, have an AUTOEXEC.BAT file that automatically sets the search path each time they boot the system so that, unless the user wishes to make a change, the path is automatically set.

Chapter Summary

1. Subdirectories are created to help organize files on a disk as well as to defeat the file limitation of the root directory.
2. Whenever a disk is formatted, one directory is always created. It is called the root directory.
3. MD is an internal command that allows the user to create a subdirectory.

4. Subdirectory-naming conventions follow DOS file-naming conventions—a limit of 8 characters in the filename and 3 characters for a file extension.
5. A <DIR> following a file name indicates that it is a subdirectory.
6. CD is an internal command that when keyed in by itself will show the user the current or default directory.
7. CD followed by a directory name will change the current directory to the named directory.
8. When managing subdirectories and file names, you must use the backslash (\) as a delimiter to separate subdirectory and/or file names.
9. You may use either the absolute path name or the relative path name. The absolute path name is the entire subdirectory name or names. The relative path only requires the path name relative to your current directory.
10. The way the prompt looks can be changed using the PROMPT command. The PROMPT command followed by a text string will show that text.
11. The PROMPT command has metastrings. When included following the PROMPT command, the metastrings will return a value. For instance, the metastrings pg will set the prompt to display the default drive and subdirectory. To return the prompt to the default value, key in PROMPT with no parameters.
12. Subdirectory markers are shortcuts to using subdirectories. The single dot (.) represents the directory itself. The double dot (..) represents the name of the parent directory.
13. You can move up the tree with subdirectory markers, but not down the tree.
14. The MOVE command, introduced in DOS 6.0, allows you to rename subdirectories.
15. The TREE command displays the structure of a disk. If you have DOS 4.0 or above, the display is graphic.
16. The /F parameter used with the TREE command displays all the files on a disk. If you have DOS 4.0 or above, you can specify a single subdirectory with the /F parameter.
17. RD is an internal command that allows users to eliminate subdirectories.
18. Subdirectories must be empty of files before using the RD command.
19. The root directory can never be eliminated.
20. DELTREE, introduced in DOS 6.0, is an external command that allows you to remove an entire directory including all its files and subdirectories with one command.
21. PATH is an internal command that allows you to tell DOS on what disk and in what subdirectory to search for command files.
22. DOS will search the path for only executable files, with the file extensions of .COM, .EXE, or .BAT.
23. PATH keyed in by itself will display the current path.
24. PATH keyed in with a semicolon will cancel the path.
25. If you have multiple search paths, subdirectory names are separated by semicolons.

Key Terms

Absolute path	Executables	Root directory
Child directory	Hierarchical	Search
Current directory	structure	Path
Customized prompt	Metastring	Subdirectory
Dot .	Parent directory	markers
Double dot . .	Relative path	Tree structure

Discussion Questions

1. List the four major categories of application software and briefly explain their functions.
2. What is the purpose and function of a program file (application program)?
3. Explain the purpose and function of DOS when working with program files and data files.
4. Explain documentation, update notices, and technical support.
5. What file extensions indicate an executable program?
6. What is the purpose and function of the root directory? What symbol is used to represent the root directory?
7. What is a subdirectory?
8. Why would you want to create a subdirectory?
9. What naming conventions must be followed when naming a subdirectory?
10. What is a parent directory?
11. Explain the purpose and function of three directory management commands.
12. Give the syntax for creating a subdirectory.
13. Give the syntax for the CD command.
14. What is the difference between the absolute path and the relative path?
15. If you wanted to create a subdirectory called JAIL under the subdirectory called COURT on Drive A:, would you get the same result by keying in either MD A:\COURT\JAIL, or MD A:\JAIL? Why or why not?
16. What are subdirectory markers? How can they be used?
17. What are metastrings?
18. How can you return the prompt to the default value?
19. Explain the purpose and function of the MOVE command. Explain each part of the syntax.
20. What is the purpose and function of the TREE command? Explain each part of the syntax.
21. How can you find out the structure of a disk?
22. Why will the RD command not remove a directory if there is a file in it?
23. What steps must be followed to remove a directory with RD?
24. What is the purpose and function of the DELTREE command?
25. What precautions might you want to take prior to using DELTREE? Why would you take them?
26. Give the syntax of the DELTREE command and explain each part of the syntax.

27. What is the purpose and function of the PATH command? Explain each part of the syntax.
28. How can you undo the path?
29. How can you set a multiple search path?
30. What is the difference between the path to a file and using the PATH command?

Chapter 6

Internal Commands: COPY and TYPE

Learning Objectives

After completing this chapter you will be able to:

1. Explain the purpose and function of internal commands.
2. Explain the purpose and function of the COPY command.
3. List the file-naming rules.
4. Explain the purpose and function of the TYPE command.
5. Explain the purpose and function of dummy files.
6. Explain when and how to use wildcards with the COPY command.
7. Explain the purpose and use of subdirectory markers.
8. Identify the commands that can be used with subdirectories.
9. Explain when and how files are overwritten.
10. Explain the function, purpose, and dangers of concatenating files.
11. Compare and contrast printing files using the TYPE, COPY, and PRINT commands.

Student Outcomes

1. Copy a file on the same disk using the COPY command.
2. Use wildcards with the COPY command to copy files on the same disk.
3. Display a text file using the TYPE command.
4. Use dummy files with the COPY and TYPE commands.
5. Use the COPY command to make additional files on the same disk but in different subdirectories.
6. Use wildcards with the COPY command to copy files on the same disk to a different subdirectory.

7. Use the COPY and DIR commands with subdirectories.
8. Use subdirectory markers with commands.
9. Overwrite a file using the COPY command.
10. Combine the contents of two or more files using the COPY command.
11. Print files using the TYPE, COPY, and PRINT commands.

Chapter Overview

As you create new files, you should know how to name, manage, and manipulate them. Specific rules must be adhered to when you choose a unique name for a file. It may be advantageous to take a quick peek inside a file to see if the file contains the information you seek. It may be necessary to transfer files within a disk, from one directory to another or from one disk to another, or even to a device such as a printer. DOS has several internal commands that will make it easy to manage and manipulate the files that you create.

In this chapter you will review the rules used to create unique names for files and learn some essential internal commands that will help you manage and manipulate your files. You will learn about the COPY command that allows you to make additional copies of files, to backup files by copying them to another disk or directory, the consequences of overwriting files and the consequences of combining the contents of files. You will copy dummy files that are in the DOS6BK directory to your DATA disk so that you can have some experience in naming, managing, manipulating, viewing, and printing files.

6.1 Why Learn DOS Commands?

In the last chapter, you learned how to manipulate directories. You learned MD, CD and RD which are directory management commands that handle subdirectories. However, directories are places to hold files. With the directory management commands, you built the book shelves, but you have not as yet put any books on them. If shelves are directories, the books are the files. In a library, you are interested in locating, reading, and using the books, not admiring the shelves. In the same way, on your computer, you are interested in locating, reading and using files, not admiring the directories you created.

You will have many files and directories on a disk. The directories will be used to organize both your program and your data files. Directories are the largest units of information management, but you need to manage information in smaller quantities—at the file level. You will generate many data files with your programs. You will need a way to perform what are called **housekeeping tasks** such as copying files from one directory or one disk to another or eliminating files you no longer need. These tasks are different from creating or changing the data in the files. You must use the application program that created the data file to change the data in the file.

For instance, if you are the accountant who created Ms. Woo's tax return, you know how to manage the information correctly in her tax return. You also have other clients for whom you perform the same service. The accountant is analogous to an application program such as TurboTax. The data for Ms. Woo is the data file that will be created by TurboTax. That data file will have to be named according to the rules of DOS. The other clients such as Mr. Rodriguez and Mr. Markiw will also need separate data files which will be generated in TurboTax. Naming and saving the data files will come under the rules of DOS.

In addition to doing the work, there are the housekeeping tasks that must be performed. For instance, Ms. Woo might get married and want her data file under her married name. You, as the accountant, do not need to perform those low level tasks. You hire a clerk to perform those tasks. In the computer world, you hire DOS to perform those tasks.

Several major internal commands will help manage your files on disks and in directories. These are the file management commands. They include DIR, COPY, REN, DEL, and TYPE. These commands are internal, meaning that once you have booted the system, they are always available to you. You neither have to change the directory to the DOS directory nor do you need to have the path set to the DOS subdirectory. These commands deal only with files; you are not working with the contents of the files, just manipulating them. The commands allow you to see what files you have on a disk or in a directory (DIR), copy files from here to there (COPY), change their names (REN), throw files away (DEL), and take a quick peek at what is inside a file (TYPE). The following activities in this chapter will show you how to use the COPY and TYPE commands.

6.2 The COPY Command

COPY, one of the most frequently used internal commands, is used to copy files from one place to another. COPY does exactly what it says—it takes an original **source file**, makes an identical copy of that file, and places the copy where you want it to go. In a sense, it is similar to a photocopy machine. You place your original on the copy plate, press the appropriate button, and receive a copy of your document. Nothing has happened to your original document. If it has a smudge on it, so does your copy. The same thing is true with the COPY command. It makes an exact copy of the file, and the original file remains the same. Copying a file does not alter the original file in any way.

Why might you want to copy files? You might want to copy a file from one disk to another. For example, you might create an inventory of all your household goods for your homeowner's insurance policy. It would be stored as a file on your disk. If your home burned down, so would your disk with your inventory file. Thus, it makes sense to copy this file to another disk and store it somewhere else, perhaps in a safe-deposit box.

You might want to make a second copy of an existing file on the same disk. Why would you want to do this? If you are going to be making changes to a data file with the program that created it, you might like a copy of the original just in case you do not like the changes you made to the data file.

You might want to copy a file to a device. One of the most common devices is the printer. You can use the COPY command to copy a file to the printer to get a hard copy but it must be an **ASCII** file—a special kind of text file.

You have used the HPB program and The THINKER program. You might wish to make another copy of those program files, in case something happens to the original, presuming that you are the legal owner. Those programs also had data files with information in them. You might like to have another copy, a backup copy of the various data files, so that if anything goes wrong, you still have another copy to work with.

COPY has a very specific syntax. Its basic syntax is always:

```
COPY  [d:][path]filename]  [d:][path]filename]
```

or conceptually:

COPY *source destination*

COPY is the command or the work you want the system to do. The source is *what* you want copied, your original. The destination is *where* you want it copied. In the formal syntax, the variables are as follows: [*d:*] stands for the drive letter where the file is located; [*path*] is the subdirectory where the file is located; and *filename* is the name of the file you wish to copy. The file name is made up of two parts, the file name and the file extension. If a file has an extension, it is separated from the file name by the period or dot. When you key in a file name, you must have no spaces between the file name and the file extension. That is why the syntax is written as *file name*. COPY, a **source file** name, and a **destination file** name are mandatory. Drive and path do not need to be specified if you are using the default drive and subdirectory.

You use the file management commands to manage files. When you are learning how to use these commands, you do not want to worry about harming your "real" program or "real" data files. The DOS6BK subdirectory, therefore, contains practice data files and program files. In the following activities, you will write data to your DATA disk only. You will never write to the hard disk. Thus, you can enjoy the next activities and not have to worry about making mistakes. Mistakes are part of the learning process.

6.3 *Review of File-naming Rules*

To name any file, whether it is an application or a data file, you must follow the DOS file-naming rules. A file name is technically called a file specification. The file specification is comprised of two parts, the file name itself and the file extension. The file-naming rules are:

1. The names of files in a directory must be unique.
2. No file name can be longer than eight characters.
3. File extensions are optional, but an extension cannot be longer than three characters.
4. A file name must be separated from its extension with a period, called a dot.

5. All alphanumeric characters can be used in file names and file extensions *except* the following illegal or forbidden characters:

```
<space> . " / \ [ ] : ; | < > + = , * ?
```

You cannot alter the rules. Usually, you will not get an opportunity to name program files. You purchase these programs, and the file names are those that were assigned by a programmer. Remember, a program file always has the file extension of .COM, .EXE, or .BAT. However, you will be naming your data files all the time. You name the data file from within the application program, usually when you save it to disk.

You should apply some common sense when you are naming files. For instance, naming a file ABCDEF.GHI does not tell you much about the contents of the file but a file named TAXES95.TKR does give you a clear idea of what is in the data file. File names should reflect file contents. However, you must know how your application program works. Many application programs let you assign the file name, but they will assign the file extension.

6.4 *Activity: Making Copies of Files*

Note 1:   The DATA disk is in Drive A. Be sure it is the DATA disk and not the APPLICATIONS DISK.

Note 2:   The C:\> is displayed as the default drive and the default directory. Remember to check your Configuration Table in Chapter 2.8 if your system configuration varies from the textbook.

Note 3:   It is assumed that the DOS6BK directory with its files has been installed on the hard disk. If it has not, refer to Appendix A for instructions on how to install it.

Correcting Keystroke Errors

When keying in commands, you may use the function keys to correct typographical errors. To edit command lines fully, you may use DOSKEY. For instructions on how to use DOSKEY, see Chapter 14, sections 14.1–14.2.

Step 1   Key in the following: C:\>**CD DOS6BK** [Enter]

Step 2   Key in the following: C:\DOS6BK>**DIR *.TMP** [Enter]

```
C:\DOS6BK>DIR *.TMP


Volume in drive C has no label
Volume Serial Number is 1CD1-5E42
Directory of C:\DOS6BK
```

```
     APRIL    TMP               70 01-23-93  11:49a
     GOODBYE  TMP               32 11-23-94   7:07a
     BONJOUR  TMP               51 10-12-94   7:09a
     JANUARY  TMP               71 01-23-93  11:48a
     MARCH    TMP               69 01-23-93  11:49a
     JAN      TMP               72 11-23-95  10:41a
     FEB      TMP               74 11-23-95  10:41a
     MAR      TMP               70 11-23-95  10:42a
     APR      TMP               71 11-23-95  10:42a
            9 file(s)                580 bytes
                          82,321,408 bytes free

   C:\DOS6BK>_
```

WHAT'S HAPPENING? You changed the default directory to DOS6BK. You then used the DIR command to see what files had a .TMP file extension in this directory. You want to make a copy of the file called JAN.TMP and place it on the DATA disk. You are going to use the absolute path for both the source and the destination file.

Step 3   Key in the following:

C:\DOS6BK>**COPY C:\DOS6BK\JAN.TMP A:\JAN.TMP** Enter

```
   C:\DOS6BK>COPY C:\DOS6BK\JAN.TMP A:\JAN.TMP
          1 file(s) copied

   C:\DOS6BK>_
```

WHAT'S HAPPENING? You see a message on the screen telling you that the file was copied. If you look at your command, following the syntax diagram, COPY is the command and JAN.TMP is the source file or what you want to copy. It is located in the subdirectory called DOS6BK, which is under the root directory of the hard disk. The C: was substituted for the [*d:*]. The subdirectory name \DOS6BK was substituted for the [*path*] (remembering that the \ indicates the root directory). The next \ is a delimiter separating the subdirectory name from the file name. The second backslash (\) is only a separator. JAN.TMP was substituted for the *filename*. A . (dot), not a space, separates the file name from the file extension.

The destination file also followed the syntax diagram. A: was substituted for the [*d:*]; \ was substituted for the [*path*] and JAN.TMP was substituted for the *filename*. Each file followed the file-naming rules; each is a unique name no longer than eight characters with no illegal characters. Each file extension is no longer than three characters with no illegal characters. You used a period to separate the file name from the file extension. The period is *not* part of the file specification. It is a delimiter telling DOS that you are done with the file name; get ready for the file extension. Thus, JAN is the source file name and .TMP is the source file extension. JAN is the destination file name, and .TMP is the destination file extension.

Step 4   Key in the following: C:\DOS6BK>**DIR A:** Enter

```
C:\DOS6BK>DIR A:

 Volume in drive A is DATADISK
 Volume Serial Number is 2F26-1901
 Directory of A:\

POLYSCI        <DIR>         06-20-94    5:59p
JAN       TMP            72 11-23-95   10:41a
         2 file(s)              72 bytes
                      1,211,904 bytes free

C:\DOS6BK>_
```

WHAT'S HAPPENING? You used the DIR command to confirm that you copied JAN.TMP to the DATA disk. You have one file and one subdirectory in the root directory of the DATA disk. Notice that on the directory display, the period or the dot is not displayed. However, remember that when you key in the file name, you *must* use the dot to separate the file name from the file extension. In Step 3 you used the absolute path name. You can save yourself a lot of time by using the relative path names and the defaults.

Step 5   Key in the following: C:\DOS6BK>**COPY FEB.TMP A:** [Enter]

Step 6   Key in the following: C:\DOS6BK>**COPY MAR.TMP A:** [Enter]

Step 7   Key in the following: C:\DOS6BK>**COPY APR.TMP A:** [Enter]

Step 8   Key in the following: C:\DOS6BK>**DIR A:** [Enter]

```
C:\DOS6BK>DIR A:

 Volume in drive A is DATADISK
 Volume Serial Number is 2F26-1901
 Directory of A:\

POLYSCI        <DIR>         06-20-94    5:59p
JAN       TMP            72 11-23-95   10:41a
FEB       TMP            74 11-23-95   10:41a
MAR       TMP            70 11-23-95   10:42a
APR       TMP            71 11-23-95   10:42a
         5 file(s)             287 bytes
                      1,210,368 bytes free

C:\DOS6BK>_
```

WHAT'S HAPPENING? You executed several copy commands and used DIR to confirm that you copied the files. You copied the file called FEB.TMP to the root directory of the DATA disk, but you did not need to key in all the information. Since the default drive and directory are already C:\DOS6BK, DOS will always look in the default drive and directory and no place else, unless you tell it otherwise. Since the destination you wanted the file copied to was the DATA disk, which in this case is Drive A, you *had* to key in the drive letter followed by a colon. The colon lets DOS know it is a drive. If you just keyed in A, DOS would think that you wanted to name the file A. You did not give the destination file a name, because, if you do not supply a file name, DOS will use the source file name as the destination file name. In this case the source file name was FEB.TMP, and that is what DOS called the copy of the file on the DATA disk. You then proceeded to perform the same task with MAR.TMP and APR.TMP. Next, you will give the destination file a different name and override the defaults.

Step 9   Key in the following: C:\DOS6BK>**COPY MAR.TMP A:\MARCH.FIL**
           Enter

Step 10   Key in the following: C:\DOS6BK>**DIR A:** **Enter**

```
C:\DOS6BK>COPY MAR.TMP A:\MARCH.FIL
        1 file(s) copied


C:\DOS6BK>DIR A:

 Volume in drive A is DATADISK
 Volume Serial Number is 2F26-1901
 Directory of A:\

POLYSCI        <DIR>         06-20-94    5:59p
JAN       TMP            72 11-23-95   10:41a
FEB       TMP            74 11-23-95   10:41a
MAR       TMP            70 11-23-95   10:42a
APR       TMP            71 11-23-95   10:42a
MARCH     FIL            70 11-23-95   10:42a
        6 file(s)              357 bytes
                        1,209,856 bytes free


C:\DOS6BK>_
```

WHAT'S HAPPENING? You executed the COPY command and used DIR to confirm that you copied the file. Following the syntax diagram, COPY is the command. MAR.TMP is the source file or what you want to copy. MARCH.FIL is the new destination file name. The destination file name followed the file-naming rules; it is a unique name no longer than eight characters with no illegal characters. You used a period to separate the file name from the file extension. The period is not part of the file specification. It is a delimiter. You did not need to use the drive letter or path name (subdirectory name) in the source file, but you did need to specify the drive letter in the destination. DOS always assumes the default drive and subdirectory, unless you tell it otherwise. In this case, you overrode the defaults by telling DOS to call the destination file on the DATA disk `MARCH.FIL`.

6.5   Using Wildcards with the COPY Command

In Chapter 3, you used global file specifications or wildcards (* and ?) with the DIR command so that you could display a group of files. You can also use the wildcards to copy files. In the previous activity you copied one file at a time, for example, `COPY JAN.TMP A:\`. You then proceeded to key in a command line for each file you wanted copied. Since each of the files you wished to copy had the same file extension, `.TMP`, instead of keying in each source file and destination file, you could have used the wildcards to key in the command line and reduced three commands to one.

6.6   Activity: Using Wildcards with the COPY Command

Note: The DATA disk is in Drive A. The `C:\DOS6BK>` is displayed.

Step 1   Key in the following: `C:\DOS6BK>`**COPY *.TMP A:*.NEW** `Enter`

```
C:\DOS6BK>COPY *.TMP A:*.NEW
APRIL.TMP
GOODBYE.TMP
BONJOUR.TMP
JANUARY.TMP
MARCH.TMP
JAN.TMP
FEB.TMP
MAR.TMP
APR.TMP
        9 file(s) copied

C:\DOS6BK>_
```

WHAT'S HAPPENING? As each file is copied, it is displayed on the screen. Your command line says COPY any file in the `DOS6BK` subdirectory that has the file extension `.TMP`, regardless of its file name, to a new set of files that will have the same file name but a different extension, `.NEW`. The * represented any file name. DOS knew that you were referring to file extensions because you preceded the file extension with the delimiter, the period. These files will be copied to the DATA disk. You could have keyed in the absolute path name, `COPY C:\DOS6BK\*.TMP A:\*.NEW`. Once again, it is unnecessary to specify the source drive (default drive) and source subdirectory (default directory). Since you did not tell it otherwise, DOS assumed the default drive and default subdirectory for the source. You need to key in the destination drive and the destination file extension since you were not using the default values.

Step 2   Key in the following: `C:\DOS6BK>`**DIR A:*.NEW** `Enter`

```
C:\DOS6BK>DIR A:*.NEW

 Volume in drive A is DATADISK
 Volume Serial Number is 2F26-1901
 Directory of A:\

APRIL     NEW            70 01-23-93  11:49a
GOODBYE   NEW            32 11-23-94   7:07a
BONJOUR   NEW            51 10-12-94   7:09a
JANUARY   NEW            71 01-23-93  11:48a
MARCH     NEW            69 01-23-93  11:49a
JAN       NEW            72 11-23-95  10:41a
FEB       NEW            74 11-23-95  10:41a
MAR       NEW            70 11-23-95  10:42a
APR       NEW            71 11-23-95  10:42a
         9 file(s)              580 bytes
                        1,205,248 bytes free

C:\DOS6BK>_
```

WHAT'S HAPPENING? You keyed in the command DIR *.NEW. You used the
wildcards to display the .NEW files, instead of displaying the entire directory. You
also used the wildcard * to make copies of the .TMP files. The file names are identical,
but the extensions are different. You successfully copied nine files with the
extension .TMP to nine new files with the extension .NEW from the hard disk to the
DATA disk. However, the directory display merely shows that the files are there.
How can you tell if the contents of the files are the same? You can use the TYPE
command.

6.7   The TYPE Command

The DIR command allowed you to determine that, indeed, there are "file folders"
with the .TMP and .NEW extension on the DATA disk. Using the DIR command is
like opening your file drawer (the disk) and looking at the labels on the file folders.
DIR does not show you what is in the file folder. An internal command called TYPE
opens the file folder and displays the contents of the file on the screen. The TYPE
command displays the file on the screen without stopping (scrolling). If the file is
longer than one full screen, you can stop the scrolling by pressing **Ctrl** + S or the
Pause key.

The syntax is:

TYPE   [*drive:*][*path*]*filename*

TYPE is the command or the work you want the system to do. The brackets [ ]
indicate that what is between the brackets is optional. You do not key in the
brackets, only what is inside them. [*drive:*] represents the drive letter. You do not

key in "drive:." You must substitute the drive letter where the file is located (A: or B: or C:). Another name for the drive letter is designated disk drive. This letter tells DOS on which disk drive to look for the information. [*path*] is the name of the subdirectory where the file is located. You do not key in "path" but substitute the name of the path or subdirectory name, as in \DOS or \PHONE. The file name is mandatory. If the file has an extension, it must be included as part of the file name. You substitute the file name you are interested in. You do not key in "file name." *File name* is the parameter that the TYPE command expects. You can display only one file at a time on the screen. You may not use wildcards or global file specifications with the TYPE command. In addition, the file must be a text file to be readable.

6.8 *Activity: Displaying Files Using the TYPE Command*

Note: The DATA disk is in Drive A. The C:\DOS6BK> is displayed.

Step 1   Key in the following: C:\DOS6BK>**TYPE** Enter

```
C:\DOS6BK>TYPE
Required parameter missing

C:\DOS6BK>_
```

WHAT'S HAPPENING? The message displayed on the screen is telling you that TYPE does not know what to do. DOS is asking you, "TYPE" or display what? Since you did not give a file name as the parameter as the syntax mandates, the TYPE command cannot show the contents of this file. If you have a version of DOS earlier than DOS 4.0, the message could say, Invalid number of parameters.

Step 2   Key in the following: C:\DOS6BK>**TYPE PHONE\HPB.EXE** Enter

WHAT'S HAPPENING? What you see displayed on the screen is, indeed, the contents of a file named HPB.EXE in the PHONE subdirectory. It is a program that you executed in Chapter 5. This program or executable code is in machine language and not meaningful to you in this format. However, the TYPE command will display the contents of any file, even if it looks like nonsense characters to you. Remember, when you keyed in HPB, the program executed and allowed you to look at some data—names and addresses, but when you used TYPE, looking at the contents of the program was not meaningful. Because HPB is a program file and *not* a text file, using the TYPE command has no value.

Programs or executable code are recognized by their file extensions. If you see the file extension .COM, .EXE, or .SYS, it tells you that the file is a program. COM stands for command file. EXE stands for executable code. SYS stands for system file. However, the TYPE command will do whatever you ask, even if it means displaying nonsense. Remember, a file must be a text file to be readable.

Another name for a text file is an ASCII file, pronounced as-key. ASCII is an acronym for American Standard Code for Information Interchange. ASCII is a code that translates the bits of information into readable letters. All you need to remember is that an ASCII file is a readable text file. Another name for an ASCII file is an **unformatted text file**. ASCII files are a like a common language that almost all programs can recognize.

The data files that the programs generate are usually not readable either. Each program has a special way of reading and writing the information in the data file so that the program knows what to do with the data. Usually no other program can read the data file except the program that generated it. It would be like wanting to write a letter in Japanese when you neither speak, read or write Japanese. Thus, you hire a translator (the program). He writes the letter (the data file). You still cannot read the letter. You must give it to the translator to know what is in the letter. Furthermore, if you have another translator—say a French translator (another program), you cannot give your Japanese letter (data file) to the French translator. She will not be able to read it either.

Step 3   Key in the following: C:\DOS6BK>**TYPE PHONE\HPB.DAT** [Enter]

```
                                                              04231994
          Smith                    Jane Doe     1111195141622233334444Joh
n       12121952416555666667777123 Sunset Road
                                   Toronto            ON5H5 6Y2   Cana
da              416888888801011975Dear John & Jane,   X   Sample record for co
uple with different last namesDelete it for practice!
Joe             01011971Joan           02021972
                                                   07041993           The
Book Biz
                   498 North Street
                        Orange              CA92669    USA
     7145559997                    B

                                   04231994          Tuttle
          Mary Brown    12201963             Steven        0514196371455593
77    444 Sweetheart Lane
            Tustin          CA92670    USA                714555888907
311994             FX
                                        Walter        10121995
                   12121996
C:\DOS6BK>
```

WHAT'S HAPPENING? You are looking at the data file for the `HPB.EXE` program in its rawest form when you keyed in `TYPE PHONE\HPB.DAT`. This program has its data in a somewhat recognizable form, in that you can at least read some of it. But as you can see the format of the data is not nicely laid out as it is when you use the data file with the program file. Format, in this case, does not mean format as in format a disk but format in the sense of how the data is arranged. Only the program HPB.EXE knows how to arrange this data so it is meaningful to you. TYPE can be useful with data files like these because it gives you an idea of what information the file actually holds. Nearly all the files in the `DOS6BK` directory are ASCII files, which means that you can read them using the TYPE command.

Step 4   Key in the following: `C:\DOS6BK>`**TYPE JAN.TMP** Enter

```
C:\DOS6BK>TYPE JAN.TMP
This is my January file.
It is my first dummy file.
This is file 1.

C:\DOS6BK>_
```

WHAT'S HAPPENING? In this case, the above is a text file (ASCII file) and, thus, you can read it. Using the TYPE command, you "opened" your file folder, `JAN.TMP`, and saw the contents displayed on the screen. Whenever a file is readable on the screen as this one is, you know it is an ASCII file. You did not need to include the drive or path since `JAN.TMP` was on the hard disk in the `DOS6BK` subdirectory, and DOS used the default values. You copied this file to the DATA disk in Activity 6.4. Is the content of the file the same on the DATA disk as it is in the `DOS6BK` subdirectory? If it is, you will know that the COPY command makes no changes to any information in a file when it copies it.

Step 5   Key in the following: C:\DOS6BK>**TYPE A:JAN.TMP** [Enter]

```
C:\DOS6BK>TYPE A:JAN.TMP
This is my January file.
It is my first dummy file.
This is file 1.

C:\DOS6BK>_
```

WHAT'S HAPPENING? The contents of the files are the same. Copying the file from one disk to another had no impact on the contents. However, you did need to include the drive designator, A: in front of the file name JAN.TMP because that told DOS which disk drive to select. Had you not included the drive designator, DOS would have looked for the file JAN.TMP on the default hard disk and in the default subdirectory \DOS6BK. After DOS has executed the TYPE command, it returns to the system prompt, ready for the next command.

Step 6   Key in the following: C:\DOS6BK>**CD ** [Enter]

```
C:\DOS6BK>CD \

C:\>_
```

WHAT'S HAPPENING? You have returned to the root directory of the hard disk.

6.9 Dummy Files

You are going to use some **dummy files**. "Dummy" means that these files have no particular meaning. You can use these files to practice the file management commands without worrying about harming your "real" program and data files. The concept of dummy files and/or dummy data is common in data processing. Often data processing professionals wish to test different portions of systems or programs. For instance, if you were writing a program about employee benefits, rather than looking at every employee, you would create dummy files and data in order to have a smaller representative sample that is manageable and easily tested. Not only are the files smaller, they are samples. If the data gets harmed in any way, it has no impact on the "real" data.

The following activities allow you to do the same. Following the instructions, you will use the COPY command to make copies of different files either on the DATA disk or from the DOS6BK subdirectory to the DATA disk. You will then display the contents of the file on the screen with the TYPE command.

You often want to have extra copies of the same files on the same disk. Often, you may wish to make copies of files created when you use other software application packages. You choose to make copies because you want to leave your original files intact. For instance, if you created an extensive client list with a database management package and needed to update it, rather than working on the original file, you could rekey in the entire client list. If you made a mistake, you would still have your original list. However, an easier method would be to copy the client list, stored as a file, to a new file with a new name and make changes to the new file. When you make a copy of a file on the same disk in the same subdirectory, you must give it a different name. Every file name in a directory must be unique.

6.10 Activity: Using the COPY and TYPE Commands

Note 1: The C:\> is displayed and the DATA disk is in Drive A.

Note 2: Remember that if your DATA disk is in a drive other than A, you will have to substitute the proper drive letter. Check your Configuration Table in Chapter 2.8 for the appropriate substitutions.

Step 1   Key in the following: C:\>**A:** [Enter]

```
C:\>A:

A:\>_
```

WHAT'S HAPPENING? You changed the default drive so that all activities will automatically occur or default to the DATA disk.

Step 2   Key in the following: A:\>**COPY JAN.TMP JAN.OLD** [Enter]

```
A:\>COPY JAN.TMP JAN.OLD
        1 file(s) copied

A:\>_
```

WHAT'S HAPPENING? You told DOS the work you want to do by keying in the command and its required parameters. You did not need to specify the drive letter or the path name preceding either the source file nor destination file name. Because you did not, DOS automatically read JAN.TMP and wrote JAN.OLD to the default drive and directory which was the root directory of the DATA disk.

Step 3   Key in the following: A:\>**TYPE JAN.TMP** [Enter]

Step 4   Key in the following: A:\>**TYPE JAN.OLD** [Enter]

```
A:\>TYPE JAN.TMP
This is my January file.
It is my first dummy file.
This is file 1.
```

```
A:\>TYPE JAN.OLD
This is my January file.
It is my first dummy file.
This is file 1.

A:\>_
```

WHAT'S HAPPENING? You can see that you made a copy of the JAN.TMP file to a new file called JAN.OLD, but the contents of the files are identical.

Step 5   Key in the following: A:\>**COPY MAR.TMP MAR.TMP** [Enter]

```
A:\>COPY MAR.TMP MAR.TMP
MAR.TMP
File cannot be copied onto itself
        0 file(s) copied

A:\>_
```

WHAT'S HAPPENING? You must give new files on the same disk and in the same subdirectory unique names. Just as you should not label two file folders the same in a file drawer, you would not label two disk files the same.

Step 6   Key in the following: A:\>**COPY MAR.TMP MARCH.TXT** [Enter]

```
A:\>COPY MAR.TMP MARCH.TXT
        1 file(s) copied

A:\>_
```

WHAT'S HAPPENING? Here, you are making a copy of the contents of the file on the DATA disk called MAR.TMP, copying the contents to the DATA disk, and calling this new file MARCH.TXT. You could have keyed in A:\>COPY A:\MAR.TXT A:\MARCH.TXT. Either is correct, but it is not necessary to specify the disk drive since the default drive is assumed. Nor is it necessary to specify the path or directory because the root directory (\) is the default directory.

Step 7   Key in the following: A:\>**TYPE MARCH.TXT** [Enter]

Step 8   Key in the following: A:\>**TYPE MAR.TMP** [Enter]

```
A:\>TYPE MARCH.TXT
This is my March file.
It is my third dummy file.
This is file 3.
```

```
A:\>TYPE MAR.TMP
This is my March file.
It is my third dummy file.
This is file 3.

A:\>_
```

WHAT'S HAPPENING? The contents of each file are identical even though the file names are different. The COPY command does nothing to the original; the contents of the original file remain the same. As far as DOS is concerned, what makes a file different is its unique file name. To DOS, MAR.TMP and MARCH.TXT are unique, separate files.

Step 9　Key in the following: A:\>**COPY　JAN.TMP　JANUARY.TXT** ⌷Enter⌷

Step 10　Key in the following: A:\>**COPY　FEB.TMP　FEBRUARY.TXT** ⌷Enter⌷

Step 11　Key in the following: A:\>**COPY　APR.TMP　APRIL.TXT** ⌷Enter⌷

```
A:\>COPY JAN.TMP JANUARY.TXT
        1 file(s) copied

A:\>COPY FEB.TMP FEBRUARY.TXT
        1 file(s) copied

A:\>COPY APR.TMP APRIL.TXT
        1 file(s) copied

A:\>_
```

Step 12　Key in the following: A:\>**DIR** *.TMP ⌷Enter⌷

Step 13　Key in the following: A:\>**DIR** *.TXT ⌷Enter⌷

```
Volume in drive A is DATADISK
 Volume Serial Number is 2F26-1901
 Directory of A:\

JAN      TMP           72 11-23-95   10:41a
FEB      TMP           74 11-23-95   10:41a
MAR      TMP           70 11-23-95   10:42a
APR      TMP           71 11-23-95   10:42a
        4 file(s)            287 bytes
                   1,202,688 bytes free

A:\>DIR *.TXT
```

```
Volume in drive A is DATADISK
Volume Serial Number is 2F26-1901
Directory of A:\

MARCH     TXT           70 11-23-95  10:42a
JANUARY   TXT           72 11-23-95  10:41a
FEBRUARY  TXT           74 11-23-95  10:41a
APRIL     TXT           71 11-23-95  10:42a
       4 file(s)             287 bytes
                      1,202,688 bytes free

A:\>_
```

WHAT'S HAPPENING? You had four files with the extension . TMP. You still have those files, but, in addition, you now have four more files that you just copied or "created" with the extension . TXT. DOS keeps track of all these files.

6.11 *Making Additional Files on the Same Disk*

You often want to have extra copies of files on the same disk but in a different subdirectory. You may want to keep your backup files in the same file cabinet (disk) but in a different drawer (subdirectory). Thus, you can group similar files together. When you make a copy of a file on the same disk, in a different subdirectory, it may have the same file name. Every file on a disk must have a unique name. However, if it is in a subdirectory, even though the file name is the same, the path name makes the file name unique.

6.12 *Activity: Using the COPY Command*

Note: The DATA disk is in Drive A. The A:\> is displayed.

Step 1   Key in the following: A:\>**MD \CLASS** [Enter]

```
A:\>MD \CLASS

A:\>_
```

WHAT'S HAPPENING? You created a subdirectory called CLASS on the DATA disk. MD, which means Make Directory, is the command to create a place for additional files. The first backslash (\) is the name of the root directory. CLASS is the name of the subdirectory. The only reserved name for a directory is the \. You can use any name for the subdirectory you create, provided that you follow the DOS file-naming rules.

Step 2   Key in the following: A:\>**DIR** [Enter]

```
POLYSCI      <DIR>          06-20-94    5:59p
JAN      TMP          72 11-23-95   10:41a
FEB      TMP          74 11-23-95   10:41a
MAR      TMP          70 11-23-95   10:42a
APR      TMP          71 11-23-95   10:42a
MARCH    FIL          70 11-23-95   10:42a
APRIL    NEW          70 01-23-93   11:49a
GOODBYE  NEW          32 11-23-94    7:07a
BONJOUR  NEW          51 10-12-94    7:09a
JANUARY  NEW          71 01-23-93   11:48a
MARCH    NEW          69 01-23-93   11:49a
JAN      NEW          72 11-23-95   10:41a
FEB      NEW          74 11-23-95   10:41a
MAR      NEW          70 11-23-95   10:42a
APR      NEW          71 11-23-95   10:42a
JAN      OLD          72 11-23-95   10:41a
MARCH    TXT          70 11-23-95   10:42a
JANUARY  TXT          72 11-23-95   10:41a
FEBRUARY TXT          74 11-23-95   10:41a
APRIL    TXT          71 11-23-95   10:42a
CLASS        <DIR>          06-21-94    1:02a
        21 file(s)          1,296 bytes
                        1,202,176 bytes free

A:\>_
```

WHAT'S HAPPENING? The directory display shows the subdirectory called
CLASS. You know it is a subdirectory because it has <DIR> following the file name.
To see what is inside the file cabinet, you must use DIR with the path name. A review
of the syntax is:

DIR   [*drive:*][*path*][*filename*]

You do not need to include the drive letter since the default drive is where the DATA
disk is. Nor do you need to include the \ for the root directory, since the root directory
of the DATA disk is the default. You do need to include the path name. The path
name is the subdirectory name, CLASS.

Step 3   Key in the following: A:\>**DIR CLASS** Enter

```
A:\>DIR CLASS

 Volume in drive A is DATADISK
 Volume Serial Number is 2F26-1901
 Directory of A:\CLASS
```

```
    .              <DIR>           06-21-94    1:02a
    ..             <DIR>           06-21-94    1:02a
         2 file(s)                      0 bytes
                            1,202,176 bytes free

A:\>_
```

WHAT'S HAPPENING? This directory listing is not for the root directory. DOS tells you what you are looking at. The third line of the display says `Directory of A:\CLASS`, telling you that you are looking at the subdirectory called `CLASS` on the DATA disk. There is nothing yet in this subdirectory. The `.` and the `..` are created when you create a subdirectory. The `.` tells DOS that this is a subdirectory. The `..` is a shorthand name for the directory above `CLASS`, the root (`\`). How do you copy a file into this subdirectory? You can always correctly use the absolute path. You do this by following the syntax of the COPY command:

```
COPY   [drive:][path]file name]   [drive:][path]file name]
```

Step 4   Key in the following:

A:\>**COPY A:\JAN.TMP A:\CLASS\JAN.PAR** Enter

WHAT'S HAPPENING? You copied the source file, JAN.TMP, from the root directory on the DATA disk, to the destination, the subdirectory CLASS; you also gave the destination file a new name, JAN.PAR. By looking at the syntax diagram, you can follow how you substituted the values you wanted:

In the destination syntax, what is the second backslash? The first backslash is the name of the root directory. The second backslash is used as a delimiter between the subdirectory name and the file name. This delimiter tells DOS that the subdirectory name is over and the file name is about to begin. Backslashes are used as delimiters separating subdirectory and file names.

Keying in the absolute path is not as easy as using the relative path and with the default assumptions that DOS will make. You must include the command, COPY. Since the DATA disk is the default drive, you do not need to include the drive letter. Since the root directory is the default directory, you do not need to include the first `\`. However, you do need to include the source file name. The same is true with the destination file. You do not need to include the drive letter or root directory, but you must include the path name and the new file name. Thus, the shorthand way of copying a file would be the following:

Step 5   Key in the following: A:\>**COPY FEB.TMP CLASS\FEB.PAR** [Enter]

```
A:\>COPY FEB.TMP CLASS\FEB.PAR
       1 file(s) copied

A:\>_
```

WHAT'S HAPPENING? In this case, you kept your typing to a minimum by observing your default drive and directory and keying in only what was necessary to execute the command.

Step 6   Key in the following: A:\>**DIR CLASS** [Enter]

```
A:\>DIR CLASS

 Volume in drive A is DATADISK
 Volume Serial Number is 2F26-1901
 Directory of A:\CLASS

 .              <DIR>         06-21-94    1:02a
 ..             <DIR>         06-21-94    1:02a
 JAN      PAR          72 11-23-95   10:41a
 FEB      PAR          74 11-23-95   10:41a
       4 file(s)             146 bytes
                       1,201,152 bytes free

A:\>_
```

WHAT'S HAPPENING? You copied the files JAN.TMP and FEB.TMP from the root directory to the subdirectory CLASS on the DATA disk. You gave the copies new names, JAN.PAR and FEB.PAR. Are the files the same? You can use the TYPE command to compare the contents visually. But since TYPE does not support the use of wildcards, you must look at each file individually. Again, since you want to look at the contents of two files in different subdirectories, you must follow the TYPE syntax:

> TYPE   [*drive:*][*path*]*filename*[*.ext*]

Step 7   Key in the following: A:\>**TYPE JAN.TMP** [Enter]

Step 8   Key in the following: A:\>**TYPE CLASS\JAN.PAR** [Enter]

```
A:\>TYPE JAN.TMP
This is my January file.
It is my first dummy file.
This is file 1.
```

```
A:\>TYPE CLASS\JAN.PAR
This is my January file.
It is my first dummy file.
This is file 1.

A:\>_
```

WHAT'S HAPPENING? The contents of the files are the same, even though they are in different directories. The same is true for the FEB files.

Step 9   Key in the following: A:\>**TYPE FEB.TMP** [Enter]

Step 10   Key in the following: A:\>**TYPE CLASS\FEB.PAR** [Enter]

```
A:\>TYPE FEB.TMP
This is my February file.
It is my second dummy file.
This is file 2.

A:\>TYPE CLASS\FEB.PAR
This is my February file.
It is my second dummy file.
This is file 2.

A:\>_
```

WHAT'S HAPPENING? The file contents are the same.

6.13 Using Wildcards with the COPY Command

You can also use wildcards to copy files on the same drive to a different subdirectory. Again, the important point to remember when using DOS commands is that you can never violate syntax. It is always COPY *source destination*. Computers and commands always do what you tell them to. Users sometimes think that the "computer lost their files." More often than not, the file or files is misplaced because the user gave an instruction that he or she thought meant one thing but, in reality, meant something else. For instance, the default drive and directory was A:\>, and you keyed in COPY THIS.FIL YOUR.FIL. You wanted YOUR.FIL to be copied to the root of Drive C. Since you did not key that in (C:\YOUR.FIL), DOS used the defaults, and YOUR.FIL was copied to the default drive and directory (A:\).

6.14 Activity: Using Wildcards with the COPY Command

Note: The DATA disk is in Drive A. The A:\> is displayed.

Step 1   Key in the following: A:\>**COPY *.TMP CLASS*.ABC** [Enter]

```
A:\>COPY *.TMP CLASS\*.ABC
JAN.TMP
FEB.TMP
MAR.TMP
APR.TMP
        4 file(s) copied

A:\>_
```

WHAT'S HAPPENING? As each file is copied, it is displayed on the screen. Your command line says COPY any file on the DATA disk in the root directory (the default directory) that has the file extension .TMP, regardless of its file name, to a new set of files that will have the same file name but a different extension, .ABC. These files will be copied to the DATA disk and to the subdirectory called CLASS. You could have keyed in A:\>COPY A:*.TMP A:\CLASS*.ABC. Once again, for the source files (*.TMP), it is unnecessary to specify the designated drive and directory. Since you did not tell it otherwise, DOS assumed the default drive and default directory. However, for the destination you had to include the subdirectory name, CLASS; otherwise, DOS would have assumed the default directory and drive.

Step 2   Key in the following: A:\>**DIR** *.TMP Enter

Step 3   Key in the following: A:\>**DIR CLASS*.ABC** Enter

```
 Volume in drive A is DATADISK
 Volume Serial Number is 2F26-1901
 Directory of A:\

JAN       TMP         72 11-23-95  10:41a
FEB       TMP         74 11-23-95  10:41a
MAR       TMP         70 11-23-95  10:42a
APR       TMP         71 11-23-95  10:42a
        4 file(s)          287 bytes
                     1,199,104 bytes free

A:\>DIR CLASS\*.ABC

 Volume in drive A is DATADISK
 Volume Serial Number is 2F26-1901
 Directory of A:\CLASS

JAN       ABC         72 11-23-95  10:41a
FEB       ABC         74 11-23-95  10:41a
MAR       ABC         70 11-23-95  10:42a
APR       ABC         71 11-23-95  10:42a
        4 file(s)          287 bytes
                     1,199,104 bytes free

A:\>_
```

WHAT'S HAPPENING? You keyed in two separate commands, DIR *.TMP and DIR CLASS*.ABC. You used the wildcards to display the .ABC files in the subdirectory CLASS and the .TMP files in the root directory. You also used the wildcard * to make copies of the .TMP files. The file names are identical, but the extensions are different. The files were copied to the subdirectory CLASS. However, the directory display merely shows that the files are there. To see that the contents of the original files and copied files are the same, use the TYPE command. Remember, you must specify the subdirectory where the .ABC files are located. Also remember that you cannot use wildcards with the TYPE command.

Step 4   Key in the following: A:\>**TYPE FEB.TMP** `Enter`

Step 5   Key in the following: A:\>**TYPE CLASS\FEB.ABC** `Enter`

```
A:\>

A:\>TYPE FEB.TMP
This is my February file.
It is my second dummy file.
This is file 2.

A:\>TYPE CLASS\FEB.ABC
This is my February file.
It is my second dummy file.
This is file 2.

A:\>_
```

WHAT'S HAPPENING? The file contents are identical even though the file names are different and the files are in different directories.

6.15 Using COPY and DIR with Subdirectories

You are going to see how the DOS commands work with subdirectories by using the COPY command to place files in the subdirectories and by using the DIR command to see that the files were copied.

6.16 Activity: Using COPY with Subdirectories

Note: The DATA disk is in Drive A. The A:\> is displayed.

Step 1   Key in the following: A:\>**CD POLYSCI\USA** `Enter`

Step 2   Key in the following: A:\POLYSCI\USA>**DIR** `Enter`

```
A:\>CD POLYSCI\USA
```

```
A:\POLYSCI\USA>DIR


 Volume in drive A is DATADISK
 Volume Serial Number is 2F26-1901
 Directory of A:\POLYSCI\USA


 .              <DIR>        06-20-94    6:08p
 ..             <DIR>        06-20-94    6:08p
      2 file(s)                   0 bytes
                        1,199,104 bytes free


A:\POLYSCI\USA>_
```

WHAT'S HAPPENING? You changed the default directory to the USA directory, which is under the POLYSCI directory under the root of the DATA disk. The prompt should display A:\POLYSCI\USA> as the default drive and subdirectory. The prompt is quite lengthy because it shows you the default drive as well as the default subdirectory. All activities will occur in the subdirectory \POLYSCI\USA, unless you specify another path. When you keyed in DIR, it showed you the contents of only the current default directory. The directory is empty of files but has the two subdirectory markers, dot and double dot.

Step 3   Key in the following:

A:\POLYSCI\USA>**COPY \CLASS\JAN.PAR FINAL.RPT** Enter

```
A:\POLYSCI\USA>COPY \CLASS\JAN.PAR FINAL.RPT
        1 file(s) copied

A:\POLYSCI\USA>_
```

WHAT'S HAPPENING? Spacing is very important when keying in commands.

Command	Space	Source (no spaces)	Space	Destination (no spaces)
COPY		\CLASS\JAN.PAR		FINAL.RPT

The file called JAN.PAR in the subdirectory \CLASS was successfully copied to the subdirectory \POLYSCI\USA but is now called FINAL.RPT.

The syntax of the COPY command remained the same—COPY *source destination.* First, you issued the COPY command, but it was not enough to list just the file name JAN.PAR as the source. You had to include the path so that DOS would know in which subdirectory the file was located; hence, the source was \CLASS\JAN.PAR. Users often get confused when using the \. Here is a simple rule: The first \ in any command line always means the root directory. Any other \ in the command is simply a delimiter. Thus, in our example, the first \ tells DOS to go to the root and

then go down to CLASS. The second \ is the delimiter between the subdirectory **name and the file name,** JAN.PAR. The destination is a file called FINAL.RPT. You **did not have to key in** the path for the destination because the default (\POLYSCI\USA) **was assumed. If you** were going to key in the absolute path in using the COPY **command, the command** would read as follows:

```
COPY  A:\CLASS\JAN.PAR  A:\POLYSCI\USA\FINAL.RPT
```

You did not **need to key in the drive** letter because the default drive is assumed. If you had keyed in COPY JAN.PAR FINAL.RPT, you would have gotten the error message, File not found, **because DOS would have looked only in the current** directory (\POLYSCI\USA) **for the file and would not have found it. Next, you are** going to make a copy of the file in the current directory, so you do not need to include the absolute path name; here, you can use the relative path name.

Step 4   Key in the following:

A:\POLYSCI\USA>**COPY FINAL.RPT NOTE2.TMP** Enter

Step 5   Key in the following:

A:\POLYSCI\USA>**COPY FINAL.RPT NOTE3.TMP** Enter

```
A:\POLYSCI\USA>COPY FINAL.RPT NOTE2.TMP
        1 file(s) copied

A:\POLYSCI\USA>COPY FINAL.RPT NOTE3.TMP
        1 file(s) copied

A:\POLYSCI\USA>_
```

WHAT'S HAPPENING? You copied two files. You did not have to include the absolute path name because the default path was assumed. You used the relative path name. DOS always assumes the default drive and directory, unless you tell it otherwise. Technically, the commands looked like this:

```
COPY  A:\POLYSCI\USA\FINAL.RPT  A:\POLYSCI\USA\NOTE2.TMP
COPY  A:\POLYSCI\USA\FINAL.RPT  A:\POLYSCI\USA\NOTE3.TMP
```

You can see that using the relative path eliminates a lot of typing.

Step 6   Key in the following: A:\POLYSCI\USA>**DIR** Enter

```
A:\POLYSCI\USA>DIR

 Volume in drive A is DATADISK
 Volume Serial Number is 2F26-1901
 Directory of A:\POLYSCI\USA
```

```
    .              <DIR>          06-20-94    6:08p
    ..             <DIR>          06-20-94    6:08p
 FINAL    RPT           72 11-23-95   10:41a
 NOTE2    TMP           72 11-23-95   10:41a
 NOTE3    TMP           72 11-23-95   10:41a
          5 file(s)             216 bytes
                         1,197,568 bytes free

 A:\POLYSCI\USA>_
```

WHAT'S HAPPENING? You see only the files that are in the default subdirectory. You can create subdirectories from the current directory.

Step 7   Key in the following: A:\POLYSCI\USA>**MD \WORK** ⌈Enter⌉

Step 8   Key in the following: A:\POLYSCI\USA>**MD \WORK\CLIENTS** ⌈Enter⌉

Step 9   Key in the following: A:\POLYSCI\USA>**MD \WORK\ADS** ⌈Enter⌉

```
 A:\POLYSCI\USA>MD \WORK

 A:\POLYSCI\USA>MD \WORK\CLIENTS

 A:\POLYSCI\USA>MD \WORK\ADS

 A:\POLYSCI\USA>
```

WHAT'S HAPPENING? You had to include the first backslash so that the WORK directory would be under the root. WORK had to be created before you could create its subdirectories, CLIENTS and ADS. Now that you have created the directories of interest, you can use wildcards to copy files to them.

Step 10   Key in the following:

A:\POLYSCI\USA>**COPY *.* \WORK\CLIENTS** ⌈Enter⌉

```
 A:\POLYSCI\USA>COPY *.* \WORK\CLIENTS
 FINAL.RPT
 NOTE2.TMP
 NOTE3.TMP
         3 file(s) copied

 A:\POLYSCI\USA>_
```

WHAT'S HAPPENING? As the files were copied to the \WORK\CLIENTS subdirectory, they were listed on the screen. Again, the syntax is the same: the command,

COPY, the *source*, * . * (all the files in the default subdirectory \POLYSCI\USA), to the *destination*, \WORK\CLIENTS. You had to include the absolute path name in the destination. The first \ in the destination is very important because it tells DOS to go to the top of the tree and then go down to the \WORK\CLIENTS subdirectory. If you had not included that first backslash, DOS would have looked under the subdirectory \POLYSCI\USA. Since you wanted to have the files with the same name in the destination subdirectory, \WORK\CLIENTS, you did not have to specify new file names. DOS used or defaulted to the current file names.

Step 11   Key in the following:

A:\POLYSCI\USA>**DIR \WORK\CLIENTS** Enter

```
A:\POLYSCI\USA>DIR \WORK\CLIENTS

 Volume in drive A is DATADISK
 Volume Serial Number is 2F26-1901
 Directory of A:\WORK\CLIENTS

 .                <DIR>         06-21-94  10:30a
 ..               <DIR>         06-21-94  10:30a
 FINAL    RPT           72 11-23-95  10:41a
 NOTE2    TMP           72 11-23-95  10:41a
 NOTE3    TMP           72 11-23-95  10:41a
         5 file(s)              216 bytes
                          1,194,496 bytes free

A:\POLYSCI\USA>_
```

WHAT'S HAPPENING? You can copy files from anywhere to anywhere provided you give the source and destination location. If you use the relative path, be sure you are aware of the current default drive and directory.

Step 12   Key in the following:

A:\POLYSCI\USA>

COPY \WORK\CLIENTS\NOTE?.TMP \WORK\ADS\EXAM?.QZ Enter

```
A:\POLYSCI\USA>COPY \WORK\CLIENTS\NOTE?.TMP \WORK\ADS\EXAM?.QZ
A:\WORK\CLIENTS\NOTE2.TMP
A:\WORK\CLIENTS\NOTE3.TMP
        2 file(s) copied

A:\POLYSCI\USA>_
```

WHAT'S HAPPENING? DOS displayed the entire path name as it copied all the . TMP files from the subdirectory \WORK\CLIENTS to the subdirectory \WORK\ADS.

So that you could retain the number in the source file name in the destination file names (NOTE1.TMP and NOTE2.TMP), you used the ? wildcard as a place holder. Thus NOTE2.TMP got copied as EXAM2.QZ, and NOTE3.TMP got copied EXAM3.QZ. To see if the files were copied correctly, you will use the DIR command.

Step 13 Key in the following:
    A:\POLYSCI\USA>**DIR \WORK\ADS** [Enter]

```
A:\POLYSCI\USA>DIR \WORK\ADS

 Volume in drive A is DATADISK
 Volume Serial Number is 2F26-1901
 Directory of A:\WORK\ADS

 .               <DIR>         06-21-94  10:30a
 ..              <DIR>         06-21-94  10:30a
 EXAM2    QZ              72 11-23-95  10:41a
 EXAM3    QZ              72 11-23-95  10:41a
         4 file(s)              144 bytes
                       1,193,472 bytes free

A:\POLYSCI\USA>_
```

WHAT'S HAPPENING? You successfully copied the files because you used the proper path name. You have been using the COPY and DIR commands to exemplify how to use the path. Any DOS command will work if you use the proper syntax and the proper path.

Step 14 Key in the following: A:\POLYSCI\USA>**C:** [Enter]

Step 15 Key in the following: C:\>**CD \DOS6BK** [Enter]

```
A:\POLYSCI\USA>C:

C:\>CD DOS6BK

C:\DOS6BK>_
```

WHAT'S HAPPENING? You changed the default drive to C. In this example, you were in the root directory of C. You then changed the default directory to DOS6BK. Note that it took two steps. You must change drives, then directories.

Step 16 Key in the following: C:\DOS6BK>**COPY DRESS.UP A:** [Enter]

```
C:\DOS6BK>COPY DRESS.UP A:
        1 file(s) copied

C:\DOS6BK>_
```

WHAT'S HAPPENING? You executed a simple COPY command. You asked that DOS copy the file called DRESS.UP from the \DOS6BK directory to the DATA disk. But where on the DATA disk did the file get copied? Since the last place you were on the DATA disk was the USA subdirectory (under POLYSCI, under the root), that is where the file was copied. If you wanted the file copied to the root directory of the DATA disk, you would have had to key in COPY DRESS.UP A:\.

Step 17   Key in the following: C:\DOS6BK>**DIR A:DRESS.UP** Enter

Step 18   Key in the following: C:\DOS6BK>**DIR A:\DRESS.UP** Enter

```
C:\DOS6BK>DIR A:DRESS.UP

 Volume in drive A is DATADISK
 Volume Serial Number is 2F26-1901
 Directory of A:\POLYSCI\USA

DRESS    UP               25 05-07-94  11:06a
        1 file(s)                25 bytes
                         1,192,960 bytes free

C:\DOS6BK>DIR A:\DRESS.UP

 Volume in drive A is DATADISK
 Volume Serial Number is 2F26-1901
 Directory of A:\

File not found

C:\DOS6BK>_
```

WHAT'S HAPPENING? The last place you were on the DATA disk was in the subdirectory \POLYSCI\USA. DOS "remembered" where you last were and copied the file to the USA subdirectory, not to the root directory. When you asked DIR to locate the file DRESS.UP and preceded DRESS.UP only with the A:, DOS looked in the last place you were—\POLYSCI\USA. In order to look at the root directory, you had to request A:\DRESS.UP.

Step 19   Key in the following: C:\DOS6BK>**A:** Enter

```
C:\DOS6BK>A:

A:\POLYSCI\USA>_
```

WHAT'S HAPPENING? Your default drive is now the DATA disk. Now look at your default directory. Note that you are *not* in the root directory of the DATA disk, but were returned to the USA subdirectory (under the POLYSCI, under the root directory). Thus, if you change drives during various activities, DOS will remember the last default subdirectory of the drive you were on. On the hard disk, the default directory is still \DOS6BK.

Step 20   Key in the following: A:\POLYSCI\USA>**CD C:** [Enter]

```
A:\POLYSCI\USA>CD C:\

A:\POLYSCI\USA>_
```

WHAT'S HAPPENING? You issued the command to change the directory to the root on the hard disk, in this case Drive C, but your prompt shows that you are still in the USA subdirectory on the DATA disk. Did you accomplish anything with the command?

Step 21   Key in the following: A:\POLYSCI\USA>**DIR C:DO*.*** [Enter]

```
A:\POLYSCI\USA>DIR C:DO*.*

 Volume in drive C has no label
 Volume Serial Number is 1CD1-5E42
 Directory of C:\

DOS          <DIR>        02-22-93   1:14p
DOS6BK       <DIR>        06-19-94  10:32a
       2 file(s)              0 bytes
               82,247,680 bytes free

A:\POLYSCI\USA>_
```

WHAT'S HAPPENING? Your display may vary, but notice the directory line Directory of C:\. You did indeed accomplish something. When you issued the command CD C:\, you changed the default directory on the hard disk to the root from \DOS6BK to the root of C on the hard disk without leaving the DATA disk.

6.17 Using Subdirectory Markers with the COPY Command

As you can see, the command line can get unwieldy. This situation is another reason for using the subdirectory markers dot and double dot, as a shorthand way of writing the commands. The . . represents the parent of a directory. The only directory that does not have a parent is the root directory because it is the parent of all the directories on a disk. You are going to use COPY as an example, but any DOS command works with subdirectory markers.

6.18 Activity: Using Shortcuts: The Subdirectory Markers

Note: The DATA disk is in Drive A. The A:\POLYSCI\USA> is displayed.

Step 1   Key in the following:

A:\POLYSCI\USA>**COPY FINAL.RPT ..\FIRST.TST** ⸢Enter⸣

```
A:\POLYSCI\USA>COPY FINAL.RPT ..\FIRST.TST
     1 file(s) copied

A:\POLYSCI\USA>_
```

WHAT'S HAPPENING? You copied the file called FINAL.RPT located in the current directory, USA to the parent of USA, which is POLYSCI. You gave it a new name, FIRST.TST. Instead of having to key in, as the destination file path, \POLYSCI\FIRST.TST, you used the shorthand name for \POLYSCI, which is .. and means the parent of USA. You included the \ between the .. and FIRST.TST as a delimiter.

Step 2   Key in the following:

A:\POLYSCI\USA>**COPY ..\FIRST.TST ..\FRANCE\LAST.TST**

```
A:\POLYSCI\USA>COPY ..\FIRST.TST ..\FRANCE\LAST.TST
     1 file(s) copied

A:\POLYSCI\USA>_
```

WHAT'S HAPPENING? You copied the file called FIRST.TST from the POLYSCI subdirectory to the FRANCE subdirectory, which is a child directory of POLYSCI. The long way to key in the command is to use the absolute path. If you issued the command using the absolute path, it would look like the following:

```
COPY A:\POLYSCI\FIRST.TST    A:\POLYSCI\FRANCE\LAST.TST
```

Because you used the subdirectory markers in the source file, the first .. represented the parent of USA. You did not have to key in \POLYSCI. However, you did need to key in the \ preceding the file name. This \ is a delimiter. You also did not need to key in \POLYSCI in the destination file. Instead you used the .., the subdirectory markers. You did need to key in the \ preceding FRANCE and the \ preceding LAST.TST because they were needed as delimiters to separate subdirectory names and file names. You can use subdirectory markers to save keystrokes. You can now verify that the files are in the FRANCE subdirectory.

Step 3   Key in the following: A:\POLYSCI\USA>**DIR ..\FRANCE** ⸢Enter⸣

```
A:\POLYSCI\USA>DIR ..\FRANCE

 Volume in drive A is DATADISK
 Volume Serial Number is 2F26-1901
 Directory of A:\POLYSCI\FRANCE

 .               <DIR>         06-20-94    6:11p
 ..              <DIR>         06-20-94    6:11p
 LAST    TST        72 11-23-95   10:41a
        3 file(s)              72 bytes
                       1,191,936 bytes free

A:\POLYSCI\USA>_
```

WHAT'S HAPPENING? You used the DIR command with the subdirectory markers to verify that you successfully copied the file using subdirectory markers.

Step 4   Key in the following: A:\POLYSCI\USA>**CD** \ Enter

```
A:\POLYSCI\USA>CD \

A:\>_
```

WHAT'S HAPPENING? You have returned to the root directory of the DATA disk.

6.19 Overwriting Files with the COPY Command

When you made copies of files, you gave the files on the same disk and in the same subdirectory unique names. One of the reasons for doing this is that, when you tried to use the same file name on the same disk and directory, you got this error message:

```
File cannot be copied onto itself, 0 file(s) copied.
```

DOS would not permit you to make that error.

However, the rule of unique file names is true only if the files are on the same disk and in the same subdirectory. If you are using more than one disk or more than one subdirectory, DOS will let you use the same file name. There have been no problems so far because, when you copied the source file from one disk to the destination file on another disk, it was a new file on the destination disk. Prior to DOS 6.2, if you already had a file on the destination disk with the same file name, DOS would *not* give you the error message saying, File cannot be copied onto itself, 0 file(s) copied. It would merely overwrite the destination file with the contents of the source file.

Overwrite means just what it says; it writes over or replaces what used to be in that file. Hence, if the contents of the source file are different from the contents of the destination file, the destination and source file will now have not only the same file name but also the same file contents. The previous contents of the destination file will be gone. Overwriting also happens on the same disk when the destination file name already exists. The same rules apply to subdirectories. See Figure 6.2 for a graphic representation of this.

```
A:THIS.FIL

This data will overwrite any
data in the destination file.
```

```
A:THIS.FIL

This data will overwrite any
data in the destination file.
```

`C:\>COPY A:THIS.FIL B:`

```
B:THIS.FIL

This data will be replaced by
the data in the source file.
```

```
B:THIS.FIL

This data will overwrite any
data in the destination file.
```

BEFORE

AFTER

Figure 6.2   **Overwriting Files**

The overwrite process seems dangerous because you could lose the data in a file. Why does DOS not protect you from this error? You were not protected from this potential error until the release of MS-DOS 6.2. If you have that version, you will be warned that you are about to overwrite a file. You then make the decision of whether or not you want to overwrite the file. However, in working with computers, typically, you *do* want to overwrite files.

Data changes all the time. For example, if you have a customer list stored as a file named CUSTOMER.LST on a disk, the information in the file (the data) changes as you add customers, delete customers, and update information about customers. When you have completed your work for the day, you want to **back up** your file or copy it to another disk, because you are working with it on a daily basis. Thus, you have a file called CUSTOMER.LST on your source disk and a file called CUSTOMER.LST on your destination disk. Since CUSTOMER.LST is a clearly descriptive file name, you really do not want to create a new file name every time you copy the file to the destination disk because creating new file names and then tracking current files can be time-consuming and confusing. In addition, if you are working with a file on a daily basis, you could end up with hundreds of files. In reality, you do not care about last week's or yesterday's customer information, or the old file; you care about the current version and its backup file. When copying a file for backup purposes, you do want the source file to overwrite the destination file. With DOS 6.2 and 6.22, you are warned that this is an overwrite. Remember, earlier versions of DOS simply overwrite the destination file contents with the source file contents without a warning.

6.20 Activity: Overwriting Files Using the COPY Command

Note: The DATA disk is in Drive A. The A:\> is displayed.

Step 1   Key in the following: A:\>**TYPE GOODBYE.NEW** [Enter]

Step 2   Key in the following: A:\>**TYPE JAN.OLD**

```
A:\>TYPE GOODBYE.NEW
THIS IS GOODBYE
AND FAREWELL.

A:\>TYPE JAN.OLD
This is my January file.
It is my first dummy file.
This is file 1.

A:\>_
```

WHAT'S HAPPENING? The contents of the files are different.

Step 3   Key in the following: A:\>**COPY GOODBYE.NEW JAN.OLD** [Enter]

```
A:\>COPY GOODBYE.NEW JAN.OLD
Overwrite JAN.OLD (Yes/No/All)?_
```

WHAT'S HAPPENING? In DOS 6.2, you get a message. The message is telling you that you already have a file by the name of JAN.OLD. Remember, in earlier versions of DOS, you will not get this message; you will see only the message of 1 file(s) copied.

Step 4   Key in the following: **Y** [Enter]

```
A:\>COPY GOODBYE.NEW JAN.OLD
Overwrite JAN.OLD (Yes/No/All)?y
        1 file(s) copied

A:\>_
```

WHAT'S HAPPENING? The file GOODBYE.NEW was successfully copied to the file called JAN.OLD, but what about the contents of the file? Did anything change?

Step 5   Key in the following: A:\>**TYPE GOODBYE.NEW** [Enter]

Step 6   Key in the following: A:\>**TYPE JAN.OLD**

```
A:\>TYPE GOODBYE.NEW
THIS IS GOODBYE
AND FAREWELL.

A:\>TYPE JAN.OLD
THIS IS GOODBYE
AND FAREWELL.

A:\>_
```

WHAT'S HAPPENING? The file contents are identical. What used to be inside the file called JAN.OLD located on the DATA disk has been overwritten or replaced (gone forever) by the contents of the file called GOODBYE.NEW also located on the DATA disk. You should be aware of how this procedure works so that you do not overwrite a file accidentally. Overwriting files is the norm.

DOS does not allow you to overwrite or copy a file when the source file and the destination file on the same disk and same subdirectory have *exactly* the same file name. All you get is the error message. This process works the same when dealing with subdirectories. In Activity 6.12, you copied JAN.TMP and FEB.TMP to the CLASS directory with the same file names, but different extensions so that in the CLASS directory the files were now called JAN.PAR and FEB.PAR. You are going to use wildcards to copy the rest of the .TMP files to the CLASS directory. In the process, you will overwrite the existing files.

Step 7   Key in the following: A:\>**COPY *.TMP CLASS*.PAR** [Enter]

```
A:\>COPY *.TMP CLASS\*.PAR
Overwrite CLASS\JAN.PAR (Yes/No/All)?_
```

WHAT'S HAPPENING? DOS does not know the contents of the file; it only knows you already have a file by that name. Rather than prompting you each time, one of the choices is A for all. Thus, if you intend to overwrite, you can choose A.

Step 8   Key in the following: **A** [Enter]

```
A:\>COPY *.TMP CLASS\*.PAR
Overwrite CLASS\JAN.PAR (Yes/No/All)?A
FEB.TMP
MAR.TMP
APR.TMP
        4 file(s) copied

A:\>_
```

WHAT'S HAPPENING? DOS has overwritten the JAN.PAR and FEB.PAR files in the CLASS directory with the JAN.TMP and FEB.TMP files in the root directory. You can prove this occurred by using the TYPE command.

Step 9   Key in the following: A:\>**TYPE JAN.TMP** [Enter]

Step 10   Key in the following: A:\>**TYPE CLASS\JAN.PAR** [Enter]

```
A:\>TYPE JAN.TMP
This is my January file.
It is my first dummy file.
This is file 1.

A:\>TYPE CLASS\JAN.PAR
This is my January file.
It is my first dummy file.
This is file 1.

A:\>_
```

WHAT'S HAPPENING? The contents of the two files are identical. You did overwrite the destination file with the contents of the source file. You can see that all the files have been copied by using the DIR command.

Step 11   Key in the following: A:\>**DIR CLASS*.PAR** [Enter]

```
A:\>DIR CLASS\*.PAR

  Volume in drive A is DATADISK
  Volume Serial Number is 2F26-1901
  Directory of A:\CLASS

JAN       PAR          72 11-23-95   10:41a
FEB       PAR          74 11-23-95   10:41a
MAR       PAR          70 11-23-95   10:42a
APR       PAR          71 11-23-95   10:42a
        4 file(s)             287 bytes
                    1,190,912 bytes free

A:\>_
```

WHAT'S HAPPENING? Now all the .TMP files are in the CLASS directory. They have the same file names but different file extensions.

6.21 Combining Text Files with the COPY Command

Sometimes, but rarely, it is useful to combine the contents of two or more text (ASCII) files. This process is known as concatenation of files. **Concatenation** means to put together. You might wish to concatenate when you have several short text files that would be easier to work with if they were combined into one file. When you combine files, nothing happens to the original files; they remain intact. You just create another new file from the original files.

However, most often users concatenate files accidentally and are unaware of it until they attempt to retrieve the file. Concatenation should never be done with either program files or the data files that the programs generate. Programs are binary code and combining any of these files makes the binary code useless and the program incapable of being executed. The same is true for the data files that programs generate. When you create a data file with a program, that program "formats" the data in such a way that the program knows how to interpret that data. That data file format is different for each program. A data file can be read only by the program that created it. If another program can read a *foreign* data file, it is because the program converts the *foreign* data into its own *native* format.

Why learn concatenation if you should not use it? You need to learn concatenation because accidental concatenation of files can occur very easily. The clue is to read the messages DOS places on the screen. In the following activity you will see the results of concatenation. The COPY command never changes. The syntax never changes. It is always COPY *source destination*. Look at the full syntax diagram:

```
COPY   [/A | /B]   source [/A | /B] [+ source [/A | /B] [+ ...]]
[destination [/A | /B]] [/V]
```

The /A indicates an ASCII file, whereas a /B indicates a binary file. In addition, whenever you see the notation in a syntax diagram of two or more items separated by the | as in [/A | /B], it is an *either/or* choice. *Either* you may use the /A *or* you may use the /B, but not both together.

6.22 Activity: Combining Files Using the COPY Command

Note: The DATA disk is in Drive A. The A:\> is displayed.

Step 1   Key in the following:

        A:\>**TYPE C:\DOS6BK\EMPLOYEE.ONE** [Enter]

Step 2   Key in the following:

        A:\>**TYPE C:\DOS6BK\EMPLOYEE.TWO** [Enter]

```
A:\>TYPE C:\DOS6BK\EMPLOYEE.ONE
This is employee file one.
It is the first file.

A:\>TYPE C:\DOS6BK\EMPLOYEE.TWO
This is employee file two.
It is the second file.

A:\>_
```

WHAT'S HAPPENING? You have displayed the contents of two files on the screen. Each file is unique with different file names and different file contents. You are going to place the contents of these two files into a new file called JOINED.SAM that will consist of the contents of the first file, EMPLOYEE.ONE, followed by the contents of the second file, EMPLOYEE.TWO. The new file will reside on the DATA disk. The command line is one line. There is one space between EMPLOYEE.TWO and JOINED.SAM.

Step 3 Key in the following (Do not press **Enter** until you see **Enter** in the step):

    A:\>COPY C:\DOS6BK\EMPLOYEE.ONE +

    C:\DOS6BK\EMPLOYEE.TWO JOINED.SAM **Enter**

```
A:\>COPY C:\DOS6BK\EMPLOYEE.ONE + C:\DOS6BK\EMPLOYEE.TWO JOINED.SAM
C:\DOS6BK\EMPLOYEE.ONE
C:\DOS6BK\EMPLOYEE.TWO
        1 file(s) copied

A:\>
```

WHAT'S HAPPENING? The message says 1 file(s) copied. It seems as if you have too many parameters because the syntax is COPY *source destination*. However, you are still following the correct syntax for the COPY command. You are making one destination file out of two source files. What you did here was to say COPY (the command) the contents of the file called C:\DOS6BK\EMPLOYEE.ONE and the contents of the file called C:\DOS6BK\EMPLOYEE.TWO (*source*) to a new file called JOINED.SAM that will reside on the DATA disk (*destination*). The + (plus sign) told DOS that the source had more to it than just one file. It also told DOS that you were joining files. The destination file is the last file name on the command line that does not have a plus sign in front. Look at Step 3 and note that JOINED.SAM has a space in front of it, not a plus sign, making JOINED.SAM the destination.

Step 4 Key in the following: A:\>**TYPE JOINED.SAM** **Enter**

```
A:\>TYPE JOINED.SAM
This is employee file one.
It is the first file.
This is employee file two.
It is the second file.

A:\>_
```

WHAT'S HAPPENING? The contents of the file JOINED.SAM consist of the contents of the file EMPLOYEE.ONE, followed immediately by the contents of the file EMPLOYEE.TWO. The contents in JOINED.SAM do not show any file names. You do not know where one file ended and the next began. JOINED.SAM is a new file, but you did not destroy or in any way alter the two original source files, EMPLOYEE.ONE or EMPLOYEE.TWO. You can prove this by using the TYPE command.

Step 5   Key in the following:

A:\>**TYPE C:\DOS6BK\EMPLOYEE.ONE** Enter

Step 6   Key in the following:

A:\>**TYPE C:\DOS6BK\EMPLOYEE.TWO** Enter

```
A:\>TYPE C:\DOS6BK\EMPLOYEE.ONE
This is employee file one.
It is the first file.

A:\>TYPE C:\DOS6BK\EMPLOYEE.TWO
This is employee file two.
It is the second file.

A:\>_
```

WHAT'S HAPPENING? As you can see, the source files remain unchanged. You merely created a third file from the contents of two files. You can join many files with the plus sign, but this is only useful for text files. If you try to join two data files created by an application program using the COPY command, the application program will no longer be able to read the combined data file.

Step 7   Key in the following: A:\>**C:** Enter

Step 8   Key in the following: C:\>**CD \DOS6BK\FINANCE** Enter

Step 9   Key in the following (Do not press Enter until you see Enter in the step):

C:\DOS6BK\FINANCE>**COPY BUDGET.TKR + HOMEBUD.TKR A:\TEST.TKR**

Enter

```
A:\>C:

C:\>CD \DOS6BK\FINANCE

C:\DOS6BK\FINANCE>COPY BUDGET.TKR + HOMEBUD.TKR A:TEST.TKR
BUDGET.TKR
HOMEBUD.TKR
        1 file(s) copied

C:\DOS6BK\FINANCE>_
```

WHAT'S HAPPENING? You have changed the drive and directory to the FINANCE directory under the DOS6BK directory on the hard disk. You then concatenated or combined the contents of two data files, BUDGET.TKR and HOMEBUD.TKR, generated by The THINKER program and placed the contents on the DATA disk in one file called TEST.TKR. Notice the message on the screen, 1 file(s) copied. You are now going to try to retrieve this joined file, TEST.TKR, in The THINKER program.

Step 10   Key in the following: C:\DOS6BK\FINANCE>**THINK** **Enter**

Step 11   Press **Enter**

Step 12   Press **/**

Step 13   Press **F**

Step 14   Press **R**

```
A1:
Enter name of file to retrieve:():
                                                    Status:ENTER
         A        B        C        D        E        F        G        H
 1
 2
 3
 4
 5
 6
 7
 8
 9
10
11
12
13
14
15
16
17
18
19
20
/-Command F1-Help F2-Edit F5-GOTO F9-Recalc           The Thinker(c)82,86
```

WHAT'S HAPPENING? You have loaded The THINKER program and have issued the command to load a data file. A prompt asks you what data file you wish to load. You are going to try to load the TEST.TKR file on the DATA disk.

Step 15   Key in the following: **A:\TEST.TKR** **Enter**

```
A1:
Enter name of file to retrieve:():A:\TEST.TKR
                                                        Status:WAIT
ERROR IN TRYING TO GET FILE, TRY AGAIN...    E        F        G        H
RETURN without GOSUB in line 31992 of module THINK    at address 23AB:48CB
2
Hit any key to return to system
4
5
6
7
8
9
10
11
12
13
14
15
16
17
18
19
20
/-Command F1-Help F2-Edit F5-GOTO F9-Recalc            The Thinker(c)82,86
```

WHAT'S HAPPENING? The THINKER program cannot recognize the joined data file and informs you with a message. (*Note:* sometimes the program finds the error so severe, it kicks you out of the program and returns you to the DOS system level. If that happens to you, simply press **Enter** and proceed to Step 20.)

Step 16   Press **Enter**

Step 17   Press **/**

Step 18   Press **Q**

Step 19   Press **Y**

```
C:\DOS6BK\FINANCE>_
```

WHAT'S HAPPENING? You have exited the program and returned to the system level.

Step 20   Key in the following: C:\DOS6BK\FINANCE>**CD \ Enter**

Step 21   Key in the following: C:\>**A: Enter**

```
C:\DOS6BK\FINANCE>CD \

C:\>A:

A:\>_
```

WHAT'S HAPPENING? Now you know that you should not combine data or program files. You may say to yourself that by never including the +, you cannot make that mistake. However, there is more to the story. You can also use wildcards to join files, which eliminates the need to key in all the file names. If you wanted to join all the files with a .TMP file extension and place them into a new file called MONTHS.SAM, located on the DATA disk, you would have to key in

```
COPY JAN.TMP + FEB.TMP + MAR.TMP + APR.TMP   A:MONTHS.SAM
```

You can save many keystrokes by using wildcards.

Step 22 Key in the following: A:\>**COPY** *.TMP **MONTHS.SAM** [Enter]

```
A:\>COPY *.TMP MONTHS.SAM
JAN.TMP
FEB.TMP
MAR.TMP
APR.TMP
        1 file(s) copied

A:\>_
```

WHAT'S HAPPENING? Using the wildcard has the same effect as keying in all the file names and connecting the source files with plus signs. DOS found each file with a .TMP file extension and wrote the contents of those files to a new file called MONTHS.SAM. Note the message 1 file(s) copied. Four files were combined into one file.

Step 23 Key in the following: A:\>**TYPE MONTHS.SAM** [Enter]

```
A:\>TYPE MONTHS.SAM
This is my January file.
It is my first dummy file.
This is file 1.
This is my February file.
It is my second dummy file.
This is file 2.
This is my March file.
It is my third dummy file.
This is file 3.
This is my April file.
It is my fourth dummy file.
This is file 4.

A:\>_
```

WHAT'S HAPPENING? As you can see, you joined together the contents of all the .TMP files into a new file called MONTHS.SAM. Again, since the .TMP files are ASCII files, the text is readable on the screen. How then can you make an error? A typical activity is to copy files from a hard disk to a floppy disk for backup purposes.

Wildcards are very useful to back up groups of files. You may choose to place the copies in a subdirectory. If you make only a one character error, you will combine the files into one file, making the file useless.

Step 24   Key in the following:

A:\>**COPY C:\DOS6BK\FINANCE\B*.TKR CLASX** Enter

```
A:\>COPY C:\DOS6BK\FINANCE\B*.TKR CLASX
C:\DOS6BK\FINANCE\BALANCE.TKR
C:\DOS6BK\FINANCE\BUDGET.TKR
        1 file(s) copied

A:\>_
```

WHAT'S HAPPENING? Again, note the message that only one file is being copied. Your intention was to copy the .TKR files that begin with B to the CLASS directory. You made a small typographical error. You keyed in CLASX instead of CLASS, so instead of two files being copied to the CLASS directory, you have one file called CLASX.

Step 25   Key in the following: A:\>**DIR CLASS\B*.*** Enter

Step 26   Key in the following: **DIR CLASX** Enter

```
A:\>DIR CLASS\B*.*

 Volume in drive A is DATADISK
 Volume Serial Number is 2F26-1901
 Directory of A:\CLASS

File not found

A:\>DIR CLASX

 Volume in drive A is DATADISK
 Volume Serial Number is 2F26-1901
 Directory of A:\

CLASX                15,108 06-21-94  11:17a
        1 file(s)        15,108 bytes
                     1,157,632 bytes free

A:\>_
```

WHAT'S HAPPENING? There are no files with the .TKR extension in the CLASS subdirectory, but there is one file called CLASX in the root directory. Again, DOS did exactly what you told it to do. In this case, however, what you said is not what you meant. This is why reading the messages on the screen is so important. The message you should have seen, if you had not made an error, was 2 file(s) copied. The minute you see the message 1 file(s) copied, you should realize that you joined the files into one file instead of copying each to the subdirectory called CLASS.

6.23 Printing Files

So far, you have not printed the contents of any files. You have redirected the output of the DIR command to the printer, but not any file contents. You could key in TYPE MY.FIL, and, if you were not on a network, print the screen, but this method of printing has several disadvantages. When you print the screen, you get *everything* that is displayed on the screen: the prompts, the commands, as well as the contents of the file. In addition, these text files have been very short and have fit entirely on the screen, but what if the contents of the file were longer than the number of lines available on your screen? There are easier ways to print the contents of text files. However, these techniques work *only* for ASCII files. Again, data files generated by application programs can be printed *only* from within the application program because the application program must send special signals to the printer so that the data prints correctly.

There are times you will wish to print an ASCII file. You will learn later about the ASCII files CONFIG.SYS and AUTOEXEC.BAT. You often want a hard copy of these files. There are also other reasons for printing text files. For instance, if you have a printer problem from within an application program, the first thing that you want to do is verify that it is a software problem, not a hardware problem. To test this, you return to the DOS system level and print an ASCII file. If the ASCII file prints, you now know you have a software problem within the application program.

There are four ways to print a text file from the DOS system level.

❑ Print the screen.

❑ Use redirection as you did in Chapter 3 with the DIR command.

❑ Copy the contents of a file to a printer. The destination is a device, instead of a file. The device is the printer. Since the printer is a device, it has a reserved name: PRN. You can also use LPT1 for Line Printer 1. If you use LPT1, be sure to key in the letter L, the letter P, the letter T, and the number 1. You cannot use the letter l ("ell") as the number 1.

❑ Use the PRINT command. The PRINT command, an external command, will print an ASCII file and automatically eject the page.

Before proceeding with this activity, check with your lab instructor to see if there are any special procedures in your lab or if, in fact, you are to do the activity at all.

6.24 Activity: Printing Files

WARNING: Do not do this activity if you are on a network unless instructed to do so.

Note 1:   The DATA disk is in Drive A. The A:\> is displayed.
Note 2:   Check with your lab instructor for any special instructions.
Note 3:   Sometimes, in a lab environment, you cannot use PRN. If PRN does not work, substitute LPT1.

Step 1   Key in the following: A:\>**TYPE JANUARY.TXT** `Enter`

```
A:\>TYPE JANUARY.TXT
This is my January file.
It is my first dummy file.
This is file 1.

A:\>_
```

WHAT'S HAPPENING? The contents of the TYPE command are written to the standard device, the screen. Since this is true, you can redirect the output to the printer.

Step 2:   Turn the printer on. Make sure the printer is online.

Step 3:   Key in the following: A:\>**TYPE JANUARY.TXT > PRN** `Enter`

```
A:\>TYPE JANUARY.TXT > PRN

A:\>_
```

WHAT'S HAPPENING? Nothing was written to the screen because you redirected the output to the printer. Now you want to eject the page. (*Note:* Remember, the notation `Ctrl` + **L** means press them at the same time.)

Step 4   Key in the following: A:>**ECHO** `Ctrl` + **L** > **PRN** `Enter`

```
A:\>ECHO ^L > PRN

A:\>_
```

WHAT'S HAPPENING? The page was ejected. You should have the following printout on your printer.

```
This is my January file.
It is my first dummy file.
This is file 1.
```

WHAT'S HAPPENING? It would seem that, if this works as it did, you could do the same with the COPY command. But you cannot. The only screen output from the copy command is 1 file(s) copied. If you redirected the output, you would only have printed the message 1 file(s) copied, not the contents of the file. Instead of redirection, you copy the file to a device, the printer.

Step 5   Key in the following: A:\>**COPY JANUARY.TXT PRN** Enter

WHAT'S HAPPENING? Even though you are using a device, the syntax remains the same. COPY is the command, the work you want done. JANUARY.TXT is the source, the file you want copied. You do not need to enter a drive designator in front of the file name because DOS will assume the default. PRN is the device name for the printer. The printer is the destination, where you want the contents of the file to go. As soon as you press Enter, you should hear/see the printer begin to print. The hard copy or output is at the printer. Your screen displays the message 1 file(s) copied. You see on the printed paper the following words:

```
      This is my January file.
      It is my first dummy file.
      This is file 1.
```

WHAT'S HAPPENING? All that was written to the screen was the message 1 file copied. You copied the contents of the file to a device, the printer. Now you want to eject the page.

Step 6   Key in the following: A:>**ECHO** Ctrl **+ L > PRN** Enter

```
A:\>ECHO ^L > PRN

A:\>_
```

WHAT'S HAPPENING? The page was ejected. However, you may get tired of always having to take two steps—printing the file and ejecting the page. Thus, there is a command that combines both of those steps, the PRINT command. The PRINT command is an external command that will print a page and then eject it. The basic syntax is:

```
PRINT [drive:][path]filename
```

Step 7   Key in the following: A:\>**PRINT JANUARY.TXT** Enter

```
A:\>PRINT JANUARY.TXT
Name of list device [PRN]:
```

WHAT'S HAPPENING? The first time you use PRINT in a DOS session, it is loaded into memory as are all external commands. Since your path is set to the DOS subdirectory, you do not need to change default drives or directories. PRINT is asking you for the name of the device that the output should be sent to. Once PRINT has this information, it will not ask for it again during this work session.

Step 8   Press **Enter**

```
A:\>PRINT JANUARY.TXT
Name of list device [PRN]:
Resident part of PRINT installed


   A:\JANUARY.TXT is currently being printed

A:\>_
```

WHAT'S HAPPENING? Now that the device is noted by the PRINT command, the file will print and the page will be ejected.

```
   This is my January file.
   It is my first dummy file.
   This is file 1.
```

WHAT'S HAPPENING? You have printed your file and ejected the page with one command.

Chapter Summary

1. One of the major reasons people buy computers is for application programs that assist people in different tasks.
2. Application software usually generates data. Both application software and data are stored as disk files.
3. Usually, only a program can use its data file. A data file without the application program cannot be used.
4. Another component of DOS are the commands that allow the user to manage and manipulate program and data files.
5. The internal commands DIR, COPY, and TYPE allow you to manage the files on a disk.
6. The file extensions .COM (command file) and .EXE (executable code) tell DOS that the file is a program.
7. COPY allows you to copy files selectively.
8. The syntax of the copy command is:

```
COPY  [d:][path][file name]   [d:][path][file name]
```

A simple way to remember the COPY syntax is

```
COPY    source    destination.
```

Source is what you want to copy. *Destination* is where you want it copied.

9. The COPY command never changes the source file.
10. When naming files, it is best to stick to alphanumeric characters. Certain characters are illegal, such as the colon : and the <Space>.
11. A dummy file is created for test purposes.
12. When copying a file to a subdirectory, you must include the path name. The path name and the file name are separated by the backslash. The backslash is used as a delimiter. The one exception is that the root directory's name is \ (backslash).
13. Wildcards may be used with the COPY command.
14. Files must have unique names on the same drive and subdirectory, but those files that are copied to a subdirectory may have identical names because the path makes those file names unique.
15. TYPE allows you to display the contents of a file on the screen. The syntax is:

```
TYPE    [drive:][path]filename
```

16. Wildcards may not be used with the TYPE command.
17. You may use subdirectory markers with the DIR, COPY, and TYPE commands.
18. If you use *.* with a command, it chooses all the files. Thus, DIR *.* would display all the files. COPY C:\WHAT*.* A:\ would copy all the files in the WHAT directory to the disk in Drive A.
19. When you move between drives, DOS remembers the last directory you were in.
20. Overwriting files with the COPY command is the process where the contents of the source file copies over the contents of the destination file. MS-DOS 6.2 or 6.22 will prompt you before you overwrite an existing file. Earlier versions of DOS will not.
21. Concatenation means combining the contents of files using the COPY command with either the + sign or a wildcard. The key is that there is only one destination file. You should not concatenate program files or data files generated from program files.
22. You may print the contents of ASCII files by using COPY *filename* PRN or COPY *filename* LPT1.
23. You may also print ASCII files by keying in TYPE *filename* > PRN or TYPE *filename* > LPT1.
24. If you wish to eject a page using either COPY file name PRN or TYPE file name > PRN, you must redirect the **Ctrl** + L command to the printer as ECHO **Ctrl** + **L** > PRN.
25. If you wish to print files and have the pages eject automatically, use the PRINT command.

Key Terms

ASCII	Destination file	Overwrite
Back up	Dummy files	Source file
Concatenation	Housekeeping tasks	Unformatted text file

Discussion Questions

1. Explain the function and purpose of internal commands.
2. Give two reasons for making a copy of a file on the same disk.
3. Give the syntax for the COPY command and explain each part of the syntax.
4. Is a file extension mandatory when naming a file?
5. What is the maximum number of characters that may be used when naming a file? A file extension?
6. List three characters that cannot be used when naming files.
7. List three examples of legal file names.
8. When would you use a wildcard with the COPY command?
9. What is the purpose and function of the TYPE command? Explain each part of the syntax diagram.
10. How can you recognize that a file is a program or executable?
11. What are ASCII files?
12. What is the purpose and function of dummy files?
13. Every file on a disk must have a unique name. Yet, when you make a copy of a file on the same disk, in a different subdirectory, it may have the same file name. Explain.
14. Under what circumstances could a user think that the computer has "lost his files"?
15. Can you use wildcards with the TYPE command? Why or why not?
16. What does the first \ in any command line mean?
17. What does it mean to "overwrite a file"? What are some of the dangers of overwriting files?
18. Why would you make a copy of a file on the same disk? On another disk?
19. What would happen if you tried to copy a file from one disk to another and the destination disk already had a file with the same name? Does the version of DOS make a difference in the results?
20. How would you combine the contents of two files? Why would you?
21. What happens to the original files when you combine two or more files?
22. What are some of the dangers of concatenating program files or data files?
23. What message on the screen informs you that you have concatenated several files?
24. What are some of the disadvantages of printing the screen to have a printout of an ASCII file?
25. Compare and contrast printing a file using redirection with the TYPE command, the COPY command, and the PRINT command.

Chapter 7

Using ERASE, DEL, UNDELETE, DELTREE, RENAME, and MOVE

7. Use the MOVE command to move files and rename directories.
8. Use DELTREE to delete files and directories.
9. Use the RD command to delete directories.
10. Back up a data disk using the DISKCOPY command.
11. Back up files using the COPY command.

Chapter Overview

The more work you do with computers, the greater number of files you create. The more files and/or disks you have, the harder it is to manage them. It becomes increasingly difficult to keep track of what disks have which files and which files are needed. In addition, as new data is keyed into existing files, the name given to the file may no longer be appropriate. It is also important to be able to make a copy of an entire disk or specific files on a disk so that data is not lost due to a power failure, surge, or a bad disk.

In this chapter you will continue to work with commands that help you manage and manipulate your files. This chapter will focus on the DEL and ERASE commands, which allow you to delete files you no longer need or want, the UNDELETE command, which will let you recover files you have accidentally deleted, the RENAME command, which is used to rename files, the MOVE command, which allows you to move files from one location to another as well as to rename a directory (introduced in Chapter 5). In addition, you will look at the DELTREE command, which allows you to eliminate a subdirectory with all its files quickly. You will also learn why and how to back up specific files or an entire disk so that you do not lose important data.

7.1   Eliminating Files with the ERASE and DEL Commands

In the various activities completed previously, you copied many files. The DATA disk began as a disk absent of files. As you have been working, the number of files on the disk has increased dramatically, typical when working with computers. There is a kind of Murphy's Law that says you create as many files as you have disk space. However, you do not want to keep files forever. The more files and/or disks you have, the harder it is to keep track of what disks have which files and which files are the ones you need. If you have floppy disks, you end up with many floppies, and if you have a hard disk, you end up with many subdirectories and many files. Often, you are not quite sure what files are where. Thus, keeping only the files you need on your disk will decrease the number of files you have to manage.

Logic should tell you that, if you can copy and create files, you should be able to eliminate files by deleting or erasing them. You can do these tasks with the ERASE or the DEL command. These commands are internal, always resident in memory. You do need to be careful with these commands. Once you press **Enter** after the ERASE or DEL command, the file is gone forever. DOS does not ask you if this is really the file you want to get rid of; it simply obeys your instructions.

A deleted file cannot be recovered except by certain special utility programs; even then, recovery is not necessarily complete. Technically, when you delete a file, DOS does not actually remove the file from the disk physically. Instead, it replaces the first character of the file name with a special byte that marks the file as deleted in the directory table—the symbol σ. It then places a zero in each cluster entry in the FAT (File Allocation Table). The value of 0 in each cluster means to DOS that the space is now available for reuse by other files. This is true even though, in fact, the data is still on the disk. When you create the next file, DOS sees that there is space available in the directory table and FAT and may assign the new file to that space. DOS then overwrites the old file with the new file.

Special utility programs, such as Norton Utilities or the UNDELETE command, introduced in DOS 5.0, can occasionally help you recover deleted files, particularly if you realize immediately that you inadvertently erased a file. However, once a file is overwritten by new data, nothing can recover the previous data. It is gone forever. DOS 6 introduced some higher levels of security that, when installed, allow a better chance of restoring deleted files. On the whole, though, when you use the ERASE or DEL commands, you cannot count on recovering deleted files. Thus, you should consider that when you use DEL, you have indeed removed the file or files.

Both ERASE and DEL work in precisely the same way. The syntax of each command is:

```
DEL [drive:][path]filename [/P]
```

or

```
ERASE [drive:][path]filename [/P]
```

The /P parameter, introduced in DOS 4.0, prompts you before a file is deleted. ERASE is spelled out and DEL is an abbreviation for delete. You can neither abbreviate ERASE as ERA, nor can you spell DELETE for DEL. The commands must be used as they are specified. Most computer users key in DEL instead of ERASE for the simple reason that DEL has fewer characters. Computer users are big on saving keystrokes.

7.2 Activity: Using the ERASE and DEL Commands

Correcting Keystroke Errors

When keying in commands, you may use the function keys to correct typographical errors. To edit command lines fully, you may use DOSKEY. For instructions on how to use DOSKEY, see Chapter 14, sections 14.1–14.2.

Note 1: Be sure the DATA disk, not the APPLICATIONS DISK, is in Drive A.

Note 2: The DATA disk is in Drive A. The C:\> is displayed as the default drive and the default directory.

Step 1   Key in the following: C:\>**A:** [Enter]

Step 2   Key in the following: A:\>**COPY C:\DOS6BK*.DOS *.AAA** [Enter]

```
C:\>A:

A:\>COPY C:\DOS6BK\*.DOS *.AAA
C:\DOS6BK\WILDONE.DOS
C:\DOS6BK\WILDTHR.DOS
C:\DOS6BK\WILDTWO.DOS
        3 file(s) copied

A:\>_
```

WHAT'S HAPPENING? You changed the default drive to A. You then copied the files with a .DOS extension from the \DOS6BK directory, kept the same file name, but gave them a different extension—.AAA on the DATA disk.

Step 3   Key in the following: A:\>**DIR *.AAA** [Enter]

```
A:\>DIR *.AAA

 Volume in drive A is DATADISK
 Volume Serial Number is 2F26-1901
 Directory of A:\

WILDONE  AAA            180 05-07-93    9:02a
WILDTHR  AAA            180 05-07-93    9:03a
WILDTWO  AAA            181 05-07-93    9:03a
        3 file(s)            541 bytes
                       1,156,096 bytes free

A:\>_
```

WHAT'S HAPPENING? You used the DIR command to confirm that the .AAA files are on the DATA disk. The work you wish to do is erase or delete files. The DEL and ERASE commands are internal and were installed in memory (RAM) when you booted the system. They will remain in memory until you turn off the power.

Step 4   Key in the following: A:\>**DIR WILDONE.AAA** [Enter]

```
A:\>DIR WILDONE.AAA

 Volume in drive A is DATADISK
 Volume Serial Number is 2F26-1901
 Directory of A:\
```

```
WILDONE   AAA          180 05-07-93    9:02a
        1 file(s)               180 bytes
                        1,156,096 bytes free

A:\>_
```

WHAT'S HAPPENING? The DIR command verified the file called WILDONE.AAA is located on the DATA disk.

Step 5   Key in the following: A:\>**ERASE WILDONE.AAA** [Enter]

```
A:\>ERASE WILDONE.AAA

A:\>_
```

WHAT'S HAPPENING? You are asking the ERASE command to eliminate the file called WILDONE.AAA, located on the DATA disk. You did not need to include the drive letter or the \ because DOS assumed the default drive and directory and looked only for the file called WILDONE.AAA on the DATA disk in the root. However, it appears that nothing happened. All you got on the screen was the system prompt.

Step 6   Key in the following: A:\>**DIR WILDONE.AAA** [Enter]

```
A:\>DIR WILDONE.AAA

 Volume in drive A is DATADISK
 Volume Serial Number is 2F26-1901
 Directory of A:\

File not found

A:\>_
```

WHAT'S HAPPENING? The DIR command confirmed that the file is gone. You now know that DOS executed the ERASE command and removed the file called WILDONE.AAA. It is no longer on the DATA disk.

Step 7   Key in the following: A:\>**DIR WILDTWO.AAA** [Enter]

```
A:\>DIR WILDTWO.AAA

 Volume in drive A is DATADISK
 Volume Serial Number is 2F26-1901
 Directory of A:\
```

```
WILDTWO   AAA              181 05-07-93     9:03a
         1 file(s)                181 bytes
                          1,156,608 bytes free

A:\>_
```

WHAT'S HAPPENING? The screen display indicates that the file named WILDTWO.AAA is on the DATA disk. Before you delete a file, it is always a good practice to verify that the file is on the disk and that you really want to remove it.

Step 8   Key in the following: A:\>**DEL WILDTWO.AAA** [Enter]

```
A:\>DEL WILDTWO.AAA

A:\>_
```

WHAT'S HAPPENING? The system prompt is displayed on the screen, indicating that the file was deleted. You can verify deletion using the DIR command.

Step 9   Key in the following: A:\>**DIR WILDTWO.AAA** [Enter]

```
A:\>DIR WILDTWO.AAA

 Volume in drive A is DATADISK
 Volume Serial Number is 2F26-1901
 Directory of A:\

File not found

A:\>_
```

WHAT'S HAPPENING? The file called WILDTWO.AAA is gone from the DATA disk. As you can see, the ERASE command and the DEL command do exactly the same thing. What if the file you want to erase is not on the disk?

Step 10   Key in the following: A:\>**DEL NOFILE.XXX** [Enter]

```
A:\>DEL NOFILE.XXX
File not found

A:\>_
```

WHAT'S HAPPENING? In order for DOS to execute the command DEL, it must be able to find the file to delete. Here, the file was not found.

Step 11   Key in the following: A:\>**DEL** [Enter]

```
A:\>DEL
Required parameter missing

A:\>_
```

WHAT'S HAPPENING? Not only must DOS find the file, it must also have a file to find. Remember, the syntax is DEL *filename.* The Required parameter missing message is the computer equivalent of "Get rid of what file?" If you are using DOS 3.3 or below, the message is Invalid number of parameters. It means the same as the message from later versions of DOS. However, the new message is more explicit. One of the things that happen when software is upgraded is that improvements are made. The old message did not give you as much information as the new message.

7.3 Deleting Files on Other Drives and Directories

Using the DEL command to eliminate files works exactly the same on other drives and subdirectories as it did in the previous activity. The syntax of the command remains DEL *[drive:][path]filename.* The only difference is that you must specify which disk drive and which directory you want DOS to look on. Once again, DOS follows your instructions exactly as keyed in; it does not check with you to see if you are deleting the correct file. One of the most common mistakes computer users make is placing the drive designator or subdirectory in the wrong place, completely changing the instructions. Again, the syntax of the command is:

```
DEL [drive:][path]filename
```

DEL is the command. *drive:* represents the designated drive. *path* represents any subdirectory. *filename* represents the name of the file you wish to delete. For example, if the file you want to delete is on Drive A, you would substitute A: for *drive:.* If the file you want to delete is on Drive C, you would substitute C: for the *drive:.* If the path name was \DOS, you would substitute \DOS for *path. filename* is the name of the file—the file specification. For example, if the default drive is A:\> and you want to delete a file on the disk in Drive B called GONE.FIL, a common error is to key in the command as:

```
A:\>DEL  GONE.FIL B:
```

This sequence is *wrong* because you did not use the proper syntax, DEL *d:filename.* The command should have been keyed in as:

```
A:\>DEL B:GONE.FIL.
```

Not only is the command wrong, but it is also illogical, the equivalent of sending someone to throw away a file folder and not telling that person which file cabinet to look in. What are the results of incorrectly keying in the command? It depends on the version of DOS. If you have a version prior to 3.3, DOS will delete the file on the disk in Drive A, the default drive, and will not pay attention to the B: because it is in the wrong place. If you have DOS 4.0 or above, it will tell you that you have too many parameters. Remember to be aware of the default drive and directory.

7.4 Activity: Using the DEL Commands with Individual Files

Note: The DATA disk is in Drive A. The A:\> is displayed.

Step 1   Key in the following: A:\>**MD TRIP** **Enter**

Step 2   Key in the following: A:\>**COPY C:\DOS6BK*.99 TRIP** **Enter**

Step 3   Key in the following: A:\>**COPY C:\DOS6BK*.JAZ TRIP** **Enter**

```
A:\>MD TRIP

A:\>COPY C:\DOS6BK\*.99 TRIP
C:\DOS6BK\APR.99
C:\DOS6BK\FEB.99
C:\DOS6BK\JAN.99
C:\DOS6BK\MAR.99
        4 file(s) copied

A:\>COPY C:\DOS6BK\*.JAZ TRIP
C:\DOS6BK\BLUE.JAZ
C:\DOS6BK\GREEN.JAZ
        2 file(s) copied

A:\>_
```

WHAT'S HAPPENING? You created another subdirectory on the DATA disk called TRIP. You then copied files from the \DOS6BK subdirectory on the hard disk to the subdirectory called TRIP on the DATA disk. You used the COPY command. You had to specify where the source files were located, which was C:\DOS6BK. However, for the destination of these files, since the default drive is A and the default directory is the root, the default is assumed, and you did not have to specify either the destination drive or the root directory in the destination. If you had not included the name of the subdirectory TRIP, where you wanted the files copied, DOS would have assumed the default and copied the files to the root directory of the DATA disk. The longhand version of the command is A:\>COPY C:\DOS6BK*.99 A:\TRIP*.99.

Step 4   Key in the following: A:\>**DIR TRIP\JAN.99** **Enter**

```
A:\>DIR TRIP\JAN.99
```

```
    Volume in drive A is DATADISK
    Volume Serial Number is 2F26-1901
    Directory of A:\TRIP

JAN      99             72 11-23-95  10:41a
         1 file(s)             72 bytes
                       1,153,536 bytes free

A:\>_
```

WHAT'S HAPPENING? The file is there. You successfully copied it.

Step 5   Key in the following: A:\>**DEL TRIP\JAN.99** [Enter]

```
A:\>DEL TRIP\JAN.99

A:\>_
```

WHAT'S HAPPENING? You had to provide the proper syntax to tell the DEL command where the JAN.99 file is located. It was located in the subdirectory TRIP under the root directory on the DATA disk. Since the default drive is A, you did not need to include the drive letter because it is the default drive. Since the default subdirectory is the root (\), the \ is assumed and does not need to be keyed in. However, the \ between the subdirectory TRIP and the file name JAN.99 does need to be keyed in. In this case the \ is used as a delimiter between the subdirectory name and the file name. Has the file been deleted?

Step 6   Key in the following: A:\>**DIR TRIP\JAN.99** [Enter]

```
A:\>DIR TRIP\JAN.99

 Volume in drive A is DATADISK
 Volume Serial Number is 2F26-1901
 Directory of A:\TRIP

File not found

A:\>_
```

WHAT'S HAPPENING? The file called JAN.99 is gone from the subdirectory called TRIP on the DATA disk. Look at the display. The third line, Directory of A:\TRIP, tells you that DIR looked only in the subdirectory called TRIP.

Step 7   Key in the following: A:\>**C:** [Enter]

Step 8   Key in the following: C:\>**CD \DOS6BK** [Enter]

Step 9   Key in the following: C:\DOS6BK>**COPY HELLO.TXT A:** [Enter]

```
A:\>C:

C:\>CD \DOS6BK

C:\DOS6BK>COPY HELLO.TXT A:\
        1 file(s) copied

C:\DOS6BK>_
```

WHAT'S HAPPENING? You changed the default drive to the hard disk. You then changed the default subdirectory from the root of the hard disk to the subdirectory called \DOS6BK. You then copied the file called HELLO.TXT from the \DOS6BK directory to the root directory of the DATA disk. The purpose of this activity is to have two identically named files on different drives.

Step 10   Key in the following: C:\DOS6BK>**DIR HELLO.TXT** Enter

Step 11   Key in the following: C:\DOS6BK>**DIR A:\HELLO.TXT** Enter

```
C:\DOS6BK>DIR HELLO.TXT

 Volume in drive C has no label
 Volume Serial Number is 1CD1-5E42
 Directory of C:\DOS6BK

HELLO    TXT            52 11-23-95  10:44a
        1 file(s)              52 bytes
                   82,321,408 bytes free

C:\DOS6BK>DIR A:\HELLO.TXT

 Volume in drive A is DATADISK
 Volume Serial Number is 2F26-1901
 Directory of A:\

HELLO    TXT            52 11-23-95  10:44a
        1 file(s)              52 bytes
                    1,153,536 bytes free

C:\DOS6BK>_
```

WHAT'S HAPPENING? You have two files called HELLO.TXT. One file is on the hard disk in the subdirectory \DOS6BK. The other file is on the DATA disk. You want to delete the file on the DATA disk, not on the hard disk.

Step 12   Key in the following: C:\DOS6BK>**DEL A:\HELLO.TXT** Enter

```
C:\DOS6BK>DEL A:\HELLO.TXT

C:\DOS6BK>_
```

WHAT'S HAPPENING? You asked DEL to erase the file on the DATA disk called
HELLO.TXT. The file should be gone from the DATA disk, but the file called
HELLO.TXT on the hard disk (Drive C, subdirectory \DOS6BK) should still be there.

Step 13   Key in the following: C:\DOS6BK>**DIR HELLO.TXT** Enter

Step 14   Key in the following: C:\DOS6BK>**DIR A:\HELLO.TXT** Enter

```
C:\DOS6BK>DIR HELLO.TXT

 Volume in drive C has no label
 Volume Serial Number is 1CD1-5E42
 Directory of C:\DOS6BK

HELLO     TXT          52 11-23-95  10:44a
        1 file(s)              52 bytes
                      82,272,256 bytes free

C:\DOS6BK>DIR A:\HELLO.TXT

 Volume in drive A is DATADISK
 Volume Serial Number is 2F26-1901
 Directory of A:\

File not found

C:\DOS6BK>_
```

WHAT'S HAPPENING? The file called HELLO.TXT is still in the subdirectory
\DOS6BK on the hard disk, but the file called HELLO.TXT on the DATA disk is gone.

Step 15   Key in the following: C:\DOS6BK>**DIR A:\TRIP\BLUE.JAZ** Enter

```
C:\DOS6BK>DIR A:\TRIP\BLUE.JAZ

 Volume in drive A is DATADISK
 Volume Serial Number is 2F26-1901
 Directory of A:\TRIP

BLUE      JAZ          18 10-12-94  10:40a
        1 file(s)              18 bytes
                       1,154,048 bytes free

C:\DOS6BK>_
```

WHAT'S HAPPENING? There is a file called BLUE.JAZ in the subdirectory TRIP on the DATA disk. To delete this file, you once again follow the syntax of the DEL command, substituting the values you want for the variable parameters.

Step 16   Key in the following: C:\DOS6BK>**DEL A:\TRIP\BLUE.JAZ** Enter

```
C:\DOS6BK>DEL A:\TRIP\BLUE.JAZ

C:\DOS6BK>_
```

WHAT'S HAPPENING? The syntax is DEL *[drive:][path]filename*. You substituted the drive letter of the DATA disk for the *[drive:]*. You then substituted TRIP for the *[path]*. You did not need to key in the first backslash because the root directory of the DATA disk is the default directory. In order to ensure that you indeed meant the root directory of the DATA disk and to be on the safe side, you included the \ for the root directory. You then substituted BLUE.JAZ for the *filename*. The second backslash was mandatory because you need a delimiter between the file name and the subdirectory name. This backslash is just like the period that you used to separate the file name from the file extension. Is the file gone?

Step 17   Key in the following: C:\DOS6BK>**DIR A:\TRIP\BLUE.JAZ** Enter

```
C:\DOS6BK>DIR A:\TRIP\BLUE.JAZ

 Volume in drive A is DATADISK
 Volume Serial Number is 2F26-1901
 Directory of A:\TRIP

File not found

C:\DOS6BK>_
```

WHAT'S HAPPENING? The file BLUE.JAZ from the directory TRIP on the DATA disk is gone.

Step 18   Key in the following: C:\DOS6BK>**CD ** Enter

Step 19   Key in the following: C:\>**A:** Enter

```
C:\DOS6BK>CD \

C:\>A:

A:\>_
```

WHAT'S HAPPENING? You returned to the root directory of the hard disk. You then made the root directory of DATA disk the default drive and directory.

7.5 Using Wildcards with the DEL Command

You have been erasing or deleting individual files one file at a time. Often you want to erase many files. It is tedious to erase many files one at a time. Just as you can use the global file specifications with the DIR and COPY commands, you can also use the wildcards with the ERASE or DEL command. Wildcards allow you to erase a group of files with a one-line command. However, be *exceedingly careful* when using wildcards with the DEL command. Once again, the strength of wildcards is also their weakness. Global means *global*. You can eliminate a group of files very quickly. If you are not careful, you could erase files you want to keep. In fact, you probably will some day. "Oh, no, not *those* files gone." However, this does not mean you should not use wildcards. They are far too useful. Just be careful.

7.6 Activity: Using the ERASE and DEL Commands

Note 1:   The DATA disk is in Drive A. The A:\> is displayed.
Note 2:   If the .TMP files are not on the DATA disk, they may be copied from the
           \DOS6BK subdirectory to the DATA disk.

Step 1   Key in the following: A:\>**DIR *.TMP** [Enter]

```
A:\>DIR *.TMP


 Volume in drive A is DATADISK
 Volume Serial Number is 2F26-1901
 Directory of A:\

 JAN       TMP            72 11-23-95  10:41a
 FEB       TMP            74 11-23-95  10:41a
 MAR       TMP            70 11-23-95  10:42a
 APR       TMP            71 11-23-95  10:42a
         4 file(s)            287 bytes
                       1,154,560 bytes free

A:\>_
```

WHAT'S HAPPENING? You should see four files with .TMP as the file extension displayed on the screen. Prior to a global erase, it is *always* wise to key in DIR with the global file specification you are going to use. This process allows you to confirm visually that you are not going to erase a file you want to retain.

Step 2   Key in the following: A:\>**DEL *.TMP** [Enter]

```
A:\>DEL *.TMP

A:\>_
```

WHAT'S HAPPENING? You asked DEL to erase or delete *every* file on the DATA disk that has the file extension .TMP in the root directory. The wildcard * represented any file name. Only the system prompt appears on the screen. The DEL command executed, erasing those *.TMP files quickly and permanently. To verify this, use the DIR command.

Step 3   Key in the following: A:\>**DIR** *.**TMP** Enter

```
A:\>DIR *.TMP

 Volume in drive A is DATADISK
 Volume Serial Number is 2F26-1901
 Directory of A:\

File not found

A:\>_
```

WHAT'S HAPPENING? Those *.TMP files are, indeed, gone from the root directory on the DATA disk. They are not recoverable by DOS except with the UNDELETE command introduced in DOS 5.0. Again, let it be emphasized that, before you use a wildcard to delete groups of files, you should use the DIR command to see the files you are going to delete. For instance, if you had a file called TEST.TMP that you had forgotten about, the directory display would include it as follows:

```
A:\>DIR *.TMP

  Volume in drive A is DATA DISK
  Volume Serial Number is 3839-0EC8
  Directory of A:\

JAN       TMP     72     11-23-92      7:04a
FEB       TMP     74     11-23-92      7:04a
MAR       TMP     70     11-23-92      7:04a
APR       TMP     71     11-23-92      7:04a
TEST      TMP    110     11-23-92      7:10a
        5 file(s)           397 bytes
                     232448 bytes free
```

Using the DIR command with wildcards will let you display on the screen all the files that have been selected by *.TMP, which includes the TEST.TMP file that you do not want to erase. If you had keyed in DEL *.TMP, all those .TMP files would have been deleted. Remember, the computer does not come back and tell you, "Oh, by the way, TEST.TMP is also included with the *.TMP files; did you want to erase that file?" The DEL command simply eliminates all the .TMP files because that is what you told it to do. You can also use wildcards when files are in a subdirectory.

Step 4   Key in the following: A:\>**DIR TRIP*.99** **Enter**

```
A:\>DIR TRIP\*.99

 Volume in drive A is DATADISK
 Volume Serial Number is 2F26-1901
 Directory of A:\TRIP

APR       99             71 11-23-95  10:42a
FEB       99             74 11-23-95  10:41a
MAR       99             70 11-23-95  10:42a
         3 file(s)            215 bytes
                       1,156,608 bytes free

A:\>_
```

WHAT'S HAPPENING? There are three files with the extension .99 on the DATA disk in the subdirectory TRIP. The DEL command works the same way, but you must be sure to include the path name.

Step 5   Key in the following: A:\>**DEL TRIP*.99** **Enter**

```
A:\>DEL TRIP\*.99

A:\>_
```

WHAT'S HAPPENING? You asked DEL to erase or delete *every* file on the DATA disk in the subdirectory TRIP that has any file name and has the file extension .99. The wildcard * represented any file name. Only the system prompt appears on the screen. The DEL command executed, erasing those *.99 files quickly and permanently. To verify this, you can use the DIR command.

Step 6   Key in the following: A:\>**DIR TRIP*.99** **Enter**

```
A:\>DIR TRIP\*.99

 Volume in drive A is DATADISK
 Volume Serial Number is 2F26-1901
 Directory of A:\TRIP

File not found

A:\>_
```

WHAT'S HAPPENING? The files are indeed gone.

7.7 The /P Parameter with the DEL Command

The problem with earlier versions of the DEL command was that there was no way for you to confirm deletions. DOS simply erased. In DOS 4.0 an enhancement was introduced, the /P. This parameter allows you to tell the DEL command to prompt you with the file name prior to deleting the file. The syntax is:

```
DEL [drive:][path]filename [/P]
```

or

```
ERASE [drive:][path]filename [/P]
```

The last statement, /P, is an optional fixed parameter. Its purpose is to display each file name to verify that you really want to delete it. You can think of the P standing for "prompt you for an answer." This parameter is particularly useful when using wildcards. You cannot accidentally eliminate a file. It minimizes file deletions.

7.8 Activity: Using /P with the DEL Command

Note 1:   The DATA disk is in Drive A. The A:\> is displayed.

Step 1   Key in the following: **A:\>COPY C:\DOS6BK*.99** [Enter]

```
A:\>COPY C:\DOS6BK\*.99
C:\DOS6BK\APR.99
C:\DOS6BK\FEB.99
C:\DOS6BK\JAN.99
C:\DOS6BK\MAR.99
        4 file(s) copied

A:\>_
```

WHAT'S HAPPENING? You have copied the files with the .99 extension from the DOS6BK directory to the root of the DATA disk and kept the file names the same.

Step 2   Key in the following: A:\>**COPY *.99 TRIP** [Enter]

Step 3   Key in the following: A:\>**DIR TRIP** [Enter]

```
A:\>COPY *.99 TRIP
APR.99
FEB.99
JAN.99
MAR.99
        4 file(s) copied

A:\>DIR TRIP
```

```
Volume in drive A is DATADISK
Volume Serial Number is 2F26-1901
Directory of A:\TRIP

.              <DIR>           06-21-94  10:58p
..             <DIR>           06-21-94  10:58p
APR       99              71  11-23-95  10:42a
FEB       99              74  11-23-95  10:41a
JAN       99              72  11-23-95  10:41a
MAR       99              70  11-23-95  10:42a
GREEN     JAZ             18  10-12-94  10:40a
        7 file(s)            305 bytes
                    1,154,048 bytes free

A:\>_
```

WHAT'S HAPPENING? You copied the files with the extension of .99 to the TRIP subdirectory on the DATA disk and confirmed that they are there. In addition, the file called GREEN.JAZ is also in that subdirectory. Next you are going to choose some of the .99 files to delete.

Step 4   Key in the following: A:\>**DEL TRIP*.99** /P **Enter**

```
A:\>DEL TRIP\*.99 /P

A:\TRIP\APR.99,    Delete (Y/N)?_
```

WHAT'S HAPPENING? The /P parameter, when included in the command line, prompts you by asking if you want to delete the file called APR.99 in the subdirectory TRIP on the DATA disk. When you have a Y/N choice, press either the Y or the N key. Pressing **Enter** is not necessary.

Step 5   Key in the following: **Y**

```
A:\>DEL TRIP\*.99 /P

A:\TRIP\APR.99,    Delete (Y/N)?Y
A:\TRIP\FEB.99,    Delete (Y/N)?_
```

WHAT'S HAPPENING? DEL found the next file and asked if you want to delete the file called FEB.99.

Step 6   Key in the following: **N**

```
A:\>DEL TRIP\*.99 /P

A:\TRIP\APR.99,    Delete (Y/N)?Y
A:\TRIP\FEB.99,    Delete (Y/N)?N
A:\TRIP\JAN.99,    Delete (Y/N)?_
```

WHAT'S HAPPENING? DEL found the next file and asked if you want to delete the file called JAN.99.

Step 7   Key in the following: **Y**

```
A:\>DEL TRIP\*.99 /P

A:\TRIP\APR.99,    Delete (Y/N)?Y
A:\TRIP\FEB.99,    Delete (Y/N)?N
A:\TRIP\JAN.99,    Delete (Y/N)?Y
A:\TRIP\MAR.99,    Delete (Y/N)?_
```

WHAT'S HAPPENING? DEL found the next file and asked you if you want to delete the file called MAR.99.

Step 8   Key in the following: **N**

```
A:\>DEL TRIP\*.99 /P

A:\TRIP\APR.99,    Delete (Y/N)?Y
A:\TRIP\FEB.99,    Delete (Y/N)?N
A:\TRIP\JAN.99,    Delete (Y/N)?Y
A:\TRIP\MAR.99,    Delete (Y/N)?N

A:\>_
```

WHAT'S HAPPENING? DOS returned you to the system prompt because there were no more files with the extension .99 on the DATA disk in the subdirectory TRIP. You were able to delete files selectively. You deleted the files JAN.99 and APR.99 but kept the files FEB.99 and MAR.99. You can verify this by using the DIR command.

Step 9   Key in the following: A:\>**DIR TRIP** Enter

```
A:\>DIR TRIP

 Volume in drive A is DATADISK
 Volume Serial Number is 2F26-1901
 Directory of A:\TRIP

 .            <DIR>          06-21-94  10:58p
 ..           <DIR>          06-21-94  10:58p
 FEB      99             74  11-23-95  10:41a
 MAR      99             70  11-23-95  10:42a
 GREEN    JAZ            18  10-12-94  10:40a
         5 file(s)             162 bytes
                       1,155,072 bytes free

A:\>_
```

WHAT'S HAPPENING? You retained the files FEB.99 and MAR.99 but deleted JAN.99 and APR.99. The file GREEN.JAZ was not deleted because it did not have the file extension .99.

7.9 Recovering Deleted Files

It is fairly easy to delete a file accidentally, so there are many utility programs in the market place, such as Norton Utilities or PC Tools, which make deleted file recoveries possible. DOS 5.0 introduced a utility for recovering deleted files. DOS 6.0 expanded on the power of recovering deleted files. This external command is called UNDELETE. If the command looks like UNDELETE from PC Tools, it is for good reason. Microsoft licensed UNDELETE and UNFORMAT from Central Point Software, the manufacturer of PC Tools.

To refresh your memory, when DOS deletes a file, it simply replaces the first character in the file name in the directory table with the special symbol, the σ. It also zeroes out the cluster entries in the FAT (File Allocation Table) freeing those clusters for other files entries. However, the data still remains on the disk. The best time to undelete a file is as soon as possible. Remember, DOS thinks the space is available on the disk and will write to the first available cluster. Once the data is overwritten, your chances of successfully undeleting the file or files diminishes significantly.

DOS 6.0 offers three levels of deletion protection: Delete Sentry, Delete Tracker, and Standard. DOS 5.0 only offers two levels of protection: Standard and Delete Tracker. The Standard Undelete protection is always on after you boot the system. When you invoke the UNDELETE command, DOS scans the disk's directory table for a file name whose first character is σ and whose remaining characters match what you asked for. DOS will then ask you for the first character of the file's name and then finds the starting cluster number for the file and determine how many bytes it occupied. It can then reconstruct the file chain. However, this level of protection assumes that all the file clusters were stored contiguously, or next to each other. If that was not so, then the recovery of the file will be less likely.

Thus, the second method of security is the Delete Tracker. Delete Tracker is not installed when you boot the system. You must install this feature of the program. Whenever Delete Tracker is enabled, every time you delete a file, DOS copies information about the file, including the clusters it occupies, to a hidden file called a deletion tracking file. When you want to undelete a file later, DOS uses the information in this file to find all the clusters of the file. It will not even ask you for the first character of the file name because that is also stored in the file. In DOS 5.0, to use this level of protection, you must install a program called MIRROR /TC. In DOS 6.0, you install this file by using the command line UNDELETE /TC for Drive C. Delete Tracker requires about 13.5 K of memory and some disk space. This level of protection still does not protect your data if it has been overwritten by other data. Still the best time to recover a deleted file is as soon as you discover you have accidentally deleted it.

Introduced in DOS 6.0 is the highest level of protection—Delete Sentry. You must install this level of protection using the command line UNDELETE /SC for

Drive C. This level of protection creates a hidden subdirectory named SENTRY. When you delete a file, UNDELETE moves the file from its current location to the SENTRY directory without changing the record of the file's location in the FAT. When you undelete the file, it is moved back to its original location. The SENTRY directory will occupy about seven percent of your hard disk space. If you exceed this limit, undelete purges the oldest deleted files to make room for the new deleted files. Delete Sentry also requires about 13.5 K of memory in addition to the disk space.

The syntax of the command in DOS 6.0 is as follows:

```
UNDELETE [[drive:][path]filename] [/DT | /DS | /DOS]
UNDELETE [/LIST | /ALL | /PURGE[DRIVE] | /STATUS | /LOAD | /UNLOAD
/UNLOAD | /S[DRIVE] | /T[DRIVE]-entrys ]]
```

```
/LIST             Lists the deleted files available to be recovered.
/ALL              Recovers files without prompting for confirmation.
/DOS              Recovers files listed as deleted by MS-DOS.
/DT               Recovers files protected by Delete Tracker.
/DS               Recovers files protected by Delete Sentry.
/LOAD             Loads Undelete into memory for delete protection.
/UNLOAD           Unloads Undelete from memory.
/PURGE[drive]     Purges all files in the Delete Sentry directory.
/STATUS           Display the protection method in effect for each drive.
/S[drive]         Enables Delete Sentry method of protection.
/T[drive][-entrys] Enables Delete Tracking method of protection.
```

UNDELETE, and UNFORMAT Copyright (C) 1987-1993 Central Point Software.

In the next activity, you will work with the simplest level of UNDELETE, the Standard UNDELETE using the /LIST parameter. The UNDELETE command undeletes files—not directories. If you remove a directory, you will not be able to recover a file that was in the directory.

7.10 Activity: Using UNDELETE

Note 1:   The DATA disk is in Drive A. The A:\> is displayed.

Note 2:   You are going to change the default directory to the directory where the DOS system utility files are located, typically called \DOS. You are going to do this even though your path is set to \DOS. There may be other directories that will be searched before the DOS directory. If this occurred, you could be using the Norton Utilities Undelete program or the PC Tools Undelete program or some other file recovery utility program. It is even possible that, if you are on a network, you may not be able to do this activity at all. If you can do this activity, you want to use the DOS UNDELETE program and no other.

Step 1   Key in the following: A:\>**C:**

Step 2   Key in the following: C:\>**CD DOS** [Enter]

```
A:\>C:

C:\>CD DOS

C:\DOS>_
```

WHAT'S HAPPENING? You are in the DOS subdirectory, which guarantees that you are using the DOS UNDELETE program.

Step 3   Key in the following: C:\DOS>**UNDELETE A:\TRIP /LIST** [Enter]

```
C:\DOS>UNDELETE A:\TRIP /LIST

UNDELETE - A delete protection facility
Copyright (C) 1987-1993 Central Point Software, Inc
All rights reserved.

Directory: A:\TRIP
File Specifications: *.*

    Delete Sentry control file not found.

    Deletion-tracking file not found.

    MS-DOS directory contains    3 deleted files.
    Of those,    3 files may be recovered.

Using the MS-DOS directory method.

        ?PR        99        71 11-23-95 10:42a  ...A
        ?AN        99        72 11-23-95 10:41a  ...A
        ?LUE       JAZ       18 10-12-94 10:40a  ...A

C:\DOS>_
```

WHAT'S HAPPENING? By using the /LIST parameter with UNDELETE for the TRIP subdirectory on the DATA disk, you see what files can be recovered. The information on the screen is telling you that you are using neither the Delete Sentry method nor the Deletion Tracking method. However, since you just deleted the files in the TRIP directory, each may be recovered. You are going to undelete the file called ?LUE.JAZ. In this case, the missing letter is B.

Step 4   Key in the following:C:\DOS>**UNDELETE A:\TRIP\BLUE.JAZ** [Enter]

```
UNDELETE - A delete protection facility
Copyright (C) 1987-1993 Central Point Software, Inc.
All rights reserved.
```

```
Directory: A:\TRIP
File Specifications: BLUE.JAZ

    Delete Sentry control file not found.

    Deletion-tracking file not found.

    MS-DOS directory contains     1 deleted files.
    Of those,     1 files may be recovered.

Using the MS-DOS directory method.

    ?LUE      JAZ       18 10-12-94 10:40a  ...A  Undelete (Y/N)?_
```

WHAT'S HAPPENING? Even though you gave the entire file name, UNDELETE looked for ?LUE.JAZ. It found the specific file of interest. It is now asking you if you want to undelete the file.

Step 5   Press **Y**

```
Using the MS-DOS directory method.

    ?LUE      JAZ       18 10-12-94 10:40a  ...A  Undelete (Y/N)?Y
    Please type the first character for ?LUE    .JAZ:_
```

WHAT'S HAPPENING? UNDELETE is now asking you for the first character of the file name.

Step 6   Press **B**

```
Using the MS-DOS directory method.

    ?LUE      JAZ       18 10-12-94 10:40a  ...A  Undelete (Y/N)?Y
    Please type the first character for ?LUE    .JAZ: B

File successfully undeleted.


C:\DOS>_
```

WHAT'S HAPPENING? The message tells you that the file was successfully undeleted. You can prove that by using the DIR command.

Step 7   Key in the following: C:\DOS>**DIR A:\TRIP** [Enter]

```
    C:\DOS>DIR A:\TRIP
```

```
Volume in drive A is DATADISK
Volume Serial Number is 2F26-1901
Directory of A:\TRIP

.               <DIR>           06-21-94  10:58p
..              <DIR>           06-21-94  10:58p
FEB      99                 74 11-23-95  10:41a
MAR      99                 70 11-23-95  10:42a
BLUE     JAZ                18 10-12-94  10:40a
GREEN    JAZ                18 10-12-94  10:40a
         6 file(s)              180 bytes
                        1,154,560 bytes free

C:\DOS>_
```

WHAT'S HAPPENING? The file BLUE.JAZ has indeed been recovered. You can also recover all the files in a directory by using the /ALL parameter with UNDE-LETE. When you use this parameter, you will not be prompted for the first character for each file name.

Step 8   Key in the following: C:\DOS>**UNDELETE A:\TRIP /ALL**

```
All rights reserved.

Directory: A:\TRIP
File Specifications: *.*

    Delete Sentry control file not found.

    Deletion-tracking file not found.

    MS-DOS directory contains    2 deleted files.
    Of those,    2 files may be recovered.

Using the MS-DOS directory method.

     ?PR      99          71 11-23-95 10:42a  ...A

File successfully undeleted.

     ?AN      99          72 11-23-95 10:41a  ...A

File successfully undeleted.



C:\DOS>_
```

WHAT'S HAPPENING? As you can see, UNDELETE recovered all the files you deleted in the TRIP directory, but you did not give UNDELETE the first character in the file name. What character did UNDELETE use?

Step 9   Key in the following: C:\DOS>**DIR A:\TRIP*.99** **Enter**

```
C:\DOS>DIR A:\TRIP\*.99

 Volume in drive A is DATADISK
 Volume Serial Number is 2F26-1901
 Directory of A:\TRIP

#PR      99            71 11-23-95  10:42a
FEB      99            74 11-23-95  10:41a
#AN      99            72 11-23-95  10:41a
MAR      99            70 11-23-95  10:42a
         4 file(s)           287 bytes
                       1,153,536 bytes free

C:\DOS>_
```

WHAT'S HAPPENING? Since UNDELETE did not know what character to place in the first position, it used the pound sign— #. If you happened to have a file named that already, UNDELETE would keep trying other characters until it found a unique character. Regardless of UNDELETE's character choice, the file contents remain the same. Recovering a file means recovering the file's contents.

Step 10   Key in the following: C:\DOS>**TYPE A:\TRIP\#AN.99** **Enter**

Step 11   Key in the following: C:\DOS>**TYPE A:\JAN.99** **Enter**

```
C:\DOS>TYPE A:\TRIP\#AN.99
This is my January file.
It is my first dummy file.
This is file 1.

C:\DOS>TYPE A:\JAN.99
This is my January file.
It is my first dummy file.
This is file 1.

C:\DOS>_
```

WHAT'S HAPPENING? As you can see, the file contents are unchanged. By using UNDELETE, you may recover accidentally deleted files. Remember that any time you delete a file, recovery of data is always chancy. Rather than relying on UNDELETE, the best method for ensuring the preservation of your data is to back up your files.

Step 12   Key in the following: C:DOS\>**CD** \ [Enter]

Step 13   Key in the following: C:\>**A:** [Enter]

```
C:\DOS>CD \

C:\>A:

A:\>_
```

WHAT'S HAPPENING? You returned to the root directory of the hard disk and then made the DATA disk the default drive.

7.11 Changing the Names of Files

Often, when you are working with files, you find that you want to change a file name. For example, you may wish to change the name of a file to indicate an older version. You might also think of a more descriptive file name. As the contents of a file change, the old name may no longer reflect the contents. When you make a typographical error, you want to be able to correct it. In the last activity, a file was named #AN.99. Changing the name to JAN.99 would make more sense.

DOS supplies a way to change existing file names using the RENAME command, an internal command. RENAME does exactly what it says; it changes the name of a file. The contents of the file do not change, only the name of the file.

Using RENAME is different from copying a file. When copying a file, you retain the original and make a copy; you start with one file and end with two. With the RENAME command you start with one file under one name and end up with the same file under a new name. The syntax for this command is:

    RENAME [*drive:*][*path*] *filename1 filename2*

or

    REN [*drive:*][*path*]*filename1 filename2*

RENAME does not let you specify a new drive or path for filename2. Remember, you are not making a copy of a file but using the same "file folder." It is like pasting a new label on an existing file folder. That file folder does not get moved in the process. You are only dealing with one file when using REN. In the syntax diagram, *filename1* and *filename2* refer to the same file. *filename1* will be changed to *filename2*. You are only changing the file name, not creating another copy of it with a new name.

The RENAME command has two forms, RENAME or REN, with exactly the same syntax. Most computer users choose REN, simply because it has fewer keystrokes. The syntax is the command REN, the first parameter or the old file name, and the second parameter or the new file name.

7.12 Activity: Using the REN Command

Note: The DATA disk is in Drive A. The A:\> is displayed.

Step 1   Key in the following: A:\>**COPY C:\DOS6BK\MEDIA\TV** [Enter]

```
A:\>COPY C:\DOS6BK\MEDIA\TV
C:\DOS6BK\MEDIA\TV\COMEDY.TV
C:\DOS6BK\MEDIA\TV\DRAMA.TV
        2 file(s) copied

A:\>_
```

WHAT'S HAPPENING? You copied two files from the hard disk subdirectory \DOS6BK\MEDIA\TV to the root directory of the DATA disk. Notice that after the TV you did not have to specify a file name. When you key in a command like that, *.* is assumed. The destination is also assumed. It is the default drive and directory—in this case the root directory of the DATA disk.

Step 2   Key in the following: A:\>**TYPE COMEDY.TV** [Enter]

```
A:\>TYPE COMEDY.TV

COMEDY TELEVISION SERIES

Cheers
MASH
SOAP
Home Improvement
Leave it to Beaver
I Love Lucy
Roseanne
TAXI
The Mary Tyler Moore Show
Wings
The Dick Van Dyke Show


A:\>_
```

WHAT'S HAPPENING? You are displaying the contents of the file called COMEDY.TV located in the root directory on the DATA disk. You opened the file folder called COMEDY.TV and looked inside.

Step 3   Key in the following: A:\>**REN COMEDY.TV COMEDY.TV** [Enter]

```
A:\>REN COMEDY.TV COMEDY.TV
Duplicate file name or file not found

A:\>_
```

WHAT'S HAPPENING? The message tells you that two files on the same disk and same directory cannot have the same name (Duplicate file name), or that DOS could not find a file called COMEDY.TV (file not found). In this example, the broken rule is Duplicate file name. You already have a file on the DATA disk called COMEDY.TV.

Step 4 Key in the following: A:\>**REN COMEDY.TV FUNNY.TV** [Enter]

```
A:\>REN COMEDY.TV FUNNY.TV

A:\>_
```

WHAT'S HAPPENING? Using the command REN changed the name of the file called COMEDY.TV to FUNNY.TV. Since the default is the DATA disk and the default directory is the root, DOS will look only on the root directory of the DATA disk for the file called COMEDY.TV. Once you pressed [Enter], you got back only the system prompt. Did anything happen?

Step 5 Key in the following: A:\>**DIR COMEDY.TV** [Enter]

```
A:\>DIR COMEDY.TV

 Volume in drive A is DATADISK
 Volume Serial Number is 2F26-1901
 Directory of A:\

File not found

A:\>_
```

WHAT'S HAPPENING? Once you have renamed a file, it no longer exists under its old file name.

Step 6 Key in the following: A:\>**DIR FUNNY.TV** [Enter]

```
A:\>DIR FUNNY.TV

 Volume in drive A is DATADISK
 Volume Serial Number is 2F26-1901
 Directory of A:\
```

```
FUNNY     TV           180 11-23-94  10:19a
          1 file(s)              180 bytes
                        1,152,512 bytes free


A:\>_
```

WHAT'S HAPPENING? The above display demonstrates that the file called FUNNY.TV is on the DATA disk in the root directory. You know that the file named COMEDY.TV is no longer on the DATA disk. Are the contents of the file FUNNY.TV the same as the contents of the file that was named COMEDY.TV?

Step 7   Key in the following: A:\>**TYPE FUNNY.TV** Enter

```
A:\>TYPE FUNNY.TV

COMEDY TELEVISION SERIES

Cheers
MASH
SOAP
Home Improvement
Leave it to Beaver
I Love Lucy
Roseanne
TAXI
The Mary Tyler Moore Show
Wings
The Dick Van Dyke Show



A:\>_
```

WHAT'S HAPPENING? As you can see, you changed the file name from COMEDY.TV to FUNNY.TV, but the contents of the file did not change. REN works the same way with a file in a subdirectory. You just have to follow the syntax:

    REN [drive:][path]oldfile.ext newfile.ext

Step 8   Key in the following: A:\>**DIR TRIP\GREEN.JAZ** Enter

```
A:\>DIR TRIP\GREEN.JAZ

  Volume in drive A is DATADISK
  Volume Serial Number is 2F26-1901
  Directory of A:\TRIP
```

```
    GREEN     JAZ          18 10-12-94  10:40a
          1 file(s)             18 bytes
                        1,152,512 bytes free

    A:\>_
```

WHAT'S HAPPENING? The file called GREEN.JAZ is in the subdirectory called TRIP on the DATA disk. Using REN is different from using COPY. The COPY syntax requires that you place the path name in front of the source file and destination file. You are dealing with two files; thus, each file could be in a separate location. This situation is not true with REN. You are dealing with only one file and are changing only one file name. You are not moving the file; thus, the path name is only placed in front of the source file.

Step 9   Key in the following:

    A:\>**REN TRIP\GREEN.JAZ TRIP\RED.JAZ** [Enter]

```
    A:\>REN TRIP\GREEN.JAZ TRIP\RED.JAZ
    Invalid filename or file not found

    A:\>_
```

WHAT'S HAPPENING? The message is really not very descriptive. Invalid filename really refers to the TRIP\RED.JAZ. TRIP\RED.JAZ, the portion that is incorrect. It is incorrect because you do not place a drive or subdirectory preceding the new filename.

Step 10   Key in the following: A:\>**REN TRIP\GREEN.JAZ RED.JAZ** [Enter]

```
    A:\>REN TRIP\GREEN.JAZ RED.JAZ

    A:\>_
```

WHAT'S HAPPENING? You received no error message, indicating that this command was executed. You will confirm that the file name was changed from GREEN.JAZ to RED.JAZ using the DIR command.

Step 11   Key in the following: A:\>**DIR TRIP*.JAZ** [Enter]

```
    A:\>DIR TRIP\*.JAZ

      Volume in drive A is DATADISK
      Volume Serial Number is 2F26-1901
      Directory of A:\TRIP
```

```
   BLUE      JAZ           18 10-12-94  10:40a
   RED       JAZ           18 10-12-94  10:40a
             2 file(s)              36 bytes
                            1,152,512 bytes free


   A:\>_
```

WHAT'S HAPPENING? There are two files with a .JAZ extension in the subdirectory TRIP on the DATA disk. One is called BLUE.JAZ and the other that you renamed is now called RED.JAZ instead of GREEN.JAZ.

7.13 Using RENAME with Wildcards

When you wish to change the names of a group of files, you can use the REN or RENAME command with the wildcards, ? and *, allowing you to change many file names with a one-line command. The wildcards or global file specifications are so "global" that, prior to renaming files, it is wise to do a directory display with the wildcards you want to use so that you can see what files are going to be renamed. You do not want to rename a file accidentally. Once a file is renamed, you cannot find the file under its old name, *ever*. This rule has caused havoc for users because it seems as if the file is lost. The file is still on the disk, but you cannot find it unless you know the new name.

7.14 Activity: Using RENAME with Wildcards

Note 1:   The DATA disk is in Drive A. The A:\> is displayed.

Note 2:   This activity assumes you have files on the DATA disk with the file extension .NEW. If you do not, you may copy them from \DOS6BK to the DATA disk.

Step 1   Key in the following: A:\>**DIR ???.NEW** [Enter]

```
A:\>DIR ???.NEW

   Volume in drive A is DATADISK
   Volume Serial Number is 2F26-1901
   Directory of A:\

   JAN       NEW           72 11-23-95  10:41a
   FEB       NEW           74 11-23-95  10:41a
   MAR       NEW           70 11-23-95  10:42a
   APR       NEW           71 11-23-95  10:42a
             4 file(s)             287 bytes
                            1,152,512 bytes free


   A:\>_
```

WHAT'S HAPPENING? You have four files with file names of three characters or fewer (???) and with the extension .NEW. You used the ??? instead of the *. When you use ???.NEW, the ??? selected only files that had a file name of three characters or less . Had you used the * instead of ???, you would have selected all file names that had an extension of .NEW. That would have included such files as BONJOUR.NEW or any other file with a file name longer than three characters. Your objective is to retain these four files, keep their file names, and change the file extension from .NEW to .BUD. You could rename these files one at a time, REN JAN.NEW JAN.BUD, then REN FEB.NEW FEB.BUD, then REN MAR.NEW MAR.BUD and REN APR.NEW APR.BUD. However, this repetition becomes very tiresome. Using wildcards will allow you to rename these four files at one time.

Step 2   Key in the following: A:\>**REN ???.NEW *.BUD** **[Enter]**

```
A:\>REN ???.NEW *.BUD

A:\>_
```

WHAT'S HAPPENING? All that is displayed is the system prompt. Was the work done? Are the files renamed? To verify that you did rename these files, use the DIR command.

Step 3   Key in the following: A:\>**DIR ???.NEW** **[Enter]**

Step 4   Key in the following: A:\>**DIR *.BUD**

```
A:\>DIR ???.NEW

 Volume in drive A is DATADISK
 Volume Serial Number is 2F26-1901
 Directory of A:\

File not found

A:\>DIR *.BUD

 Volume in drive A is DATADISK
 Volume Serial Number is 2F26-1901
 Directory of A:\

JAN      BUD          72 11-23-95   10:41a
FEB      BUD          74 11-23-95   10:41a
MAR      BUD          70 11-23-95   10:42a
APR      BUD          71 11-23-95   10:42a
        4 file(s)            287 bytes
                       1,152,512 bytes free

A:\>_
```

WHAT'S HAPPENING? Files with file names of three characters or fewer with the extension .NEW no longer exist on the DATA disk. With the REN command and the use of the wildcards, you renamed four files with one command. You can also use wildcards with subdirectories.

Step 5   Key in the following: A:\>**COPY *.BUD TRIP** Enter

```
A:\>COPY *.BUD TRIP
JAN.BUD
FEB.BUD
MAR.BUD
APR.BUD
        4 file(s) copied

A:\>_
```

WHAT'S HAPPENING? You copied files with the .BUD extension from the root directory of the DATA disk to a subdirectory called TRIP on the DATA disk.

Step 6   Key in the following: A:\>**REN TRIP*.BUD *.PEN** Enter

Step 7   Key in the following: A:\>**DIR TRIP*.BUD** Enter

Step 8   Key in the following: A:\>**DIR TRIP*.PEN** Enter

```
A:\>REN TRIP\*.BUD *.PEN

A:\>DIR TRIP\*.BUD

 Volume in drive A is DATADISK
 Volume Serial Number is 2F26-1901
 Directory of A:\TRIP

File not found

A:\>DIR TRIP\*.PEN

 Volume in drive A is DATADISK
 Volume Serial Number is 2F26-1901
 Directory of A:\TRIP
```

```
    JAN        PEN              72 11-23-95   10:41a
    FEB        PEN              74 11-23-95   10:41a
    MAR        PEN              70 11-23-95   10:42a
    APR        PEN              71 11-23-95   10:42a
               4 file(s)              287 bytes
                            1,150,464 bytes free

    A:\>_
```

WHAT'S HAPPENING? You successfully renamed all the files with the .BUD extension in the subdirectory TRIP on the DATA disk to a new set of files with the same file name but with the file extension of .PEN.

7.15 Using RENAME on Different Drives and Directories

Since REN is an internal command, you can use it at any time, for any file, in any drive, and in any directory. If you wish to rename a file on a different drive, you must specify on which drive the old file is located. If you want the file renamed in a different directory, you must specify in which directory the file is located. In the syntax of REN *oldfile.ext newfile.ext*, DOS looks only for *oldfile.ext* on the designated drive and directory. It renames the file and leaves the file where it found it. If you do not preface *oldfile.ext* with a drive letter, DOS looks only on the default drive. When you key in the command REN B:OLDFILE.EXT NEWFILE.EXT, DOS will look only on the disk in Drive B for the file called OLDFILE.EXT. If a directory is involved, you must also include the name, so the command would read:

        REN C:\JUNK\OLDFILE.EXT NEWFILE.EXT.

In addition, there is a substantial difference between the COPY command and the REN command. With the COPY command, you can copy a file from one disk to another disk or one directory to another directory, ending up with two identical files in different locations. You cannot do this with the REN command because it changes the names of files in only one directory or disk at a time. Remember, with REN you are changing the name of an existing file in a specific location. REN finds a file on the designated disk or directory and renames it. REN cannot move a file from one location to another.

7.16 Activity: Using RENAME on Different Drives

Note: The DATA disk is in Drive A. The A:\> is displayed.

Step 1   Key in the following: A:\>**C:** **Enter**

Step 2   Key in the following: C:\>**CD \DOS6BK** **Enter**

```
A:\>C:

C:\>CD \DOS6BK

C:\DOS6BK>_
```

WHAT'S HAPPENING? You have changed the default drive to C: and have made \DOS6BK the default directory.

Step 3   Key in the following: C:\DOS6BK>**DIR APRIL.TXT** [Enter]

Step 4   Key in the following: C:\DOS6BK>**DIR A:\APRIL.TXT** [Enter]

Note: If you do not have APRIL.TXT on your DATA disk, copy it there now.

```
C:\DOS6BK>DIR APRIL.TXT

 Volume in drive C has no label
 Volume Serial Number is 1CD1-5E42
 Directory of C:\DOS6BK

APRIL    TXT            71 11-23-95  10:42a
        1 file(s)              71 bytes
                     82,313,216 bytes free

C:\DOS6BK>DIR A:\APRIL.TXT

 Volume in drive A is DATADISK
 Volume Serial Number is 2F26-1901
 Directory of A:\

APRIL    TXT            71 11-23-95  10:42a
        1 file(s)              71 bytes
                      1,150,464 bytes free

C:\DOS6BK>_
```

WHAT'S HAPPENING? The directory display tells you that the file called APRIL.TXT does exist on both the DATA disk and in the \DOS6BK subdirectory.

Step 5   Key in the following: C:\DOS6BK>**TYPE A:\APRIL.TXT** [Enter]

```
C:\DOS6BK>TYPE A:\APRIL.TXT
This is my April file.
It is my fourth dummy file.
This is file 4.

C:\DOS6BK>_
```

WHAT'S HAPPENING? You used the TYPE command to see the contents of the file called APRIL.TXT located on the DATA disk.

Step 6   Key in the following:

C:\DOS6BK>**REN A:\APRIL.TXT A:\APR.TST** [Enter]

```
C:\DOS6BK>REN A:\APRIL.TXT A:\APR.TST
Invalid parameter

C:\DOS6BK>_
```

WHAT'S HAPPENING? The syntax of this command is:

        REN [*drive:*] [*path*]*oldfile.ext newfile.ext*

Since DOS knows you cannot change a file name on any other disk except where the original file is located, it will not allow you to put a drive designator before the new file name.

Step 7   Key in the following:

C:\DOS6BK>**REN A:\APRIL.TXT APR.TST** [Enter]

```
C:\DOS6BK>REN A:\APRIL.TXT APR.TST

C:\DOS6BK
```

WHAT'S HAPPENING? You see no messages because the syntax is correct. The file called APRIL.TXT is in the root directory of the DATA disk. You requested that REN change the name of this file from APRIL.TXT to a new file name APR.TST.

Step 8   Key in the following: C:\DOS6BK>**DIR APRIL.TXT** [Enter]

Step 9   Key in the following: C:\DOS6BK>**DIR A:\APRIL.TXT** [Enter]

```
C:\DOS6BK>DIR APRIL.TXT

  Volume in drive C has no label
  Volume Serial Number is 1CD1-5E42

  Directory of C:\DOS6BK
```

```
APRIL      TXT                71 11-23-95  10:42a
        1 file(s)                  71 bytes
                        66,256,896 bytes free

C:\DOS6BK>DIR A:\APRIL.TXT

 Volume in drive A is DATA DISK
 Volume Serial Number is 2F26-1901
 Directory of A:\

File not found

C:\DOS6BK>_
```

WHAT'S HAPPENING? You did not rename the file APRIL.TXT on the hard disk in the \DOS6BK directory, only the one on the DATA disk. You got the message File not found on the DATA disk because the file no longer exists under the file name A:\APRIL.TXT.

Step 10 Key in the following: C:\DOS6BK>**DIR A:\APR.TST** [Enter]

```
C:\DOS6BK>DIR A:\APR.TST

 Volume in drive A is DATADISK
 Volume Serial Number is 2F26-1901
 Directory of A:\

APR        TST                71 11-23-95  10:42a
        1 file(s)                  71 bytes
                         1,150,464 bytes free

C:\DOS6BK>_
```

WHAT'S HAPPENING? You successfully renamed the file in the root directory of the DATA disk from APRIL.TXT to APR.TST. Does the file APR.TST have the same contents as APRIL.TXT? It should because renaming changes only the file name, not the contents. To verify this, you can use the TYPE command.

Step 11 Key in the following: C:\DOS6BK>**TYPE A:\APR.TST** [Enter]

```
C:\DOS6BK>TYPE A:\APR.TST
This is my April file.
It is my fourth dummy file.
This is file 4.

C:\DOS6BK>_
```

WHAT'S HAPPENING? If you check the screen display following Step 5, you will see that the file contents are identical. REN works the same way with subdirectories on other drives. In Activity 7.14, you copied the files with the .BUD extension to the subdirectory TRIP on the DATA disk; you then renamed them with the same file name but with the .PEN file extension.

Step 12   Key in the following: C:\DOS6BK>**DIR A:\TRIP*.PEN** [Enter]

```
C:\DOS6BK>DIR A:\TRIP\*.PEN

 Volume in drive A is DATADISK
 Volume Serial Number is 2F26-1901
 Directory of A:\TRIP

JAN       PEN           72 11-23-95   10:41a
FEB       PEN           74 11-23-95   10:41a
MAR       PEN           70 11-23-95   10:42a
APR       PEN           71 11-23-95   10:42a
        4 file(s)           287 bytes
                      1,150,464 bytes free

C:\DOS6BK>_
```

WHAT'S HAPPENING? The files are there in the subdirectory TRIP on the DATA disk.

Step 13   Key in the following: C:\DOS6BK>**REN A:\TRIP*.PEN *.INK** [Enter]

```
C:\DOS6BK>REN A:\TRIP\*.PEN *.INK

C:\DOS6BK>_
```

WHAT'S HAPPENING? Once again, all that appears is the system prompt. Notice how you placed the drive and path in front of only the file names that you wanted to change (the old file names). These files can only be renamed on the DATA disk in the subdirectory TRIP. The REN command does not move files; it only changes file names.

Step 14   Key in the following: C:\DOS6BK>**DIR A:\TRIP*.PEN** [Enter]

Step 15   Key in the following: C:\DOS6BK>**DIR A:\TRIP*.INK** [Enter]

```
C:\DOS6BK>DIR A:\TRIP\*.PEN

 Volume in drive A is DATADISK
 Volume Serial Number is 2F26-1901
 Directory of A:\TRIP

File not found
```

```
C:\DOS6BK>DIR A:\TRIP\*.INK

 Volume in drive A is DATADISK
 Volume Serial Number is 2F26-1901
 Directory of A:\TRIP

 JAN     INK          72 11-23-95  10:41a
 FEB     INK          74 11-23-95  10:41a
 MAR     INK          70 11-23-95  10:42a
 APR     INK          71 11-23-95  10:42a
         4 file(s)            287 bytes
                      1,150,464 bytes free

C:\DOS6BK>_
```

WHAT'S HAPPENING? You successfully renamed all the .PEN files in the subdirectory TRIP on the DATA disk. These files no longer exist with the .PEN file extension.

Step 16   Key in the following: C:\DOS6BK>**CD** \ Enter

Step 17   Key in the following: C:\>**A:** Enter

```
C:\DOS6BK>CD \

C:\>A:

A:\>_
```

WHAT'S HAPPENING? You have returned to the root directory of the hard disk and also changed the default drive to where the DATA disk is located.

7.17 Moving Files and Renaming Directories

You learned in Chapter 5 that you could use the MOVE command to rename a directory. The REN command renames files; it does not move them from one location to another. If you wanted to move files prior to DOS 6.0 you had to COPY the files from the old location to the new location and then delete the files from the old location.

The MOVE command was introduced in DOS 6.0. MOVE, as you learned in Chapter 5, allows you to rename a directory. It also lets you move files. If you move files individually, you can change the name of the moved file. If you move a group of files, you cannot change their file names. Prior to DOS 6.2, if you moved a file and you already had a file with that name, the MOVE command would not warn you. It would simply overwrite the file. DOS 6.22 includes a prompt that will warn you that you are about to overwrite a file. However, if you desire, you can turn off the warning. The syntax to the command is:

To move one or more files:

```
MOVE [/Y | /-Y] [drive:][path]filename1[,...] destination
```

To rename a directory:

```
MOVE [/Y | /-Y] [drive:][path]dirname1 dirname2
```

[drive:][path]filename1	Specifies the location and name of the file or files you want to move.
destination	Specifies the new location of the file. Destination can consist of a drive letter and colon, a directory name, or a combination. If you are moving only one file, you can also include a filename if you want to rename the file when you move it.
[drive:][path]dirname1	Specifies the directory you want to rename.
dirname2	Specifies the new name of the directory.
/Y	Suppresses prompting to confirm creation of a directory or overwriting of the destination.
/-Y	Causes prompting to confirm creation of a directory or overwriting of the destination.

The MOVE command will not only move files from one directory to another but will also allow you to move files from one drive to another. This feature is especially useful in maintaining your hard disk.

7.18 Activity: Moving Files and Renaming Directories

Note: The DATA disk is in Drive A. The A:\> is displayed.

Step 1   Key in the following: A:\>**MD FILES** **Enter**

Step 2   Key in the following: A:\>**COPY *.99 FILES*.FIL** **Enter**

Step 3   Key in the following: A:\>**MD FILES\ROOM** **Enter**

Step 4   Key in the following: A:\>**COPY GOODBYE.NEW FILES** **Enter**

```
A:\>MD FILES

A:\>COPY *.99  FILES\*.FIL
APR.99
FEB.99
JAN.99
MAR.99
        4 file(s) copied

A:\>MD FILES\ROOM

A:\>COPY GOODBYE.NEW FILES
        1 file(s) copied

A:\>_
```

WHAT'S HAPPENING? You have created the FILES directory with a directory beneath it called ROOM. You copied some files from the root directory of the DATA disk into the FILES directory.

Step 5   Key in the following: A:\>**DIR FILES** Enter

```
A:\>DIR FILES

 Volume in drive A is DATADISK
 Volume Serial Number is 2F26-1901
 Directory of A:\FILES

.              <DIR>         06-21-94  11:49p
..             <DIR>         06-21-94  11:49p
APR      FIL        71 11-23-95  10:42a
FEB      FIL        74 11-23-95  10:41a
JAN      FIL        72 11-23-95  10:41a
MAR      FIL        70 11-23-95  10:42a
ROOM           <DIR>         06-21-94  11:50p
GOODBYE  NEW        32 11-23-94   7:07a
        8 file(s)            319 bytes
                       1,146,880 bytes free

A:\>_
```

WHAT'S HAPPENING? You have a subdirectory called ROOM under the FILES directory on the DATA disk. You decide that you no longer care for the name ROOM and wish to call the directory PLACE.

Step 6   Key in the following:

A:\>**MOVE FILES\ROOM FILES\PLACE** Enter

```
A:\>MOVE FILES\ROOM FILES\PLACE
a:\files\room => a:\files\place [ok]

A:\>_
```

WHAT'S HAPPENING? You have renamed a subdirectory from FILES\ROOM to FILES\PLACE.

Step 7   Key in the following: A:\>**DIR FILES** Enter

```
A:\>DIR FILES

 Volume in drive A is DATADISK
 Volume Serial Number is 2F26-1901
 Directory of A:\FILES

 .               <DIR>         06-21-94   11:49p
 ..              <DIR>         06-21-94   11:49p
 APR      FIL          71     11-23-95   10:42a
 FEB      FIL          74     11-23-95   10:41a
 JAN      FIL          72     11-23-95   10:41a
 MAR      FIL          70     11-23-95   10:42a
 PLACE           <DIR>         06-21-94   11:50p
 GOODBYE  NEW          32     11-23-94    7:07a
         8 file(s)            319 bytes
                       1,146,880 bytes free

A:\>_
```

WHAT'S HAPPENING? The directory name has changed. Now you want to move a file. You should use MOVE to move files from one location to another. If you MOVE a file in the same drive and the same directory, it is equivalent to copying the contents of the file. In the next steps you will see the results of such a task.

Step 8   Key in the following: A:\>**TYPE FILES\APR.FIL** Enter

Step 9   Key in the following: A:\>**TYPE FILES\JAN.FIL** Enter

```
A:\>TYPE FILES\APR.FIL
This is my April file.
It is my fourth dummy file.
This is file 4.

A:\>TYPE FILES\JAN.FIL
This is my January file.
It is my first dummy file.
This is file 1.

A:\>_
```

WHAT'S HAPPENING? You can see that the contents are different as well as the file names.

Step 10   Key in the following:

A:\>**MOVE FILES\APR.FIL FILES\JAN.FIL** [Enter]

```
A:\>MOVE FILES\APR.FIL FILES\JAN.FIL
Overwrite a:\files\jan.fil (Yes/No/All)?_
```

WHAT'S HAPPENING? Because this is DOS 6.22, the MOVE command warns you that it is about to overwrite the contents of JAN.FIL with the contents of APR.FIL. If this was an earlier version of DOS, it would simply overwrite the file.

Step 11   Press **Y** [Enter]

```
A:\>MOVE FILES\APR.FIL FILES\JAN.FIL
Overwrite a:\files\jan.fil (Yes/No/All)?y
a:\files\apr.fil => a:\files\jan.fil [ok]

A:\>_
```

WHAT'S HAPPENING? Because you entered Y for yes, the file was overwritten.

Step 12   Key in the following: A:\>**TYPE FILES\APR.FIL** [Enter]

Step 13   Key in the following: A:\>**TYPE FILES\JAN.FIL** [Enter]

```
A:\>TYPE FILES\APR.FIL
File not found - FILES\APR.FIL

A:\>TYPE FILES\JAN.FIL
This is my April file.
It is my fourth dummy file.
This is file 4.

A:\>_
```

WHAT'S HAPPENING? The file APR.FIL no longer exists, but JAN.FIL now holds the contents of the old APR.FIL. The old contents of JAN.FIL are gone. If this sounds confusing, it is. The lesson here is do not use MOVE when you mean REN. The following steps will show you how MOVE is extremely useful and how it should be used.

Step 14   Key in the following:

A:\>**MOVE FILES\FEB.FIL FILES\PLACE\FEB.NEW** [Enter]

```
A:\>MOVE FILES\FEB.FIL FILES\PLACE\FEB.NEW
a:\files\feb.fil => a:\files\place\feb.new [ok]

A:\>_
```

WHAT'S HAPPENING? You have, in essence, copied the file called `FEB.FIL` located in the `FILES` directory to the `FILES\PLACE` directory, gave it a new name `FEB.NEW`, and deleted `FEB.FIL` from the `FILES` directory. All this occurred using one command, MOVE, not two—COPY and DEL.

Step 15   Key in the following: `A:\>`**DIR FILES** `Enter`

Step 16   Key in the following: `A:\>`**DIR FILES\PLACE** `Enter`

```
Volume Serial Number is 2F26-1901
 Directory of A:\FILES


.               <DIR>        06-21-94   11:49p
..              <DIR>        06-21-94   11:49p
JAN      FIL          71 11-23-95   10:42a
MAR      FIL          70 11-23-95   10:42a
PLACE           <DIR>        06-21-94   11:50p
GOODBYE  NEW          32 11-23-94    7:07a
        6 file(s)            173 bytes
                   1,147,392 bytes free


A:\>DIR FILES\PLACE

 Volume in drive A is DATADISK
 Volume Serial Number is 2F26-1901
 Directory of A:\FILES\PLACE


.               <DIR>        06-21-94   11:50p
..              <DIR>        06-21-94   11:50p
FEB      NEW          74 11-23-95   10:41a
        3 file(s)             74 bytes
                   1,147,392 bytes free

A:\>_
```

WHAT'S HAPPENING? The file called `FEB.FIL` is no longer in the `FILES` directory. It is, however, in the `FILES\PLACE` directory with the name of `FEB.NEW`. MOVE also works well with wildcards. However, when you use wildcards, you cannot change file names.

Step 17   Key in the following:

      `A:>`**MOVE FILES*.FIL FILES\PLACE*.TXT** `Enter`

```
A:\>MOVE FILES\*.FIL FILES\PLACE\*.TXT
Make directory "a:\files\place\*.txt"? [yn]_
```

WHAT'S HAPPENING? The MOVE command thinks that you want to create a directory.

Step 18   Press **Y** **Enter**

```
A:\>MOVE FILES\*.FIL FILES\PLACE\*.TXT
Make directory "a:\files\place\*.txt"? [yn] y
Cannot move multiple files to a single file

A:\>_
```

WHAT'S HAPPENING? As the message states, MOVE cannot combine the contents of files (concatenate files) and therefore cannot place these files into one file called *.TXT.

Step 19   Key in the following: A:\>**MOVE FILES*.FIL FILES\PLACE** **Enter**

```
A:\>MOVE FILES\*.FIL FILES\PLACE
a:\files\jan.fil => a:\files\place\jan.fil [ok]
a:\files\mar.fil => a:\files\place\mar.fil [ok]

A:\>_
```

WHAT'S HAPPENING? Now that you have issued the command correctly, the files with the .FIL extension are no longer in the FILES directory but in the PLACE directory.

Step 20   Key in the following: A:\>**DIR FILES** **Enter**

Step 21   Key in the following: A:\>**DIR FILES\PLACE*.FIL** **Enter**

```
A:\>DIR FILES

 Volume in drive A is DATADISK
 Volume Serial Number is 2F26-1901
 Directory of A:\FILES

.              <DIR>        06-21-94   11:49p
..             <DIR>        06-21-94   11:49p
PLACE          <DIR>        06-21-94   11:50p
GOODBYE  NEW              32 11-23-94    7:07a
        4 file(s)              32 bytes
                       1,147,392 bytes free
```

```
A:\>DIR FILES\PLACE\*.FIL

 Volume in drive A is DATADISK
 Volume Serial Number is 2F26-1901
 Directory of A:\FILES\PLACE

JAN      FIL           71 11-23-95  10:42a
MAR      FIL           70 11-23-95  10:42a
         2 file(s)             141 bytes
                        1,147,392 bytes free

A:\>_
```

WHAT'S HAPPENING? The files with the .FIL extension were successfully moved from one location to another. You can move files from one drive to another and from one directory to another.

Step 22   Key in the following:

      A:\>**MOVE FILES\PLACE*.FIL CLASS** Enter

```
A:\>MOVE FILES\PLACE\*.FIL CLASS
a:\files\place\jan.fil => a:\class\jan.fil [ok]
a:\files\place\mar.fil => a:\class\mar.fil [ok]

A:\>_
```

WHAT'S HAPPENING? The files with the .FIL extension are no longer located in the FILES\PLACE directory but were moved to the CLASS directory, keeping the same file names.

Step 23   Key in the following: A:\>**DIR FILES\PLACE*.FIL** Enter

Step 24   Key in the following: A:\>**DIR CLASS*.FIL** Enter

```
A:\>DIR FILES\PLACE\*.FIL

 Volume in drive A is DATADISK
 Volume Serial Number is 2F26-1901
 Directory of A:\FILES\PLACE

File not found

A:\>DIR CLASS\*.FIL

 Volume in drive A is DATADISK
 Volume Serial Number is 2F26-1901
 Directory of A:\CLASS
```

```
JAN        FIL              71 11-23-95  10:42a
MAR        FIL              70 11-23-95  10:42a
           2 file(s)             141 bytes
                           1,147,392 bytes free


A:\>_
```

WHAT'S HAPPENING? The files were successfully moved. You can see what a welcome addition the MOVE command was to the DOS system utility files.

7.19 DELTREE Revisited

In Chapter 5, you learned two ways to remove a directory. One by using the RD command. This was the bottom up approach. Since you create directories from the top down, you had to delete directories from the bottom up. If the subdirectory you wished to remove had more subdirectories beneath it, you had to remove those subdirectories first. DELTREE, introduced in DOS 6.0, finally allowed you to delete directories from the top down with one command. In addition, when you use RD, not only must you remove any subdirectories, but you must first delete any files that are in each subdirectory. Thus, removing directories with RD is a two step process—first delete files (DEL), then eliminate the directory (RD). DELTREE has the advantage that in one fell swoop, you eliminate files and directories.

However, MS-DOS 6.0 had a fatal flaw and did not require a parameter. Thus, you could eliminate all the directories and files on a hard disk. *Always* use a parameter with DELTREE.

7.20 Activity: Using RD and DELTREE

Note: The DATA disk is in Drive A. The A:\> is displayed.

Step 1 Key in the following: A:\>**RD FILES\PLACE** [Enter]

```
A:\>RD FILES\PLACE
Invalid path, not directory,
or directory not empty


A:\>_
```

WHAT'S HAPPENING? The portion of the message that applies here is that the FILES\PLACE directory is not empty of files. Thus, you have to take a step preceding the RD command.

Step 2 Key in the following: A:\>**DEL FILES\PLACE** [Enter]

```
A:\>DEL FILES\PLACE
All files in directory will be deleted!
Are you sure (Y/N)?_
```

WHAT'S HAPPENING? You had to use the DEL command to eliminate the files. The command DEL FILES\PLACE implied or defaulted to *all* the files in the PLACE directory. You could have keyed in DEL FILES\PLACE*.*, but the *.* was not necessary since, if you do not include a value with DEL, the default is all files.

Step 3   Press **Y** **Enter**

Step 4   Key in the following: A:\>**RD FILES\PLACE** **Enter**

Step 5   Key in the following: A:\>**DIR FILES** **Enter**

```
A:\>RD FILES\PLACE

A:\>DIR FILES

 Volume in drive A is DATADISK
 Volume Serial Number is 2F26-1901
 Directory of A:\FILES

 .              <DIR>         06-21-94   11:49p
 ..             <DIR>         06-21-94   11:49p
GOODBYE   NEW            32 11-23-94    7:07a
        3 file(s)              32 bytes
                       1,148,416 bytes free

A:\>_
```

WHAT'S HAPPENING? Once you eliminated the files from the PLACE directory using DEL, you could remove the directory using RD. If you wanted to eliminate the FILES directory using RD, you would still have to delete any files that were in it. In this case, using DELTREE is much faster because it is a one-step process.

Step 6   Key in the following: A:\>**DELTREE FILES** **Enter**

```
A:\>DELTREE FILES
Delete directory "files" and all its subdirectories? [yn]_
```

WHAT'S HAPPENING? As you can see, DELTREE is offering to delete files and directories. FILES is the parameter you included with DELTREE. Had you not included FILES and you had MS-DOS 6.0, you would have eliminated *every* directory and file on the DATA disk if you had pressed Y for yes.

Step 7   Press **Y** **Enter**

```
Delete directory "files" and all its subdirectories? [yn] y
Deleting files...

A:\>_
```

WHAT'S HAPPENING? The message stated that the files were deleted. But was the subdirectory removed?

Step 8   Key in the following: A:\>**DIR FILES** [Enter]

```
A:\>DIR FILES

 Volume in drive A is DATADISK
 Volume Serial Number is 2F26-1901
 Directory of A:\

 File not found

A:\>_
```

WHAT'S HAPPENING? The directory FILES was removed. DELTREE is fast but can be dangerous. In addition, any version of DOS will let you use RD, whereas you must have DOS 6.0 or above to use DELTREE.

7.21 Backing Up Your DATA Disk

You should get into the habit of *always* backing up your data files so that, if something happens to the original data, you will have a copy of the original material. In data-processing circles, this habit is called **Disaster and Recovery Planning**. It means exactly what it says. If there is a disaster—fire, flood, power surge, theft, head crash, coffee spilled on a disk—what is your plan to recover your programs and data? Nowadays, the term that is used is **Business Resumption Plan**, to cover more than data processing and include the entire business spectrum. However, backing up programs on application disks can be tricky, especially on **copy-protected** disks (which means you cannot back them up with regular DOS commands). You should never back up your program or software application disks until you understand how the application programs work. All application software comes with documentation that instructs you how to back up the specific application program disk you own. Backing up a hard disk is a special circumstance, using special DOS commands. You cannot and should not back up the hard disk using the techniques that will be described here because the contents of a hard disk will not fit on one floppy disk.

However, you can and should back up all the data on any data disk with the following techniques. There are three ways to back up data files. One way is to back up the entire data disk. You will get all the files and all the subdirectories. To do this, you use the DISKCOPY command, which makes an identical copy of a disk, track for track and sector for sector. However, remember that DISKCOPY cannot be used to back up the hard disk.

You can also use the COPY command, which backs up files from floppy disk to floppy disk or specific files in specific directories on the hard disk. Later, we will discuss the third method, using the XCOPY command. The MOVE command, although useful in copying files to a floppy disk from a hard disk, removes the files from their original location. Thus, you end up with only one copy of your data files.

Typically, data files are backed up at the end of every work session so that you can keep your data files current. It is very important to acquire a regular backup routine so that it becomes an automatic process.

Usually, with application software, you are not so worried about backing up the programs. If something happens to the hard disk, you can recover and reinstall the programs from the original purchased floppy disks. However, the data that you create is unrecoverable, unless you have backed it up. A common technique to back up data from a hard disk is to purchase a device called a tape backup. This device allows the user the ease of backing up the hard disk without having to sit in front of the computer and keep inserting blank floppy disks. However, the important message is, whatever technique you use, **BACK UP YOUR DATA FILES**.

In this text, you have been placing all your data files on a floppy disk. This is the easiest kind of back up to perform. It is also extremely useful. With a backup copy of the DATA disk, if you should have a problem, you would not have to go back to Chapter 2 and redo all the activities and homework. In the next activity, you will back up your DATA disk.

7.22 Activity: Backing Up with the DISKCOPY Command

Note 1:   The DATA disk is in Drive A. The A:\> is displayed.

Note 2:   DISKCOPY requires that media types be the same. See Table 7.1.

Data Disk Media Type	Blank Floppy Disk To Use
5¼-inch 360 KB double-density disk	5¼-inch 360 KB double-density disk
5¼-inch 1.2 MB high-density disk	5¼-inch 1.2 MB high-density disk
3½-inch 720 KB double-density drive disk	3½-inch 720 KB double-density disk
3½-inch 1.44 MB high-density drive disk	3½-inch 1.44 MB high-density disk

Table 7.1   *Matching Media Types*

Step 1   Get a blank disk, one that has not been used or one that has data on it that you no longer want. Write BACKUP DATA DISK on the label.

Step 2   Key in the following: A:\>**DISKCOPY A: A:** [Enter]

```
A:\>DISKCOPY A: A:

Insert SOURCE diskette in drive A:

Press any key to continue . . .
```

WHAT'S HAPPENING? You are asked to put the SOURCE disk that you wish to copy in Drive A. In this case, the DATA disk, which you want to copy, is already in Drive A. You keyed in two disk drives, A and A, to ensure that you do not accidentally copy the hard disk. You are telling DISKCOPY to make a copy from the disk in Drive A to the disk in Drive A.

Step 3   Press **Enter**

```
Copying 80 tracks, 15 sectors per track, 2 side(s)

Reading from source diskette . . .
```

WHAT'S HAPPENING? The number of tracks and sectors will vary depending on the disk media type. The DISKCOPY command tells DOS to copy everything on the disk in Drive A (the SOURCE) to RAM. While this program is doing the copying, the cursor flashes on the screen. When the command is completed or the program has finished executing (copying), you need to take another step. You receive the following prompt:

```
Insert TARGET diskette in drive A:

Press any key to continue . . .
```

WHAT'S HAPPENING? This prompt tells you to remove the SOURCE disk from Drive A and insert the blank or TARGET disk in Drive A so DOS has a place to copy the information.

Step 4   Remove your original DATA disk from Drive A. Insert the blank disk labeled BACKUP DATA DISK into Drive A. The BACKUP DATA DISK is your target disk. Close or latch the drive door. Press **Enter**.

```
Writing to target diskette . . .

Formatting while copying
```

WHAT'S HAPPENING? Again, you see the flashing cursor. Now, whatever was copied into RAM is being copied or written to the blank disk in Drive A. The message you see depends on the version of DOS you are using and whether or no the disk is new.

For DOS Versions Prior to 6.2

Remember, if you are using a version of DOS earlier than 6.2, and you are using a high-density disk, you will receive additional prompts like the one shown below.

```
Insert SOURCE diskette in drive A:

Press any key to continue...
```

This prompt tells you to remove the TARGET disk from Drive A and insert the original DATA disk back into Drive A. Do this and press **Enter** until you get the message Insert TARGET diskette in drive A. You continue to swap disks until DISKCOPY has finished and given you this message:

```
Volume Serial Number is 1DE2-136A

Copy another diskette (Y/N)?_
```

```
Do you wish to write another duplicate of this disk (Y/N)?_
```

WHAT'S HAPPENING? The prompt tells you that the program has finished executing and now asks you a question. Do you want to create another identical copy of the DATA disk? In this case, you do not.

Step 5   Press N

```
Volume Serial Number is 1F00-100E

Copy another diskette (Y/N)?_
```

WHAT'S HAPPENING? You see another question: Do you want to execute DISKCOPY again to make another copy of another disk? In this case, you do not wish to make another copy, so you key in N. The Volume Serial Number, by the way, changes each time you use the DISKCOPY command.

Step 6   Press N

```
Copy another diskette (Y/N)? N

A:\>_
```

WHAT'S HAPPENING? Because of the DISKCOPY command, you now have two copies of the DATA disk, the original and the backup. At the end of each work session, you should follow these steps to back up your DATA disk. You do not need a new backup disk each time. Keep using the same backup disk over and over. You are merely keeping current by today's date; you do not need an archival or historical record of each day's work. However, if you wish to be prudent, it is wise to have more than one backup copy of your data. As you can imagine, the only time you need your copy of the data is when something has gone wrong. This is not the time you want to find out that your only copy of the data is bad. It is also a good idea to check your backed up data periodically to ensure that it is good data and that you can recover it if you need to.

Some organizations, such as banks and the IRS, may need to recreate records so they will have not only a Disaster and Recovery Plan but also **archival data** or an **archival backup**. This is sometimes called a transaction history. Organizations like this need far more than a simple backup copy. For instance, if you go into the bank today and say you are missing the $100.00 deposit you made last week, the bank cannot tell you that they do not know what happened last week. The bank needs to be able to recreate all the transactions that occurred on the day in question. Just having a back up copy of your account for today or even yesterday is not sufficient. Most users, however, do not need archival data. Simply backing up their data is sufficient.

Step 7   Remove the disk labeled BACKUP DATA DISK and keep it in a safe place until you need it again to make another backup.

WHAT'S HAPPENING? You now have a backup copy of your DATA disk. Every time you complete a chapter, it is a good idea to update your BACKUP DATA DISK so that it is current.

7.23 Backing Up Files with the COPY Command

Note: The following material is informational and meant only to be read. It is not an activity.

Using the DISKCOPY command backs up an entire floppy disk. More often than not, however, you only need to back up specific files or you want to back up files from the hard disk to a floppy disk. Remember that you can also use the COPY command to back up specific files. The syntax does not change. It is:

```
COPY    [drive:][path]source.fil    [drive:][path]destination.fil
```

You can also back up files from one disk to another with the COPY command. Be sure that the destination disk is already formatted, because COPY does not format a new disk as DISKCOPY does. This command can only be used if you have two floppy disk drives. In addition, the disk media types do not have to be identical. For example, you can copy from a 5¼-inch 360 KB disk to a 3½-inch 1.44 MB disk. You would place the source disk in Drive A and the destination disk in Drive B and key in:

```
A:\>COPY *.* B:\
```

A:\> is the default drive. COPY is the command. *.* means every file with every file extension, the first * represents any file name, the second * represents any file extension. COPY goes to the source disk to find each file in the root directory. As it copies the source file, it lists the file name on the screen. B:\ represents the root directory of the destination disk. Since you give no file names following B:\, COPY assumes that you want the same file name on the destination disk. If there is a file with the same name on the destination disk, COPY overwrites it.

If you want to back up files from a hard disk, you can also use this command to copy the files in the individual subdirectories. However, you must be sure that there are not too many files in a subdirectory to fit on a floppy disk. DOS 5.0 and above tells you how many bytes are in a subdirectory when you use the DIR command. For instance, look at the following display:

```
C:\DOS6BK>DIR *.TMP

   Volume in drive C has no label
   Volume Serial Number is 1B93-9D8B
   Directory of C:\DOS6BK

APRIL      TMP          70 01-23-93   11:49a
GOODBYE    TMP          32 11-23-94    7:07a
BONJOUR    TMP          51 10-12-94    7:09a
JANUARY    TMP          71 01-23-93   11:48a
MARCH      TMP          69 01-23-93   11:49a
JAN        TMP          72 11-23-95   10:41a
FEB        TMP          74 11-23-95   10:41a
MAR        TMP          70 11-23-95   10:42a
APR        TMP          71 11-23-95   10:42a
         9 file(s)           580 bytes
                   73,048,064 bytes free

C:\DOS6BK>_
```

After 9 file(s), the number is 580 bytes. This tells you that these nine files require only 580 bytes and will easily fit on a floppy disk. On the other hand, if you get a display like the one that follows:

```
DEFAULT    BAK       4,205 01-12-94    8:53p
DEFAULT    SLT       4,080 01-12-94    8:52p
DEFAULT    SET       4,205 01-12-94    8:54p
DEFAULT    SAV       4,080 01-12-94    8:50p
DEFAULT    CAT          66 01-12-94    8:53p
CC40112B   FUL       6,368 01-12-94    8:53p
MSBACKUP   INI          43 06-14-93   12:12p
MSBACKUP   LOG     119,755 01-13-94   11:25p
MSBACKUP   TMP       5,010 01-12-94    8:54p
BBCECPDK                0 10-24-93    5:36p
MSAV       INI         248 01-10-94   12:37a
MSBACKUP   RST         224 01-13-94   11:33p
```

```
RESTORE   TMP         6,176 01-12-94    8:54p
BBCECPDP                 13 10-24-93    5:36p
MWAV      INI            24 10-24-93    5:46p
AUTO          <DIR>        02-25-94    4:21p
~INS0363  ~MP        9,728 02-26-94   12:22a
DOSSHELL INI       16,343 03-03-94    6:55p
AUTOEXEC UMB          494 03-15-94    3:26p
CONFIG   UMB          339 03-17-94   11:10p
MEMMAKER STS        1,455 03-17-94   11:15p
      154 file(s)      4,941,428 bytes
                      72,892,416 bytes free


C:\DOS>_
```

The number is now `154 file(s)` that occupy over `4,941,428` bytes, which will not fit on a single floppy disk. However, if the files will fit on a floppy disk, you could use the COPY command. Thus, if you wanted to back up the subdirectory \DOS6BK, the command would be keyed in as: `C:\>COPY C:\DOS6BK\*.* A:` This command, however, would not copy files in any subdirectories under the \DOS6BK subdirectory, only the files in the \DOS6BK directory. You would have to key in another command such as: `C:\ >COPY \DOS6BK\DATA\*.* A:`

You *cannot* and *must not* copy all the files from a hard disk to a floppy disk with the COPY command. There are too many files on the hard disk, and they will not fit on a single floppy disk. Other commands in DOS, such as MSBACKUP (BACKUP and RESTORE in versions of DOS below 6.0), are designed to back up a hard disk.

A question that arises is how often should you back up data? If you have backed up files to floppies or a tape and have not changed them, you do not need to back them up again and again. The files you are interested in backing up are those that have changed or those that are new. A rule of thumb to follow is how long would it take you to recreate your data. If you think in those terms, you will make regular backups.

Chapter Summary

1. DEL or ERASE eliminates files.
2. Deleting files helps you manage your disks and directories.
3. The syntax for the DEL and ERASE commands are:

    ERASE [*drive:*][*path*]*filename*

   or

    DEL [*drive:*][*path*]*filename*

4. Wildcards can be used with DEL or ERASE.
5. DEL or ERASE does not eliminate the data on the disk, only the entry in the directory table.

6. In DOS versions prior to 5.0, there is no way to recover a deleted file. The entry in the FAT is freed up when you delete a file, and thus the next time DOS writes to the disk, it overwrites the file with the new data.

7. Once a file has been deleted, it cannot be recovered except with special utility programs such as UNDELETE.

8. UNDELETE will allow you to recover deleted files if they have not been overwritten.

9. The syntax for UNDELETE is UNDELETE [*drive:*] [*path*]*filename*

10. Before you use wildcards with DEL or ERASE, it is wise to use the DIR command to see what is going to be erased.

11. The /P parameter that became available in DOS 4.0 prompts you to confirm whether or not you wish to delete a file.

12. The /P parameter in DOS 4.0 and above is an example of an enhancement in a new release of software.

13. You can change the names of files with the RENAME or REN command.

14. The syntax for renaming files is:

        REN [*drive:*] [*path*]oldfile.ext newfile.ext

    or

        RENAME [*drive:*] [*path*]oldfile.ext newfile.ext

15. Renaming can only be done on one drive or directory. RENAME does not move files.

16. Renaming changes only file names; not contents of files.

17. With the REN command, you start with one file and end up with the same file with a new name.

18. Wildcards can be used with the REN command.

19. Before you use wildcards with the REN command, it is wise to use the DIR command to see what files are going to be affected by renaming.

20. Once a file is renamed, it cannot be found under the old name.

21. The MOVE command can be used either to change the name of a subdirectory or to move files from one location to another. When you use MOVE, two steps are taken. The files are copied to the new location and deleted from the old location.

22. The syntax of MOVE is to move one or more files:

        MOVE [*drive:*] [*path*]filename1[,...] *destination*

    To rename a directory:

        MOVE [*drive:*] [*path*]dirname1 dirname2

23. You may remove directories with either RD or DELTREE. With RD, you must first remove files and any directories. DELTREE does it all.

24. It is wise to make backup copies of data files so that, if something happens, you have another source of data.
25. You can back up a floppy disk with the DISKCOPY command, or you can back up files on your disk using the COPY command. The wildcard *.* allows you to back up all the files in a directory.

Key Terms

Archival data
Archival backup
Business Resumption Plan

Copy-protected
Disaster and Recovery Plan

Discussion Questions

1. Explain why you may want to eliminate files from a disk.
2. When you delete a file, the file is not actually removed from the disk. What really happens?
3. What is the difference between the DEL and ERASE commands?
4. Give the syntax of the DEL/ERASE command and explain each part of the syntax.
5. The strength of wildcards is also a weakness. Explain this statement when using DEL or ERASE.
6. When deleting files why should you key in DIR with global file specifications first?
7. Explain the purpose and function of the /P parameter with the DEL command.
8. Name and explain the levels of deletion protection offered by DOS 6.0
9. Give the syntax of the UNDELETE command and explain each part of the syntax.
10. Why would you want to change the name of a file?
11. Explain the purpose and function of the RENAME or REN command.
12. Give the syntax of the REN command and explain each part of the syntax.
13. What is the difference between the REN and RENAME commands?
14. What is the difference between the RENAME and COPY commands?
15. If you are using the REN command and get the message, Duplicate file name or file not found, what could it mean?
16. What is the function and purpose of the MOVE command?
17. Give the syntax of the MOVE command and explain each part of the syntax.
18. Compare and contrast MOVE and COPY.
19. What is the difference between the MOVE and the REN commands?
20. Compare and contrast the DELTREE command with the RD command.
21. What process could you use to back up specific files?
22. What process could you use to back up a subdirectory?
23. Why would you not copy all the files from the hard disk to a floppy disk with the DISKCOPY command?
24. Why would you not copy all the files from a hard disk to a floppy disk with the COPY command?

Chapter 8

Informational Commands: CHKDSK, ATTRIB, SCANDISK, DEFRAG, FC, and More DIR

8. Be able to use the F/ parameter with CHKDSK to convert lost clusters into files, if necessary.
9. Use the SCANDISK command to repair disk problems.
10. Use the DEFRAG command to optimize performance on disks.

Chapter Overview

By using different commands, you can reveal much information about your disks and files. You can discover how much room is left on a disk for new files. You can repair disk errors. You can see if files are being stored efficiently on a disk. If they are not, you can take steps to store them more efficiently, a process called optimizing a disk. You can easily discover if files are alike. In addition, you will learn what file attributes are and how to manipulate them.

In this chapter you will learn to use the ATTRIB command to manipulate file attributes, the FC command to compare files, the CHKDSK command to obtain statistical information about a disk and to repair some disk errors, the SCANDISK command to get additional information about a disk and do other kinds of disk repairs, and the DEFRAG command to optimize a disk.

8.1 File Attributes and the ATTRIB Command

The root directory keeps track of information about every file on a disk. The information for every file it tracks is the file name, file extension, file size, date and time the file was last modified, and a pointer to the file's starting cluster in the File Allocation Table. In addition, each file in the directory has "attributes." Attributes are bits that are either on or off. **File attributes** describe the status of a file. These attributes include whether or not a file is a system file, a hidden file, read-only file, or an archived file. Attributes are sometimes called **flags**.

The **system attribute** is a special signal to DOS that the file is a system file. This bit is usually reserved for the DOS system files, but some application programs may set a bit to indicate that a particular program is a system file. The **hidden attribute** means that, when you use the DIR command, the file name is not displayed. Hidden files cannot be deleted, copied, or renamed. For example, hidden files such as the operating system files, IO.SYS and MSDOS.SYS, are on a disk, but, when you execute DIR, they are not displayed.

When a file is marked as read-only, it means exactly that. A user can only read the file, not modify or delete it. Sometimes, application programs will mark a file with a **read-only attribute** bit so that a user cannot delete the file.

Last, the **archive attribute** is used to indicate the backup history (archive status) of a file. When you create or modify a file, an **archive bit** is turned on or set. Certain DOS commands can modify the archive bit and reset it (turn off or clear it).

DOS has a command that allows you to manipulate file attributes. It is called the ATTRIB command. You can view, set, and reset all the file attributes for one file or many files. Prior to DOS 5.0, you could only set the archive bit and the read-only bit, but now you can mark files as hidden or system files. ATTRIB is an external command. The syntax for the ATTRIB command is:

```
ATTRIB [+R | -R] [+A | -A] [+S | -S] [+H | -H]
[[drive:][path]filename] [/S]
```

When you see a parameter in brackets, as you know, it is an optional parameter. When you see a parameter displayed as [+R | -R], the bar acts like a toggle switch. The parameter can be one thing or the other, not both—the choices are mutually exclusive. Thus, you can set a file with +R *or* -R but not both at the same time. The parameters are as follows:

```
+           Sets an attribute.
-           Clears an attribute.
R           Read-only file attribute.
A           Archive file attribute.
S           System file attribute.
H           Hidden file attribute.
/S          Processes files in the current directory and all
            of its subdirectories.
```

The attributes that you will find most useful to set or unset are read-only (R) and hidden (H). By making a file read-only, no one, including you, will be able to delete or overwrite the file accidentally. If a data file is marked read-only, even when you are in an application program, you cannot alter the data.

When you use the H attribute to make a file hidden, it will not be displayed when using the DIR command. If you cannot see a file displayed in the directory listing, you also cannot copy, delete, or rename it. This feature, as you will see, will allow you great flexibility in manipulating and managing files.

The A attribute is called the archive bit. Any file marked with the A attribute is a signal that the file has not been backed up. However, merely using the COPY command does not turn off the A attribute. You must use certain programs, such as XCOPY, which can read the archive bit. Unlike COPY, XCOPY will determine whether or not a file has changed since the last time it was backed up, based on whether or not the archive bit is set. Then XCOPY can make a decision on whether or not the file needs to be backed up. Rarely, if ever, will you use the ATTRIB command to change the attribute of a file marked as a system file (S).

8.2 *Activity: Using ATTRIB to Make Files Read-only*

Note 1: Be sure the DATA disk is in Drive A and the A:\> is displayed.
Note 2: It is assumed that the path is set to the \DOS subdirectory.
Note 3: If specific files are not on your DATA disk, you can copy them from the \DOS6BK subdirectory.

Step 1   Key in the following: A:\>**ATTRIB** *.99 [Enter]

```
A:\>ATTRIB *.99
  A            A:\APR.99
  A            A:\FEB.99
  A            A:\JAN.99
  A            A:\MAR.99

A:\>_
```

WHAT'S HAPPENING? You asked the ATTRIB command to show you the file with the .99 extension in the root directory of the DATA disk. The only file attribute that is visible or "on" for these files is the A, or the archive bit.

Step 2   Key in the following: A:\>**ATTRIB C:*.*** [Enter]

```
A:\>ATTRIB C:\*.*
      SHR      C:\IO.SYS
      SHR      C:\MSDOS.SYS
      SHR      C:\DRVSPACE.BIN
  A            C:\CONFIG.SYS
      SHR      C:\DRVSPACE.MR1
  A   SH       C:\386SPART.PAR
        R      C:\COMMAND.COM
        R      C:\WINA20.386
        R      C:\DBLSPACE.WIN
      SHR      C:\DRVSPACE.INI
  A   SHR      C:\IBMBIO.COM
  A   SHR      C:\IBMDOS.COM
        R      C:\DBLSPACE.INF
      SHR      C:\DBLSPACE.BIN
      SHR      C:\DRVSPACE.001
      SHR      C:\DRVSPACE.002
               C:\AUTOEXEC.BAT
A:\>_
```

WHAT'S HAPPENING? You are looking at the files in the root directory of C. Your display will be different depending on what files are in your root directory. Also, if you are using a network, you may not be able to access the root directory of the network drive. If you cannot access the root directory of Drive C on your system, just look at the above example. You can see that IO.SYS and MSDOS.SYS are marked with an S for system attribute an H for hidden attribute and an R for the read-only attribute. Since you cannot boot the computer from the hard disk without these files, they are triply protected. In addition, other critical files are marked with the S, H, and R attributes.

Step 3   Key in the following: A:\>**COPY C:\DOS6BK*.FIL** [Enter]

```
A:\>COPY C:\DOS6BK\*.FIL
C:\DOS6BK\PERSONAL.FIL
C:\DOS6BK\Y.FIL
C:\DOS6BK\STEVEN.FIL
C:\DOS6BK\MARK.FIL
C:\DOS6BK\FRANK.FIL
C:\DOS6BK\CAROLYN.FIL
C:\DOS6BK\CASES.FIL
C:\DOS6BK\SECOND.FIL
        8 file(s) copied

A:\>_
```

WHAT'S HAPPENING? You have copied all the files with the .FIL extension from the \DOS6BK subdirectory.

Step 4   Key in the following: A:\>**ATTRIB** *.**FIL** (Enter)

```
A:\>ATTRIB *.FIL
   A          A:\MARCH.FIL
   A          A:\PERSONAL.FIL
   A          A:\Y.FIL
   A          A:\STEVEN.FIL
   A          A:\MARK.FIL
   A          A:\FRANK.FIL
   A          A:\CAROLYN.FIL
   A          A:\CASES.FIL
   A          A:\SECOND.FIL

A:\>_
```

WHAT'S HAPPENING? The only attribute that is set (turned on) for these files is the archive bit (A).

Step 5   Key in the following: A:\>**ATTRIB** **+R** **STEVEN.FIL** (Enter)

```
A:\>ATTRIB +R STEVEN.FIL

A:\>_
```

WHAT'S HAPPENING? You asked the ATTRIB command to make STEVEN.FIL a read-only file.

Step 6   Key in the following: A:\>**ATTRIB** **STEVEN.FIL** (Enter)

```
A:\>ATTRIB STEVEN.FIL
   A    R     A:\STEVEN.FIL

A:\>_
```

WHAT'S HAPPENING? Now you have flagged or marked STEVEN.FIL as a read-only file.

Step 7 Key in the following: A:\>**DEL STEVEN.FIL** **Enter**

```
A:\>DEL STEVEN.FIL
Access denied

A:\>_
```

WHAT'S HAPPENING? You cannot delete this file because it is marked read-only. You can also protect against other kinds of file destruction. Once a file is marked read-only, even when you are in an application program, DOS will stop you from overwriting the file.

Step 8 Key in the following: A:\>**C:** **Enter**

Step 9 Key in the following: C:\>**CD \DOS6BK\FINANCE** **Enter**

Step 10 Key in the following:
C:\DOS6BK\FINANCE>**COPY HOMEBUD.TKR A:** **Enter**

Step 11 Key in the following:
C:\DOS6BK\FINANCE>**ATTRIB +R A:\HOMEBUD.TKR** **Enter**

Step 12 Key in the following:
C:\DOS6BK\FINANCE>**ATTRIB A:\HOMEBUD.TKR** **Enter**

```
A:\>C:

C:\>CD \DOS6BK\FINANCE

C:\DOS6BK\FINANCE>COPY HOMEBUD.TKR A:\
        1 file(s) copied

C:\DOS6BK\FINANCE>ATTRIB +R A:\HOMEBUD.TKR

C:\DOS6BK\FINANCE>ATTRIB A:\HOMEBUD.TKR
    A    R    A:\HOMEBUD.TKR

C:\DOS6BK\FINANCE>_
```

WHAT'S HAPPENING? You have taken several steps. You changed your default drive to the hard disk. You changed directories. You then copied the HOMEBUD.TKR file to the DATA disk and made it a read-only file. Although you can alter the data in the file, if you try to save the altered file to disk, the read-only attribute will prohibit you from overwriting the original data.

Step 13   Key in the following: C:\DOS6BK\FINANCE>**THINK** Enter

Step 14   Press Enter

WHAT'S HAPPENING? You are in The Thinker program. You are going to load the read-only file from the DATA disk.

Step 15   Press **/**

Step 16   Press **F**

Step 17   Press **R**

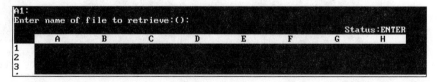

WHAT'S HAPPENING? You issued the command to retrieve a file. Now you must enter the file name.

Step 18   Be sure to include the DATA disk drive letter in front of the file name.
          Key in the following: **A:\HOMEBUD** Enter

WHAT'S HAPPENING? You have loaded the data file HOMEBUD.TKR from the DATA disk. You are going to change the file and try to save the changed file to the DATA disk.

Step 19   Key in the following: tttt **Enter**

```
A1:
                                                              Status:ENTER
              A            B          C          D          E
1    tttt                  JANUARY    FEBRUARY   MARCH
2
3    RENT                  450.00     450.00     450.00
4    ELECTRICITY            35.00      39.00
5    GAS                    25.45      23.74
6    PHONE                  32.98      34.75
7    CABLE                  14.50      14.50      14.50
8    FOOD                  257.98     233.45
9    PERSONAL               37.50      41.25
10   ENTERTAINMENT          78.00      85.00
11   TRANSPORTATION        110.00     113.00
12
13   TOTAL                1041.41    1034.69     464.50
14
15
16
17
18
19
20
/-Command F1-Help F2-Edit F5-GOTO F9-Recalc          The Thinker(c)82,86
```

WHAT'S HAPPENING? You have keyed in some characters, tttt.

Step 20   Press /

Step 21   Press **F**

Step 22   Press **S**

Step 23   Press **Enter**

```
A1:'tttt
Cancel Replace
                                                              Status:ENTER
              A            B          C          D          E
1    tttt                  JANUARY    FEBRUARY   MARCH
2
3    RENT                  450.00     450.00     450.00
4    ELECTRICITY            35.00      39.00
5    GAS                    25.45      23.74
```

WHAT'S HAPPENING? This program asks if you want to replace an existing file.

Step 24   Press **R**

```
A1:'tttt
ERROR SAVING FILE, TRY AGAIN
                                                      Status:ENTER
            A           B          C          D          E
1   tttt              JANUARY   FEBRUARY    MARCH
2
3   RENT              450.00     450.00     450.00
4   ELECTRICITY        35.00      39.00
5   GAS                25.45      23.74
```

WHAT'S HAPPENING? The ERROR SAVING FILE, TRY AGAIN message indicates that on the DATA disk, the data file A:\HOMEBUD.TKR was flagged with the read-only attribute and cannot be overwritten.

Step 25   Press **/**

Step 26   Press **Q**

Step 27   Press **Y**

```
C:\DOS6BK\FINANCE>_
```

WHAT'S HAPPENING? You have exited The Thinker and returned to the system level. Your data file has not been changed on the DATA disk.

Step 28   Key in the following: C:\DOS6BK\FINANCE>**CD \ Enter**

Step 29   Key in the following: C:\>**A: Enter**

```
C:\DOS6BK\FINANCE>CD \

C:\>A:

A:\>_
```

WHAT'S HAPPENING? You have returned to the root directory of the DATA disk.

8.3   Using the Hidden and Archive Attributes with ATTRIB

The purpose of the H attribute is to hide a file so that when you use the DIR command, you will not see it displayed. Why would you want to hide a file? The most likely person you are going to hide the file from is yourself, and this seems to make no logical sense. The real advantage to using the hidden attribute is that it allows you to manipulate files. For instance, when you use the COPY or the MOVE command with wildcards, you may not want to move or copy specific files. When you hide files, neither COPY nor MOVE can see them so they are protected from manipulation.

The purpose of the A attribute is to flag a file as changed since the last time you backed it up using certain commands. These commands can read the attribute bit

(A) and can identify if it has been set. If it is set (on), the commands that can read the archive bit know that the file has changed since the last time it was copied. With the ATTRIB command, you can set and unset this flag to help identify what files you changed since the last time that you backed them up. The following activity will demonstrate how you can use the H and A attributes.

8.4 Activity: Using the H and the A Attributes

Note 1: The DATA disk is in Drive A. The A:\> is displayed.
Note 2: It is assumed that the path is set to the DOS subdirectory on the hard disk.

Step 1   Key in the following: A:\>**COPY C:\DOS6BK\FI*.*** Enter

```
A:\>COPY C:\DOS6BK\FI*.*
C:\DOS6BK\FILE2.CZG
C:\DOS6BK\FILE2.FP
C:\DOS6BK\FILE2.SWT
C:\DOS6BK\FILE3.CZG
C:\DOS6BK\FILE3.FP
C:\DOS6BK\FILE3.SWT
C:\DOS6BK\FILE4.FP
        7 file(s) copied

A:\>_
```

Step 2   Key in the following: A:\>**DIR F*.*** Enter

```
A:\>DIR F*.*

 Volume in drive A is DATADISK
 Volume Serial Number is 2F26-1901
 Directory of A:\

FEB        99          74 11-23-95   10:41a
FEB        BUD         74 11-23-95   10:41a
FEBRUARY   TXT         74 11-23-95   10:41a
FUNNY      TV         180 11-23-94   10:19a
FRANK      FIL         42 11-23-94    7:13a
FILE2      CZG         18 12-06-94   10:45a
FILE2      FP          18 12-06-94   10:46a
FILE2      SWT         18 12-06-94   10:46a
FILE3      CZG         18 12-06-94   10:46a
FILE3      FP          18 12-06-94   10:46a
FILE3      SWT         18 12-06-94   10:47a
FILE4      FP          18 12-06-94   10:47a
       12 file(s)           570 bytes
                      1,131,520 bytes free

A:\>_
```

WHAT'S HAPPENING? You copied all the files that begin with FI and have any file name and any file extension from the DOS6BK subdirectory to the root directory of the DATA disk. Now you want to move all the files that begin with F to the TRIP subdirectory, but you do not want to move the files you just copied. The problem is that, if you use MOVE F*.* TRIP, all the files that begin with F will be moved, not just the ones you desire. You cannot say, "Move all the files that begin with F *except* the files that begin with FI*.*." Here, the ability to hide files is useful.

Step 3   Key in the following: A:\>**ATTRIB +H FI*.*** [Enter]

Step 4   Key in the following: A:\>**DIR F*.*** [Enter]

```
A:\>ATTRIB +H FI*.*


A:\>DIR F*.*

 Volume in drive A is DATADISK
 Volume Serial Number is 2F26-1901
 Directory of A:\

FEB        99          74 11-23-95   10:41a
FEB        BUD         74 11-23-95   10:41a
FEBRUARY   TXT         74 11-23-95   10:41a
FUNNY      TV         180 11-23-94   10:19a
FRANK      FIL         42 11-23-94    7:13a
        5 file(s)            444 bytes
                       1,131,520 bytes free


A:\>_
```

WHAT'S HAPPENING? The files that begin with FI*.* are hidden and will not be displayed by the DIR command. Now when you use the MOVE command, none of the hidden files, the FI*.* files, will be moved.

Step 5   Key in the following: A:\>**MOVE F*.* TRIP** [Enter]

```
A:\>MOVE F*.* TRIP
Overwrite a:\trip\feb.99 (Yes/No/All)?_
```

WHAT'S HAPPENING? You are being warned that you are about to overwrite a file. In this case, you do want to overwrite.

Step 6   Press A [Enter]

```
A:\>MOVE F*.* TRIP
Overwrite a:\trip\feb.99 (Yes/No/All)?a
a:\feb.99 => a:\trip\feb.99 [ok]
```

```
a:\feb.bud => a:\trip\feb.bud [ok]
a:\february.txt => a:\trip\february.txt [ok
a:\funny.tv => a:\trip\funny.tv [ok]
a:\frank.fil => a:\trip\frank.fil [ok]
Cannot move file2.czg - Permission denied
Cannot move file2.fp - Permission denied
Cannot move file2.swt - Permission denied
Cannot move file3.czg - Permission denied
Cannot move file3.fp - Permission denied
Cannot move file3.swt - Permission denied
Cannot move file4.fp - Permission denied

A:\>_
```

WHAT'S HAPPENING? You see that you accomplished your mission. The files you hid were not moved. What if you forget which files you hid? The /A parameter which can be used with the DIR command was introduced in DOS 5.0. It allows you to specify the kind of file you want to look for. The attributes choices are:

```
D   Directories
R   Read-only files
H   Hidden files
A   Files ready to archive
```

Step 7   Key in the following: A:\>**DIR /AH** Enter

```
A:\>DIR /AH

 Volume in drive A is DATADISK
 Volume Serial Number is 2F26-1901
 Directory of A:\

FILE2     CZG         18 12-06-94   10:45a
FILE2     FP          18 12-06-94   10:46a
FILE2     SWT         18 12-06-94   10:46a
FILE3     CZG         18 12-06-94   10:46a
FILE3     FP          18 12-06-94   10:46a
FILE3     SWT         18 12-06-94   10:47a
FILE4     FP          18 12-06-94   10:47a
        7 file(s)            126 bytes
                       1,132,032 bytes free

A:\>_
```

WHAT'S HAPPENING? The attribute you wanted to use was the hidden attribute (H). As you can see, the DIR /AH command displays only the hidden files. Now you can "unhide" the files.

Step 8   Key in the following: A:\>**ATTRIB -H FI*.*** Enter

```
A:\>ATTRIB -H FI*.*

A:\>_
```

WHAT'S HAPPENING? The FI*.* files are no longer hidden. You can manipulate other file attributes to assist you in managing your files. You can indicate to yourself what files have changed since the last time you copied them by changing the A or archive bit. When you create a file, DOS automatically turns on the A attribute or "flags" it as new and not backed up. When you use certain DOS commands, such as XCOPY, that specific command will turn off the A flag to indicate that the file has been backed up. Whenever you make a change to a file, the A attribute bit is turned on again or "reflagged" to indicate that there has been a change since the last time you backed it up. You will learn later how this works when using the XCOPY command. However, you can also manipulate the archive bit directly with the ATTRIB command to let you know if you changed the file.

Step 9   Key in the following: A:\>**TYPE STEVEN.FIL** Enter

Step 10   Key in the following: A:\>**ATTRIB STEVEN.FIL** Enter

```
A:\>TYPE STEVEN.FIL
Hi, my name is Steven.
What is your name?

A:\>ATTRIB STEVEN.FIL
   A    R     A:\STEVEN.FIL

A:\>_
```

WHAT'S HAPPENING? This is a text file that you protected with the R attribute. You can see the contents of it using the TYPE command. You set the R attribute. DOS automatically set the A attribute.

Step 11   Key in the following: A:\>**ATTRIB -A -R STEVEN.FIL** Enter

Step 12   Key in the following: A:\>**ATTRIB STEVEN.FIL** Enter

```
A:\>ATTRIB -A -R STEVEN.FIL

A:\>ATTRIB STEVEN.FIL
             A:\STEVEN.FIL

A:\>_
```

WHAT'S HAPPENING? You have turned off all the attributes of this file.

Step 13   Key in the following:

A:\>**COPY TRIP\FRANK.FIL STEVEN.FIL** [Enter]

```
A:\>COPY TRIP\FRANK.FIL STEVEN.FIL
Overwrite STEVEN.FIL (Yes/No/All)?_
```

WHAT'S HAPPENING? Since the file is no longer read-only, you are asked if you want to overwrite the contents of STEVEN.FIL with FRANK.FIL.

Step 14   Press **Y** [Enter]

Step 15   Key in the following: A:\>**TYPE STEVEN.FIL** [Enter]

```
Overwrite STEVEN.FIL (Yes/No/All)?Y
        1 file(s) copied

A:\>TYPE STEVEN.FIL
Hi, my name is Frank
What is your name?

A:\>_
```

WHAT'S HAPPENING? The file contents have clearly changed. This is an ASCII or text file and can be read on the screen with the TYPE command. If this were a data file generated by a program, you could not use the TYPE command to see if the contents changed. By looking at the attributes of a data file you could see that the file had changed.

Step 16   Key in the following: A:\>**ATTRIB STEVEN.FIL** [Enter]

```
A:\>ATTRIB STEVEN.FIL
  A            A:\STEVEN.FIL

A:\>_
```

WHAT'S HAPPENING? The A attribute or archive bit is once again turned on so that you know the file has changed. Another way of saying it is that STEVEN.FIL is flagged with the archive bit. If you had protected STEVEN.FIL with the read-only attribute, you would be protected from accidentally overwriting the file. Other operations do not work the same way. If you rename the file, it keeps the same file attributes, but, if you copy the file, it does not carry the read-only attribute to the copy. However, since this is a "new" file, the archive bit will be set automatically by DOS.

Step 17   Key in the following: A:\>**ATTRIB +R -A STEVEN.FIL** [Enter]

Step 18   Key in the following: A:\>**ATTRIB STEVEN.FIL** [Enter]

```
A:\>ATTRIB +R -A STEVEN.FIL

A:\>ATTRIB STEVEN.FIL
      R     A:\STEVEN.FIL

A:\>
```

WHAT'S HAPPENING? STEVEN.FIL is now read-only and has had the A flag turned off.

Step 19   Key in the following: A:\>**REN STEVEN.FIL THIS.ONE** [Enter]

Step 20   Key in the following: A:\>**ATTRIB THIS.ONE** [Enter]

```
A:\>REN STEVEN.FIL THIS.ONE

A:\>ATTRIB THIS.ONE
      R     A:\THIS.ONE

A:\>_
```

WHAT'S HAPPENING? Even though you renamed STEVEN.FIL to THIS.ONE, THIS.ONE retained the same file attributes that STEVEN.FIL had. However, things change when you copy a file.

Step 21   Key in the following: A:\>**COPY THIS.ONE STEVEN.FIL** [Enter]

Step 22   Key in the following: A:\>**ATTRIB STEVEN.FIL** [Enter]

Step 23   Key in the following: A:\>**ATTRIB THIS.ONE** [Enter]

```
A:\>COPY THIS.ONE STEVEN.FIL
        1 file(s) copied

A:\>ATTRIB STEVEN.FIL
   A          A:\STEVEN.FIL

A:\>ATTRIB THIS.ONE
      R     A:\THIS.ONE

A:\>
```

WHAT'S HAPPENING? When you copied THIS.ONE, which had a read-only file attribute, to a new file called STEVEN.FIL, DOS copied it but removed the read-only attribute of the new file. STEVEN.FIL is not read-only. Thus, setting the read-only attribute is really most valuable for protecting you against accidental erasure of a file, not for any particular security reason. The same was true for the A attribute. When you renamed the file STEVEN.FIL to THIS.ONE, the A attribute was not set. But when you copied THIS.ONE to STEVEN.FIL, STEVEN.FIL now has the A attribute set. Remember that you set file attributes with the plus sign (+). You can unset file attributes with the minus (-) sign. You can eliminate or add several file attributes with a one-line command, but there must be a space between each parameter so follow the spacing of the command line carefully.

8.5 Comparing Files

In the preceding activities, you made copies of many files. As you may have noticed, the number of files on the disk continues to grow. The more files you have, the harder it is to remember which file is which. Many times you will want to know if two files with different names or two files with the same name have the same contents. One method of checking the contents is to use the TYPE command with each file name (TYPE *filename*) and compare the contents visually on the screen. Another way is to send the contents of each file to the printer and compare them visually (COPY *filename* PRN). Neither process is too difficult when dealing with the dummy files, because the contents of these files are brief, but brevity is *not* the norm for files. Furthermore, if the files of interest are data files generated from program files, they can neither be viewed on the screen with the TYPE command nor printed with the COPY command.

Usually, file contents are extensive, so visual checks would be time-consuming. In addition, it would be very easy to miss small differences. Also, programs are in binary format, "nonsense characters," and there is no way to compare these files visually. It would be useful to have a command that allows you to compare files quickly. There are file compare commands. Depending on which version of DOS you have, you could have the external commands COMP or FC for file compare. In DOS 5.0, you get both the COMP and the FC commands. The COMP command has fewer options than the FC command. Beginning with DOS 6.0, you get only the FC command.

FC is an external command which allows you to compare the contents of any two files very quickly. The command does the work for you and compares the files to see if they are identical. If you compare files that are different or have been modified, even by one character, you will get an error message. FC, when it finds a difference, resynchronizes the files. This means if it finds one character difference, such as a space, FC then attempts to see if the files return to being the same.

The syntax for the FC command is as follows:

```
FC  [/A]  [/C]  [/L]  [/LBn]  [/N]  [/T]  [/W]  [/nnnn]
[drive1:][path1]filename1 [drive2:][path2]filename2
```

If you wish to compare binary files, such as application programs, use the following syntax:

FC /B [*drive1:*][*path1*]*filename1* [*drive2:*][*path2*]*filename2*

The parameters are as follows:

/A	Displays only first and last lines for each set of differences.
/B	Performs a binary comparison.
/C	Disregards the case of letters.
/L	Compares files as ASCII text.
/LBn	Sets the maximum consecutive mismatches to the specified number of lines.
/N	Displays the line numbers on an ASCII comparison.
/T	Does not expand tabs to spaces.
/W	Compresses white space (tabs and spaces) for comparison.
/nnnn	Specifies the number of consecutive lines that must match after a mismatch.

8.6 Activity: Using the FC Command

Note 1:   The DATA disk is in Drive A. The A:\> is displayed.

Step 1   Key in the following: A:\>**C:** [Enter]

Step 2   Key in the following: C:\>**CD \DOS6BK**

```
A:\>C:

C:\>CD \DOS6BK

C:\DOS6BK>_
```

WHAT'S HAPPENING? You have changed default drives and directories so that the hard disk is the default drive and \DOS6BK is the default subdirectory.

Step 3   Key in the following: C:\DOS6BK>**TYPE APRIL.TXT** [Enter]

Step 4   Key in the following: C:\DOS6BK>**TYPE WILDTWO.DOS** Enter

```
C:\DOS6BK>TYPE APRIL.TXT
This is my April file.
It is my fourth dummy file.
This is file 4.

C:\DOS6BK>TYPE WILDTWO.DOS
This is a file created to demonstrate how to
use wildcards.  Wildcards allow me to copy a
group of files using the wildcards symbols, * and ?.
It is the second wildcard file.

C:\DOS6BK>_
```

WHAT'S HAPPENING? The file names are different, and the file contents are different. Remember, FC compares the contents of the files. FC is an external command. However, the path is set to the DOS subdirectory so that DOS can find the FC command.

Step 5   Key in the following:
          C:\DOS6BK>**FC APRIL.TXT WILDTWO.DOS** Enter

```
C:\DOS6BK>FC APRIL.TXT WILDTWO.DOS
Comparing files APRIL.TXT and WILDTWO.DOS
***** APRIL.TXT
This is my April file.
It is my fourth dummy file.
This is file 4.
***** WILDTWO.DOS
This is a file created to demonstrate how to
use wildcards.  Wildcards allow me to copy a
group of files using the wildcards symbols, * and ?.
It is the second wildcard file.
*****



C:\DOS6BK>_
```

WHAT'S HAPPENING? The FC command literally showed you the contents of each file on the screen. You can see that the files are different.

Step 6   Key in the following: C:\DOS6BK>**TYPE STATE.CAP** Enter

Step 7   Key in the following: C:\DOS6BK>**TYPE STATE2.CAP** Enter

```
California       Sacramento
Michigan         Lansing
Arizona          Phoenix
New York         Albany
Florida          Tallahassee
Oregon           Salem
Louisiana        Baton Rouge
Nebraska         Lincoln
Colorado         Denver
Ohio             Columbus


C:\DOS6BK>TYPE STATE2.CAP

California       Sacramento
Michigan         Lansing
Arizona          Phoenix
Illinois         Springfield
Florida          Tallahassee
Oregon           Salem
Louisiana        Baton Rouge
Nebraska         Lincoln
Colorado         Denver
Ohio             Columbus

C:\DOS6BK>_
```

WHAT'S HAPPENING? Here there is a difference. Instead of New York, the state of Illinois is listed.

Step 8   Key in the following:
C:\DOS6BK>**FC STATE.CAP STATE2.CAP** [Enter]

```
C:\DOS6BK>FC STATE.CAP STATE2.CAP
Comparing files STATE.CAP and STATE2.CAP
***** STATE.CAP
Arizona          Phoenix
New York         Albany
Florida          Tallahassee
***** STATE2.CAP
Arizona          Phoenix
Illinois         Springfield
Florida          Tallahassee
*****


C:\DOS6BK>_
```

WHAT'S HAPPENING? These two files are nearly identical, except that one lists New York and the other lists Illinois. The FC command shows each file with the lines before and after the line(s) that differ. FC uses this method for ASCII files. If the files are binary, as are most program files and related data files, you would use the /B parameter. You can also use wildcards with the FC command.

Step 9   Key in the following: C:\DOS6BK>**FC *.FP *.SWT** **Enter**

```
C:\DOS6BK>FC *.FP *.SWT
Comparing files FILE2.FP and FILE2.SWT
FC: no differences encountered

Comparing files FILE3.FP and FILE3.SWT
FC: no differences encountered

Comparing files FILE4.FP and FILE4.SWT
FC: cannot open FILE4.SWT - No such file or directory


C:\DOS6BK>_
```

WHAT'S HAPPENING? You have three files with the .FP extension, FILE2.FP, FILE3.FP, and FILE4.FP. Beginning at the top, you are asking FC to take FILE2.FP, find a file that has an identical file name with the extension .SWT (FILE2.SWT), and compare the two files. When the comparison is complete, FC will go to the next file, FILE3.FP, and do the same (FC FILE3.FP FILE3.SWT). FC carries out the instructions. However, when it gets to FILE4.FP, it cannot find a corresponding file, FILE4.SWT. Therefore, FC cannot compare these files (FC cannot open file: FILE4.SWT—No such file or directory). Since the files that did compare are identical, you get the message FC: No differences encountered. Comparing files is mostly "negative" information. If the files are identical, you can safely delete a copy if you wish. If they are different, you will need to explore further to identify the differences.

Step 10   Key in the following: C:\DOS6BK>**CD ** **Enter**

Step 11   Key in the following: C:\>**A:** **Enter**

```
C:\DOS6BK>CD \

C:\>A:

A:\>_
```

WHAT'S HAPPENING? You have made the root directory of the DATA disk the default.

8.7 Checking a Disk and Memory

There is information about your disks you often need. You need to know how much room is left on the disk so that you can add a new file. You want to know if there are any bad spots on a disk, which can mean the loss of a file. Bad spots can come from a variety of sources such as a mishandled disk or a manufacturing defect. You may want to know if the files are being stored efficiently on a disk. You may have installed such RAM-resident programs as SideKick and Gofer and want to know how much RAM you have for a program.

These tasks can be accomplished by using a utility program called the CHKDSK command, an external command, located in the \DOS subdirectory. In addition to showing the system files, which let you know that a disk is a system disk, CHKDSK also gives other statistical information about a disk and about computer memory as well. The CHKDSK command analyzes the directory on a disk, making sure that the directory entries match the location and lengths of files with the File Allocation Table on the default drive (or designated drive). It makes sure that all the directories are readable. After checking the disk, CHKDSK reports any errors and gives information about the disk's total capacity—how many files are on a disk and how much space is taken. CHKDSK establishes the space left on the disk for additional files and displays the size of the computer's memory in terms of bytes. Thus, the command supplies a disk and memory status report. You should run the CHKDSK command occasionally for each disk to ensure that your file structures have integrity.

CHKDSK informs you of errors. The two kinds of errors are **cross-linked files** and **lost clusters**. Cross-linked files means that two files claim the same sectors in the File Allocation Table. Different files cannot share clusters. Lost clusters indicates sectors that have no directory entry and are "orphans;" that is, they do not belong to any file that DOS knows about.

The syntax for CHKDSK is:

```
CHKDSK [drive:][[path]filename] [/F] [/V]
```

SCANDISK, introduced in MS-DOS 6.2, is intended as a replacement for CHKDSK, and it is better at fixing the disk problems mentioned above. SCANDISK scans the surface of the disk, looks for bad sectors, and fixes other disk problems as well. However, SCANDISK does not really replace CHKDSK because SCANDISK does not give you the reports that CHKDSK does. So, although SCANDISK may be a better command for repairing disk errors, CHKDSK still is a viable command because of its reporting functions.

8.8   Activity: Using the CHKDSK Command

Note: The DATA disk is in Drive A. The A:\> is displayed.

Step 1   Key in the following: A:\>C: [Enter]

Step 2   Key in the following: C:\>CD \DOS [Enter]

Step 3   Key in the following: C:\DOS>DIR CHKDSK*.* [Enter]

```
A:\>C:

C:\>CD \DOS

C:\DOS>DIR CHKDSK*.*

 Volume in drive C has no label
 Volume Serial Number is 1CD1-5E42
 Directory of C:\DOS

CHKDSK    EXE        12,241 05-31-94    6:22a
          1 file(s)          12,241 bytes
                     82,051,072 bytes free

C:\DOS>_
```

WHAT'S HAPPENING? You changed the default drive and directory to the hard disk and subdirectory with the DOS system utility programs. The DIR command told you that the program CHKDSK.EXE is stored as a file in the \DOS subdirectory. CHKDSK is an external command. In order to execute or run this program, DOS has to be able to find it on a disk and load it into memory. By keying in DIR CHKDSK*.*, you have verified that the file is on the disk. However, to execute the command or program, you have to load it into memory or call it. In some versions of DOS, CHKDSK.EXE is called CHKDSK.COM.

Step 4   If you are on a network, you cannot do Step 4. You cannot check a network drive. You should read the information that follows Step 4, then go on to Step 5. If you are not on a network, key in the following:

C:\DOS>CHKDSK [Enter]

```
Volume Serial Number is 1CD1-5E42

 527,138,816 bytes total disk space
 374,628,352 bytes in 26 hidden files
     761,856 bytes in 90 directories
  69,681,152 bytes in 2,032 user files
  82,059,264 bytes available on disk
```

```
      8,192 bytes in each allocation unit
     64,348 total allocation units on disk
     10,017 available allocation units on disk

    655,360 total bytes memory
    606,336 bytes free

Instead of using CHKDSK, try using SCANDISK. SCANDISK can reliably detect
and fix a much wider range of disk problems. For more information,
type HELP SCANDISK from the command prompt.


C:\DOS>_
```

WHAT'S HAPPENING? Do not worry if you do not see the same numbers displayed on your screen. These numbers are related to how the disk was formatted, the size of the hard disk, and how much internal memory is installed in a specific computer. What is important is what the status report is telling you. Let us look at this example, line for line.

`527,138,816 bytes` `total disk space`	This number is the entire capacity of a specific disk. An enhancement included with MS-DOS 6.2 is the addition of commas for easier readability of numbers.
`374,628,352 bytes` `in 26 hidden files`	What are hidden files? On Drive C, in order to boot from the disk, there must be a least two hidden files: IO.SYS and MSDOS.SYS. The hidden files message informs you that this is a system or bootable disk. The other hidden files that are on this disk have to do with various system and program files. The number of hidden files will vary from disk to disk. Other application programs can also create hidden system files.
`761,856 bytes` `in 90 directories`	Nearly all hard disks have subdirectories. This number is for subdirectory entries only.
`69,681,152 bytes in` `2,032 user files`	A user file is any file that is stored on the disk. It does not have to be a file that you, the user, created. User files include all program or application files you have on a disk.
`82,059,264 bytes` `available on disk`	This line establishes how much room remains on the disk in Drive C for new data or program files in bytes. A byte is one character. It can be the letter *b*, the letter *c*, the number *3*, or the punctuation

mark *?*. To give you a rough idea of what a byte means, a page of a printed novel contains about 3,000 bytes. Thus, a disk with a total capacity of 360,000 bytes could hold or store a maximum of about 120 pages of a novel. If you had a 20 MB hard disk (one megabyte means one million bytes) it would hold approximately 20,000,000 bytes or 6,667 pages of text, and if the average novel has about 400 pages, you could store about sixteen and a half novels. You can see why people like the capacity of hard disks. Imagine the numbers with a 40 MB hard disk (33 books) or a 100 MB hard disk (83 books) or a 500 MB hard disk (415 books). This approximation is not entirely accurate because it does not take into account that often information is stored in such a way as to be compressed. However, it does give you an idea of the disk capacity in "human terms." As you work with computers, you become accustomed to thinking in bytes.

`8,192 bytes in each`
`allocation unit`

As discussed earlier, the smallest unit that DOS actually reads is a cluster. A cluster is made up of sectors. A cluster is also referred to as an allocation unit. The number of sectors that make up a cluster (allocation unit) vary depending on the type of disk. For most hard disks, like the one used in this textbook, a cluster is comprised of 16 sectors (512 x 16 = 8,192).

`64,348 total`
`allocation units`
`on disk`

This indicates the total number of clusters available. If you multiply 64,348 x 8,192, you get 527,138,816 or the capacity of this hard disk, a 500 MB hard disk.

`10,017 available`
`allocation units`
`on disk`

This line tells you how much room is available on the disk by cluster.

`655,360 total`
`bytes memory`

After all these numerical lines on the display screen, there are two blank lines. Then, the next two lines of information appear. This second group of numbers discloses the conventional internal memory (RAM) of the particular personal computer you are using. Memory and disk space are measured in bytes. Bytes are expressed in the context of the binary numbering system, as 2^0, 2^1, 2^2, and so on. Rather than being stated individually, bytes are grouped in kilobytes (KB). One kilobyte is 2^{10} or 1024. The odd 24 per thousand is dropped to simplify calculations. For all practical purposes the value of KB is equal to 1000. Thus, 64 KB technically speaking would be 64 x 1024 = 65,536. In user terms, 64 KB is translated as 64,000 bytes, even though a 64 KB memory would actually have room for 65,536 bytes. Some common internal memory sizes are shown in Table 8.1.

`606,336 bytes free` Memory available to run programs.

System Memory	Actual Number of Bytes
64 KB	65,536
128 KB	131,072
256 KB	262,144
512 KB	524,288
640 KB	655,360

Table 8.1   *Computer Memory Sizes*

When a specific computer, regardless of its disk drives, has `655,360 bytes total memory`, it is a 640 KB machine. Remember that memory refers to the work space of a computer, the place where programs and data are held while they are processed. If a computer has `655,360 bytes of total memory`, why are there only `606,366 bytes free`? Free means that you have only 606,336 bytes in conventional memory available for data and programs. You must have an operating system installed in RAM (memory) to be able to use the computer, and some of the bytes were used. When you booted the system and loaded the operating system, you loaded it into memory where the files remain resident.

Sometimes you will see a line reporting how many bad sectors a disk may have. Having bad sectors is not uncommon on hard disks. If you had bad sectors, the line might read `16,384 bytes in bad sectors`. The number would, of course, vary depending on the disk that is checked. On a 500 MB hard disk, for instance, 16,344 bytes in bad sectors is not that significant. However, if you had a smaller hard disk, the number would be significant and you might want to determine if your hard disk needs to be replaced.

mem /c command for memory summary

If you have MS-DOS 6.2 or above, you also see the following message:

```
Instead of using CHKDSK, try using SCANDISK. SCANDISK can reliably detect
and fix a much wider range of disk problems. For more information,
type HELP SCANDISK from the command prompt.
```

This is informing you of the new command, SCANDISK, that does a better job of fixing problems than CHKDSK, but, as you will see, SCANDISK does not give you the reports CHKDSK does.

Step 5   Key in the following: C:\DOS>**CHKDSK A:** [Enter]

```
C:\DOS>CHKDSK A:

Volume DATADISK     created 06-20-1994 5:55p
Volume Serial Number is 2F26-1901

  1,213,952 bytes total disk space
      4,096 bytes in 8 directories
     78,336 bytes in 73 user files
  1,131,520 bytes available on disk

        512 bytes in each allocation unit
      2,371 total allocation units on disk
      2,210 available allocation units on disk

    655,360 total bytes memory
    606,336 bytes free

Instead of using CHKDSK, try using SCANDISK. SCANDISK can reliably detect
and fix a much wider range of disk problems. For more information,
type HELP SCANDISK from the command prompt.


C:\DOS>_
```

WHAT'S HAPPENING? In Step 4, CHKDSK checked out the disk on the default drive, Drive C. Since you wanted to know about the status of the DATA disk, located in Drive A, you had to ask specifically for that information by telling CHKDSK which disk to check. In other words, you added a parameter (the parameter A:). This display looks similar to the first screen. You have 1,213,952 bytes total disk space because this is a 1.2 MB disk. If you had formatted this disk with an operating system, you would have seen the two hidden files. Since you did not, you did not see this information. If you have another capacity disk such as a 1.44 MB disk, you will have more space available. The files and bytes available will vary based on what is on the DATA disk. The last two lines displayed on the screen do not change because you are still using the same computer and the amount of internal memory (RAM) on a specific computer does not vary. However, the statistical information about the disk does change because you asked for information about a different disk. If you placed another disk in Drive A, you would get different information about files and the bytes remaining on the disk.

Step 6   Key in the following: C:\DOS>**CD** \ [Enter]

Step 7   Key in the following: C:\>**A:** [Enter]

```
C:\DOS>CD \

C:\>A:

A:\>_
```

WHAT'S HAPPENING? You have made the root directory of the DATA disk the default.

8.9 *The Verbose Parameter with the CHKDSK Command*

The CHKDSK command has an exceedingly useful parameter, /V. Using /V is known as running in **verbose** mode. This parameter, in conjunction with the CHKDSK command, not only gives the usual status report but also lists every file on the disk, including hidden files. An important thing to remember about parameters is that they are associated with specific commands and perform specific tasks for those commands. The same parameter does not do the same thing with other commands. For instance, you have used /V with the FORMAT command. When /V is used with the FORMAT command, it means put a volume label on the disk. However, when you use /V with the CHKDSK command, it displays all the files on the disk.

8.10 *Activity: Using the /V Parameter; Using DIR Parameters*

Note 1:   The DATA disk is in Drive A. The A:\> is displayed.
Note 2:   When you key in Step 2, the screen display scrolls by very quickly. You can press the [Pause] key to freeze the screen display. If that doesn't work and the screen scrolls by too quickly, you can key in the command again and press [Pause]. As an alternative, you can also hold the [Ctrl] key down and press the S key or try the [Ctrl] + [NumLock] keys if you have an older computer.

Step 1   Key in the following: A:\>**CHKDSK** **/V** [Enter]

Step 2   Press the [Pause] key.

```
A:\APRIL.NEW
A:\GOODBYE.NEW
A:\BONJOUR.NEW
A:\JANUARY.NEW
```

```
A:\MARCH.NEW
A:\JAN.BUD
A:\MAR.BUD
A:\APR.BUD
A:\JAN.OLD
A:\MARCH.TXT
A:\JANUARY.TXT
A:\APR.TST
Directory A:\CLASS
A:\CLASS\JAN.PAR
A:\CLASS\FEB.PAR
A:\CLASS\JAN.ABC
A:\CLASS\FEB.ABC
A:\CLASS\MAR.ABC
A:\CLASS\APR.ABC
A:\CLASS\MAR.PAR
A:\CLASS\APR.PAR
A:\CLASS\JAN.FIL
A:\CLASS\MAR.FIL
Directory A:\WORK
Directory A:\WORK\CL_
```

WHAT'S HAPPENING? Your display will be different, depending on where you pressed the **Pause** key and what files you have on the DATA disk. Furthermore, if you have a fast processor, you may never be able to stop the display in time. It will simply scroll to the end. If you can't catch the display, look at the example above. You see that the display shows you all the files on the disk, including the subdirectories and the files in the subdirectories.

Step 3   Press **Enter**

```
A:\FILE2.FP
A:\FILE2.SWT
A:\FILE3.CZG
A:\FILE3.FP
A:\FILE3.SWT
A:\FILE4.FP

    1,213,952 bytes total disk space
        4,096 bytes in 8 directories
       78,336 bytes in 73 user files
    1,131,520 bytes available on disk

          512 bytes in each allocation unit
        2,371 total allocation units on disk
        2,210 available allocation units on disk

      655,360 total bytes memory
      606,336 bytes free
```

```
Instead of using CHKDSK, try using SCANDISK. SCANDISK can reliably detect
and fix a much wider range of disk problems. For more information,
type HELP SCANDISK from the command prompt.


A:\>_
```

WHAT'S HAPPENING? When you pressed Enter, you allowed the command to continue executing, so the display continued scrolling. You also got the statistical and memory information at the end of the display for all the files on the disk. If you wish to use the command on a drive other than the default drive, all you need to do is specify another drive and use the /V parameter. For instance, you could key in A:\>CHKDSK C:/V. However, since the display on a hard disk is typically so large, it is not as useful as you would like. Introduced in DOS 5.0, the DIR command was enhanced with the /S parameter. This parameter allows you to look at all your subdirectories on any disk. Furthermore, the DIR command has the /P parameter to pause the display. CHKDSK does not.

Step 4   Key in the following: A:\>**DIR** /**S** /**P** Enter

```
Volume in drive A is DATADISK
 Volume Serial Number is 2F26-1901

Directory of A:\

POLYSCI        <DIR>         06-20-94   5:59p
APR        99            71 11-23-95  10:42a
STEVEN     FIL           42 11-23-94   7:13a
JAN        99            72 11-23-95  10:41a
MAR        99            70 11-23-95  10:42a
MARCH      FIL           70 11-23-95  10:42a
APRIL      NEW           70 01-23-93  11:49a
GOODBYE    NEW           32 11-23-94   7:07a
BONJOUR    NEW           51 10-12-94   7:09a
JANUARY    NEW           71 01-23-93  11:48a
MARCH      NEW           69 01-23-93  11:49a
JAN        BUD           72 11-23-95  10:41a
MAR        BUD           70 11-23-95  10:42a
APR        BUD           71 11-23-95  10:42a
JAN        OLD           32 11-23-94   7:07a
MARCH      TXT           70 11-23-95  10:42a
JANUARY    TXT           72 11-23-95  10:41a
APR        TST           71 11-23-95  10:42a
Press any key to continue . . .
```

WHAT'S HAPPENING? So far it looks like the standard DIR display.

Step 5   Press Enter

Step 6   Press Enter

```
(continuing A:\)
FILE3    SWT             18 12-06-94  10:47a
FILE4    FP              18 12-06-94  10:47a
        42 file(s)         44,512 bytes

Directory of A:\CLASS

    .            <DIR>        06-21-94   1:02a
    ..           <DIR>        06-21-94   1:02a
JAN      PAR             72 11-23-95  10:41a
FEB      PAR             74 11-23-95  10:41a
JAN      ABC             72 11-23-95  10:41a
FEB      ABC             74 11-23-95  10:41a
MAR      ABC             70 11-23-95  10:42a
APR      ABC             71 11-23-95  10:42a
MAR      PAR             70 11-23-95  10:42a
APR      PAR             71 11-23-95  10:42a
JAN      FIL             71 11-23-95  10:42a
MAR      FIL             70 11-23-95  10:42a
        12 file(s)            715 bytes

Directory of A:\POLYSCI

Press any key to continue . . .
```

WHAT'S HAPPENING? This parameter allows you to view the files in all your directories and pause the display.

Step 7   Press Enter until you reach the system prompt.

Step 8   Key in the following: A:\>**DIR *.TXT /S**

```
A:\>DIR *.TXT /S

  Volume in drive A is DATADISK
  Volume Serial Number is 2F26-1901

  Directory of A:\

MARCH    TXT             70 11-23-95  10:42a
JANUARY  TXT             72 11-23-95  10:41a
        2 file(s)            142 bytes

Directory of A:\TRIP
```

```
    FEBRUARY TXT                74 11-23-95  10:41a
              1 file(s)                 74 bytes

  Total files listed:
              3 file(s)                216 bytes
                          1,131,520 bytes free

    A:\>
```

WHAT'S HAPPENING? This command allows you to be even more specific and locate a file anywhere on the disk by searching all the subdirectories. Thus, DIR /S supplants CHKDSK /V in its ability to show every file on the disk in every subdirectory.

The CHKDSK /V command will also show you any hidden files, but again the new parameters in the DIR command are better for that purpose. By using the /A parameter (attribute) with the attribute you wish, you can determine what you will see. You can use D (directories), R (read-only files), H (hidden files), S (system files), A (files ready to archive), or, if you use the -, you will select all the files *except* those attributes.

Step 9   Key in the following: A:\>**DIR /AD** [Enter]

```
  A:\>DIR /AD

    Volume in drive A is DATADISK
    Volume Serial Number is 2F26-1901
    Directory of A:\

  POLYSCI       <DIR>         06-20-94    5:59p
  CLASS         <DIR>         06-21-94    1:02a
  WORK          <DIR>         06-21-94   10:30a
  TRIP          <DIR>         06-21-94   10:58p
            4 file(s)                0 bytes
                        1,131,520 bytes free

    A:\>_
```

WHAT'S HAPPENING? You selected the /A parameter and used the D attribute for directories only.

8.11 Contiguous and Noncontiguous Files

Contiguous means being in contact or touching. What does this have to do with files? As far as DOS is concerned, data is a string of bytes that DOS keeps track of by grouping it into a file. In order to manage the storing and retrieving of files, DOS divides a disk into numbered blocks called sectors. Sectors are then grouped into clusters. A cluster is the smallest unit that DOS will deal with. A cluster is always a set of contiguous sectors. Clusters on a 360 KB floppy disk are made of two 512-

byte sectors, whereas on a 1.2 MB floppy disk a cluster consists of one 512-byte sector. The number of sectors that make up a cluster on a hard disk varies depending on the size of the hard disk and the version of DOS being used, but is generally between eight and sixteen sectors. Most often, a file full of information will take up more space on a disk than one cluster. Thus, DOS has to keep track of the location of all the parts of the file that are on the disk. It does so by means of the directory and the FAT.

The FAT (File Allocation Table) keeps a record of the cluster numbers each file occupies. As DOS begins to write files on a new disk, it makes an entry in the disk's directory for that file and updates the FAT with the cluster numbers used to store that file. DOS writes the data to the disk based on the next empty cluster. As DOS begins to write the file to a disk, it writes the information in adjacent clusters. As a matter of fact, DOS wants all the file information to be next to each other and tries to write to adjacent clusters because it is easier to retrieve or store information when it is together. When this occurs, the file is considered contiguous. For example, if you began writing a letter to your United States senator, it would be stored on your disk in the manner shown in Figure 8.1.

Figure 8.1   *One File in Clusters*

The clusters with nothing in them are simply empty spaces on the disk. If you now decide to write a letter to your mother, DOS writes this new file to the next adjacent cluster, which would begin with cluster 4 as shown in Figure 8.2.

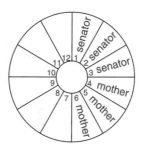

Figure 8.2   ***Contiguous Files in Clusters***

These two files, SENATOR and MOTHER, are contiguous. Each part of each file follows on the disk. Now, you decide to add a comment to your senator letter, making the SENATOR file bigger. When DOS goes to write the letter to the disk, it looks for the next empty cluster, which is cluster 7. It would appear as shown in Figure 8.3.

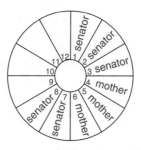

Figure 8.3   ***Noncontiguous Files in Clusters***

The parts of the file named SENATOR are separated, making this file **noncontiguous** or **fragmented**. The process becomes more complicated as you add and delete files. For example, if you delete the file SENATOR, the FAT marks clusters 1, 2, 3, 7, and 8 as available even though the data actually remains on the disk. You then decide to develop a PHONE file, shown in Figure 8.4.

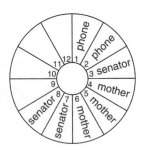

Figure 8.4 **Adding a File**

Next, you decide to write a letter to your friend Joe, to write a letter to your friend Mary, to add to the PHONE file and to add to the letter to your mother. The disk would look like Figure 8.5.

Figure 8.5 **Adding More Files**

The parts of these files are broken up and are no longer stored in adjacent clusters. They are now known as noncontiguous or fragmented files. If the disk is comprised of noncontiguous files, it can be called a **fragmented disk**. DOS will take longer to read noncontiguous files because the read/write heads must move around the disk to find all the parts of a file. You can see if files are contiguous or noncontiguous by using a parameter with the CHKDSK command.

8.12 Activity: Using CHKDSK to See If Files Are Contiguous

Note: The DATA disk is in Drive A. The A:\> is displayed.

Step 1 Key in the following: A:\>**CHKDSK MARCH.TXT** [Enter]

```
A:\>CHKDSK MARCH.TXT

Volume DATADISK     created 06-20-1994 5:55p
Volume Serial Number is 2F26-1901

    1,213,952 bytes total disk space
        4,096 bytes in 8 directories
       78,336 bytes in 73 user files
    1,131,520 bytes available on disk

          512 bytes in each allocation unit
        2,371 total allocation units on disk
        2,210 available allocation units on disk

      655,360 total bytes memory
      606,336 bytes free

All specified file(s) are contiguous

Instead of using CHKDSK, try using SCANDISK. SCANDISK can reliably detect
and fix a much wider range of disk problems. For more information,
type HELP SCANDISK from the command prompt.


A:\>_
```

WHAT'S HAPPENING? The screen display supplies all the statistical information about the DATA disk and memory. In addition, the last line states, All specified file(s) are contiguous. By adding the parameter of the file name MARCH.TXT after the CHKDSK command, you asked not only to check the disk but also to look at the file MARCH.TXT to see if all the parts of this file are next to one another on the DATA disk. Are they contiguous? The message said, "Yes."

Step 2 Key in the following: A:\>**CHKDSK *.TXT** [Enter]

```
A:\>CHKDSK *.TXT

Volume DATADISK     created 06-20-1994 5:55p
Volume Serial Number is 2F26-1901
```

```
      1,213,952 bytes total disk space
          4,096 bytes in 8 directories
         78,336 bytes in 73 user files
      1,131,520 bytes available on disk

            512 bytes in each allocation unit
          2,371 total allocation units on disk
          2,210 available allocation units on disk

        655,360 total bytes memory
        606,336 bytes free

All specified file(s) are contiguous

Instead of using CHKDSK, try using SCANDISK. SCANDISK can reliably detect
and fix a much wider range of disk problems. For more information,
type HELP SCANDISK from the command prompt.


A:\>_
```

WHAT'S HAPPENING? CHKDSK not only gave you the usual statistical information but also checked to see if all the files that have .TXT as an extension are
contiguous in the root directory of the DATA disk. By using wildcards, you can check
a group of files with a common denominator. In this case, the common denominator
is the file extension .TXT. The message on the screen verifies that all the files with
the extension .TXT are contiguous.

Step 3   Key in the following: A:\>**CHKDSK** *.* **Enter**

```
Volume DATADISK     created 06-20-1994 5:55p
Volume Serial Number is 2F26-1901

      1,213,952 bytes total disk space
          4,096 bytes in 8 directories
         78,336 bytes in 73 user files
      1,131,520 bytes available on disk

            512 bytes in each allocation unit
          2,371 total allocation units on disk
          2,210 available allocation units on disk

        655,360 total bytes memory
        606,336 bytes free

A:\CLASX Contains 3 non-contiguous blocks
A:\PERSONAL.FIL Contains 4 non-contiguous blocks
```

```
Instead of using CHKDSK, try using SCANDISK. SCANDISK can reliably detect
and fix a much wider range of disk problems. For more information,
type HELP SCANDISK from the command prompt.


A:\>
```

WHAT'S HAPPENING? The screen display shows two non-contiguous files. CLASX has three non-contiguous blocks and PERSONAL.FIL has two noncontiguous blocks. Your screen display can vary. It may not show the same files as noncontiguous. If you have no fragmented files, you would have received the message, All specified file(s) are contiguous. The CHKDSK command, followed by star dot star (*.*), checked every file in the root directory on the DATA disk to see if all the files were contiguous. The *.* represents *all* files in the root directory.

Step 4   Key in the following: A:\>**CHKDSK CLASS*.*** [Enter]

```
A:\>CHKDSK CLASS\*.*

Volume DATADISK     created 06-20-1994 5:55p
Volume Serial Number is 2F26-1901

    1,213,952 bytes total disk space
        4,096 bytes in 8 directories
       78,336 bytes in 73 user files
    1,131,520 bytes available on disk

          512 bytes in each allocation unit
        2,371 total allocation units on disk
        2,210 available allocation units on disk

      655,360 total bytes memory
      606,336 bytes free

All specified file(s) are contiguous

Instead of using CHKDSK, try using SCANDISK. SCANDISK can reliably detect
and fix a much wider range of disk problems. For more information,
type HELP SCANDISK from the command prompt.


A:\>_
```

WHAT'S HAPPENING? You are checking to see if all the files in the subdirectory CLASS are contiguous. If a subdirectory has any noncontiguous files, the screen display would look as follows:

```
A:\>CHKDSK \CLASS\*.*

Volume DATA DISK   created 03-29-1994 8:31p
Volume Serial Number is 2B24-1BE8

    1,213,952 bytes total disk space
        5,120 bytes in 9 directories
       50,176 bytes in 79 user files
    1,158,656 bytes available on disk

          512 bytes in each allocation unit
        2,371 total allocation units on disk
        2,263 available allocation units on disk

      655,360 total bytes memory
      602,240 bytes free

A:\CLASS\FILE2   Contains 2 non-contiguous blocks
A:\CLASS\FILE3   Contains 1 non-contiguous blocks
A:\CLASS\FILE4   Contains 3 non-contiguous blocks

Instead of using CHKDSK, try using SCANDISK.  SCANDISK can reliably detect
and fix a much wider range of disk problems.  For more information,
type HELP SCANDISK from the command prompt.


A:\>_
```

WHAT'S HAPPENING? What difference does it make if files are contiguous or not? It matters to the extent that noncontiguous files or a fragmented disk can slow performance. In other words, if a file is contiguous, DOS can find all its parts quickly, minimizing the amount of time the head needs to read and write to the disk. If files are noncontiguous, DOS has to look for all the parts of the file, causing the read/write heads to fly about the disk. Furthermore, the longer the disk is used, the more fragmented it becomes, slowing its performance. However, there is a way to solve the problem with a floppy-based system—format a new disk. Then place the newly formatted disk in Drive B, the old, fragmented disk in Drive A, and key in A:\>COPY *.* B:. As DOS executes the command, it finds the first file, including all the associated clusters, on the disk in Drive A and copies that file contiguously to the disk in Drive B. Next, it goes to the second file and so on. Remember, the disk in Drive B must be newly formatted. Furthermore, do *not* use the DISKCOPY command. DISKCOPY makes an identical, track for track, cluster for cluster, sector for sector copy of a disk. You want to make your newly formatted disk a contiguous copy of the old, noncontiguous disk. However, performance on a floppy disk is usually not that important because most of the time you are working on the hard disk.

Where you notice a big decline in performance is on a hard disk system. Before DOS 6.0, you could back up the hard disk, reformat the hard disk—not a task to be taken lightly—and then copy all the files back to the hard disk using the special backup and restore commands. However, that does not really solve the long-term problem because, as you continue to work with the hard disk, you are again making the files on the hard disk noncontiguous.

The solution most hard disk users opt for is to purchase a special type of utility program that in the past was not included with the DOS system utility files. The programs, referred to generically as **disk optimization** programs, rearrange the storage on the hard disk so that each file is stored in sequentially numbered clusters. Norton Utilities and PC Tools include optimization programs. These special programs make all the files contiguous by reading clusters into memory and then writing the clusters back to the hard disk contiguously. Introduced in DOS 6.0 is a command that does this task. It is called DEFRAG which you will examine shortly.

8.13 Using the /F Parameter with CHKDSK

The File Allocation Table (FAT) and directory work in conjunction. Every file has an entry in the directory table. The file entry in the directory table points to the first starting cluster in the FAT. If the file is longer than one cluster, which it usually is, the File Allocation Table has a pointer that leads it to the next cluster, then the next cluster and so on. These pointers **chain** all the data together in a file. If the chain is broken (a lost pointer), the disk ends up with lost clusters, which means that these clusters are marked as used in the FAT and not available for new data. Look at Figure 8.6. Clusters 3, 4, and 6 are a chain, but the FAT does not know to which file this chain belongs. There is no entry in the root directory. Hence, these are lost clusters.

Root Directory Table

File Name	File Extension	Date	Time	Other Info	Starting Cluster Number

File Allocation Table

Cluster Number	Status
1	in use
2	in use
3	4
4	6
5	in use
6	end

Clusters 3, 4, and 6 have data, are linked together, but have no file entry in the directory table.

Figure 8.6   *Lost Clusters*

Since these lost clusters belong to no specific file, they cannot be retrieved. The data becomes useless, yet DOS cannot write other data to these lost clusters. Thus, you lose space on the disk. This phenomenon occurs for a variety of reasons. The most common reason is that a user does not exit a program properly. When you exit a program, you should end up at the DOS system level. If you simply turn off the computer, you are interrupting the shut-down process of the application program. Often, when you interrupt this process, the data will not be properly written to the disk. Other times power failures or power surges are the cause.

If one of these events happens, when you execute the CHKDSK command, you will get a message similar to the following:

```
Volume Serial Number is 1B93-9D8B
Errors found, F parameter not specified
Corrections will not be written to disk


    2 lost allocation units found in 2 chains.
        16,384 bytes disk space would be freed
```

This message means that DOS will turn these lost clusters into files with the file name FILE000n.CHK (where n is a number such as 1, 2 or 3). However, you cannot convert these lost clusters into files unless you used CHKDSK with the /F parameter. **WARNING:** *Never* run CHKDSK /F if you are in Windows or if you are using a caching program. Should you get the Errors found message, you would key in CHKDSK /F to get the following message.

```
10 lost allocation units found in 3 chains.
Convert lost clusters to files? (Y/N)_
```

You have a choice of keying in Y for Yes or N for No. If you key in Y for Yes, Figure 8.7 is a graphic example of what happens.

Root Directory Table   **File Allocation Table**

File Name	File Extension	Date	Time	Other Info	Starting Cluster Number
FILE0000	CHK	4-15-94	11:23		3

Cluster Number	Status
1	in use
2	in use
3	4
4	6
5	in use
6	end

Clusters 3, 4, and 6 now belong to FILE0000.CHK after you choose Y.

Figure 8.7   ***Repairing Lost Clusters with /F and Yes***

Now, there is a new file called `FILE0000.CHK` in the root directory. The clusters are no longer lost. They have a file entry in the root directory table called `FILE0000.CHK`. You have recovered your data because you have the necessary components—a file name and a pointer to the clusters. You can use the TYPE command to see if there is data in `FILE0000.CHK` that you want to recover. Usually data recovered in `*.CHK` files is what is euphemistically called garbage data; it cannot be read. Typically you delete the files (`DEL \*.CHK`) because your objective is to recapture disk space.

The other alternative is to answer N to the question `Convert lost chains to clusters`. If you choose N, CHKDSK simply places an 0 in each lost cluster making the clusters available for new data. However, since the clusters never have a file entry, there is no way to see the data in the lost clusters. You have recaptured the disk space, not the data. Figure 8.8 demonstrates this.

Root Directory Table

File Name	File Extension	Date	Time	Other Info	Starting Cluster Number

File Allocation Table

Cluster Number	Status
1	in use
2	in use
3	0
4	0
5	in use
6	0

Choosing N frees up clusters 3, 4, and 6 for data but does not assign a file entry for them in the root directory table.

Figure 8.8   Repairing Lost Clusters with /F and No

The preferred method with DOS 6.2 and above is to use SCANDISK for repairing lost clusters.

8.14 SCANDISK

The SCANDISK command was introduced in DOS 6.2. Although intended as a replacement for CHKDSK, it is actually an enhancement to CHKDSK. CHKDSK does a better job of displaying information about how much conventional memory you have as well as the total number of files on a disk. SCANDISK, however, does a much better job fixing disk problems. The only problem that CHKDSK can fix is a lost cluster. SCANDISK can find and repair the following disk problems:

❑   File allocation table (FAT)

❑   File system structure (lost clusters, cross-linked files)

❑   Directory tree structure

❑   Physical surface of the drive (bad clusters)

❑   Various DriveSpace or DoubleSpace compressed disk drives

Kinds of disks that can be checked and fixed by SCANDISK:

❑   Hard drives

❑   DriveSpace drives (if DriveSpace is installed)

❑   DoubleSpace drives (if DoubleSpace is installed)

❑ Floppy disk drives

❑ RAM drives

❑ Memory cards

Kinds of disks that *cannot* be checked and fixed by SCANDISK:

❑ CD-ROM drives

❑ Network drives

❑ Drives created by using the ASSIGN, SUBST, or JOIN commands

❑ Drives created by using INTERLNK

AN IMPORTANT WARNING ABOUT SCANDISK—Do not use SCANDISK when other programs are running. It is designed for use when files on a disk are in an unchanging state. When you are using a file, MS-DOS updates the file allocation table (FAT) and the directory structure to reflect changes. Such updates are not always made immediately. If you run SCANDISK when other programs are running, files might still be open. SCANDISK interprets differences between the directory structure and the file allocation table as errors. This can result in corruption or loss of data.

It should be clear to you that you must exit Windows before running SCANDISK. What may not be clear to you is that you may have what are called memory resident programs, particularly caching programs, that are running that can affect the outcome of running SCANDISK. If you do not know if you are running memory resident programs, do not run SCANDISK on your hard disk until you learn about a clean boot (Chapter 10). You can run SCANDISK safely on a floppy disk regardless of whether or not you have a caching program running.

Some of these error fixing capabilities need explanation. Cross-linked files is one of them. **Cross-linked files** are two files that claim the same cluster.

Root Directory Table

File Name	File Extension	Date	Time	Other Info	Starting Cluster Number
MY	FIL	4-15-94	11:23		1
HIS	FIL	4-15-94	11:23		3

File Allocation Table

Cluster Number	Status
1	MY.FIL
2	MY.FIL
3	HIS.FIL
4	MY.FIL HIS.FIL
5	HIS FIL
6	MY.FIL

Figure 8.9   Cross-linked Files

In Figure 8.9, MY.FIL thinks it owns clusters 1, 2, 4 and 6. HIS.FIL thinks it owns clusters 3, 4, and 5. Thus, both MY.FIL and HIS.FIL think that cluster 4 is part of their chain. If you edit MY.FIL, the files will contain its own data as well as some part of HIS.FIL. Even worse, if you delete MY.FIL, you will be deleting part of the HIS.FIL data. Usually, to recover data from cross-linked files, you copy each file to a new name. One of the files is usually bad, but at least you have one file that is good. SCANDISK automates this process and will create two separate files for you.

Another error fixing ability that needs to be understood is the DoubleSpace or DriveSpace errors. As you work with computers, you will discover that you always seem to need more hard disk space as programs and files get bigger and bigger. One of the ways to increase disk space, other than purchasing a new hard disk, is through what are known as **disk compression** programs. A disk compression program is a software solution that increases disk space. A disk compression program does not actually make your hard disk larger, but, instead, pulls some software tricks to make it seem as if you disk is larger. For instance, if you take the following sentence, "What is the cost of the newest hard disk and the newest software?" the word "the" is repeated many times. A disk compression program essentially takes that redundant, repetitive data in a file, stores it one time and makes a note to itself how many times and where the data needs to be repeated. When you need the data, it is uncompressed. This is known as on-the-fly compression. You, as the user, only see and manipulate uncompressed data.

There are many after-market disk compression programs such as Stacker and SuperStor, but, with the introduction of MS-DOS 6.0, Microsoft included its own disk compression utility called DoubleSpace. DoubleSpace must be invoked and installed in order to be used. If it has been installed on your computer, you cannot use CHKDSK to check that disk drive because it is compressed. You must use SCANDISK. SCANDISK can also repair problems with DoubleSpace drives. Because of legal problems with the company that produces Stacker, Microsoft removed DoubleSpace beginning with MS-DOS 6.21. However, if you already owned the version of MS-DOS 6.0 or 6.2 that had DoubleSpace, you may use it. If you have MS-DOS 6.22, you have the replacement for DoubleSpace which is called DriveSpace. If you installed DoubleSpace and upgraded to MS-DOS 6.22, you can safely use DoubleSpace. If you wish, you can convert DoubleSpace drives to DriveSpace drives, but it is not necessary.

SCANDISK also provides an undo feature for the errors it corrects.

The syntax for SCANDISK is as follows:

To Check and Repair a Drive

```
SCANDISK [drive: [drive: ...]|/ALL] [/CHECKONLY | /AUTOFIX
[/NOSAVE] | /CUSTOM] [/SURFACE] [/MONO] [/NOSUMMARY]
```

To Check an Unmounted Compressed Volume File for Errors

```
SCANDISK volume-name [/CHECKONLY | /AUTOFIX [/NOSAVE] | /CUSTOM]
[/MONO] [/NOSUMMARY]
```

To Check a File or Files for Fragmentation

```
SCANDISK /FRAGMENT [drive:][path]filename
```

To Undo Repairs You Made Previously

```
SCANDISK /UNDO [undo-drive:] [/MONO]
```

In the next activity you will use some of the features of SCANDISK, but you will only use it to check your floppy disk. Remember, you cannot use SCANDISK whenever a program is running. If, for example, you were in Windows, you would have to exit Windows and return to the DOS system level to run SCANDISK. You cannot run SCANDISK on network drives.

In addition, do not use SCANDISK if you have any drives created by ASSIGN, JOIN, or SUBST. SCANDISK can be run *from* a network drive, but it *cannot* be run *on* a network drive. Please check with your instructor before doing this activity. If you are on a network, you may not be able to do this activity.

for windows 95.
↓   ↳ *Defrag*

8.15 Activity: Using SCANDISK on the DATA Disk

Note 1:   The DATA disk is in Drive A. The A:\> is displayed.
Note 2:   Please check with your lab instructor before proceeding with this activity.

Step 1   Key in the following: A:\>**SCANDISK A:** [Enter]

WHAT'S HAPPENING? The program immediately starts checking the DATA disk. As it finishes each test, it moves to the next test. As you can see, it is checking the type of disk you have, the File Allocation Table, the directory structure, and the files.

WHAT'S HAPPENING? When it has finished testing the areas mentioned above, it now asks you if you want it to test the surface of the disk (Surface Scan). It will look for any bad spots on a disk. It also tells you the length of time it will take. In this example, it will take about 5 minutes.

Step 2   Press **Y**

WHAT'S HAPPENING? As it examines the clusters on the disk, it displays a graphical picture. The bar at the bottom of the screen is telling you what percent is complete. Remember, if you were to perform this task on a hard disk, it would take a long time. In addition, you should not run SCANDISK on a network drive. When the task is complete, the following screen appears.

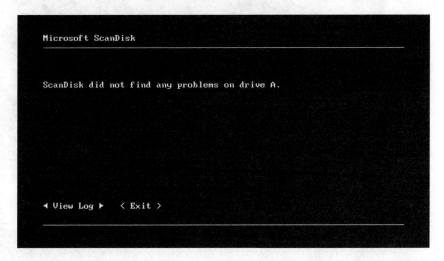

WHAT'S HAPPENING? On this disk, there are no errors. If you want, you may look at the log which is a report of what it found.

Step 3   Press **V**

WHAT'S HAPPENING? As the report indicates, there are no problems on this disk. You do not want to save the log file.

Step 4   Press **O**

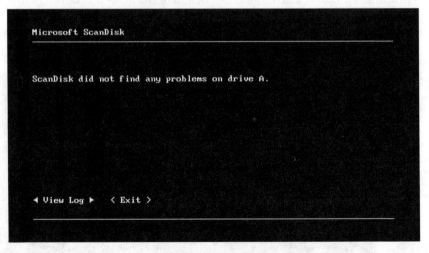

Step 5   Press **X**

```
A:\>_
```

WHAT'S HAPPENING? You have returned to the root directory of the DATA disk. Although SCANDISK is a very useful tool for fixing disk problems, CHKDSK is still useful for finding out how much room you have on a disk. Remember, if you are working with compressed drives that are created by such programs as DoubleSpace or DriveSpace, you can only use SCANDISK, never CHKDSK.

8.16 Optimizing Performance on Disks

As you add to files, add new files, or remove files, DOS places the information in the first available clusters. As discussed earlier, DOS wants to write the files contiguously, but as time goes on, this becomes impossible. Thus, all hard disk files end up in some way fragmented. Since fragmented files take longer to read and write, especially on a hard disk, performance is slowed.

Prior to MS-DOS 6.0, users had to turn to third party utility programs, such as Norton Utilities or PC Tools for a defragmenting utility program sometimes called a defragger or a disk optimization program. Sometimes, these programs are called disk compression programs but that is a misnomer. These programs do not compress data. A defragging program literally moves data around the disk so that files are contiguous, and rewrites the directory table and the FAT. Figure 8.10 shows what a disk looks like before and after you run a defragging program. EOF stands for the special End of File marker.

Before Defragmentation			After Defragmentation		
FAT Clusters	Pointers	Data	FAT Clusters	Pointers	Data
1	2	MYFILE.TXT	1	2	MYFILE.TXT
2	4	MYFILE.TXT	2	3	MYFILE.TXT
3	5	YOUR.FIL	3	4	MYFILE.TXT
4	9	MYFILE.TXT	4	EOF	MYFILE.TXT
5	7	YOUR.FIL	5	6	YOUR.FIL
6	8	THIS.ONE	6	7	YOUR.FIL
7	EOF	YOUR.FIL	7	EOF	YOUR.FIL
8	10	THIS.ONE	8	9	THIS.ONE
9	EOF	MYFILE.TXT	9	10	THIS.ONE
10	EOF	THIS.ONE	10	EOF	THIS.ONE

Figure 8.10   The Results of Running DEFRAG

DEFRAG was introduced in MS-DOS 6.0. It was licensed from Norton Utilities. DEFRAG allows you to optimize files on disk to improve disk performance.

The syntax for DEFRAG is:

```
DEFRAG [drive:] [/F] [/Sorder] [/B] [/SKIPHIGH] [/LCD | /BW | /G0] [/H]
DEFRAG [drive:] [/U] [/B] [/SKIPHIGH] [/LCD | /BW | /G0] [/H]
```

[*drive:*]	The drive letter of the disk to be optimized.
/F	Fully optimizes the specified disk.
/U	Unfragments files, leaving space between files.
/S	Sorts files by specified order.
order	
N	By Name (alphabetic)
E	By extension (alphabetic)
D	By date & time (earliest first)
S	By size (smallest first)
-	Suffix to reverse order
/B	Restarts your computer after optimization.
/SKIPHIGH	Prevents Defrag from using extended or upper memory.
/LCD	Runs Defrag using an LCD color scheme.
/BW	Runs Defrag using a black and white color scheme.
/G0	Disables the graphic mouse and graphic character set.
/H	Moves hidden files.

You can specify what you want DEFRAG to accomplish. Full optimization (/F) can take a long time because it moves files until all the files are stored contiguously on the disk. In addition, during a full optimization all files with data in them are moved to the front of the disk for fastest access time which leaves no spaces between files.

If you select only to unfragment the files (/U), DEFRAG will also make the files contiguous. However, it will not move the files to the front of the disk. It will leave spaces between the files, if necessary, to save time. This option will execute much more quickly than a full optimization.

When you execute the DEFRAG command, it will recommend the preferred defragmentation method. However, if you do not care for the recommendation, you can make your own selection.

When you run DEFRAG, you can choose to have your files physically arranged in alphabetic order by file name (/SN), in alphabetic order by file extension (/SE), by the size of the file (/SS), or by the date of the file (/SD). The first time you run DEFRAG on a hard disk it could take several hours or even overnight, especially if you have a large hard disk. If you run DEFRAG regularly, depending on your computer use, the time to execute diminishes because file fragmentation is not as great.

It is imperative that you back up your hard disk prior to running DEFRAG. DEFRAG, although an extremely useful command to improve disk performance, is also a very dangerous command because you are physically rearranging files on your disk and rewriting the directory and the FAT. For instance, if you had a power outage, in the middle of defragging your disk, you would no longer have a directory nor a FAT which means you would not be able to access *any* file on your hard disk.

You *cannot* run DEFRAG on a network drive or on any drive that was created with the INTERLINK command. However, you can use DEFRAG on compressed disks, but prior to running DEFRAG, you should run CHKDSK /F or SCANDISK to ensure that you have no lost clusters or cross-linked files. Furthermore, you should never run DEFRAG if you are in Windows or if you have any memory resident programs loaded. If you are in a lab environment, check with your instructor before proceeding with the next activity.

8.17 Activity: Using DEFRAG on the Data Disk

Note 1:   The DATA disk is in Drive A. The A:\> is displayed.
Note 2:   Please check with your lab instructor before proceeding with this activity.

Step 1   Key in the following: A:>**C:** **Enter**

Step 2   Key in the following: C:\>**CD \DOS** **Enter**

```
A:\>C:

C:\>CD \DOS

C:\DOS>_
```

WHAT'S HAPPENING? You are going to defrag the DATA disk, so you moved to the DOS directory on the hard disk. This is not a mandatory step, but you want to be sure about what it is you are optimizing. You do not want to optimize your hard disk, only the DATA disk.

Step 3   Key in the following: C:\DOS>**DEFRAG A:** **Enter**

WHAT'S HAPPENING? Since you specified which drive to optimize, the DEFRAG program went to work. You then see the following screen:

WHAT'S HAPPENING? This disk is not very fragmented, so the recommendation is to unfragment the files only. However, you can override this recommendation.

Step 4 Press the [Tab] key so the Configure button is highlighted. Then press [Enter]. If you have a mouse, you can click the Configure button.

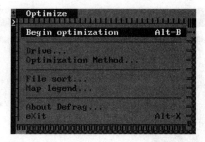

WHAT'S HAPPENING? You have dropped down the Optimize menu. You are going to select Optimization Method.

Step 5   Press the ⬇ arrow key until Optimization Method is highlighted. Press **Enter**

WHAT'S HAPPENING? You are presented with a dialog box. A dialog box either gives you information or asks for information. In this case, it is asking you what optimization method you wish to use. Full Optimization has already been selected. If Full Optimization has not been selected, you must select it. Press the ⬆ arrow key to move to the Full Optimization button; then, press the **Space Bar** bar to "check" it.

Step 6   Press the **Tab** key to move to the OK button. Press **Enter**. (If OK is not selected, press the arrow key to toggle between the OK and Cancel buttons.)

WHAT'S HAPPENING? You returned to the menu.

Step 7   Move the ⬆ arrow key until Begin optimization is selected. Then press **Enter**. (You could, instead, press the highlighted letter B. If you have a mouse, you can click Begin optimization.)

WHAT'S HAPPENING? DEFRAG gets to work. It begins by optimizing the directories. You see the following screen.

WHAT'S HAPPENING? After DEFRAG finishes with the directories, it begins with the files. If you look at the bottom of the screen, you will see messages as it does tasks. In this example, it is Writing directories... .

```
┌─Optimize──────────────────────────────────────────────Esc=Stop Defrag─┐
│•••••••••••••••••••••••••••••••••••••••••••••••••••••••••••••••••••••••••│
│••••                                                                    │
│                                                                        │
│                                                                        │
│                                                                        │
│                                                                        │
│                                                                        │
│          ┌──────Status───────┐  ┌──────Legend──────┐                   │
│          │ Cluster 134    82%│  │ ▪ - Used     ▒ - Unused │            │
│          │                   │  │ r - Reading  W - Writing│            │
│          │ Elapsed Time: 00:00:29│ B - Bad      X - Unmovable│          │
│          │ Full Optimization │  │ Drive A:   1 block = 2 clusters│      │
│          └───────────────────┘  └──────────────────┘                   │
└────────────────────────────────────────────────────────────────────────┘
```

WHAT'S HAPPENING? When DEFRAG is finished, you see the following dialog box.

```
┌─Optimize──────────────────────────────────────────────Esc=Stop Defrag─┐
│•••••••••••••••••••••••••••••••••••••••••••••••••••••••••••••••••••••••••│
│••••                                                                    │
│                                                                        │
│                 ┌────────────────────┐                                 │
│                 │ Finished condensing│                                 │
│                 │      ┌────────┐     │                                 │
│                 │      │   OK   │     │                                 │
│                 │      └────────┘     │                                 │
│                 └────────────────────┘                                 │
│          ┌──────Status───────┐  ┌──────Legend──────┐                   │
│          │ Cluster 162   100%│  │ ▪ - Used     ▒ - Unused │            │
│          │                   │  │ r - Reading  W - Writing│            │
│          │ Elapsed Time: 00:01:49│ B - Bad      X - Unmovable│          │
│          │ Full Optimization │  │ Drive A:   1 block = 2 clusters│      │
│          └───────────────────┘  └──────────────────┘                   │
└────────────────────────────────────────────────────────────────────────┘
```

WHAT'S HAPPENING? DEFRAG tells you that the task is complete.

Step 8   Press **Enter**

```
┌──────────────────────────────────────────────────────────┐
│           Optimization for Drive A: Complete               │
│                                                            │
│              You may optimize another drive or             │
│              reconfigure optimization for the              │
│                      current drive.                        │
│                                                            │
│   ┌─Another Drive─┐    ┌──Configure──┐    ┌─Exit DEFRAG─┐  │
│   └───────────────┘    └─────────────┘    └─────────────┘  │
└──────────────────────────────────────────────────────────┘
```

WHAT'S HAPPENING? You are given an opportunity to optimize another drive.

Step 9 Press the [Tab] key until Exit DEFRAG is highlighted.

```
Optimization for Drive A: Complete

You may optimize another drive or
reconfigure optimization for the
current drive.

    Another Drive        Configure        Exit DEFRAG
```

WHAT'S HAPPENING? You may now exit the program.

Step 10 Press [Enter]

```
C:\DOS>_
```

WHAT'S HAPPENING? You have returned to the system level.

Step 11 Key in the following: C:\DOS>**DIR A: /P** [Enter]

```
Volume in drive A is DATADISK
 Volume Serial Number is 2F26-1901
 Directory of A:\

POLYSCI      <DIR>          06-20-94    5:59p
CLASS        <DIR>          06-21-94    1:02a
WORK         <DIR>          06-21-94   10:30a
TRIP         <DIR>          06-21-94   10:58p
APR     99             71   11-23-95   10:42a
STEVEN  FIL            42   11-23-94    7:13a
JAN     99             72   11-23-95   10:41a
MAR     99             70   11-23-95   10:42a
MARCH   FIL            70   11-23-95   10:42a
APRIL   NEW            70   01-23-93   11:49a
GOODBYE NEW            32   11-23-94    7:07a
BONJOUR NEW            51   10-12-94    7:09a
JANUARY NEW            71   01-23-93   11:48a
MARCH   NEW            69   01-23-93   11:49a
JAN     BUD            72   11-23-95   10:41a
MAR     BUD            70   11-23-95   10:42a
APR     BUD            71   11-23-95   10:42a
JAN     OLD            32   11-23-94    7:07a
MARCH   TXT            70   11-23-95   10:42a
Press any key to continue . . .
```

WHAT'S HAPPENING? Now that the disk has been optimized, all the directories are at the front of the disk. The files, however, are arranged as they were originally found on the disk. You can change this order, if you like.

Step 12   Press **Enter** until you return to the system prompt.

```
C:\DOS>
```

WHAT'S HAPPENING? You are now going to optimize the DATA disk, but this time place the files in alphabetical order by file extension.

Step 13   Key in the following: C:\DOS>**DEFRAG A:/F/SE** **Enter**

WHAT'S HAPPENING? DEFRAG again begins by Optimizing the Directories. You then see the next screen.

WHAT'S HAPPENING? If you look at the message at the bottom of the screen, you see that it says `Sorting.....` When DEFRAG is complete, it returns you to the system level.

```
C:\DOS>_
```

Step 14   Key in the following: `C:\DOS>`**DIR A:/P** [Enter]

```
Volume in drive A is DATADISK
 Volume Serial Number is 2F26-1901
 Directory of A:\

POLYSCI      <DIR>           06-20-94    5:59p
CLASS        <DIR>           06-21-94    1:02a
WORK         <DIR>           06-21-94   10:30a
TRIP         <DIR>           06-21-94   10:58p
CLASX                 15,108 06-21-94   11:17a
APR       99              71 11-23-95   10:42a
JAN       99              72 11-23-95   10:41a
MAR       99              70 11-23-95   10:42a
WILDTHR   AAA            180 05-07-93    9:03a
APR       BUD             71 11-23-95   10:42a
JAN       BUD             72 11-23-95   10:41a
MAR       BUD             70 11-23-95   10:42a
FILE2     CZG             18 12-06-94   10:45a
FILE3     CZG             18 12-06-94   10:46a
Y         FIL              3 05-14-93   11:00a
MARK      FIL             73 04-30-94    3:35p
CAROLYN   FIL             45 11-23-94    7:13a
CASES     FIL            315 11-23-94    7:04a
PERSONAL  FIL          2,305 12-06-93    4:45p
Press any key to continue . . .
```

WHAT'S HAPPENING? Now, not only are your directories first, but your files are alphabetically in order by file extension.

Step 15   Press [Enter] until you return to the system prompt.

Step 16   Key in the following: `C:\DOS>`**CD ** [Enter]

Step 17   Key in the following: `C:\>`**A:** [Enter]

```
C:\DOS>CD \

C:\>A:

A:\>_
```

WHAT'S HAPPENING? You have returned to the root directory of the DATA disk. As you can see, DEFRAG is a useful command. You should use it on your hard disk on a regular basis, but back up your hard disk first.

Chapter Summary

1. File attributes are tracked by DOS in the directory table.
2. There are four file attributes that DOS tracks: whether a file is a system file, a hidden file, a read-only file, or the archive status of a file.
3. The ATTRIB command allows you to manipulate file attributes.
4. The FC command compares the contents of files. Both text and program files can be compared. The COMP command compares files in earlier versions of DOS.
5. The CHKDSK command allows you to get statistical information about disks and memory.
6. CHKDSK will tell you whether or not the disk has hidden files, how much room is left on the disk in bytes, how many files are on the disk, if there are any bad spots on the disk, how much total memory is in the computer, and how much memory is available.
7. Files that are contiguous have been written to the disk in adjacent clusters. Noncontiguous files are those that have been written to the disk in nonadjacent clusters and cause a fragmented disk. Using a file specification with the CHKDSK command will verify whether or not specified files are contiguous.
8. Clusters are made up of sectors. Clusters are the smallest unit written to or read from a disk. The number of sectors in a cluster can vary. Clusters on a double-sided disk consist of two 512-byte sectors. Clusters on a high-density disk consist of one 512 byte sector. The number of sectors that make up a cluster on a hard disk can vary.
9. If you use the /V parameter with the CHKDSK command, it not only checks the disk but also lists all the files and subdirectories on that disk.
10. If you use the /F parameter with the CHKDSK command, it not only checks the disk but also writes any lost sectors to files that have the .CHK file extension. You can then delete these files to free up disk space.
11. SCANDISK, introduced in DOS 6.0, is an intended replacement for CHKDSK. SCANDISK can repair more types of disk errors than CHKDSK, but SCANDISK does not give the statistical information that CHKDSK does.
12. You must not use either SCANDISK or CHKDSK /F while in Windows, on a network drive, nor on any substituted, assigned or joined drives.
13. Prior to running SCANDISK, back up your disk. In addition, do not run SCANDISK when there are any other programs running, especially memory-resident programs.
14. DEFRAG was introduced in DOS 6.0 to optimize performance of a disk by rewriting files so the clusters are contiguous. When files are contiguous, computer performance is increased.

Key Terms

Archive attribute	Disk optimization	Lost clusters
Archive bit	File attributes	Noncontiguous
Chain	Flags	Read-only attribute
Contiguous	Fragmented disks	System attribute
Cross-linked files	Fragmented files	Verbose
Disk compression	Hidden attribute	

Discussion Questions

1. What is the purpose and function of the ATTRIB command? Explain each part of the syntax diagram.
2. Give two parameters for the ATTRIB command and describe the function and purpose of each.
3. What are file attributes?
4. What effect does a file marked "hidden" have for a user? Once a file is "hidden," is there a way to "unhide" the file? If so, how can this be done?
5. What does a file marked "read-only" mean to a user?
6. What is the function of the archive bit?
7. What is the purpose and function of the FC (COMP) command?
8. Give the syntax of the FC command and explain each part of the syntax.
9. What type of statistical information about a disk and about computer memory might be useful to you?
10. What is the function and purpose of the CHKDSK command?
11. CHKDSK informs you of two types of errors. Explain.
12. What is a lost cluster? a cross-linked file? What impact does either of these conditions have on available disk space?
13. Give the syntax for CHKDSK and explain each part of the syntax.
14. What is the verbose mode? Explain the use of the /V parameter with the CHKDSK command.
15. Compare and contrast contiguous files with noncontiguous (fragmented) files.
16. Why would you use the parameter of the file name after the CHKDSK command?
17. What is the purpose and function of the /F parameter when it is used with the CHKDSK command?
18. Explain the purpose and function of the SCANDISK command.
19. Compare the SCANDISK and CHKDSK commands.
20. Explain the purpose and function of a disk compression program.
21. Give the syntax of the SCANDISK command to examine a file for fragmentation and explain each part of the syntax.
22. Explain the function and purpose of disk optimization programs.
23. Give the syntax of the DEFRAG command and explain two parts of the syntax diagram.
24. Explain the ways you can arrange files on a disk with the DEFRAG command.
25. Under what circumstances should you execute or not execute the DEFRAG command?

Chapter 9

Organizing the Hard Disk

Learning Objectives

After completing this chapter, you will be able to:

1. Explain the purpose for organizing a hard disk.
2. List criteria for organizing a hard disk efficiently and logically.
3. Explain the purpose and function of the XCOPY command.
4. Explain the purpose and function of the REPLACE command.
5. Compare and contrast the strengths and weaknesses of the COPY, XCOPY, and REPLACE commands.
6. Explain the purposes and functions of the MOVE command.
7. List three suggestions for safeguarding programs when organizing a hard disk.
8. Explain the function and purpose of utility programs.
9. Explain the function and purpose of a logical disk drive.
10. Explain the purpose and function of the three pretender commands: SUBST, ASSIGN, and JOIN.
11. Explain the purpose and function of the APPEND command.
12. Compare and contrast the APPEND command with the PATH command and determine when each should be used.

Student Outcomes

1. Reorganize the DATA disk.
2. Use the XCOPY command with its parameters to copy files.
3. Use the REPLACE command with its parameters to update and add files to subdirectories.

4. Use the MOVE command to move files and rename subdirectories.
5. Use a utility program (RNS) to rename subdirectories.
6. Use the SUBST command to substitute a drive letter for a path name.

Chapter Overview

The more efficiently and logically a hard disk is organized, the easier it becomes for you to know where to store a new file or how to access an existing one. Subdirectories (which are files grouped together under one heading) help you organize a hard disk so that you can easily locate a specific file.

An inefficient but typical hard-disk organizational scheme is to divide the disk into major application programs (i.e., word processing program, spreadsheet program, etc.) and place the data files for those applications in the same subdirectory. This organizational scheme can create problems when you try to locate a specific data file. To locate a specific data file, you have to remember under which program the data file was listed. It also makes more sense never to place program files and data files in the same subdirectory because program files rarely change and data files are always changing. The majority of people using a computer are working on projects and are using application programs to help them do their work more easily and efficiently. It makes better sense to organize the disk the way most people work—by project, not by software application.

This chapter demonstrates ways to use the hard disk efficiently. You will learn how to organize a hard disk to serve your specific needs, use the directory to keep track of the files on your disk, determine the best command to use to locate a specific file, and learn what a logical disk is and the commands that can be used with a logical disk. In addition, you will learn some useful commands to manage the hard disk.

9.1 Why Organize a Hard Disk?

The initial response of most people with a hard disk, no matter what size, is to place program files and/or data files into the root directory. When they purchase a new program, the users will either copy the files from the floppy disks to the hard disk or use the now standard SETUP or INSTALL routines to place the application program on the hard disk. These routines are programs that usually create a subdirectory for that application program and then copy the files from the floppy disks to the named subdirectory on the hard disk. Many application programs have such huge files that, when they are placed by the manufacturer on the disk, the files are compressed. In the process of copying the files to the named subdirectory, the SETUP or INSTALL programs must first decompress those program files.

When you use the DIR command, the many, many files and subdirectory names in the root directory scroll by seemingly endlessly. In fact, it becomes very difficult to know what files are on the hard disk and where they are located. You spend your time looking for data files instead of doing work with data files.

If you copy all the program files from floppy disks to the root directory of the hard disk, you are going to have a major problem knowing to which program those files belong. There are also technical reasons for not placing all files in the root directory on a hard disk. No matter what size a hard disk is, the root directory can hold a maximum of only 512 file entries. If all files are placed in the root directory, it quickly becomes full. When the root directory table is full, then DOS thinks the disk is full, even if there is actually room on the disk.

Thus, subdirectories become mandatory if for no other reason than the limitations of the root directory. Remember, when you create a subdirectory, it counts as one entry in the root directory even though the subdirectory itself may hold hundreds of files. Your only limitation becomes the physical size of your hard disk. However, once again, when users discover subdirectories, the norm is to create lump subdirectories by dividing the disk into major applications such as a word processing subdirectory, a spreadsheet subdirectory, and a database subdirectory. The installation programs encourage this tendency. For example, when you install a program like Word, using the setup program, a subdirectory is created called WORD, and all the Word program files are placed in that subdirectory.

You typically have more than one program on your computer system. The programs may have come with the computer when you purchased it or you may have purchased additional programs. For instance, a typical user might have a word processing program (Word), a spreadsheet program (Lotus 1-2-3), a database program (FoxPro), DOS, and a checkbook management program (Quicken). Thus, if you were that user, your hard disk might look like Figure 9.1.

Figure 9.1   A Typical Hard-Disk Organization

In the above figure, the ellipsis (...) represents the rest of the files. You or the program would create each subdirectory and place the program files that belong to the application program in the proper subdirectory. Some programs, like Quicken, will automatically create a subdirectory for data files.

The point is, you want to use the programs to do work. As an example, you are a sales person, and you have two products to sell: Widgets and Bangles. You use Word to write letters to clients and to make proposals. You use Lotus 1-2-3 to do budget projections for clients. You use Quicken to manage your expenses. You use DOS to manage your files and disks. You use FoxPro to manage your client's names and addresses (a database) and to work with those data files. You know enough that you know you do not want the data files (such as `report.doc` or `clients.dbf`) in the root directory. You could use the MOVE command to move the `report.doc` file to the WORD subdirectory and to move `clients.dbf` to the FOXPRO subdirectory.

However, you realize that you do not want to place your data files in the program subdirectory. There are several reasons for this. The major reason is that program files do not change. Data files are always changing as you add information or delete information. Within this process you are also adding and deleting files. Thus, when you want to backup your data files, you have to sort through many program files to do so. Furthermore, part of the rationale for subdirectories is to categorize information; data files are information. It would be easier to locate the file of interest if you know what subdirectory it might be in.

When creating file names, you always attempt to create a meaningful name. For example, you are using your database program, and you want to keep track of your clients for the BANGLES product line. You name the data file `clients.dbf`. However, you have two products to sell, BANGLES and WIDGETS. Each product has different clients, so each product requires a separate client file. Since `clients.dbf` is a meaningful file name, you now have two files you want to call `clients.dbf`. You do not want to overwrite one file with another, so you must uniquely identify each file. An efficient way to do this is to create a subdirectory called BANGLES and a subdirectory called WIDGETS and place each `clients.dbf` file in the appropriate subdirectory. It is the subdirectory name that clarifies which product client file you work with. An example of an inefficient but typical hard disk organizational scheme with subdirectories for data might look like Figure 9.2.

Figure 9.2   *Organizing a Disk by Software Application Package*

Although this organizational scheme is better than placing the data files in the root directory or in the program subdirectories, it is still very inefficient. There are too many repeated subdirectory names. In addition, every time you want a data file, you will have to remember not only what application you are working on but also where the appropriate data file is located. Furthermore, at this point you must key in long path names. For example, when you want to retrieve report.doc in Word, you would need to key in C:\WORD\WIDGETS\REPORT.DOC. In addition, when you need to find a file two or three levels down the hierarchical tree, DOS must look at every subdirectory on the way down. The heads on the disk drive are constantly going back and forth reading the entries and looking for the files.

As you become a more sophisticated user, you will find that you can use data files in conjunction with different application programs. For instance, you could use FoxPro to generate a mailing list from your clients.dbf file so that you can use it with Word to send out a form letter. When you begin doing this, you end up with data in two places: the word processing subdirectory and the database subdirectory. More importantly, when you find a new program you want to purchase, such as a presentation package like Harvard Graphics, you need to add a new subdirectory for that program and you need to add further subdirectories for your products, BANGLES and WIDGETS. Or you could decide that you want a different word processor such as WordPerfect. How do you handle those data files in the WIDGETS and BANGLES subdirectories? You do not want to delete them because WordPerfect will be able to read them. An even worse nightmare is if you, as in this example, pick up a new product line such as BEADS. Now you have to create a BEADS subdirectory under each application program. You have created a logistic nightmare finding out where the files are located and deciding what data files should be kept.

However, the real problem with this all too typical organizational scheme is the logic behind it. Remember, programs are tools. Before computers, you still used tools—a pencil, a calculator, a typewriter. But did you file your output from these tools by the tool name? When you wrote a letter using a typewriter, did you file it in a folder labeled TYPEWRITER? When you calculated some numbers with your calculator, did you place your totals in a file folder called CALCULATOR? Of course not. It sounds silly to even suggest that. But in the above organizational scheme, that is *exactly* what you are doing!

Programs are simply tools. People do not work by software package; they work by projects. Software is a tool to help do work easily and efficiently. Hence, it makes much more sense to organize a hard disk by the way you work rather than by the application package—the tool. In addition, with an efficient organizational scheme, it is easier to add and delete projects and software. The following section will recommend some guidelines to assist you in organizing your hard disk. However, you must always remember that any organization scheme you devise is to assist you in saving, retrieving, and backing up your data files easily. A good organizational scheme for one user will not work for another.

9.2 Methods of Organizing a Hard Disk

Certain criteria can give a hard disk an efficient and logical organization. These include the following suggestions:

❏ The root directory should be a map to the rest of the disk. The only files that should be in the root directory are COMMAND.COM, AUTOEXEC.BAT, and CONFIG.SYS. All other files in the root directory should be subdirectory listings. Look at the root directory as the index or table of contents to your entire hard disk. Ideally, when you execute the DIR command, you should not see more than a screenful of information.

❏ Create subdirectories that are shallow and wide instead of compact and deep. The reason is that it is easier for DOS to find files that are not buried several levels down. Also, it is much easier for you to keep track of the subdirectories when the organizational scheme is simple. Remember the old programmer's principle: KISS—Keep It Simple, Stupid. Short path names are easier to key in than long path names.

❑ Plan the organization of your hard disk. Think about the work you do and how it would be easiest for you to find it. This is especially true prior to installing new software. Create as many subdirectories as you need *before* copying files into subdirectories.

❑ Do not place data files in the same subdirectory as program files. Although you are constantly changing the information in data files, creating and deleting data files, you rarely, if ever, create or delete program files.

❑ Many small subdirectories with few files are better than a large subdirectory with many files. Remember, you are categorizing data. If you begin to get too many files in a subdirectory, think about breaking the subdirectory into two or more subdirectories. It is easier to manage and update a subdirectory with a limited number of files because there is less likelihood of having to determine on a file-by-file basis which file belongs where.

❑ Keep subdirectory names short but descriptive. Try to stay away from generic and meaningless subdirectory names such as DATA. The shorter the subdirectory name, the less there is to key in. For instance, using the subdirectory name WIDGETS for your WIDGETS data files is easy. If you simply use W, that is too short and cryptic for you to remember easily what the W subdirectory holds. On the other hand, using the name WIDGETS.FIL is a little long to key in. You rarely, if ever, use extensions with subdirectory names. Again, remember, you will be keying in these path names.

❑ Create a separate subdirectory containing all the application software you will use. This program subdirectory will be a map to all the software application programs on the disk. Popular names for this subdirectory are PROG (for programs) or BIN (for binary files).

❑ Create a separate subdirectory for the DOS system utility files. This subdirectory may be placed either under the root directory or under the program directory.

❑ Create a separate subdirectory for batch files. Batch files are files that you will learn to write. They help automate processes you do often. Place this subdirectory under either the root directory or the program directory. A popular name for this subdirectory is BATCH.

❑ Create a subdirectory called UTILS (utilities) in which you will create further separate subdirectories for each utility program you own or purchase. As you work with computers, you start collecting utility software. Utility software programs provide commonly needed services. Examples of these include Norton Utilities, PC Tools, and shareware that you might acquire. In many instances, software utility and shareware packages have similar file names, making it imperative that each has its own separate and readily identifiable subdirectory. You can place this subdirectory either under the root directory or under the program directory.

❑ Learn how to use the application package and also learn how the application package works. For instance, find out if the application package assigns a file extension. Lotus 1-2-3 assigns an extension of `.WK1` for its files, whereas WordPerfect 5.1 does not assign a file extension. If an application does not assign file extensions to data files, you can be extremely flexible and create file extensions that will apply to the work that you do with that application program's data files. For instance, you could assign the file extension `.LET` to WordPerfect data files that deal with all your correspondence or `.MYS` for WordPerfect data files that deal with a mystery book you are writing.

❑ Find out how the application package works with subdirectories. For instance, does it recognize subdirectories for data files? Some do and some do not. Although you are going to learn some DOS tricks to force applications to recognize subdirectories, there are application packages that insist on being directly off the root directory. If that is the case, you have no choice but to place them in the root directory.

❑ Analyze the way you work. If you always use an application program's default data directory when you save and retrieve files, then organizing your hard disk around projects will not work for you. In that case, perhaps you do want to create data directories. Figure 9.3 is another way to organize your hard disk.

Figure 9.3   Another Organizational Scheme

❑ Analyze your environment. If, for instance, you are in an educational environment, organization by application package makes sense. You are teaching only the package, and all data created by students will be saved to floppy disks. Hence, your focus is the package, and organizing around the application package makes sense.

An organizational scheme following the project logic and based on our sales person scenario could look something like Figure 9.4.

Figure 9.4 **Organization by Project**

In this organizational scheme, you know where all your software application programs are located. In addition, it is much easier to add a new software package or to update an existing one because all the program files are located in one place. For instance, when you want to add a presentation software application program, such as Harvard Graphics, you can create a subdirectory called `C:\PROG\HG` and install all the files in that location. Also, since this scheme is organized by project, it is easy to add a new project or delete an old one. If, for example, you are now selling beads, you can create a subdirectory called `C:\BEADS`. If you no longer are selling widgets, you can use DELTREE and eliminate the `WIDGETS` subdirectory. It is also easy to know which data files belong to what project. You also can tell which data file belongs to which program by virtue of the file extension. In this example, if you look at the subdirectory called `WIDGETS`, you know that the data files `present.doc` and `report.doc` were created with Word. You know that the data files `bud.wk1` and `94bud.wk1` were created with Lotus 1-2-3, whereas `clients.dbf` was created with FoxPro. The same would be true for the `BANGLES` subdirectory. This example also shows that you leave the `DATA` subdirectory as is for Quicken because that is where Quicken prefers the data files.

This, of course, is not the only way to organize a hard disk. You can organize your hard disk any way you wish, but there should be organization. Although it may take some time in the beginning, ultimately organization will make more effective use of the hard disk. The two major considerations for any organizational scheme are first, how do you work, and second, how do the application programs work?

9.3   Organizing a Disk

Most users do not begin with an organized hard disk. What may seem organized to one user is chaos to another. In this instance the user needs to reorganize the hard disk, a process that can be done without reformatting the hard disk. To master this process, you are going to take the DATA disk and reorganize it. This exercise will give you some idea of how the process works without having to worry about inadvertently deleting files from the hard disk. Prior to reorganizing it, however, you will make a backup copy of the DATA disk.

9.4   Activity: Making a Copy of the DATA Disk

Note 1:   The `C:\>` is displayed and the DATA disk is in Drive A. The path is set to `\DOS`.

Note 2:   You will also have a blank disk or one you no longer want. Remember, with DISKCOPY you must use identical media. See Table 9.1.

DATA Disk Media Types	Needed Blank Disk Media Types
5¼-inch 360 KB DS/DD	5¼-inch 360 KB DS/DD
5¼-inch 1.2 MB DS/HD	5¼-inch 1.2 MB DS/HD
3½-inch 720 KB DS/DD	3½-inch 720 KB DS/DD
3½-inch 1.44 MB DS/HD	3½-inch 1.44 MB DS/HD

Figure 9.1   ***Floppy Disk Media Types***

Step 1   Key in the following: `C:\>`**DISKCOPY A: A:** Enter

```
C:\>DISKCOPY A: A:

Insert SOURCE diskette in drive A:

Press any key to continue . . .
```

WHAT'S HAPPENING? Since the DATA disk is the SOURCE disk, it is already in the proper drive. If it is not, place it there.

Step 2   Press **Enter**

```
C:\>DISKCOPY A: A:

Insert SOURCE diskette in drive A:

Press any key to continue . . .

Copying 80 tracks, 15 sectors per track, 2 side(s)

Reading from source diskette . . .

Insert TARGET diskette in drive A:

Press any key to continue . . .
```

Step 3   Remove the DATA disk from Drive A. Get a blank disk. Write on the label BACKUP DATA disk. Apply the label to the disk. Insert this blank disk in Drive A. Press any key.

```
C:\>DISKCOPY A: A:

Insert SOURCE diskette in drive A:

Press any key to continue . . .

Copying 80 tracks, 15 sectors per track, 2 side(s)

Reading from source diskette . . .

Insert TARGET diskette in drive A:

Press any key to continue . . .

Writing to target diskette . . .

Do you wish to write another duplicate of this disk (Y/N)?
```

Step 4   Press **N**

```
Volume Serial Number is 1DE0-0B39

Copy another diskette (Y/N)?_
```

Step 5   Press **N**

```
Copy another diskette (Y/N)? N

C:\>_
```

WHAT'S HAPPENING? You made a backup of the DATA disk.

Step 6   Remove the BACKUP DATA disk and put it in a safe place. Insert the
          DATA disk into Drive A.

WHAT'S HAPPENING? Now, you can safely work on the DATA disk because you
have a backup copy of it.

9.5   Organizing the DATA Disk

The DATA disk has minimal organization. The . . . represents file names. (Note: If
you did not do all the chapter activities, your disk could look different.) Its structure
is as follows:

In addition to organizing this disk, you are also going to copy some programs from
the \DOS6BK directory to the disk so that there will be programs as well as data files
on it. At this moment, you really cannot tell what is on this disk. In addition, there
are so many files in the root directory that when you key in DIR, you see many, many

files scrolling by on the screen. Therefore, you are going to reorganize the disk so that it will be easier to manage. When complete, the new structure will look as follows:

You are going to create the necessary subdirectories and copy the appropriate files to the correct subdirectories. The PROG subdirectory will be the map to the programs on the DATA disk. In the PROG subdirectory you will have the subdirectory GAMES for the different games you will copy from the \DOS6BK directory and UTILS for the RNS.EXE program. In addition, you are going to copy the MEDIA directory with its subdirectories from the \DOS6BK subdirectory to the DATA disk.

9.6 Activity: Setting up the PROG Subdirectory

Note: The DATA disk is in Drive A. The C:\> is displayed as the default drive and the default directory.

Step 1   Key in the following: C:\>**A:** [Enter]

Step 2   Key in the following: A:\>**MD PROG** [Enter]

Step 3   Key in the following: A:\>**MD PROG\GAMES** [Enter]

Step 4   Key in the following: A:\>**MD PROG\UTILS** [Enter]

```
C:\>A:

A:\>MD PROG

A:\>MD PROG\GAMES
```

```
A:\>MD PROG\UTILS

A:\>_
```

WHAT'S HAPPENING? You created a generic program subdirectory and identified the specific subdirectories that reflect the programs on the DATA disk. Now you need to copy the proper files to the proper subdirectory and, if necessary, delete them from their original location.

Step 5   Key in the following:

         A:\>**COPY C:\DOS6BK\GAMES\M*.* PROG\GAMES** Enter

```
A:\>COPY C:\DOS6BK\GAMES\M*.* PROG\GAMES
C:\DOS6BK\GAMES\MLSHUT.DOC
C:\DOS6BK\GAMES\MLSHUT.EXE
C:\DOS6BK\GAMES\MAZE.EXE
        3 file(s) copied

A:\>_
```

WHAT'S HAPPENING? You copied all the programs that begin with M from the \DOS6BK\GAMES directory to the PROG\GAMES subdirectory on the DATA disk.

Step 6   Key in the following: A:\>**DIR C:\DOS6BK\GAMES** Enter

```
A:\>DIR C:\DOS6BK\GAMES

 Volume in drive C has no label
 Volume Serial Number is 1CD1-5E42
 Directory of C:\DOS6BK\GAMES

.               <DIR>         01-14-95   10:32a
..              <DIR>         01-14-95   10:32a
MLINK           <DIR>         01-14-95   10:32a
CHEK            <DIR>         01-14-95   10:32a
MLSHUT   DOC        15,049    08-14-89   10:48p
MLSHUT   EXE        43,776    08-14-89   10:31p
MAZE     EXE        34,645    05-09-89    3:51p
LS       PAS         8,404    06-23-89   11:41p
LS       DOC         2,611    06-23-89   11:34p
LS       EXE        12,576    06-23-89   11:40p
3DTICTAC EXE        37,760    10-08-85   11:13p
ARGH     DOC         8,729    08-19-90    4:00a
ARGH     EXE        69,728    08-19-90    4:00a
       13 file(s)          233,278 bytes
                        82,214,912 bytes free

A:\>_
```

WHAT'S HAPPENING? When you used the COPY command and requested all the files that begin with M, the subdirectory called MLINK and its files were not copied to the DATA disk. COPY only copies files, not subdirectories. What if you wanted to copy a subdirectory structure such as MEDIA from the DOS6BK directory to the DATA disk? It seems very time-consuming and inconvenient to key in all the necessary commands—MD \MEDIA, MD \MEDIA\BOOKS, MD \MEDIA\TV, and MD \MEDIA\MOVIES—and then issue the COPY command for the files in each subdirectory. There must be an easier way to copy a directory structure and its files. There is. You can use the XCOPY command.

9.7 The XCOPY Command

Although COPY is a useful internal command, it has some drawbacks as you have seen. COPY copies one file at a time, even with wildcards, so it is a slow command. In addition, you cannot copy a subdirectory structure. If you have disks with different formats such as a 3½-inch and a 5¼-inch, you cannot use DISKCOPY because the media types must be the same. You can, however, use XCOPY. When DOS 3.2 was released the XCOPY command was added to the DOS system utility programs. Unlike COPY, XCOPY is an external command that allows you to copy files that exist in different subdirectories, as well as to copy the contents of a subdirectory including both files and subdirectories beneath the parent subdirectory. It allows you to specify a drive as a source and assumes you want to copy all files on the drive in the default directory. With XCOPY you can copy files created on or after a certain date, or files with the archive bit set. In MS-DOS 6.2, overwrite protection was added so that, if there is a file with the same name, XCOPY will ask you before you overwrite the destination file with the source file. Furthermore, XCOPY operates faster than the COPY command. The COPY command reads and copies one file at a time, even if you use wildcards. XCOPY first reads all the source files into memory and subsequently copies them as one group of files. XCOPY will not copy system or hidden files. The syntax is:

```
XCOPY source [destination] [/A | /M] [/D:date] [/P] [/S] [/E] [/V] [/W]
```

The parameters include the following definitions:

source	Specifies the file(s) to copy.
destination	Specifies the location and/or name of new files.
/A	Copies files with the archive attribute bit set to 1 and does not change the attribute of the source files. These are files that have been either created or modified since the last backup.
/M	Copies files with the archive attribute set. Most often the archive bit is set by the program being run. If the archive bit is set to 0, it means that the file has already been backed up and has not been changed since the last backup.

/D:*date*   Copies files changed on or after the specified
                 date. The *date* parameter is entered as:
                 /D:mm-dd-yy. A specific date such as November 23,
                 1995 would look like: /D:11-23-95.
/P   Prompts you before creating each destination file
                 with a Y or N.
/S   Copies directories and subdirectories, except
                 empty ones. Copies files in the source directory
                 and in all subdirectories beneath the starting
                 directory maintaining the same tree structure of
                 the parent. If you do not include the /S
                 parameter, DOS stops copying after the first
                 subdirectory. If you wish to include any empty
                 subdirectories, you must also include the /E
                 parameter.
/E   Creates a subdirectory on the target disk even if
                 there are no files in it.
/V   Verifies each new file.
/W   Prompts you to press any key before copying.
/Y   Suppresses prompting to confirm you want to
                 overwrite existing destination file. If you do
                 not want to be prompted for every file overwrite
                 confirmation, you would use this parameter. This
                 is new in MS-DOS 6.2.
/-Y   Causes prompting to confirm you want to overwrite
                 existing destination file. Also new in MS-DOS
                 6.2. This is the default setting.

9.8 Activity: Using the XCOPY Command

Note: You have the DATA disk in Drive A with the A:\> displayed.

Step 1   Key in the following: A:\>**DIR C:\DOS6BK\MEDIA** [Enter]

Step 2   Key in the following: A:\>**DIR C:\DOS6BK\MEDIA\BOOKS** [Enter]

```
Directory of C:\DOS6BK\MEDIA

     .           <DIR>         12-06-93   10:32a
     ..          <DIR>         12-06-93   10:32a
MOVIES           <DIR>         12-06-93   10:32a
TV               <DIR>         12-06-93   10:32a
BOOKS            <DIR>         12-06-93   10:32a
        5 file(s)                 0 bytes
                      81,895,424 bytes free


A:\>DIR C:\DOS6BK\MEDIA\BOOKS

  Volume in drive C has no label
```

```
Volume Serial Number is 1CD1-5E42
Directory of C:\DOS6BK\MEDIA\BOOKS

.              <DIR>        12-06-93  10:32a
..             <DIR>        12-06-93  10:32a
AME-LIT  BKS            186 05-07-94   4:44p
MYSTERY  BKS            190 05-07-94   4:44p
PULITZER BKS            382 05-07-94   4:45p
        5 file(s)              758 bytes
                      81,895,424 bytes free

A:\>_
```

WHAT'S HAPPENING? As you can see, the MEDIA subdirectory has three subdirectories: BOOKS, TV, and MOVIES. Each subdirectory has files in it as well. If you were going to use the COPY command to recreate this structure on your DATA disk, you would have to create the directories with the MD command, and then copy the files in the BOOKS, TV, and MOVIES subdirectories. XCOPY can do all this work for you. You are still copying files, but you can consider that XCOPY is a smart COPY command. When working with computers, you want the computer to do the work, if possible. Remember that XCOPY is an external command, so you *must* have the path set to where the DOS system utility files are located.

Step 3 Key in the following:

A:\>**XCOPY C:\DOS6BK\MEDIA MEDIA /S** Enter

```
A:\>XCOPY C:\DOS6BK\MEDIA MEDIA /S
Does MEDIA specify a file name
or directory name on the target
(F = file, D = directory)?_
```

WHAT'S HAPPENING? You asked XCOPY to copy all the files from the DOS6BK\MEDIA subdirectory located on the hard disk to the \MEDIA subdirectory under the root directory of the DATA disk. In this case, XCOPY is a smart command. It asks you if you want to place all these files in one file or to create a subdirectory structure. In this case, you want to create the subdirectory structure. The /S parameter means to copy *all* the subdirectories and their files to the MEDIA subdirectory on the DATA disk. XCOPY is a command that does not care where you place the /S. The command could have been written as XCOPY /S C:\DOS6BK\MEDIA MEDIA, and it would also be correct.

Step 4 Key in the following: **D**

```
A:\>XCOPY C:\DOS6BK\MEDIA MEDIA /S
Does MEDIA specify a file name
or directory name on the target
(F = file, D = directory)?D
Reading source file(s)...
```

```
C:\DOS6BK\MEDIA\MOVIES\DRAMA.MOV
C:\DOS6BK\MEDIA\MOVIES\MUSIC.MOV
C:\DOS6BK\MEDIA\MOVIES\OTHER.MOV
C:\DOS6BK\MEDIA\TV\COMEDY.TV
C:\DOS6BK\MEDIA\TV\DRAMA.TV
C:\DOS6BK\MEDIA\BOOKS\AME-LIT.BKS
C:\DOS6BK\MEDIA\BOOKS\MYSTERY.BKS
C:\DOS6BK\MEDIA\BOOKS\PULITZER.BKS
        8 File(s) copied

A:\>_
```

WHAT'S HAPPENING? Since you included the /S parameter, XCOPY copied all the files from the subdirectory \DOS6BK\MEDIA, including the subdirectories called BOOKS, TV, and MOVIES and their contents.

Step 5   Key in the following: A:\>**DIR MEDIA** [Enter]

Step 6   Key in the following: A:\>**DIR MEDIA\BOOKS** [Enter]

```
Directory of A:\MEDIA

.              <DIR>         06-25-94   12:03p
..             <DIR>         06-25-94   12:03p
MOVIES         <DIR>         06-25-94   12:03p
TV             <DIR>         06-25-94   12:03p
BOOKS          <DIR>         06-25-94   12:03p
        5 file(s)                0 bytes
                        1,029,632 bytes free


A:\>DIR MEDIA\BOOKS

 Volume in drive A is DATADISK
 Volume Serial Number is 2F26-1901
 Directory of A:\MEDIA\BOOKS

.              <DIR>         06-25-94   12:03p
..             <DIR>         06-25-94   12:03p
AME-LIT  BKS      186 05-07-94    4:44p
MYSTERY  BKS      190 05-07-94    4:44p
PULITZER BKS      382 05-07-94    4:45p
        5 file(s)              758 bytes
                        1,029,632 bytes free

A:\>_
```

WHAT'S HAPPENING? All the files and subdirectories were copied, and retained their structures. As you can see, XCOPY is a smart command which has many useful parameters. One of the more useful ones is copying files modified or created after a certain date.

Step 7   Key in the following: A:\>**DIR C:\DOS6BK*.TXT** [Enter]

```
A:\>DIR C:\DOS6BK\*.TXT

 Volume in drive C has no label
 Volume Serial Number is 1CD1-5E42
 Directory of C:\DOS6BK

GOODBYE    TXT          32 11-23-94    7:07a
DANCES     TXT          70 08-08-95    5:34p
JANUARY    TXT          72 11-23-95   10:41a
FEBRUARY   TXT          74 11-23-95   10:41a
MARCH      TXT          70 11-23-95   10:42a
APRIL      TXT          71 11-23-95   10:42a
HELLO      TXT          52 11-23-95   10:44a
BYE        TXT          44 11-23-95   10:45a
TEST       TXT          64 03-14-93   11:07a
         9 file(s)             549 bytes
                     81,887,232 bytes free

A:\>_
```

WHAT'S HAPPENING? You want to copy all the .TXT files that were created on or after 11-23-95 to the root directory of the DATA disk. You do not want to copy the files TEST.TXT, GOODBYE.TXT, or DANCES.TXT. XCOPY allows you to make choices by date.

Step 8   Key in the following:

        A:\>**XCOPY C:\DOS6BK*.TXT /D:11-23-95** [Enter]

```
A:\>XCOPY C:\DOS6BK\*.TXT /D:11-23-95
Reading source file(s)...
Overwrite \JANUARY.TXT (Yes/No/All)?_
```

WHAT'S HAPPENING? Remember the default for XCOPY in MS-DOS 6.2 and above is to confirm overwrites. The command is telling you that JANUARY.TXT already exists. In this case, you do want to overwrite all the files.

Step 9   Press **A** [Enter]

```
A:\>XCOPY C:\DOS6BK\*.TXT /D:11-23-95
Reading source file(s)...
Overwrite \JANUARY.TXT (Yes/No/All)?A
C:\DOS6BK\FEBRUARY.TXT
C:\DOS6BK\MARCH.TXT
C:\DOS6BK\APRIL.TXT
C:\DOS6BK\HELLO.TXT
C:\DOS6BK\BYE.TXT
```

```
        6 File(s) copied

A:\>_
```

WHAT'S HAPPENING? You copied only the six files of interest, and not all nine that were in the `\DOS6BK` subdirectory and that were created before 11-23-95. Furthermore, you can use the XCOPY command to copy only files that have changed since the last time you copied them with XCOPY. Remember, XCOPY can manipulate the A attribute (archive bit).

Step 10 Key in the following: A:\>**ATTRIB *.BUD** [Enter]

```
A:\>ATTRIB *.BUD
  A              A:\APR.BUD
  A              A:\MAR.BUD
  A              A:\JAN.BUD

A:\>_
```

WHAT'S HAPPENING? The files with the extension of `.BUD` have the archive attribute turned on.

Step 11 Key in the following: A:\>**XCOPY /M *.BUD CLASS** [Enter]

Step 12 Key in the following: A:\>**ATTRIB *.BUD** [Enter]

```
A:\>XCOPY /M *.BUD  CLASS
Reading source file(s)...
APR.BUD
MAR.BUD
JAN.BUD
        3 File(s) copied

A:\>ATTRIB *.BUD
              A:\APR.BUD
              A:\MAR.BUD
              A:\JAN.BUD

A:\>_
```

WHAT'S HAPPENING? When you used the /M parameter, it read the attribute bit for the `*.BUD` files, and, as it copied each file to the CLASS directory, it turned off the archive bit. To see how XCOPY can use the archive bit, you are going to make a change to the `APR.BUD` file by using COPY to copy over the contents of `APR.BUD` with the contents of `FILE2.FP`. You will then use the ATTRIB command to see that the A bit is back on because the file contents changed. When you next use XCOPY with the /M parameter, it will copy only the file that changed.

Step 13   Key in the following: A:\>**COPY FILE2.FP APR.BUD** Enter

Step 14   Press **Y** Enter

Step 15   Key in the following: A:\>**ATTRIB *.BUD** Enter

```
A:\>COPY FILE2.FP APR.BUD
Overwrite APR.BUD (Yes/No/All)?y
        1 file(s) copied

A:\>ATTRIB *.BUD
  A           A:\APR.BUD
              A:\MAR.BUD
              A:\JAN.BUD

A:\>_
```

WHAT'S HAPPENING? Since APR.BUD already existed, COPY asked if you really wanted to overwrite it. You said yes. The APR.BUD file has changed since the last time you used XCOPY. When you used the ATTRIB command, you see that the A bit is turned back on for APR.BUD.

Step 16   Key in the following: A:\>**XCOPY *.BUD CLASS /M** Enter

Step 17   Press **Y** Enter

Step 18   Key in the following: A:\>**ATTRIB *.BUD** Enter

```
A:\>XCOPY *.BUD  CLASS /M
Reading source file(s)...
Overwrite CLASS\APR.BUD (Yes/No/All)?y
        1 File(s) copied

A:\>ATTRIB *.BUD
              A:\APR.BUD
              A:\MAR.BUD
              A:\JAN.BUD

A:\>_
```

WHAT'S HAPPENING? Once again, XCOPY informed you that you were about to overwrite an existing file in the CLASS subdirectory. You told XCOPY you wanted to do that. Notice that only one file was copied, APR.BUD, to the CLASS subdirectory. XCOPY read the attribute bit, saw that only APR.BUD had changed and, therefore, copied only one file, not all of the .BUD files. XCOPY then turned off the A attribute so that if you make any further changes to any BUD file, XCOPY will know to copy only the files that changed. In addition to the "smart" XCOPY command, there is another "smart" copy command called REPLACE.

9.9 The REPLACE Command

You have used the XCOPY command to copy files and subdirectories, to copy files specifically by date, and to copy only files that have changed since the last time you used XCOPY. There is another command called REPLACE, an external command, that also copies files. You may ask yourself why there are three commands to copy files—COPY, XCOPY, and now REPLACE. Ultimately, all three commands do the same job—copy files from one place to another, but each command has slightly different capabilities; you choose which is the appropriate command for the job. You want the command to do as much of your work as possible.

COPY has the advantage of always being available because it is an internal command. You might consider COPY the least sophisticated of the copy commands. It does the job but slowly and one file at a time. XCOPY, as you have seen, is faster (but an external command) and allows you to recreate subdirectory structures as well as choose to copy by a specific date or to copy files with the attribute bit set.

The REPLACE command is another way to copy files. But it offers different choices than either COPY or XCOPY. For instance, you often keep multiple copies of files, so that you have both the original files and backup files in case anything happens to the original. These backup files can be on a floppy disk or even in another subdirectory on the hard disk. One of the dilemmas with backup files is that you want to keep them current. You do not want to assess which is the most current file by using the DIR command to look at dates. Furthermore, if you only created one or two new files in a subdirectory, you do not want to copy all the files in the subdirectory, only the new ones or only the ones that have been updated since the last time you did a backup.

The REPLACE command, with no parameters, allows you to replace an entire set of old files with new files. It also lets you add a new file and/or replace a file that was changed since the last time you backed up the files. The syntax for REPLACE is:

```
REPLACE [drive1:][path1]filename [drive2:][path2] [/A] [/P] [/R] [/W]
REPLACE [drive1:][path1]filename [drive2:][path2] [/P] [/R] [/S] [/W] [/U]
```

The syntax is given twice to indicate which parameters cannot be used with one another. You can see in the first line /A is listed, but not /U. In the second syntax line, /U is listed, but not /A. What this means is that you cannot use /A and /U together. The parameters are as follows:

[drive1:][path1]filename	Specifies the source file or files.
[drive2:][path2]	Specifies the directory where files are to be replaced.

/A	Adds new files to destination directory. Cannot be used with /S or /U switches.
/P	Prompts for confirmation before replacing a file or adding a source file.
/R	Replaces read-only files as well as unprotected files.
/S	Replaces files in all subdirectories of the destination directory. Cannot be used with the /A switch.
/W	Waits for you to insert a disk before beginning.
/U	Replaces (updates) only files that are older than source files. Cannot be used with the /A switch.

9.10 Activity: Using the REPLACE Command

Note: You have the DATA disk in Drive A with the A:\> displayed.

Step 1   Key in the following: A:\>**DIR MEDIA\MOVIES** [Enter]

```
A:\>DIR MEDIA\MOVIES

 Volume in drive A is DATADISK
 Volume Serial Number is 2F26-1901
 Directory of A:\MEDIA\MOVIES

.             <DIR>        06-25-94   12:03p
..            <DIR>        06-25-94   12:03p
DRAMA    MOV        240 11-23-94    7:15a
MUSIC    MOV        224 11-23-93    7:11a
OTHER    MOV        212 11-23-94    7:16a
         5 file(s)             676 bytes
                     1,026,048 bytes free

A:\>_
```

WHAT'S HAPPENING? You can see that you have three files in the MEDIA\MOVIES subdirectory.

Step 2   Key in the following:

A:\>**COPY C:\DOS6BK\MEDIA\MOVIES MEDIA\MOVIES** [Enter]

```
A:\>COPY C:\DOS6BK\MEDIA\MOVIES MEDIA\MOVIES
Overwrite MEDIA\MOVIES\DRAMA.MOV (Yes/No/All)?_
```

WHAT'S HAPPENING? You did not need to key in the *.* after the source. When you use only a subdirectory name, all the files (*.*) are assumed. COPY is smarter in MS-DOS 6.2 and above. It tells you that the files already exist and asks you before it overwrites them.

Step 3   Press A **Enter**

```
A:\>COPY C:\DOS6BK\MEDIA\MOVIES MEDIA\MOVIES
Overwrite MEDIA\MOVIES\DRAMA.MOV (Yes/No/All)?A
C:\DOS6BK\MEDIA\MOVIES\MUSIC.MOV
C:\DOS6BK\MEDIA\MOVIES\OTHER.MOV
        3 file(s) copied

A:\>_
```

WHAT'S HAPPENING? You have used COPY to copy the files with the .MOV extension to the \MEDIA\MOVIES subdirectory. Now you are going to use the REPLACE command. With REPLACE you must use a file specification after the source directory; otherwise, REPLACE does not know which files you wish to replace.

Step 4   Key in the following:

A:\>

REPLACE C:\DOS6BK\MEDIA\MOVIES*.MOV MEDIA\MOVIES **Enter**

Step 5   Key in the following: A:\>**DIR MEDIA\MOVIES** **Enter**

```
A:\>REPLACE C:\DOS6BK\MEDIA\MOVIES\*.MOV  MEDIA\MOVIES

Replacing A:\MEDIA\MOVIES\DRAMA.MOV

Replacing A:\MEDIA\MOVIES\MUSIC.MOV

Replacing A:\MEDIA\MOVIES\OTHER.MOV

3 file(s) replaced

A:\>DIR MEDIA\MOVIES

 Volume in drive A is DATADISK
 Volume Serial Number is 2F26-1901
 Directory of A:\MEDIA\MOVIES


        .          <DIR>         06-25-94   12:03p
        ..         <DIR>         06-25-94   12:03p
 DRAMA     MOV           240 11-23-94    7:15a
```

```
MUSIC    MOV        224 11-23-93    7:11a
OTHER    MOV        212 11-23-94    7:16a
         5 file(s)          676 bytes
                     1,026,048 bytes free

A:\>_
```

WHAT'S HAPPENING? The REPLACE command replaced globally all the .MOV files in the MEDIA\MOVIES subdirectory with those .MOV files from the C:\DOS6BK\MEDIA\MOVIES directory, but this seems no different from simply copying files. It did you give one advantage—you were not prompted for overwrite confirmation. In the next step, you will see another difference when you copy a file that is not in the \MEDIA\MOVIES subdirectory.

Step 6   Key in the following:

A:\>**REPLACE C:\DOS6BK*.MOV MEDIA\MOVIES /A** Enter

Step 7   Key in the following: A:\>**DIR MEDIA\MOVIES** Enter

```
A:\>REPLACE C:\DOS6BK\*.MOV  MEDIA\MOVIES /A

Adding A:\MEDIA\MOVIES\AWARD.MOV

1 file(s) added

A:\>DIR MEDIA\MOVIES

 Volume in drive A is DATADISK
 Volume Serial Number is 2F26-1901
 Directory of A:\MEDIA\MOVIES

 .              <DIR>        06-25-94    12:03p
 ..             <DIR>        06-25-94    12:03p
 DRAMA    MOV        240 11-23-94    7:15a
 MUSIC    MOV        224 11-23-93    7:11a
 OTHER    MOV        212 11-23-94    7:16a
 AWARD    MOV         41 11-23-93   12:57p
         6 file(s)          717 bytes
                     1,025,536 bytes free

A:\>_
```

WHAT'S HAPPENING? In this case, because you included the /A parameter for add, the REPLACE command looked at the files in the \MEDIA\MOVIES subdirectory and realized that only AWARD.MOV was missing. Thus, it added only that file. The REPLACE command is also very useful if you change a file and only want to replace it.

In the next step, you will use the editor called EDIT, which was introduced in DOS 5.0. EDIT allows you to create and change data in a text or ASCII file. It is a very simple program (see Appendix B). You use the menu commands to create, edit, and save files. If you have a mouse, you can click the menu commands. In this example, you will be shown only the keystrokes.

Step 8   Key in the following: A:\>**COPY   C:\DOS6BK\AWARD.MOV** Enter

Step 9   Key in the following: A:\>**TYPE   AWARD.MOV** Enter

Step 10   Key in the following:

   A:\>**TYPE   MEDIA\MOVIES\AWARD.MOV** Enter

```
A:\>COPY C:\DOS6BK\AWARD.MOV
        1 file(s) copied

A:\>TYPE AWARD.MOV
Rain Man
Dances with Wolves
Platoon


A:\>TYPE MEDIA\MOVIES\AWARD.MOV
Rain Man
Dances with Wolves
Platoon


A:\>
```

WHAT'S HAPPENING? You copied the file called AWARD.MOV to the root directory of the DATA disk from the \DOS6BK subdirectory on the hard disk. You did this so that you could make changes to the file on the DATA disk, not on the hard disk. You then used the TYPE command to see the contents of the file AWARD.MOV in both the root directory of the DATA disk and the MEDIA\MOVIES directory. You can see that the contents are the same—a list of some Academy award winning movies. Now, you are going to make changes to the AWARD.MOV in the root directory.

Step 11   Key in the following: A:\>**EDIT   AWARD.MOV** Enter

WHAT'S HAPPENING? This program allows you to change data. You can use the ⬆ and ⬇ arrow keys, and the **Home** and **End** keys to move around the document. EDIT is known as a full-screen editor because you can move around the screen. If you have a mouse, you will see an arrow—known as the pointer, and, by clicking it, you can position the cursor any where on the screen.

Step 12   Press the ⬇ arrow key three times until you are on the line under *Platoon*. The cursor will be aligned with the *P* in *Platoon*. Then key in the following:

> **Driving Miss Daisy** **Enter**
> **Out of Africa** **Enter**
> **Schindler's List** **Enter**

WHAT'S HAPPENING? You made some changes to the file. Now, you want to save the file to the root directory of the disk.

Step 13   Press **Alt**

Step 14   Press **F**

WHAT'S HAPPENING? By pressing the **Alt** and F keys, you dropped down the File menu. You could have also just clicked File on the menu bar.

Step 15   Press **X**

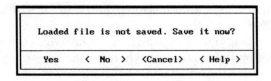

```
Loaded file is not saved. Save it now?

Yes     < No >   <Cancel>   < Help >
```

WHAT'S HAPPENING? You are presented with a dialog box that tells you that the file has not been saved. You want to save it.

Step 16   Press **Y**

```
A:\>_
```

WHAT'S HAPPENING? You changed the contents of the file AWARD.MOV using the EDIT program, saved it, and returned to the system level. Now, you are going to use the REPLACE command to update the MEDIA\MOVIES subdirectory using the /U parameter with the newly edited file.

Step 17   Key in the following:

   A:\>**REPLACE *.MOV MEDIA\MOVIES /U** **Enter**

Step 18   Key in the following:

   A:\>**TYPE MEDIA\MOVIES\AWARD.MOV** **Enter**

```
A:\>REPLACE *.MOV MEDIA\MOVIES /U

Replacing A:\MEDIA\MOVIES\AWARD.MOV

1 file(s) replaced
```

```
A:\>TYPE MEDIA\MOVIES\AWARD.MOV
Rain Man
Dances with Wolves
Platoon
Driving Miss Daisy
Out of Africa
Schindler's List


A:\>_
```

WHAT'S HAPPENING? Again, the REPLACE command selectively replaced only the file that was updated or changed since the last time you copied it. When you used the TYPE command, you could see that the correct file was updated in the MEDIA\MOVIES subdirectory. You let the command decide which files had changed since the last time you copied them. Again, you are saving yourself work by allowing the command to do the work for you. The REPLACE command gives you much more flexibility than the COPY command. It also does things the XCOPY command does not do. You now have three ways to copy files. Each has its strengths and weaknesses. You decide which command best suits your needs.

9.11 The MOVE Command Revisited

In the last activities you used XCOPY and REPLACE. Although certainly extremely useful commands, they are forms of the COPY command. These commands are excellent for day-to-day use in maintaining the organization of your disk. Indeed, when reorganizing your hard disk, you sometimes do need to copy files and/or subdirectory structures from one place to another and replace existing files. In terms of reorganizing your hard disk, you do not necessarily want to copy files and directories. What you often really need to do is either move files from one location to another or simply rename the subdirectory.

You have used the MOVE command in previous chapters to both rename directories and to move files from one directory to another. Clearly using the MOVE command is an easy way to manipulate your files. However, there is an important warning prior to moving files and directories wholesale. Moving data files and renaming data file directories are usually fairly safe and foolproof procedures which usually do not impact how your programs work. Nevertheless, moving program files and renaming program directories is not that "safe." It is not that there is a problem *per se*, but often when you install a program, the program installation routine will perform the following steps:

❑ Make note of what directory the program files are in.

❑ Modify the path with the program subdirectory name.

❑ Modify the AUTOEXEC.BAT file and the CONFIG.SYS files (you will learn about these later).

When you move program files and rename program subdirectories, you could find that, because you have changed the information, the programs no longer work. If you move program files and rename program directories, you also need to modify files like AUTOEXEC.BAT and CONFIG.SYS, and, if you are in the Windows environment, you need to modify several files. Does this mean that you should not organize your hard disk? It does not, but you must do it with caution. Some suggestions for safeguarding your programs are listed below:

1. Create your program subdirectories as suggested but use them only to install new programs in this location.
2. Know what files are affected if you rename a program subdirectory or move program files. Know what changes you must make to these files *before* you move files or rename program subdirectories.
3. A drastic, but effective, means of moving your programs or renaming the program subdirectories is to delete the old program subdirectories and reinstall your programs, giving them the new and proper location.

Now that you know the warnings, in the next activity you will move files and rename subdirectories so you can see how easy it is with data files.

9.12 Activity: Using MOVE to Organize Your Disk

Note: You have the DATA disk in Drive A with the A:\> displayed.

Step 1   Key in the following: A:\>**MOVE BON*.* POLYSCI\FRANCE** [Enter]

```
A:\>MOVE BON*.* POLYSCI\FRANCE
a:\bonjour.new => a:\polysci\france\bonjour.new [ok]

A:\>_
```

WHAT'S HAPPENING? You quickly copied the BONJOUR.NEW file to the POLYSCI\FRANCE subdirectory and deleted it from the root directory at the same time. That is what a move is.

Step 2   Key in the following: A:\>**DIR M*.*** [Enter]

```
A:\>DIR M*.*

  Volume in drive A is DATADISK
  Volume Serial Number is 2F26-1901
  Directory of A:\


MAR        99            70  11-23-95   10:42a
MAR        BUD           70  11-23-95   10:42a
MARK       FIL           73  04-30-94    3:35p
MARCH      FIL           70  11-23-95   10:42a
```

```
MARCH     NEW          69 01-23-93  11:49a
MONTHS    SAM         284 06-21-94  11:16a
MARCH     TXT          70 11-23-95  10:42a
MEDIA          <DIR>      06-25-94  12:03p
          8 file(s)          706 bytes
                      1,025,024 bytes free

A:\>_
```

WHAT'S HAPPENING? You want to move all the files that begin with M to the POLYSCI\USA directory. But what will happen to the MEDIA directory? Will it also be moved?

Step 3   Key in the following: A:\>**MOVE M*.* POLYSCI\USA** Enter

```
A:\>MOVE M*.* POLYSCI\USA
a:\mar.99 => a:\polysci\usa\mar.99 [ok]
a:\mar.bud => a:\polysci\usa\mar.bud [ok]
a:\mark.fil => a:\polysci\usa\mark.fil [ok]
a:\march.fil => a:\polysci\usa\march.fil [ok]
a:\march.new => a:\polysci\usa\march.new [ok]
a:\months.sam => a:\polysci\usa\months.sam [ok]
a:\march.txt => a:\polysci\usa\march.txt [ok]
a:\media => a:\polysci\usa\media [Unable to open source]

A:\>_
```

WHAT'S HAPPENING? The MOVE command moved the files, but was not able to move the subdirectory called MEDIA. What if you did want to move a directory? You can do it. In the next step, you are going to move the BOOKS subdirectory, which is under the MEDIA subdirectory, to the TRIP subdirectory with its directory name and files intact.

Step 4   Key in the following:

A:\>**MOVE MEDIA\BOOKS*.* TRIP\BOOKS** Enter

```
A:\>MOVE MEDIA\BOOKS\*.* TRIP\BOOKS
Make directory "a:\trip\books"? [yn]_
```

WHAT'S HAPPENING? The MOVE command knows that you do not have a subdirectory called BOOKS under TRIP, so it is asking you if you want to create one.

Step 5   Press **Y** Enter

```
A:\>MOVE MEDIA\BOOKS\*.* TRIP\BOOKS
Make directory "a:\trip\books"? [yn] y
a:\media\books\ame-lit.bks => a:\trip\books\ame-lit.bks [ok]
```

```
a:\media\books\mystery.bks => a:\trip\books\mystery.bks [ok]
a:\media\books\pulitzer.bks => a:\trip\books\pulitzer.bks [ok]

A:\>_
```

WHAT'S HAPPENING? It seems that the move was successful. Well, was it?

Step 6   Key in the following: A:\>**DIR TRIP\BOOKS** Enter

Step 7   Key in the following: A:\>**DIR MEDIA** Enter

```
Directory of A:\TRIP\BOOKS

.               <DIR>           06-25-94    8:25p
..              <DIR>           06-25-94    8:25p
AME-LIT  BKS          186 05-07-94    4:44p
MYSTERY  BKS          190 05-07-94    4:44p
PULITZER BKS          382 05-07-94    4:45p
        5 file(s)             758 bytes
                       1,024,000 bytes free


A:\>DIR MEDIA

 Volume in drive A is DATADISK
 Volume Serial Number is 2F26-1901
 Directory of A:\MEDIA

 .              <DIR>           06-25-94   12:03p
 ..             <DIR>           06-25-94   12:03p
 MOVIES         <DIR>           06-25-94   12:03p
 TV             <DIR>           06-25-94   12:03p
 BOOKS          <DIR>           06-25-94   12:03p
        5 file(s)               0 bytes
                 1,024,000 bytes free

 A:\>_
```

WHAT'S HAPPENING? The files and BOOKS subdirectory did get moved, but why is BOOKS still in the MEDIA subdirectory? What is in it?

Step 8   Key in the following: A:\>**DIR MEDIA\BOOKS** Enter

```
A:\>DIR MEDIA\BOOKS

 Volume in drive A is DATADISK
 Volume Serial Number is 2F26-1901
 Directory of A:\MEDIA\BOOKS
```

```
.            <DIR>          06-25-94   12:03p
..           <DIR>          06-25-94   12:03p
     2 file(s)                     0 bytes
                          1,024,000 bytes free

A:\>_
```

WHAT'S HAPPENING? Moving files is easy, and so was creating the subdirectory called BOOKS under the TRIP subdirectory. Nonetheless, the MOVE command has no way of removing a directory after you empty it. You must use a separate command to remove the BOOKS directory under MEDIA. You must understand how a command works. The bad news is that a command does not always do what you expect or want it to do. The MOVE command did not remove the directory, but the good news is the command will always behave the same way once you know what the "way" is. Thus, now you know that if you move files, you will need to issue another command to remove the empty directory. Another example is using MOVE to rename a directory.

Step 9   Key in the following: A:\>**MOVE TRIP*.* NEWSTUFF** Enter

```
A:\>MOVE TRIP\*.* NEWSTUFF
Make directory "a:\newstuff"? [yn]_
```

WHAT'S HAPPENING? Here, because you included the *.* after TRIP, the MOVE command assumed that you wanted to create a new directory called NEWSTUFF and move the TRIP files into it. The TRIP directory would remain in the root directory empty of files. The files would be moved to a new directory called NEWSTUFF, but this is not what you want to do. You want to rename the TRIP directory NEWSTUFF.

Step 10   Press **N** Enter

```
A:\>MOVE TRIP\*.* NEWSTUFF
Make directory "a:\newstuff"? [yn] n
Cannot move multiple files to a single file

A:\>_
```

WHAT'S HAPPENING? Because you keyed in N for no, no directory was created and no files were moved.

Step 11   Key in the following: A:\>**MOVE TRIP NEWSTUFF** Enter

Step 12   Key in the following: A:\>**DIR TRIP** Enter

```
A:\>MOVE TRIP NEWSTUFF
a:\trip => a:\newstuff [ok]
```

```
A:\>DIR TRIP

 Volume in drive A is DATADISK
 Volume Serial Number is 2F26-1901
 Directory of A:\

File not found

A:\>_
```

WHAT'S HAPPENING? You successfully renamed the TRIP directory NEWSTUFF. You may say to yourself that the MOVE command can be confusing given that, if you key it in one way, you move files, but, if you key it another way, you rename subdirectories. You might wish that MS-DOS had given you two commands—one for renaming a subdirectory and one for moving files. Well, MS-DOS did not, but there are utility programs that can do that for you.

9.13 A Utility Program—RNS.EXE

Many utility programs come with DOS. These include all the external commands such as XCOPY, REPLACE, and MOVE. As you may have noticed, each new edition of DOS comes with more utility programs. XCOPY, for instance, was not available when DOS 1.0 was introduced, primarily because XCOPY is most useful with subdirectories and the ability to create and use subdirectories did not exist in DOS 1.0. In addition to all the new commands that DOS introduces, there are also other commands that DOS has *not* included. Thus, a market has developed for commands not yet available within the standard DOS utility programs. Some of these programs are given away; others are released as shareware, and others are commercially packaged and sold. Some of the better known commercial utility software includes Norton Utilities and PC Tools. Why do computer users buy these utility programs? Each program does something useful that DOS does not yet allow you to do.

The program RNS.EXE was written by Nick Markiw and is included on the ACTIVITIES disk. This program was written and given to you when you purchased this textbook to demonstrate the use of utility programs that are not available in DOS. This utility only renames subdirectories. It does not move files. Its syntax is:

RNS [*drive:*][*path*]*oldname* [*drive:*][*path*]*newname*

9.14 Activity: Using RNS, a Rename Subdirectory Utility

Note 1:   You have the DATA disk in Drive A with the A:\> displayed.
Note 2:   In Activity 9.6, you created the PROG\UTILS subdirectory. If you did not do so then, do so now.

Step 1   Key in the following:

A:\>**COPY C:\DOS6BK\RNS.EXE PROG\UTILS** [Enter]

Step 2   Key in the following: A:\>**DIR PROG\UTILS** Enter

```
A:\>COPY C:\DOS6BK\RNS.EXE   PROG\UTILS
        1 file(s) copied


A:\>DIR PROG\UTILS

 Volume in drive A is DATADISK
 Volume Serial Number is 2F26-1901
 Directory of A:\PROG\UTILS

 .             <DIR>         06-25-94  11:58a
 ..            <DIR>         06-25-94  11:58a
 RNS      EXE        7,269 11-22-89  10:35p
        3 file(s)           7,269 bytes
                    1,016,320 bytes free

A:\>_
```

WHAT'S HAPPENING? You copied the file RNS.EXE from the \DOS6BK subdirectory to the PROG\UTILS subdirectory on the DATA disk. You should recognize that any file with an .EXE extension is a program. As you have been cleaning up the DATA disk, some of the activities included creating a subdirectory and then copying the appropriate files into it. Some of you may have thought that this was a lot of work when, in reality, all you were doing was changing the name of the subdirectory. If you want to change the name of a file, it is very easy. You use the RENAME command. DOS provides no equivalent command for renaming subdirectories until MS-DOS 6.0 and the MOVE command. If you had a version of DOS prior to that, your only choice was to create a new subdirectory and copy files into it. The RNS.EXE program allows you to rename directories in any version of DOS. Furthermore, if you do have DOS 6.0 and above, if you like this program, you can copy it to your DOS subdirectory and use RNS for renaming subdirectories and MOVE for moving files.

Step 3   Key in the following: A:\>**CD PROG\UTILS** Enter

Step 4   Key in the following: A:\PROG\UTILS>**DIR \NEWSTUFF** Enter

```
 #AN      99           72 11-23-95  10:41a
 MAR      99           70 11-23-95  10:42a
 FEB      BUD          74 11-23-95  10:41a
 FRANK    FIL          42 11-23-94   7:13a
 MAR      INK          70 11-23-95  10:42a
 FEB      INK          74 11-23-95  10:41a
 APR      INK          71 11-23-95  10:42a
 JAN      INK          72 11-23-95  10:41a
 RED      JAZ          18 10-12-94  10:40a
 BLUE     JAZ          18 10-12-94  10:40a
```

```
FUNNY     TV              180 11-23-94  10:19a
FEBRUARY  TXT              74 11-23-95  10:41a
BOOKS            <DIR>        06-19-94  11:14a
         17 file(s)            980 bytes
                        1,016,320 bytes free


A:\PROG\UTILS>_
```

WHAT'S HAPPENING? The first thing you did was change the directory to the place where the program RNS.EXE is located so that you can execute it. You could have changed the path, but since this is a one-time experiment, you do not want to do that. The second thing you did was look at the contents of the subdirectory called NEWSTUFF. You decided that NEWSTUFF was not a descriptive name for the subdirectory, and you want to change the subdirectory name from NEWSTUFF to TRIP. With DOS prior to 6.0, you would have to take four steps. First, you would key in MD \TRIP, and second, you would key in COPY \NEWSTUFF\TRIP. Then, you would key in DEL \NEWSTUFF*.*. The last step to remove the subdirectory NEWSTUFF would be to key in RD \NEWSTUFF. With DOS 6.0 and above, it is much easier. You would just key in MOVE \NEWSTUFF \TRIP. However, you are going to use the utility program RNS instead.

Step 5   Key in the following:

           A:\PROG\UTILS>**RNS \NEWSTUFF \TRIP** Enter

```
A:\PROG\UTILS>RNS \NEWSTUFF \TRIP
RNS VER. 1.05


A:\PROG\UTILS>_
```

WHAT'S HAPPENING? This seemed easy enough. Did it work?

Step 6   Key in the following: A:\PROG\UTILS>**DIR \TRIP** Enter

Step 7   Key in the following: A:\PROG\UTILS>**DIR \NEWSTUFF** Enter

```
#AN       99               72 11-23-95  10:41a
MAR       99               70 11-23-95  10:42a
FEB       BUD              74 11-23-95  10:41a
FRANK     FIL              42 11-23-94   7:13a
JAN       INK              72 11-23-95  10:41a
MAR       INK              70 11-23-95  10:42a
FEB       INK              74 11-23-95  10:41a
```

```
    APR        INK        71  11-23-95   10:42a
    RED        JAZ        18  10-12-94   10:40a
    BLUE       JAZ        18  10-12-94   10:40a
    FUNNY      TV        180  11-23-94   10:19a
    FEBRUARY   TXT        74  11-23-95   10:41a
    BOOKS          <DIR>      06-25-94    8:25p
           17 file(s)            980 bytes
                           1,016,320 bytes free


A:\PROG\UTILS>DIR \NEWSTUFF

  Volume in drive A is DATADISK
  Volume Serial Number is 2F26-1901
  Directory of A:\

File not found

A:\PROG\UTILS>_
```

WHAT'S HAPPENING? The RNS command did rename the subdirectory
\NEWSTUFF to \TRIP. It was much easier to use this command then to have to make
and delete a subdirectory and copy and delete files. Even if you have DOS 6.0 and
the MOVE command, you might prefer to separate the functions and use MOVE for
moving files and RNS for renaming subdirectories. People write utility programs
like RNS to extend the power of DOS. Although utility programs often have
overlapping commands, users still purchase more than one utility program because
each one has certain useful functions not yet available in DOS.

Step 8   Key in the following: A:\PROG\UTILS>**CD** \ Enter

```
A:\PROG\UTILS>CD \

A:\>_
```

WHAT'S HAPPENING? You have returned to the root directory of the DATA disk.

9.15 The Pretender Commands—SUBST, ASSIGN, and JOIN

Throughout this textbook, you have been acting as if you were always accessing
actual physical disk drives. If you were using your own computer, you were talking
about "real" drives. When Drive A, B, or C were discussed, they were being discussed
as devices that are physically attached to the computer via cables. These are
examples of peripheral hardware. You perceive these as physical entities.

DOS views peripherals in a much more generic way. DOS treats all devices (keyboard, monitor, disk drives, etc.) as logical devices. DOS relies on **device drivers** to handle the input/output to the peripheral hardware in a way that the device can understand. Device drivers are special files that know how to handle the device. Since DOS views physical disk drives as logical devices, you can manipulate these devices. Thus, in addition to physical disk drives, there are **logical disk drives**. Logical disk drives are not necessarily physically attached to the computer. If you have been working on a network and have been seeing drive letters such as P or F, it was not a "real" drive, but a logical drive. DOS treats a logical drive in the same way it treats a physical drive. DOS can read and write to a logical disk drive, and, therefore, application programs can read and write to logical drives. In the famous data processing words, "It is transparent to the user." This means that you were not really accessing Drive P or Drive F, but a directory on Drive C that was masked to appear as Drive P or Drive F or any other drive letter the network administrator assigned.

A logical disk drive can provide benefits to the user. In fact, networks cannot be run without logical disk drives. You, on your own computer, can also use an alias for another disk drive, or you can use a disk drive letter for a subdirectory name. DOS has three commands to take advantage of drives. The SUBST command allows you to treat a subdirectory as a disk drive or, in other words, to pretend that a subdirectory is a disk drive. The ASSIGN command reroutes requests for one disk drive to another disk drive or, in other words, pretends that one disk drive is another. Last, the JOIN command allows you to make two disk drives one disk drive or, in other words, to pretend that two disk drives are really one disk drive. These are grouped as the **pretender commands**.

There are several reasons why these commands were included with the DOS system utility files. Some older application programs know *only* about physical Drive A and/or physical Drive B and do not recognize the subdirectories on a hard disk, or even the hard disk itself. You need some way to use your hard disk with these older programs. In addition, you can use these commands as shortcuts to avoid having to key in long path names. Sometimes, older programs know about Drives A and B and a hard disk but do not recognize any other drive letters.

Today, it is not unusual to have a computer with two 3½-inch internal floppy drives (Drives A and B) and one hard drive (Drive C). Some users have one 5¼-inch external floppy disk drive (Drive D) for all those older 360 KB disks. If your application program cannot recognize Drive D, you have a real problem. You can place the 5¼-inch disk in Drive D, but the program will not be able to access the files on that disk because it cannot recognize Drive D. At times, if you have a notebook computer with two 3½-inch floppy drives and no hard drive, and you have a very large program, you may want the two disk drives to appear as one disk drive.

Although these pretender commands can assist you in solving these problems, there are pitfalls to using them. For instance, some application programs do what is called **direct read** and **direct write** to a disk drive. In this case, you cannot fool the application program with DOS; you are just out of luck. A direct read and a direct write will bypass DOS. This situation is particularly true with copy-protected programs.

Sometimes, you can fool not only DOS, but also yourself by not remembering which drive is which. If you create logical drives with SUBST or ASSIGN and then try to JOIN them together, not only is this incorrect, but DOS will behave in a confusing and unpredictable manner. There are also other commands that cannot be used when SUBST, JOIN, or ASSIGN are in effect. In fact, you cannot use SUBST, JOIN, or ASSIGN on network drives since the network already has a scheme to assign drive letters that supersedes the DOS commands. Furthermore, you cannot use JOIN or ASSIGN if you are using Windows, even if you are not on a network. In light of this, in MS-DOS 6.0, ASSIGN and JOIN are no longer included on the disk. If you upgraded to DOS 6.0 or 6.22, if JOIN and ASSIGN were already in the DOS subdirectory, the install program did not delete them. If you would like ASSIGN and JOIN, you need to order what is called the MS-DOS Resource Kit. This kit includes the technical reference manual and supplementary disks. The supplementary disks will include ASSIGN and JOIN.

In general, SUBST is the intended replacement for ASSIGN and works fairly well. If you have a really stubborn older program, you might find that ASSIGN is the only command that will work. JOIN, on the whole, will not be missed. If you have some special circumstances, it too can be useful. If you use any of these pretender commands, use them one at a time. Do not use ASSIGN, SUBST, and JOIN at the same time. You will not only confuse yourself, but DOS as well. In fact, in this text, JOIN and ASSIGN will be discussed but there will be no activities to follow.

In the next activity, you will take a look at SUBST. Please check with your lab instructor prior to doing this activity. The SUBST drive letter you will be using will be Drive E:. Most networks, but not all, do not start drive letter assignments until Drive F. Thus, you can actually use Drive E, but again this varies from network to network. Do check with your lab instructor before proceeding. In addition, if you have two floppy drives, you can try this activity using Drive A and Drive B. Even on a network, this will work. But again, take no steps unless cleared by your lab instructor.

9.16 The SUBST Command

SUBST is an external command that allows you to substitute a drive letter for a path name. This command can be used to shorten keying in a long path name or with programs that do not recognize a subdirectory but do recognize a disk drive. You can also use SUBST if you need information from a drive that a program does not recognize. Be cautious when you use SUBST with a network drive. You may not be able to use SUBST on the network.

On a stand-alone system, when you use SUBST and while a substitution is in effect, be very careful when using CD, MD, RD, PATH, APPEND, and LABEL. Furthermore, do not use the commands CHKDSK, FORMAT, DISKCOPY, DISKCOMP, FDISK, PRINT, BACKUP, or RESTORE while a substitution is in effect. You may use SUBST with Windows, if you perform the substitution *prior* to executing Windows. The syntax for the SUBST command is:

```
SUBST [drive1: [drive2:]path]
```

or to undo a substitution:

```
SUBST    drive1:    /D
```

and to see what you have substituted:

```
SUBST
```

9.17 Activity: Using SUBST

Note 1:   You have the DATA disk in Drive A with the A:\> displayed.
Note 2:   Do not proceed with this activity until you have checked with your lab
           instructor.

Step 1   Key in the following:

          A:\>**TYPE MEDIA\MOVIES\DRAMA.MOV** [Enter]

```
A:\>TYPE MEDIA\MOVIES\DRAMA.MOV

CAROLYN'S FAVORITE MOVIE DRAMAS

Citizen Kane
The African Queen
Gone With the Wind
Flame and the Arrow
One Flew Over the Cuckoo's Nest
Chinatown
The Bridge on the River Kwai
The Women
An Officer and a Gentleman
Casablanca


A:\>_
```

WHAT'S HAPPENING? You displayed the contents of the file called DRAMA.MOV
in the subdirectory called MOVIES under the subdirectory called MEDIA in the root
directory. Even though you left the first backslash off, since the default directory is
the root, you still have a lot of keying in to do. If you use the SUBST command, you
need to key in only the logical drive letter. In this example, E: is selected. Be sure
to use a drive letter that is not being used by a physical disk drive.

Step 2   Key in the following: A:\>**SUBST E: A:\MEDIA\MOVIES** [Enter]

Step 3   Key in the following: A:\>**TYPE E:DRAMA.MOV** Enter

```
A:\>SUBST E: A:\MEDIA\MOVIES

A:\>TYPE E:DRAMA.MOV

CAROLYN'S FAVORITE MOVIE DRAMAS

Citizen Kane
The African Queen
Gone With the Wind
Flame and the Arrow
One Flew Over the Cuckoo's Nest
Chinatown
The Bridge on the River Kwai
The Women
An Officer and a Gentleman
Casablanca


A:\>_
```

WHAT'S HAPPENING? You first set up the substitution. Then, the SUBST command could be executed because the path was set to C:\DOS. You said substitute the letter E for the path name A:\MEDIA\MOVIES. Now, every time you want to refer to the subdirectory called A:\MEDIA\MOVIES, you can just use the letter E:, which refers to logical Drive E:. You can use this logical drive just like a physical drive. You can use the DIR command, the COPY command, the DEL command, and any other DOS command you wish.

Step 4   Key in the following: A:\>**SUBST** Enter

```
A:\>SUBST
E: => A:\MEDIA\MOVIES

A:\>_
```

WHAT'S HAPPENING? SUBST, when used alone, tells you what substitution you have used. If you are using DOS 4.0 or above, there is an additional command that will indicate the same information—the internal command called TRUENAME. It is an undocumented command. An **undocumented command** is one that exists but is not listed in the manual. It is not unusual for software to have undocumented features. The programmers may have decided that the new feature was not quite ready or not quite perfect. It can be used, but there are no guarantees that it will work properly. TRUENAME does exactly what it says. It gives you the actual drive and/or path name of whatever you have substituted, assigned, or joined. It has the advantage of being an internal command.

Step 5   Key in the following: A:\>**TRUENAME E:** [Enter]

```
A:\>TRUENAME E:

A:\MEDIA\MOVIES

A:\>_
```

WHAT'S HAPPENING? As you can see, the TRUENAME command did indeed tell you the true name of E:.

Step 6   Key in the following: A:\>**SUBST E: /D** [Enter]

Step 7   Key in the following: A:\>**SUBST** [Enter]

```
A:\>SUBST E: /D

A:\>SUBST

A:\>_
```

WHAT'S HAPPENING? The /D parameter disabled or undid the SUBST command so that logical Drive E no longer refers to the subdirectory A:\MEDIA\MOVIES. The SUBST that was keyed in with no parameters showed that no substitution was in effect. Most software today is quite sophisticated. For instance, if you have an older program that comes on a 5¼-inch disk and insists on running from Drive A, but Drive A is a 3½ inch disk drive, you can solve the problem with SUBST. The biggest offenders are game programs and older installation programs. The solution would be as follows:

```
SUBST  A:  B:\
```

This command would reroute every disk request intended for Drive A to Drive B. The only thing tricky about this command is that you must include the \ after the B:. SUBST does not recognize just a drive letter as a destination.

9.18 The ASSIGN Command

ASSIGN is no longer included with MS-DOS 6.0 and above. If you upgraded and ASSIGN was already in the DOS subdirectory, the install program did not delete it. If you would like ASSIGN, you need to order the MS-DOS Resource Kit. The supplementary disks will include ASSIGN.

ASSIGN, an external command, allows you to assign one disk drive to another disk drive. ASSIGN works only with physical disk drives. Thus, both drives must physically exist. Logical drives cannot be assigned. You cannot use ASSIGN on a network. If you are working on a stand-alone computer system, you can.

When you assign Drive A to Drive C, every time DOS or an application program wants to access Drive A, it will instead look to Drive C. This command is extremely useful for older programs that do not recognize a hard drive. They want to look only on a floppy disk drive. Thus, by using the command ASSIGN A=C, every time the program looks for a file on Drive A, it will look instead on Drive C. ASSIGN refers to drive letters only and cannot specify a drive with a subdirectory.

Do not assign the drive letter of the hard disk to another drive. If possible, use SUBST instead of ASSIGN. While an assignment is in effect, be very careful using CD, MD, RD, PATH, or APPEND. Do not use the commands FORMAT, DISKCOPY, DISKCOMP, FDISK, FORMAT, PRINT, BACKUP, RESTORE, LABEL, JOIN or SUBST while an assignment is in effect. Furthermore, be very careful with the ASSIGN command. If you assign an application disk to C:, you will not be able to get back to \DOS. DOS will not recognize the ASSIGN because it will look only on the application disk. The only way to resolve this problem is to reboot the system. When you reboot the system, all assignments are canceled. The syntax for the ASSIGN command is:

```
ASSIGN   [x[:]=y[:][...]]
ASSIGN   /STATUS
```

The parameters are as follows:

x	Specifies the drive letter to reassign and represents the drive that currently gets the I/O requests.
y	Specifies the drive that x: will be assigned to and represents the drive letter where you want the I/O requests to be sent.
/STATUS	Displays current drive assignments. This can be abbreviated as /S or /STA. This is new to DOS 5.0.

Key in ASSIGN with no parameters to reset the default drive letters to the original and undo the assignments.

You may have more than one assignment on the command line, i.e.,

```
ASSIGN A=C B=C
```

This command would send all requests for information on Drives A or B to Drive C. If you wanted to assign one floppy drive to another, you would use the command line

```
ASSIGN A=B
```

This command would reroute every disk request intended for Drive A to Drive B. Remember, that SUBST is the preferred method.

9.19 The JOIN Command

JOIN is no longer included with MS-DOS 6.0 and above. If you upgraded and JOIN was already in the DOS subdirectory, the install program did not delete it. If you would like JOIN, you need to order the MS-DOS Resource Kit. The supplementary disks will include JOIN.

JOIN, an external command, allows you to make two separate disks appear to be one disk. It is as if a disk is a subdirectory on another drive. JOIN can be useful when you have software that does not let you work easily between two disk drives.

The purpose of this command is limited. It could be useful if you had a hard drive partitioned into four logical drives. If you were looking for a particular file, such as MY.TXT, you would have to key in four separate commands: DIR C:\MY.TXT /S, DIR D:\MY.TXT /S, DIR E:\MY.TXT /S, and DIR F:\MY.TXT /S. If you joined the drives together, you could issue the command as DIR MY.TXT /S, and all your drives would be searched as if they were one drive. A graphic example is helpful here. Assume that Drive C is structured as follows:

After you join Drive A to Drive C, your structure looks as follows:

While a JOIN is in effect, be very careful using CD, MD, RD, PATH or APPEND. Do not use the commands ASSIGN, CHKDSK, FORMAT, DISKCOPY, DISKCOMP, FDISK, MIRROR, RECOVER, SYS, PRINT, BACKUP, RESTORE, or LABEL while a JOIN is in effect. Furthermore, if you join an application disk to C:, you will not be able to get back to DOS. DOS will not recognize the JOIN because it will only look on the application disk. The only way to resolve this problem is to reboot the system. When you reboot the system, all joins will be canceled. In order to use the JOIN command, you must first create an empty directory on the disk you intend to use. The syntax of JOIN is:

```
JOIN [drive1: [drive2:]path]
```

with the parameters as follows:

drive1:	Specifies a disk drive that will appear as a directory on *drive2*.
drive2:	Specifies a drive to which you want to join *drive1*.

path	Specifies the directory to which you want to join *drive1*. It must be empty and cannot be the root directory.
JOIN	With no parameters will show any joins in effect.
JOIN *drive1:* /D	Disables JOIN.

Again, this command is hardly ever used, but if you have a need for it, you should not delete it from your DOS directory; otherwise you will have to order the supplemental disks.

9.20 The APPEND Command

APPEND is a command that should not be used with networks or with Windows. The APPEND command solves some of the problems you might encounter when you use the PATH command. Although the PATH command is very useful, it has shortcomings. One of the major shortcomings is that the PATH command only looks for program files—those files that are executable. Executable files always have the file extensions of .COM, .EXE, or .BAT. Even though you set the path, DOS will not search for any data files.

Most application programs have auxiliary files that the program uses, often called **overlay files**. To see how this process works (Figure 9.5) assume that you are working on a report for a class. Your default directory, from the organizational scheme you designed, is the subdirectory called SCHOOL. You set the path to PATH=C:\PROG\WORD. You key in WORD. Because the path is set to \PROG\WORD and WORD is an executable file (WORD.EXE), the WORD program is loaded. Then the WORD program asks you what file you want to work on. You key in REPORT.FIL. Since the default subdirectory is SCHOOL and that is where the REPORT.FIL is located, the WORD program, through DOS, can find the data file when it looks in the default subdirectory.

Figure 9.5   Shortcomings of the PATH Command

So far, everything is working fine. Now, you decide that you want to use the spell checker to look for any typographical errors. You instruct the word processing program to spell check, but, instead of the word processor spell checking your document, you get a message: `File not found`. Why? The spell checker is an overlay file. Overlay files are used to keep the maximum amount of memory free. Thus, when you loaded the word processing program, it only placed in memory the part of the program it needed. Now, you want to do another task, so the word processing program must load the spell checker program. Unfortunately, the word processing program cannot find it.

Remember, the word processing program turns to DOS to get what it needs. The word processing program tells DOS to get the overlay file. Because the overlay file does not have the appropriate file extension, DOS tells the word processor that it cannot find the spell checker file. Even though the path is set to `\PROG\WORD`, that only works for the executable file—`WORD.EXE`, not `SPELL.OVL`.

To solve these kinds of problems internally, the APPEND command was introduced in DOS 3.3. The APPEND command works much like the PATH command, but APPEND is not limited to searching for only `.COM`, `.EXE`, and `.BAT` files. The APPEND command will search for all other files. Although the APPEND command is an external command, once it is loaded, it remains resident in memory until the computer is turned off. In other words, once loaded, APPEND becomes an internal command. Hence, you can change your appends during your work session without having to reload the APPEND command. The syntax for first loading APPEND is:

```
APPEND [[drive:]path[;...]] [/X[:ON | :OFF]] [/PATH:ON | /PATH:OFF] [/E]
APPEND ;
```

Where the parameters are:

`[drive:]path`	Specifies a drive and directory to append.
`/X:ON`	Applies appended directories to file searches and application execution.
`/X:OFF`	Applies appended directories only to requests to open files. /X:OFF is the default setting.
`/PATH:ON`	Applies appended directories to file requests that already specify a path. /PATH:ON is the default setting.
`/PATH:OFF`	Turns off the effect of /PATH:ON.
`/E`	Stores a copy of the appended directory list in an environment variable named APPEND. /E may only be used the first time you use APPEND after starting your system.
`APPEND;`	Separates the APPEND paths or will clear the appended directory list.
`APPEND`	With no parameters displays the appended directory list.

Once again, there are some warnings about using APPEND. First and foremost, do not use APPEND with network drives or when you are in Windows. APPEND can create havoc in either Windows or on a network drive.

On the other hand, if you are working only with DOS-based programs, you can use APPEND, but you must be very careful. Data files are always written to the current default subdirectory. Thus, looking at Figure 9.5, if you made \PROG\WORD the default subdirectory and used APPEND to append the data subdirectory SCHOOL to access REPORT.FIL, the process would work correctly. When you wanted to save the edited REPORT.FIL to disk, it would be saved to the default directory— \PROG\WORD. Therefore, you would have your original file in \SCHOOL and the edited copy in \PROG\WORD.

This process occurs because APPEND works only at the time you look for and load the data file. Thus, when you told DOS to APPEND \SCHOOL and you loaded WORD and asked for REPORT.FIL the first time, APPEND was happy to comply with WORD's request. APPEND located and loaded a copy of REPORT.FIL in the \SCHOOL directory. Now, APPEND is out of the picture, and WORD is in charge. You make editing changes to REPORT.FIL with WORD. Now you want to save the edited REPORT.FIL to disk. WORD does not know that you originally retrieved the file from \SCHOOL. When you save your file and you do not specify that you want the changed REPORT.FIL to be saved to \SCHOOL, WORD will use, as do all programs, the default directory \PROG\WORD. You now have two copies of REPORT.FIL. One that is uncorrected in \SCHOOL\REPORT.FIL and the corrected copy in \PROG\WORD\REPORT.FIL.

You can resolve this confusion by making \SCHOOL the default directory and appending \PROG\WORD. Since your default directory is \SCHOOL, you are only working with the same copy of REPORT.FIL. When you save the edited copy of

REPORT.FIL, it will be written to the default directory \SCHOOL and overwrite the old version. By appending \PROG\WORD, WORD can find any overlay files it needs, be it a spell checker or grammar checker, since APPEND is not limited to .COM, .EXE, or .BAT files. See Figure 9.6.

In addition, there are some application programs that will ignore APPEND or will not work properly when APPEND is invoked. Thus, if an application program begins to act "funny," undo the APPEND to see if that solves the problem. In general, APPEND can create problems. The best solution is to organize your hard disk effectively.

beginning with \SCHOOL as
the default subdirectory

beginning with \PROG\WORD as
the default subdirectory

if we append the \PROG\WORD subdirectory
C:\SCHOOL>APPEND \PROG\WORD

if we append the \SCHOOL subdirectory
C:\PROG\WORD>APPEND \SCHOOL

and edit REPORT.FIL

C:\SCHOOL>WORD REPORT.FIL

C:\PROG\WORD>WORD REPORT.FIL

DOS retrieves the WORD program from \PROG\WORD,
and retrieves REPORT.FIL from \SCHOOL

when ready to save, DOS will save REPORT.FIL
back into the *default* subdirectory, \SCHOOL

when ready to save, DOS will save REPORT.FIL
back into the *default* subdirectory, \PROG\WORD

Figure 9.6   *Differences in Using APPEND*

Chapter Summary

1. All disks should be organized. All programs and data should not be in the root directory.
2. The root directory of a hard disk holds only 512 files.
3. Many users inefficiently organize their disk by application program. Too often it becomes a repetition of subdirectory names. Users must remember where they placed their files and must key in long path names. DOS must search every subdirectory. It is difficult to add and delete application programs and data files.
4. One way to organize a hard disk is by project.
5. Some guidelines to organizing a disk:
   a. The root directory is a map to the rest of the disk.
   b. Subdirectories should be shallow and wide.
   c. Plan the organization before installing software.
   d. Do not place data files in program subdirectories.
   e. It is better to have small subdirectories with only a few files.
   f. Keep subdirectory names short and descriptive.
   g. Create a separate subdirectory that will contain all software packages.
   h. Create a separate subdirectory for the DOS system utility files, batch files, and any other utility programs you own.
   i. Learn how the application program works.
   j. Analyze the way you work.
6. If a disk is not organized, you can organize it by planning it—creating the new organizational scheme, copying files to the new subdirectories, and deleting them from the old subdirectories.
7. The XCOPY command allows you to copy files and the subdirectories beneath them. You may choose:
   a. to be prompted (/P).
   b. to copy by date (/D).
   c. to be instructed to insert another disk (/W).
   d. to copy subdirectories and the files in them (/S).
   e. to create an empty subdirectory (/E).
   f. to verify that sectors are written correctly (/V).
   g. to copy files whose archive bit is set (/M).
   h. to copy only files that have been created or modified since the last backup (/A).
8. The REPLACE command is similar to the COPY and XCOPY commands because it copies files. However, it is much more flexible than COPY. REPLACE allows you to keep files updated and copy selected files as a group. You may choose:
   a. to update only files that have been changed by using the /U parameter.
   b. to add only new files by using the /A parameter.
   c. to be prompted for a confirmation prior to replacing a file using the /P parameter.

    d. to also replace read-only files by using the /R parameter.
    e. to search all subdirectories for replacement files using the /S parameter.
    f. to be prompted to insert a disk if you are copying to a floppy disk by using the /W parameter.

9. EDIT is a full screen editor that allows you to modify text files. It is a menu-driven program.
10. MOVE is used to move files and rename directories. However, you must be cautious when you use it to ensure you are performing the task that you wish.
11. Utility programs include the ones that come with DOS such as all DOS external commands.
12. There are commercial software packages that add enhancements to DOS. These are either given away, sold, or are shareware
13. RNS (rename subdirectory) is an example of a DOS utility program that only renames directories and works with any version of DOS.
14. Physical disk drives are attached to the computer. Logical disk drives are "imaginary" drives that act exactly like real disk drives. DOS looks at peripheral devices as logical devices.
15. The pretender commands are JOIN, ASSIGN, and SUBST.
16. The pretender commands help you work with older application programs that do not recognize subdirectories. They let you do things like abbreviate path names.
17. The SUBST command allows you to treat a subdirectory as a disk drive. SUBST is the preferred replacement for ASSIGN.
18. TRUENAME is an internal, undocumented command that will let you see the actual name of the drive in question.
19. An undocumented command is one that is provided with software but is not officially included in the list of commands. There are no guarantees that the undocumented command will work correctly.
20. The ASSIGN command reroutes requests from one disk drive to another. ASSIGN is no longer included in DOS 6.0 and above.
21. The JOIN command allows you to make two disk drives one disk drive. JOIN is no longer included in DOS 6.0 and above.
22. The APPEND command allows DOS to search for other than program files. PATH searches for program files (`.COM`, `.EXE`, and `.BAT`). Many application files have auxiliary data files, often called overlay files, that the PATH command cannot locate. APPEND will look for these files. APPEND should not be used if you are in Windows. Many programs will not work successfully with APPEND.

Key Terms

Device drivers
Direct read
Direct write
Logical disk drives
Overlay files

Pretender commands
Undocumented command

Discussion Questions

1. Why would you want to organize a hard disk?
2. What are the advantages/disadvantages of organizing a hard disk by application program or by project?
3. Why would you not want to place data files in the program subdirectory?
4. List five criteria that can be used for organizing a hard disk and explain the rationale for each.
5. What are two major considerations for any disk organizational scheme?
6. What are some of the drawbacks of using the COPY command?
7. What is the purpose and function of the XCOPY command? Give the syntax and explain each part.
8. Would you use the COPY or the XCOPY command to copy a directory structure and its files from a hard disk to a floppy disk? Why?
9. When would you use the REPLACE command?
10. Explain the purpose and function of the REPLACE command. Explain each part of the syntax. Why are two syntax diagrams shown?
11. Compare the strengths and weaknesses of the COPY, XCOPY, and REPLACE commands.
12. Why are moving program files and renaming program directories not as "safe" as moving data files and renaming data file directories?
13. What steps would you take to move a directory?
14. Why would you want to own utility programs that do not come with DOS?
15. What is the purpose and function of the program RNS.EXE?
16. What are logical devices?
17. What are device drivers?
18. What are pretender commands? Why are they used?
19. Explain the purpose and function of pretender commands.
20. What kinds of problems can you have with pretender commands?
21. Why can you not use APPEND, JOIN, or ASSIGN on network drives? In Windows?
22. Explain the purpose and function of the SUBST command.
23. Explain how the SUBST command can be used with Windows.
24. Give the syntax of the SUBST command and explain each part of the syntax.
25. What is an undocumented command? Give an example of an undocumented command.
26. Explain the purpose and function of the ASSIGN command.
27. Explain the purpose and function of the JOIN command.
28. How do the PATH and APPEND commands differ? When should each be used?
29. What are overlay files? How do they affect application programs?
30. When using the pretender commands, what problems can you have? Are there any pretender commands that should not be used? Why?

Chapter 10

Introduction to Batch Files

After completing this chapter you will be able to:

1. Compare and contrast batch and interactive processing.
2. Explain how batch files work.
3. Explain the purpose and function of the REM, ECHO, and PAUSE commands.
4. Explain how to stop or interrupt the batch file process.
5. Explain the function and use of replaceable parameters in batch files.
6. Explain the function and use of menu systems.
7. Explain the purpose and function of AUTOEXEC.BAT.
8. Explain the purpose and function of interactive booting.
9. Explain how to bypass CONFIG.SYS and AUTOEXEC.BAT files.

Student Outcomes

1. Use EDIT to write batch files.
2. Use COPY CON to write batch files.
3. Write and execute a simple batch file.
4. Write a batch file to load an application program.
5. Use the REM, PAUSE, and ECHO commands in batch files.
6. Terminate a batch file while it is executing.
7. Write batch files using replaceable parameters.

8. Write a menu system using batch files.
9. Write and use AUTOEXEC.BAT.
10. Be able to bypass AUTOEXEC.BAT.

Chapter Overview

You have used DOS commands throughout the text. Many of the DOS commands you have learned are repeated in the same sequence. If more than one command is needed to execute a program, you have to key in each command at the system prompt. This repetitive, time-consuming process increases the possibility of human error.

A batch file enables the computer to execute a series of commands with a minimum number of keystrokes. A batch file is a text file that contains a series of commands stored in the order the user wants them carried out. By using batch files it is possible to automate a DOS process and, at the same time, create a more powerful command, which increases the productivity of the computer user.

In this chapter you will learn to create batch files to automate the sequence of DOS commands, to write and execute an AUTOEXEC.BAT file for start-up routines, to write and use batch files for complex tasks, to use batch file subcommands, to halt the execution of a batch file, to write batch files using replaceable parameters, and to create your own menu system using batch files.

10.1 Concepts of Batch and Interactive Processing

DOS commands are programs that are executed or run when you key in the command name. If you wish to run more than one command, you need to key in each command at the system prompt. You can customize or automate the sequence of DOS commands by writing a command sequence that DOS will execute with a minimum number of keystrokes. This process is called a **batch file**. Sometimes you will hear it referred to as a batch program or a command file. Any command you can enter at the system prompt can also be included in a batch file. You can even execute an application program from a batch file. When you string together a sequence of steps in an application program, it is called a **macro**. A macro is conceptually similar to a batch file.

A batch file contains one or more commands. To create this file of commands, you write a text file using EDIT, COPY CON, or a text editor. You cannot use a word processor unless the word processor has a "Save as text file" option. The file that you write and name will run any command that DOS can execute. This file must have the file extension .BAT. Once you have written this command file, you execute or run it by simply keying in the name of the batch file, just as you key in the name of a DOS command. DOS reads and executes each line of the batch file. It is as if you sat in front of the terminal and separately keyed in each command line. Once you start running a batch file, DOS does not need your attention or input until the batch file has finished executing.

Batch files are used for several reasons. They allow you to minimize keystrokes. They also allow you the freedom to walk away from your computer when it runs a long series of commands. Batch files are used to put together a complex sequence of commands and store them under an easily remembered name. They automate any frequent and/or consistent procedures that you always want to do in the same manner. In addition, you can execute your application programs by calling them with a batch file.

Batch is an old data processing term. In the early days of computing, all work was done by submitting a job (or all the instructions needed to run the job successfully) to the data processing department, which would run these jobs in batches. There was no chance for anyone to interact with the program. The job was run, and the output was delivered. Thus, when you run a batch job, you are running a computer routine without interruption.

Batch jobs are still run today. An example of a batch job would be running a payroll—issuing paychecks. The computer program that calculates and prints paychecks is run without interruption. The output or results are the paychecks. This job can be run at any time. If a company decides that payday will be Friday, the data processing department can run the payroll Thursday night. If the company decides payday will be Monday, the data processing department can run the payroll Sunday night. This is **batch processing**.

Batch processing is in contrast to an interactive mode of data processing. Interactive means that you are interacting directly with the computer. Sometimes this is called online, real-time mode because you are actually talking to a computer as the event occurs. An automatic teller machines (ATM) that a bank uses so that you can withdraw or deposit money without human intervention is an example of **interactive processing**. The bank needs instant updating of its records. It cannot wait until next week to run a batch job to find out how much money you have deposited or withdrawn. If you withdraw $100, the bank first wants to be sure that you have $100 in your account, and then it wants the $100 subtracted immediately from your balance. You are dealing with the computer in an interactive, real-time mode. Real-time means the information is processed as it occurs.

In the DOS world, you can work in an interactive mode, but this usually requires a connection to another computer, often over phone lines. Commercial services called bulletin boards allow you to communicate directly with other computers and perform such functions as reviewing airline flight schedules. Although interactive mode can be exciting, most of the time you are working one-on-one with your computer and are not in an interactive mode. Hence, the batch mode will be the area of emphasis.

10.2 How DOS Batch Files Work

You will be creating and executing batch files in this chapter. By now you should know that data and programs are stored as files. How does DOS know the difference between a data file and a program file? It knows the difference based on the file extension. When you key in something at the prompt, DOS first checks in RAM to compare what you keyed in to the internal table of commands. If it finds a match, DOS executes that program.

If what you keyed in does not match an internal command, DOS has an order it uses to search for program files. DOS next looks for the extension .COM. The extension .COM means command file. DOS looks on the default drive and directory for what you keyed in with the file extension .COM. If it finds a match, it loads the program and runs it.

If not, DOS goes through the same process but looks for the file extension is .EXE. The extension .EXE means executable file. This is how you load and execute not only the DOS utility programs but also most application software. Application software usually has the file extension .EXE, such as LOTUS.EXE.

If what you keyed in does not match these scenarios, DOS's last looks for the file extension .BAT. The extension .BAT means batch file. It looks on the default drive and directory for what you keyed in with the file extension .BAT. If it finds a match, it loads and executes the batch file, one line at a time. If what you keyed in does not match any of the above criteria, DOS sends back the message, Bad command or file name.

What if you had files on a disk that had the same file name but three different file extensions such as CHKDSK.COM, CHKDSK.EXE, and CHKDSK.BAT? How would DOS know which program to load and execute? DOS follows the rules. It would find and load the program with the .COM file extension first and would never get to the other files. However, if you were more specific and keyed in both the file name AND the file extension, such as CHKDSK.BAT, DOS would then execute the file name that you specified.

Remember that, since the batch file is a program, the .BAT file must be either on the default drive and directory or the path set to the location of the batch file so you may invoke it. Most importantly, each line in a batch file must contain only *one* command.

10.3 Using EDIT to Write Batch Files

You need a mechanism to write or create batch files. A batch file is an ASCII text file. ASCII is a code used by DOS to interpret the letters, numbers, and punctuation marks that you key in. In simple terms, if you can read a file with the TYPE command, it is an ASCII text file. You can also use a word processing program to write a batch file if it has a nondocument or text mode. However, most word processing programs are quite large and take time to load into memory. Most batch files are not very long, nor do they need the features of a word processor. Using a word processor to write a batch file is much like using a sledge hammer to kill a fly.

Having a small, simple text editor is so important that DOS includes one as part of the system utility programs. Prior to DOS 5.0, the text editor was EDLIN. In DOS 5.0, although EDLIN was also included, the text editor of choice was EDIT because it is a full-screen editor. EDIT is simple to use and universal. Everyone who has DOS 5.0 or above has EDIT. Beginning with MS-DOS 6.2, EDLIN was no longer included. If you want EDLIN, you will find it on the MS-DOS Resource Kit supplemental disks.

You are going to write some batch files using EDIT. Remember, EDIT is only a tool to create the file; it does not run or execute it. You will execute the file when you key in the file name at the DOS command prompt. Each line in a batch file must contain only one command. A batch file can have any legal DOS file name but the file extension must always be .BAT.

10.4 Activity: Writing and Executing a Batch File

Note 1:   The DATA disk is in Drive A. The A:\> is displayed.
Note 2:   Be sure the path is set to the DOS subdirectory. To use EDIT, DOS must be able to find QBASIC, which usually is in the DOS subdirectory. If you are working with an earlier version of DOS, use EDLIN.
Note 3:   Although you may use a mouse with EDIT, the instructions will show the keystrokes steps, not the mouse steps.

Step 1   Key in the following: A:\>**EDIT EXAMPLE.BAT** [Enter]

WHAT'S HAPPENING? You are now using EDIT. You are going to create a batch file named EXAMPLE. The file extension must be .BAT.

Step 2   Key in the following: **DIR *.99** [Enter]
                                DIR C:*.99

WHAT'S HAPPENING? Look at this file line by line. Each line is a legitimate and separate DOS command that could be keyed in at the prompt. Each command is on a separate line. The first line asks for a listing of all the files on the disk in the default drive that have the file extension .99. The second line asks for all the files in the root directory of C that have the file extension .99. At this point, you have written the batch file. Next, you need to exit EDIT and save the file to disk.

Step 3   Press **Alt** + **F**

Step 4   Press **X**

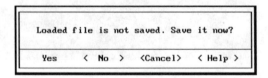

WHAT'S HAPPENING? Since you have not saved the file, EDIT reminds you with a dialog box that, if you want this file on the disk, you must save it.

Step 5   Press **Y**

```
A:\>EDIT EXAMPLE.BAT

A:\>_
```

WHAT'S HAPPENING? You returned to the system prompt.

Step 6   Key in the following: A:\>**DIR EXAMPLE.BAT** [Enter]

```
A:\>DIR EXAMPLE.BAT

 Volume in drive A is DATADISK
 Volume Serial Number is 2F26-1901
 Directory of A:\

EXAMPLE   BAT            23 06-26-94  11:22a
        1 file(s)              23 bytes
                        1,015,808 bytes free

A:\>_
```

WHAT'S HAPPENING? You exited the EDIT program and returned to the system prompt. The DIR EXAMPLE.BAT command shows that there is a file on the DATA disk called EXAMPLE.BAT. It is like any other file. How do you make DOS treat it like a program so that you can execute it? To run or execute this batch file, you key in the name of the file at the prompt. DOS then looks for a file in its internal table called EXAMPLE. It does not find it. It then looks for a file called EXAMPLE.COM on the default disk, the DATA disk. No file exists called EXAMPLE.COM. Next, DOS looks for a file on the default disk called EXAMPLE.EXE. No file exists called EXAMPLE.EXE.

Finally, DOS looks for a file called EXAMPLE.BAT on the default disk. It does find a file by this name. It loads it into memory and executes each line, one at a time. Thus, to execute the batch file called EXAMPLE, key in the name of the file at the prompt. Watch what happens on the screen after you key in the file name.

Step 7   Key in the following: A:\>**EXAMPLE** Enter

```
A:\>EXAMPLE

A:\>DIR *.99

 Volume in drive A is DATADISK
 Volume Serial Number is 2F26-1901
 Directory of A:\

APR      99             71 11-23-95  10:42a
JAN      99             72 11-23-95  10:41a
        2 file(s)             143 bytes
                        1,015,808 bytes free

A:\>DIR C:\*.99

 Volume in drive C has no label
 Volume Serial Number is 1CD1-5E42
 Directory of C:\
```

```
File not found

A:\>
A:\>_
```

WHAT'S HAPPENING? DOS read and executed each line of the batch file you wrote, one line at a time. The screen displayed each command line, and the results of the command line as it executed. Each line executed as if you had sat in front of the keyboard and keyed in each command individually. You did key in the commands when you wrote the batch file, but you only had to key them in once.

The first line was DIR *.99. When DOS read that line, it executed it and showed on the screen both files on the DATA disk with the file extension .99. It read the next line of the batch file and looked in the root directory of Drive C for any file that had the file extension .99. Since there were no files on that drive with the extension .99, it gave the message, File not found. Now that you have written the file EXAMPLE.BAT, you can execute this batch file over and over again by keying in EXAMPLE at the prompt. By keying in one command, you can execute two DOS commands.

10.5 Writing and Executing a Batch File to Save Keystrokes

The previous example showed you how to write and execute a batch file, but that file is not especially useful. The next batch file to be written will allow you to key in only one keystroke instead of seven. The command DIR /AD will quickly show you any subdirectories on the DATA disk. The /A switch means attribute, and the attribute you want displayed is D for directories. This command is composed of seven keystrokes, and you must have the proper parameters. With a batch file, you can do the same task by pressing only one key.

The DIR command has other parameters that are very useful. One of these is O for order. There are many kinds of order you can achieve, but one that is useful is to arrange files by size. The command line would be DIR /OS. The "O" is for order, and the "S" is to arrange by size from the smallest to the largest file. If you wanted to reverse the order so that the files would be displayed from the largest to the smallest, the command would be DIR /O-S. The "O" is still for order, but the (-) is for reverse order, placing smallest files at the end of the listing. The "S" is for file size. This command would take seven keystrokes. You can reduce it to one.

These batch files you are going to write are very small—one line. It seems like a lot of trouble to load EDIT just to accomplish this task. If you would rather not load EDIT, you can use the COPY command to write a simple ASCII file. The syntax is:

```
COPY CON filename
```

What you are doing here is copying what you key in (CON) to a file name. You are still following the syntax of the COPY command; it is just that now you are copying from a device—the console (CON) to a file. Remember that in an early chapter, you copied to a device, the printer (COPY *filename* PRN). Just as PRN, LPT1, and LPT2 are reserved device names, so is CON. CON means the console (the keyboard and the monitor).

When you are done keying in text, you must tell the COPY command you are done. You do this by pressing the F6 key and then the **Enter** key. This writes the data you keyed in to the file name you specified. This is what you have been doing in your application assignments when you entered data in the NAME.FIL. The only problem with COPY CON, as it is informally referred to, is that you cannot correct errors once you press **Enter** at the end of a command line. Nor can you use COPY CON to correct errors in an existing file. To do that, you need an editor, such as EDIT. But nothing is faster than using COPY CON.

10.6 Activity: Writing and Executing a One-letter Batch File

Note 1:   The DATA disk is in Drive A. The A:\> is displayed.

Note 2:   For these examples, the use of COPY CON will be shown. If you make errors, you can either rekey in the data or use EDIT to correct the errors.

Note 3:   In earlier chapters you may have used DOSKEY and the function keys to correct errors. Either of these methods will work with COPY CON.

Step 1   Key in the following: A:\>**COPY CON D.BAT Enter**

```
A:\>COPY CON D.BAT
_
```

WHAT'S HAPPENING? When you keyed in COPY CON D.BAT, you were informing the COPY command that you wanted to make the keyboard the *source*. The cursor is blinking right below the prompt, and the screen is blank.

Step 2   Key in the following: **DIR /AD Enter**

```
A:\>COPY CON D.BAT
DIR /AD
_
```

WHAT'S HAPPENING? You have one line. You are finished keying in data and you wish this line to be saved to a file called D.BAT. First, however, you must tell COPY you are finished.

Step 3   Press **F6 Enter**

```
A:\>COPY CON D.BAT
DIR /AD
^Z
        1 file(s) copied

A:\>
```

WHAT'S HAPPENING? By pressing F6 and then Enter, you sent a signal to COPY that you were done. The F6 appeared on the screen as ^z. Pressing Ctrl + Z will produce the same results as F6. You then got the message 1 file(s) copied and were returned to the system level.

Step 4   Key in the following: A:\>**TYPE D.BAT** Enter

```
A:\>TYPE D.BAT
DIR /AD

A:\>_
```

WHAT'S HAPPENING? You wrote a one-line batch file named D.BAT with COPY CON and saved the file D.BAT to disk. Once you returned to the DOS system prompt, you displayed the contents of D.BAT with the TYPE command. The fact that you could display this file with the TYPE command is another indication that it is indeed an ASCII file. All COPY CON did was allow you to create the file, and TYPE merely displayed what is inside the file. To execute the file, you must key in the file name. Now, whenever you want to see the subdirectories on the DATA disk in Drive A, you only have to key in one letter to execute this command.

Step 5   Key in the following: A:\>**D** Enter

```
A:\>D

A:\>DIR /AD

 Volume in drive A is DATADISK
 Volume Serial Number is 2F26-1901
 Directory of A:\

POLYSCI      <DIR>        06-20-94    5:59p
CLASS        <DIR>        06-21-94    1:02a
WORK         <DIR>        06-21-94   10:30a
TRIP         <DIR>        06-21-94   10:58p
PROG         <DIR>        06-25-94   11:58a
MEDIA        <DIR>        06-25-94   12:03p
        6 file(s)              0 bytes
                      1,015,296 bytes free

A:\>
A:\>_
```

WHAT'S HAPPENING? Your display may vary based on what subdirectories are on the DATA disk and in what order they were created. As you can see, you set up a command sequence in a batch file called D.BAT. You can run this batch file whenever the need arises, simply by keying in the name of the batch file at the system prompt. You can also display the files by size, with the smallest file at the end of the list.

Step 6 Key in the following: A:\>**COPY CON S.BAT** [Enter]
DIR /O-S [Enter]

```
A:\>COPY CON S.BAT
DIR /O-S
_
```

WHAT'S HAPPENING? You have written another simple one line batch file.

Step 7 Press [F6] [Enter]

Step 8 Key in the following: A:\>**TYPE S.BAT** [Enter]

```
A:\>COPY CON S.BAT
DIR /O-S
^Z
        1 file(s) copied

A:\>TYPE S.BAT
DIR /O-S

A:\>_
```

WHAT'S HAPPENING? You created another batch file called S.BAT using COPY CON. The purpose of this batch file is to arrange the files by size with the smallest file at the end of the directory listing. You then saved the file to disk and looked at its contents with the TYPE command. To execute the batch file, you must key in the batch file name (S) at the DOS system prompt.

Step 9 Key in the following: A:\>**S** [Enter]

```
GOODBYE   NEW         32 11-23-94    7:07a
JAN       OLD         32 11-23-94    7:07a
EXAMPLE   BAT         23 06-26-94   11:22a
APR       BUD         18 12-06-94   10:46a
FILE2     CZG         18 12-06-94   10:45a
FILE3     CZG         18 12-06-94   10:46a
FILE4     FP          18 12-06-94   10:47a
FILE3     FP          18 12-06-94   10:46a
FILE2     FP          18 12-06-94   10:46a
FILE2     SWT         18 12-06-94   10:46a
FILE3     SWT         18 12-06-94   10:47a
S         BAT         10 06-26-94   11:28a
D         BAT          9 06-26-94   11:26a
Y         FIL          3 05-14-93   11:00a
```

```
    POLYSCI        <DIR>           06-20-94    5:59p
    CLASS          <DIR>           06-21-94    1:02a
    WORK           <DIR>           06-21-94   10:30a
    TRIP           <DIR>           06-21-94   10:58p
    PROG           <DIR>           06-25-94   11:58a
    MEDIA          <DIR>           06-25-94   12:03p
           44 file(s)             44,079 bytes
                               1,014,784 bytes free


A:\>
A:\>_
```

WHAT'S HAPPENING? The files are listed by size, and all the subdirectories are grouped at the bottom of the display. Because directories have no size, they are listed last as the smallest files.

10.7 Using Batch Files To Load Application Software

One of the common uses of batch files is to load application software, particularly on a hard disk. Usually, application software programs are stored in a subdirectory. When you want to use a program, you have to change the directory to the proper subdirectory, load the program, and, when you are finished using the application program, return to the system level. You usually want to change the default subdirectory to the root directory. This process can be easier with a batch file. First you will run through the process of working with application software, and then you will create a batch file to load the application software.

10.8 Activity: Using the HPB Application Package

Note: The DATA disk is in Drive A. The A:\> is displayed.

Step 1   Key in the following:

A:\>**XCOPY C:\DOS6BK\PHONE*.* HPB** [Enter]

```
A:\>XCOPY C:\DOS6BK\PHONE\*.* HPB
Does HPB specify a file name
or directory name on the target
(F = file, D = directory)?_
```

WHAT'S HAPPENING? You are copying the PHONE directory and its files from the \DOS6BK subdirectory to the DATA disk. You are placing the files in a subdirectory you called HPB.

Step 2   Press **D**

```
A:\>XCOPY C:\DOS6BK\PHONE\*.* HPB
Does HPB specify a file name
```

```
or directory name on the target
(F = file, D = directory)?D
Reading source file(s)...
C:\DOS6BK\PHONE\FILE_ID.DIZ
C:\DOS6BK\PHONE\HPB.DAT
C:\DOS6BK\PHONE\HPB.EXE
C:\DOS6BK\PHONE\HPB.SLC
C:\DOS6BK\PHONE\README.HPB
C:\DOS6BK\PHONE\HPB.CFG
        6 File(s) copied

A:\>_
```

WHAT'S HAPPENING? You have copied the files to the new HPB subdirectory on the DATA disk.

Step 3   Key in the following: A:\>**CD HPB** [Enter]

Step 4   Key in the following: A:\HPB>**DIR HPB.EXE** [Enter]

Step 5   Key in the following: A:\HPB>**DIR HPB.DAT** [Enter]

```
A:\>CD HPB

A:\HPB>DIR HPB.EXE

 Volume in drive A is DATADISK
 Volume Serial Number is 2F26-1901
 Directory of A:\HPB

HPB      EXE        164,420 07-03-93   8:01a
        1 file(s)         164,420 bytes
                          826,368 bytes free

A:\HPB>DIR HPB.DAT

 Volume in drive A is DATADISK
 Volume Serial Number is 2F26-1901
 Directory of A:\HPB

HPB      DAT          4,368 12-12-96  10:46p
        1 file(s)           4,368 bytes
                          826,368 bytes free

A:\HPB>_
```

WHAT'S HAPPENING? You are looking at the file HPB.EXE in the subdirectory HPB on the DATA disk. You are going to load the program called HPB.EXE that is a simple address book. You are going to use the data file called HPB.DAT also in the subdirectory HPB. This program automatically loads its data file when you load the program.

Step 6   Key in the following: A:\HPB>**HPB** [Enter]

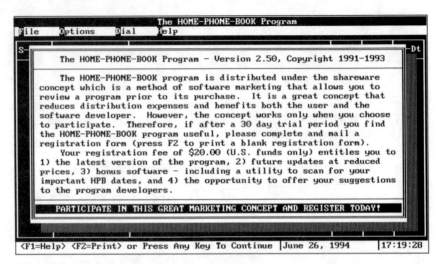

WHAT'S HAPPENING? You see the opening screen introducing you to shareware and to the details for registering the program.

Step 7   Press [Enter]

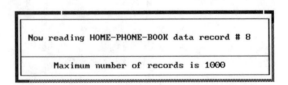

WHAT'S HAPPENING? You see a quick message that this program is automatically loading the data file. The data file is called HPB.DAT. Then the following screen appears.

WHAT'S HAPPENING? This is a database program called Home Phone Book. It has a menu bar across the top with specific choices. To access the menu, you press the [Alt] key and the first letter of your menu choice.

Step 8   Press [Alt] + **O**

WHAT'S HAPPENING? You dropped down the Options menu, which has many choices. A database program is comprised of records and fields. A record is a new entry in the file. Add a new record... is already highlighted and is the default choice. It also has a keyboard shortcut—pressing the [Shift] + [F2] keys.

Step 9   Press [Enter]

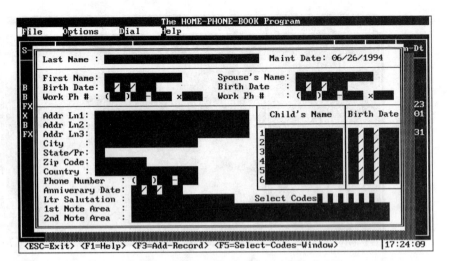

WHAT'S HAPPENING? You are presented with a screen in which you can fill out information. Each item on the screen is a field. A collection of fields makes up a record. A collection of records is the data file.

Step 10   In the `Last Name    :` field, key in your last name.

Step 11   Press the **Tab** key. That will move you to `First Name    :`

Step 12   Key in your first name.

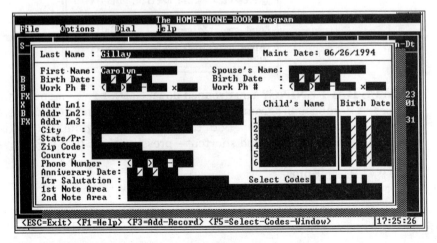

WHAT'S HAPPENING? You have keyed in some information in the appropriate fields. At the bottom of the screen are the instructions for using this program. You are going to choose `Add Record`. This means that you will save the information you just keyed in.

Step 13   Press the F3 key.

```
                        The HOME-PHONE-BOOK Program
 File      Options      Dial      Help

 S-Code  Phone Number   Last Name, First Name(s)              F-Bdt S-Bdt An-Dt

         (800) 888-8888 Acme Fly-By-Night, Inc.
         (   )    -     Bonitz, Tom
 B       (503) 682-7668 Franklin, Beedle & Associates
         (   )    -     Gillay, Carolyn
 B       (800) 462-9673 Microsoft
 FX      (714) 555-7777 Panezich, Carolyn Gillay & Frank      05/07 12/06 11/23
 X       (416) 888-8888 Smith, Jane Doe & John                11/11 12/12 01/01
 B       (714) 555-9997 The Book Biz
 FX      (714) 555-8889 Tuttle, Mary Brown & Steven           12/20 05/14 07/31




 <F1=Help><Alt-f/o/d/h=Menu><Any-Alpha-Char=Browse>|June 26, 1994    |17:27:10
```

WHAT'S HAPPENING? You returned to the main screen. Your name should be highlighted. Now, you are going to exit the program.

Step 14   Press Alt + **F**

WHAT'S HAPPENING? You have dropped down the File menu. You press X to exit the program.

Step 15   Press **X**

```
        Resequencing the HPB data file prior to exit

             Record #  3
```

WHAT'S HAPPENING? You see what is called a housekeeping detail on the screen. The housekeeping here is placing the records in the file in order.

```
 A:\HPB>_
```

WHAT'S HAPPENING? You quit the program HPB.EXE and returned to the system level. However, you are still in the subdirectory HPB.

Step 16 Key in the following: A:\HPB>**CD ** [Enter]

```
A:\HPB>CD \

A:\>_
```

WHAT'S HAPPENING? You returned to the root directory of the DATA disk so that you can do other work.

10.9 Writing a Batch File to Load an Application Program

In the previous activity, in order to execute the database program called HPB, you needed to take three steps. First, you went from the root directory to the subdirectory called HPB. Then you had to load HPB.EXE. When you exited HPB, you wanted to return to the root directory. A batch file is an ideal place to put all of these commands.

10.10 Activity: Writing a Batch File to Execute HPB

Note 1: The DATA disk is in Drive A. The A:\> is displayed.
Note 2: You may use any text editor you wish for creating the batch files. You may use COPY CON, but when you have more than one line, using an editor is easier. The EDIT instructions for keyboard use will be shown, but, if you prefer using a mouse, do so.

Step 1 Key in the following: A:\>**EDIT HPB.BAT** [Enter]

Step 2 Key in the following: **CD \HPB** [Enter]
HPB [Enter]
**CD **

WHAT'S HAPPENING? You have just written a batch file to load the HPB application program. You can give the file the name `HPB.BAT`, because it is in the root directory and `HPB` is in a subdirectory. The two files will not conflict, and you will not have to be specific and key in `HPB.BAT`. Furthermore, the first line states `CD \HPB`. Although the backslash is not necessary in this instance, you want the batch file to run no matter where you are, so the CD command includes the \.

Step 3   Press **Alt** + **F**

Step 4   Press **X**

Step 5   Press **Y**

Step 6   Key in the following: `A:\>`**TYPE HPB.BAT** **Enter**

```
A:\>TYPE HPB.BAT
CD \HPB
HPB
CD \

A:\>_
```

WHAT'S HAPPENING? You created the batch file `HPB.BAT` in EDIT and then returned to the system prompt. Now, you can execute this file.

Step 7   Key in the following: `A:\>`**HPB** **Enter**

Step 8   Press **Enter**

```
                       The HOME-PHONE-BOOK Program
 File      Options     Dial     Help

 S-Code  Phone Number    Last Name, First Name(s)            F-Bdt S-Bdt An-Dt

         (800) 888-8888 Acme Fly-By-Night, Inc.
         (   )    -     Bonitz, Tom
 B       (503) 682-7668 Franklin, Beedle & Associates
         (   )    -     Gillay, Carolyn
 B       (800) 462-9673 Microsoft
 FX      (714) 555-7777 Panezich, Carolyn Gillay & Frank   05/07 12/06 11/23
 X       (416) 888-8888 Smith, Jane Doe & John             11/11 12/12 01/01
 B       (714) 555-9997 The Book Biz
 FX      (714) 555-8889 Tuttle, Mary Brown & Steven        12/20 05/14 07/31




 <F1=Help><Alt-f/o/d/h=Menu><Any-Alpha-Char=Browse> June 26, 1994   17:41:58
```

WHAT'S HAPPENING? When you keyed in HPB at the root directory, DOS looked for HPB.BAT and found it. It read the first line, which said to change the directory to the HPB subdirectory. DOS did that. It then read the second line which said look for a program called HPB.EXE and loaded HPB. You then got the program HPB on the screen.

Step 9   Press **Alt** + **F**

Step 10   Press **X**

```
A:\HPB>CD \

A:\>
A:\>_
```

WHAT'S HAPPENING? It does not matter if you are in the application program one minute, one hour, or one day. Whenever you exit an application program, DOS continues with the batch file where it last was and simply reads the next line. DOS finished executing your batch file by changing the directory to the root.

10.11 Special Batch File Commands

There are nine commands specifically designed to be used in batch files. These commands can make batch files extremely versatile. They are:

CALL   Allows you to call one batch file from another without causing the first batch file to stop.

CHOICE   Allows user to make a choice in a batch file (new in 6.0).

ECHO   Displays or hides display of commands or text in batch files when batch file is running. When used on command line, will display status of ECHO.

FOR   Runs a specified command for each file in a set of files. Can be used on command line.

GOTO   Directs DOS to a line in a batch file that is marked by a label you specify.

IF   Performs conditional processing in a batch file. If the condition is true, DOS carries out the command that follows the condition. If the condition is false, DOS ignores the command that follows the condition.

PAUSE   Suspends processing of a batch file and displays a message that prompts the user to press any key to continue.

REM   Allows you to include comments in a batch file or in CONFIG.SYS. Can also be used to disable commands in a batch file or in CONFIG.SYS.

SHIFT   Changes the position of replaceable parameters in a batch file.

In this chapter, you will use only REM, ECHO, and PAUSE.

10.12 The REM Command

The REM command, which stands for remarks, is a special command that allows the user to key in explanatory text that will be displayed on the screen. Nothing else happens. REM does not cause DOS to take any action, but it is very useful. When DOS sees REM, it knows that anything following the REM is not a command and, thus, is not supposed to be executed, just displayed on the screen. REM allows a batch file to be **documented**. In a data processing environment, "to document" means to give an explanation about the purpose of the program. This process can be very important when there are many batch files on a disk, especially when someone who did not write the batch file would like to use it. The REM statements should tell anyone what the purpose of the batch file is. The remarks can also include the name of the batch file, the time and date it was last updated, and the author of the batch file.

10.13 Activity: Using REM

Note 1:   The DATA disk is in Drive A. The A:\> is displayed.
Note 2:   If JAN.BUD is not on the DATA disk, you can copy \DOS6BK\JAN.TMP to the DATA disk as JAN.BUD.

Step 1   Key in the following: A:\>**EDIT TEST.BAT** [Enter]

        REM This is a test file [Enter]

        REM to see how the REM [Enter]

        REM command works. [Enter]

        TYPE JAN.BUD [Enter]

        COPY JAN.BUD JAN.XYZ

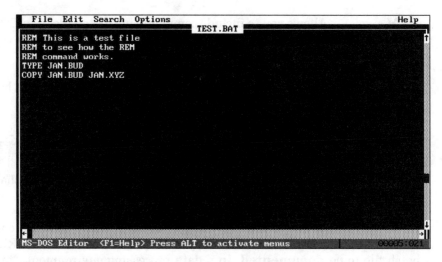

WHAT'S HAPPENING? You are using EDIT to write another batch file called TEST.BAT. You have inserted some text with REM preceding each line. Then, you keyed in two DOS commands, TYPE and COPY. Now, you want to save this file to disk and return to the DOS system level.

Step 2   Press **Alt** + **F**

Step 3   Press **X**

Step 4   Press **Y**

Step 5   Key in the following: A:\>**TYPE TEST.BAT** **Enter**

```
A:\>TYPE TEST.BAT
REM This is a test file
REM to see how the REM
REM command works.
TYPE JAN.BUD
COPY JAN.BUD JAN.XYZ

A:\>_
```

WHAT'S HAPPENING? This batch file was created to be used as a test case. The remarks just keyed in explain the purpose of this batch file. You created TEST.BAT in EDIT and returned to the system prompt. You then displayed TEST.BAT with the TYPE command. To execute the TEST.BAT batch file, you must run it.

Step 6   Key in the following: A:\>**TEST** **Enter**

```
A:\>TEST

A:\>REM This is a test file

A:\>REM to see how the REM

A:\>REM command works.

A:\>TYPE JAN.BUD
This is my January file.
It is my first dummy file.
This is file 1.

A:\>COPY JAN.BUD JAN.XYZ
        1 file(s) copied

A:\>
A:\>_
```

WHAT'S HAPPENING? When you keyed in TEST, the batch file was executed. DOS read the first line of the batch file, REM This is a test file. DOS knew that it was supposed to do nothing but display the text following REM on the screen. DOS then read the next line in the batch file, REM to see how the REM and did the same. DOS kept reading and displaying the REM lines until it got to the line that had the command TYPE. To DOS, TYPE is a command, so it executed or ran the TYPE command with the parameter JAN.BUD. DOS read the next line, which was another command, COPY and copied the file JAN.BUD to a new file called JAN.XYZ. Then, DOS looked for another line in the batch file but could find no more lines, so it returned to the system level. The purpose of REM is to provide explanatory remarks about the batch file.

10.14 The ECHO Command

Usually a command is displayed, then the results of that command are displayed. ECHO is a command that means "echo" or display the command and the output of the command to the screen. The default value for ECHO is on. The ECHO command is normally *always* on. The only time it is off is if you turn it off. In a batch file, you can turn off the *display of the command* and see only the *output of a command*. For instance, COPY THIS.FIL THAT.FIL is a command. The output of the command is 1 file(s) copied. The work of the command is the actual copying of the file. See Table 10.1.

	ECHO ON Screen Display	ECHO OFF Screen Display
Command:	COPY THIS.FIL THAT.FIL	
Output:	1 file(s) copied.	1 file(s) copied.

Table 10.1 **ECHO On or Off**

If the purpose of the REM command is to document a batch file, what is the purpose of the ECHO command? One of the purposes you saw in an earlier chapter was to redirect a special character to the printer so that the printer would eject a page. Another purpose of the ECHO command is to minimize screen clutter. For instance, although you want to use the REM command to document your batch file, you really do not need to see your documentation on the screen every time you run the batch file. ECHO OFF allows you to suppress the display of the commands.

10.15 Activity: Using ECHO

Note: The DATA disk is in Drive A. The A:\> is displayed.

Step 1   Key in the following: A:\>**COPY TEST.BAT TESTING.BAT** [Enter]

```
A:\>COPY TEST.BAT TESTING.BAT
        1 file(s) copied

A:\>_
```

WHAT'S HAPPENING? You made a copy of the file TEST.BAT.

Step 2   Key in the following: A:\>**EDIT TESTING.BAT** [Enter]
                                       ECHO OFF [Enter]

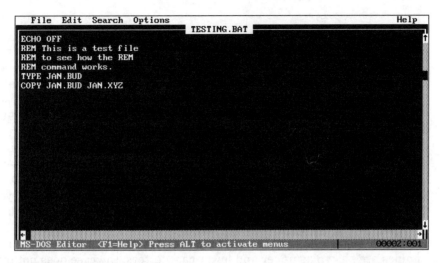

```
 File  Edit  Search  Options                                    Help
┌─────────────────────────────── TESTING.BAT ──────────────────────────────┐
│ECHO OFF                                                                  ↑│
│REM This is a test file                                                    │
│REM to see how the REM                                                     │
│REM command works.                                                        ▓│
│TYPE JAN.BUD                                                               │
│COPY JAN.BUD JAN.XYZ                                                       │
│                                                                           │
│                                                                           │
│                                                                           │
│                                                                           │
│                                                                           │
│                                                                           │
│                                                                          ↓│
│←                                                                        →▐│
 MS-DOS Editor  <F1=Help> Press ALT to activate menus  │        00002:001
```

WHAT'S HAPPENING? You are using a copy of the batch file from the previous activity. The only difference is that you added one line at the top of the batch file to turn ECHO OFF. You are going to run the batch file so that only the output of each command is displayed, not the actual commands. First you must exit EDIT and save the file to disk.

Step 3   Press **Alt** + **F**. Press **X**

Step 4   Press **Y**

Step 5   Key in the following: A:\>**TYPE TESTING.BAT** **Enter**

```
A:\>TYPE TESTING.BAT
ECHO OFF
REM This is a test file
REM to see how the REM
REM command works.
TYPE JAN.BUD
COPY JAN.BUD JAN.XYZ

A:\>_
```

WHAT'S HAPPENING? You saved the file as TESTING.BAT and displayed the contents on the screen. Now, you wish to execute the file.

Step 6   Key in the following: A:\>**TESTING** **Enter**

```
A:\>ECHO OFF
This is my January file.
It is my first dummy file.
This is file 1.
```

```
          1 file(s) copied
  A:\>_
```

WHAT'S HAPPENING? The batch file TESTING.BAT has the same commands as TEST.BAT. You saw only the output of the commands, not the actual commands. You saw the ECHO OFF command on the screen, but you did not see the REM command displayed on the screen. You saw the results of the TYPE JAN.BUD command, the contents of the file on the screen, but you never saw the TYPE JAN.BUD command on the screen. You also did not see the COPY JAN.BUD JAN.XYZ command, only the results of the command—the message 1 file(s) copied.

You already have a file by the name of JAN.XYZ, but, even though you are using the COPY command in DOS 6.22, the COPY command did not tell you that the file already exists (overwrite protection). The differences between ECHO ON and ECHO OFF are exemplified in Table 10.2. (*Note:* Although commands and file names are shown as upper and lower case letters, the case does not matter.)

	TEST.BAT ECHO ON Screen Display	TESTING.BAT ECHO OFF Screen Display
Command:	ECHO ON	ECHO OFF
Command:	REM This is a test file	
Command:	REM to see how the REM	
Command:	REM command works.	
Command:	TYPE MAR.BUD	
Output:	This is my March file. It is my third dummy file. This is file 3.	This is my March file. It is my third dummy file. This is file 3.
Command:	COPY MAR.BUD MAR.XYZ	
Output:	1 file(s) copied	1 file(s) copied

Table 10.2   *ECHO ON and ECHO OFF: A Comparison of Screen Displays*

The batch file TEST.BAT and TESTING.BAT executed the same commands. The only difference is that when ECHO was on, which it was for TEST.BAT, you saw the remarks as well as the commands. When you executed TESTING.BAT, you only saw the output of the commands displayed on the screen, not the actual commands because ECHO was off. If you did not want to see the ECHO OFF on the screen, you could have entered the command as @ECHO OFF. The @ suppresses the display of ECHO OFF.

10.16 The PAUSE Command

Another batch file command is PAUSE, which does exactly what it says: it tells the batch file to stop executing until the user takes some action. No other batch command will be executed until the user presses a key. The PAUSE command will wait forever until the user takes some action.

10.17 Activity: Using PAUSE

Note: The DATA disk is in Drive A. The A:\> is displayed.

Step 1   Key in the following: A:\> **EDIT TEST.BAT** [Enter]

Step 2   Press [Ctrl] + [End]

Step 3   Key in the following: **PAUSE You are going to delete JAN.XYZ**[Enter]
                          DEL JAN.XYZ

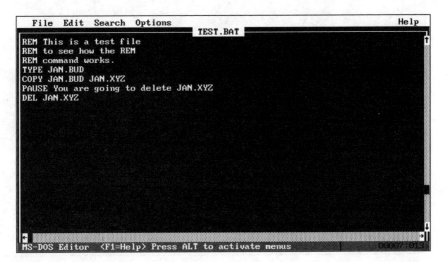

WHAT'S HAPPENING? You edited the batch file TEST.BAT. When the file is executed, the first three lines of the file, the REM statements, explain the purpose of TEST.BAT. Then the batch file displays the contents of JAN.BUD on the screen and copies the file JAN.BUD to a new file, JAN.XYZ. The PAUSE statement tells you that the file is going to be deleted and gives you a chance to change your mind. After you take action by pressing a key, the file JAN.XYZ is erased.

Step 4   Press [Alt] + **F**. Press **X**

Step 5   Press **Y**

Step 6   Key in the following: A:\>**TYPE TEST.BAT** [Enter]

```
A:\>TYPE TEST.BAT
REM This is a test file
REM to see how the REM
REM command works.
TYPE JAN.BUD
COPY JAN.BUD JAN.XYZ
PAUSE You are going to delete JAN.XYZ
DEL JAN.XYZ

A:\>
```

WHAT'S HAPPENING? You saved the file to disk with the changes you made. You then looked at the contents of the file with the TYPE command. To execute TEST.BAT, you must key in TEST at the prompt.

Step 7   Key in the following: A:\>**TEST** [Enter]

```
A:\>TEST

A:\>REM This is a test file

A:\>REM to see how the REM

A:\>REM command works.

A:\>TYPE JAN.BUD
This is my January file.
It is my first dummy file.
This is file 1.

A:\>COPY JAN.BUD JAN.XYZ
        1 file(s) copied

A:\>PAUSE You are going to delete JAN.XYZ
Press any key to continue . . .
```

WHAT'S HAPPENING? If you have a version of DOS before 4.0, the message will read Strike a key when ready.... The batch file TEST has stopped running or "paused." It has halted execution until some action is taken. When you press a key, DOS will read and execute the next line of the batch file. PAUSE just stops; it is not an order. If ECHO was off, all you would see is the message, Press any key to continue .... You would not see your message You are going to delete JAN.XYZ.

Step 8   Press any key.

```
A:\>PAUSE You are going to delete JAN.XYZ
Press any key to continue . . .



A:\>DEL JAN.XYZ


A:\>
A:\>_
```

WHAT'S HAPPENING? The batch file continued executing all the steps and deleted the file called JAN.XYZ.

Step 9   Key in the following: A:\>**DIR JAN.XYZ** [Enter]

```
A:\>DIR JAN.XYZ

 Volume in drive A is DATADISK
 Volume Serial Number is 2F26-1901
 Directory of A:\

File not found

A:\>_
```

WHAT'S HAPPENING? The file JAN.XYZ was deleted.

10.18 Stopping a Batch File from Executing

In the above activity, you pressed a key after the PAUSE command was displayed so that the batch file continued to execute. What if you wanted to stop running the batch file? You can interrupt or exit from a batch file. You do this by pressing the Control key, and while pressing the Control key, press the letter C ([Ctrl] + C or [Ctrl] + [Break]). At whatever point [Ctrl] + C is pressed, you leave the batch file and return to the system prompt. The rest of the lines in the batch file do not execute.

10.19 Activity: Quitting a Batch File

Note: The DATA disk is in Drive A. The A:\> is displayed.

Step 1   Key in the following: A:\>**TEST** [Enter]

```
A:\>TEST

A:\>REM This is a test file

A:\>REM to see how the REM
```

```
A:\>REM command works.

A:\>TYPE JAN.BUD
This is my January file.
It is my first dummy file.
This is file 1.

A:\>COPY JAN.BUD JAN.XYZ
        1 file(s) copied

A:\>PAUSE You are going to delete JAN.XYZ
Press any key to continue . . .
```

WHAT'S HAPPENING? You are at the same point as you were in the last activity. The batch file reached the PAUSE command. It stopped running. You do not want to erase JAN.XYZ. You want the batch file to cease operation. Previous experience with the PAUSE command showed that pressing any key would continue running the program. If any key were pressed here, the next line in the file, DEL JAN.XYZ would execute and the file JAN.XYZ would be erased. To stop this from happening, another action must be taken to interrupt the batch file process.

Step 2   Press the **Ctrl** key. While pressing the **Ctrl** key, press the letter **C**

```
A:\>PAUSE You are going to delete JAN.XYZ
Press any key to continue . . .
^C

Terminate batch job (Y/N)?_
```

WHAT'S HAPPENING? The message is giving you a choice: either stop the batch file from running (Y for yes), or continue with the batch file (N for no). If you press Y for yes, the last line in the batch file, DEL JAN.XYZ, will not execute.

Step 3   Press **Y**

```
A:\>PAUSE You are going to delete JAN.XYZ
Press any key to continue . . .
^C

Terminate batch job (Y/N)?Y

A:\>_
```

WHAT'S HAPPENING? The system prompt is displayed. If the batch file was interrupted properly, JAN.XYZ should not have been deleted because the line, DEL JAN.XYZ should not have executed.

Step 4   Key in the following: A:\>**DIR JAN.XYZ** Enter

```
A:\>DIR JAN.XYZ

  Volume in drive A is DATADISK
  Volume Serial Number is 2F26-1901
  Directory of A:\

JAN       XYZ             72 11-23-95  10:41a
         1 file(s)              72 bytes
                          818,688 bytes free


A:\>_
```

WHAT'S HAPPENING? The file JAN.XYZ is still on the DATA disk. Pressing Ctrl + C at the line PAUSE You are going to delete JAN.XYZ broke into the batch file TEST.BAT and stopped it from running. Because TEST.BAT stopped executing and returned you to the system prompt, it never got to the command line DEL JAN.XYZ. Therefore, the file JAN.XYZ is still on the DATA disk. Although you broke into the batch file at the PAUSE statement, you can press Ctrl + C any time during the execution of a batch file. The batch file will stop the first chance it gets.

10.20 *Replaceable Parameters in Batch Files*

In the same way that you use parameters with DOS commands, parameters can be used effectively in batch files. Parameters are information that you want the command to have. The commands or programs use the information in the parameter. For instance, look at the command, DIR A:/W.

Command   **Command Line Parameter**
DIR   A:/W

In the above example, the space and the / are delimiters. DIR is the command. A: and W are parameters that tell DOS that you want a directory of A: and that you want it displayed in a wide mode. Parameters tell DIR what to do. When you use the DIR command as used above, the /W parameter is fixed; you cannot choose another letter.

DOS commands also use variable or replaceable parameters. An example of where a replaceable parameter can be used is with TYPE. TYPE requires one parameter, a file name. The command TYPE remains the same, but the file name you use will vary; hence, it is a variable parameter. TYPE uses the parameter that you keyed in to choose the file to display on the screen. You can key in TYPE THIS.FIL or TYPE TEST.TXT or whatever file name you want. You replace the file name for the parameter.

Command	Replaceable command line parameter
TYPE	THIS. FIL

or

Command	Replaceable command line parameter
TYPE	TEST.TXT

Batch files can also use **replaceable parameters**, also called **dummy parameters**, **substitute parameters** or **positional parameters**. When you key in the name of the batch file to execute, you can also key in, at the same time, additional information on the command line that your batch file can use. When you write the batch file, you supply the markers or place holders to let the batch file know that something, a variable, will be keyed in with the batch file name. The place holder, marker, or blank parameter used in a batch file is the percent sign (%) followed by a number from 0 through 9. The % sign is the signal to DOS that a parameter is coming. The numbers indicate what position the parameter is on the command line. The command itself is always %0.

The batch files that you have written so far deal with specific commands and specific file names, but the real power of batch files is their ability to use replaceable parameters. You are going to write a batch file in the usual way with specific file names and then use the batch file to see how replaceable parameters work.

10.21 Activity: Using Replaceable Parameters

Note: The DATA disk is in Drive A. The A: \> is displayed.

Step 1   Key in the following: A:\>**TYPE JAN.XYZ** [Enter]

Step 2   Key in the following: A:\>**DIR JAN.XYZ** [Enter]

```
A:\>TYPE JAN.XYZ
This is my January file.
It is my first dummy file.
This is file 1.

A:\>DIR JAN.XYZ

  Volume in drive A is DATADISK
  Volume Serial Number is 2F26-1901
  Directory of A:\

JAN        XYZ              72 11-23-95  10:41a
           1 file(s)              72 bytes
                          818,688 bytes free

A:\>_
```

WHAT'S HAPPENING? This file was created in the last activity. It has data in it and occupies 72 bytes of space on the disk. If you remember, when you delete a file, the data is still on the disk. What if you wanted a way to delete the data completely so that it cannot be recovered? You can effectively fool UNDELETE. One of the pieces of information that UNDELETE uses to recreate the data is the length of the file. If you can set the length of the file to 0 bytes, prior to deleting the file, the UNDELETE command has no way to recover the data. You have an "empty" file. How can you make a file 0 bytes long? You can redirect the output of the REM command (REM has nothing in it) to your file making it 0 bytes long. You are going to try this at the command line.

Step 3   Key in the following: A:\>**REM > JAN.XYZ** [Enter]

Step 4   Key in the following: A:\>**TYPE JAN.XYZ** [Enter]

Step 5   Key in the following: A:\>**DIR JAN.XYZ** [Enter]

```
A:\>REM > JAN.XYZ

A:\>TYPE JAN.XYZ

A:\>DIR JAN.XYZ

 Volume in drive A is DATADISK
 Volume Serial Number is 2F26-1901
 Directory of A:\

JAN     XYZ             0 06-26-94   6:58p
        1 file(s)            0 bytes
                       819,200 bytes free

A:\>_
```

WHAT'S HAPPENING? It worked. You have really deleted this file. Even if you use UNDELETE, there is no data in the file to recover. This command would be useful in a batch file.

Step 6   Key in the following: A:\>**EDIT KILLIT.BAT** [Enter]
                                REM > JAN.XYZ [Enter]
                                DEL JAN.XYZ

WHAT'S HAPPENING? You created a simple batch file that sends 0 bytes to JAN.XYZ and, then, deletes the file called JAN.XYZ. Remember that EDIT is the tool to write a batch file. You must still save KILLIT.BAT to disk before you can execute it.

Step 7   Press [Alt] + **F**. Press **X**

Step 8   Press **Y**

Step 9   Key in the following: A:\>**TYPE KILLIT.BAT** [Enter]

```
A:\>TYPE KILLIT.BAT
REM > JAN.XYZ
DEL JAN.XYZ

A:\>_
```

WHAT'S HAPPENING? You saved the file to disk. To execute this batch file, you must call it, which is another way of saying key in the command name.

Step 10   Key in the following: A:\>**KILLIT** [Enter]

```
A:\>KILLIT

A:\>REM > JAN.XYZ

A:\>DEL JAN.XYZ
```

```
A:\>
A:\>_
```

WHAT'S HAPPENING? The batch file called KILLIT ran successfully. However, it can only be used for the file called JAN.XYZ. You have deleted JAN.XYZ so now KILLIT.BAT is no longer useful. What if you wanted to do the same sequence of commands for a file called JAN.TMP or PERSONAL.FIL or any other file on the disk? Until now, you would have to create another batch file using JAN.TMP instead of JAN.XYZ. You would write another batch file for PERSONAL.FIL. You can quickly clutter up your disks with many batch files, all doing the same thing but using different file names and havin no value after they have executed. An easier way is to have a batch file that does the same steps—a generic batch file. When you execute it, you supply the specific parameter or file name that interests you.

You are going to edit KILLIT.BAT but use replaceable parameters. In addition, you will document it and add some protection for yourself. When you key in the replaceable parameters, be sure to use the percent sign (%), then the number 1. There is no space between the % and the number 1. Be sure you use the number 1, not the lower case letter l.

Step 11 Key in the following: A:\> **EDIT KILLIT.BAT** [Enter]

        REM This batch file will make [Enter]

        REM the data in a file unrecoverable. [Enter]

        DIR %1 [Enter]

        PAUSE You are going to kill the file, %1. Are you sure? [Enter]

Step 12 Replace REM > JAN.XYZ with **REM > %1**

Step 13 Replace DEL JAN.XYZ with **DEL %1**

```
 File  Edit  Search  Options                                      Help
                          KILLIT.BAT
REM This batch file will make                                          ↑
REM the data in a file unrecoverable.
DIR %1
PAUSE You are going to kill the file, %1. Are you sure?
REM > %1
DEL %1




















MS-DOS Editor  <F1=Help> Press ALT to activate menus        00006:007
```

WHAT'S HAPPENING? Your edited file should look like the above screen. You must save the file to disk.

Step 14   Press **Alt** + **F**. Press **X**

Step 15   Press **Y**

Step 16   Key in the following: A:\>**TYPE KILLIT.BAT** **Enter**

```
A:\>TYPE KILLIT.BAT
REM This batch file will make
REM the data in a file unrecoverable.
DIR %1
PAUSE You are going to kill the file, %1. Are you sure?
REM > %1
DEL %1

A:\>_
```

WHAT'S HAPPENING? You used EDIT to edit the file KILLIT.BAT. You then saved it to disk. You displayed the contents of the file on the screen. The contents of the batch file KILLIT.BAT is different from the previous version of KILLIT.BAT. By using the place holder %1, instead of a specific file name, you are saying that you do not yet know what file name (%1) you want these commands to apply to. When you run the batch file KILLIT, you will provide a value or parameter on the command line that the batch file will substitute for %1. For instance, if you keyed in on the command line, KILLIT MY.FIL, KILLIT is in the zero position on the command line (%0 replaceable parameter), and MY.FIL is in the first position on the command line (%1 replaceable parameter).

For you to understanding the purpose of replaceable parameters, you need to view them as positional parameters, their other name. DOS gets the information or knows what to substitute by the position on the command line. The first piece of data on the command line is always in position 0; the second piece of data on the command line is always in position 1; the third piece of data on the command line is always in position 2, and so on.

Step 17 Key in the following: A:\>**KILLIT JAN.BUD** Enter

```
A:\>KILLIT JAN.BUD

A:\>REM This batch file will make

A:\>REM the data in a file unrecoverable.

A:\>DIR JAN.BUD

 Volume in drive A is DATADISK
 Volume Serial Number is 2F26-1901
 Directory of A:\

JAN        BUD            72 11-23-95  10:41a
        1 file(s)              72 bytes
                         819,688 bytes free

A:\>PAUSE You are going to kill the file, JAN.BUD. Are you sure?
Press any key to continue . . .
```

WHAT'S HAPPENING? In the command line KILLIT JAN.BUD, KILLIT is position 0 and JAN.BUD is position 1. The batch file KILLIT executed each command line. However, when it found %1 in the batch file, it looked for the first position after KILLIT on the command line, which was JAN.BUD. It substituted JAN.BUD every time it found %1. You placed the DIR %1 in the batch file to confirm that it is on the disk. The PAUSE statement allows you to change your mind. The %1 in the PAUSE line identifies which file is to be killed.

Step 18 Press Enter

```
A:\>PAUSE You are going to kill the file, JAN.BUD. Are you sure?
Press any key to continue . . .

A:\>REM > JAN.BUD

A:\>DEL JAN.BUD

A:\>
A:\>
```

WHAT'S HAPPENING? You have deleted the file. Even if you, or anyone else tries to undelete it, the data is truly gone. You have written a generic or "plain wrap" batch file that allows you to use the same batch file over and over. All you have to supply is a value or parameter after the batch file name on the command line. Thus, you could key in KILLIT BUSINESS.APP, KILLIT SALES.LET, KILLIT FEB.99, KILLIT TELE.SET, or any other file name. The batch file will execute the same commands over and over, using the position 1 value (the file name) you keyed in after the batch file name.

10.22 Multiple Replaceable Parameters in Batch Files

In the above example, you used one replaceable parameter. What happens if you need more than one parameter? For instance, if you want to include the COPY command in a batch file, COPY needs two parameters: *source* and *destination*. Many commands require more than one parameter. You may also use multiple parameters in batch files. You can have up to ten dummy parameters (%0 through %9). Replaceable parameters are sometimes called positional parameters because DOS uses the position number in the command line to determine which parameter to use. The parameters are placed in order from left to right. For example, if you had the command line:

```
COPY MYFILE.TXT YOUR.FIL
```

COPY is in position one, %0 (computers always start with 0, not 1) MYFILE.TXT is in position two, %1, and YOUR.FIL is in position three, %2.

The next activity will allow you to create a simple batch file with multiple replaceable parameters so you will how the positional process works. Then, you will write another batch file, and in it you will create a command that DOS does not have. Your new command will copy all files *except* the ones you specify.

10.23 Activity: Using Multiple Replaceable Parameters

Note: The DATA disk is in Drive A. The A:\> is displayed.

Step 1   Key in the following: A:\>**EDIT MULTI.BAT** [Enter]

REM This is a sample batch file [Enter]

REM using more than one replaceable parameter. [Enter]

TYPE %3 [Enter]

COPY %1 %2 [Enter]

TYPE %1

Step 2   Press [Alt] + **F**. Press **X**

Step 3   Press **Y**

Step 4   Key in the following: A:\>**TYPE MULTI.BAT** [Enter]

```
A:\>TYPE MULTI.BAT
REM This is a sample batch file
REM using more than one replaceable parameter.
TYPE %3
COPY %1 %2
TYPE %1


A:\>_
```

WHAT'S HAPPENING? You are displaying the contents of MULTI.BAT. To execute it you must not only key in the command name MULTI but must also provide the command with the positional parameters. In the next step, you will key in MULTI APR.99 LAST.ONE FILE2.SWT. The batch file knows what to put in each percent sign because it looks at the *position* on the command line. It does not matter what the %1 or %2 or %3 order is in the batch file, only the order on the command line. See Table 10.3

Position 0 on the command line	Position 1 on the command line	Position 2 on the command line	Position 3 on the command line
MULTI	**APR.99**	**LAST.ONE**	**FILE2.SWT**
When batch file needs a value for %0, it uses **MULTI**	When batch file needs a value for %1, it uses **APR.99**	When batch file needs a value for %2, it uses **LAST.ONE**	When batch file needs a value for %3, it uses **FILE2.SWT**
COMMAND	PARAMETER	PARAMETER	PARAMETER

Table 10.3   *Positional Parameters*

Step 5   Key in the following:

A:\>**MULTI APR.99 LAST.ONE FILE2.SWT** [Enter]

```
A:\>MULTI APR.99 LAST.ONE FILE2.SWT

A:\>REM This is a sample batch file

A:\>REM using more than one replaceable parameter.

A:\>TYPE FILE2.SWT
This is file 2.

A:\>COPY APR.99 LAST.ONE
        1 file(s) copied

A:\>TYPE APR.99
This is my April file.
It is my fourth dummy file.
This is file 4.

A:\>
A:\>
A:\>_
```

WHAT'S HAPPENING? Each time the batch file came to a command line and needed a value for a replaceable parameter (%1, %2, or %3), it looked to the command line and counted over until it found the value to replace for the percent sign. NOCOPY.BAT is actually in the first position, which is counted as %0. The command itself is always first, or %0. Thus, to indicate the position of the replaceable parameters, %1 refers to the *first* position after the command, not the first item on the command line. %2 refers to the *second* position after the command, not the second item on the command line, and so on. Hence, when you refer to %1, you are referring to the first position after the command. When it needed a value for %1, it used APR.99 because that was in the first position on the command line. When it needed a value for %2, it used LAST.ONE because that was in the second position on the command line, and, when it needed a value for %3, it used FILE2.SWT because that was in the third position on the command line. Instead calling them replaceable parameters, it is easier to remember them as positional parameters because it is the *position* on the command line that matters, not where it occurs in the batch file. Although this batch file may show you how the positional parameters work, it is not very useful. You are going to use the same principle to create a command that DOS does not have.

Step 6   Key in the following: A:\>**EDIT NOCOPY.BAT** [Enter]

REM This batch file, NOCOPY.BAT, will hide specified files, [Enter]

REM then copy all other files from one location to another, [Enter]

REM then unhide the original files. [Enter]

ATTRIB +H %1 [Enter]

COPY %3*.* %2 [Enter]

ATTRIB -H %1

```
 File   Edit   Search   Options                                    Help
                          NOCOPY.BAT
REM This batch file, NOCOPY.BAT, will hide specified files,
REM then copy all other files from one location to another,
REM then unhide the original files.
ATTRIB +H %1
COPY %3\*.* %2
ATTRIB -H %1




                                                         00006:013
```

WHAT'S HAPPENING? You created a batch file called NOCOPY.BAT using multiple positional parameters. You have created a command that DOS does not have. It copies files selectively, allowing you to copy all files *except* those you hid. You must save the file to disk.

Step 7   Press **Alt** + **F**. Press **X**

Step 8   Press **Y**

Step 9   Key in the following: A:\>**TYPE NOCOPY.BAT** **Enter**

```
A:\>TYPE NOCOPY.BAT
REM This batch file, NOCOPY.BAT, will hide specified files,
REM then copy all other files from one location to another,
REM then unhide the original files.
ATTRIB +H %1
COPY %3\*.* %2
ATTRIB -H %1


A:\>_
```

WHAT'S HAPPENING? You are displaying the contents of NOCOPY.BAT. To execute it, you must not only key in the command name—NOCOPY—but also provide the command with the positional parameters. You want to copy all the files from the CLASS directory to the TRIP subdirectory *except* the files that have the .ABC file extension.

Step 10   Key in the following:

A:\>**NOCOPY CLASS*.ABC TRIP CLASS** **Enter**

```
A:\>NOCOPY CLASS\*.ABC TRIP CLASS

A:\>REM This batch file, NOCOPY.BAT, will hide specified files,

A:\>REM then copy all other files from one location to another,

A:\>REM then unhide the original files.

A:\>ATTRIB +H CLASS\*.ABC

A:\>COPY CLASS\*.* TRIP
CLASS\MAR.FIL
CLASS\JAN.FIL
CLASS\FEB.PAR
CLASS\JAN.PAR
CLASS\MAR.PAR
CLASS\APR.PAR
CLASS\APR.BUD
```

```
CLASS\JAN.BUD
CLASS\MAR.BUD
        9 file(s) copied

A:\>ATTRIB -H CLASS\*.ABC

A:\>
A:\>
A:\>
```

WHAT'S HAPPENING? You ran the batch file called NOCOPY. You substituted or provided the values: CLASS*.ABC (%1), TRIP (%2), and CLASS (%3). To check that the *.ABC files are not hidden in the CLASS directory and that they have not been copied to the TRIP directory, do the following:

Step 11 Key in the following: A:\>**DIR CLASS*.ABC** [Enter]

Step 12 Key in the following: A:\>**DIR TRIP*.ABC** [Enter]

```
A:\>DIR CLASS\*.ABC

 Volume in drive A is DATADISK
 Volume Serial Number is 2F26-1901
 Directory of A:\CLASS

APR        ABC          71 11-23-95  10:42a
FEB        ABC          74 11-23-95  10:41a
JAN        ABC          72 11-23-95  10:41a
MAR        ABC          70 11-23-95  10:42a
        4 file(s)            287 bytes
                         813,056 bytes free

A:\>DIR TRIP\*.ABC

 Volume in drive A is DATADISK
 Volume Serial Number is 2F26-1901
 Directory of A:\TRIP

File not found

A:\>_
```

WHAT'S HAPPENING? Your goal was achieved. To DOS, the command sequence or string of commands looked like this:

```
ATTRIB +H CLASS\*.ABC
COPY CLASS\*.* TRIP
ATTRIB -H CLASS\*.ABC
```

When you keyed in `NOCOPY CLASS\*.ABC TRIP CLASS`, you asked DOS to load the batch file called `NOCOPY.BAT`. The first position after `NOCOPY` has the value of `CLASS\*.ABC`. The second position has the value of `TRIP`, and the third position has the value of `CLASS`. DOS then executed the first line, which is:

1. `REM This batch file, NOCOPY.BAT, will hide specified files,`
   This line is information for you to know why you wrote the batch file.

2. `REM then copy all other files from one location to another,`
   This line is information for you to know why you wrote the batch file.

3. `REM then unhide the original files.`
   This line is a continuation of the information for you to know why you wrote this batch file.

4. `ATTRIB +H CLASS\*.ABC`
   This line tells ATTRIB to hide all the files in the `CLASS` directory with the file extension of .ABC. DOS knew which file and which directory were %1 and could substitute `CLASS\*.ABC` for %1 because `CLASS\*.ABC` held the first position (%1) after the command NOCOPY.

5. `COPY CLASS\*.* TRIP`
   This line tells DOS to copy files in a directory. It knew which directory to go to get the files because `CLASS` was %3. It substituted `CLASS` for `%3`. DOS knew it could substitute `CLASS` for %3 because `CLASS` was in the third position after NOCOPY. It knew to copy *all* the files because you included `*.*`. DOS knew which directory to copy the files to because it substituted `TRIP` for %2. It could substitute `TRIP` for %2 because `TRIP` was in the second position after NOCOPY.

6. `ATTRIB -H CLASS\*.ABC`
   This line tells DOS to unhide all the files in the `CLASS` directory with the file extension of .ABC. DOS knew which file and which directory were %1 and could substitute `CLASS\*.ABC` for %1 because `CLASS\*.ABC` held the first position after the command NOCOPY.

   This command, which you just wrote as a batch file with replaceable parameters, can be very useful. You can use it to copy files selectively from one disk to another or from one subdirectory to another. You do not need to take separate steps because all the steps are included in the batch file.

10.24 Creating Menus with Batch Files

You can use batch files to create menus that relate to your applications. A menu is exactly what it sounds like. In a restaurant, you look at a menu and then pick your selection. In this case, instead of picking out something to eat, you are picking a task to do. A menu system presents a "main menu" with choices in it. Each choice has a corresponding batch file. When you pick a choice from the menu, it runs the batch file that corresponds to the letter or number you picked. When you are done with the program, you are returned to the menu batch file. It is a chain where one batch file calls another batch file.

On your DATA disk you have copied the program called HPB to the HPB subdirectory. You are going to copy the games from the \DOS6BK\GAMES subdirectory to the subdirectory called GAMES on the DATA disk under the directory PROG which you created in Chapter 9. In the next activity, you are going to create a menu system to access easily a game you want to play or information you want from the HPB program. In addition, you will have a choice of exiting back to the system level.

10.25 Activity: Writing Menus

Note 1:   The DATA disk is in Drive A. The A:\> is displayed.
Note 2:   If you do not have a subdirectory under PROG called GAMES, create it now.

Step 1   Key in the following:

A:\>**XCOPY C:\DOS6BK\GAMES*.* PROG\GAMES** [Enter]

```
A:\>XCOPY C:\DOS6BK\GAMES\*.* PROG\GAMES
Reading source file(s)...
Overwrite PROG\GAMES\MLSHUT.DOC (Yes/No/All)?_
```

WHAT'S HAPPENING? Since you have some files in the PROG\GAMES subdirectory, XCOPY is asking you if you want to overwrite them. You do.

Step 2   Press **A** [Enter]

```
A:\>XCOPY C:\DOS6BK\GAMES\*.* PROG\GAMES
Reading source file(s)...
Overwrite PROG\GAMES\MLSHUT.DOC (Yes/No/All)?A
C:\DOS6BK\GAMES\MLSHUT.EXE
C:\DOS6BK\GAMES\MAZE.EXE
C:\DOS6BK\GAMES\LS.PAS
C:\DOS6BK\GAMES\LS.DOC
C:\DOS6BK\GAMES\LS.EXE
C:\DOS6BK\GAMES\3DTICTAC.EXE
C:\DOS6BK\GAMES\ARGH.DOC
C:\DOS6BK\GAMES\ARGH.EXE
        9 File(s) copied

A:\>_
```

WHAT'S HAPPENING? You copied the games from the \DOS6BK\GAMES subdirectory to the PROG\GAMES subdirectory on the DATA disk.

Step 3   Key in the following: A:\>**MD \BATCH** Enter

Step 4   Key in the following: A:\>**CD \BATCH** Enter

```
A:\>MD BATCH

A:\>CD BATCH

A:\BATCH>_
```

WHAT'S HAPPENING? You created a subdirectory called BATCH where you will keep all your batch files and any associated files. It is always wise to keep like files together. You then changed the default directory to BATCH where you are going to write the necessary files.

Step 5   *Note:* When you see Enter, press the Enter key. When you see Tab, press the Tab key.

Key in the following: A:\BATCH>**EDIT MENU.TXT** Enter

Enter

Enter

MY MENU SYSTEM Enter

Enter

Enter

A. Tab **HOME PHONE BOOK** Enter

B. Tab **THE GAME CALLED MAZE** Enter

E. Tab **EXIT TO DOS** Enter

Enter

Enter

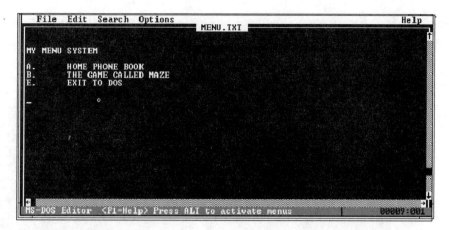

WHAT'S HAPPENING? You are using EDIT to write a text file that will be used in the batch file. You must now save this file to disk.

Step 6   Press **Alt** + **F**. Press **X**

Step 7   Press **Y**

Step 8   Key in the following: A:\BATCH>**TYPE MENU.TXT** **Enter**

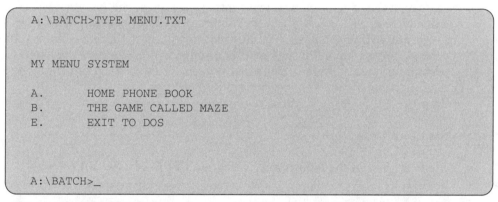

```
A:\BATCH>TYPE MENU.TXT


MY MENU SYSTEM

A.       HOME PHONE BOOK
B.       THE GAME CALLED MAZE
E.       EXIT TO DOS


A:\BATCH>_
```

WHAT'S HAPPENING? The file you just created is not a batch file. It is simply a text file which displays your choices. It will be displayed in the menu batch file with the TYPE command. It is easier to create a separate text file than it is to put these text lines in a batch file. If you put text lines in a batch file, every line would have to be preceded by a REM, or an ECHO if you used ECHO OFF, so that DOS would not try to execute the line. The next step is to create the MENU.BAT file.

Step 9   Key in the following: A:\BATCH>**EDIT MENU.BAT** Enter
                             TYPE MENU.TXT Enter
                             PROMPT Select a letter. SpaceBar SpaceBar

WHAT'S HAPPENING? This batch file has two lines. The first command line will display the contents of the MENU.TXT file. The MENU.TXT file simply tells you what the choices are. The second command line changes the way the prompt looks. Instead of the prompt being a drive letter such as A> or A:\BATCH> or C:\>, it will now read Select a letter. You pressed the SpaceBar twice after Select a letter so that you have a visually pleasing prompt. Since it is the command line prompt, any command issued at this prompt will perform in the same way. The prompt just looks different. You must save the file before you test the menu system.

Step 10   Press Alt + **F**. Press **X**

Step 11   Press **Y**

Step 12   Key in the following: A:\BATCH>**TYPE MENU.BAT** Enter

```
A:\BATCH>TYPE MENU.BAT
TYPE MENU.TXT
PROMPT   SELECT A LETTER

A:\BATCH>_
```

WHAT'S HAPPENING? You saved the file to disk. The next step is to execute it.

Step 13   Key in the following: A:\BATCH>**MENU** Enter

```
A:\BATCH>MENU
```

```
A:\BATCH>TYPE MENU.TXT

MY MENU SYSTEM



A.         HOME PHONE BOOK
B.         THE GAME CALLED MAZE
E.         EXIT TO DOS




A:\BATCH>PROMPT   SELECT A LETTER

SELECT A LETTER
SELECT A LETTER _
```

WHAT'S HAPPENING? DOS read and executed each line of the batch file. Notice that the prompt looks different. It will behave the same as any prompt. However, if you try to select one of the choices from the menu by keying in A, B, or E, all that will happen is that you will get the `Bad command or file name` message. When you key something in at the command line prompt, DOS looks for a program to execute. Thus, if you key in A, it will be to no purpose since, as of yet, you have no program called `A.COM`, `A.EXE`, or `A.BAT`. If DOS cannot find a program, it cannot execute it.

Step 14   Key in the following: **A** **Enter**

Step 15   Key in the following: **DIR** **Enter**

```
Select a letter.   A
Bad command or file name

Select a letter.   DIR

 Volume in drive A is DATADISK
 Volume Serial Number is 2F26-1901
 Directory of A:\BATCH


 .              <DIR>         07-01-94    5:10p
 ..             <DIR>         07-01-94    5:10p
MENU    TXT          102 07-01-94    5:12p
MENU    BAT           43 07-01-94    5:18p
        4 file(s)            145 bytes
                      669,696 bytes free

Select a letter._
```

WHAT'S HAPPENING? When you keyed in A at the prompt Select a letter, DOS looked for a file called A.COM, then A.EXE and last, A.BAT. There are no programs with those names. You must write a batch file called A.BAT, B.BAT, and E.BAT in order to be able to select the choices. However, DIR did execute. How the prompt looks makes no difference in executing commands, when there is a command to execute.

Step 16   Key in the following: **PROMPT pg** [Enter]

```
SELECT A LETTER      PROMPT $p$g

A:\BATCH>_
```

WHAT'S HAPPENING? The prompt has been changed from Select a letter to a prompt that identifies the default drive and subdirectory. Now, you are going to write some other batch files. Each of the batch files will contain the steps necessary to accomplish running the application programs. For instance, you know that on this disk the HOME PHONE BOOK program is called HPB.EXE and is located in the subdirectory \HPB. Thus, you must change directories before you issue the HPB command. In addition, when you have finished using the phone book program, not only do you want to return to the system level, but you also want to return to the menu system. You are, in essence, **chaining batch files** together.

Step 17   Key in the following: A:\BATCH>**EDIT A.BAT** [Enter]

                             PROMPT pg [Enter]

                             CD \HPB [Enter]

                             HPB [Enter]

                             CD \BATCH [Enter]

                             MENU

WHAT'S HAPPENING? Each line in the A.BAT file takes you through the steps that you need to access the phone book program. First you change the prompt so that it reflects the current drive and subdirectory. Then you change the default directory to the \HPB subdirectory. You next issue the HPB command that will execute the phone book program. You then can do work in the phone book for an hour, a minute, or a day. Time does not matter. When you exit the phone book program, DOS returns to the next line in the batch file, which returns you to the \BATCH subdirectory. It then executes the next line, which calls the MENU.BAT program. Do not forget to save the A.BAT file to disk.

Step 18   Press **Alt** + **F**. Press **X**

Step 19   Press **Y**

Step 20   Key in the following: A:\BATCH>**TYPE A.BAT** **Enter**

```
A:\BATCH>TYPE A.BAT
PROMPT $p$g
CD \HPB
HPB
CD \BATCH
MENU

A:\BATCH>_
```

WHAT'S HAPPENING? You now have saved the file. To see both MENU.BAT and A.BAT in action, you must begin with MENU.

Step 21   Key in the following: A:\BATCH>**MENU** **Enter**

```
A:\BATCH>TYPE MENU.TXT

MY MENU SYSTEM



A.        HOME PHONE BOOK
B.        THE GAME CALLED MAZE
E.        EXIT TO DOS


A:\BATCH>PROMPT   SELECT A LETTER

SELECT A LETTER
SELECT A LETTER_
```

WHAT'S HAPPENING? The menu system looks the same. Now that you have written the batch file called A.BAT, when you key in A at the Select a letter prompt, DOS will find A.BAT and execute it. Watch the screen closely in the next step. Notice how quickly you will be in the phone book program.

Step 22   Key in the following: A Enter

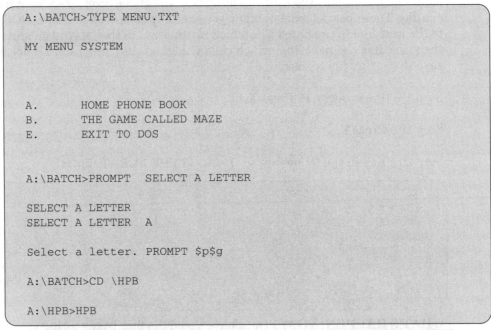

```
A:\BATCH>TYPE MENU.TXT

MY MENU SYSTEM


A.        HOME PHONE BOOK
B.        THE GAME CALLED MAZE
E.        EXIT TO DOS


A:\BATCH>PROMPT  SELECT A LETTER

SELECT A LETTER
SELECT A LETTER  A

Select a letter. PROMPT $p$g

A:\BATCH>CD \HPB

A:\HPB>HPB
```

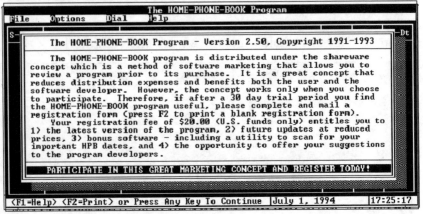

WHAT'S HAPPENING? By selecting the letter A, you ended up in the application program, The HOME-PHONE-BOOK Program (HPB).

Step 23   Press Enter

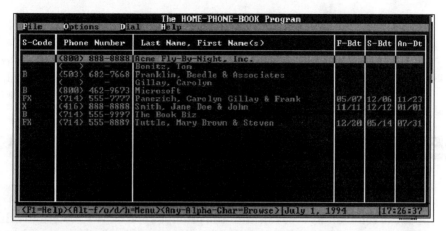

WHAT'S HAPPENING? You are now in the main screen of the program. You could stay here and look up a phone number or edit a phone number or whatever work you planned to do. Sooner or later, you would be finished working and would want to exit the program. The batch file, MENU.BAT, is still poised on the line HPB. The minute you exit the phone program, DOS will read the next line CD \BATCH. Again, watch the screen carefully in the next step because the screen display will execute very quickly.

Step 24   Press **Alt** + **F**. Press **X**

```
A:\HPB>CD \BATCH

A:\BATCH>MENU

A:\BATCH>TYPE MENU.TXT

MY MENU SYSTEM



A.        HOME PHONE BOOK
B.        THE GAME CALLED MAZE
E.        EXIT TO DOS



A:\BATCH>PROMPT   SELECT A LETTER
```

```
SELECT A LETTER
SELECT A LETTER _
```

WHAT'S HAPPENING? You exited The HOME-PHONE-BOOK Program. The next line in the batch file was read and executed (CD \BATCH), and then the next line was read and executed (MENU). Now, you are ready for the next step. You need to write the rest of the batch files, B.BAT, E.BAT, and END.TXT.

10.26 Completing the Menu

In order to complete your menu system, you need to write more files. You need to write B.BAT and E.BAT. The file called E.BAT will, like MENU.BAT, use a file called MENU.TXT. You must also write that. In addition, you may have noticed that you can see the commands. It seems that the prompt appears twice. Actually that is not so. What happens is that DOS really is reading each line in the batch file as if you were keying it in. It has no way to know when there are no more lines to read. It finds out when it tries to put a batch file line at the prompt. There is no line, so DOS exits the batch file and returns to the "real" prompt, thus giving the appearance of two prompts.

You can make the menu system more appealing by using ECHO OFF and CLS to eliminate that problem. If you do not even want to see ECHO OFF as the first line in the batch file, you can suppress its display by preceding it with the @ sign, as in @ECHO OFF. Then, ECHO OFF will not appear on the screen.

In the next activity, you will be shown each batch file that is needed to complete the menu system. You use EDIT to create or edit the files as necessary.

10.27 Activity: Completing the Menu

Note: The DATA disk is in Drive A. The A:\BATCH> is displayed.

Step 1   Key in the following: **PROMPT pg** [Enter]

```
SELECT A LETTER
SELECT A LETTER      PROMPT $p$g

A:\BATCH>_
```

WHAT'S HAPPENING? You changed the prompt so that it displays the default drive and subdirectory. Be sure you are in the BATCH subdirectory on the DATA disk. You are going to write the rest of the files needed for the menu system as well as discover how to make the menu system more aesthetically pleasing. You will use EDIT to create or alter the files. MENU.TXT is the only file that does not change. All files must be in the BATCH subdirectory. Using the editor of your choice, create the following files.

MENU.BAT

```
@ECHO OFF
CLS
TYPE MENU.TXT
PROMPT SELECT A LETTER
```

A.BAT

```
@ECHO OFF
CLS
PROMPT $p$g
CD \HPB
HPB
CD \BATCH
MENU
```

B.BAT

```
@ECHO OFF
CLS
CD \PROG\GAMES
MAZE
CD \BATCH
MENU
```

E.BAT

```
@ECHO OFF
CLS
PROMPT $p$g
CD \
TYPE \BATCH\END.TXT
```

END.TXT

```
You have exited the MENU program. If you wish to
return to the MENU system, you must key in the following:
```

CD\BATCH
MENU

WHAT'S HAPPENING? The files you need are complete.

Step 2:   Key in the following: A:\BATCH>**DIR** Enter

```
A:\BATCH>DIR

 Volume in drive A is DATADISK
 Volume Serial Number is 2F26-1901
 Directory of A:\BATCH

 .              <DIR>        07-01-94    5:10p
 ..             <DIR>        07-01-94    5:10p
 MENU    TXT            102  07-01-94    5:12p
 MENU    BAT             59  07-02-94   11:38a
 A       BAT             60  07-02-94   11:39a
 B       BAT             55  07-02-94   11:39a
 E       BAT             60  07-02-94   11:40a
 END     TXT            166  07-02-94   11:41a
         8 file(s)            502 bytes
                         667,648 bytes free

A:\BATCH>_
```

WHAT'S HAPPENING? Each file has purpose. MENU.BAT is the program that sets up the menu system. MENU.TXT is an easy way to give instructions. A.BAT takes you to the HPB program, and its last line is MENU, which, once again, runs the MENU.BAT program. B.BAT takes you to the MAZE program, and its last line is MENU which runs the MENU.BAT program. E.BAT changes the prompt and takes you to the root directory. It then displays the END.TXT file, which is an easy way to give instructions. These are all the files that make the menu system work. Now, you are going to see how it works.

Step 3   Key in the following: A:\BATCH>**MENU** [Enter]

```
MY MENU SYSTEM




 A.      HOME PHONE BOOK
 B.      THE GAME CALLED MAZE
 E.      EXIT TO DOS




 SELECT A LETTER
```

WHAT'S HAPPENING? By turning ECHO OFF and clearing the screen, your menu looks much more attractive. If you wanted, you could add characters like the asterisk to set it off more or indent the choices. You would do this in the MENU.TXT file.

Step 4   Press **A** [Enter]

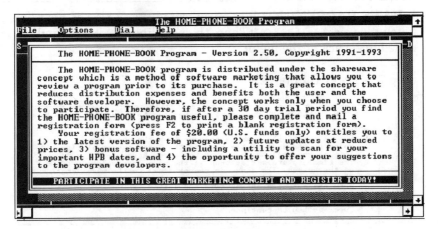

WHAT'S HAPPENING? By selecting A, you executed A.BAT, which changed directories and loaded the HPB.EXE program.

Step 5   Press [Enter]

S-Code	Phone Number	Last Name, First Name(s)	F-Bdt	S-Bdt	An-D
	(800) 888-8888	Acme Fly-By-Night, Inc.			
	( ) -	Bonitz, Tom			
B	(503) 682-7668	Franklin, Beedle & Associates			
	( ) -	Gillay, Carolyn			
B	(800) 462-9673	Microsoft			
FX	(714) 555-7777	Panezich, Carolyn Gillay & Frank	05/07	12/06	11/2
X	(416) 888-8888	Smith, Jane Doe & John	11/11	12/12	01/0
B	(714) 555-9997	The Book Biz			
FX	(714) 555-8889	Tuttle, Mary Brown & Steven	12/20	05/14	07/3

WHAT'S HAPPENING? You are in the phone book program. Now you want to return to the menu program (MENU.BAT).

Step 6   Press [Alt] + **F**. Press **X**

```
MY MENU SYSTEM




A.      HOME PHONE BOOK
B.      THE GAME CALLED MAZE
E.      EXIT TO DOS
```

```
SELECT A LETTER
```

WHAT'S HAPPENING? When you exited HPB.EXE, the next line in the A.BAT batch file was CD \BATCH. Then, the next line was MENU, and that is where you ended up—back at the menu.

Step 7   Press **B** **Enter**

```
M A Z E    (SHAREWARE Version 1.00) written by Garry Spencer - Memphis, TN

NOTES:
1) The object of the game is to move from the starting
   point to the exit of the maze in the least amount of time.
   This is accomplished by using the arrow keys.
2) The timer is started as soon as the maze is completely drawn
   on the screen. The score is proportional to the maze length.
3) If you have trouble with a particular maze, the computer will
   show the solution if you type the letter 'S' .
4) Type 'Q' or 'ESCape' to Quit

   Type any key to continue
```

WHAT'S HAPPENING? By selecting B, you executed B.BAT, which changed directories and loaded the MAZE.EXE program.

Step 8   Press **Enter**

WHAT'S HAPPENING? You are in the MAZE game. If you want to play it, use your arrow keys to move the happy face out of the maze.

Step 9   Press **Esc**

```
MY MENU SYSTEM
```

```
A.        HOME PHONE BOOK
B.        THE GAME CALLED MAZE
E.        EXIT TO DOS




SELECT A LETTER
```

WHAT'S HAPPENING? When you exited MAZE.EXE, the next line in the B.BAT batch file was CD \BATCH. The next line was MENU, and that is where you ended up—back at the menu. Now, you want to exit the menu program.

Step 10 Press E **Enter**

```
        You have exited the MENU program. If you wish to
        return to the MENU system, you must key in the following:

        CD \BATCH
        MENU


A:\>_
```

WHAT'S HAPPENING? You exited the menu system and are back at the root directory of the DATA disk. When you pressed E, you were executing the program called E.BAT, which returned you to the root directory and displayed the contents of \BATCH\END.TXT. Your introduction to writing menus is complete.

10.28 Understanding AUTOEXEC.BAT

AUTOEXEC.BAT, which means automatically execute, is a unique batch file. When the system is booted and the operating system is loaded into memory, one of the last things DOS does is to look for a file called AUTOEXEC.BAT on the booting disk. If DOS finds it, this file takes precedence and DOS automatically runs it. The AUTOEXEC.BAT file is just a batch file. The only thing special about it is the time it is run. It always runs when you boot the system. Thus, only one AUTOEXEC.BAT file can be on any one booting disk. In order for AUTOEXEC.BAT to be automatic, it must be on the booting disk, Drive A or Drive C. It must also be located in the root directory of the booting disk.

The AUTOEXEC.BAT file is typically used for start-up routines. It contains specific commands that a user chooses to run. In other words, it is a custom program designed by the user. Typical lines that a user puts in the AUTOEXEC.BAT file include the PROMPT pg, the PATH statement, and any program needed to begin a work session. If, when you boot your system, you automatically are in Windows or DOS Shell, it is because the last line in the AUTOEXEC.BAT file is WIN (for Windows—the program called WIN.COM) or DOSSHELL (for the program called

DOSSHELL.EXE). If you do not want to load Windows automatically, you could edit AUTOEXEC.BAT and either delete the line WIN or place a REM in front of it as in REM WIN. Remember, when you place a REM in front of a line, DOS only displays the line, it does not execute it. If ECHO OFF is in the AUTOEXEC.BAT file, you will not see any line prefaced by a REM.

In MS-DOS 6.2, a new feature was added. It is called **interactive booting**. There are two ways to use it. One is called a **clean boot**. A clean boot means that both your CONFIG.SYS file and your AUTOEXEC.BAT file are bypassed and not executed. The CONFIG.SYS file is a file that configures your system and sets up different hardware and software specific to your computer. The other choice is truly interactive. You will be asked by DOS if you want each line in the CONFIG.SYS file and the AUTOEXEC.BAT to execute. If you are having trouble with your computer, this allows you to troubleshoot the problem by trying out different combinations of commands so that you can pinpoint the troublemaker. If you do a "clean" boot and/ or bypass your CONFIG.SYS file and AUTOEXEC.BAT files, MS-DOS will not load installable device drivers so that, if you have a CD-ROM drive, for example, it will not work.

Before doing the next activity, you should check with your instructor. If you are on a network, the instructor may not want you to do this activity. If you are working on your own computer, you may proceed.

You are going to create an AUTOEXEC.BAT file on a newly formatted floppy disk that has the operating system files copied to it. This is known as a bootable floppy. You will place it in Drive A and then boot from Drive A. You can boot only from Drive A or Drive C. If there is a bootable floppy in Drive A, your computer will boot from that disk and never go to Drive C. A bootable floppy is an emergency disk. If something goes wrong with your hard disk so you cannot boot from it, you need a way to get into your system.

WARNING: CHECK WITH YOUR INSTRUCTOR BEFORE PROCEEDING. YOU MAY BE INSTRUCTED TO READ THE ACTIVITY AND NOT DO IT.

10.29 Activity: Writing and Using an AUTOEXEC.BAT File

Note: The DATA disk is in Drive A. The A:\> is displayed.

Step 1   Remove the DATA disk from Drive A. Label a new blank disk or a disk with data you no longer want, "Bootable DOS System Disk." Insert this disk in Drive A. Remember that the blank disk must be compatible with your disk drive. IT MUST BE DRIVE A.

Step 2   Key in the following: A:\>C: **Enter**

Step 3   Key in the following: C:\>**FORMAT A:/S/U** **Enter**

```
C:\>FORMAT A:/S/U
Insert new diskette for drive A:
and press ENTER when ready...
```

WHAT'S HAPPENING? You are going to format a disk with an operating system. The /S parameter copies the two hidden files IO.SYS and MS.DOS to the disk in Drive A. It then copies the file called COMMAND.COM to the disk in Drive A. The /U parameter for unconditional means that FORMAT will not even try to make this disk unformattable.

Step 4   Press **Enter**

```
C:\>FORMAT A:/S/U
Insert new diskette for drive A:
and press ENTER when ready...

Formatting 1.2M
Format complete.
System transferred

Volume label (11 characters, ENTER for none)?_
```

WHAT'S HAPPENING? You see a new message System transferred. System transferred means that IO.SYS, MSDOS.SYS, and COMMAND.COM were copied to the disk in Drive A. This is now a bootable system disk.

Step 5   Key in the following at the Volume Label prompt: **DOS SYSTEM** **Enter**

```
Volume label (11 characters, ENTER for none)? DOS SYSTEM

    1,213,952 bytes total disk space
      200,704 bytes used by system
    1,013,248 bytes available on disk

        512 bytes in each allocation unit.
      1,979 allocation units available on disk.

Volume Serial Number is 383E-12FE

Format another (Y/N)?_
```

WHAT'S HAPPENING? You now have a volume label on the disk. You can also see that the operating system files take a lot of room on the disk. Thus, you rarely make data disks bootable. You do not want to format another.

Step 6   Press N **Enter**

```
Format another (Y/N)?N



C:\>_
```

WHAT'S HAPPENING? Now that you have formatted a disk with an operating system on it, you are ready to write an AUTOEXEC.BAT file.

Step 7   Key in the following: C:\>**A:** Enter

Step 8   Key in the following: **EDIT A:\AUTOEXEC.BAT**

WHAT'S HAPPENING? You should have a blank EDIT screen. If it is not blank, exit now and repeat Steps 7 and 8.

Step 9   Key in the following: **PROMPT pg** Enter
                                 PATH A:\GAMES Enter
                                 DIR Enter
                                 VER

WHAT'S HAPPENING? You have written a simple AUTOEXEC.BAT file with EDIT. Now, you need to save the file to disk.

Step 10   Press $\boxed{\text{Alt}}$ + **F**. Press **X**

Step 11   Press **Y**

Step 12   Key in the following: A:\>**TYPE AUTOEXEC.BAT** $\boxed{\text{Enter}}$

```
A:\>TYPE AUTOEXEC.BAT
PROMPT $p$g
PATH A:\GAMES
DIR
VER


A:\>_
```

WHAT'S HAPPENING? You have written a batch file named AUTOEXEC.BAT using EDIT. When you completed writing the batch file, you exited EDIT and returned to the system prompt. You then displayed the contents of the file with the TYPE command. The batch file will then execute the first line which asks for changes in the prompt so that it will reflect the current drive and subdirectory. Then the path will be set to GAMES on Drive A. Next, you will see a DIR of the root directory. Last, it will show you the version of DOS you are working with. What makes AUTOEXEC.BAT unique is that it executes automatically when you boot the system. However, before you do that, you are going to create the GAMES directory on the disk and copy the files from the C:\DOS6BK\GAMES subdirectory to the GAMES directory on the bootable floppy disk.

Step 13   Key in the following:

A:\>**XCOPY C:\DOS6BK\GAMES*.* GAMES** $\boxed{\text{Enter}}$

```
A:\>XCOPY C:\DOS6BK\GAMES\*.*  GAMES
Does GAMES specify a file name
or directory name on the target
(F = file, D = directory)?_
```

WHAT'S HAPPENING? You are using XCOPY to copy the games and to create a directory called GAMES.

Step 14   Press **D**

```
Reading source file(s)...
C:\DOS6BK\GAMES\MLSHUT.DOC
C:\DOS6BK\GAMES\MLSHUT.EXE
C:\DOS6BK\GAMES\MAZE.EXE
C:\DOS6BK\GAMES\LS.PAS
C:\DOS6BK\GAMES\LS.DOC
C:\DOS6BK\GAMES\LS.EXE
```

```
C:\DOS6BK\GAMES\3DTICTAC.EXE
C:\DOS6BK\GAMES\ARGH.DOC
C:\DOS6BK\GAMES\ARGH.EXE
        9 File(s) copied

A:\>_
```

WHAT'S HAPPENING? Using XCOPY, you created a subdirectory and copied files to it. If you are on a network and have permission to do this activity, you should log off the network before proceeding.

Step 15　Log off the network, if you are on a network. Then, reboot the system by pressing the Ctrl, Alt, and Delete keys. Your display will vary depending on your computer brand. The following example is rebooting a Dell computer.

```
Phoenix 80486 ROM BIOS PLUS Version 1.10 A16
Copyright (C) 1985-1988 Phoenix Technologies Ltd.
Copyright (C) 1990-1993 Dell Computer Corporation
All Rights Reserved

Quadtel S3 86C801/805 Enhanced VGA BIOS, Version 2.13.06
Copyright 1987-1992 Phoenix Technologies Ltd.
Copyright 1992-1993 S3 Inc.
All Rights Reserved

Dell Embedded Diagnostics Version 1.11
Copyright 1992-1993 Dell Computer Corporation
All Rights Reserved

Dell System 466/M

Starting MS-DOS...

A:\>PROMPT $p$g

A:\>PATH A:\GAMES

A:\>DIR

 Volume in drive A is DOS SYSTEM
 Volume Serial Number is 383E-12FE
 Directory of A:\

COMMAND  COM        54,645 05-31-94   6:22a
AUTOEXEC BAT            38 07-02-94  12:02p
GAMES        <DIR>        07-02-94  12:10p
```

```
        3 file(s)          54,683 bytes
                          776,192 bytes free


 A:\>VER

 MS-DOS Version 6.22


 A:\>
 A:\>_
```

WHAT'S HAPPENING? You did not have to key in the file name to execute this batch file because it is called AUTOEXEC.BAT and always automatically executes when you boot the system. It followed the instructions you included in it. It changed the prompt, set the path, ran the command DIR, and indicated what version of DOS you are running. Since the last command in AUTOEXEC.BAT was VER, DOS returns control from the batch file to DOS, ready for you to key in the next command.

10.30 Controlling the Boot Process

It is always good to have a bootable floppy system disk so that, when or if something goes wrong, you can always reboot. When you are experiencing problems that could be related to the statements in the CONFIG.SYS or AUTOEXEC.BAT file, you want a way to bypass the computer following the instructions in either CONFIG.SYS or AUTOEXEC.BAT. That is the purpose of the bootable floppy system disk.

Beginning with MS-DOS 6.0, a new procedure is included that allows you to bypass both files. In addition, the new procedure allows you to install lines selectively in the CONFIG.SYS file and, beginning with MS-DOS 6.2, allows you to install lines selectively in AUTOEXEC.BAT. This procedure involves certain function keys the moment you see the line displayed on your computer:

```
 Starting MS-DOS ...
```

When you see that message, you can use the function keys. When you use these keys the results are:

F5	You will bypass both the CONFIG.SYS and AUTOEXEC.BAT files.
F8	You will be prompted whether or not you want to process each line in the CONFIG.SYS and AUTOEXEC.BAT files.
Ctrl + **F5**	You will bypass both the CONFIG.SYS and AUTOEXEC.BAT files and not install either DOUBLESPACE or DRIVESPACE.
Ctrl + **F8**	You will be prompted whether or not you want to process each line in the CONFIG.SYS and AUTOEXEC.BAT files. You will not load DOUBLESPACE or DRIVESPACE.

Pressing the [F5] key is known as a clean boot, and pressing the [F8] key is known as an interactive boot. In the next activity, you will try both of these scenarios. You will not use the [Ctrl] key in conjunction with either the [F5] or [F8] key.

WARNING: CHECK WITH YOUR INSTRUCTOR BEFORE PROCEEDING. YOU MAY BE INSTRUCTED TO READ THE ACTIVITY ONLY.

10.31 Activity: Bypassing AUTOEXEC.BAT

Note: The Bootable DOS System Disk is in Drive A. The A:\> is displayed.

Step 1   Reboot the system by pressing the [Ctrl] + [Alt] + [Delete] keys. If you have a reset button, you may use it instead of keystrokes.

Step 2   The moment you see the prompt Starting MS-DOS..., press the [F5] key.

```
Phoenix 80486 ROM BIOS PLUS Version 1.10 A16
Copyright (C) 1985-1988 Phoenix Technologies Ltd.
Copyright (C) 1990-1993 Dell Computer Corporation
All Rights Reserved

Quadtel S3 86C801/805 Enhanced VGA BIOS, Version 2.13.06
Copyright 1987-1992 Phoenix Technologies Ltd.
Copyright 1992-1993 S3 Inc.
All Rights Reserved

Dell Embedded Diagnostics Version 1.11
Copyright 1992-1993 Dell Computer Corporation
All Rights Reserved

Dell System 466/M

640 K Base Memory, 15648K Extended

Starting MS-DOS...

MS-DOS is bypassing your CONFIG.SYS and AUTOEXEC.BAT files.

Microsoft (R) MS-DOS (R) Version 6.22
            (C) Copyright Microsoft Corp. 1981-1994.

A:\>
```

WHAT'S HAPPENING? There is no CONFIG.SYS file on this disk. Furthermore, the commands in the AUTOEXEC.BAT file were not executed. You do not see the DIR command nor the VER command displayed. If you boot from a floppy system disk from Drive A, no path is set. If you boot with no disk in drive A, MS-DOS will automatically set the path to C:\DOS.

Step 3   Reboot the system by pressing the $\boxed{\text{Ctrl}}$ + $\boxed{\text{Alt}}$ + $\boxed{\text{Delete}}$ keys or the reset button.

Step 4   The moment you see the prompt Starting MS-DOS..., press the $\boxed{\text{F8}}$ key.

```
Phoenix 80486 ROM BIOS PLUS Version 1.10 A16
Copyright (C) 1985-1988 Phoenix Technologies Ltd.
Copyright (C) 1990-1993 Dell Computer Corporation
All Rights Reserved

Quadtel S3 86C801/805 Enhanced VGA BIOS, Version 2.13.06
Copyright 1987-1992 Phoenix Technologies Ltd.
Copyright 1992-1993 S3 Inc.
All Rights Reserved

Dell Embedded Diagnostics Version 1.11
Copyright 1992-1993 Dell Computer Corporation
All Rights Reserved

Dell System 466/M

640 K Base Memory, 15648K Extended

Starting MS-DOS...

MS-DOS will prompt you to confirm each CONFIG.SYS command.
Process AUTOEXEC.BAT [Y,N]?
```

WHAT'S HAPPENING? This bootable floppy DOS System Disk had no CONFIG.SYS file, so MS-DOS proceeded to the AUTOEXEC.BAT file.

Step 5   Press **Y** (*Do not* press $\boxed{\text{Enter}}$)

```
A:\>PROMPT $p$g
PROMPT $p$g [Y/N]?_
```

WHAT'S HAPPENING? The AUTOEXEC.BAT file is asking you whether or not you want to change the prompt.

Step 6   Press **Y**

```
A:\>PATH A:\GAMES
PATH A:\GAMES [Y/N]?_
```

WHAT'S HAPPENING? The AUTOEXEC.BAT file is asking you whether or not you want to set the path.

Step 7   Press **Y**

```
A:\>DIR
DIR [Y/N]?_
```

WHAT'S HAPPENING? The AUTOEXEC.BAT file is asking you whether or not you execute the DIR command.

Step 8   Press **N**

```
A:\>VER
VER [Y/N]?_
```

WHAT'S HAPPENING? The AUTOEXEC.BAT file is asking you whether or not you want to execute the VER command.

Step 9   Press **Y**

```
MS-DOS Version 6.22

A:\>
A:\>_
```

WHAT'S HAPPENING? There are no more commands to process.

10.32 Running a Program When You Boot

Often, you want to work on the same program every time you start up. For instance, you might always want the MENU program to run. To ensure this process, you place this command as the last line in the AUTOEXEC.BAT file. When you no longer want that program to run every time you boot the computer, you remove the line from AUTOEXEC.BAT.

In the next activity, you are going to execute the Shut the Box program automatically. However, you no longer have an editor available to you since this AUTOEXEC.BAT did not set the path to C:\DOS where EDIT is located. If you are on your own computer, you can regain access to C:\DOS by keying in PATH C:\DOS. On some networks, you can also use a command like C:\DOS\EDIT A:\AUTOEXEC.BAT, if the computer you are working on has a stand-alone hard disk. If you are on a network, you cannot just set the path. You cannot access the network drives unless you boot off the network disk.

There is a solution. You can create a text file by using COPY CON. Knowing about COPY CON is very useful. As you learned earlier, when you use the COPY CON AUTOEXEC.BAT command, whatever you key in at the console (CON—the source file), will be written to the destination file. Since COPY is an internal command, you do not need access to the DOS system utility files. The downfall of using COPY CON is that, if you make a mistake, you have no way to correct it. You must begin again.

**WARNING: CHECK WITH YOUR INSTRUCTOR BEFORE PROCEEDING.
YOU MAY BE INSTRUCTED TO READ THE ACTIVITY ONLY.**

10.33 Activity: Loading a Program Automatically

Note: The Bootable DOS System Disk is in Drive A. The A:\> is displayed.

Step 1   Key in the following: A:\>**COPY CON AUTOEXEC.BAT**

```
A:\>COPY CON AUTOEXEC.BAT
Overwrite AUTOEXEC.BAT (Yes/No/All)?_
```

WHAT'S HAPPENING? COPY knows you are about to overwrite AUTOEXEC.BAT
and is asking your permission.

Step 2   Press **Y** [Enter]

```
A:\>COPY CON AUTOEXEC.BAT
Overwrite AUTOEXEC.BAT (Yes/No/All)?y
_
```

WHAT'S HAPPENING? The cursor is blinking, waiting for you to key something
in.

Step 3   Key in the following: **PROMPT pg** [Enter]
                                              PATH A:\GAMES [Enter]
                                              MLSHUT [Enter]

```
A:\>COPY CON AUTOEXEC.BAT
Overwrite AUTOEXEC.BAT (Yes/No/All)?y
PROMPT $p$g
PATH A:\GAMES
MLSHUT
_
```

WHAT'S HAPPENING? Since COPY has no way of knowing if you finished keying
in your data, you must give it a signal. The signal is to press the [F6] key and [Enter].
That will write the file to disk. (*Note:* If you make a mistake, you cannot correct it.
Press [F6] and [Enter] to begin again.)

Step 4   Press [F6] and [Enter]

```
A:\>COPY CON AUTOEXEC.BAT
Overwrite AUTOEXEC.BAT (Yes/No/All)?y
PROMPT $p$g
PATH A:\GAMES
MLSHUT
^Z
        1 file(s) copied

A:\>
```

WHAT'S HAPPENING? The ^Z is the result of pressing [F6]. Then, you get the message 1 file(s) copied.

Step 5   Key in the following: A:\>**TYPE AUTOEXEC.BAT** [Enter]

```
A:\>TYPE AUTOEXEC.BAT
PROMPT $p$g
PATH A:\GAMES
MLSHUT

A:\>_
```

WHAT'S HAPPENING? Now, when you boot your system, the Shut the Box program will automatically be loaded.

Step 6   Reboot the system by pressing the [Ctrl] + [Alt] + [Delete] keys or pressing the reset button.

```
Phoenix 80486 ROM BIOS PLUS Version 1.10 A16
Copyright (C) 1985-1988 Phoenix Technologies Ltd.
Copyright (C) 1990-1993 Dell Computer Corporation
All Rights Reserved

Quadtel S3 86C801/805 Enhanced VGA BIOS, Version 2.13.06
Copyright 1987-1992 Phoenix Technologies Ltd.
Copyright 1992-1993 S3 Inc.
All Rights Reserved

Dell Embedded Diagnostics Version 1.11
Copyright 1992-1993 Dell Computer Corporation
All Rights Reserved

Dell System 466/M

Starting MS-DOS...
```

```
A:\>PROMPT $p$g

A:\>PATH A:\GAMES

A:\>MLSHUT
```

WHAT'S HAPPENING? You have changed the prompt, set the path and automatically loaded MLSHUT.EXE.

Step 7   Press **Enter**

WHAT'S HAPPENING? You are in the opening screen of the game.

Step 8   Press **Esc**

Step 9   Press **Esc**

WHAT'S HAPPENING? By pressing **Esc** twice, you are telling the game that you wish to exit.

Step 10:   Press **Y**

WHAT'S HAPPENING? You have returned to the system level. If you no longer want this (or any other program) to load automatically when you boot the system, you would remove the line MLSHUT from AUTOEXEC.BAT. You could also place a REM in front of the line so it reads REM MLSHUT. By "remming" out a command, DOS will read it but not execute it. This alternate method allows you to keep lines in your batch file that you are presently not using. If you need them to execute again, you remove REM from each line

Chapter Summary

1. Batch processing means running a series of instructions without interruption.
2. Interactive processing allows the user to interface directly with the computer and update records immediately.
3. Batch files allow a user to put together a string of commands and execute them with one command.
4. Batch files must have the .BAT file extension.
5. DOS first looks internally for a command, then for a .COM file extension, then for an .EXE file extension, and finally for a .BAT file extension.
6. EDIT is a full-screen text editor used to write batch files.
7. A word processor, if it has a means to save files in ASCII, can be used to write batch files. ASCII files are also referred to as unformatted text files.
8. Batch files must be in ASCII.

9. A quick way to write an ASCII file is to use COPY CON. You copy from the console to a file.
10. Batch files are executed from the system prompt by keying in the batch file name.
11. Batch files are used for many purposes such as to save keystrokes and load application packages.
12. To document means to explain the purpose a file serves.
13. REM allows the user to document a batch file.
14. When DOS sees REM, it displays on the screen whatever text follows the REM but does not execute it as a command.
15. ECHO OFF turns off the display of commands. Only the messages from the commands are displayed on the screen.
16. PAUSE allows the user to take some action before the batch file continues to execute.
17. PAUSE does not force the user to do anything. The batch file just stops running until the user presses a key.
18. To stop a batch file from executing, press the **Ctrl** key and the letter C (**Ctrl**+C).
19. Replaceable parameters allow the user to write batch files that can be used with many different parameters. The replaceable parameters act as place holders for values that the user will substitute when executing the batch file.
20. Replaceable parameters are sometimes called dummy, positional, or substitute parameters.
21. The percent (%) sign followed immediately by a numerical value, 0 to 9, indicates a replaceable parameter in a batch file.
22. You can create a menu system using batch files.
23. A batch file menu system is an on-screen display that lists available choices. When you choose an option, you are actually choosing to run another batch file.
24. In essence, when writing a batch file menu system, you are chaining files together.
25. A batch file called AUTOEXEC.BAT can be created.
26. An AUTOEXEC.BAT file will execute automatically when the system is booted.
27. There can only be one AUTOEXEC.BAT file per booting disk.
28. You may control the boot process.
29. By pressing **F5** when you see Starting MS-DOS..., you will bypass both CONFIG.SYS and AUTOEXEC.BAT.
30. By pressing **F8** when you see Starting MS-DOS..., you will interactively be asked which commands you want to process in CONFIG.SYS and AUTOEXEC.BAT.

Key Terms

Batch file	Interactive booting	Replaceable
Batch processing	Interactive	parameters
Chaining batch files	processing	Substitute
Clean boot	Macro	parameters
Documented	Positional	
Dummy parameters	parameters	

Discussion Questions

1. Explain the purpose and function of batch files.
2. Compare and contrast batch processing with interactive processing.
3. You have a batch file called `CHECK.BAT`. You key in `CHECK` at the prompt. What does DOS do? Where does DOS look for the file?
4. What is an ASCII file? Why is it important in batch processing?
5. Under what circumstances can a word processor be used to write batch files?
6. Compare and contrast using EDIT and COPY CON to write batch files.
7. Explain the purpose and function of the O and A parameters when it is used with the DIR command.
8. Explain the purpose and function of the REM command. What happens when DOS sees REM in a batch file?
9. In a data processing environment, what does it mean to document a batch file? Why would it be important to document a batch file?
10. Explain the purpose and function of the ECHO command.
11. Explain the purpose and function of the PAUSE command.
12. Why does the PAUSE command require user intervention?
13. How can you stop a batch file from executing, once it has begun?
14. What are parameters?
15. What is a replaceable parameter? Describe how it might be used.
16. What indicates to DOS that there is a replaceable parameter in a file?
17. What advantages are there to using replaceable parameters in a batch file?
18. Replaceable parameters are sometimes called positional parameters. Explain.
19. What is a menu system?
20. How can you create a menu system using batch files?
21. There appear to be two prompts when you do not use the `ECHO OFF`. Explain.
22. Explain the purpose and function of an `AUTOEXEC.BAT` file.
23. Why can only one `AUTOEXEC.BAT` file be on any booting disk?
24. Explain two ways that interactive booting may be used.
25. Explain the purpose and function of the bootable floppy system disk.

Chapter *11*

Pipes, Filters, and Redirection

Learning Objectives

After completing this chapter you will be able to:

1. List the standard input and output devices.
2. Explain redirection.
3. Explain what filters are and when they are used.
4. Formulate and explain the syntax of the filter commands SORT, FIND, and MORE.
5. Explain when and how to use the SORT, FIND, and MORE commands.
6. Explain what pipes are and how they are used.
7. Explain how batch files can be written using pipes, filters, and redirection.

Student Outcomes

1. Use > and >> to redirect standard output.
2. Use < to redirect standard input.
3. Use filter commands to manipulate information.
4. Combine commands using pipes, filters, and redirection.
5. Write a batch file using pipes and filters.

Chapter Overview

DOS usually expects to read information from the keyboard, the standard input device. DOS usually expects to write to the display screen, the standard output device. However, there are times when it is desirable to redirect input and output.

DOS allows you to use devices other than the standard input/output devices—a process known as redirection. DOS also has three external commands, called filters, which allow the user to manipulate data. Pipes, used with filters, allow the user to link commands. Pipes, filters, and redirection give the user choices in determining where information is read from (input) and written to (output). Using pipe, filter, and redirection management commands makes DOS more powerful.

In this chapter you will learn how to use redirection. You will learn to use pipes to connect programs and filters to manipulate data. Then, you will write batch files using pipes, filters, and redirection.

11.1 Redirection of Standard I/O (Input/Output)

You have already used input and output with DOS. When you keyed in something, DOS recognized it as input. After DOS processed the input, it wrote it to an output device—usually the screen. In other words, if you key in TYPE MYFILE.TXT, the input is what you key in. The output is the content of the file that is displayed on the screen. See Figure 11.1.

Figure 11.1   Input and Output Devices

In the data processing world, this **input/output** process is commonly referred to as **I/O**.

DOS gets information from or sends information to three places: **standard input**, **standard output,** and **standard error**. Standard input is the keyboard, from which DOS (and programs that you use) expects to get data. Standard output is the display screen, to which DOS (and programs) expects to write. Standard error is the place where DOS writes error messages to the screen, e.g., File not found.

Not all commands deal with standard input and standard output. For instance, the result or output of many of the DOS commands you have used has been some action that occurred, such as copying a file with the COPY command. There is no standard input or output except the messages written to the screen. See Figure 11.2.

```
A:\>  COPY MY.TXT  ONE.FIL   ◄──── INPUT from user


             1 file(s) copied ◄──── OUTPUT from COPY command
A:\>
```

Figure 11.2   *Results of COPY Command*

On the other hand, the output of commands like DIR has been a screen display of all the files on the disk. DOS received information from the standard input device, the keyboard, and sent the results of the DIR command to the standard output device, the screen. I/O **redirection** means that you tell DOS you want information read from or written to a device other than the standard ones. With the DIR command, you can write the output to some other device such as a printer or another file. This process is called redirecting the output of a command. See Figure 11.3.

STANDARD INPUT

STANDARD OUTPUT
from DIR expects to
display on screen

```
A:\>DIR > PRN

A:\>_
```

STANDARD OUTPUT
from DIR is redirected
to the printer

```
Volume in Drive A is DATA DISK
Volume Serial Number is 1E73-1234
Directory of A:\
```

Figure 11.3   *Redirecting Standard Output*

Redirection works only when the command expects to send its output to standard devices or receive the information from standard input.

The symbols used for redirection are:

>   The greater than symbol redirects the output of a command to some other device or file.

<   The less than symbol tells DOS to get its input from somewhere other than the keyboard.

>> The double greater than symbol redirects the output of a command but does not overwrite the existing file. It appends the output to the bottom of the existing file.

As a matter of fact, you have already used these redirection principles if you did the Application Assignments. You redirected output to a file, appended the files together, and redirected the output to the printer.

11.2 Activity: Using the > to Redirect Standard Output

Note: The DATA disk is in Drive A with the A:\> displayed. Be sure the path is set to C:\DOS.

Step 1 Key in the following: A:\>**DIR C:\DOS6BK*.TXT** [Enter]

```
A:\>DIR C:\DOS6BK\*.TXT

 Volume in drive C has no label
 Volume Serial Number is 1CD1-5E42
 Directory of C:\DOS6BK

GOODBYE   TXT           32 11-23-94    7:07a
DANCES    TXT           70 08-08-95    5:34p
JANUARY   TXT           72 11-23-95   10:41a
FEBRUARY  TXT           74 11-23-95   10:41a
MARCH     TXT           70 11-23-95   10:42a
APRIL     TXT           71 11-23-95   10:42a
HELLO     TXT           52 11-23-95   10:44a
BYE       TXT           44 11-23-95   10:45a
TEST      TXT           64 03-14-93   11:07a
          9 file(s)            549 bytes
                       76,152,832 bytes free

A:\>_
```

WHAT'S HAPPENING? This command behaved in the "normal" way. You asked for a display of all the files in the DOS6BK directory that had a .TXT file extension. The selected files were displayed on the screen. Because the DIR command writes its results to the screen, a standard output device, redirection can be used with this command.

Step 2 If you are on a network, check with your lab instructor to see if you can do this activity in the lab. Be sure the printer is turned on. Key in the following: A:\>**DIR C:\DOS6BK*.TXT > PRN** [Enter]

WHAT'S HAPPENING? The output of the command has been sent to the printer. Nothing appears on the screen. When you key in DIR C:\DOS6BK*.TXT, you normally see the directory listing of all the *.TXT files on the screen, as you did in the display following Step 1. The > sign tells DOS that instead of sending the standard output to the screen, you want to redirect that output elsewhere. PRN, an output device, tells DOS where to redirect the output, so you redirected the output to the printer. Redirection is very useful. For example, if you wanted a hard copy of the directory of a disk, you *could not* key in COPY DIR PRN because DIR is a command, not a file. You cannot copy a command to the printer. COPY is for files only. Redirection used properly gets you that printed copy.

The output that you sent to the printer did not print an entire page. Again, you can use the technique you have learned to send a form feed to the printer. On some networks you cannot use PRN. You must instead use LPT1.

Step 3   Key in the following: A:\>**ECHO** **Ctrl** + **L** > **PRN** **Enter**

```
A:\>ECHO ^L > PRN

A:\>_
```

WHAT'S HAPPENING? You have ejected the printed page.

11.3 Activity: Using the < to Redirect Standard Input

Note: The DATA disk is in Drive A with the A:\> displayed.

Step 1   Key in the following: A:\>**MD TEST** **Enter**

Step 2   Key in the following: A:\>**COPY C:\DOS6BK*.NEW TEST** **Enter**

```
A:\>MD TEST

A:\>COPY C:\DOS6BK\*.NEW TEST
C:\DOS6BK\JAN.NEW
C:\DOS6BK\FEB.NEW
C:\DOS6BK\MAR.NEW
C:\DOS6BK\APR.NEW
        4 file(s) copied

A:\>_
```

WHAT'S HAPPENING? You have a created a subdirectory called TEST on the DATA disk and copied four files into it.

Step 3   Key in the following: A:\>**DEL TEST*.*** **Enter**

```
A:\>DEL TEST\*.*
All files in directory will be deleted!
Are you sure (Y/N)?_
```

WHAT'S HAPPENING? You asked the DEL command to delete all the files in the TEST subdirectory. DEL is asking you if you are really sure that you want to delete these files. DEL is expecting input from the standard input device, the keyboard.

Step 4 Key in the following: **N** **Enter**

```
A:\>DEL TEST\*.*
All files in directory will be deleted!
Are you sure (Y/N)?N
A:\>_
```

WHAT'S HAPPENING? You were returned to the system prompt without deleting the files in the TEST subdirectory because you answered N for "No, don't delete." As you can see, DOS took no action until it received input from you via the keyboard, N. The input was N. You can prove that the files are still there by keying in DIR TEST.

Step 5 Key in the following: A:\>**DIR TEST** **Enter**

```
A:\>DIR TEST

 Volume in drive A is DATADISK
 Volume Serial Number is 2F26-1901
 Directory of A:\TEST

 .             <DIR>          07-30-94  12:00p
 ..            <DIR>          07-30-94  12:00p
 JAN     NEW            71 01-23-93  11:48a
 FEB     NEW            73 01-23-93  11:48a
 MAR     NEW            69 01-23-93  11:49a
 APR     NEW            70 01-23-93  11:49a
        6 file(s)            283 bytes
                      665,088 bytes free

A:\>_
```

WHAT'S HAPPENING? You did not delete the files in the TEST directory.

Step 6 Key in the following: A:\>**TYPE Y.FIL** **Enter**

```
A:\>TYPE Y.FIL
Y

A:\>_
```

WHAT'S HAPPENING? The Y.FIL file is a simple file whose contents are the letter Y followed by a carriage return (**Enter**). If you do not have this file on the DATA disk, you can copy it from the DOS6BK directory to the DATA disk.

Step 7   Key in the following: A:\>**DEL TEST*.* < Y.FIL** [Enter]

```
A:\>DEL TEST\*.* < Y.FIL
All files in directory will be deleted!
Are you sure (Y/N)?Y

A:\>_
```

WHAT'S HAPPENING? This time you told DOS to get the input from a file called Y.FIL (< Y.FIL), instead of from the standard input device, the keyboard. Then, when DOS executed DEL TEST*.TXT and displayed the message Are you sure (Y/N)?, it still needed input, a Y or N followed by [Enter]. DOS found the file you told it to look for, Y.FIL, which had the "Y [Enter]" answer. Since DOS got a response to its question, it proceeded to delete the files in the subdirectory TEST.

You must be very careful with redirection of input. When you tell DOS to take input from a file, you are telling DOS to ignore any input from the keyboard. In this example, if the Y.FIL contents were "X", this would not be a valid answer to the question DOS posed, Are you sure (Y/N)? DOS wants only Y or N. Any other letter would be unacceptable, and DOS would keep asking the same question over and over. You could not correct the problem by keying in Y or N because DOS would never look to the keyboard. You told DOS not to. If you ever got into this situation, you could not even use [Ctrl] + [Break] or [Ctrl] + C because DOS would not recognize any input from the keyboard. Your only recourse would be to reboot.

Step 8   Key in the following: A:\>**DIR TEST** [Enter]

```
A:\>DIR TEST

 Volume in drive A is DATADISK
 Volume Serial Number is 2F26-1901
 Directory of A:\TEST

.           <DIR>         07-30-94  12:00p
..          <DIR>         07-30-94  12:00p
      2 file(s)              0 bytes
                      667,136 bytes free

A:\>_
```

WHAT'S HAPPENING? The files were deleted. You did it with one command line, and you did not have to key in the Y. The Y came from the file Y.FIL.

11.4 Activity: Using the >> to Add Redirected Output to a File

Note: The DATA disk is in Drive A with the A:\> displayed.

Step 1   Key in the following: A:\>**TYPE JANUARY.TXT** [Enter]

Step 2   Key in the following: A:\>**TYPE FEBRUARY.TXT** [Enter]

```
A:\>TYPE JANUARY.TXT
This is my January file.
It is my first dummy file.
This is file 1.

A:\>TYPE FEBRUARY.TXT
This is my February file.
It is my second dummy file.
This is file 2.

A:\>_
```

WHAT'S HAPPENING? You have two files. You want to add FEBRUARY.TXT to the end of JANUARY.TXT. If you keyed in TYPE FEBRUARY.TXT > JANUARY.TXT, you would overwrite the contents of JANUARY.TXT with the contents of FEBRUARY.TXT. To append to the end of an existing file, you use the double >>. Again, in a previous application assignment, you used a batch file to do this for you.

Step 3   Key in the following:

     A:\>**TYPE FEBRUARY.TXT >> JANUARY.TXT** [Enter]

Step 4   Key in the following: A:\>**TYPE JANUARY.TXT** [Enter]

```
A:\>TYPE FEBRUARY.TXT >> JANUARY.TXT

A:\>TYPE JANUARY.TXT
This is my January file.
It is my first dummy file.
This is file 1.
This is my February file.
It is my second dummy file.
This is file 2.

A:\>_
```

WHAT'S HAPPENING? Instead of overwriting the contents of JANUARY.TXT with the contents of FEBRUARY.TXT, the contents of FEBRUARY.TXT were added to the end of the JANUARY.TXT file.

11.5 Filters

Filter commands manipulate information. **Filters** read information from the keyboard (standard input), change the input in a specified way, and write the results to the screen (standard output). Filters function like filters in a water purification system. They remove the unwanted elements from the water (data) and send the purified water (data) on its way. There are three DOS filters, all of which are external commands:

SORT   Arranges lines in ascending or descending order.

FIND   Searches for a particular group of characters, also called a character string.

MORE   Temporarily halts the screen display after each screenful.

DOS creates temporary files while it "filters" data, so during this process DOS reads from and writes to the disk. It is important that DOS have access to the disk and the filters. You must not only set the path to C:\DOS but also be sure that the floppy disk is not write-protected. If a disk is write-protected, DOS cannot execute the command.

11.6 The SORT Command

The SORT filter command arranges or sorts lines of input text and sends them to standard output (the screen), unless you redirect it. The default SORT is in ascending order (A to Z or lowest to highest numbers), starting in the first column. The syntax for the command is:

```
SORT [/R] [/+n] < [drive1:][path1]filename1 [> [drive2:][path2]filename2]
    [command ¦]
SORT [/R] [/+n] [> [drive2:][path2]filename2]
```

/R	Reverses the sort order; that is, sorts Z to A, then 9 to 0.
/+n	Sorts the file according to characters in column n.
[drive1:][path1]filename1	Specifies a file to be sorted.
[drive2:][path2]filename2	Specifies a file where the sorted input is to be stored.
command	Specifies a command whose output is to be sorted.

11.7 Activity: Using SORT

Note: The DATA disk is in Drive A with the A:\> displayed.

Step 1   Key in the following: A:\>**SORT** `Enter`
                                 beta `Enter`
                                 omega `Enter`
                                 chi `Enter`
                                 alpha `Enter`
                                 `F6` `Enter`

```
A:\>SORT
beta
omega
chi
alpha
^Z
alpha
beta
chi
omega

A:\>_
```

WHAT'S HAPPENING? As you can see, the SORT command took input from the keyboard. When you pressed the [F6] key (identical to pressing [Ctrl] + Z), you told the SORT command that you were finished entering data. Then, the SORT command "filtered" the data and wrote the keyboard input alphabetically. See Figure 11.4 for a graphical representation of this filter.

Figure 11.4   Filtering Data

Step 2   Key in the following: A:\>**SORT** [Enter]
                            333 [Enter]
                            3 [Enter]
                            23 [Enter]
                            124 [Enter]
                         [F6] [Enter]

```
A:\>SORT
333
3
23
124
^Z
124
```

```
23
3
333

A:\>_
```

WHAT'S HAPPENING? The SORT command does not seem very smart because these numbers are not in order. Numbers in this case are really character data and not numbers that are manipulated mathematically. Numbers are often used as character data. For instance, a zip code or a phone number, although they use numbers, really are character data and are not treated mathematically. You would not think of adding your address to your phone number and dividing by your zip code.

Character data is sorted from left to right. This is called left-justified. Numeric data is sorted from right to left. This is called right-justified. Thus, if you look at "Smith" and "Smythe," you read character data from left to right and would place "Smith" before "Smythe." Conversely, if you look at "12" and "13," you read numeric data from right to left and place "12" before "13" because the rightmost "2" comes before the rightmost "3."

A human *knows* that "12" comes before "13" because a person has learned how numbers work. DOS is different. DOS relies on something called the **ASCII sort sequence**. ASCII is a standard code that assigns values to letters, numbers, and punctuation marks. The ASCII sort sequence is determined by the number assigned to the ASCII character. The sort order is punctuation marks, including the space, then numbers, then uppercase letters, and finally lowercase letters. If you had a series of characters such as BB, aa, #, 123, bb, 13, and AA, the ASCII sort order would be:

```
#    123    13    AA    aa    BB    bb
```

Although DOS, and hence the SORT command, follows the ASCII sort sequence, there is one exception when using DOS 4.0 and above. These DOS versions equate lowercase and uppercase letters so that the sort would look like this:

```
#    123    13    aa    AA    BB    bb
```

There is another point about using the SORT command. Not only does it follow the ASCII sort sequence, but it also sorts entire lines from left to right. Thus, the sort sequence of "Carolyn Smith" and "Robert Nesler" is:

```
Carolyn Smith
Robert Nesler
```

Because the SORT command looks at the entire line, "Carolyn" comes before "Robert."

In our numeric example, SORT looked at the entire line, and, since the "1" in "124" preceded the "2" in "23," it placed the "124" before the "23." You force DOS to sort numbers correctly using the following technique.

Step 3   Key in the following: A:\>**SORT** [Enter]

                                          333 [Enter]

                                          [Space Bar] [Space Bar] 3 [Enter]

                                          [Space Bar] 23 [Enter]

                                          124 [Enter]

                                          [F6] [Enter]

```
A:\>SORT
333
   3
  23
124
^Z
   3
  23
124
333

A:\>_
```

WHAT'S HAPPENING? By entering spaces, you forced the lines to be the same length. Since spaces precede numbers in the ASCII sort sequence, the SORT command could sort the entire line and place it in proper numeric order. Indeed, you made numeric data character data. Essentially, you left-justify character data and right-justify numeric data.

11.8 Filters and Redirection

The standard output of filters is a screen display. Hence, you can redirect both the output and input of these filter commands. The filter commands are not usually used with actual keyboard input, but with the input redirected to a file, device, or another command.

11.9 Activity: Using the SORT Command with Redirection

Note: The DATA disk is in Drive A with the A:\> displayed.

Step 1   Key in the following: A:\>**COPY C:\DOS6BK\STATE.CAP** [Enter]

Step 2   Key in the following: A:\>**SORT < STATE.CAP** [Enter]

```
A:\>COPY C:\DOS6BK\STATE.CAP
        1 file(s) copied

A:\>SORT < STATE.CAP

Arizona         Phoenix
California      Sacramento
Colorado        Denver
Florida         Tallahassee
Louisiana       Baton Rouge
Michigan        Lansing
Nebraska        Lincoln
New York        Albany
Ohio            Columbus
Oregon          Salem

A:\>_
```

WHAT'S HAPPENING? You copied the STATE.CAP file from the DOS6BK directory to the DATA disk. You then keyed in the SORT command. You used the symbol (<) for taking data from a source other than the keyboard, the file called STATE.CAP, and fed it into the SORT command. Displayed on your screen (the standard output) is the STATE.CAP file arranged in alphabetical order, with ARIZONA and PHOENIX at the top. Another SORT command feature is the /R parameter, which allows you to sort in reverse or descending order (Z to A).

Step 3   Key in the following: A:\>**SORT /R < STATE.CAP** [Enter]

```
A:\>SORT /R < STATE.CAP
Oregon          Salem
Ohio            Columbus
New York        Albany
Nebraska        Lincoln
Michigan        Lansing
Louisiana       Baton Rouge
Florida         Tallahassee
Colorado        Denver
California      Sacramento
Arizona         Phoenix

A:\>_
```

WHAT'S HAPPENING? The file STATE.CAP that the SORT command used as input is displayed on the screen in reverse alphabetical order. The standard output, the results of the SORT command, is written to the screen. The SORT parameter that sorts by a column number is /+n.

Step 4   Key in the following: A:\>**SORT /+17 < STATE.CAP** [Enter]

```
A:\>SORT /+17 < STATE.CAP

New York        Albany
Louisiana       Baton Rouge
Ohio            Columbus
Colorado        Denver
Michigan        Lansing
Nebraska        Lincoln
Arizona         Phoenix
California      Sacramento
Oregon          Salem
Florida         Tallahassee

A:\>_
```

WHAT'S HAPPENING? This time you sorted by column number, the seventeenth position in the list in this example. The file is now ordered by city rather than by state. An important point is that the SORT command does not understand columns in the usual sense. A person would say that the "city column" is the second column going from left to right. The SORT command counts each character (letters and spaces) from left to right, not each column. Thus, "city" is located by counting the number of characters to the ones you want to sort, including the spaces between the characters. The total number was 17.

In these examples, you have been "massaging the data." The actual data in STATE.CAP has not changed. The only thing that has changed is the way it is displayed. This alphabetic arrangement is temporary. If you want to change the data in the file, you need to save the altered data to a new file.

Step 5   Key in the following:

        A:\>**SORT < STATE.CAP > SORTED.CAP** [Enter]

Step 6   Key in the following: A:\>**TYPE SORTED.CAP** [Enter]

```
A:\>SORT < STATE.CAP > SORTED.CAP

A:\>TYPE SORTED.CAP

Arizona         Phoenix
California      Sacramento
Colorado        Denver
Florida         Tallahassee
Louisiana       Baton Rouge
Michigan        Lansing
Nebraska        Lincoln
New York        Albany
```

```
    Ohio          Columbus
    Oregon        Salem

    A:\>_
```

WHAT'S HAPPENING?   You saved the sorted output to a new file called
SORTED.CAP. The standard output of the command SORT < STATE.CAP will
normally be written to the screen (standard output). Since standard output is
written to the screen, you can redirect it to a file called SORTED.CAP, or the
command line SORT < STATE.CAP > SORTED.CAP. If you did not want a permanent copy of it but wanted a printed copy of the file, you could have written the
command as SORT < STATE.CAP > PRN.

11.10 The FIND Filter

The FIND command allows you to search a file for a specific **character string,**
which is a string of characters enclosed in quotation marks. This command is **case
sensitive**, but introduced in DOS 5.0 is a new parameter /I, which means ignore
case. The syntax is:

```
    FIND [/V] [/C] [/N] [/I] "string" [[drive:][path]filename[ ...]]
```

/V	Displays all lines NOT containing the specified string.
/C	Displays only the count of lines containing the string.
/N	Displays line numbers with the displayed lines.
/I	Ignores the case of characters when searching for the string.
"string"	Specifies the text string to find.
[drive:][path]filename	Specifies a file or files to search.

If a *pathname* is not specified, FIND searches the text typed at the prompt or piped
from another command.

11.11 Activity: Using the FIND Filter

Note 1:   The DATA disk is in Drive A with the A:\> displayed.

Note 2:   If PERSONAL.FIL is not on the DATA disk, it can be copied from the
DOS6BK directory to the DATA disk.

Note 3:   You must use the double quotes. Single quotes are invalid.

Step 1   Key in the following: A:\>**FIND "Smith" PERSONAL.FIL** [Enter]

```
A:\>FIND "Smith" PERSONAL.FIL

------- PERSONAL.FIL
Smith      Gregory  311 Orchard   Ann Arbor    MI  Engineer
Smith      Carolyn  311 Orchard   Ann Arbor    MI  Housewife
Smith      David    120 Collins   Orange       CA  Chef

A:\>_
```

WHAT'S HAPPENING? The FIND command found every occurrence of the character string `Smith` in `PERSONAL.FIL` on the DATA disk. A character string *must* be enclosed in quotation marks. Since FIND is case sensitive, you must key in exactly as it appears in the file. The character string `SMITH` would not be found because FIND would be looking for lowercase letters. If you have DOS 5.0 or above and you wanted to ignore the case, you would use the parameter /I. The FIND command "filtered" the file `PERSONAL.FIL` to extract the character string that matched the specification. With the use of the /V parameter, you can search a file for anything *except* what is in quotation marks.

Step 2   Key in the following: A:\>**FIND /V "Smith" PERSONAL.FIL** ⌷Enter⌷

```
Brogan     Sally     111 Miller    Santa Cruz     CA  Account Manager
Babchuk    Nicholas  13 Stratford  Sun City West  AZ  Professor
Babchuk    Bianca    13 Stratford  Sun City West  AZ  Professor
Rodriguez  Bob       20 Elm        Ontario        CA  Systems Analyst
Helm       Milton    333 Meadow    Sherman Oaks   CA  Consultant
Suzuki     Charlene  567 Abbey     Rochester      MI  Day Care Teacher
Markiw     Nicholas  354 Bell      Phoenix        AZ  Engineer
Markiw     Emily     10 Zion       Sun City West  AZ  Retired
Nyles      John      12 Brooks     Sun City West  AZ  Retired
Nyles      Sophie    12 Brooks     Sun City West  AZ  Retired
Markiw     Nick      10 Zion       Sun City West  AZ  Retired
Washingon  Tyrone    345 Newport   Orange         CA  Manager
Jones      Steven    32 North      Phoenix        AZ  Buyer
Babchuk    Walter    12 View       Thousand Oaks  CA  President
Babchuk    Deana     12 View       Thousand Oaks  CA  Housewife
Jones      Cleo      355 Second    Ann Arbor      MI  Clerk
Gonzales   Antonio   40 Northern   Ontario        CA  Engineer
JONES      JERRY     244 East      Mission Viejo  CA  Systems Analyst
Lo         Ophelia   1213 Wick     Phoenix        AZ  Writer
Jones      Ervin     15 Fourth     Santa Cruz     CA  Banker
Perez      Sergio    134 Seventh   Ann Arbor      MI  Editor
Yuan       Suelin    56 Twin Leaf  Orange         CA  Artist
Markiw     Nicholas  12 Fifth      Glendale       AZ  Engineer

A:\>_
```

WHAT'S HAPPENING? FIND located everyone *except* `Smith`. Furthermore, you can find the specific line number of each occurrence by using the /N parameter.

Step 3   Key in the following: A:\>**FIND /N "Smith" PERSONAL.FIL** `Enter`

```
A:\>FIND /N "Smith" PERSONAL.FIL

─────── PERSONAL.FIL
[6]Smith       Gregory  311 Orchard  Ann Arbor    MI  Engineer
[7]Smith       Carolyn  311 Orchard  Ann Arbor    MI  Housewife
[27]Smith      David    120 Collins  Orange       CA  Chef

A:\>_
```

WHAT'S HAPPENING? Displayed on the screen are not only all the Smiths but also the line numbers where their names appear in the file. You can also have a numeric count of the number of times a specific character string appears in a file. The FIND command will not display the actual lines, but it will tell you how many occurrences there are of that specific string.

Step 4   Key in the following: A:\>**FIND /C "Smith" PERSONAL.FIL** `Enter`

```
A:\>FIND /C "Smith" PERSONAL.FIL

─────── PERSONAL.FIL: 3

A:\>_
```

WHAT'S HAPPENING? The number three follows the file name. The name Smith appears three times in the file PERSONAL.FIL. If you have DOS 5.0 or above, you can tell the FIND command to ignore case.

Step 5   Key in the following: A:\>**FIND /I "Jones" PERSONAL.FIL** `Enter`

```
A:\>FIND /I "Jones" PERSONAL.FIL

─────── PERSONAL.FIL
Jones      Steven   32 North     Phoenix       AZ  Buyer
Jones      Cleo     355 Second   Ann Arbor     MI  Clerk
JONES      JERRY    244 East     Mission Viejo CA  Systems Analyst
Jones      Ervin    15 Fourth    Santa Cruz    CA  Banker

A:\>_
```

WHAT'S HAPPENING? By using the /I parameter, which told the FIND command to ignore the case, it found both Jones and JONES.

11.12 Pipes

Pipes allow the standard output of one program to be used as the standard input to the next program. When you use pipes, you are not limited to two programs. You may pipe together many programs. The term *pipe* reflects the flow of information from one command to the next. Pipes are used with filter commands. You may take any DOS command that has standard output and pipe it to a filter. The filter will "do" something to the standard output of the previous command, such as sort it. Since filters always write to standard output, you may use pipes and filters to further refine your data. Essentially, you may use filters to transform data to your needs.

The pipe symbol is the vertical broken bar ¦ used between two commands. DOS takes the standard output from a command and writes it to a temporary file. Then the next command in the pipeline, typically a filter, reads the temporary file as standard input. See Figure 11.5.

Figure 11.5   Piping Commands

On the original IBM PC keyboard, the pipe symbol is located between the **Shift** and the letter Z. On some newer computers, the pipe symbol is located below the **Backspace** key. Some other keyboards have the ¦ symbol next to the **Ctrl** and **Alt** keys on the right side of the keyboard. The location of the ¦ symbol is not standard and could appear in other locations. The symbol ¦ is the connection between the two commands, like a pipe in a water system. Since filters are external commands, DOS must be able to access the commands. If a disk is write-protected, filter commands will not work because these commands read and write temporary files to the disk.

After using pipes with filters, you may see some "strange" files on the directory labeled:

```
%PIPE1.$$$
%PIPE2.$$$
%PIPE3.$$$
```
or
```
11002649
1100274E
```

All files must be named, even temporary files. These are the names DOS gives for the files that it creates when you use piping. These temporary files "hold" the data until the next command can process it. These temporary files are automatically deleted by DOS when you have finished your chain of commands. Newer versions of DOS do not display those "funny" file names on the screen.

11.13 The MORE Filter

The MORE command displays one screenful of data at a time with a prompt that says `-- More --`. The MORE command pauses after the screen is full. When any key is pressed, the MORE command displays the next screenful of information, once again pausing so you can read the screen display. When there is no more data in the file, the MORE command finishes by returning you to the system prompt. The purpose of the MORE command is to allow you to be able to read a long text file that would not fit onto the screen one screenful at a time. The syntax is:

```
MORE < [drive:][path]filename command-name | MORE
```

`[drive:][path]filename`	Specifies a file to display one screen at a time.
`command-name`	Specifies a command whose output will be displayed.

The syntax diagram indicates that MORE can be both redirected and used with a pipe.

11.14 Activity: Using the MORE Filter

Note: The DATA disk is in Drive A with the `A:\>` displayed.

Step 1   You will use the pipe symbol |, so be sure you locate it on the keyboard. Key in the following: `A:\>`**DIR | MORE** [Enter]

```
    Volume in drive A is DATADISK
    Volume Serial Number is 2F26-1901
    Directory of A:\

    POLYSCI        <DIR>          06-20-94    5:59p
    CLASS          <DIR>          06-21-94    1:02a
    WORK           <DIR>          06-21-94   10:30a
    TRIP           <DIR>          06-21-94   10:58p
    CLASX                 15,108  06-21-94   10:38a
    APR      99               71  11-23-95   10:42a
    JAN      99               72  11-23-95   10:41a
    EXAMPLE  BAT              23  06-26-94   11:22a
    WILDTHR  AAA             180  05-07-93    9:03a
    APR      BUD              18  12-06-94   10:46a
    MULTI    BAT             111  06-26-94    7:05p
    D        BAT               9  06-26-94   11:26a
    FILE2    CZG              18  12-06-94   10:45a
    FILE3    CZG              18  12-06-94   10:46a
    Y        FIL               3  05-14-93   11:00a
    S        BAT              10  06-26-94   11:28a
    CAROLYN  FIL              45  11-23-94    7:13a
```

```
 PERSONAL     FIL            2,305 12-06-93    4:45P
 -- More --
```

WHAT'S HAPPENING? Your files may vary. By using the pipe symbol, you asked that the output of the DIR command be used as input to the MORE command. The -- More -- on the bottom of the screen tells you that there are "more" screens of data. Press any key and the next screen of data will display.

Step 2   Press any key until you are back at the system prompt. You may have to press several times until you are returned to the system prompt.

```
 TEST      TKR          16,516 06-21-94   10:37a
 HOMEBUD   TKR           8,064 02-28-94    6:19p
 APR       TST              71 11-23-95   10:42a
 DRAMA     TV              198 11-23-94   10:19a
 JANUARY   TXT             144 07-31-94   10:33p
 -- More --

 TESTING   BAT             117 06-26-94    5:42p
 PROG           <DIR>          06-25-94   11:58a
 MEDIA          <DIR>          06-25-94   12:03p
 FEBRUARY  TXT              74 11-23-95   10:41a
 APRIL     TXT              71 11-23-95   10:42a
 HELLO     TXT              52 11-23-95   10:44a
 BYE       TXT              44 11-23-95   10:45a
 AWARD     MOV              94 06-25-94   12:10p
 KILLIT    BAT             153 06-26-94    7:02p
 NOCOPY    BAT             203 06-26-94    7:10p
 BATCH          <DIR>          07-01-94    5:10p
 TEST           <DIR>          07-30-94   12:00p
 STATE     CAP             260 05-14-94    5:11p
 SORTED    CAP             260 07-31-94   11:00p
        55 file(s)           45,431 bytes
                           666,112 bytes free

 A:\>_
```

WHAT'S HAPPENING? You returned to the system level. You may ask yourself, why do this when I get the same effect by using DIR /P? There are two reasons. The first is that you can connect several commands with pipes and filters. The second is that /P works only with the DIR command.

Step 3   Key in the following: A:\>**DIR ¦ SORT ¦ MORE** Enter

```
                        666,112 bytes free
        55 file(s)           45,431 bytes
 Directory of A:\
 Volume in drive A is DATADISK
```

```
 Volume Serial Number is 2F26-1901
APR        99            71 11-23-95  10:42a
APR        BUD           18 12-06-94  10:46a
APR        TST           71 11-23-95  10:42a
APRIL      NEW           70 01-23-93  11:49a
APRIL      TXT           71 11-23-95  10:42a
AWARD      MOV           94 06-25-94  12:10p
BATCH         <DIR>         07-01-94   5:10p
BYE        TXT           44 11-23-95  10:45a
CAROLYN    FIL           45 11-23-94   7:13a
CASES      FIL          315 11-23-94   7:04a
CLASS         <DIR>         06-21-94   1:02a
CLASX              15,108 06-21-94  10:38a
D          BAT            9 06-26-94  11:26a
DRAMA      TV           198 11-23-94  10:19a
EXAMPLE    BAT           23 06-26-94  11:22a
FILE2      CZG           18 12-06-94  10:45a
-- More --
```

WHAT'S HAPPENING? You now have an alphabetically sorted directory. If you have a version of DOS previous to DOS 5.0, this was the only way you could get a sorted directory. The reason the volume label, files, and numbers are at the top is that, as we discussed in the ASCII sort sequence, spaces are listed before numbers.

Step 4   Continue pressing any key until you have returned to the system prompt.

```
LAST       ONE           71 11-23-95  10:42a
MEDIA         <DIR>         06-25-94  12:03p
MULTI      BAT          111 06-26-94   7:05p
NOCOPY     BAT          203 06-26-94   7:10p
PERSONAL   FIL        2,305 12-06-93   4:45p
-- More --

POLYSCI       <DIR>         06-20-94   5:59p
PROG          <DIR>         06-25-94  11:58a
S          BAT           10 06-26-94  11:28a
SECOND     FIL           73 11-23-94   7:04a
SORTED     CAP          260 07-31-94  11:00p
STATE      CAP          260 05-14-94   5:11p
STEVEN     FIL           42 11-23-94   7:13a
TEST          <DIR>         07-30-94  12:00p
TEST       BAT          157 06-26-94   5:39p
TEST       TKR       16,516 06-21-94  10:37a
TESTING    BAT          117 06-26-94   5:42p
THIS       ONE           42 11-23-94   7:13a
TRIP          <DIR>         06-21-94  10:58p
WILDTHR    AAA          180 05-07-93   9:03a
```

```
WORK            <DIR>           06-21-94  10:30a
Y         FIL           3 05-14-93  11:00a

A:\>_
```

WHAT'S HAPPENING? You returned to the system prompt. Pipes are extremely useful with long text files. If you have a text file that is more than one screenful of data, you cannot use TYPE /P *filename.ext* because /P is not a valid TYPE parameter. You can use the MORE command with a file as input. You can either redirect the input of any text file to the MORE command, or you can pipe it. Here redirection will be used first.

Step 5   Key in the following: A:\>**MORE** < **PERSONAL.FIL** Enter

```
Gillay     Carolyn   699 Lemon     Orange         CA  Professor
Panezich   Frank     689 Lake      Orange         CA  Teacher
Tuttle     Steven    356 Embassy   Mission Viejo  CA  Juggler
Maurdeff   Kathryn   550 Traver    Ann Arbor      MI  Teacher
Maurdeff   Sonia     550 Traver    Ann Arbor      MI  Student
Smith      Gregory   311 Orchard   Ann Arbor      MI  Engineer
Smith      Carolyn   311 Orchard   Ann Arbor      MI  Housewife
Winter     Jim       333 Pick      Garden Grove   CA  Key Grip
Winter     Linda     333 Pick      Garden Grove   CA  Teacher
Tran       Tai Chan  345 Lakeview  Orange         CA  Doctor
Golden     Jane      345 Lakeview  Orange         CA  Nurse
Chang      Wendy     356 Edgewood  Ann Arbor      MI  Librarian
Brogan     Lloyd     111 Miller    Santa Cruz     CA  Vice-President
Brogan     Sally     111 Miller    Santa Cruz     CA  Account Manager
Babchuk    Nicholas  13 Stratford  Sun City West  AZ  Professor
Babchuk    Bianca    13 Stratford  Sun City West  AZ  Professor
Rodriguez  Bob       20 Elm        Ontario        CA  Systems Analyst
Helm       Milton    333 Meadow    Sherman Oaks   CA  Consultant
Suzuki     Charlene  567 Abbey     Rochester      MI  Day Care Teacher
Markiw     Nicholas  354 Bell      Phoenix        AZ  Engineer
Markiw     Emily     10 Zion       Sun City West  AZ  Retired
Nyles      John      12 Brooks     Sun City West  AZ  Retired
Nyles      Sophie    12 Brooks     Sun City West  AZ  Retired
Markiw     Nick      10 Zion       Sun City West  AZ  Retired
-- More --
```

WHAT'S HAPPENING? You asked that the file from the DATA disk called PERSONAL.FIL be redirected as input into (<) the command MORE. The MORE command then displayed a screenful of this file.

Step 6   Continue to press any key until you have returned to the system prompt.

```
Rodriguez  Bob       20 Elm        Ontario        CA  Systems Analyst
Helm       Milton    333 Meadow    Sherman Oaks   CA  Consultant
Suzuki     Charlene  567 Abbey     Rochester      MI  Day Care Teacher
```

```
Markiw      Nicholas 354 Bell       Phoenix          AZ  Engineer
Markiw      Emily    10 Zion        Sun City West    AZ  Retired
Nyles       John     12 Brooks      Sun City West    AZ  Retired
Nyles       Sophie   12 Brooks      Sun City West    AZ  Retired
Markiw      Nick     10 Zion        Sun City West    AZ  Retired
-- More --

WashingtonTyrone     345 Newport    Orange           CA  Manager
Jones       Steven   32 North       Phoenix          AZ  Buyer
Smith       David    120 Collins    Orange           CA  Chef
Babchuk     Walter   12 View        Thousand Oaks    CA  President
Babchuk     Deana    12 View        Thousand Oaks    CA  Housewife
Jones       Cleo     355 Second     Ann Arbor        MI  Clerk
Gonzales    Antonio  40 Northern    Ontario          CA  Engineer
JONES       JERRY    244 East       Mission Viejo    CA  Systems Analyst
Lo          Ophelia  1213 Wick      Phoenix          AZ  Writer
Jones       Ervin    15 Fourth      Santa Cruz       CA  Banker
Perez       Sergio   134 Seventh    Ann Arbor        MI  Editor
Yuan        Suelin   56 Twin Leaf   Orange           CA  Artist
Markiw      Nicholas 12 Fifth       Glendale         AZ  Engineer

A:\>_
```

WHAT'S HAPPENING? You returned to the system prompt. There is an alternative way to produce the same results. You can pipe the output of the file to the MORE command.

Step 7   Key in the following: A:\>**TYPE PERSONAL.FIL ¦ MORE** ⌞Enter⌟

```
Gillay      Carolyn   699 Lemon      Orange          CA  Professor
Panezich    Frank     689 Lake       Orange          CA  Teacher
Tuttle      Steven    356 Embassy    Mission Viejo   CA  Juggler
Maurdeff    Kathryn   550 Traver     Ann Arbor       MI  Teacher
Maurdeff    Sonia     550 Traver     Ann Arbor       MI  Student
Smith       Gregory   311 Orchard    Ann Arbor       MI  Engineer
Smith       Carolyn   311 Orchard    Ann Arbor       MI  Housewife
Winter      Jim       333 Pick       Garden Grove    CA  Key Grip
Winter      Linda     333 Pick       Garden Grove    CA  Teacher
Tran        Tai Chan  345 Lakeview   Orange          CA  Doctor
Golden      Jane      345 Lakeview   Orange          CA  Nurse
Chang       Wendy     356 Edgewood   Ann Arbor       MI  Librarian
Brogan      Lloyd     111 Miller     Santa Cruz      CA  Vice-President
Brogan      Sally     111 Miller     Santa Cruz      CA  Account Manager
Babchuk     Nicholas  13 Stratford   Sun City West   AZ  Professor
Babchuk     Bianca    13 Stratford   Sun City West   AZ  Professor
Rodriguez   Bob       20 Elm         Ontario         CA  Systems Analyst
Helm        Milton    333 Meadow     Sherman Oaks    CA  Consultant
Suzuki      Charlene  567 Abbey      Rochester       MI  Day Care Teacher
Markiw      Nicholas  354 Bell       Phoenix         AZ  Engineer
```

```
Markiw      Emily       10 Zion        Sun City West   AZ   Retired
Nyles       John        12 Brooks      Sun City West   AZ   Retired
Nyles       Sophie      12 Brooks      Sun City West   AZ   Retired
Markiw      Nick        10 Zion        Sun City West   AZ   Retired
-- More --
```

WHAT'S HAPPENING? You took the output from the TYPE command, which is normally a screen display, and piped it as input to the MORE command. The MORE command then displayed a screenful of this file. Remember that there must be a command on either side of the pipe. You could not key in PERSONAL.FIL ¦ MORE because PERSONAL.FIL is a file and not a command.

Step 8   Continue to press any key until you have returned to the system prompt.

```
Rodriguez Bob       20 Elm        Ontario        CA   Systems Analyst
Helm      Milton    333 Meadow    Sherman Oaks   CA   Consultant
Suzuki    Charlene  567 Abbey     Rochester      MI   Day Care Teacher
Markiw    Nicholas  354 Bell      Phoenix        AZ   Engineer
Markiw    Emily     10 Zion       Sun City West  AZ   Retired
Nyles     John      12 Brooks     Sun City West  AZ   Retired
Nyles     Sophie    12 Brooks     Sun City West  AZ   Retired
Markiw    Nick      10 Zion       Sun City West  AZ   Retired
-- More --

WashingtonTyrone    345 Newport   Orange         CA   Manager
Jones     Steven    32 North      Phoenix        AZ   Buyer
Smith     David     120 Collins   Orange         CA   Chef
Babchuk   Walter    12 View       Thousand Oaks  CA   President
Babchuk   Deana     12 View       Thousand Oaks  CA   Housewife
Jones     Cleo      355 Second    Ann Arbor      MI   Clerk
Gonzales  Antonio   40 Northern   Ontario        CA   Engineer
JONES     JERRY     244 East      Mission Viejo  CA   Systems Analyst
Lo        Ophelia   1213 Wick     Phoenix        AZ   Writer
Jones     Ervin     15 Fourth     Santa Cruz     CA   Banker
Perez     Sergio    134 Seventh   Ann Arbor      MI   Editor
Yuan      Suelin    56 Twin Leaf  Orange         CA   Artist
Markiw    Nicholas  12 Fifth      Glendale       AZ   Engineer

A:\>_
```

WHAT'S HAPPENING? You returned to the system prompt.

11.15 Combining Commands with Pipes and Filters

You can use the pipe symbol to join commands where the standard output of one command is the standard input of the next command. The pipe symbol allows you to connect two or more programs and create a flow of data. When you use the pipe symbol, there must be a command on both sides of the actual symbol. If you use redirection with the "pipeline," a command does not have to be on either side of the > or >>. Remember, when you are redirecting output from a command, it is an "instead of" process. For instance, instead of writing the output of a command to the screen, you are redirecting the output to a file or a device. When you combine the use of pipes and the >, the redirection becomes the end of the pipeline, the last step in the process.

11.16 Activity: Combining Commands

Note: The DATA disk is in Drive A. The `A:\>` is displayed.

Step 1   Key in the following:

A:\> **FIND "Teacher" PERSONAL.FIL ¦ FIND "CA"** Enter

```
A:\>FIND "Teacher" PERSONAL.FIL ¦ FIND "CA"
Panezich   Frank    689 Lake    Orange         CA   Teacher
Winter     Linda    333 Pick    Garden Grove   CA   Teacher

A:\>_
```

WHAT'S HAPPENING? Only the teachers who live in California are displayed. You asked FIND first to locate the character string `Teacher` in the file called PERSONAL.FIL on the DATA disk. Then out of that group or subset of `Teacher`, you wanted displayed only those who lived in California (`CA`). Remember, the data in PERSONAL.FIL has not changed. You are merely changing the way the data is displayed. If you want to save the data in this format, you must save it to a file.

Step 2   Key in the following:

A:\> **FIND "Teacher" PERSONAL.FIL ¦ FIND "CA" > TEACHER.FIL** Enter

Step 3   Key in the following: A:\> **TYPE TEACHER.FIL** Enter

```
A:\>FIND "Teacher" PERSONAL.FIL ¦ FIND "CA" > TEACHER.FIL

A:\>TYPE TEACHER.FIL
Panezich   Frank    689 Lake    Orange         CA   Teacher
Winter     Linda    333 Pick    Garden Grove   CA   Teacher

A:\>_
```

WHAT'S HAPPENING? You used FIND to locate all the teachers in California. Since the FIND command writes its output to the screen, you could redirect it. The results of the command did not appear on the screen because you redirected the output to a file called TEACHER.FIL. You then used the TYPE command to display that file on the screen. You can also use the same filter more than one time, or use other filters in the command line.

Step 4   Key in the following:

A:\>**FIND "Professor" PERSONAL.FIL ¦ FIND "AZ" ¦ SORT** [Enter]

```
A:\>FIND "Professor" PERSONAL.FIL ¦ FIND "AZ" ¦ SORT
Babchuk    Bianca    13 Stratford   Sun City West   AZ   Professor
Babchuk    Nicholas  13 Stratford   Sun City West   AZ   Professor

A:\>_
```

WHAT'S HAPPENING? You asked FIND to locate all occurrences of Professor in the file called PERSONAL.FIL. You then piped (had the standard output of the FIND command sent as standard input to the next FIND command) to select only those who lived in Arizona. You then piped the standard output of FIND to the SORT command because you wanted all the professors who live in Arizona sorted in alphabetical order.

If you wanted a permanent copy of this list, you could have redirected the standard output (normally displayed on the screen) to a file. If you wanted only a printout, you could have redirected the standard output (normally displayed on the screen) to the printer. You could not do both.

For instance, if you had keyed in the command as FIND "Professor" PERSONAL.FIL ¦ FIND "AZ" ¦ SORT > AZ.FIL > PRN, you would have only a hard copy of the output, not a saved file called AZ.FIL. You can consider the > as the "end of the line." The secret, when combining filters and redirection, is to break the command line down into separate components and determine whether each part of the command works. Furthermore, you should know that if you keyed in AZ.FIL > PRN at the system prompt, it would not work. You would get an error message of Bad command or file name because no command was issued. AZ.FIL is not a command and neither is PRN. Just because you use pipes, filters, and redirection, the rules of DOS are not suspended. You must always have a command. Similarly, the command line FIND "Professor" PERSONAL.FIL ¦ FIND "AZ" ¦ SORT ¦ PRN also would not work. Again, you should know that if you keyed in SORT ¦ PRN at the system prompt, it would not work because, although SORT is a command, PRN is a device. What is SORT supposed to sort? You have given the SORT command no data. It cannot sort the printer.

Perhaps the easiest way to remember the rules of pipes, filters, and redirection is that, when you use a pipe, there must be a command on either side of the pipe. Remember, you are taking the standard output of a command and using it as standard input to the next command. Remember also that not every command has standard output. For instance, when you key in DEL *filename* at the system level, there is no output that appears or is written to the screen. The file is simply deleted. When you key in COPY myfile yourfile, the only item written to the screen is the message 1 file(s) copied. The standard output from the COPY command is the message 1 file(s) copied. Nothing else is written to the screen.

Conversely, when you use redirection, it is an "instead of" action. Instead of the standard output being written to the screen, you are redirecting (sending) it somewhere else, such as a file or a device. You only get "one" somewhere else. Since it is an "instead of" action, you cannot say instead of displaying the output of the DIR command on the screen, redirect the output to a file *and* redirect the output to the printer. Your choice is *either* the printer *or* a file, not both. The primary use of pipes and filters is manipulating the standard output and standard input of DOS commands. You rarely use pipes and filters to sort or find data in text or data files.

Step 5   Key in the following: A:\>**DIR** ¦ **SORT /+9** ¦ **MORE** [Enter]

```
                           665,600 bytes free
     CLASX                 15,108 06-21-94   10:38a
     POLYSCI     <DIR>            06-20-94    5:59p
     CLASS       <DIR>            06-21-94    1:02a
     WORK        <DIR>            06-21-94   10:30a
     TRIP        <DIR>            06-21-94   10:58p
     PROG        <DIR>            06-25-94   11:58a
     MEDIA       <DIR>            06-25-94   12:03p
     HPB         <DIR>            06-26-94    5:03p
     BATCH       <DIR>            07-01-94    5:10p
     TEST        <DIR>            07-30-94   12:00p
     APR     99                71 11-23-95   10:42a
     JAN     99                72 11-23-95   10:41a
     WILDTHR AAA              180 05-07-93    9:03a
     D       BAT                9 06-26-94   11:26a
     S       BAT               10 06-26-94   11:28a
     HPB     BAT               20 06-26-94    5:38p
     EXAMPLE BAT               23 06-26-94   11:22a
     MULTI   BAT              111 06-26-94    7:05p
     TESTING BAT              117 06-26-94    5:42p
     KILLIT  BAT              153 06-26-94    7:02p
     TEST    BAT              157 06-26-94    5:39p
     -- More --
```

Note: Your screen display will vary based on the work you did as well as the date and time you created the files.

WHAT'S HAPPENING? You took the directory display and piped the output to the SORT command. You then sorted by the file extension. How did you know that the file extension was in the ninth column? Since you know that all files can have no more than 8 characters, the extension must start at 9. You then piped the output to the MORE command so that you could see the output one screenful at a time. Now you can perform the same task with the newer parameters of the DIR command. The command line DIR /OE would provide the same results.

Step 6   Continue pressing [Enter] until you have returned to the system prompt.

Step 7   Key in the following: A:\>**DIR** ¦ **FIND "<DIR>"** ¦ **SORT** [Enter]

```
A:\>DIR | FIND "<DIR>" | SORT
BATCH          <DIR>          07-01-94    5:10p
CLASS          <DIR>          06-21-94    1:02a
HPB            <DIR>          06-26-94    5:03p
MEDIA          <DIR>          06-25-94   12:03p
POLYSCI        <DIR>          06-20-94    5:59p
PROG           <DIR>          06-25-94   11:58a
TEST           <DIR>          07-30-94   12:00p
TRIP           <DIR>          06-21-94   10:58p
WORK           <DIR>          06-21-94   10:30a

A:\>_
```

WHAT'S HAPPENING? You sent the output of DIR to FIND. You were looking for any file that had <DIR> in it. You used uppercase letters since everything in the directory is in uppercase. You had to use quotation marks to enclose the<DIR>. Had you not done that, the command line would have read the < and the > as redirection symbols. By enclosing them, you ensured those symbols were read as character data. You then sent that output to the SORT command. Now you have an alphabetical list of the subdirectories on your DATA disk. Again, you can do the same task with the newer parameters of the DIR command. The command line DIR /AD /ON would provide the same results.

11.17 Batch Files with Pipes and Filters

You can use batch files to automate these processes. Instead of having to key in the commands, you can save them in an easily remembered batch file name. There are many useful batch files that can be written using pipes, filters, and redirection.

11.18 Activity: Writing a Batch File with Pipes and Filters

Note: The DATA disk is in Drive A with the A:\> displayed.

Step 1   Key in the following: A:\>**PATH > ORIGPATH.BAT** [Enter]

Step 2   Key in the following: A:\>**TYPE ORIGPATH.BAT** [Enter]

```
A:\>PATH > ORIGPATH.BAT

A:\>TYPE ORIGPATH.BAT
PATH=C:\WINDOWS;C:\DOS;C:\PROG\MOUSE;C:\PROG\BATCH;H:\UTILS\ZIP

A:\>_
```

WHAT'S HAPPENING? Your path will vary depending on how it is set on your system. Since the PATH command, when keyed in by itself, displays (writes) the currently set path to the screen, you can redirect the output to a file. You redirected the output to a batch file by naming the file with the `.BAT` file extension. The advantage to this batch file is twofold. First, if you ever set the path incorrectly or in a way you no longer desire, you can return to your default path (usually set in `AUTOEXEC.BAT`) by keying in `ORIGPATH`. You no longer have to remember what was in your original path statement. Secondly, if you ever want to add a subdirectory to your path, rather than having to key in the entire path name, you can use EDIT to edit `ORIGPATH.BAT` and easily alter the path statement.

The next batch file you will write will solve a problem. For backup purposes, you often have the same files on more than one subdirectory or floppy disk. You may want to compare which files are in which directory or on which disk. This normally would involve using the DIR command to view each directory or disk, or redirecting the output of the DIR command to the printer and comparing them. Why not let the computer do the work?

Step 3   Key in the following: `A:\>`**EDIT DCOMP.BAT** Enter

REM This batch file will compare the file names Enter

REM in two directories. Enter

DIR %1 ¦ FIND /V "e" ¦ FIND /V "<DIR>" ¦ SORT > SOURCE.TMP Enter

DIR %2 ¦ FIND /V "e" ¦ FIND /V "<DIR>" ¦ SORT > OTHER.TMP Enter

FC SOURCE.TMP OTHER.TMP ¦ MORE Enter

PAUSE You are about to delete the files SOURCE.TMP and OTHER.TMP
Enter

DEL SOURCE.TMP Enter

DEL OTHER.TMP Enter

```
   File   Edit   Search   Options                                    Help
══════════════════════════════════DCOMP.BAT═══════════════════════════════════
REM   This batch file will compare the file names
REM   in two directories.
DIR %1 ¦ FIND /V "e" ¦ FIND /V "<DIR>" ¦ SORT > SOURCE.TMP
DIR %2 ¦ FIND /V "e" ¦ FIND /V "<DIR>" ¦ SORT > OTHER.TMP
FC SOURCE.TMP OTHER.TMP ¦ MORE
PAUSE You are about to delete the files SOURCE.TMP and OTHER.TMP
DEL   SOURCE.TMP
DEL   OTHER.TMP




 MS-DOS Editor   <F1=Help> Press ALT to activate menus              00009:001
```

Step 4   Press Alt + **F**. Press **X**

Step 5   Press **Y**

WHAT'S HAPPENING? This batch file will compare file names in directories. Rather then writing the command line as `DIR | SORT > SOURCE.TMP`, the command line was written as `DIR %1 | FIND /V "e" | FIND /V "<DIR>" | SORT > SOURCE.TMP`. Why?

`DIR %1 |`   This command will display a specified directory and send the standard output to

`FIND /V "e" |`   the FIND command. The /V will exclude any line that has a lower case "e" in it. Since you are interested only in the file names and since file names are always displayed in upper case letters, what are you excluding? You are excluding such lines as

```
Volume in drive A is DATADISK
Volume Serial Number is 2F26-1901
Directory of A:\
```

Each of the above lines has a lower case "e" somewhere in the text. Now that you have "filtered" out those lines, you are sending the standard output to the next command, which is another FIND.

`FIND /V "<DIR>" |`   This command excludes any line with `<DIR>` in it, because every subdirectory will have at least two of these lines. You do not need to compare these lines. Once you have "filtered" out `<DIR>`, you are piping the standard output to the next command, which is the SORT command.

`SORT >`   This will take the filtered data, sort it, and redirect the standard output to a file called `SOURCE.TMP`.

`SOURCE.TMP`   This file can now be compared to some other file.

In addition, you took care to clean up by deleting both `SOURCE.TMP` and `OTHER.TMP` when the program finished executing. You are now going to test this batch file.

Step 6   Key in the following:

A:\>**DCOMP PROG\GAMES C:\DOS6BK\GAMES** Enter

```
A:\>DCOMP PROG\GAMES   C:\DOS6BK\GAMES

A:\>REM  This batch file will compare the file names

A:\>REM  in two directories.
```

```
A:\>DIR PROG\GAMES ¦ FIND /V "e" ¦ FIND /V "<DIR>" ¦ SORT > SOURCE.TMP

A:\>DIR C:\DOS6BK\GAMES ¦ FIND /V "e" ¦ FIND /V "<DIR>" ¦ SORT > OTHER.TMP

A:\>FC SOURCE.TMP OTHER.TMP ¦ MORE

Comparing files SOURCE.TMP and OTHER.TMP
FC: no differences encountered


A:\>PAUSE You are about to delete the files SOURCE.TMP and OTHER.TMP
Press any key to continue . . .
```

WHAT'S HAPPENING? The same files are on the DATA disk in the PROG\GAMES subdirectory and in the C:\DOS6BK\GAMES subdirectory.

Step 7   Press **Enter**

```
A:\>DEL   SOURCE.TMP

A:\>DEL   OTHER.TMP

A:\>
A:\>
A:\>_
```

WHAT'S HAPPENING? You have deleted the SOURCE.TMP and OTHER.TMP files. What if there were differences?

Step 8   Key in the following: A:\>**DCOMP HPB C:\DOS6BK\PHONE** **Enter**

```
A:\>FC SOURCE.TMP OTHER.TMP ¦ MORE

Comparing files SOURCE.TMP and OTHER.TMP
      SOURCE.TMP
HPB       CFG          230 04-23-94   10:47p
HPB       DAT        4,914 06-26-94    5:36p
HPB       EXE      164,420 07-03-93    8:01a
HPB       OLD        4,914 06-26-94    5:36p
HPB       SLC          448 04-23-94   10:30p
      OTHER.TMP
HPB       CFG          230 04-23-94   10:47p
HPB       DAT        4,368 12-12-96   10:46p
HPB       EXE      164,420 07-03-93    8:01a
HPB       SLC          448 04-23-94   10:30p
```

```
A:\>PAUSE You are about to delete the files SOURCE.TMP and
OTHER.TMP
Press any key to continue . . .
```

WHAT'S HAPPENING? There are differences. The DATA disk has one more file
(HPB.OLD) than the C:\DOS6BK\PHONE subdirectory. There is also a difference in
dates between the two versions of HPB.DAT.

Step 9   Press **Enter**

```
A:\>DEL    SOURCE.TMP

A:\>DEL    OTHER.TMP

A:\>
A:\>
A:\>_
```

WHAT'S HAPPENING? You can also use this batch file to determine which file is
most current.

Step 10   Key in the following:

A:\>**DCOMP HPB*.DAT C:\DOS6BK\PHONE*.DAT** **Enter**

```
A:\>REM  This batch file will compare the file names

A:\>REM  in two directories.

A:\>DIR HPB\*.DAT | FIND /V "e" | FIND /V "<DIR>" | SORT > SOURCE.TMP

A:\>DIR C:\DOS6BK\PHONE\*.DAT | FIND /V "e" | FIND /V "<DIR>" | SORT


A:\>FC SOURCE.TMP OTHER.TMP | MORE

Comparing files SOURCE.TMP and OTHER.TMP
     SOURCE.TMP

HPB       DAT         4,914 06-26-94    5:36p
     OTHER.TMP

HPB       DAT         4,368 12-12-96   10:46p



A:\>PAUSE You are about to delete the files SOURCE.TMP and OTHER.TMP
Press any key to continue . . .
```

WHAT'S HAPPENING? In this example, the HPB.DAT file with the 12-12-96 date is the most current.

Step 11   Press **Enter**

```
A:\>DEL   SOURCE.TMP

A:\>DEL   OTHER.TMP

A:\>
A:\>
A:\>_
```

WHAT'S HAPPENING? You now have an easy way to compare the files in directories or on disks. You could, of course, add an @ECHO OFF statement at the beginning of the batch file so you see only the results of the command.

Chapter Summary

1. The redirection symbols are the >, the <, and the >>.
2. The >> appends output to the end of a file.
3. Redirection, pipes, and filters have to do with standard input and standard output.
4. Any command that expects its input from the keyboard has standard input.
5. Any command that normally displays its output on the screen has standard output.
6. Standard error means that DOS writes error messages to the screen.
7. You can redirect standard input and output to and from devices or files.
8. The pipe symbol is the ¦.
9. The pipe takes standard output from one command and uses it as standard input into the next command.
10. You can pipe many programs together.
11. Filters take data, change it in some fashion, and send the output to the screen.
12. The three DOS filters are SORT, FIND, and MORE.
13. SORT has two parameters: /R for reverse order and /+*n* for column number.
14. FIND has three parameters: /V for everything except, /C for counting occurrences of the item, and /N for line number where the item appears in the file. DOS 5.0 and above also has the parameter /I for ignore case.
15. MORE lets you look at any text file one screenful at a time. It has no parameters.
16. You must have a command on both ends of the pipe.
17. Redirection is the last action you can take. You either write to the screen *or* to a file device. You either accept input from the keyboard *or* from a file.
18. You can string together pipes and filters to create your own commands.
19. Each part of the command must be able to stand alone on the command line.
20. You can use pipes and filters in batch files.

Key Terms

ASCII sort sequence	I/O	Standard error
Case sensitive	Input/output	Standard input
Character string	Pipes	Standard output
Filters	Redirection	

Discussion Questions

1. Explain redirection.
2. Explain the terms standard input, standard output, and standard error.
3. Does every DOS command use standard input and standard output? If not, why not?
4. What is the difference between > and >> when redirecting output?
5. Explain how the symbol < is used.
6. Keying in COPY DIR PRN will not give you a printout of the directory. Why?
7. What are filters?
8. Give the syntax of the SORT command.
9. What do the parameters in the SORT syntax represent?
10. Explain how the SORT command works. Describe any limitations of the SORT command.
11. Identify one place that standard output can be written.
12. Give the syntax for the FIND command.
13. What is the purpose of the FIND command?
14. What are the three parameters that are used with the FIND command and what do they represent?
15. Why must the character string be enclosed in quotation marks when using the FIND command?
16. What are pipes?
17. Are there any restrictions on the use of pipes? If so, what are they?
18. How is the MORE command used?
19. Give the syntax of the MORE command.
20. How may pipes, filters, and redirection be used in batch files?

Chapter 12

Advanced Batch Files

Learning Objectives

After completing this chapter you will be able to:

1. List the commands used in batch files.
2. List and explain batch file rules.
3. Explain the purpose and function of the REM, PAUSE, and ECHO commands.
4. Explain the purpose and function of the CTTY command.
5. Explain the purpose and function of the GOTO command.
6. Explain the purpose and function of the SHIFT command.
7. Explain the purpose and function of the IF command.
8. Explain the purpose and function of the IF EXIST/IF NOT EXIST command.
9. Explain the purpose and function of the IF ERRORLEVEL command.
10. Explain the purpose and function of writing programs.
11. Explain the purpose of DEBUG.
12. Explain the purpose and function of the CHOICE command.
13. Explain the purpose and function of the environment and environmental variables.
14. Explain the purpose and function of the DIRCMD environmental variable.
15. Explain the purpose and function of the FOR..IN..DO command.
16. Explain the purpose and function of the CALL command.

Student Outcomes

1. Use the ECHO command to place a blank line in a batch file.
2. Use the GOTO command in conjunction with a label to create a loop.
3. Use the SHIFT command to move parameters.
4. Use the IF command with strings for conditional processing.
5. Test for null values in a batch file.
6. Use the IF EXIST/IF NOT EXIST command to test for the existence of a file or a subdirectory.
7. Use SET, the environment, and environmental variables in batch files.
8. Use the IF ERRORLEVEL with XCOPY to write a batch file for testing exit codes.
9. Write a script file and redirect it to a batch file that checks the scan codes.
10. Use the CHOICE command in a batch file.
11. Use the DIRCMD environmental variable in a batch file.
12. Use the FOR..IN..DO command for repetitive processing.
13. Use the CALL command in a batch file.

Chapter Overview

You learned in Chapter 10 how to write simple batch files, use replaceable parameters, and write menus as well as create an AUTOEXEC.BAT file. You can write even more powerful batch files that act like sophisticated programs. There are commands that can be used in batch files that allow you this capability.

This chapter focuses on introducing the remaining batch file commands as well as learning to use them. This will allow you the capability to write sophisticated batch files. You will also be introduced to DEBUG to assist you in creating powerful batch files. You will further refine your techniques in working with the environment. You will learn how to manipulate a special environmental variable—DIRCMD.

12.1 Batch File Commands

You can do many things with batch files. A quick summary of batch file rules remind us that any batch file must have the file extension of .BAT. It must always be an ASCII file. A batch file must include legitimate commands. Only one batch file has a predetermined name, AUTOEXEC.BAT. This batch file is designed to execute when you initially boot the system. You may create or alter AUTOEXEC.BAT to customize the way you want your system to appear when you boot it. In addition, you can use replaceable or "positional" parameters to create generic batch files. Batch file commands are not case sensitive. You may use only the following commands in batch files. Table 12.1 lists all the batch file commands.

CALL	Allows you to call one batch file from another without causing the first batch file to stop.
CHOICE	Allows user to make a choice in a batch file (new in DOS 6.0).
ECHO	Displays or hides the display of commands or text in batch files when they are running. At command line, will display status of ECHO (either ON or OFF).
FOR	Runs a specified command for each file in a set of files. Can be used on command line.
GOTO	Directs MS-DOS to a line in a batch file that is marked by a label you specify.
IF	Performs conditional processing in a batch file. If the condition is true, MS-DOS carries out the command that follows the condition. If the condition is false, MS-DOS ignores the command that follows the condition.
PAUSE	Suspends processing of a batch file and displays a message that prompts the user to press any key to continue.
REM	Allows you to include comments in a batch file or in CONFIG.SYS. Can also be used to disable commands in a batch file or in CONFIG.SYS.
SHIFT	Changes the position of replaceable parameters in a batch file.

Table 12.1   Batch File Commands

You have already used ECHO, PAUSE, and REM. You will now learn the remaining batch file commands. These commands allow you to create complex batch files. Using these commands is similar to using a programming language. Batch files have a limited vocabulary (the commands listed above), a syntax, and programming logic. Batch files are also limited in the kinds of programming you can do. They do not have the power or the flexibility of a "real" programming language such as Visual Basic or C++. Batch files, however, accomplish many things in the DOS environment.

12.2 A Review of the REM, PAUSE, and ECHO Commands

The REM command in a batch file indicates to DOS that whatever text follows the REM is to be displayed, but only if ECHO has not been turned off. If it is a command, it will be displayed but not executed. Remarks can be any string of characters up to 123. Remarks are typically used to document batch files. Placing a REM in front of a command will allow you to execute a batch file or the CONFIG.SYS file without executing that command. This allows you to disable a line or lines without having to delete them.

The PAUSE command stops a batch file from continuing to execute until you press any key. The PAUSE command informs you to press any key to continue but does not do any conditional processing.

Remember, to interrupt a batch file, you can always press Ctrl + C or Ctrl + Break. Pressing this key combination will interrupt the execution of the batch file. There is one warning—if DOS is in the middle of executing a command such as FORMAT or DISKCOPY, it will finish executing the command before exiting the batch file.

The ECHO command can be used either on a command line or in a batch file. The ECHO command is a special command that turns on or turns off the echoing of commands to the screen . If you key in ECHO on the command line or include it in a batch file, you will see the status of ECHO: either ECHO is on or ECHO is off. When ECHO is on, all the commands in a batch file are displayed on the screen. When ECHO is off, you see the output of the command but not the command itself. Normally ECHO is on, which is particularly useful when you want to track the operation of a batch file. However, when a batch file runs successfully, the display of commands can clutter the screen.

In a batch file, if you do not wish to see each command on the screen, you can issue the command ECHO OFF. The commands are not displayed, but any messages that a command issues are displayed, i.e., 1 file(s) copied. Depending on your preferences, you can key in ECHO ON or ECHO OFF within the batch file to display or not display the commands. In addition, if you precede ECHO OFF with @, ECHO OFF will not appear on the screen.

12.3 Advanced Features of ECHO and REM

There are some interesting features and variations you can implement with both REM and ECHO. One problem with REM is that DOS recognizes it as a command and must take time to process it. A shortcut is to precede a remark with a double colon (::) instead of REM. This will save valuable processing time because DOS treats all lines beginning with a colon as a label and ignores them unless they "called" elsewhere in the batch file. This will be further explained later.

When you turn ECHO OFF, you still get the display of messages such as 1 file(s) copied. Sometimes you do not wish to see messages. You can use redirection with standard output and redirect the output of a command to a device called NUL. As the name implies, NUL means send it to "nothing." When you send the output to NUL, it goes nowhere, and it is not displayed on the screen.

Although redirecting the output of a command to the NUL device will suppress messages such as 1 file(s) copied, it will not suppress a message like File not found. You can suppress those messages by using another command, CTTY. This command allows you to specify what device DOS will use as the console (the place where you input commands and where DOS sends output). Usually it is the keyboard and the monitor. It has a reserved name—CON.

You can use the NUL device with the CTTY command by using the command CTTY NUL. When you use this command in a batch file, you are essentially telling DOS to accept what you keyed in and send all the screen output to nowhere. You should use this command *only* in a batch file, because if you use it at the command line, you will not be able to enter any other commands, forcing you to reboot the system. You should also use CTTY NUL in tandem with CTTY CON. CTTY CON passes control back to the console so when you exit the batch file, you have control of the console. Whenever you use CTTY NUL in a batch file, be sure the last line is always CTTY CON to ensure that control is returned to the console.

You often want to place a blank line in a batch file for aesthetic purposes or to highlight particular commands. There is, of course, no such thing as a blank line. In the word processing world, when you want a blank line, you press the **Enter** key, which places a carriage return in the document and prints as a blank line. This does not work in batch files. In a batch file, DOS simply ignores it when you press **Enter**. Pressing **Enter** does not leave a blank line. If you use REM, you will see nothing if ECHO is off. If you place the word ECHO in the batch file, it will report whether ECHO is on or off. An easy method to get a blank line is to key in ECHO, followed by a period. There can be no space between ECHO and the period.

12.4 Activity: Using ::, ECHO, CTTY, and NUL

Note: The DATA disk is in Drive A. The A:\> is displayed.

Step 1   Use an editor to create and save the following batch file called ONE.BAT. Press **Enter** where indicated.

:: **This is a test of a batch file using** **Enter**

:: **different features.** **Enter**

COPY CAROLYN.FIL BOOK.FIL **Enter**

Enter

TYPE BOOK.FIL **Enter**

ECHO **Enter**

DEL BOOK.FIL **Enter**

COPY NO.FIL BOOK.FIL **Enter**

Step 2   Key in the following: A:\>**TYPE ONE.BAT** **Enter**

```
::   This is a test of a batch file using
::   different features.
COPY  CAROLYN.FIL  BOOK.FIL

TYPE BOOK.FIL
ECHO
DEL BOOK.FIL
COPY  NO.FIL  BOOK.FIL

A:\>_
```

WHAT'S HAPPENING? You have created a batch file without any of the suggested improvements. You are now going to see how it looks when it executes.

Step 3   Key in the following: A:\>**ONE** **Enter**

```
A:\>ONE
A:\>COPY  CAROLYN.FIL  BOOK.FIL
   1 file(s) copied
A:\>
A:\>TYPE BOOK.FIL
Hi, my name is Carolyn.
What is your name?

A:\>ECHO
ECHO is on

A:\>DEL BOOK.FIL

A:\>COPY  NO.FIL  BOOK.FIL
File not found - NO.FIL
         0 file(s) copied


A:\>
A:\>
A:\>_
```

WHAT'S HAPPENING? You see messages as well as the output. Your blank line presented only the prompt.

Step 4   Edit and save ONE.BAT so it looks as follows:

> **@ECHO OFF**
> **:: This is a test of a batch file using**
> **:: different features.**
> **COPY CAROLYN.FIL BOOK.FIL > NUL**
> **ECHO.**
> **TYPE BOOK.FIL**
> **ECHO.**
> **DEL BOOK.FIL**
> **COPY NO.FIL BOOK.FIL > NUL**

Step 5   Key in the following: A:\>**ONE** **Enter**

```
A:\>ONE

Hi, my name is Carolyn.
What is your name?

File not found - NO.FIL
A:\>_
```

WHAT'S HAPPENING? You now do not see your messages or remarks. You also get some blank lines. The COPY command could not find NO.FIL and you did not suppress the display of the message `File not found - NO.FIL.` **CTTY NUL** is useful here.

Step 6   Edit and save `ONE.BAT` so it looks as follows:

   @ECHO OFF
   :: This is a test of a batch file using
   :: different features.
   COPY CAROLYN.FIL BOOK.FIL > NUL
   ECHO.
   TYPE BOOK.FIL
   ECHO.
   DEL BOOK.FIL
   CTTY NUL
   COPY NO.FIL BOOK.FIL > NUL
   CTTY CON

Step 7   Key in the following: `A:\>`**ONE** **Enter**

```
A:\>ONE

Hi, my name is Carolyn.
What is your name?

A:\>_
```

WHAT'S HAPPENING? You no longer display any messages. Note that `CTTY CON` is at the end of the batch file. These techniques will be used in the batch files you are going to create.

12.5 The GOTO Command

By using the GOTO command, a batch file can be constructed to behave like a program written in a programming language such as BASIC or C++. The GOTO command will branch to a specific part within a batch file, creating a loop. A **loop** is an operation that will repeat steps until you stop the loop either by using an IF statement or by breaking into the batch file with **Ctrl** + C.

  The GOTO command works in conjunction with a label. This label is not to be confused with a volume label on a disk. A label is any name you choose to flag a location in a batch file. A label in a batch file indicates a specific location in the batch file. A label is preceded by a colon (`:`) and is ignored by DOS until called with the GOTO command. A double colon (`::`), used earlier for REM staements, ensures that DOS will always disregard the line since a colon may not be used as a label name. A label can be no longer than 8 characters. The label itself is not a command, it just identifies a location in a batch file. When a batch file goes to a label, it carries out whatever command follows the label. GOTO has one parameter, GOTO *label*. Earlier versions of DOS were case sensitive and both the label and the GOTO *label* had to be identical. Although this is not true with newer DOS versions, it is still wise to make them the same case.

12.6 Activity: Using the GOTO Command

Note: The DATA disk should be in Drive A with the A:\> displayed.

Step 1   Use any text editor to create and save a batch file called REPEAT.BAT. Key in the following using exactly the same case:

> **REM This file displays many times the contents**
> **REM of a file.**
> **:REPEAT**
> **TYPE %1**
> **PAUSE**
> **GOTO REPEAT**

WHAT'S HAPPENING? You have written a small batch file. The first two lines are remarks that will not execute. You are not including ECHO OFF, because you want to see what is happening in your batch file. Omitting ECHO OFF is a way to "debug" a batch file program. **Debug** means to see and repair any errors. The third line (:REPEAT) is a label which must be preceded by a colon. The fourth line is a simple TYPE command with a replaceable parameter. The PAUSE command is placed on the fifth line so you may see what is happening. The sixth and last line is the loop. The GOTO tells the batch file to return to the label (:REPEAT). It will then return to line three and execute the TYPE command. It will then read lines 5 and 6 and continually repeat the process.

Step 2:   You must be at the system prompt, not in the editor. Key in the following:

> A:\>**REPEAT APRIL.TXT** [Enter]

```
A:\>REPEAT APRIL.TXT

A:\>REM This file displays many times the

A:\>REM contents of a file.

A:\>TYPE APRIL.TXT
This is my April file.
It is my fourth dummy file.
This is file 4.

A:\>PAUSE
Press any key to continue . . .
```

WHAT'S HAPPENING? The first two lines displayed are remarks. The label was ignored, but the TYPE command was executed. The next line has paused the batch file. You need to press [Enter] to continue.

Step 3   Press **Enter**

```
A:\>GOTO REPEAT

A:\>TYPE APRIL.TXT

This is my April file.
It is my fourth dummy file.
This is file 4.

A:\>PAUSE
Press any key to continue . . .
```

WHAT'S HAPPENING? The next line in the batch file was GOTO REPEAT. The batch file was sent back to the label :REPEAT. The batch file read the next line after the label, which was the TYPE command, then the next line, which is PAUSE. When you press a key, you will again be returned to the label. Now you see a loop in action.

Step 4   Press **Enter** a few times to see the loop in action. Then press **Ctrl** + **C** to break out of the batch file. It will ask you if you want to terminate the batch job. Key in **Y** for yes. You will be returned to the A:\> prompt.

WHAT'S HAPPENING? A loop can be very useful. For instance, if you wanted to delete all the files from many floppy disks, you could write a batch file that would look like this:

> @ECHO OFF
> :TOP
> CLS
> ECHO Place the disk with the files you no longer want in
> Drive A.
> PAUSE
> ECHO Y | DEL A:*.*
> ECHO Press Ctrl + C to stop executing this batch file.
> ECHO otherwise, press any key to continue deleting files.
> PAUSE > NUL
> GOTO TOP

The ECHO Y | DEL A:*.* is a way to send the Y character to the prompt that DEL A:*.* will ask for. You could have used DEL A:*.* < Y.FIL, but the ECHO method has the advantage of not requiring a file called Y.FIL. You did not want to see the output of the PAUSE command, so you redirected it to the NUL device.

12.7 The SHIFT Command

When you have written a batch file with positional parameters, you key in the batch file name followed by a series of values. When the batch file is executed, DOS looks to the command line for the values it needs to plug into the batch file. It does this based on the position of particular parameters in the command line. If you had a batch file called LIST.BAT with the lines TYPE %1 and TYPE %2, you would key in the following command line: TYPE ARPIL.TXT MAY.TXT

DOS READS		DOS SUBSTITUTES
TYPE %1	DOS needs a value for %1. It looks to the command line and sees that APRIL.TXT occupies position 1.	**TYPE APRIL.TXT**
TYPE %2	DOS needs a value for %2. It looks to the command line and sees that MAY.TXT occupies position 2.	**TYPE MAY.TXT**

With this generic batch file, you could key in only two file names. If you wanted more file names, you would have to reexecute the batch file. You are limited to 10 parameters on a command line—%0 through %9. The SHIFT command allows you to shift the parameters over one by one, making the number of parameters on a line limitless. The SHIFT command shifts the contents of the parameters to the left. Parameter 2 becomes parameter 1, parameter 3 becomes parameter 2, and so on. This allows the batch file to process all the parameters on the command line.

12.8 Activity: Using the SHIFT Command

Note: The DATA disk should be in Drive A with the A:\> displayed.

Step 1   Key in the following: A:\>**ECHO a b c d e** [Enter]

```
A:\>ECHO a b c d e
a b c d e
A:\>_
```

WHAT'S HAPPENING? ECHO on a command line just "echoed" what you keyed in. Thus, the parameters a, b, c, d, and e on the command line were repeated on the screen. If you wanted to display more than five parameters and place the echoing parameters in a batch file, you would need to use the SHIFT command.

Step 2   Use any text editor to create and save the file ALPHA.BAT follows:

```
@ECHO OFF
ECHO %0 %1 %2 %3
SHIFT
ECHO %0 %1 %2 %3
SHIFT
ECHO %0 %1 %2 %3
SHIFT
ECHO %0 %1 %2 %3
```

WHAT'S HAPPENING? You have created a batch file with replaceable parameters. The purpose of the batch file is to demonstrate the SHIFT command. Remember that ECHO just "echoes" what you keyed in. In your command line, however, even though you have only four parameters (0 through 3), you want to key in more than four values.

Step 3   Remember, you must be at the system prompt, not in the editor. Key in the following: A:\>**ALPHA a b c d e f g** Enter

```
A:\>ALPHA a b c d e f g
ALPHA a b c
a b c d
b c d e
c d e f
A:\>_
```

WHAT'S HAPPENING? Notice the output. In each case, when the batch file read SHIFT, it moved each parameter over by one position. You keyed in on the command line: ALPHA a b c d e f g

Batch File	Supplied Value From Command Line	Screen Display
@ECHO OFF		
ECHO %0 %1 %2 %3	ALPHA is %0 a is %1 b is %2 c is %3	ALPHA a b c
SHIFT	ALPHA is dropped as %0 a becomes %0 b becomes %1 c becomes %2 d becomes %3	
ECHO %0 %1 %2 %3	a is %0 b is %1 c is %2 d is %3	a b c d
SHIFT	a is dropped as %0 b becomes %0 c becomes %1 d becomes %2 e becomes %3	
ECHO %0 %1 %2 %3	b is %0 c is %1 d is %2 e is %3	b c d e
SHIFT	b is dropped as %0	
ECHO %0 %1 %2 %3	c becomes %0 d becomes %1 e becomes %2 f becomes %3	c d e f

You should see that you are indeed shifting parameters, but how is this useful? You will write some batch files that use SHIFT so you can see how this technique can be used.

As you know, DOS stamps each file with the current date and time when it is created or modified . Most often, this means that each file has a unique time and date based on the last time you modified or created the file. Sometimes, you want to place a specific time and date stamp on a file or group of files. For example, if you sell software and you have customers to whom you send files, you might like to ascertain which version of the file they have. By having a particular date and/or time on the file, you can easily keep a date log that is not dependent on the file modification date. Commands such as XCOPY can back up files after or before a certain date. To ensure that you are backing up all the files you want, you can set the date, update the date stamp on your files, and then update from that date. You need a way to update the dates. You can do this by using the following command:

```
COPY  filename  /b  +
```

Remember, the + sign tells DOS to concatenate files. The first thing DOS does when copying files is create a file name with the current time and date in the directory . At first, the new file is empty. Since there is no specific destination file name, COPY will default to the source file name. It then proceeds to concatenate (add) the existing file to the "new" file name and the new date and time. In essence, it is copying a file onto itself. Since it is a new entry in the directory table, it has the current date and time.

The /b switch tells DOS to copy the file in binary mode. When you concatenate files with no switches, DOS will copy a file in text mode. The COPY command knows the contents of the file has ended when it sees a special mark called an **EOF** (**end of file**) mark. Typically, the EOF mark is a [Ctrl] Z. The instant COPY sees this special signal, it thinks there is no more information to copy and will place its own EOF mark at the end of the file—another [Ctrl] Z. Unfortunately, this "extra" EOF mark is sometimes interpreted by a program or a data file as something other than the end of the file. Thus, you could be in the situation of not copying the entire file. The alternative is to copy the file in binary mode. When you choose this option—the /b switch—COPY will not read the file but will copy everything in the file, ensuring that the entire file contents are copied without adding an extra [Ctrl] Z to a file. An extra [Ctrl] Z can create problems when you are trying to use the copied file.

Now that you know how and why to update file dates and times, it is easy to place these commands in a batch file. Since you may have more than one file you wish to "stamp," you want to allow for many file names, so you will use the SHIFT command.

Step 4   Use any text editor. Name the file UPDATE.BAT and then key in the following:

:DOIT
COPY %1 /b + > NUL

       SHIFT
       PAUSE
       GOTO DOIT

Step 5   Key in the following: A:\>**DIR APR.99** Enter

Step 6   Key in the following: A:\>**DIR APR.BUD** Enter

```
A:\>DIR APR.99

 Volume in drive A is DATADISK
 Volume Serial Number is 2F26-1901
 Directory of A:\

APR        99            71 11-23-95  10:42a
        1 file(s)              71 bytes
                         662,528 bytes free


A:\>DIR APR.BUD

 Volume in drive A is DATADISK
 Volume Serial Number is 2F26-1901
 Directory of A:\

APR        BUD           18 12-06-94  10:46a
        1 file(s)              18 bytes
                         662,528 bytes free


A:\>_
```

WHAT'S HAPPENING? You want the files APR.99 and APR.BUD to have today's date and time on them.

Step 7   Key in the following: A:\>**UPDATE APR.99 APR.BUD** Enter

```
A:\>UPDATE APR.99 APR.BUD

A:\>COPY APR.99 /b + > NUL

A:\>SHIFT

A:\>PAUSE
Press any key to continue . . .
```

WHAT'S HAPPENING? The batch file copied APR.99, went to the SHIFT, and is now going to copy the next parameter it shifted, APR.BUD.

Step 8   Press Enter

```
A:\>GOTO DOIT

A:\>COPY APR.BUD /b + > NUL

A:\>SHIFT

A:\>PAUSE
Press any key to continue . . .
```

WHAT'S HAPPENING? It now copied APR.BUD.

Step 9 Press **Enter**

```
A:\>GOTO DOIT

A:\>COPY  /b + > NUL
Required parameter missing

A:\>SHIFT

A:\>PAUSE
Press any key to continue . . .
```

WHAT'S HAPPENING? This batch file seemed to work effectively when you first initiated it. It copied APR.99. It then shifted over to APR.BUD and copied that. However, you created an endless loop. When the batch file finished copying APR.BUD, it again shifted parameters, but there was nothing to shift to. The batch file informed you that the file name is missing (Required parameter missing). It will continue to do this forever. There is something missing here: a condition which you need to insert. First, though, you must break into the batch file.

Step 10 Press **Ctrl** + **C** and answer **Y** to the prompt.

Step 11 Key in the following: A:\>**DIR APR.99** **Enter**

Step 12 Key in the following: A:\>**DIR APR.BUD** **Enter**

```
A:\>DIR APR.99

 Volume in drive A is DATADISK
 Volume Serial Number is 2F26-1901
 Directory of A:\

APR      99           71 08-14-94  9:18p
        1 file(s)              71 bytes
                        662,528 bytes free

A:\>DIR APR.BUD
```

```
Volume in drive A is DATADISK
Volume Serial Number is 2F26-1901
Directory of A:\

APR      BUD           18 08-14-94   9:20p
         1 file(s)               18 bytes
                       662,528 bytes free

A:\>_
```

WHAT'S HAPPENING? The file worked—the date and time should be the current date and time. You can create a batch file and use shift to identify the size and number of files in a directory so you can determine whether the files will fit on a floppy disk.

Step 13   Use any text editor. Name the file SIZE.BAT and then key in the following:

> :TOP
> **DIR %1 ⋮ FIND "Directory" >> TEMP.FIL**
> **DIR %1 ⋮ FIND "bytes" ⋮ FIND /V "free" >> TEMP.FIL**
> **SHIFT**
> **GOTO TOP**
> **TYPE TEMP.FIL**
> **PAUSE**
> **DEL TEMP.FIL**

WHAT'S HAPPENING? Since you do not care about the names of the files, only the size and the directory they are in, you "filtered" the output from the DIR command to include only the items that you wanted. You used the double >> so that you would see both the name of the directory and the bytes in the directory. Had you not used the >>, you would have overwritten TEMP.FIL. At the end of your work, delete TEMP.FIL so it will not take space on your disk.

Step 14   Key in the following: A:\>**SIZE CLASS TRIP** [Enter]

WHAT'S HAPPENING? Your batch file is running endlessly. You again created an endless loop.

Step 15   Press [Ctrl] + **C** and answer **Y** to the prompt.

```
A:\>GOTO TOP

A:\>DIR ⋮ FIND "Directory" >> TEMP.FIL
A:\>DIR ⋮ FIND "bytes" ⋮ FIND /V "free" >> TEMP.FIL

A:\>SHIFT
```

```
A:\>GOTO TOP

A:\>DIR | FIND "Directory" >> TEMP.FIL

A:\>DIR | FIND "bytes" | FIND /V "free" >> TEMP.FIL

A:\>SHIFT

A:\>GOTO TOP

A:\>DIR | FIND "Directory" >> TEMP.FIL

A:\>DIR ^C

Terminate batch job (Y/N)?y

A:\>_
```

WHAT'S HAPPENING? Your display may look different depending on where you broke into the batch file.

Step 16   Key in the following: A:\>**TYPE TEMP.FIL** [Enter]

```
A:\>TYPE TEMP.FIL
  Directory of A:\CLASS
       15 file(s)              875 bytes
  Directory of A:\TRIP
       26 file(s)            1,568 bytes
  Directory of A:\
       64 file(s)           46,711 bytes
  Directory of A:\
       64 file(s)           46,770 bytes
  Directory of A:\

A:\>_
```

WHAT'S HAPPENING? You got more information than you wanted. You now know the size of the CLASS and TRIP directories, but the other information is useless. You are missing **conditional processing**.

12.9 The IF Command

The IF command allows for conditional processing. Conditional processing is a powerful tool in programming. Conditional processing allows a comparison between two items. To determine whether the items are identical or whether one is greater than another. A comparison test will yield one of two values—true or false. If the items are identical, the condition is true. If the items are not identical the condition is false. Once you establish a true or false value, you can then direct the program to do something based on that value. Conditional processing is often expressed as *IF* the condition is true, *THEN* do something; *IF* the condition is false, *THEN* do nothing.

In batch files, the IF command will test for some logical condition and then, if the condition is true, the batch file will execute the command. If the test is false, the command will not be executed and the batch file will fall through to the next command line in the batch file. The IF command in batch file processing can check for three conditions:

1. Whether two sets of characters are identical or not. The characters are called a "string," as in string of data (sometimes referred to as a character string).
2. Whether or not a file exists.
3. The value of the variable in ERRORLEVEL. An ERRORLEVEL is a number that a program can set. ERRORLEVEL can check that number.

The syntax reads:

```
IF [NOT] ERRORLEVEL number command
IF [NOT] string1==string2 command
IF [NOT] EXIST filename command
```

NOT	Specifies that MS-DOS should carry out the command only if the condition is false.
ERRORLEVEL number	Specifies a true condition if the last program run returned an exit code equal to or greater than the number specified.
command	Specifies the command to carry out if the condition is met.
string1==string2	Specifies a true condition if the specified text strings match.
EXIST filename	Specifies a true condition if the specified filename exists.

12.10 IF Command Using Strings

You can use the IF command with character strings to test whether or not one string is exactly the same as another. You can tell the IF statement to GOTO a label or to perform an operation when the strings match and the condition is true. Conversely, you can tell the IF statement to GOTO a label or perform an operation when the strings do not match and the condition is false. What is to be compared is separated by two equal signs (==).

12.11 Activity: Using the IF Command with Strings

Note: The DATA disk should be in Drive A. The default drive and directory should be A:\>.

Step 1   Use any text editor to create and save a file called GREET.BAT. Key in the following:

IF %1==Carolyn GOTO Carolyn
IF %1==Steven GOTO Steven
ECHO Isn't anyone there?
GOTO FINISH
:Carolyn
ECHO Greetings, Ms. Carolyn.
GOTO FINISH
:Steven
ECHO Greetings, Mr. Steven.
:FINISH

WHAT'S HAPPENING? You have created a batch file to test the IF statement using character strings. You did not place the ECHO OFF at the beginning of the file so you can see what happens when it executes.

Step 2   Key in the following: A:\>**GREET Carolyn** [Enter]

```
A:\>GREET Carolyn

A:\>IF Carolyn==Carolyn GOTO Carolyn

A:\>ECHO Greetings, Ms. Carolyn.
Greetings, Ms. Carolyn.

A:\>GOTO FINISH

A:\>

A:\>_
```

WHAT'S HAPPENING? You keyed in GREET Carolyn. The first line in the batch file was executed. When Carolyn took the place of %1, the line read IF Carolyn==Carolyn, which is a true statement because the "strings" of data matched exactly. Since it is true, it performed the GOTO Carolyn command. The line after the label :Carolyn was then displayed: Greetings, Ms. Carolyn. The line following said GOTO FINISH, which it did. After the label :FINISH, there were no more lines, and you were returned to the system prompt.

Step 3   Key in the following: A:\>**GREET Steven** [Enter]

```
A:\>GREET Steven

A:\>IF Steven==Carolyn GOTO Carolyn

A:\>IF Steven==Steven GOTO Steven

A:\>ECHO Greetings, Mr. Steven.
    Greetings, Mr. Steven.

A:\>

A:\>
```

WHAT'S HAPPENING? When you keyed in GREET Steven, it read the first line as IF Steven==Carolyn GOTO Carolyn. Steven does not equal Carolyn, so it is a false statement. Therefore, the batch file did not go to the label :Carolyn but fell through to the next line. The line then read as IF Steven==Steven, which is a true statement because the strings of data matched exactly. Since it is true, it performed the GOTO Steven command. The line after the label :Steven was then displayed: Greetings, Mr. Steven. The line following said :FINISH, which it did. After the label: FINISH, there were no more lines, and you were returned to the system prompt.

Step 4   Key in the following: A:\>**GREET Juan** `Enter`

```
A:\>GREET Juan

A:\>IF Juan==Carolyn GOTO Carolyn

A:\>IF Juan==Steven GOTO Steven

A:\>ECHO  Isn't anyone there?
 Isn't anyone there?

A:\>GOTO FINISH
A:\>
A:\>
```

WHAT'S HAPPENING? You keyed in GREET Juan. It read the first line as IF Juan==Carolyn GOTO Carolyn. Juan does not equal Carolyn, so it is a false statement. The batch file did not go to the label :Carolyn but fell through to the next line. The line then read as IF Juan==Steven. This is another false statement, so the batch file did not go to the label :Steven but fell through to the next line. The line following said ECHO Isn't anyone there? Thus, Isn't anyone there? was displayed (echoed) to the screen. It then fell through to the next line, which was GOTO FINISH. After the label :FINISH, there were no more lines, and you were returned to the system prompt.

Step 5   Key in the following: A:\>**GREET STEVEN** Enter

```
A:\>GREET STEVEN

A:\>IF STEVEN==Carolyn GOTO Carolyn

A:\>IF STEVEN==Steven GOTO Steven

A:\>ECHO  Isn't anyone there?
 Isn't anyone there?

A:\>GOTO FINISH

A:\>
A:\>
```

WHAT'S HAPPENING? You keyed in GREET STEVEN. It read the first line as IF STEVEN==Carolyn GOTO Carolyn. STEVEN does not equal Carolyn, so it is a false statement. The batch file did not go to the label :Carolyn but fell through to the next line. The line then read IF STEVEN==Steven, which is another false statement. Even though the word is the same, the case is different. Both sides of the == must match exactly. Because it was not an exact match, the batch file did not go to the label: Steven but fell through to the next line. The line following said ECHO Isn't anybody there?. Thus, Isn't anybody there? was displayed (echoed) to the screen. It then fell through to the next line, which was GOTO FINISH. It did. After the label :FINISH, there were no more lines, and you were returned to the system prompt.

12.12 Testing for Null Values

In the above example, you tested for an exact match of character strings. What if you have nothing to test for? For example, in the batch files you wrote, UPDATE.BAT and SIZE.BAT, you used SHIFT. SHIFT kept shifting parameters until all of them were used. When there were no more parameters, you were in an endless loop. You can test to see if a string matches, but what if "nothing" is there? This is called testing for a **null value**. You are literally testing for nothing. You must have "something" to test for "nothing." Thus, you place a value in the test that will give you nothing.

There are a variety of methods for testing for null values. One method is to use quotation marks so that your statement becomes IF "%1"=="" GOTO LABEL. The second set of quotation marks is keyed in with no spaces. This statement says, if nothing is there, GOTO somewhere else. You may also make the line read IF %1void==void GOTO LABEL. If you keyed in GREET Carolyn, your line would then look like Carolynvoid==void. This is not true, so it would proceed to the next line. If there was no value, your line would look like void==void. Now, this is true, and the GOTO label would execute. You may use any word; "void" was used in this example. Another method is to use the \ so that the statement would become IF \%1\==\\ GOTO LABEL. If you keyed in GREET Carolyn, your line would then look like \Carolyn\==\\. This is not true, so it would proceed to the next line. If there were no value, your line would look like \\==\\. Now, this is true and the GOTO label would execute.

12.13 Activity: Using Null Values

Note: The DATA disk should be in Drive A. The default drive and directory should be A:\>.

Step 1   Edit and save the file called UPDATE.BAT to look as follows:

```
:DOIT
IF "%1"=="" GOTO END
COPY %1 /b + > NUL
SHIFT
PAUSE
GOTO DOIT
:END
```

Step 2   Key in the following: A:\>**DIR CAROLYN.FIL** Enter

```
A:\>DIR CAROLYN.FIL

 Volume in drive A is DATADISK
 Volume Serial Number is 2F26-1901
 Directory of A:\

CAROLYN  FIL             45 11-23-94    7:13a
         1 file(s)              45 bytes
                          660,992 bytes free

A:\>_
```

WHAT'S HAPPENING? The file called CAROLYN.FIL has a date of 11-23-94. You are going to update only the date on this file. The SHIFT will still work and will shift "nothing" to %1, but now you are testing for a null value, and, once the file is updated, you will go to :END.

Step 3   Key in the following: A:\>**UPDATE CAROLYN.FIL** Enter

```
A:\>UPDATE CAROLYN.FIL

A:\>IF "CAROLYN.FIL"=="" GOTO END

A:\>COPY CAROLYN.FIL /b + > NUL
```

```
A:\>SHIFT

A:\>PAUSE
Press any key to continue . . .
```

WHAT'S HAPPENING? The batch file updated the file `CAROLYN.FIL`. Prior to your testing for a null value, the file looped endlessly. Now, you will see if your test for "nothing" works. Remember, there is a SHIFT that will shift over nothing.

Step 4   Press **Enter**

```
A:\>GOTO DOIT

A:\>IF ""=="" GOTO END

A:\>

A:\>_
```

WHAT'S HAPPENING? Since nothing, or a null value, was there, it was a true condition, and GOTO told it to go to the label called :END. Thus, it skipped the lines and went directly to the end of the batch file.

Step 5   Key in the following: A:\>**DIR CAROLYN.FIL** **Enter**

```
A:\>DIR CAROLYN.FIL

 Volume in drive A is DATADISK
 Volume Serial Number is 2F26-1901
 Directory of A:\

CAROLYN  FIL             45 08-15-94  11:00p
        1 file(s)               45 bytes
                        660,992 bytes free

A:\>_
```

WHAT'S HAPPENING? The date did change (your date will be different), and you were not in an endless loop. You are now going to try another technique to test for a null value.

Step 6   Edit and save the file called `SIZE.BAT` to look as follows:

```
:TOP
IF %1nothing==nothing  GOTO  END
DIR %1 | FIND "Directory" >> TEMP.FIL
DIR %1 | FIND "bytes" | FIND /V "free" >> TEMP.FIL
SHIFT
GOTO TOP
```

```
TYPE  TEMP.FIL
PAUSE
DEL  TEMP.FIL
:END
```

Step 7   Key in the following: A:>**DEL TEMP.FIL** [Enter]

WHAT'S HAPPENING? You wanted to eliminate TEMP.FIL, because the last time you ran this batch file, you were stuck in a loop and TEMP.FIL was not deleted.

Step 8   Key in the following: A:\>**SIZE CLASS TRIP** [Enter]

```
A:\>IF CLASSnothing==nothing GOTO END

A:\>DIR CLASS | FIND "Directory" >> TEMP.FIL

A:\>DIR CLASS | FIND "bytes" | FIND /V "free" >> TEMP.FIL

A:\>SHIFT

A:\>GOTO TOP

A:\>IF TRIPnothing==nothing GOTO END

A:\>DIR TRIP | FIND "Directory" >> TEMP.FIL

A:\>DIR TRIP | FIND "bytes" | FIND /V "free" >> TEMP.FIL

A:\>SHIFT

A:\>GOTO TOP

A:\>IF nothing==nothing GOTO END

A:\>

A:\>
```

WHAT'S HAPPENING? You did not have the problem of an endless loop, but, when you tested for a null value and there was a null value, you told the batch file to GOTO END. It did so, but, by going to the label :END, it never processed the other lines in the batch file. This is why writing batch files (and programs) is a complicated task. You have to think through what you are trying to do and what consequences your instructions will have.

Step 9   Key in the following: A:\>**TYPE TEMP.FIL** [Enter]

```
A:\>TYPE TEMP.FIL
   Directory of A:\CLASS
       15 file(s)            875 bytes
   Directory of A:\TRIP
       26 file(s)          1,568 bytes

A:\>_
```

WHAT'S HAPPENING? The batch file SIZE.BAT worked to some degree. You got the information in the file TEMP.FIL, but the file was never displayed or deleted. Thus, you must find another solution to the problem.

12.14 The IF EXIST/IF NOT EXIST Command

The IF EXIST command uses a file specification for the test. If the file exists, then the condition is true. Processing then passes to the specified GOTO location or to the command that follows the IF statement. If the file does not exist, the condition is false, and the batch process will read the next line in the file. When you use IF NOT EXIST, and the file does not exist, then the condition is true. Processing then passes to the specified GOTO location or to the command that follows the IF NOT statement. If the file does exist, the condition is false, and the batch process will fall through to the next line in the batch file. IF EXIST/IF NOT EXIST works only with file names and not with directory names.

12.15 Activity: Using IF EXIST to Test for a File

Note: The DATA disk should be in Drive A. The displayed prompt is A:\>.

Step 1   Use any text editor and create and save a file called RENDIR.BAT. Key in the following:

> IF \%1\==\\ GOTO end
> IF NOT \%2\==\\ GOTO next
> ECHO You must include a destination name
> ECHO for the new directory name.
> GOTO end
> :next
> IF EXIST %1 GOTO message
> MOVE %1 %2
> GOTO end
> :message
> ECHO This is a file, not a directory.
> :end

WHAT'S HAPPENING? This batch file will ensure that you are renaming a directory and not moving or copying a file. Analyzing the batch file one line at a time:

Batch File by Line Number	Test True	Processing	Test False
1 **IF \%1\==\\ GOTO end**	User keys in nothing for %1. Since test is true, action is to go to line 12.	Testing for null value.	User keys in value for %1. Since test is false, action is to go to line 2.
2 **IF NOT \%2\==\\ GOTO next**	User keys in nothing for %2. Since test is true, action is to go to line 3.	Testing for null value	User keys in something for %2. Since test is false, action is to go to line 6.
3 **ECHO You must include a destination name.**		Message for user that he did not include a value.	
4 **ECHO for the new directory name.**		Continuation of message.	
5 **GOTO end**		Falls through to the GOTO end statement. Action is to go to line 12.	
6 **:next**		Label referred to in line 2.	
7 **IF EXIST %1 GOTO message**	User keys in file name for %1. Since test is true, action is to go to line 10.	Testing for value for %1. Is it a file or a directory?	User keys in directory name for %1. Since test is false, action is to go to line 8.
8 **MOVE %1 %2**		Since %1 test is false (not a file), renaming directory can proceed.	
9 **GOTO end**		After directory is renamed, falls through to GOTO end.	
10 **:message**		Label referred to in line 2.	
11 **ECHO This is a file, not a directory.**		Message that user used a file name, not a directory name.	
12 **:end**			

Step 2   Key in the following: A:\>**RENDIR JAN.99 LAST** Enter

```
A:\>RENDIR JAN.99  LAST

A:\>IF \JAN.99\==\\ GOTO end

A:\>IF NOT \LAST\== \\ GOTO next

A:\>IF EXIST JAN.99 GOTO message
```

```
A:\>ECHO This is a file, not a directory.
This is a file, not a directory.

A:\>

A:\>_
```

WHAT'S HAPPENING? Since JAN.99 is a file, the line IF EXIST JAN.99 was true. Since it was true, the batch file executed the GOTO and went to the label :message. What if it is a directory and not a file?

Step 3   Key in the following: A:\>**RENDIR TEST OLDER** [Enter]

```
A:\>RENDIR TEST OLDER

A:\>IF \TEST\==\\ GOTO end

A:\>IF NOT \OLDER\== \\ GOTO next

A:\>IF EXIST TEST GOTO message

A:\>MOVE TEST OLDER

A:\test => a:\older [ok]

A:\>GOTO end

A:\>

A:\>_
```

WHAT'S HAPPENING? Each of the tests was false, so the batch file fell through to the MOVE line and successfully renamed the directory OLDER. Using the logic you just learned, you can correct (debug) SIZE.BAT so that it processes all the lines in the batch file. There is one more piece of information you need. You cannot use IF EXIST with a directory name unless you "fool" it. To check for the existence or nonexistence of a directory, you must use NUL. NUL is a device that discards anything sent to it. By using %1\NUL, you force IF EXIST/IF NOT EXIST to check for a directory name and not a file name.

Step 4   Edit and save the file called SIZE.BAT to look as follows:

```
IF EXIST TEMP.FIL DEL TEMP.FIL
:TOP
IF %1nothing==nothing GOTO END
IF NOT EXIST %1\NUL GOTO NEXT
DIR %1 ¦ FIND "Directory" >> TEMP.FIL
DIR %1 ¦ FIND "bytes" ¦ FIND /V "free" >> TEMP.FIL
```

```
:NEXT
SHIFT
GOTO TOP
:END
TYPE  TEMP.FIL
PAUSE
DEL  TEMP.FIL
```

WHAT'S HAPPENING? The first line IF EXIST TEMP.FIL DEL TEMP.FIL will
look for the file called TEMP.FIL and delete it if it exists. Then, when you create
TEMP.FIL, it will be a new file every time. The next addition, IF NOT EXIST
%1\NUL GOTO NEXT, will see if a directory exists. That is the purpose of %1\NUL.
If it is a file, the batch file will go to the :NEXT label, SHIFT, and go back to the :TOP
label. The :TOP label is not at the top of the batch file because you want to delete
TEMP.FIL only the first time you execute the batch file. Notice that you had to move
the :END label. In its previous batch file location, you would not have been able to
read TEMP.FIL.

Step 5   Key in the following: A:\>**SIZE CLASS JAN.99 TRIP** Enter

```
A:\>GOTO TOP

A:\>IF TRIPnothing==nothing GOTO END

A:\>IF NOT EXIST TRIP\NUL GOTO NEXT

A:\>DIR TRIP | FIND "Directory" >> TEMP.FIL

A:\>DIR TRIP | FIND "bytes" | FIND /V "free" >> TEMP.FIL

A:\>SHIFT

A:\>GOTO TOP

A:\>IF nothing==nothing GOTO END

A:\>TYPE TEMP.FIL
 Directory of A:\CLASS
      15 file(s)              875 bytes
 Directory of A:\TRIP
      26 file(s)            1,568 bytes

A:\>PAUSE
Press any key to continue . . .
```

WHAT'S HAPPENING? Your batch file worked correctly. It used JAN.99, knew it was a file, and did not include it in the output. The more complicated you want a batch file to be, the more you will have to analyze the logic of what you want to do and how to accomplish it.

Step 6   Press **Enter**

```
A:\>PAUSE
Press any key to continue . . .


A:\>DEL TEMP.FIL

A:\>
A:\>_
```

WHAT'S HAPPENING? You have executed your batch file and returned to the system level.

12.16 The IF ERRORLEVEL Command Testing

A program, including many DOS programs, can set an **exit code** when it finishes executing. A batch file can test this exit code with the IF ERRORLEVEL statement. Actually the name ERRORLEVEL is a misnomer because the number returned does not necessarily mean there was an error. For instance, the test IF ERRORLEVEL 3 will be true if the exit code is greater than or equal to 3. Thus, an exit code is not tested for a match with ERRORLEVEL, but to determine if it is greater than or equal to it. The test IF ERRORLEVEL 0 will always be true since every possible exit code is greater than or equal to 0. The trickiest thing about testing errorlevels in batch files is that the exit codes must be listed in descending order when you use IF ERRORLEVEL and in ascending order when you use IF NOT ERRORLEVEL. For instance, XCOPY will set one of the following exit codes:

   0   Files were copied without error.
   1   No files were found to copy.
   2   The user pressed CTRL + C to terminate XCOPY.
   4   Initialization error occurred. There is not enough memory or disk space, or you entered an invalid drive name or invalid syntax on the command line.
   5   Disk write error occurred.

You can write a batch file testing for exit codes.

12.17 Activity: Using IF ERRORLEVEL with XCOPY

Note: The DATA disk should be in Drive A. The displayed prompt is A:\>.

Step 1   Use any text editor to create and save a file called ERROR.BAT. Key in the
         following:

         XCOPY %1 %2
         IF ERRORLEVEL 2 GOTO message
         IF ERRORLEVEL 1 GOTO NOTOK
         IF ERRORLEVEL 0 GOTO OK
         :message
         ECHO You used Ctrl + Break and did not copy any files.
         GOTO END
         :NOTOK
         ECHO There are no %1 files. Try again.
         GOTO END
         :OK
         ECHO You copied the %1 files successfully.
         :END

Step 2   Key in the following: A:\>**ERROR *.TXT OLDER** Enter

```
A:\>ERROR *.TXT OLDER

A:\>XCOPY *.TXT OLDER
Reading source file(s)...
JANUARY.TXT
FEBRUARY.TXT
APRIL.TXT
HELLO.TXT
BYE.TXT
        5 File(s) copied

A:\>IF ERRORLEVEL 2 GOTO message

A:\>IF ERRORLEVEL 1 GOTO NOTOK

A:\>IF ERRORLEVEL 0 GOTO OK

A:\>ECHO You copied the *.TXT files successfully.
You copied the *.TXT files successfully.

A:\>

A:\>_
```

WHAT'S HAPPENING? You successfully copied the .TXT files to the OLDER
subdirectory. The exit code that was generated by XCOPY gave you the message
that the copy was successful.

Step 3   Key in the following: A:\>**ERROR *.NON OLDER** [Enter]

```
A:\>ERROR *.NON  OLDER

A:\>XCOPY *.NON OLDER
File not found - ????????.NON
     0 File(s) copied

A:\>IF ERRORLEVEL 2 GOTO message

A:\>IF ERRORLEVEL 1 GOTO NOTOK

A:\>ECHO There are no *.NON files. Try again.
There are no *.NON files. Try again.

A:\>GOTO END

A:\>
A:\>_
```

WHAT'S HAPPENING? Again, the exit code was correctly read. As you can see, you can use the exit codes successfully in a batch file. Since programs like XCOPY give you a message anyway when it could not find the file or files, you may ask yourself, why go to the trouble of writing a batch file? The reason is that you can write a small program to test for other kinds of information.

12.18 Writing Programs to Test for Key Codes

Rather than being limited to the exit codes that are set by DOS programs, you can write a small program that will create an exit code based on some activity. For instance, a program can be written that will identify which key was pressed and report which key it was. You can do this because every time you press a key, it is identified by a one or two-digit **scan code**. Actually, two things are reported when you press any key on the keyboard. First, it is reported that you pressed a key. Second, it is reported that you released the key. The keyboard controller tells the CPU that some keyboard activity is occurring. The stream of bytes is converted into the scan code, which identifies the specific key (see Appendix F for a list of all the scan codes for all the keys).

You are going to write a program that will report the scan code for any key that is pressed on the keyboard. Once you know the reported code, you can test for a specific key using ERRORLEVEL in the batch file. The batch file can then act, based on the reported code. In order to do this, you must write a program. Remember, to be executed, a program must be in "bits and bytes"—the 0s and 1s the computer understands.

There are several ways to write a program. One of the ways is to know a programming language and be able to turn the programming language program (source code) into executable code (object code). This is called compiling a program —turning a language into code. That task is beyond the scope of this text. Fortunately, there is an easier way that you can learn. It is by using a DOS system utility program called DEBUG.

DEBUG can directly modify bytes in a file. DEBUG allows you to test and debug executable files—those with a .COM or .EXE file extension. Remember, you cannot use TYPE to look at a file with the extension of .EXE or .COM because those file extension indicate programs which are not ASCII readable files. DEBUG is a small program that has its own commands and syntax. If you know the commands of the DEBUG program and the rules of programming, you could write a .COM program directly with DEBUG. Unless you are a programming expert, you will probably not want to do this.

The easiest way to use DEBUG is to create a **script** or a **script file.** A script is a set of instructions that you can write in any ASCII editor. Once you have written the script, you can "feed" it to the DEBUG program via redirection (DEBUG < SCRIPT.FIL). DEBUG will then convert the script file to an executable program with a .COM file extension. Once you have a .COM file, you can execute it as you do any program. This process is the simplest way to create a file that will report the scan code for any key that is pressed. The program you create will be called REPLY.COM.

Since using DEBUG directly can be tricky, the example below shows a .COM program written with DEBUG that will return the scan code of a pressed key. If you want to try to use DEBUG directly, what appears on the screen in this example will be in this *typeface* and what you would key in will be in this typeface. Instructions such as **a 100** assemble the program at memory address 100 (hexadecimal). *12B3* will vary from machine to machine. In the example shown here, *12B3:0100* represents segment/offset memory address. You must press [Enter] after each line, and also when [Enter] is specified. This is shown as an example of how to use DEBUG, but you do not have to do this. If you do, note the differences between the letter l and the number 1.

```
A:\>DEBUG
-a 100
12B3:0100 mov ah,8 [Enter]
12B3:0102 int 21 [Enter]
12B3:0104 cmp al,0 [Enter]
12B3:0106 jnz 10a [Enter]
12B3:0108 int 21 [Enter]
12B3:010A mov an,4c [Enter]
12B3:010C int 21 [Enter]
12B3:010E [Enter]
-r cx [Enter]
CX 0000
:e [Enter]
-n reply.com [Enter]
```

-w Enter
Writing 000E bytes
-q Enter

An easier way to create REPLY.COM is to create a script file. Again, a script file is merely a text file that contains a series of commands that can be redirected into DEBUG to create the .COM file. The script file is not the program. You use any text editor, name the file, in this case REPLY.SCR, and key in the following commands. Then, to make REPLY.SCR an executable program, you redirect it into DEBUG to create REPLY.COM. The next activity will show you how to create REPLY.SCR and REPLY.COM. (Note: You may want to check with your instructor to see if he or she has created REPLY.COM for you.).

12.19 Activity: Writing a Script File

Note: The DATA disk should be in Drive A. The displayed prompt is A:\>.

Step 1   Use any text editor to create and save a file called REPLY.SCR. Key in the following:

```
e 100  b4  08  cd  21  3c  00  75 02  cd  21  b4  4c  cd  21
rcx
e
n  reply.com
w
q
```

WHAT'S HAPPENING? Now that you have written REPLY.SCR, you must "assemble" it or convert it into the bytes that make it a program. You do this by redirecting the script file into DEBUG.

Step 2   Key in the following: A:\>**DEBUG < REPLY.SCR** Enter

```
A:\>DEBUG < REPLY.SCR
-e 100 b4 08 cd 21 3c 00 75 02 cd 21 b4 4c cd 21
-rcx
CX 0000
:e
-n reply.com
-w
Writing 0000E bytes
-q

A:\>_
```

WHAT'S HAPPENING? You have compiled REPLY.SCR into a program called REPLY.COM.

Step 3   Key in the following: A:\>**DIR REPLY.COM** [Enter]

```
A:\>DIR REPLY.COM

 Volume in drive A is DATADISK
 Volume Serial Number is 2F26-1901
 Directory of A:\

REPLY      COM              14 08-21-94  11:39a
         1 file(s)               14 bytes
                         656,896 bytes free

A:\>_
```

WHAT'S HAPPENING? Now that you have written a program, you want to use it in a batch file.

Step 4   Use any text editor to create and save a file called KEYS.BAT.

> **ECHO PRESS F1 TO CLEAR THE SCREEN.**
> **ECHO PRESS F2 TO DISPLAY THE DIRECTORY**
> **ECHO PRESS ANY OTHER KEY TO EXIT.**
> **REPLY**
> **IF ERRORLEVEL 61 GOTO END**
> **IF ERRORLEVEL 60 GOTO F2**
> **IF ERRORLEVEL 59 GOTO F1**
> **GOTO END**
> **:F1**
> **CLS**
> **GOTO END**
> **:F2**
> **DIR**
> **:END**

WHAT'S HAPPENING? This is a simple batch file which checks the scan codes that you generate by pressing a key. Checking IF ERRORLEVEL codes in descending order is critical because the command is tested to determine if the error code is equal to or greater than the value specified. In this program, if you press a key that returns a value of 61 or above, you exit the program. If you press [F2], it returns a code of 60. If you press [F1], it returns a code of 59. If none of those conditions exist, then you exit the batch file.

Step 5   Key in the following: A:\>**KEYS** [Enter]

```
A:\>KEYS

A:\>ECHO  PRESS F1 TO CLEAR THE SCREEN.
 PRESS F1 TO CLEAR THE SCREEN.
```

```
A:\>ECHO  PRESS F2 TO DISPLAY THE DIRECTORY
 PRESS F2 TO DISPLAY THE DIRECTORY

A:\>ECHO  PRESS ANY OTHER KEY TO EXIT.
 PRESS ANY OTHER KEY TO EXIT.

A:\>REPLY
__
```

WHAT'S HAPPENING? You have executed the KEYS batch file. The program called REPLY.COM is waiting for you to press a key.

Step 6   Press **F1**

```
A:\>
A:\>_
```

WHAT'S HAPPENING? Pressing **F1** cleared the screen.

Step 7   Key in the following: A:\>**KEYS** **Enter**

Step 8   Press **F2**

```
BATCH         <DIR>           07-01-94    5:10p
OLDER         <DIR>           07-30-94   12:00p
STATE    CAP           260 05-14-94    5:11p
SORTED   CAP           260 07-31-94   11:00p
TEACHER  FIL           122 08-03-94   12:25p
ORIGPATH BAT            65 08-03-94    6:40p
DCOMP    BAT           328 08-03-94    8:09p
ONE      BAT           211 08-14-94    5:57p
REPEAT   BAT           102 08-14-94    6:49p
ALPHA    BAT           104 08-14-94    8:32p
UPDATE   BAT            80 08-15-94   10:54p
SIZE     BAT           258 08-17-94    9:16p
ERROR    BAT           281 08-17-94   10:15p
GREET    BAT           196 08-15-94   10:29p
RENDIR   BAT           247 08-16-94   10:33a
REPLY    SCR            78 08-21-94   11:38a
REPLY    COM            14 08-21-94   11:39a
KEYS     BAT           256 08-21-94   11:46a
        69 file(s)        47,773 bytes
                         656,384 bytes free

A:\>
A:\>_
```

WHAT'S HAPPENING? Pressing [F2] gave you a directory of your disk. As you can see, REPLY.COM gave the scan code of the key you pressed and followed the instruction in the batch file based on what key you pressed. Writing .COM programs can be difficult. Thus, the CHOICE command was introduced in DOS 6.0 .

12.20 The CHOICE Command

The CHOICE command is an external command. It will display an optional message and wait for the user to press a key. If you do not specify a choice, CHOICE waits for a Y or an N but you can choose your own values. You can make CHOICE case sensitive, but by default it is not case sensitive. When you use CHOICE, an ERRORLEVEL is set to indicate which key was pressed. You can even specify a time-out period ranging from 0 to 99 seconds. Time-out means that if the time elapses and the user has not pressed a key, CHOICE will end and set the ERRORLEVEL to the default key.

CHOICE does have drawbacks. Although CHOICE accepts most keys on the keyboard, it does not support the [Space Bar], any function keys or any key combinations such as [Ctrl] + J. There is no easy way to set CHOICE to accept any key or to accept a word or phrase. In addition, CHOICE only supports a single pressed key. Nonetheless, CHOICE is very useful. The syntax is:

```
CHOICE [/C[:]choices] [/N] [/S] [/T[:]c,nn] [text]

/C[:]choices    Specifies allowable keys. Default is YN
/N              Do not display choices and ? at end of prompt
                string.
/S              Treat choice keys as case sensitive.
/T[:]c,nn       Default choice to c after nn seconds
text            Prompt string to display

ERRORLEVEL is set to offset of key user presses in choices.
```

12.21 Activity: Using CHOICE

Note: The DATA disk should be in Drive A. The displayed prompt is A:\>.

Step 1   Key in the following: A:\>**COPY KEYS.BAT KEYTWO.BAT** [Enter]

```
A:\>COPY KEYS.BAT KEYTWO.BAT
        1 file(s) copied

A:\>_
```

WHAT'S HAPPENING? You have made a copy of the KEYS.BAT file. You are going to edit KEYTWO.BAT.

Step 2   Use any text editor to edit and save KEYTWO.BAT so it looks as follows:

```
ECHO  PRESS 1 TO CLEAR THE SCREEN.
ECHO  PRESS 2 TO DISPLAY THE DIRECTORY
ECHO  PRESS 3 TO EXIT.
CHOICE /C123
IF ERRORLEVEL 3 GOTO END
IF ERRORLEVEL 2 GOTO DISP
IF ERRORLEVEL 1 GOTO CLEAR
GOTO END
:CLEAR
CLS
GOTO END
:DISP
DIR
:END
```

WHAT'S HAPPENING? You have written a batch file using CHOICE. Notice that 1 and 2 and 3 do not need to be separated by any punctuation.

Step 3   Key in the following: A:\>**KEYTWO** **Enter**

```
A:\>KEYTWO

A:\>ECHO  PRESS 1 TO CLEAR THE SCREEN.
 PRESS 1 TO CLEAR THE SCREEN.

A:\>ECHO  PRESS 2 TO DISPLAY THE DIRECTORY
 PRESS 2 TO DISPLAY THE DIRECTORY

A:\>ECHO  PRESS 3 TO EXIT.
 PRESS 3 TO EXIT.

A:\>CHOICE /C123
[1,2,3]?_
```

WHAT'S HAPPENING? The choices are displayed as [1,2,3]?_. The CHOICE command formats the choices by placing the brackets around the choices as well as including the question mark. You simply press a number as directed.

Step 4   Press 1 **Enter**

```
A:\>GOTO  END

A:\>
A:\>_
```

WHAT'S HAPPENING? Your batch file ran successfully. There is another way to use CHOICE with an IF and IF NOT ERRORLEVEL test, which saves the trouble of using a GOTO statement. You can also customize what the choice will look like. You may also use letters of the alphabet in your CHOICE statement.

Step 5   Use any text editor to create and save a batch file called MYDIR.BAT. Key in the following:

> **CLS**
> **ECHO How do you want your directory displayed?**
> **ECHO.**

ECHO	**1.**	**Files only arranged by file name.**	**A to Z**
ECHO	**2.**	**Files only arranged by file name.**	**Z to A**
ECHO	**3.**	**Files only arranged by file extension.**	**A to Z**
ECHO	**e.**	**Files only arranged by file extension.**	**Z to A**

> **ECHO.**
> **CHOICE /N /C123e Please select a number or letter.**
> **if errorlevel 1 if not errorlevel 2 DIR /ON /A-D /P**
> **if errorlevel 2 if not errorlevel 3 DIR /O-N /A-D /P**
> **if errorlevel 3 if not errorlevel 4 DIR /OE /A-D /P**
> **if errorlevel 4 if not errorlevel 5 DIR /O-E /A-D /P**

WHAT'S HAPPENING? There are several interesting items in this batch file. First, observe the IF ERRORLEVEL statement. You must test if errorlevel statements in descending order but test if not errorlevel statements in ascending order. Because you specified a range (if 1 but not 2) you have limited your choice to one answer. Hence, you can write the batch file as above. In addition, you can place the command immediately after the ERRORLEVEL statement.

Now look at the CHOICE line. The /N suppresses the default format—brackets and a question mark. You supplied the format you wanted. The Please select a number or letter is your replacement for the default message and format. You also included the letter e to show you that you may use letters as well as numbers.

Step 6   Key in the following: A:\>**MYDIR** [Enter]

```
How do you want your directory displayed?

A:\>ECHO.


A:\>ECHO    1.      Files only arranged by file name.      A to Z
   1.      Files only arranged by file name.      A to Z

A:\>ECHO    2.      Files only arranged by file name.      Z to A
   2.      Files only arranged by file name.      Z to A

A:\>ECHO    3.      Files only arranged by file extension.  A to Z
   3.      Files only arranged by file extension.  A to Z
```

```
A:\>ECHO     e.        Files only arranged by file extension.  Z to A
    e.          Files only arranged by file extension.  Z to A

A:\>ECHO.


A:\>CHOICE /N /C123e  Please select a number or letter.
Please select a number or letter. _
```

WHAT'S HAPPENING? Your choices are ready.

Step 7   Press **E**

```
Volume in drive A is DATADISK
 Volume Serial Number is 2F26-1901
 Directory of A:\

JANUARY   TXT           144 08-29-94   10:54p
FEBRUARY  TXT            74 11-23-95   10:41a
APRIL     TXT            71 11-23-95   10:42a
HELLO     TXT            52 11-23-95   10:44a
BYE       TXT            44 11-23-95   10:45a
DRAMA     TV            198 11-23-94   10:19a
APR       TST            71 11-23-95   10:42a
TEST      TKR        16,516 06-21-94   10:37a
HOMEBUD   TKR         8,064 02-28-94    6:19p
FILE2     SWT            18 12-06-94   10:46a
FILE3     SWT            18 12-06-94   10:47a
REPLY     SCR            76 09-02-94    5:30p
JOINED    SAM           104 06-21-94   10:36a
THIS      ONE            42 11-23-94    7:13a
LAST      ONE            71 11-23-95   10:42a
JAN       OLD            32 11-23-94    7:07a
GOODBYE   NEW            32 11-23-94    7:07a
JANUARY   NEW            71 01-23-93   11:48a
APRIL     NEW            70 01-23-93   11:49a
Press any key to continue . . .
```

WHAT'S HAPPENING? Your files are arranged in reverse order by file extension.

Step 8   Press **Enter** until you have returned to the prompt.

12.22 The Environment

The environment is an area that DOS sets aside in memory. It is like a scratch pad where DOS keeps notes about important items that DOS needs to know. The environment is rather like using Post-it notes. Application programs can also read any items in the environment and thus can "post" their own messages there. What

DOS keeps in the environment is the location of the file COMMAND.COM. It also keeps track of the path, if one is set; the prompt, if it is changed; and append directions, if APPEND is used. You can also leave messages there *vis-à-vis* batch files or from the command line. The default size of the environment is not very large, 256 bytes. Furthermore, you can use the syntax: %variablename%, which will use the value of the environment variable.

DOS has an internal command called SET, which allows you to display what is currently in the environment, set environmental variables, or delete environmental variables. The SET syntax is:

```
SET [variable[string]]
```

where

variable	Specifies the variable you want to set or modify.
string	Specifies the string you want to associate with the specified variable.

12.23 Activity: Using SET and the Environment in Batch Files

Note: The DATA disk should be in Drive A. The displayed prompt is A:\>.

Step 1   Key in the following: A:\>**SET** [Enter]

```
A:\>SET
COMSPEC=C:\DOS\COMMAND.COM
PROMPT=$p$g
MOUSE=C:\PROG\MOUSE /Y
PATH=C:\WINDOWS;C:\DOS;C:\PROG\MOUSE;C:\PROG\BATCH;H:\UTILS\ZIP
TEMP=C:\TEMP
BLASTER=A220 I5 D1 H5 P330 T6
SOUND=C:\SB16
windir=C:\WINDOWS

A:\>
```

WHAT'S HAPPENING? Your environment will vary based on how your computer is set up. However, you will have a COMSPEC statement and will most likely have a path statement and a prompt statement, which DOS needs to know.

Step 2   Write and save the following batch file called TESTIT.BAT.

@ECHO OFF
ECHO %PATH%
ECHO.

WHAT'S HAPPENING? This batch file will display the value of path on your system.

Step 3   Key in the following: A:\>**TESTIT** [Enter]

```
A:\>TESTIT
C:\WINDOWS;C:\DOS;C:\PROG\MOUSE;C:\PROG\BATCH;H:\UTILS\ZIP

A:\>_
```

WHAT'S HAPPENING? The screen display showed the path on your system. Notice that it did not return the word path but the value of path. You can set an environmental value and then use it in a batch file.

Step 4   Key in the following: A:\>**SET TODAY=C:\DOS6BK*.99** [Enter]

Step 5   Key in the following: A:\>**SET** [Enter]

```
A:\>SET TODAY=C:\DOS6BK\*.99

A:\>SET
COMSPEC=C:\DOS\COMMAND.COM
PROMPT=$p$g
MOUSE=C:\PROG\MOUSE /Y
PATH=C:\WINDOWS;C:\DOS;C:\PROG\MOUSE;C:\PROG\BATCH;H:\UTILS\ZIP
TEMP=C:\TEMP
BLASTER=A220 I5 D1 H5 P330 T6
SOUND=C:\SB16
windir=C:\WINDOWS
TODAY=C:\DOS6BK\*.99

A:\>_
```

WHAT'S HAPPENING? You now have a value for TODAY, which you set in the environment as C:\DOS6BK*.99. Now you can use it in a batch file.

Step 6   Write and save the following batch file called SETTING.BAT. Key in the following:

> **DIR %today%**
> **ECHO %TODAY%**

Step 7   Key in the following: A:\>**SETTING** [Enter]

```
A:\>SETTING

A:\>DIR C:\DOS6BK\*.99
```

```
 Volume in drive C has no label
 Volume Serial Number is 1CD1-5E42
 Directory of C:\DOS6BK

APR          99              71 11-23-95  10:42a
FEB          99              74 11-23-95  10:41a
JAN          99              72 11-23-95  10:41a
MAR          99              70 11-23-95  10:42a
        4 file(s)                287 bytes
                      78,323,712 bytes free


A:\>ECHO C:\DOS6BK\*.99
C:\DOS6BK\*.99


A:\>
A:\>_
```

WHAT'S HAPPENING? Your batch file needed a value for `%today%`. The percent signs indicate that the value was in the environment. It substituted `C:\DOS6BK\*.99` for `%today%` and for `%TODAY%`. Case does not matter with environmental variables. You can use another value.

Step 8   Key in the following: `A:\>`**SET today=C:\DOS6BK*.TMP** [Enter]

Step 9   Key in the following: `A:\>`**SETTING** [Enter]

```
A:\>SETTING

A:\>DIR C:\DOS6BK\*.TMP

 Volume in drive C has no label
 Volume Serial Number is 1CD1-5E42
 Directory of C:\DOS6BK

APRIL      TMP            70 01-23-93  11:49a
GOODBYE    TMP            32 11-23-94   7:07a
BONJOUR    TMP            51 10-12-94   7:09a
JANUARY    TMP            71 01-23-93  11:48a
MARCH      TMP            69 01-23-93  11:49a
JAN        TMP            72 11-23-95  10:41a
FEB        TMP            74 11-23-95  10:41a
MAR        TMP            70 11-23-95  10:42a
APR        TMP            71 11-23-95  10:42a
        9 file(s)               580 bytes
                      78,323,712 bytes free

A:\>ECHO C:\DOS6BK\*.TMP
C:\DOS6BK\*.TMP
```

```
A:\>
A:\>_
```

WHAT'S HAPPENING? Since you changed the value of %today% from C:\DOS6BK*.99 to C:\DOS6BK*.TMP, the batch file knew to get only the value in the environment called %today%. To eliminate the value, you must set it to nothing.

Step 10   Key in the following: A:\>**SET TODAY=** Enter

Step 11   Key in the following: A:\>**SET** Enter

```
A:\>SET
COMSPEC=C:\DOS\COMMAND.COM
PROMPT=$p$g
MOUSE=C:\PROG\MOUSE /Y
PATH=C:\WINDOWS;C:\DOS;C:\PROG\MOUSE;C:\PROG\BATCH;H:\UTILS\ZIP
TEMP=C:\TEMP
BLASTER=A220 I5 D1 H5 P330 T6
SOUND=C:\SB16
windir=C:\WINDOWS

A:\>_
```

WHAT'S HAPPENING? You no longer have an environmental value called today. Now you can create a more useful batch file. You often want to add a directory to your path statement. This process often involves keying in the entire path you currently have and adding your new directory to the end. There is an easier way to do it using the environment.

Step 12   Write and save the following batch file called ADD.BAT. Key in the following:

> **IF %1none==none GOTO END**
> **PATH > OLDPATH.BAT**
> **:TOP**
> **PATH %PATH%;%1**
> **SHIFT**
> **IF NOT \%1\==\\ GOTO TOP**
> **:END**

Step 13   Key in the following: A:\>**PATH > ORIGPATH.BAT** Enter

Step 14   Key in the following: A:\>**ADD A:\PROG\GAMES** Enter

```
A:\>PATH > ORIGPATH.BAT

A:\>ADD A:\PROG\GAMES
```

```
A:\>IF  A:\PROG\GAMESnone==none GOTO END

A:\>PATH  > OLDPATH.BAT

A:\>PATH
C:\WINDOWS;C:\DOS;C:\PROG\MOUSE;C:\PROG\BATCH;H:\UTILS\ZIP;A:\PROG\GAMES

A:\>SHIFT

A:\>IF NOT \\==\\  GOTO  TOP

A:\>
A:\>
A:\>_
```

WHAT'S HAPPENING? To preserve your default path, you saved it to a file called
ORIGPATH.BAT. You then used your new batch file, ADD.BAT, and added the GAMES
directory to the path. You can add more than one directory.

Step 15   Key in the following:
        A:\>**ADD A:\PROG\UTILS BATCH CLASS** [Enter]

```
A:\>PATH > OLDPATH.BAT

A:\>PATH
C:\WINDOWS;C:\DOS;C:\PROG\MOUSE;C:\PROG\BATCH;H:\UTILS\ZIP;A:\PROG\GAME
S;A:\prog\utils

A:\>SHIFT

A:\>IF NOT \BATCH\==\\ GOTO TOP

A:\>PATH
C:\WINDOWS;C:\DOS;C:\PROG\MOUSE;C:\PROG\BATCH;H:\UTILS\ZIP;A:\PROG\GAMES;A:\PROG\UTILS;BATCH

A:\>SHIFT

A:\>IF NOT \CLASS\==\\ GOTO TOP

A:\>PATH
C:\WINDOWS;C:\DOS;C:\PROG\MOUSE;C:\PROG\BATCH;H:\UTILS\ZIP;A:\PROG\GAME
S;A:\PROG\UTILS;BATCH;CLASS

A:\>SHIFT

A:\>IF NOT \\==\\ GOTO TOP

A:\>
A:\>_
```

WHAT'S HAPPENING? You have quickly added new directories to your path.

Step 16 Key in the following: A:\>**PATH** [Enter]

```
A:\>PATH
PATH=C:\WINDOWS;C:\DOS;C:\PROG\MOUSE;C:\PROG\BATCH;H:\UTILS\ZIP;
A:\PROG\GAMES;A:\PROG\UTILS;BATCH;CLASS

A:\>_
```

WHAT'S HAPPENING? You keyed in PATH to confirm that you added subdirectories. To return to your original path, you created ORIGPATH.BAT.

Step 17 Key in the following: A:\>**ORIGPATH** [Enter]

```
A:\>ORIGPATH

A:\>PATH=C:\WINDOWS;C:\DOS;C:\PROG\BATCH;H:\UTILS\ZIP

A:\>
A:\>_
```

12.24 *The DIRCMD Environmental Variable*

The environment is an area that is set aside in memory. In addition to being able to place and use variables in the environment, you can preset the DIR command parameters and switches by including the SET command with the DIRCMD environmental variable. This means that, if you prefer the DIR command to display your files in alphabetic order by name every time, you can either place a SET DIRCMD in the AUTOEXEC.BAT file or simply write a batch file to set these values. SET alone will tell you what is in the environment. You can use the DIRCMD variable and ERRORLEVEL to write a batch file that will allow you to change the way DIR displays information for the entire work session.

12.25 *Activity: Using DIRCMD*

Note: The DATA disk should be in Drive A. The displayed prompt is A:\>.

Step 1 Key in the following: A:\>**COPY MYDIR.BAT MY.BAT** [Enter]

```
A:\>COPY MYDIR.BAT MY.BAT
        1 file(s) copied

A:\>_
```

WHAT'S HAPPENING? You have made a copy of the MYDIR.BAT file. You are going to edit MY.BAT.

Step 2   Use any text editor to edit and save MY.BAT so it looks as follows:

```
@ECHO OFF
CLS
ECHO How do you want your directory displayed?
ECHO.
ECHO   1.    Files only arranged by file name.      A to Z
ECHO   2.    Files only arranged by file name.      Z to A
ECHO   3.    Files only arranged by file extension. A to Z
ECHO   4.    Files only arranged by file extension. Z to A
ECHO   5.    Directory displays in default mode.
ECHO.
CHOICE /N /C12345  Please select a number.
if errorlevel 1 if not errorlevel 2 SET DIRCMD=/ON /A-D
if errorlevel 2 if not errorlevel 3 SET DIRCMD=/O-N /A-D
if errorlevel 3 if not errorlevel 4 SET DIRCMD=/OE /A-D
if errorlevel 4 if not errorlevel 5 SET DIRCMD=/O-E /A-D
if errorlevel 5 if not errorlevel 6 SET DIRCMD=
```

WHAT'S HAPPENING? You have created a batch file to set the DIRCMD environmental variable.

Step 3   Key in the following: A:\>**MY** **Enter**

```
How do you want your directory displayed?
    1.      Files only arranged by file name.      A to Z
    2.      Files only arranged by file name.      Z to A
    3.      Files only arranged by file extension. A to Z
    4.      Files only arranged by file extension. Z to A
    5.      Directory displays in default mode.

Please select a number.  _
```

WHAT'S HAPPENING? So far this looks no different from MYDIR.BAT.

Step 4   Key in the following: A:\>**4**

Step 5   Key in the following: A:\>**SET** **Enter**

```
A:\>SET
COMSPEC=C:\DOS\COMMAND.COM
PROMPT=$p$g
MOUSE=C:\PROG\MOUSE /Y
TEMP=C:\TEMP
BLASTER=A220 I5 D1 H5 P330 T6
SOUND=C:\SB16
windir=C:\WINDOWS
```

```
PATH=C:\WINDOWS;C:\DOS;C:\PROG\MOUSE;C:\PROG\BATCH;H:\UTILS\ZIP
DIRCMD=/O-E

A:\>_
```

WHAT'S HAPPENING? Now, whenever you key in DIR, it will automatically arrange the files by extension in reverse order. You can see that you have established the environmental variable for DIRCMD to equal the switch /O-E and /A-D.

Step 6   Key in the following: A:\>**DIR CLASS** [Enter]

```
A:\>DIR CLASS

 Volume in drive A is DATADISK
 Volume Serial Number is 2F26-1901
 Directory of A:\CLASS

FEB        PAR          74 11-23-95   10:41a
JAN        PAR          72 11-23-95   10:41a
MAR        PAR          70 11-23-95   10:42a
APR        PAR          71 11-23-95   10:42a
MAR        FIL          70 11-23-95   10:42a
JAN        FIL          71 11-23-95   10:42a
APR        BUD          18 12-06-94   10:46a
JAN        BUD          72 11-23-95   10:41a
MAR        BUD          70 11-23-95   10:42a
APR        ABC          71 11-23-95   10:42a
FEB        ABC          74 11-23-95   10:41a
JAN        ABC          72 11-23-95   10:41a
MAR        ABC          70 11-23-95   10:42a
        13 file(s)            875 bytes
                        651,776 bytes free

A:\>_
```

WHAT'S HAPPENING? The files are arranged in reverse alphabetical order by file extension. Until you change the values, every time you issue the DIR command it will display file names in reverse alphabetical order by file extension.

Step 7   Key in the following: A:\>**MY** [Enter]

Step 8   Press 5

Step 9   Key in the following: A:\>**SET** [Enter]

```
A:\>SET
COMSPEC=C:\DOS\COMMAND.COM
```

```
PROMPT=$p$g
MOUSE=C:\PROG\MOUSE /Y
TEMP=C:\TEMP
BLASTER=A220 I5 D1 H5 P330 T6
SOUND=C:\SB16
windir=C:\WINDOWS
PATH=C:\WINDOWS;C:\DOS;C:\PROG\MOUSE;C:\PROG\BATCH;H:\UTILS\ZIP

A:\>_
```

WHAT'S HAPPENING? You returned the default DIRCMD environmental variable.

12.26 The FOR..IN..DO Command

The FOR..IN..DO command can be issued at the command line or placed in a batch file. This command allows repetitive processing. FOR allows you to use a single command to issue several commands at once. The command can DO something FOR every value IN a specified set. The syntax at the command line is:

```
FOR %variable IN (set) DO command [command-parameter]
```

In a batch file, the syntax is:

```
FOR %%variable IN (set) DO command [command-parameter]
```

The batch file variable is an arbitrary single letter. The double percent sign with a letter (`%%a`) distinguishes the batch file variable from the replaceable parameter (`%1`). The difference between a variable and a parameter is not complicated. The FOR statement tells DOS to get a value from the set you have chosen. After DOS executes the command that appears after DO, the FOR command looks for the next value in the set. If it finds another value, `%%a` will represent something new, and the command will be executed with the new value. If there are no more values in the set, the FOR command stops processing.

If you consider the GOTO label as a vertical loop, you can consider the FOR..IN..DO as a horizontal loop. You do not need to use the letter a. You may use any letter—a, c, x, etc. The parameter value, on the other hand, is set before the batch file begins processing. Remember, DOS gets the value from the position in the command line. The set is *always* enclosed in parentheses. The values in the set, either data or file names, will be used to DO some command. The items in the set must be separated by spaces or commas. You may also use wildcards in a set.

12.27 Activity: Using the FOR..IN..DO Command

Note: The DATA disk should be in Drive A. The displayed prompt is A:\>.

Step 1   Key in the following: A:\>**FOR %a IN (*.99) DO TYPE %a** [Enter]

```
A:\>FOR %a IN (*.99) DO TYPE %a

A:\>TYPE APR.99
This is my April file.
It is my fourth dummy file.
This is file 4.

A:\>TYPE JAN.99
This is my January file.
It is my first dummy file.
This is file 1.

A:\>_
```

WHAT'S HAPPENING? The FOR..IN..DO processed every item in the set as indicated below. Besides using wildcards, you can also be specific.

Command	Need Value for Parameter from Set	Output
TYPE %a	FOR IN DO looks for first file that meets `*.99` specification.	`TYPE APR.99`
TYPE %a	FOR IN DO looks for next file that meets `*.99` specification.	`TYPE JAN.99`
TYPE %a	There are no more files that meet the `*.99` specification.	`A:\>`

Step 2   Key in the following:
A:\>**FOR %x IN (APR.BUD NOFILE.EXT D.BAT) DO TYPE %x** `Enter`

Step 3   Key in the following:
A:\>**FOR %x IN (APR.BUD,NOFILE.EXT,D.BAT) DO TYPE %x** `Enter`

```
A:\>FOR %x IN (APR.BUD NOFILE.EXT D.BAT) DO TYPE %x

A:\>TYPE APR.BUD
This is file 2.

A:\>TYPE NOFILE.EXT
File not found - NOFILE.EXT

A:\>TYPE D.BAT
DIR /AD

A:\>FOR %x IN (APR.BUD,NOFILE.EXT,D.BAT) DO TYPE %x

A:\>TYPE APR.BUD
This is file 2.
```

```
A:\>TYPE NOFILE.EXT
File not found - NOFILE.EXT

A:\>TYPE D.BAT
DIR /AD

A:\>_
```

WHAT'S HAPPENING? There are some important things to notice about these command lines. First, either a space or a comma between items in a set work the same way. Second, the variable letter you choose is not important. In this case, x was chosen rather than a. This command line is case sensitive. If you had keyed in FOR %x IN (APR.BUD NOFILE.EXT D.BAT) DO TYPE %X, the difference between x and X would have made the command line invalid. Even when there was an invalid file (NOFILE.EXT), the command line continued processing the other file names in the command. You did not need to worry about testing for null values. This command works the same when placed in a batch file, only you must use a double %%.

Step 4   Create and save the following batch file called DO.BAT and key in the following:

FOR %%v IN (Carolyn Frank Steven Mary) DO ECHO %%v

Step 5   Key in the following: A:\>**DO** [Enter]

```
A:\>FOR %v IN (Carolyn Frank Steven Mary) DO ECHO %v

A:\>ECHO Carolyn
Carolyn

A:\>ECHO Frank
Frank

A:\>ECHO Steven
Steven

A:\>ECHO Mary
Mary


A:\>
A:\>_
```

WHAT'S HAPPENING? As you can see, the ECHO command was carried out for each item in the set. It substituted each value (Carolyn Frank Steven Mary) for the replaceable parameter in the ECHO command. In this example, spaces were used to separate the values, but you could have also used commas. The advantage to using this command is that you did not have to write it as a more complicated batch file with a command on each line, as in:

```
ECHO Carolyn
ECHO Frank
ECHO Steven
ECHO Mary
```

Another advantage of the FOR..IN..DO method is you can also set values in the environment and then call them in a batch file.

Step 6   Write and save a batch file called PASS.BAT and key in the following:

> **FOR %%a IN (%USERS%) DO IF "%1"=="%%a" GOTO OKAY**
> **:NO**
> **ECHO You, %1, are NOT allowed in the system.**
> **GOTO END**
> **:OKAY**
> **ECHO Welcome %1 to my world of computers.**
> **:END**

WHAT'S HAPPENING? You have combined several features in this FOR..IN..DO statement. You have used an environmental variable in the set (%USERS%). The percent signs surrounding the value tells the FOR command to use the environmental variable called USERS. You have also used an IF statement. If what the user keys in is in the environment, then it is a true statement and the batch file will go to the OKAY label. If what the user keys in is false and not equal to the environmental variable, then the batch file falls through to the next line. First, you need to set the environmental variable.

Step 7   Key in the following: A:\>**SET USERS=Carolyn, Frank** Enter

Step 8   Key in the following: A:\>**PASS Frank** Enter

```
A:\>SET USERS=Carolyn, Frank

A:\>PASS Frank

A:\>FOR %a IN (Carolyn, Frank) DO IF "Frank"=="%a" GOTO OKAY

A:\>IF "Frank"=="Carolyn" GOTO OKAY

A:\>IF "Frank"=="Frank" GOTO OKAY


A:\>ECHO Welcome Frank to my world of computers.
Welcome Frank to my world of computers.
```

```
A:\>
A:\>_
```

WHAT'S HAPPENING? You set the environmental values for USERS. You then executed the PASS.BAT batch file. It worked as directed because the statement was true. What if it were false?

Step 9   Key in the following: A:\>**PASS Denzel** [Enter]

```
A:\>PASS Denzel

A:\>FOR %a IN (Carolyn, Frank) DO IF "Denzel"=="%a" GOTO OKAY

A:\>IF "Denzel"=="Carolyn" GOTO OKAY

A:\>IF "Denzel"=="Frank" GOTO OKAY


A:\>ECHO You, Denzel, are NOT allowed in the system.
You, Denzel, are NOT allowed in the system.

A:\>GOTO END

A:\>
A:\>_
```

WHAT'S HAPPENING? The statement was false and the batch file behaved accordingly. FOR..IN..DO can also be used with replaceable parameters, file names, and wildcards. You are going to take another look at UPDATE.BAT.

Step 10   Use any text editor and edit and save the UPDATE.BAT file so it looks as follows:

> **:DOIT**
> **IF "%1"=="" GOTO END**
> **FOR %%v IN (%1) DO COPY %%v /b + > NUL**
> **SHIFT**
> **PAUSE**
> **GOTO DOIT**
> **:END**

WHAT'S HAPPENING? You now can process any number of parameters that appear in the command line. There can be a problem with this batch file. As written, this batch file will copy the newly updated files to the current default directory. Thus, it is a good idea, in general, to place all your batch files in a subdirectory called BATCH and set your path to include the BATCH directory.

Step 11   Key in the following: A:\>**ADD A:\BATCH** [Enter]

Step 12   Key in the following: A:\>**MOVE *.BAT BATCH** [Enter]

Step 13   Key in the following: A:\>**MOVE REPLY*.* BATCH** [Enter]

```
a:\dcomp.bat => a:\batch\dcomp.bat [ok]
a:\one.bat => a:\batch\one.bat [ok]
a:\repeat.bat => a:\batch\repeat.bat [ok]
a:\alpha.bat => a:\batch\alpha.bat [ok]
a:\update.bat => a:\batch\update.bat [ok]
a:\size.bat => a:\batch\size.bat [ok]
a:\error.bat => a:\batch\error.bat [ok]
a:\greet.bat => a:\batch\greet.bat [ok]
a:\rendir.bat => a:\batch\rendir.bat [ok]
a:\keys.bat => a:\batch\keys.bat [ok]
a:\keytwo.bat => a:\batch\keytwo.bat [ok]
a:\mydir.bat => a:\batch\mydir.bat [ok]
a:\testit.bat => a:\batch\testit.bat [ok]
a:\setting.bat => a:\batch\setting.bat [ok]
a:\add.bat => a:\batch\add.bat [ok]
a:\oldpath.bat => a:\batch\oldpath.bat [ok]
a:\my.bat => a:\batch\my.bat [ok]
a:\do.bat => a:\batch\do.bat [ok]
a:\pass.bat => a:\batch\pass.bat [ok]

A:\>MOVE REPLY*.* BATCH
a:\reply.scr => a:\batch\reply.scr [ok]
a:\reply.com => a:\batch\reply.com [ok]

A:\>_
```

WHAT'S HAPPENING? You have moved all your batch files to the BATCH subdirectory including the REPLY files, because batch files use these programs. This grouping allowed you to clean up the root directory of the DATA disk. To ensure that you can use your batch files, you first added the BATCH subdirectory to the path statement.

Step 14   Key in the following: A:\>**DIR *.SWT** [Enter]

Step 15   Key in the following: A:\>**DIR *.CAP** [Enter]

```
A:\>DIR *.SWT

 Volume in drive A is DATADISK
 Volume Serial Number is 2F26-1901
 Directory of A:\

FILE2       SWT              18 12-06-94  10:46a
FILE3       SWT              18 12-06-94  10:47a
```

```
            2 file(s)              36 bytes
                              649,728 bytes free

A:\>DIR *.CAP

 Volume in drive A is DATADISK
 Volume Serial Number is 2F26-1901
 Directory of A:\

STATE     CAP          260 05-14-94    5:11p
SORTED    CAP          260 07-31-94   11:00p
         2 file(s)              520 bytes
                              649,728 bytes free

A:\>_
```

WHAT'S HAPPENING? You can see the dates on these files. Now you are going to update them to the current date.

Step 16   Key in the following: A:\>**UPDATE** *.SWT *.CAP [Enter]

```
A:\>UPDATE *.SWT *.CAP

A:\>IF "*.SWT"=="" GOTO END

A:\>FOR %v IN (*.SWT) DO COPY %v1 /b + > NUL

A:\>COPY FILE2.SWT1 /b +

A:\>COPY FILE3.SWT1 /b +


A:\>SHIFT

A:\>PAUSE
Press any key to continue . . .
```

WHAT'S HAPPENING? You can see how FOR processed each item in the set, which it got from the command line (%1 was *.SWT). Each file that had an .SWT file extension was updated. Now the batch file is going to SHIFT and process the new item in the SET (*.CAP).

Step 17   Keep pressing [Enter] until you are back at the command prompt.

Step 18   Key in the following: A:\>**DIR** *.SWT [Enter]

Step 19   Key in the following: A:\>**DIR** *.CAP [Enter]

```
A:\>DIR *.SWT

 Volume in drive A is DATADISK
 Volume Serial Number is 2F26-1901
 Directory of A:\

FILE2     SWT            18 08-22-94  11:51p
FILE3     SWT            18 08-22-94  11:51p
          2 file(s)             36 bytes
                          649,728 bytes free

A:\>DIR *.CAP

 Volume in drive A is DATADISK
 Volume Serial Number is 2F26-1901
 Directory of A:\

STATE     CAP           260 08-22-94  11:54p
SORTED    CAP           260 08-22-94  11:54p
          2 file(s)            520 bytes
                          649,728 bytes free

A:\>_
```

WHAT'S HAPPENING? Your dates will be different, but you have successfully changed the dates of the files. You have successfully used the FOR.. IN..DO command.

Step 20   Key in the following: A:\>**ORIGPATH** [Enter]

```
A:\>ORIGPATH

A:\>PATH=C:\WINDOWS;C:\DOS;C:\PROG\MOUSE;C:\PROG\BATCH;H:\UTILS\ZIP

A:\>
A:\>_
```

WHAT'S HAPPENING? You have returned to your original path.

12.28 The CALL Command

You sometimes need to be able to execute one batch file from within another. If the second batch file is the last line in the original batch file, there is no problem. The second batch file is "invoked" or called from the first batch file. But calling a second batch file and *returning* to the first batch file, is not so simple. When DOS finishes executing a batch file, it returns control to the system level and never returns to the original batch file. To solve this problem, the CALL command was introduced in

DOS 3.3. It allows you to call (execute) another batch file and then return control to the next line in the first batch file. If you have a really early version of DOS, you do not have the CALL command and instead must use COMMAND /C *batch.bat*.

12.29 Activity: Using CALL

Note: The DATA disk should be in Drive A. The displayed prompt is A:\>.

Step 1   Key in the following: A:\>**CD BATCH** [Enter]

```
A:\>CD BATCH

A:\BATCH>_
```

WHAT'S HAPPENING? Your default directory is now the BATCH subdirectory. One of the things that you can create is a "noise" to get a user's attention. In the same way you used the [Ctrl] + L to eject a page, you can use the [Ctrl] + G to make a noise. Although the noise you create sounds like a "beep," it is referred to as a bell because, in the ASCII character set, the [Ctrl] + G is labeled BEL. By using [Ctrl]+ G with ECHO you "ring a bell." Remember that when you see [Ctrl] + G, it means to press the Control key and the letter G, and, when you see [F6], it means press the [F6] key.

Step 2   Key in the following: A:\BATCH> **COPY CON BELL.BAT** [Enter]
                              ECHO [Ctrl] + **G** [Enter]
                              ECHO [Ctrl] + **G** [Enter]
                              [F6] [Enter]

```
A:\BATCH>COPY CON BELL.BAT
ECHO ^G
ECHO ^G
^Z
        1 file(s) copied

A:\BATCH>_
```

WHAT'S HAPPENING? Now that you have written BELL.BAT, you can execute it.

Step 3   Key in the following: A:\BATCH>**BELL** [Enter]

```
A:\BATCH>BELL

A:\BATCH>ECHO


A:\BATCH>ECHO
```

```
A:\BATCH>
A:\BATCH>_
```

WHAT'S HAPPENING? You should have heard the bell "beeping" as you ran the program.

Step 4   Use any text editor to create and save a batch file called BELLING.BAT. Key in the following:

COPY *.99 *.XYZ
DEL *.XYZ
BELL [Enter]

WHAT'S HAPPENING? You wrote a very simple batch file. You are going to copy the .99 files to the BATCH subdirectory, delete them, and then ring a bell.

Step 5   Key in the following: A:\BATCH>**BELLING** [Enter]

```
A:\BATCH>BELLING

A:\BATCH>COPY \*.99 *.XYZ
A:\APR.99
A:\JAN.99
        2 file(s) copied

A:\BATCH>DEL *.XYZ

A:\BATCH>BELL

A:\BATCH>ECHO


A:\BATCH>ECHO


A:\BATCH>
A:\BATCH>_
```

WHAT'S HAPPENING? You called one batch file from another. You ran BELLING. Its last line was BELL. BELL was called and it executed as expected. However, perhaps you would like the bell to sound before the files are deleted.

Step 6   Edit and save BELLING.BAT to look as follows:

COPY *.99 *.XYZ
BELL
REM You are about to delete the *.XYZ files. Are you sure?
PAUSE
DEL *.XYZ

WHAT'S HAPPENING? You moved BELL before deleting the files, added some remarks, and entered a PAUSE.

Step 7   Key in the following: A:\BATCH>**BELLING** [Enter]

```
A:\BATCH>BELLING

A:\BATCH>COPY \*.99 *.XYZ
A:\APR.99
A:\JAN.99
        2 file(s) copied

A:\BATCH>BELL

A:\BATCH>ECHO


A:\BATCH>ECHO


A:\BATCH>
A:\BATCH>_
```

WHAT'S HAPPENING? When the BELLING batch file reached the line BELL, it called and executed BELL. It turned control over to BELL.BAT. Once BELL.BAT had control, it never returned to BELLING. Since it never returned to BELLING.BAT, your *.XYZ files were not deleted, nor did you see a message.

Step 8   Key in the following: A:\>**DIR** *.XYZ [Enter]

```
A:\BATCH>DIR *.XYZ

 Volume in drive A is DATADISK
 Volume Serial Number is 2F26-1901
 Directory of A:\BATCH

APR      XYZ          71 08-14-94   9:18p
JAN      XYZ          72 11-23-95  10:41a
        2 file(s)            143 bytes
                         647,680 bytes free

A:\BATCH>_
```

WHAT'S HAPPENING? Indeed, the files are there. This is why you need the CALL command. CALL will process the batch file BELL, but it will then return control to BELLING so that the other commands in BELLING can be executed.

Step 9   Edit and save BELLING.BAT to look as follows:

```
COPY \*.99 *.XYZ
CALL  BELL
REM You are about to delete the *.XYZ files. Are you sure?
PAUSE
DEL *.XYZ
```

Step 10   Key in the following: A:\BATCH>**BELLING** [Enter]

```
A:\BATCH>BELLING

A:\BATCH>COPY \*.99 *.XYZ
A:\APR.99
A:\JAN.99
        2 file(s) copied

A:\BATCH>CALL BELL

A:\BATCH>ECHO


A:\BATCH>ECHO


A:\BATCH>
A:\BATCH>REM You are about to delete the *.XYZ files. Are you sure?

A:\BATCH>PAUSE
Press any key to continue . . .
```

WHAT'S HAPPENING? Since you added CALL in front of BELL, the bell sounded. Once BELL was finished executing, it passed control back to BELLING so that the next commands could be executed.

Step 11   Press [Enter]

Step 12   Key in the following: A:\BATCH>**DIR *.XYZ** [Enter]

```
A:\BATCH>DIR *.XYZ

 Volume in drive A is DATADISK
 Volume Serial Number is 2F26-1901
 Directory of A:\BATCH

 File not found

A:\BATCH>_
```

WHAT'S HAPPENING? The CALL command worked as promised. Your .XYZ files are gone. A more practical example of using CALL can be seen in the next group of batch files you are going to write. You may find, as you move among directories, that you want to go "home" again. In other words, you want to return to the directory where you were previously. You can create a series of batch files that will remember the directory you were in and return you to it. Note: in the next file, it is important to press the [F6] immediately after the command. Do not press [Enter], then [F6].

Step 13   Key in the following: A:\BATCH>**COPY CON HOME.DAT** [Enter]

                                    SET HOME=<F6> [Enter]

Step 14   Use any editor to create and save a batch file called HOMETO.BAT. Key in the following:

        COPY A:\BATCH\HOME.DAT A:\BATCH\HOMESAVE.BAT
        CD >> A:\BATCH\HOMESAVE.BAT
        CALL HOMESAVE.BAT
        DEL A:\BATCH\HOMESAVE.BAT

WHAT'S HAPPENING? The HOME.DAT data file you created will create an environmental variable called HOME. The batch file you just created called HOMETO.BAT will be used to set the environmental variable to wherever you want HOME to be.

Line 1	HOME.DAT **contains** SET HOME=	HOMESAVE.BAT **now has contents of** SETHOME=
Line 2	CD >> HOMESAVE.BAT **takes whatever directory you are in and appends it to** HOMESAVE.BAT	If your current directory is GAMES, HOMESAVE.BAT **now has contents of** SET HOME=A:\GAMES
Line 3	CALL HOMESAVE.BAT HOMESAVE.BAT **now executes and sets the environmental of** HOME **to** A:\GAMES	
Line 4	**You delete** HOMESAVE.BAT **because, now that you have set the environmental variable, you no longer need the batch file** HOMESAVE.BAT	

Step 15   Use any editor to create and save a batch file called HOME.BAT. Key in the following: **CD %HOME%** [Enter]

WHAT'S HAPPENING? The batch file HOME.BAT will change your directory to whatever variable in the environment is called HOME.

Step 16 Key in the following: A:\BATCH>**SET** ⏎Enter⏎

```
A:\BATCH>SET
COMSPEC=C:\DOS\COMMAND.COM
PROMPT=$p$g
MOUSE=C:\PROG\MOUSE /Y
TEMP=C:\TEMP
BLASTER=A220 I5 D1 H5 P330 T6
SOUND=C:\SB16
windir=C:\WINDOWS
PATH=C:\WINDOWS;C:\DOS;C:\PROG\MOUSE;C:\PROG\BATCH;H:\UTILS\ZIP

A:\BATCH>_
```

WHAT'S HAPPENING? There is no environmental variable called HOME. In order for this procedure to work correctly, you must include A:\BATCH in your path statement.

Step 17 Key in the following: A:\BATCH>**ADD A:\BATCH** ⏎Enter⏎

```
A:\BATCH>ADD A:\BATCH

A:\BATCH>IF   A:\BATCHnone==none GOTO END

A:\BATCH>PATH   > OLDPATH.BAT

A:\BATCH>PATH
C:\WINDOWS;C:\DOS;C:\PROG\MOUSE;C:\PROG\BATCH;H:\UTILS\ZIP;A:\BAT
CH

A:\BATCH>SHIFT

A:\BATCH>IF NOT \\==\\   GOTO  TOP

A:\BATCH>
A:\BATCH>
A:\BATCH>_
```

WHAT'S HAPPENING? You are now ready to test "going home."

Step 18 Key in the following: A:\BATCH>**CD ** ⏎Enter⏎

Step 19 Key in the following: A:\>**CD WORK\ADS** ⏎Enter⏎

Step 20 Key in the following: A:\WORK\ADS>**HOMETO** ⏎Enter⏎

```
A:\BATCH>CD \

A:\>CD WORK\ADS

A:\WORK\ADS>HOMETO

A:\WORK\ADS>COPY A:\BATCH\HOME.DAT A:\BATCH\HOMESAVE.BAT
        1 file(s) copied

A:\WORK\ADS>CD >> A:\BATCH\HOMESAVE.BAT

A:\WORK\ADS>CALL HOMESAVE.BAT

A:\WORK\ADS>SET HOME=A:\WORK\ADS

A:\WORK\ADS>
A:\WORK\ADS>DEL A:\BATCH\HOMESAVE.BAT

A:\WORK\ADS>
A:\WORK\ADS>_
```

WHAT'S HAPPENING? You want the subdirectory \WORK\ADS to be your home
directory so you keyed in HOMETO to set up your home directory.

Step 21   Key in the following: A:\WORK\ADS>**SET** [Enter]

```
A:\WORK\ADS>SET
COMSPEC=C:\DOS\COMMAND.COM
PROMPT=$p$g
MOUSE=C:\PROG\MOUSE /Y
TEMP=C:\TEMP
BLASTER=A220 I5 D1 H5 P330 T6
SOUND=C:\SB16
windir=C:\WINDOWS
PATH=C:\WINDOWS;C:\DOS;C:\PROG\MOUSE;C:\PROG\BATCH;H:\UTILS\ZIP;A:\BATCH
HOME=A:\WORK\ADS

A:\WORK\ADS>_
```

WHAT'S HAPPENING? You now have an environmental variable named HOME
whose value is A:\WORK\ADS. You will go to another directory and then return to
A:\WORK\ADS by using the HOME command you just wrote.

Step 22   Key in the following: A:\WORK\ADS>**CD** **\MEDIA\TV** [Enter]

```
A:\WORK\ADS>CD \MEDIA\TV

A:\MEDIA\TV>_
```

WHAT'S HAPPENING? Your default directory is now A:\MEDIA\TV. You want to return "home," which is A:\WORK\ADS.

Step 23 Key in the following: A:\MEDIA\TV>**HOME** [Enter]

```
A:\MEDIA\TV>HOME

A:\MEDIA\TV>CD A:\WORK\ADS

A:\WORK\ADS>
A:\WORK\ADS>_
```

WHAT'S HAPPENING? You "went home" again. At any time during the work session, you can change the value of HOME by running HOMETO while in the directory you want "home" to be) and return to it at any time by simply keying in HOME.

Step 24 Key in the following: A:\WORK\ADS>**CD ** [Enter]

```
A:\WORK\ADS>CD \

A:\>_
```

WHAT'S HAPPENING? You have returned to root directory of the DATA disk.

Step 25 Key in the following: A:\>**ORIGPATH** [Enter]

```
A:\>ORIGPATH

A:\>PATH=C:\WINDOWS;C:\DOS;C:\PROG\MOUSE;C:\PROG\BATCH;H:\UTILS\ZIP

A:\>
A:\>
```

WHAT'S HAPPENING? You have returned the default path.

Chapter Summary

1. You may substitute a double colon (::) for the REM statement.
2. You can suppress the display of any messages by using the command CTTY CON. You return control to the console by keying in CTTY NUL. These commands are *always* used together.
3. To place a blank line in a batch file, use the ECHO command followed immediately by a period (ECHO.).
4. The GOTO command used in conjunction with a label creates a loop. The GOTO will process the command following the label.
5. The label in a batch file is not a command but identifies a location in the batch file.

6. The SHIFT command shifts over command line parameters to the left one position at a time.

7. The SHIFT command is typically used in conjunction with GOTO and a label.

8. The IF command will test for some logical condition. If the condition is true, the command is processed. If the condition is false, the batch file will fall through to the next line of the batch file.

9. The IF command can test whether or not two character strings are identical.

10. The IF command can test whether or not a file exists.

11. The IF command checks ERRORLEVEL.

12. You may also use IF with NOT. The IF NOT command will test for a NOT condition. If a condition is not true, then the command will process. If the command is true, then the batch file will fall through to the next line in the batch file.

13. You can test for a null value by using quotation marks, by using a word, or by using backslashes.

14. To use IF EXIST and to test for the existence a subdirectory, you may use IF %1\NUL.

15. Many programs set an exit code when finished executing. The IF ERRORLEVEL in a batch file will test if an exit code is equal to or greater than the one in the test.

16. When you use IF ERRORLEVEL in a batch file, the codes must be listed in descending order.

17. When you use IF NOT ERRORLEVEL in a batch file, the codes must be listed in ascending order.

18. You may write programs with DEBUG to set exit codes.

19. You can write programs directly in DEBUG, or you may write a script file that supplies input for DEBUG to create a program.

20. The CHOICE command is an external command that can be used to set exit codes for input from the keyboard.

21. Each key, when pressed, issues a scan code that can be checked by the CHOICE command or by a program written in DEBUG.

22. The environment is an area in memory where DOS leaves messages to itself, including the path and the prompt values.

23. You can create environmental variables that can be used in batch files. When using the variable in a batch file, the syntax is `%variable%`.

24. The SET command lets you view what is currently in the environment.

25. The DIRCMD command can be used to preset the DIR command parameters and switches.

26. The FOR..IN..DO command allows repetitive processing. The command will execute some command for every value in a specified set.

27. When you use FOR..IN..DO at the command line, the syntax is `FOR %variable IN (set) DO command [command-parameter]`.

28. The CALL command allows you to call one batch file from another and when the second batch file is finished executing, it returns control to the first batch file.

Key Terms

DEBUG   Exit code   Null value
EOF   Conditional processing   Scan code
End of file marker   Loop   Script file

Discussion Questions

1. What is the function of the REM, ECHO, and PAUSE commands?
2. What happens in a batch file if ECHO is set to OFF?
3. What happens in a batch file if you precede the ECHO OFF switch with the @?
4. What is the purpose and function of the CTTY command?
5. What is a NUL device? Why would you use a NUL device?
6. Why should you only use the CTTY NUL command in a batch file and not at the command line?
7. Why should you use CTTY NUL in tandem with CTTY CON?
8. How can you place a "blank" line in a batch file?
9. How can you create a loop in a batch file? How can you stop a loop from processing in a batch file?
10. What is the purpose and function of the GOTO command?
11. What is a label in a batch file?
12. What is the purpose and function of the SHIFT command?
13. Why is it useful to shift parameters?
14. How can you determine whether or not a file exists?
15. What is the purpose and function of the IF command?
16. Give the syntax of the IF command and explain each part of the syntax.
17. What does it mean to test for a null value?
18. How can you test for a null value? Why would you test for a null value?
19. What is the purpose and function of the IF EXIST/IF NOT EXIST command?
20. Explain the purpose and function of the IF ERRORLEVEL command.
21. What is a script file? How can you create one?
22. What is a scan code?
23. What is the purpose and function of the CHOICE command?
24. Give the syntax of the CHOICE command and explain each part of the syntax.
25. What are some of the drawbacks of using CHOICE?
26. Give the syntax of the SET command and explain each part of the syntax.
27. Explain the purpose and function of the DIRCMD environmental variable.
28 What is the purpose and function of the FOR..IN..DO command?
29. Give the syntax of the FOR..IN..DO command and explain each part of the syntax.
30. Explain the purpose and function of the CALL command.

Chapter *13*

Configuring the System

After completing this chapter you will be able to:

1. Explain the purpose and importance of a `CONFIG.SYS` file.
2. List and explain the commands that can only be used in `CONFIG.SYS`.
3. List the commands that can be used in `CONFIG.SYS` and at the command line.
4. Explain the purpose of the files and buffers in `CONFIG.SYS`.
5. List and explain the steps that will ensure a safe recovery if something goes wrong when editing the `CONFIG.SYS` or `AUTOEXEC.BAT`.
6. Explain two ways to create a bootable floppy disk.
7. Explain how to turn NUMLOCK off.
8. Explain the purpose and function of device drivers.
9. Explain the purpose and function of a virtual disk.
10. Compare and contrast conventional, extended, and expanded memory.
11. Explain the function of upper and high memory areas.
12. Explain the purpose and function of the MEM command.
13. Explain the purpose and function of `HIMEM.SYS`.
14. Explain the purpose of using LASTDRIVE in `CONFIG.SYS`.
15. Explain the need for conserving conventional memory.
16. Explain how SHELL can be used to alter the computer environment.
17. Explain when the SWITCHES command is needed in `CONFIG.SYS`.

Student Outcomes

1. Prepare a bootable DOS System Disk.
2. Write a CONFIG.SYS file using files and buffers.
3. Turn NUMLOCK off using CONFIG.SYS.
4. Write a CONFIG.SYS file using RAMDRIVE.SYS.
5. Use the MEM command to report the amount of used and unused memory.
6. Write a CONFIG.SYS file using HIMEM.SYS.
7. Write a CONFIG.SYS file using LASTDRIVE.
8. Be able to install more than one virtual drive.
9. Load DOS High.
10. Use SHELL so DOS can locate COMMAND.COM.
11. Use SHELL to expand the environment.
12. Use SET to view the environment.

Chapter Overview

In previous chapters you used DOS commands to manage disks and files. Each command was used in a specific manner and produced a specific result. A great deal of flexibility has been built into DOS, making it possible to maximize the performance of hardware by using configuration commands. You can also improve the performance and flexibility of your computer system by altering the internal environment in which DOS operates. It is within the system configuration file (CONFIG.SYS) that these changes are made, and, thereby, you customize the operating system environment to meet your specific needs.

In this chapter you will learn to manage and manipulate your CONFIG.SYS file to reconfigure your computer system. You will learn the commands that you may place in the CONFIG.SYS file to configure your system to meet your needs.

13.1 Customizing DOS

So far, you have learned to use DOS commands in specific ways. You key in commands and get results based on what the command does. These commands, including the batch file subcommands, tell DOS what to do. In addition, you are able to customize DOS for your computer configuration. Customizing allows you to install such devices as a mouse, an external drive, or other hardware you may purchase. Furthermore, you can "tweak the system," or use configuration commands to maximize the use of your hardware. You may need to customize your configuration because some application programs require hardware settings that are not standard DOS default settings. The configuration process is similar to setting up your office environment so that you can work efficiently. You can adjust DOS internally by setting up a CONFIG.SYS file, which will alter the environment where DOS works.

13.2 The CONFIG.SYS File

When you first power-on the computer, the microprocessor goes to the ROM-BIOS chip to do a self-test of memory and hardware. Then it checks for a disk in Drive A. If it finds a disk in Drive A, BIOS reads the first sector on the disk. If it is a DOS System Disk (bootable floppy), the system files are loaded. If there is no disk in Drive A, BIOS looks in Drive C. When it finds the system files, it loads them. After loading the system files, it looks for a file called CONFIG.SYS in the root directory of the booting disk. If it finds it, it follows the instructions in the CONFIG.SYS file. If it does not find this file, it initializes your computer based on the DOS default values. It loads COMMAND.COM and then looks for AUTOEXEC.BAT. If there is no AUTOEXEC.BAT file, DOS displays the A:\> or C:\> system prompt. In earlier versions of DOS, the date and time prompts were needed. Figure 13.1 illustrates this process.

	CPU	Power on, passes control to BIOS.
	BIOS	Does self-diagnostic routine. Looks to Drive A.
	A:	Tries to load information from disk into memory.
	BIOS	If there is no disk in Drive A, looks to Drive C.
	C:	Tries to load information from disk into memory.
		IO.SYS loaded into memory (IBMBIO.COM in PC-DOS).
		MSDOS.SYS loaded into memory (IBMDOS.COM in PC-DOS).
		CONFIG.SYS loaded into memory.
		COMMAND.COM loaded into memory.
		AUTOEXEC.BAT loaded into memory.

Figure 13.1   Order of Installation

The CONFIG.SYS file is the mechanism that DOS uses to change or add default settings. DOS has certain default values it uses when there is no CONFIG.SYS file. The only way to alter these defaults is to use a special set of commands that are stored within the CONFIG.SYS file. A CONFIG.SYS file does not come with DOS per se. Beginning with DOS 5.0, the DOS setup program would create a CONFIG.SYS file based on the standard DOS defaults.

Certain application program installation routines will also create a CONFIG.SYS file. Sometimes these application programs either add a line to the existing CONFIG.SYS file or replace the CONFIG.SYS file with the application CONFIG.SYS file. The CONFIG.SYS file is an ASCII text file which contains a list of statements that establish the operating values of the system's configuration. A CONFIG.SYS file can alter the internal environment of DOS with specific but limited commands, but it is read and activated only when the system is booted. The CONFIG.SYS commands, called **directives**, are listed in Tables 13.1, 13.2, and 13.3.

BUFFERS	Tells DOS how much memory to use for holding data. Sets number of disk buffers.
COUNTRY	Tells country's date, time, and currency formats that DOS will use. It also determines order for character sorts and which legal characters are used in file names.
DEVICE	Loads special drivers that tell DOS how to handle I/O devices such as a mouse or external drives into memory.
DEVICEHIGH	Loads device drivers into upper memory area. Introduced in DOS 5.0.
DOS	Specifies that DOS should maintain a link to the upper memory area, load part of itself into the high memory area (HMA) or both. Introduced in DOS 5.0.
DRIVPARM	Sets characteristics of a disk drive or tape drives (non-IBM releases above 3.2).
FCBS	Tells DOS how many file control blocks it can open concurrently.
FILES	Tells DOS the maximum number of files that can be accessed at one time.
INSTALL	Allows installation of specific memory-resident programs such as SHARE and FASTOPEN. Introduced in DOS 4.0.
LASTDRIVE	Tells DOS which drive letter is the last drive letter that can be used.
NUMLOCK	Specifies whether the **NumLock** key setting is on or off when you boot. Introduced to DOS 6.0.
SHELL	Tells DOS the location of the command processor, usually COMMAND.COM, and also can change the size of the environment.
STACKS	Tells DOS to increase the number and size of stacks that handle hardware interrupts.
SWITCHES	Specifies options in the MS-DOS CONFIG.SYS file. Use the following parameters:

ver /r
div ,.

/F	Skips the 2-second delay after displaying the `Starting MS-DOS ...` message during startup.
/K	Forces an enhanced keyboard to behave like a conventional keyboard.
/N	Prevents you from using the **F5** or **F8** key to bypass startup commands. (SWITCHES /N does not prevent you from pressing **Ctrl** + **F5** or **Ctrl** + **F8** to bypass `DRVSPACE.BIN`; to prevent this, use the DRVSPACE /SWITCHES command to add the SWITCHES /N setting to your `DRVSPACE.INI` file.)
/W	Specifies that the `WINA20.386` file has been moved to a directory other than the root directory. You need to use this switch only if you are using Microsoft Windows 3.0 in enhanced mode and have moved the `WINA20.386` file from the root directory to another directory.

Table 13.1   ***Commands That Can Be Used Only in CONFIG.SYS***

BREAK	Checks the keyboard to see if the you have has pressed **Ctrl** + C or **Ctrl** + **Backspace** to cancel a command.
REM	Lets you document your `CONFIG.SYS` file. DOS ignores any statement with **REM** in front of it.
SET	Sets the value of environmental variables. At command line, SET displays values in the environment.

Table 13.2   ***CONFIG.SYS Commands Used in CONFIG.SYS That Can Be Keyed in at the Command Line***

INCLUDE	Includes the contents of one configuration block within another.
MENUCOLOR	Sets text and background colors for the startup menu.
MENUDEFAULT	Specifies the default menu item on the startup menu and sets a timeout value if desired.
MENUITEM	Defines an item on the startup menu.
SUBMENU	Defines an item on a startup menu that, when selected, displays another set of choices.

Table 13.3   ***CONFIG.SYS Commands That Define Multiple Configurations***

Online help in DOS 6.0 or above will give you further details about each of these directives. New also to DOS 6.0 and above is the ability to create multiple configuration commands which are listed in Table 13.3. Some of these CONFIG.SYS commands are rather esoteric. Nonetheless, many CONFIG.SYS commands are essential to run certain application programs and/or fine-tune your computer system.

13.3 Files

As an operating system, DOS must track information in memory about which files are open, as well as which devices are used. For instance, when you use the COPY command, DOS actually keeps track of two open files: the source file and the destination file. When you use an application program, the program gives DOS the name of the file or the device it plans to use. DOS returns to the application program a **file handle**—a two-byte number which the program then uses to manipulate the file or device. But DOS is not perfect. For example, an application program like dBASE IV allows the user to open many files, so even if the application program had fifteen files open at one time and could track the open files, there would be a problem with DOS. For DOS, the maximum default value for open files is eight. In other words, DOS can keep track of no more than eight open files at a time. Furthermore, DOS needs five open files for its own use. Application programs can use the remaining three files. See Table 13.4.

stdin	Standard input; source of input.
stdout	Standard output; where DOS writes information.
stderr	Standard error; where DOS writes error messages.
stdprn	Standard printer; where DOS recognizes the printer.
stdaux	Standard auxiliary; where DOS recognizes the communication port.

Table 13.4   DOS Files

An application program, then, may use only three files. So if you are running an application program and get the error message Too many files open or Not enough file handles, that means the three remaining unassigned default file values were not enough for that application program. In the CONFIG.SYS file you can change the number of allowable open files with the FILES command. The FILES directive permits a minimum of eight and a maximum of 255 open files. The default value is eight. Each file you open after eight takes additional space in memory. The syntax is:

```
FILES=x
```

where x represents a numerical value between 8 and 255.

Many application programs recommend a specific number of files open. If you use several application programs and each recommends a different number of files open, use the highest number. If there are no file recommendations in your software applications, use at least 20. If you run database programs, spreadsheet programs, or Windows, use at least 30. You can have only one FILES statement per booting disk. You do not use the maximum number of files available because you pay a price. The price is memory. The more open files you have, the less memory you have available. Thus, you must try to maximize performance without wasting memory.

13.4 Buffers

The BUFFERS statement in a `CONFIG.SYS` file tells DOS how many **disk buffers** to use. What is a disk buffer? Buffers act as the go-betweens for the disk drive you are using and RAM. Since a disk drive is a mechanical device, it is slower for DOS to use than RAM. DOS has to go to the disk and read the information into memory. DOS reads into memory a minimum of one sector, or 512 bytes, at a time. For the sake of efficiency, DOS sets up a reserved area in RAM where it can read from and write to prior to reading from or writing to the disk. This process is called **caching**, pronounced "cashing." When the program makes a request for information from a disk, DOS reads the disk and places the entire 512 byte sector in the buffer, even if the information you need uses less than 512 bytes. When you need the next group of information, DOS reads the disk buffer in memory first and, if the information is there, places it in working memory. Thus, DOS does not have to read the disk again.

The go-between process also occurs when you write information to a disk. DOS collects the information in a buffer until it has a full sector, 512 bytes. Only then will DOS write the information to the disk. When a buffer is full and DOS begins writing the information to a disk, the process is called **flushing the buffer**. When you are using an application program and you exit properly, part of this process is telling DOS the application program is finished. At that time DOS flushes the buffer to indicate that the information is no longer needed and to free up memory.

When you are done working with an application program, do not just turn off the computer. You could still have information in the buffer that has not yet been written to the disk. For example, if you are working with an application package like ADDRESS (a database), each record (name and address) is 128 bytes long. When you want to look at the first name and address (record) that must be loaded into memory, DOS does not just read the first 128 bytes; it reads the entire 512 byte sector. You get not only the first record but also the next three. Then, when you need the second record, DOS does not have to go back to the disk. It just looks in the buffer and, in this case, finds the next record that the application program needs. When there are no more records in the disk buffer, DOS goes to the disk. In this example, instead of having to access the disk four times, DOS needs to access the disk only once. Figure 13.2 demonstrates this process.

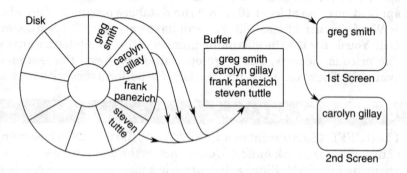

Figure 13.2   Disk Buffers and Application Programs

Remember, DOS always reads the entire sector into the disk buffer. Then, when the application needs to read the first record and display it on the screen, DOS gets it from the disk buffer. When the application needs the second record to display on the screen, DOS does not have to return to the disk which decreases the time needed to return data. It checks the disk buffer, finds the record, and passes it to the program.

DOS is improving performance by reducing the number of times it has to access the disk. You can have a minimum of 1 to a maximum of 99 buffers. The default value of the buffers ranges from 2 to 15, depending on the number of disk drives and memory. See Table 13.5.

	Buffers	Bytes
Default setting	2	
If any disk drive is greater than 360 KB but memory is less than 128 KB	3	
If memory size is between 128 KB and 255 KB	5	2672
If memory size is between 256 KB and 511 KB	10	5328
If memory size is between 512 KB and 640 KB	15	7984

Table 13.5   Default Buffers

The syntax is:

```
BUFFERS=n[,m]
```

where n specifies the numbers of disk buffers and m specifies the number of buffers in the secondary cache, called **look-ahead buffers**. Introduced in DOS 4.0, a look-ahead buffer allows DOS to read a number of sectors in advance. It acts as a secondary buffer cache, again, to reduce data retrieval time.

When working with computers, you always have trade-offs. The trade-off with buffers is that the more buffers you have, the more time DOS must spend going between or among them. DOS must read the buffers sequentially prior to reading the disk. When there are too many buffers, it is faster to go directly to the disk. A buffer also takes about 532 bytes of RAM, reducing the amount of memory available for programs. DOS uses the extra bytes above 512 for overhead. **Overhead** is what DOS needs internally to manage these buffers.

Not all programs use buffers. When an application program reads an entire file into memory, works on it, and then writes the entire file back to disk, it does not use buffers. Typically, word processing programs and spreadsheet programs are these kinds of applications. Conversely, database programs usually use buffers because they read and write information in pieces. These types of programs are **disk-intensive** because they go to the disk repeatedly and need buffers to improve their overall performance. To complicate things further, more and more software programs, including word processing software, are becoming more and more powerful and need to use overlay or auxiliary files, which use buffers. The best advice is to set the number of buffers by the guidelines found in your software application packages. If you have no software guidelines, you may use the following values in Table 13.6 based on your hard disk size:

Hard Disk Size	Buffers
Less than 40 MB	20
40—79 MB	30
80—119 MB	40
120 MB or over	50

Table 13.6   *Recommended Buffer Sizes*

Today, with extended memory becoming so important, the function of disk buffers is supplanted by the use of caching programs. Caching programs manage buffering in extended (or expanded) memory. MS-DOS provides a disk caching program called SMARTDRV.EXE. If you use SMARTDRV.EXE, you can easily minimize the number of buffers in the BUFFERS directive.

omit smartdrive.

13.5 Working with CONFIG.SYS and AUTOEXEC.BAT Files

When you begin altering the CONFIG.SYS file and the AUTOEXEC.BAT file, you want to have a way to recover the default values in case something goes wrong. You do not want to be locked out of your hard disk and/or drivers that control devices on your computer system. *Please check with your instructor for the procedures in your laboratory environment.* If you are working on your own computer system, there are some important steps to take before working with these files.

1. On the hard disk, create a subdirectory called BACK or some other appropriate name. Into this subdirectory copy the CONFIG.SYS file and the AUTOEXEC.BAT file. In addition, copy *all* drivers (files that have a .SYS extension) that reside in the root directory into the BACK subdirectory.
2. Create a bootable floppy disk that can be booted off Drive A—the bootable disk drive, sometimes called the **startup disk**. In addition, copy *all* device drivers to this floppy disk.
3. If you wish to work on the CONFIG.SYS file that is on your hard disk, copy the original CONFIG.SYS file to a new file using some other name as a file extension, such as your initials. For example, if your initials were CZG, you would key in COPY CONFIG.SYS CONFIG.CZG. The name CONFIG.CZG avoids confusion because some programs, particularly software installation programs, often use the same name to copy the current CONFIG.SYS file, such as CONFIG.BAK or CONFIG.OLD.

If you take these steps, you will always have a way to recover your default values in case disaster strikes.

13.6 The Bootable DOS System Disk—Introducing SYS

There are two ways to create a bootable floppy. One way is to take a blank disk and key in FORMAT A:/S. This will copy the two hidden files, IO.SYS and MSDOS.SYS, to the bootable floppy. If you have DOS 6.22, this command will also copy the hidden file DRVSPACE.BIN (DBLSPACE.BIN in earlier 6.0 versions) to the floppy disk, even if you have not used DriveSpace or DoubleSpace to compress your hard disk. In addition, COMMAND.COM will also be copied to the floppy. This process, of course, destroys any data on a disk. If you want to make a bootable disk without destroying the data on a disk you may do so using the SYS command.

The SYS command will create a bootable floppy by copying the hidden DOS system files (IO.SYS and MSDOS.SYS), the command interpreter (COMMAND.COM), and the part of DOS that provides access to compressed drives (DRVSPACE.BIN). In earlier versions of DOS, IO.SYS and MSDOS.SYS had to be contiguous and the first files on the disk in order to be copied, but this is no longer true. It is easy to create a bootable disk by using the SYS command. The syntax is:

```
SYS [drive1:][path] drive2:
```

```
[drive1:][path]  Specifies the location of the system files.
drive2:          Specifies the drive the files are to be copied to.
```

The first parameter specifies the location of the system file you wish to copy. If you do not specify a path, DOS searches the root directory and uses the files it finds there. Normally you issue the command as:

```
SYS  A:
```

In the following activity, you are going to use a new disk with the FORMAT A:/S command. In addition, you are going to copy some files you need in this chapter. You are not using the SYS command because all the files may not fit on the DATA disk. Please check with your lab instructor if procedures are different in your lab environment. If you are using your own computer system and wish to use the hard disk, be sure to back up the CONFIG.SYS and AUTOEXEC.BAT files.

13.7 Activity: Preparing the Bootable DOS System Disk

Note 1: No disk is in Drive A. You have booted off the hard disk, and the C:\> is displayed. Be sure the path is set to C:\DOS.

Note 2: You may use the Bootable DOS System Disk you created in Chapter 10.

Step 1 Label a new blank disk or a disk you no longer want Bootable DOS System Disk. Insert this disk in Drive A.

Step 2 Key in the following: C:\>**FORMAT A: /S/U/V:DOS_DISK** [Enter]

```
C:\>FORMAT A:/S/U/V:DOS_DISK
Insert new diskette for drive A:
and press ENTER when ready...
```

WHAT'S HAPPENING? You have used the parameters that will place the DOS operating system on the disk, format the disk unconditionally, and place a volume label on the disk.

Step 3 Press [Enter]

```
Formatting 1.2M
Format complete.
System transferred


    1,213,952 bytes total disk space
      200,704 bytes used by system
    1,013,248 bytes available on disk
```

```
          512 bytes in each allocation unit.
        1,979 allocation units available on disk.

Volume Serial Number is 1C44-19F6

Format another (Y/N)?_
```

WHAT'S HAPPENING? You have transferred the operating system to this disk.

Step 4   Press **N** ⌈Enter⌋

Step 5   Key in the following: C:\>**A:** ⌈Enter⌋

Step 6   Key in the following: A:\>**MD DOS** ⌈Enter⌋

Step 7   Key in the following: A:\>**COPY C:\DOS\CHKDSK.* DOS** ⌈Enter⌋

Step 8   Key in the following: A:\>**COPY C:\DOS\MEM.EXE DOS** ⌈Enter⌋

Step 9   Key in the following: A:\>**COPY C:\DOS\EDIT*.* DOS** ⌈Enter⌋

Step 10   Key in the following: A:\>**COPY C:\DOS\QBASIC*.* DOS** ⌈Enter⌋

Step 11   Key in the following:
          A:\>**COPY C:\DOS\RAMDRIVE.SYS DOS** ⌈Enter⌋

Step 12   Key in the following: A:\>**COPY C:\DOS\ANSI.SYS DOS** ⌈Enter⌋

Step 13   Key in the following:
          A:\>**COPY C:\DOS\HIMEM.SYS DOS** ⌈Enter⌋

Step 14   Key in the following: A:\>**COPY C:\DOS\EMM386*.* DOS** ⌈Enter⌋

Step 15   Key in the following:
          A:\>**COPY C:\DOS\DOSKEY.COM DOS** ⌈Enter⌋

```
C:\>A:

A:\>MD DOS

A:\>COPY C:\DOS\CHKDSK.* DOS
C:\DOS\CHKDSK.EXE
        1 file(s) copied

A:\>COPY C:\DOS\MEM.EXE DOS
```

```
C:\DOS\MEM.EXE
        1 file(s) copied
A:\>COPY C:\DOS\EDIT*.* DOS
C:\DOS\EDIT.COM
C:\DOS\EDIT.HLP
        2 file(s) copied

A:\>COPY C:\DOS\QBASIC*.* DOS
C:\DOS\QBASIC.EXE
C:\DOS\QBASIC.HLP
C:\DOS\QBASIC.INI
        3 file(s) copied

A:\>COPY C:\DOS\RAMDRIVE.SYS DOS
        1 file(s) copied

A:\>COPY C:\DOS\ANSI.SYS DOS
        1 file(s) copied

A:\>COPY C:\DOS\HIMEM.SYS DOS
        1 file(s) copied

A:\>COPY C:\DOS\EMM386.EXE DOS
        1 file(s) copied

A:\>COPY C:\DOS\DOSKEY.COM DOS
        1 file(s) copied

A:\>_
```

WHAT'S HAPPENING? You have copied some of the DOS system utility programs that you will need for this chapter. Next, you are going to copy some data files from the DOS6BK directory.

Step 16 Key in the following: A:\>**COPY C:\DOS6BK*.TXT** Enter

Step 17 Key in the following: A:\>**COPY C:\DOS6BK*.99** Enter

```
A:\>COPY C:\DOS6BK\*.TXT
C:\DOS6BK\GOODBYE.TXT
C:\DOS6BK\DANCES.TXT
C:\DOS6BK\JANUARY.TXT
C:\DOS6BK\FEBRUARY.TXT
C:\DOS6BK\MARCH.TXT
C:\DOS6BK\APRIL.TXT
C:\DOS6BK\HELLO.TXT
C:\DOS6BK\BYE.TXT
C:\DOS6BK\TEST.TXT
        9 file(s) copied
```

```
A:\>COPY C:\DOS6BK\*.99
C:\DOS6BK\APR.99
C:\DOS6BK\FEB.99
C:\DOS6BK\JAN.99
C:\DOS6BK\MAR.99
        4 file(s) copied

A:\>_
```

WHAT'S HAPPENING? You have copied data files to the disk.

Step 18   Use EDIT to create and save a file called AUTOEXEC.BAT on the Bootable
DOS System Disk in Drive A. Key in the following:

@ECHO OFF

PROMPT pg

PATH A:\DOS

WHAT'S HAPPENING? You have created a basic AUTOEXEC.BAT file that will set
your prompt and path to the DOS directory on the Bootable DOS System Disk. Now
you are ready to write your first CONFIG.SYS file.

13.8 Activity: Writing a CONFIG.SYS with Files and Buffers

Note 1:   The Bootable DOS System Disk is in Drive A.

Step 1   If you are on a network, log off now.

Step 2   The Bootable DOS System Disk is in Drive A. Reboot the system.

```
Starting MS-DOS....

A:\>_
```

WHAT'S HAPPENING? You have booted off the floppy disk in Drive A. Your
prompt and path are set.

Step 3   Key in the following: A:\>**CHKDSK** [Enter]

```
Volume DOS_DISK     created 08-26-1994 6:44p
Volume Serial Number is 1C44-19F6

    1,213,952 bytes total disk space
      145,920 bytes in 3 hidden files
          512 bytes in 1 directories
      623,616 bytes in 27 user files
      443,904 bytes available on disk
```

```
        512 bytes in each allocation unit
      2,371 total allocation units on disk
        867 available allocation units on disk

    655,360 total bytes memory
    538,064 bytes free

Instead of using CHKDSK, try using SCANDISK.  SCANDISK can reliably detect
and fix a much wider range of disk problems.  For more information,
type HELP SCANDISK from the command prompt.

A:\>_
```

WHAT'S HAPPENING? You numbers will vary depending your version of DOS. If you have DOS 6.0, it came with a disk compression program called DoubleSpace, if you have DOS 6.21, you have no disk compression program. If you have DOS 6.22 your disk compression program is called DriveSpace. A disk compression program "packs" the information on a disk, particularly a hard disk, giving you more space to store data. Disk compression programs will be discussed in more detail in Chapter 15. Within all versions of DOS 6.0, except 6.21, a hidden compression file will be copied to any bootable floppy disk, even if you have not used the compression program. Thus, you have a disk with three standard hidden files—the two hidden system files, IO.SYS and MSDOS.SYS, and the compression file. In addition, the amount of memory available is also impacted. The point, however, of this exercise is to note specifically how much space you have available in memory. Look at your display and make a note of the bytes free. In this example it is 538,064.

Step 4   Key in the following: A:\> **COPY CON CONFIG.SYS** [Enter]
                        FILES=20 [Enter]
                        [F6] [Enter]

```
A:\>COPY CON CONFIG.SYS
FILES=20
^Z
  1 file(s) copied

A:\>_
```

WHAT'S HAPPENING? You used COPY CON to write a simple CONFIG.SYS file. Since the CONFIG.SYS file must be an ASCII file, you used COPY CON, which writes files in ASCII. You could have used EDIT, but, because this file was so short, COPY CON was quicker. This CONFIG.SYS file sets the maximum number of open files at 20. DOS does not know this yet because DOS reads the CONFIG.SYS file only at time of bootup.

Step 5   Reboot the system.

Step 6   Key in the following: A:\>**CHKDSK** [Enter]

```
Volume DOS_DISK     created 08-26-1994 6:44p
Volume Serial Number is 1C44-19F6

  1,213,952 bytes total disk space
    145,920 bytes in 3 hidden files
        512 bytes in 1 directories
    624,128 bytes in 28 user files
    443,392 bytes available on disk

        512 bytes in each allocation unit
      2,371 total allocation units on disk
        866 available allocation units on disk

    655,360 total bytes memory
    537,360 bytes free

Instead of using CHKDSK, try using SCANDISK.  SCANDISK can reliably detect
and fix a much wider range of disk problems.  For more information,
type HELP SCANDISK from the command prompt.

A:\>_
```

WHAT'S HAPPENING? Your numbers will vary, depending on your version of DOS and how your system is set up. Look at the number of available bytes in memory where application programs run. In this example, it is 537,360 bytes free. You have lost some bytes because they were used for the FILES directive, or statement, in the CONFIG.SYS file. You are going to add a line to the CONFIG.SYS file. Because you want to add a line, it will be easier to use an editor on an existing file. That is why you copied EDIT and QBASIC to the Bootable DOS System Disk.

Step 7   Edit and save your CONFIG.SYS file and add the line at the end of the file: **BUFFERS=30**.

Step 8   Key in the following: A:\>**TYPE CONFIG.SYS** [Enter]

```
A:\>TYPE CONFIG.SYS
FILES=20
BUFFERS=30

A:\>_
```

WHAT'S HAPPENING? You edited CONFIG.SYS with EDIT. You added the line BUFFERS=30. You have now changed the buffers so that DOS will no longer use the default value but the value that you substituted, which is 30. Once again, DOS cannot make this change until you reboot the system.

Step 9   Reboot the system.

Step 10   Key in the following: A:\>**CHKDSK** [Enter]

```
Volume DOS_DISK    created 08-26-1994 6:44p
Volume Serial Number is 1C44-19F6

 1,213,952 bytes total disk space
   145,920 bytes in 3 hidden files
       512 bytes in 1 directories
   624,128 bytes in 28 user files
   443,392 bytes available on disk


       512 bytes in each allocation unit
     2,371 total allocation units on disk
       866 available allocation units on disk

   655,360 total bytes memory
   529,376 bytes free

Instead of using CHKDSK, try using SCANDISK.  SCANDISK can reliably detect
and fix a much wider range of disk problems.  For more information,
type HELP SCANDISK from the command prompt.

A:\>_
```

WHAT'S HAPPENING? Your numbers will vary, depending on the files on your disk. Look at the number of available bytes in memory. In this example, it is `529,376 bytes free`. You have lost 7984 bytes available in RAM because you have used them for the FILES and the BUFFERS statements in the CONFIG.SYS file, which took effect when you rebooted the system. Your space available for programs has diminished. You may have noticed a slightly faster performance when DOS executed the CHKDSK command.

13.9 Turning NumLock Off

Normally, when you boot the system, the NumLock light comes on indicating the numeric keypad has been activated. This makes the [Insert], [PgDn], or [Delete] keys unavailable on the numeric keypad. You may prefer to have [NumLock] turned off so you can use these keys. Newer computers will, by special hardware settings, automatically set NUMLOCK off. Prior to DOS 6.0, you would boot the system and then press the [NumLock] key to toggle it off. There is now an easier way. The NUMLOCK directive in the CONFIG.SYS file allows you to turn the [NumLock] key on or off when you boot the system. The syntax is:

```
NUMLOCK=[on|off]
```

13.10 Activity: Turning Off NumLock

Note 1:   The Bootable DOS System Disk is in Drive A.

Step 1   Edit and save your CONFIG.SYS file and add the line at the end of the file:

NUMLOCK=OFF

Step 2   Key in the following: A:\>**TYPE CONFIG.SYS** Enter

```
A:\>TYPE CONFIG.SYS
FILES=20
BUFFERS=30
NUMLOCK=OFF

A:\>_
```

WHAT'S HAPPENING? You have set the NumLock key to off. Now, when you boot the system, the NumLock key will automatically be off and your Insert, Delete, and other keys will be active.

Step 3   Reboot the system.

Step 4   Key in the following: A:\>**CHKDSK** Enter

```
Volume DOS_DISK    created 08-26-1994 6:44p
Volume Serial Number is 1C44-19F6

   1,213,952 bytes total disk space
     145,920 bytes in 3 hidden files
         512 bytes in 1 directories
     624,128 bytes in 28 user files
     443,392 bytes available on disk


         512 bytes in each allocation unit
       2,371 total allocation units on disk
         866 available allocation units on disk

     655,360 total bytes memory
     529,376 bytes free

Instead of using CHKDSK, try using SCANDISK.  SCANDISK can reliably detect
and fix a much wider range of disk problems.  For more information,
type HELP SCANDISK from the command prompt.

A:\>_
```

WHAT'S HAPPENING? Your ⟨NumLock⟩ should be toggled off, and the light indicating the status of ⟨NumLock⟩ should be off. The light off means the numbers are not active on the numeric key pad. In addition, there was no byte loss in memory for using this directive.

13.11 Device Drivers

DOS has built-in software routines to handle certain hardware. It knows how to read the keyboard, write to the screen, read and write to standard disk drives, print files, and communicate through a serial port. If you have additional nonstandard hardware devices such as a mouse or expanded memory, you must provide DOS with the proper software (device drivers) and use the DEVICE command in the CONFIG.SYS file to load them. Generally, hardware manufacturers provide this software with the hardware.

Another function of CONFIG.SYS is loading additional software drivers into memory. Device drivers remain in memory. They are programs that go between the physical device and DOS. A device driver is a software program that controls specific peripheral devices. Since DOS cannot know all the codes or programming instructions for the variety of devices available, it looks for a special driver program to handle the specific device. A device driver can enhance the keyboard, the display screen, or the disk drives, as well as other hardware relationships.

An example of a device is a mouse. A mouse is an add-on device that allows the user to move the cursor around on the screen by rolling the mouse on a flat surface. You can use the mouse instead of or in addition to the keyboard. The mouse can be used only with specific application programs designed to work with a mouse. DOS needs a special program to handle the I/O of the mouse because DOS does not know how to translate movement on a flat surface to movement of the cursor on the screen. When you purchase a mouse, you receive two items—the physical device and the software, which is called the mouse device driver and must be loaded into memory. Only after the device driver is loaded can the physical device—the mouse—be used. Today, the mouse is becoming such a common part of hardware that it may no longer need a special device driver.

Actually, when you add hardware, you need to do two things. One is to install the hardware physically, which can be as simple as plugging a cable into the back of the system unit or as complex as installing a circuit board within the system unit. Regardless, DOS will not know how to use the hardware unless you also install the software device drivers that drive the hardware. DOS itself comes with some built-in device drivers for standard devices. In addition, DOS provides additional device drivers that may be installed if you wish to use them. See Table 13.7.

Driver Name	DOS Version Introduced	Purpose
ANSI.SYS	2.0	Defines functions that change display graphics, controls cursor movement, and reassigns keys.
CHKSTATE.SYS	6.0	Used exclusively by MemMaker memory optimization program to track the optimization.
DBLSPACE.SYS	6.0	See DRVSPACE.SYS.
DRVSPACE.SYS	6.22	Replacement for DBLSPACE.SYS. Determines final memory location of DRVSPACE.BIN.
DISPLAY.SYS	3.3	Enables the display of international character sets on EGA, VGA, and LCD displays. (Primarily used for international keyboards—rarely used in the U.S.)
DRIVER.SYS	3.2	Allows you to assign logical drive letters and specifies parameters for a drive not supported by your hardware.
EGA.SYS	5.0	Allows restoration of EGA screen when using DOS 5.0 Shell—Task Swapper.
EMM386.EXE	5.0	Emulates expanded memory by using extended memory. Also provides access to upper memory on a 386 or higher microprocessor. Must have extended memory.
HIMEM.SYS	5.0	Memory manager that controls extended memory, including high memory, on a 286 or higher computer with extended memory.
INTERLNK.EXE	5.0	Used with INTERLNK so that two or more computers can be connected together via parallel or serial ports.
POWER.EXE	5.0	Reduces power consumption for use with battery-operated computers.
PRINTER.SYS	3.3	Allows you to use code page switching for printers. (Primarily used for international printing—rarely used in the U.S.)

RAMDRIVE.SYS	3.2	Allows you to create a virtual disk in memory to simulate a hard drive. IBM's DOS version is called VDISK.SYS.
SETVER.EXE	5.0	Table of DOS versions loaded into memory needed by some application programs.
SMARTDRV.SYS	4.0	Creates a disk cache in extended or expanded memory.
SMARTDRV.EXE	6.0	Replacement for SMARTDRV.SYS. The double buffering feature provides compatibility for hard-disk controllers that do not work with EMM386 or Windows running in 386 enhanced mode.
VDISK.SYS	Only IBM 3.0	Allows you to create a virtual disk in memory to simulate a hard drive. MS-DOS version is called RAMDRIVE.SYS.
XMAEM.SYS	Only IBM 4.0	Emulates expanded memory. Must have an 80386 machine.
XMA2EMS.SYS	Only IBM 4.0	Supports Lotus, Intel, and Microsoft (LIM) Expanded Memory Specification (EMS) 4.0 under DOS 4.0.

Table 13.7   *DOS-provided Device Drivers*

You may have other device drivers, depending on what pieces of hardware you have installed. One easy way to find out what device drivers you have is to use the DIR command with the .SYS file extension (DIR C:\DOS*.SYS or DIR C:*.SYS). Most standard and nonstandard drivers have a .SYS file extension. For instance, if you added a nonstandard device such as a sound card to your system, you would need to let DOS know by means of a file called SCBD.SYS. This file name is specific to this sound board (card) only. Without the device drive file SCBD.SYS installed, even though the sound card is physically installed in the system unit, DOS would not recognize it, so it could not be used. If the file were in the \SB16\DRV subdirectory, you would have to inform DOS by means of a DEVICE statement in the CONFIG.SYS file. The statement in the CONFIG.SYS file would be:

```
DEVICE=C:\SB16\DRV\SBCD.SYS /D:MSCD001 /P:220
```

The parameters would be specific to that device and would be found in the documentation for that device.

13.12 Virtual Disks

DOS includes a driver to create a **RAM disk** or **virtual disk**. The RAM disk is a logical disk drive, not a physical disk drive. One reason it is called a virtual disk is that it appears to DOS to be a "real" physical disk drive but is actually an area carved out of RAM that emulates a disk. Since accessing RAM is much faster than accessing an actual physical disk drive, processing speed increases. After you create a virtual disk and place files and/or programs the virtual drive, DOS can retrieve these "RAM" files in micro- or nanoseconds, instead of the milliseconds that a physical disk drive requires. The danger is, of course, that anything in RAM is volatile, and, if there is a power failure or if the user forgets to write files back to a real disk, the information will be lost.

The program to create a virtual disk drive is called RAMDRIVE.SYS (VDISK.SYS in IBM-PC-DOS). This device driver must be included in the CONFIG.SYS file. You can have more than one virtual disk, but each virtual disk must have a drive letter. DOS normally assigns the next available drive letter. Therefore, if you had Drive A and Drive B and installed a virtual disk, it would be Drive C. If you had a hard disk Drive C and one floppy Drive A, the RAM disk would be Drive D. If you had floppy Drive A, floppy Drive B, hard disk C, and CD-ROM Drive D, the virtual disk would be assigned the letter E. The syntax is:

```
DEVICE=[drive:][path]RAMDRIVE.SYS [DiskSize SectorSize [NumEntries]]] [/E ¦ /A]
```

[drive:][path]	Specifies the location of the RAMDRIVE.SYS file.
DiskSize	Specifies how many kilobytes of memory you want to use for the RAM drive. For example, to create a 640K RAM drive, specify 640. If you don't specify an amount, RAMDrive will create a 64K RAM drive. You can specify a value from 4 to 32767. However, you cannot specify more memory than your system has available.
SectorSize	Specifies the disk sector size in bytes. The size can be 128, 256, or 512 bytes. (If you include a SectorSize value, you must also include a value for DiskSize.)
	Generally, you should use the default sector size of 512 bytes.
NumEntries	Limits the number of files and directories you can create in the RAM drive's root directory. The limit can be from 2 to 1024 entries; the limit you specify is rounded up to the nearest sector size boundary. If you do not specify a limit, you can create up to 64 entries in the RAM drive's root directory. (If you include a value for NumEntries, you must also include values for DiskSize and SectorSize.)

```
            If there is not enough memory to create the RAM
            drive as specified, RAMDrive will try to create
            it with a limit of 16 directory entries. This may
            result in a RAM drive with a different limit from
            the one you specified.
/E          Creates the RAM drive in extended memory. For
            RAMDrive to use extended memory, your system must
            be configured so that it provides extended
            memory, and a DEVICE command for the extended-
            memory manager (such as HIMEM.SYS) must appear in
            your CONFIG.SYS file before the DEVICE command
            for RAMDRIVE.SYS. In general, it is best to
            create a RAM drive in extended memory if your
            system has extended memory.
/A          Creates the RAM drive in expanded memory. For
            RAMDrive to use expanded memory, your system must
            be configured so that it provides expanded
            memory, and the DEVICE command for the expanded-
            memory manager (such as EMM386, 386MAX, CEMM, or
            QEMM) must appear in your CONFIG.SYS file before
            the DEVICE command for RAMDRIVE.SYS.
```

Since virtual disks are temporary, it is often wise to load programs onto a virtual disk, particularly programs that use overlay files. Then, if you have a power failure, you can recover your programs from the original copy on your hard disk or your application program installation disks. Remember, if you place data files on a virtual disk, you risk losing the most current information. On the other hand, if you are using an application program that has a lot of disk access, for instance, a large database file, the risks of losing data is outweighed by the quickness of retrieving data.

13.13 Activity: Writing a CONFIG.SYS Using RAMDRIVE.SYS

Note 1: The Bootable DOS System Disk is in Drive A.

Note 2: You should not be logged into a network.

Note 3: If your file is called VDISK.SYS, you must substitute that name for RAMDRIVE.SYS.

Step 1   Using EDIT, edit the CONFIG.SYS file on the Bootable DOS System Disk. Add the following line at the end of the file and save it:

DEVICE=A:\DOS\RAMDRIVE.SYS

Step 2   Key in the following: A:\>**TYPE CONFIG.SYS** **Enter**

```
A:\>TYPE CONFIG.SYS
FILES=20
BUFFERS=30
NUMLOCK=OFF
DEVICE=A:\DOS\RAMDRIVE.SYS


A:\>_
```

WHAT'S HAPPENING? You have now added a device driver to create a virtual disk for your system. Once again, DOS cannot act until you reboot the system.

Step 3   Reboot the system.

```
Microsoft RAMDrive version 3.07 virtual disk D:
    Disk size: 64K
    Sector size: 512 bytes
    Allocation unit: 1 sectors
    Directory entries: 64

A:\>_
```

WHAT'S HAPPENING?DOS is indicating that it has created a virtual disk. In this example, the logical drive is D because you booted off the floppy disk. If you are using VDISK.SYS, the message will be slightly different. The important issue is that the virtual drive will act exactly like any other drive. Be sure to use the assigned RAM drive letter. If your system has one hard drive and one or two floppy drives, it should be D since you are booting off floppy Drive A.

Step 4   Key in the following: A:\>**DIR D:** Enter

```
A:\>DIR D:

Volume in drive D is MS-RAMDRIVE
Directory of D:\

 File not found

A:\>_
```

WHAT'S HAPPENING? As you can see, DOS treats this drive like any other disk drive. Drive D is the assigned letter in this activity. Your assigned drive letter does not have to be D, but it is important to remember what drive letter was assigned to your virtual drive. You can change the default to D, make subdirectories, or whatever else you do with a physical disk drive except format it or use DISKCOPY with it. Pay attention to how long it takes to run CHKDSK.EXE in the next step.

Step 5   Key in the following: A:\>**CHKDSK** Enter

```
Volume DOS_DISK created 08-26-1994 6:44p
Volume Serial Number is 1C44-19F6

    1,213,952 bytes total disk space
      145,920 bytes in 3 hidden files
          512 bytes in 1 directories
      624,128 bytes in 28 user files
      443,392 bytes available on disk

          512 bytes in each allocation unit
        2,371 total allocation units on disk
          866 available allocation units on disk

      655,360 total bytes memory
      462,544 bytes free

Instead of using CHKDSK, try using SCANDISK. SCANDISK can reliably detect
and fix a much wider range of disk problems. For more information,
type HELP SCANDISK from the command prompt.

A:\>_
```

WHAT'S HAPPENING? Your numbers will vary. Again, the number of available bytes for programs and data in RAM is much lower. In this example, it is `462,544 bytes free`. You have lost many bytes for the system and application programs because you have used them for the FILES statement and the BUFFERS statement and, now, you have an installed virtual disk. To see how fast a virtual disk operates, you are going to work with the new disk drive, but be sure you use the drive letter that was assigned to your virtual disk if it is not D.

Step 6   Key in the following: A:\>**D:** Enter

Step 7   Key in the following: D:\>**COPY A:\DOS\CHKDSK.*** Enter

Step 8   Key in the following: D:\>**CHKDSK** Enter

```
A:\>D:

D:\>COPY A:\DOS\CHKDSK.*
            1 file(s) copied

D:\>CHKDSK

Volume MS-RAMDRIVE      created 07-21-1992 12:00a

      62,464 bytes total disk space
      12,288 bytes in 1 user files
      50,176 bytes in 28 user files
```

```
      512 bytes in each allocation unit
      122 total allocation units on disk
       98 available allocation units on disk

  655,360 total bytes memory
  462,544 bytes free

Instead of using CHKDSK, try using SCANDISK. SCANDISK can reliably detect
and fix a much wider range of disk problems. For more information,
type HELP SCANDISK from the command prompt.

D:\>_
```

WHAT'S HAPPENING? You changed your default to D, the virtual disk. You then copied the CHKDSK.EXE program to the virtual drive. You executed the CHKDSK command from the virtual disk. Do you see how fast the command executed? If you want to add more than one virtual disk to your system, you must have two or more device statements in your CONFIG.SYS, as in:

```
DEVICE=A:\DOS\RAMDRIVE.SYS
DEVICE=A:\DOS\RAMDRIVE.SYS 360
```

Remember that, if you were booting from the hard drive, you would have to tell DOS to look on Drive C. The lines would read:

```
DEVICE=C:\DOS\RAMDRIVE.SYS
DEVICE=C:\DOS\RAMDRIVE.SYS 360
```

These entries would create two virtual drives, one 64 KB in size and the other 360 KB in size, exactly like a double-sided, double-density disk. However, if you used 424 KB (360 + 64) for virtual disks, only 180 KB would remain of RAM to run other programs. Users want to have extended and/or expanded memory so that devices such as virtual disks can be placed in extended or expanded memory and not take up room in conventional memory. Remember, conventional memory is where application programs *must* execute.

Step 9   Key in the following: D:\>**A:** **Enter**

```
D:\>A:

A:\>_
```

WHAT'S HAPPENING? You have made Drive A the default drive.

13.14 *Memory*

Memory is organized so that it is addressable. It is much like a bank of mail boxes at the post office. Each box has a unique address. You do not know if there is anything in the mail boxes, but you can locate any mail box by its address. The same is true with memory. It also has addresses that are specific locations.

Personal computers use different microprocessor chips identified by number. Early personal computers used the 8086 or 8088 Intel chip, which had 20 address pins. These address pins connect electrically to the rest of the the system. Each of these address pins, when combined with other pins, could "map" or look to many addresses. Remember, all work on a computer deals with only 0s or 1s. This translates to a binary numbering system. The number of available addresses then becomes 2^{20}. The calculation is based on the base 2 number system "powered" to the number of address pins. If you multiply out 2^{20}, your final total is 1,048,576 unique addresses (1 MB of address space). New chips have more address pins and, thus, more addressing capabilities. The Intel 80286 chip can address up to 16MB of memory. The Intel 80386 chip has 30 lines, so the mathematical calculation is 2^{30}. This computes to 4 gigabytes. A gigabyte is a billion bytes. Thus, 4 GB is 4 billion bytes. The addresses are expressed in hexadecimal notation, hexadecimal meaning a base 16 number system. One reason for using hexadecimal notation is that binary numbers become extremely cumbersome. Base 16 uses the digits 0 through 9 and the letters A through F to represent numbers. Hence, memory addresses start at 0000.

Why should you care about this "technogeek" discussion? Memory is your work area. The larger the work area, the more you can place there. More memory can mean an enormous spreadsheet or a large document. It can mean larger and much more powerful application programs. It can mean multitasking. **Multitasking** means that the computer can perform more than one task at a time, such as printing a document while you are updating your address file. In the early days of computing, 256 KB was a lot of memory. Today, people want more memory—4 MB, 8 MB or more. However, there is an catch to this. DOS and most application programs running under DOS do not recognize any memory above 640 KB.

Memory comes in three flavors—conventional, extended, and expanded. **Conventional memory** is the first 640 KB of memory on the computer. All DOS application programs must run in conventional memory. Here is where programs and data are located when you are working. Figure 13.3 shows a graphic example.

Figure 13.3 **Conventional and Extended Memory**

Conventional memory cannot exceed 640 KB, although the PC can address addresses up to 1 MB. This area of memory, which begins at the end of conventional memory and ends at the beginning of extended memory, is called the **adapter segment**. Today, it is more commonly called the **upper memory area** or **UMA**. It is also sometimes referred to as **reserved memory**. See Figure 13.4.

Figure 13.4 **Adapter Segment or Upper Memory Area**

The adapter segment or upper memory contains room for such things as ROM-BIOS routines, display adapters, and network adapters. The adapter segment is also mapped. It is always located in the same area of the computer's address space—from 640 KB to 1024 KB. There are no exceptions. Thus, when you purchase a computer with 640 KB of memory, it could have 1 MB of address space, but this does not mean that you have one megabyte of memory available to you. Adapter segment address space is reserved for these necessary computer routines. Before DOS 5.0, this is where memory ended.

13.15 Extended Memory

Extended memory is a memory board or memory chips on the system board. Extended memory is memory above 1 MB, which DOS could not address until 5.0. It is directly addressable but not by DOS below 4.0. Extended memory can be used only on a computer with an 80286, 80386, 80486, or a Pentium processor. A 286 can use up to 16 MB of extended memory. A 386 or 486 can use up to 4 GB (4 gigabytes—4 billion bytes) of extended memory. An 8086 or 8088 cannot have extended memory. Extended memory can be used only by applications that know about extended memory. Programs that do use extended memory need special instructions to recognize the higher addresses in extended memory. Extended memory is fast and efficient for programs that can use it. Newer versions of DOS let you make use of extended memory with some commands like RAMDRIVE.SYS. If you use the /E parameter and if you have extended memory, DOS will place the virtual disk in extended memory, saving conventional memory for the application programs that need it. DOS 5.0 and above can run in extended memory, leaving more conventional memory available for programs. Windows 3.1 also works in extended memory. Currently, programs written to use extended memory run program instructions in conventional memory but can load data in extended memory. To use extended memory most efficiently, certain rules are set out in the Extended Memory Specification (XMS) must be followed, and special device drivers must be installed to manage that memory (see Figure 13.5). In DOS 5.0 and above, this manager is HIMEM.SYS.

Figure 13.5   **Programs Written for Extended Memory**

13.16 Expanded Memory

Expanded memory can be used in almost any computer system. You can purchase an expanded memory card that contains more memory. In order to use this memory, you must load a device driver called an Expanded Memory Manager (EMM). The EMM establishes a page frame in an empty area of the adapter segment. Each 16 KB is called a **page**, and the area of memory that receives the page is called a **page frame**. The page frame is the place where the EMM maps information in and out of the expanded memory card. The needed information is not physically copied from the card to memory. The device driver changes the page register to make the page frame point to the data on the expanded memory card. The data appears in the page frame so that DOS can access it. This process is called **bank switching** (see Figure 13.6).

Figure 13.6   Bank Switching

The number and locations vary from machine to machine. The standard is the LIM (Lotus Intel Microsoft) EMS (Expanded Memory Specification) 3.2 and 4.0, which a software manufacturer can use when writing programs. Lotus is an example of an application program that can directly manipulate expanded memory to handle large spreadsheets. LIM 3.2 supported only four fixed-size 16 KB page frames. The maximum amount of expanded memory that could be accessed is 8 MB. The page frames have to map to a memory location above 640 KB and below 1024 KB. LIM standard 4.0, to be compatible with LIM 3.2, also requires four 16 KB page frames, but it has more flexibility and allows for any number of additional page frames of any size in any memory location. The maximum amount of memory that can be addressed is 32 MB. However, a program must know about expanded memory in order to use it. Programs that use expanded memory may run more slowly because of all the bank switching.

DOS above 4.0 can use expanded memory. You can place virtual disks in expanded memory with the /A parameter for RAMDRIVE.SYS. Again, however, you are maximizing your use of conventional memory.

If you purchase a third party expanded memory board, you must tell DOS the device driver for that expanded memory so that DOS can turn control over to the software memory manager. You may do this with the DEVICE directive or statement in the CONFIG.SYS file. You need to know the file name, the file location, and the parameters for that device driver file in order to install it in your CONFIG.SYS file. To make this more confusing, on 80386 machines you can configure a part of extended memory to emulate expanded memory with special device drivers that are placed in the CONFIG.SYS file. The reason you must turn extended memory into expanded memory is that older programs use expanded memory rather than extended memory.

13.17 Upper Memory Area

Another kind of memory becomes important when using DOS 5.0 or above. It is called the upper memory area, the area immediately adjacent to the 640 KB of conventional memory. This area in reserved memory is not considered part of conventional memory. It is normally reserved for running hardware such as the monitor. However, information can be mapped from another kind of memory to the upper memory areas that are unused by your system. The unused portions are called **upper memory blocks** (**UMB**). If you have a 386 or above and DOS 5.0 and above, you may, with the assistance of the device driver provided with DOS 5.0 and above, EMM386.EXE, use the upper memory area for device drivers and memory-resident programs. This will free conventional memory. See Figure 13.7.

0 KB	640 KB	700 KB		1024 KB	16 MB (286)	4 GB (386 or 486)
Conventional memory	Reserved for hardware code and system data	Upper memory area (UMB)	Hardware code and system data	Extended memory		

Figure 13.7 **Upper Memory Area**

13.18 High Memory Area

If you have extended memory, you can run DOS 5.0 or above in the **high memory area** (**HMA**). The high memory area is the first 64 KB of extended memory. Very few programs use this area, so it is a good location for DOS. If you used the DOS SETUP program, it will normally install DOS in the HMA (see Figure 13.8).

0 KB	640 KB	960 KB	1024 KB	1068 KB	16 MB (286)	4 GB (386 or 486)
Conventional memory	Reserved	ROM-BIOS	High memory area (HMA)	Extended memory		

Figure 13.8 **High Memory Area**

13.19 Using Extended and Expanded Memory

Although all these techniques allow DOS, and hence programs, to take advantage of breaking the 640 KB barrier, they still have limitations. Most of the time, only the data from a program can be stored in either extended or expanded memory. The actual program instructions still must be stored below 1024 KB. The microprocessors above 286 have two modes of operation—real mode and protected mode. DOS runs in real mode. **Real mode** means that program instructions must run under 1024 KB. Other operating systems such as UNIX or other operating environments such as Windows 3.1 (running in 386 enhanced mode) can run in protected mode. **Protected mode** allows programs and data to reside above 1024 KB because the processor can form higher-numbered addresses, which means it can reach beyond 1 MB. Since many programs and DOS prior to 4.0 cannot use extended or expanded memory, extended and/or expanded memory commonly holds certain configuration commands that place virtual drives and large disk buffers called disk caches there.

How do you know if you have expanded or extended memory? You can check the documentation for your computer to see what you have. If you have purchased your computer in the last few years, chances are that it has extended memory but no expanded memory. DOS has an external command called MEM that will tell you what you have.

13.20 The MEM Command

The CHKDSK command gives you a report about disks and conventional memory. Because users always need more information about memory, the MEM command was introduced in DOS 4.0. The MEM command reports the amount of used and unused memory. It will report extended memory if memory above 1 MB is installed and will report expanded memory if the memory device driver is installed. The MEM command is much improved in the DOS 6.0 versions. The syntax is:

```
MEM [/CLASSIFY ¦ /DEBUG ¦ /FREE ¦ /MODULE modulename] [/PAGE]
```

/CLASSIFY or /C	Classifies programs by memory usage. Lists the size of programs, provides a summary of memory in use, and lists largest memory block available.
/DEBUG or /D	Displays status of all modules in memory, internal drivers, and other information.
/FREE or /F	Displays information about the amount of free memory left in both conventional and upper memory.
/MODULE or /M	Displays a detailed listing of a module's memory use.

> This option must be followed by the name of a
> module, optionally separated from /M by a co-
> lon.
>
> /PAGE or /P   Pauses after each screenful of information.

The MEM command gives you much more information about memory on your computer system.

13.21 Activity: Using the MEM Command

Note: The Bootable DOS System Disk is in Drive A with the A:\> displayed. You have booted from it and not the hard disk or network.

Step 1   Key in the following: A:\>**MEM** [Enter]

```
A:\>MEM

Memory Type          Total   =    Used   +    Free
                     _____        _____       _____
Conventional          639K         187K        452K
Upper                   0K           0K          0K
Reserved               97K          97K          0K
Extended (XMS)      15,648K      15,648K         0K
                    _____      _____       _____
Total memory        16,384K      15,932K        452K

Total under 1 MB      639K         187K         452K

Largest executable program size      452K  (462,448 bytes)
Largest free upper memory block        0K        (0 bytes)

A:\>_
```

WHAT'S HAPPENING? Your display will vary if you are using DOS 4.0 or 5.0. In addition, the numbers will vary depending on how much, if any, extended memory you have installed on your computer system or if you have installed expanded memory. Compare the lines showing conventional and extended memory. In this example, you have much extended memory, and none of it is being used. Furthermore, look at the line that states Largest executable program size. You have only 452K to run programs. Programs can run in conventional memory only.

Step 2   Key in the following: A:\>**MEM /C** [Enter]

NAME	Total	=	Conventional	+	Upper Memory	
MSDOS	67,933	(66K)	67,933	(66K)	0	(0K)
RAMDRIVE	66,736	(65K)	66,736	(65K)	0	(0K)

```
  DRVSPACE    52,064    (51K)      52,064    (51K)           0    (0K)
  COMMAND      4,992     (5K)       4,992     (5K)            0    (0K)
  Free        462,544   (452K)     462,544   (452K)          0    (0K)

Memory Summary:

  Type of Memory        Total    =    Used    +    Free
  _____        _____        _____       _____

  Conventional          654,336       191,792      462,544
  Upper                       0             0            0
  Reserved               99,328        99,328            0
  Extended (XMS)     16,023,552    16,023,552            0
  _____     _____    _____       _____

  Total memory       16,777,216    16,314,672      462,544


  Total under 1 MB      654,336       191,792      462,544


  Largest executable program size         462,448    (452K)
  Largest free upper memory block               0     (0K)

A:\>_
```

WHAT'S HAPPENING? By looking at these reports, you can see that on this computer there is 16 MB of memory, but it is not being used. If you look at the line, Largest executable program size, you see that you have only 452K to run programs because you have taken up conventional memory with FILES, BUFFERS, and RAM drives. (Your numbers will vary based on how much memory you have on your computer.) Although you may not have any extended memory, chances are that, if the computer you are working on was purchased in the last few years, it probably has at least 4 MB of extended memory. If you have extended memory, you would like to be able to use it. If, for instance, you wanted to place the RAMDRIVE.SYS file in extended memory prior to rebooting, you would have to modify your CONFIG.SYS file to include the following statement:

    DEVICE=A:\DOS\RAMDRIVE.SYS /E

It is not enough to place that statement in the CONFIG.SYS file. You must first prepare memory.

13.22 MS-DOS Provided Memory Manager—HIMEM.SYS

In order to use extended, expanded, or upper memory, you must first install a memory manager. A **memory manager** is a software program that controls the access to the kind of memory you have. MS-DOS 5.0 and above provides two memory managers, HIMEM.SYS and EMM386.EXE.

HIMEM.SYS provides extended memory access to programs that use XMS (Extended Memory Specification). Windows is an example of such a program.

`HIMEM.SYS` insures that no two programs will simultaneously use the same portion of extended memory. It allows a 286 or above microprocessor to access the HMA (High Memory Area).

You must use the most recent version of `HIMEM.SYS`. This file can be located in both the `WINDOWS` and `DOS` subdirectories. The safest bet is to check file creation dates and use the most current version of these drivers in your DEVICE statement within your `CONFIG.SYS` file. Since you are booting off a floppy, you will be using the `HIMEM.SYS` file is in the `DOS` subdirectory on the bootable floppy disk.

Remember that you must have a 286 or above system in order to install `HIMEM.SYS`. You must have extended memory in order to manage it. For DOS to take advantage of extended memory, you must install `HIMEM.SYS` via the `CONFIG.SYS` file. The basic syntax for `HIMEM.SYS` is:

```
DEVICE=[drive:][path]HIMEM.SYS
```

Order is absolutely critical when using `HIMEM.SYS`. Without exception `HIMEM.SYS` must be the first item in the `CONFIG.SYS` file. Be sure you know the location of the `HIMEM.SYS` file. There are a number of parameters, which you will have to check for on your specific system. For example, if you had a IBM PS/2, you would write the statement as `DEVICE=C:\DOS\HIMEM.SYS /M:ps2`. The /M switch refers to a handler that accesses high memory. The `ps2` specifies the IBM PS/2 computer.

Once you have installed `HIMEM.SYS`, you can then place your RAM drive in extended memory. You get the advantage of a RAM disk without losing conventional memory for the programs you want to execute.

13.23 Understanding LASTDRIVE

DOS allows you to have more than one virtual disk. Once again, there is a catch. DOS, as you know, recognizes disk drives by letters of the alphabet. The first floppy drive is *always* Drive A. The first hard drive is *always* Drive C. If you have only one floppy drive and one hard drive, you have a logical Drive B. That is, you can treat the single floppy drive as one logical drive so that you can issue a command such as `COPY A:MYFILE.TXT B:MYFILE.TXT`. DOS will then prompt you to swap disks when it needs access to Drive B. DOS knows you have only one floppy disk drive but lets you pretend you have two.

In order to track your disk drives, DOS must keep an area of memory available to store the number of disk drives you have. Although DOS can recognize up to 26 drives (A to Z), it does not want to use memory for tracking drives you do not have. In DOS 5.0 and above, the last default drive letter that DOS tracks in memory is one more than the number of your physical drives. Thus, if you computer system has two floppy drives, two hard drives, and a CD-ROM drive, DOS assigns drives letters A through E, and reserves enough space in memory to track drives A through E, plus one extra—F. This seems straightforward enough, so it may seem to be nothing to worry about, but it is.

In addition to your physical disk drives, you may have many logical drives that are not allocated space in memory by DOS. For instance, when you initially install DOS, you can divide the hard drive into smaller logical drives, a process called **partitioning**. You can partition your hard drive so that it is two, three, or more logical drives, i.e., Drives C, D, and E. If you had a computer system with two floppy drives—A and B—and a fixed disk that was logically partitioned into logical drives C and D, and you wanted to have three virtual drives—E, F, and G—you would have a problem. The default value that DOS used for drives on this system was a last recognizable drive letter of D. You are out of drive letters. To solve the problem, DOS permits you to place a LASTDRIVE statement in the CONFIG.SYS file to tell DOS how many drive letters you want recognized.

13.24 Activity: Installing HIMEM.SYS and LASTDRIVE

Note 1:   The Bootable DOS System Disk is in Drive A with the A:\> displayed.

Note 2:   If your virtual disk file name is different from the one used here, use the correct file name.

Note 3:   If you do not have any extended memory, you will not be able to do this activity.

Step 1   Using EDIT, edit and save the CONFIG.SYS file on the Bootable DOS System Disk so it looks as follows:

DEVICE=A:\DOS\HIMEM.SYS
FILES=20
BUFFERS=30
NUMLOCK=OFF
DEVICE=A:\DOS\RAMDRIVE.SYS /E
DEVICE=A:\DOS\RAMDRIVE.SYS 360 512 112 /E
LASTDRIVE=H

Step 2   Key in the following:

A:\> **TYPE CONFIG.SYS** **Enter**

```
A:\>TYPE CONFIG.SYS
DEVICE=A:\DOS\HIMEM.SYS
FILES=20
BUFFERS=30
NUMLOCK=OFF
DEVICE=A:\DOS\RAMDRIVE.SYS /E
DEVICE=A:\DOS\RAMDRIVE.SYS 360 512 112 /E
LASTDRIVE=H


A:\>_
```

WHAT'S HAPPENING? You have now included the memory manager `HIMEM.SYS` so that you can use extended memory for your virtual drives. You have expanded the drive letters that DOS will recognize, and you added two device statements, which will create two virtual disks in extended memory for your system. The second virtual disk emulates a double-sided, double-density disk of 360 KB—sector size is 512 and directory size is 112 file entries. You have also increased the number of drives DOS can recognize up to Drive H. Once again, DOS cannot act until you reboot the system.

Step 3   Reboot the system.

```
Starting MS-DOS...

HIMEM is testing extended memory...done.

Microsoft RAMDrive version 3.07 virtual disk D:
    Disk size: 64K
    Sector size: 512 bytes
    Allocation unit: 1 sectors
    Directory entries: 64

Microsoft RAMDrive version 3.07 virtual disk E:
    Disk size: 360K
    Sector size: 512 bytes
    Allocation unit: 1 sectors
    Directory entries: 112

A:\>_
```

WHAT'S HAPPENING? DOS first indicated that it was installing the `HIMEM.SYS` memory manager. It then indicated that it had created two virtual disks. In this example, the logical virtual drives are D and E.

Step 4   Key in the following: `A:\>`**MEM /C** [Enter]

```
    MSDOS      68,045   (66K)    68,045   (66K)       0   (OK)
    HIMEM       3,728    (4K)     3,728    (4K)       0   (OK)
    RAMDRIVE    2,400    (2K)     2,400    (2K)       0   (OK)
    DRVSPACE   52,064   (51K)    52,064   (51K)       0   (OK)
    COMMAND     4,992    (5K)     4,992    (5K)       0   (OK)
    Free      523,072  (511K)   423,072  (511K)       0   (OK)

    Memory Summary:
```

```
Type of Memory          Total    =    Used    +    Free

Conventional          654,336        131,264        523,072
Upper                       0              0              0
Reserved               99,328         99,328              0
Extended (XMS)     16,023,552        499,712     15,523,840

Total memory       16,777,216        730,304     16,046,912

Total under 1 MB      654,336        131,264        523,072

Largest executable program size        522,976    (511K)
Largest free upper memory block              0    (OK)
The high memory area is available.

A:\>_
```

WHAT'S HAPPENING? You have accomplished a lot. You have recovered conventional memory by loading the memory manager HIMEM.SYS and by placing the RAM drives in extended memory after HIMEM.SYS prepared them for use. If you look at the line Largest executable program size, you now have 511K available in conventional memory for executable programs. LocateRAMDRIVE at the top of the display. RAMDRIVE does occupy some space in memory; it needs a "hook" in conventional memory. Before you installedHIMEM.SYS, RAMDRIVE occupied 65K of conventional memory. Now it occupies only 2K. These virtual drives are very, very fast. In the next steps, notice the difference in response time between a physical disk drive and a virtual disk drive.

Step 5   Key in the following: A:\>**D:** [Enter]

Step 6   Key in the following: D:\>**COPY A:*.*** [Enter]

Step 7   Key in the following: D:\>**COPY *.* E:** [Enter]

```
A:\CONFIG.SYS
       16 file(s) copied
COMMAND.COM
GOODBYE.TXT
DANCES.TXT
JANUARY.TXT
FEBRUARY.TXT
MARCH.TXT
APRIL.TXT
HELLO.TXT
BYE.TXT
TEST.TXT
APR.99
FEB.99
```

```
JAN.99
MAR.99
AUTOEXEC.BAT
CONFIG.SYS
        16 file(s) copied

D:\>_
```

WHAT'S HAPPENING? You should be able to see a significant increase in speed between copying files from a physical disk (Drive A) to a virtual disk (Drive D) and copying between two virtual disks (Drive D and Drive E). Here is the true reason why computer users like virtual disks. They are most effective when they are placed in extended memory because you can have full use of conventional memory for application programs. That way, you get the advantages of virtual disks without having to sacrifice conventional memory. There is a way to save even more conventional memory.

Step 8   Key in the following: D:\>A: **Enter**

```
D:\>A:

A:\>_
```

WHAT'S HAPPENING? You have made Drive A the default drive.

13.25 The DOS Command

When you installed HIMEM.SYS, you let programs that know about extended memory, such as RAMDRIVE.SYS, use it. One objective in maximizing your system is to conserve conventional memory. You want to conserve conventional memory because that is where your application programs run. If you can place items such as drivers like RAMDRIVE.SYS in extended memory, you can use them without sacrificing program space. The more conventional memory you have available, the bigger application programs you can run. If you ever get an out of memory error message, you become exceedingly interested in conserving conventional memory.

In the memory report in the above activity, one line stated that The high memory area is available. You may ask yourself "available for what?" The high memory area (HMA) is the first 64 KB of extended memory. A good portion of DOS itself can be loaded there. Only a very small part of the operating system needs to be in conventional memory. The rest of it can be in the HMA. Once HIMEM.SYS is installed, you can accomplish this by the following directive in CONFIG.SYS:

```
DOS=HIGH
```

13.26 Activity: Loading DOS High

Note: The Bootable DOS System Disk is in Drive A with the A:\> displayed.

Step 1 Using EDIT, edit and save the CONFIG.SYS file on the Bootable DOS System Disk so it looks as follows:

DEVICE=A:\DOS\HIMEM.SYS
DOS=HIGH
FILES=20
BUFFERS=30
NUMLOCK=OFF
DEVICE=A:\DOS\RAMDRIVE.SYS /E
DEVICE=A:\DOS\RAMDRIVE.SYS 360 512 112 /E
LASTDRIVE=H

Step 2 Key in the following: A:\>**TYPE CONFIG.SYS** **Enter**

```
A:\>TYPE CONFIG.SYS
DEVICE=A:\DOS\HIMEM.SYS
DOS=HIGH
FILES=20
BUFFERS=30
NUMLOCK=OFF
DEVICE=A:\DOS\RAMDRIVE.SYS /E
DEVICE=A:\DOS\RAMDRIVE.SYS 360 512 112 /E
LASTDRIVE=H

A:\>_
```

Step 3 Reboot the system.

```
Starting MS-DOS

HIMEM is testing extended memory...done.

Microsoft RAMDrive version 3.07 virtual disk D:
    Disk size: 64K
    Sector size: 512 bytes
    Allocation unit: 1 sectors
    Directory entries: 64

Microsoft RAMDrive version 3.07 virtual disk E:
    Disk size: 360K
    Sector size: 512 bytes
    Allocation unit: 1 sectors
    Directory entries: 112

A:\>_
```

WHAT'S HAPPENING? DOS first indicated that it was installing the HIMEM.SYS memory manager. It then indicated that it had created two virtual disks. In this example, the logical virtual drives are D and E.

Step 4   Key in the following: A:\> **MEM /C** Enter

```
    MSDOS       14,925   (15K)      14,925    (15K)           0    (OK)
    HIMEM        1,104   (1K)        1,104    (1K)            0    (OK)
    RAMDRIVE     2,400   (2K)        2,400    (2K)            0    (OK)
    DRVSPACE    51,312   (50K)      51,312    (50K)           0    (OK)
    COMMAND      2,928   (3K)        2,928    (3K)            0    (OK)
    Free       581,632  (568K)     581,632   (568K)           0    (OK)

Memory Summary:

  Type of Memory        Total   =   Used    +    Free

  Conventional          654,336     72,704       581,632
  Upper                       0          0             0
  Reserved               99,328     99,328             0
  Extended (XMS)     16,023,552    499,712    15,523,840

  Total memory       16,777,216    671,744    16,105,472

  Total under 1 MB      654,336     72,704       581,632

  Largest executable program size      581,536   (568K)
  Largest free upper memory block            0   (OK)
  MS-DOS is resident in the high memory area

A:\>_
```

WHAT'S HAPPENING? You now have loaded DOS high. The last line in the memory report tells you so—MS-DOS is resident in the high memory area. In addition, where you used to have 511K available for executable programs in conventional memory, you now have 568K available.

13.27 The Shell

The SHELL configuration command, available with DOS 2.0 and above, is another command you can place in the CONFIG.SYS file. It was originally designed so that programmers could use command processors other than COMMAND.COM. Since most people do not want to write their own command processor, this directive still serves two other useful purposes. One is to allow the user to place COMMAND.COM in any subdirectory and remove it from the root, and the second is to expand the size of the environment.

You have used the environment when you were writing batch files. It is an area that DOS sets aside in memory. DOS keeps the location of the command processor in the environment; the path, if one is set; the prompt, if it is changed; and append directions, if APPEND is used. Most of the time, you are concerned about the environment only when you get the message Out of environment space. If you have DOS 3.1 or above, you can increase the environment size.

COMMAND.COM, usually located in the root directory of the booting disk, is essentially divided into two parts—the resident portion and the transient portion. The transient portion is the area of DOS that holds internal commands such as DIR, COPY, and so on. It is also the part of DOS that displays the system prompt. When an application program needs the memory that the transient portion of DOS uses, it overwrites this portion of DOS in memory. When the program is completed and turns control back to DOS, it turns control back to the resident part of DOS. This resident portion of DOS reloads COMMAND.COM into memory (see Figure 13.9). If you ever receive the message Insert disk with \COMMAND.COM in Drive A and press any key to continue..., it means that DOS went to reload COMMAND.COM and could not find it on the disk. DOS maintains the location of COMMAND.COM in the environment.

The question is why would you want to place COMMAND.COM in a location other than the root directory of the booting disk? There are several reasons. One reason could be that you are working with more than one version of DOS. Often, before you upgrade DOS, you want to test your programs prior to installing the new version of DOS permanently. Remember, DOS loads into memory the version of DOS it finds on the booting disk. Thus, if DOS 5.0 was on the hard disk and you placed a bootable system disk in Drive A with DOS 6.0, DOS 6.0 would be the version of DOS installed in memory.

Another reason for placing COMMAND.COM in another location is that it makes the root directory look neater. The most important reason is to protect yourself from losing COMMAND.COM. Some programs you use will write a different version of COMMAND.COM to your disk. Most likely, you could accidentally delete COMMAND.COM. These events can make your system unusable. If you hide COMMAND.COM in a subdirectory, no other programs can overwrite it, nor can you accidentally delete it. The syntax for the SHELL command is:

```
SHELL=drive:\path\COMMAND.COM   drive:\path   /P   /E:size
```

The first drive:\path tells DOS where COMMAND.COM is located. The next item is the name of the command processor itself. If you had another command processor, you would tell DOS its name here. The next drive:\path tells DOS the path to the command processor. DOS uses it to set the COMSPEC variable. **COMSPEC** stands for command processor specification (location). You *must* use the /P switch because it means *stay* permanent. This statement instructs DOS to load and keep resident a copy of COMMAND.COM. Without the /P, DOS would load COMMAND.COM, execute any AUTOEXEC.BAT file, and immediately exit, leaving you without a command processor. With no command processor, you cannot use any commands—you have no prompt. To recover the command processor, you would have to reboot the system with another booting disk. In addition, you can increase the size of the environment.

Figure 13.9   ***Reloading COMMAND.COM***

13.28 Activity: Using SET and SHELL

Note: The Bootable DOS System Disk is in Drive A with A:\> displayed.

Step 1   Key in the following: A:\>**SET** **Enter**

```
A:\>SET
COMSPEC=A:\COMMAND.COM
PROMPT=$p$g
PATH A:\DOS


A:\>_
```

WHAT'S HAPPENING? The environment has the location of COMMAND.COM in the root directory of A. The default value of COMSPEC is always the root directory of the booting disk. Remember COMSPEC means the location of the command specification file (command processor). In addition, since this disk has an AUTOEXEC.BAT file that tells DOS to change the prompt and to set the path to the \DOS subdirectory on Drive A, DOS reminds itself in the environmental scratch pad what the values for prompt and path are. In the next steps, you are going to copy COMMAND.COM to the DOS subdirectory on Drive A and delete it from the root directory of A. When you do that , you must tell DOS that you are booting from Drive A, and that you want the booting process to find COMMAND.COM in the DOS subdirectory on Drive A. Furthermore, every time it reloads COMMAND.COM, it will know it is in the DOS subdirectory on Drive A. *You must know the correct location of* COMMAND.COM. Along with relocating COMMAND.COM, you are going to increase the size of the environment to 256 bytes.

Step 2   Using EDIT, edit and save the CONFIG.SYS file on the Bootable DOS System Disk. Add the following line to the end of the file, and do *not* leave a space between E: and 256:

SHELL=A:\DOS\COMMAND.COM A:\DOS /P /E:256

Step 3   Save the file and key in the following: A:\>**TYPE CONFIG.SYS** [Enter]

```
A:\>TYPE CONFIG.SYS
DEVICE=A:\DOS\HIMEM.SYS
DOS=HIGH
FILES=20
BUFFERS=30
NUMLOCK=OFF
DEVICE=A:\DOS\RAMDRIVE.SYS /E
DEVICE=A:\DOS\RAMDRIVE.SYS 360 512 112 /E
LASTDRIVE=H
SHELL=A:\DOS\COMMAND.COM A:\DOS /P /E:256

A:\>_
```

WHAT'S HAPPENING? You are confirming that the CONFIG.SYS file has the correct commands in it. You tell DOS to find COMMAND.COM in a location other than the root directory of the booting disk (Drive A). Instead of looking there, you are directing DOS, when it first boots, to load COMMAND.COM from the DOS subdirectory on Drive A. Then, when it needs to reload COMMAND.COM, it will find it in the subdirectory DOS on the disk in Drive A. In addition, you increased the size of the environment. Be sure that the spacing is identical to the example. If you want to try this with your hard disk, remember that if COMMAND.COM is in another location, you *must* specify that location. For example, if COMMAND.COM were in the DOS subdirectory, the CONFIG.SYS file would look as follows:

```
SHELL=C:\DOS\COMMAND.COM C:\DOS /P /E:256
```

Step 4   Key in the following: A:\>**COPY COMMAND.COM DOS** Enter

Step 5   Key in the following: A:\>**DEL COMMAND.COM** Enter

```
A:\>COPY COMMAND.COM DOS
        1 file(s) copied

A:\>DEL COMMAND.COM

A:>_
```

WHAT'S HAPPENING? You have copied COMMAND.COM to the subdirectory called DOS and deleted it from the root directory of A:\. You could not use the MOVE command because you do not have access to it.

Step 6   Reboot the system.

Step 7   Key in the following: A:\>**SET** Enter

```
A:\>SET
COMSPEC=A:\DOS\COMMAND.COM
PROMPT=$p$g
PATH C:\DOS

A:\>_
```

WHAT'S HAPPENING? The environment now has the location of COMMAND.COM in the DOS subdirectory located on Drive A. When DOS did not find COMMAND.COM in the root directory of the booting disk, it checked the SHELL directive in CONFIG.SYS to find the location of the command processor. You changed the default value of COMSPEC and at the same time increased the size of the environment. In addition, since this disk has an AUTOEXEC.BAT file that tells DOS to change the prompt and to set the path to the \DOS subdirectory on Drive A, DOS reminds itself in the environmental scratch pad what the values for PROMPT and PATH are.

13.29 The SWITCHES Command

The SWITCHES command is another DOS command introduced in MS-DOS 5.0 and enhanced in DOS 6.0. Its original purpose was to help with programs that recognized only the old-style keyboard. The old-style keyboard had the function keys on the left side. Today, the most common keyboard sold is the enhanced keyboard, which has the function keys across the top. Often, software programs assign functions to certain keys. The key assignments vary from program to program. For example, when using WordPerfect 5.1, pressing the **F3** key brings you help while pressing **Shift** + **F7** gives you a print menu. These key assignments are made by keyboard drivers. Some older programs cannot use or recognize the placement of the new keyboard locations, making the program unusable. Thus, if you have an older program, DOS may not be able to use the old-style keyboard. The SWITCHES command in the CONFIG.SYS file forces DOS to recognize the old-style conventional keyboard. You need to place this in your CONFIG.SYS file, only if you have an older program that will not operate with the new keyboard.

DOS 6.0 included some new enhancements such as eliminating the two second delay when starting MS-DOS and eliminating the ability to use the **F5** or **F8** key to bypass CONFIG.SYS or AUTOEXEC.BAT. It also has a switch if you are using Windows 3.0. The syntax is:

```
SWITCHES= /F /K /N /W
```

/F	Skips the 2-second delay after displaying the "Starting MS-DOS ..." message during startup.
/K	Forces an enhanced keyboard to behave like a conventional keyboard.
/N	Prevents you from using the F5 or F8 key to bypass startup commands. (SWITCHES /N does not prevent you from pressing CTRL+F5 or CTRL+F8 to bypass DRVSPACE.BIN; to prevent this, use the <DRVSPACE / SWITCHES> command to add the SWITCHES /N setting to your DRVSPACE.INI file.)
/W	Specifies that the WINA20.386 file has been moved to a directory other than the root directory. You need to use this switch only if you are using Microsoft Windows 3.0 in enhanced mode and have moved the WINA20.386 file from the root directory to another directory.

It would go into the CONFIG.SYS file as

```
SWITCHES=/F
```

If you wanted multiple switches, you may combine them as

```
SWITCHES=/F /W
```

Chapter Summary

1. DOS allows you to customize your system by writing a special file called CONFIG.SYS.

2. When you boot the computer, the ROM-BIOS does a self-test and checks for the DOS system files on Drive A. If there is no disk in Drive A, it looks to Drive C, then looks for and loads CONFIG.SYS, then loads COMMAND.COM, and last looks for and loads AUTOEXEC.BAT.

3. The CONFIG.SYS file is the mechanism DOS uses to change default settings or add settings for different devices.

4. CONFIG.SYS, which is an ASCII file, does not come with DOS. It is created by the user or by certain programs. Some later versions of DOS will create a CONFIG.SYS file when you use the DOS installation program.

5. The CONFIG.SYS file contains a list of statements that define the values that the user needs to define a nonstandard configuration. These are called directives.

6. The only time the commands are read in CONFIG.SYS is at the time the system is booted.

7. DOS keeps track of the number of open files. The default value for open files is eight. DOS uses five of the eight files for tracking standard input, standard output, standard error, standard printer, and standard auxiliary.

8. In CONFIG.SYS you can change the values for the files open from 8 to 255. The syntax is: FILES=*x*.

9. The BUFFERS statement or directive tells DOS how many disk buffers to use. The minimum value is 2.

10. Disk buffers act as disk and RAM go-betweens.

11. The reserved area of RAM where DOS reads from and writes to prior to reading the disk is the disk buffer area. This process is called caching.

12. If you do not exit an application properly, DOS does not flush the buffers, leaving information in memory that is not written to disk.

13. DOS uses buffers to reduce the time it needs to access the disk to improve performance.

14. Buffers can range from a minimum of 2 to a maximum of 99. The syntax is: BUFFERS=*n*[,*m*]

15. If you have too many buffers or files open, you use conventional memory and have less memory for applications.

16. You should always have a floppy DOS system disk that you can boot from.

17. Before you begin to alter the CONFIG.SYS file and/or AUTOEXEC.BAT, you should always back them up. You should also back up all device driver files.

18. If you wish to make a disk bootable, you may use the SYS command. This command copies the operating system files to a disk. The syntax is SYS drive:

19. If you want the NumLock to be set to the function keys rather than the number keys when you boot the system, you can use the NUMLOCK directive. The syntax is NUMLOCK [on|off]

20. If you have nonstandard devices, you must provide DOS with software called device drivers that must be loaded into memory prior to using the device.

21. Device drivers are installed in the CONFIG.SYS file by means of the DEVICE= statement.

22. Device drivers are special software programs that you provide to DOS for handling nonstandard I/O.

23. DOS comes with some device drivers. Other device drivers are dependent on the specific system hardware.

24. Virtual disks are logical disk drives that are placed in RAM and are much faster than physical drives, but virtual drives are volatile.

25. You can have several virtual disk drives. The syntax is:

```
DEVICE=[d:][path]RAMDRIVE.SYS  [DiskSize  SectorSize] [/E] [/A]
```

26. If you have extended or expanded memory you can place virtual drives there.

27. DOS below 5.0 cannot recognize any memory above 640 KB.

28. Memory comes in three types: conventional, expanded, and extended.

29. Conventional memory is the first 640 KB of memory.

30. The adapter segment is the area between 640 KB and 1 MB of memory which is reserved for such information as display adapters and network adapters. It is also called reserved memory and upper memory.

31. Extended memory is memory above 1 MB.

32. Most application programs cannot directly use extended memory. However, if you have DOS 4.0 and above, you can place virtual disks there.

33. Expanded memory can be used in any computer system. An expanded memory card must be purchased and installed. You must use a device driver to make expanded memory work.

34. The expanded memory driver makes use of the adapter segment area to create a page frame. The EMM (expanded memory manager) pages information in and out of the page frame from the expanded memory board. This process is called bank switching.

35. Extended memory can be turned into expanded memory by means of software drivers, because more programs can recognize expanded memory than extended memory.

36. The upper memory area becomes important if you use DOS 5.0 or above. Upper memory is the area immediately adjacent to the first 640 KB of conventional memory. Unused portions are called upper memory blocks (UMB). If you have DOS 5.0 or above, you can place memory resident programs and device drivers in upper memory with the assistance of the HIMEM.SYS and EMM386.EXE memory drivers.

37. The high memory area is the first 64 KB of extended memory. If you have DOS 5.0 or above, you can run DOS in high memory.

38. Real mode means that programs must run in the first 1 MB of memory. Protected mode means that both programs and data can use extended memory. DOS runs in real mode.

39. The MEM command, introduced in DOS 4.0, gives information on extended and expanded memory. The syntax is:

```
MEM  [/CLASSIFY  |  /DEBUG  |  /FREE | MODULE MODULENAME] [/PAGE]
```

40. In order to use extended memory, you must install a memory manager in CONFIG.SYS. The extended memory manager provided with DOS is HIMEM.SYS. It must go first in the CONFIG.SYS file and is loaded with a DEVICE= directive. The syntax is:

```
DEVICE=[drive:][path]HIMEM.SYS
```

41. The default value for the last drive DOS recognizes is one more drive than you have installed physically. By means of the LASTDRIVE statement, you can increase the number of drives DOS can recognize up to Drive Z. The syntax is:

```
LASTDRIVE=x
```

42. If you have extended memory, you can load DOS itself in the High Memory Area (HMA). The syntax is DOS=HIGH.

43. The SHELL statement or directive allows you to place COMMAND.COM in a directory other than the root directory of the booting disk. You may also expand the size of the environment. The syntax for SHELL is:

```
SHELL=drive:\path\COMMAND.COM  drive:\path\  /P  /E:size
```

44. DOS must keep track of two parts of COMMAND.COM—resident and transient. When application programs need memory, DOS allows them to overwrite the transient part of DOS. When the application finishes, DOS must reload COMMAND.COM and, hence, must know its location.

45. A SWITCHES statement or directive forces DOS to use the old-style keyboard, eliminates the two-second delay, turns off the F5 or F8 keys, and indicates the location of WINA20.386 in Windows 3.0. The syntax for SWITCHES is:

```
SWITCHES /F  /K  /N  /W
```

Key Terms

Adapter segment	Flushing the buffer	Protected mode
Bank switching	High memory area	RAM disk
Caching	(HMA)	Real mode
COMSPEC	Look-ahead buffers	Reserved memory
Conventional memory	Memory manager	Startup disk
Directives	Multitasking	Upper memory area
Disk buffers	Overhead	(UMA)
Disk intensive	Page	Upper memory
Expanded memory	Page frame	blocks (UMB)
Extended memory	Partitioning	Virtual disk
File handle		

Discussion Questions

1. What is the function of CONFIG.SYS?
2. List and explain the function of five of the commands that can only be used in CONFIG.SYS.
3. Describe the five open files that DOS uses. Explain the function of two of these files.

4. Give the syntax of the FILES command and explain each part of the syntax.
5. Why is it unwise to use the maximum number of files available to you?
6. What is the purpose and function of disk buffers?
7. Explain the purpose and function of caching.
8. Before you alter the CONFIG.SYS or AUTOEXEC.BAT files, what steps should you take and why?
9. Give the syntax of the SYS command and explain each part of the syntax.
10. Why would you want to set NUMLOCK to off?
11. Explain the purpose and function of device drivers.
12. Give the syntax of the DEVICE command and explain each part of the syntax.
13. Explain the purpose and function of a virtual disk.
14. What problems can occur when using a virtual disk?
15. Explain the purpose and function of conventional memory and upper memory.
16. Explain the purpose and function of extended and expanded memory.
17. What is upper memory? What is high memory? When and why is each used?
18. Compare and contrast real mode with protected mode.
19. Why do users want to have expanded/extended memory installed on their computers?
20. What is the purpose and function of the MEM command?
21. Give the syntax of the MEM command and explain each part of the syntax.
22. What is the purpose and function of the memory manager?
23. How can you install a memory manager in CONFIG.SYS?
24. Explain the purpose and function of the LASTDRIVE command.
25. DOS can be loaded into high memory. Why would you want to do this? How would you do this?
26. When would you use the SET command?
27. What is the purpose and function of the SHELL command?
28. Give two reasons for moving COMMAND.COM from the root directory of the booting disk to another location.
29. What is the environment and how is it used?
30. What is the purpose and function of the SWITCHES command?

Chapter 14

Utility Programs

After finishing this chapter, you will be able to:

1. Explain the purpose and function of DOSKEY.
2. Explain the purpose and function of DOSKEY macros.
3. Explain how replaceable parameters are used in macros and how to save macros.
4. Explain the purpose and function of ANSI.SYS.
5. Explain why you would want to change screen colors or remap a key.
6. Explain the purpose and function of the MODE command.
7. Compare and contrast serial and parallel communication.
8. Explain how to use the MODE command to change characteristics of the printer, the typematic rate, and the monitor, and be able to check the status of devices attached to the system.
9. Explain what computer viruses are, how they are transmitted, and how they can be detected.
10. Explain the purpose and function of MSAV and VSAFE.
11. Explain the purpose and function of MSBACKUP.
12. Compare and contrast full, incremental, and differential backups.

Student Outcomes

1.   Load and use DOSKEY to recall and edit DOS command lines, keep a command history, and write macros.
2.   Create and save macros.
3.   Use replaceable parameters in macros.
4.   Use ANSI.SYS to set foreground and background colors on the screen.
5.   Use ANSI.SYS to remap keys.
6.   Use the MODE command to change the display and typematic rate.
7.   Use the MODE command to check the status of devices.
8.   Use MSAV to check for any viruses.
9.   Use MSBACKUP to backup and restore files.

Chapter Overview

In addition to the commands you have learned, DOS provides other utility programs that go beyond manipulating files and disks, providing informational reports, and customizing your system. Many DOS system utility programs increase the usefulness of DOS. These programs include one that allows you to correct keyboard errors easily as well as write commands faster (macros) using DOSKEY. You may also alter screen colors and change keys on the keyboard using ANSI.SYS. You may control the different peripheral devices on your computer with variations of the MODE command. MSAV, introduced in DOS 6.0, ensures that your computer does not have any viruses. If you wish to monitor the possibility of viruses invading your computer, you may use VSAFE. The MSBACKUP program provides an easy way to back up and restore files. In this chapter, you will take a look at all these programs.

14.1 DOSKEY

DOSKEY, introduced in DOS 5.0, brought a much needed tool for working with DOS commands. You may have already used it to correct keystroke errors. Because DOSKEY is an external, **memory-resident command**, you must load it into memory. Once it is loaded into memory, it remains in memory and acts like an internal command, which means that you need not to reload it from disk when you wish to access it. Memory-resident commands are also referred to as **TSRs** (Terminate and Stay Resident). The normal process with any external command (program) is to execute it by keying in the command name. DOS goes to the disk and looks for a program with that name, loads it into memory, and turns control over to that program. When loaded, that program occupies and uses RAM. When you exit the program, DOS reclaims the memory (see Figure 14.1).

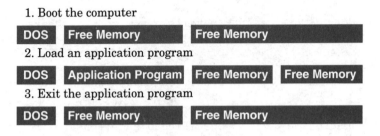

Figure 14.1   Normal Operating Procedure

When you load a TSR, the process works initially as it does with any external command. You still execute it by keying in the command name. DOS goes to the disk and looks for a program with that name, loads it into memory, and turns control over to that program. That program occupies and uses RAM. However, the TSR holds on to the memory it occupies. It does not release the memory for the work session of the computer. When you need to use the TSR, DOS no longer has to go to the disk, but, instead, goes directly to memory. Thus, the "external" command acts like an internal command. You may still load application programs as desired, but the application program cannot use the memory that the TSR has claimed (see Figure 14.2).

Figure 14.2   Loading a TSR Procedure

DOSKEY is a DOS-provided TSR that, once loaded into memory, remains there until you turn off the computer or reboot. Some TSRs allow you to unload them in the middle of a work session so you do not have to reboot to reclaim memory. DOSKEY does not allow this. DOSKEY lets you recall DOS command lines, edit them, keep a command history, and write macros. The syntax is:

```
DOSKEY [/REINSTALL] [/BUFSIZE=size] [/MACROS] [/HISTORY] [/INSERT
I OVERSTRIKE] [macroname=[text]]
```

/REINSTALL	Installs a new copy of Doskey.
/BUFSIZE=size	Sets size of command history buffer.
/MACROS	Displays all Doskey macros.
/HISTORY	Displays all commands stored in memory.
/INSERT	Specifies that new text you type is inserted in old text.
/OVERSTRIKE	Specifies that new text overwrites old text.
macroname	Specifies a name for a macro you create.
text	Specifies commands you want to record.

⬆ and ⬇ recall commands; **Esc** clears the command line; **F7** displays command history; **Alt** + **F7** clears command history; **F8** searches command history; **F9** selects a command by number; **Alt** + **F10** clears macro definitions.

The following are some special codes in DOSKEY macro definitions:

$T	Command separator. Allows multiple commands in a macro.
$1-$9	Batch parameters. Equivalent to %1-%9 in batch programs.
$*	Symbol replaced by everything following macro name on command line.

14.2 Activity: Loading and Using DOSKEY

Note: A:\> is displayed and the path is set to C:\DOS. The DATA disk, not the Bootable DOS System Disk you used in Chapter 13, is in Drive A.

Step 1   Key in the following: A:\>**DOSKEY /BUFSIZE=2048** **Enter**

```
A:\>DOSKEY /BUFSIZE=2048

A:\>_
```

WHAT'S HAPPENING? You have installed DOSKEY in memory. The default value that DOS allocates in memory is 512 bytes. Since that is really not enough to use DOSKEY effectively, you increased the size to 2 K.

Step 2   Key in the following:

A:\>**DIR *.TXT** **Enter**

A:\>**DIR C:\DOS6BK*.99** **Enter**

A:\>**TYPE AWARD.MOV** **Enter**

A:\>**VOL** **Enter**

A:\>**TYPE C:\DOS6BK\SPORTS\FOOT-PRO.TMS** **Enter**

```
        Driving Miss Daisy
        Out of Africa
        Schindler's List


        A:\>VOL

          Volume in drive A is DATADISK
          Volume Serial Number is 2F26-1901

        A:\>TYPE C:\DOS6BK\SPORTS\FOOT-PRO.TMS
        PROFESSIONAL FOOTBALL TEAMS

        Los Angeles Rams
        Chicago Bears
        Dallas Cowboys
        Pittsburg Steelers
        San Francisco 49'ers
        Detroit Lions
        Denver Broncos
        New York Jets
        St. Louis Browns
        New Orleans Saints

        A:\>_
```

WHAT'S HAPPENING? You have executed several commands and can now use the DOSKEY editing keys to recall and edit commands. The following tables illustrate the keys you may use to edit a command history.

F7	Displays a list of commands.
Alt + **F7**	Clears the list of commands.
↑	Allows you to scroll up through the commands.
↓	Allows you to scroll down through the commands.
F8	Searches the list for command that starts with text you provide.
F9	Selects the command from list by number.
PgUp	Displays the oldest command in list.
PgDn	Displays the newest command in list.
Esc	Erases the displayed command from screen.
Alt + **F10**	Clears the macros.

Table 14.1   **DOSKEY Command Summary**

[Home]	Moves cursor to beginning of displayed command.
[End]	Moves cursor to end of displayed command.
[←]	Moves cursor back one character.
[→]	Moves cursor forward one character.
[Ctrl] + [←]	Moves cursor back one word.
[Ctrl] + [→]	Moves cursor forward one word.
[Backspace]	Moves cursor back one character. If you are in insert mode, will also delete character preceding cursor.
[Delete]	Deletes character at cursor.
[Ctrl] + [End]	Deletes all characters from cursor to end of line.
[Ctrl] + [Home]	Deletes all characters from cursor to beginning of line.
[Esc]	Clears command.
[Insert]	Toggles between insert and overstrike mode.

Table 14.2 **Editing Key Summary**

Step 3 Press the [↑] arrow three times.

```
A:\>TYPE AWARD.MOV_
```

Step 4 Press the [Backspace] key to delete AWARD.MOV. Key in **JAN.TXT** [Enter]

```
A:\>TYPE JAN.TXT
File not found - JAN.TXT

A:\>_
```

WHAT'S HAPPENING? You edited the line by deleting AWARD.MOV and keying in JAN.TXT.

Step 5 Press [F7]

```
A:\>
1: DIR *.TXT
2: DIR C:\DOS6BK\*.99
3: TYPE AWARD.MOV
```

```
    4: VOL
    5: TYPE C:\DOS6BK\SPORTS\FOOT-PRO.TMS
    6: TYPE JAN.TXT
    A:\>_
```

WHAT'S HAPPENING? Pressing the F7 key lists all the commands that you have keyed in. You may edit any line you wish by selecting the line number, but you must press the F9 key first.

Step 6   Press F9. Press 5

```
    A:\>
    1: DIR *.TXT
    2: DIR C:\DOS6BK\*.99
    3: TYPE AWARD.MOV
    4: VOL
    5: TYPE C:\DOS6BK\SPORTS\FOOT-PRO.TMS
    6: TYPE JAN.TXT
    A:\>Line number: 5
```

WHAT'S HAPPENING? By pressing F9, you saw the `Line number:` prompt. You then keyed in the line number (5) of the command you wished to edit.

Step 7   Press Enter

```
    A:\>TYPE C:\DOS6BK\SPORTS\FOOT-PRO.TMS_
```

WHAT'S HAPPENING? You can edit this line or simply execute it again.

Step 8   Press the **Backspace** key to delete PRO.TMS. Key in **COL.TMS** Enter

```
    A:\>TYPE C:\DOS6BK\SPORTS\FOOT-COL.TMS
    COLLEGE FOOTBALL TEAMS

    Michigan Wolverines
    USC Trojans
    UCLA Bruins
    Purdue Boilermakers
    Michigan State Spartans
    Standford Cardinal
    Ohio Buckeyes
    Notre Dame's Fighting Irish
    Nebraska's Cornhuskers
    Princeton Tigers

    A:\>_
```

WHAT'S HAPPENING? You displayed the list of commands in numerical order. You selected a command, by number, that you were interested in. You then edited the line. If you wish to delete a line quickly, there is a shortcut—the **Esc** key.

Step 9   Press the ⬆ one time.

Step 10   Press **Esc**

```
A:\>_
```

WHAT'S HAPPENING? You quickly deleted the command that was there. You can also search for a previously entered command by pressing the first letter or letters of the command you are interested in.

Step 11   Press **D**. Press **F8**

```
A:\>DIR C:\DOS6BK\*.99_
```

WHAT'S HAPPENING? You selected a command by keying in the first letter and then pressing **F8**. With DOSKEY, you can also have more than one command on a line. In order to do this, you must use special keys—you must press the **Ctrl** + T between commands.

Step 12   Press **Esc**

Step 13   Key in the following:

A:\>**CD BATCH** **Ctrl** + T **DIR** *.TXT **Ctrl** + T **CD** \ **Enter**

```
A:\>CD BATCH ¶ DIR *.TXT ¶ CD \
A:\>CD BATCH

A:\BATCH> DIR *.TXT

 Volume in drive A is DATADISK
 Volume Serial Number is 2F26-1901
 Directory of A:\BATCH

MENU     TXT          102 07-01-94   5:12p
END      TXT          166 07-02-94  11:41a
         2 file(s)            268 bytes
                         647,168 bytes free

A:\BATCH> CD \

A:\>_
```

WHAT'S HAPPENING? You executed three commands on one command line by separating each command with ⌷Ctrl⌷ + T. If you want to clear all the commands, you may do so.

Step 14   Press ⌷Alt⌷ + ⌷F7⌷

Step 15   Press the ⌷↑⌷ arrow one time.

```
A:\>_
```

WHAT'S HAPPENING? You cleared all the commands that were in the buffer. There are no remaining commands to scroll through.

14.3 DOSKEY Macros

Macros are a series of commands that, like batch files, can be executed with a single command. A DOSKEY macro allows you to assign a shortcut name to a command or series of commands so you can quickly recall the command later. Since macros are stored in memory, they run much faster than batch files. Macros are stored in memory, so they are lost each time you reboot the system and must be reinstalled each time you boot. Macros also occupy space in memory whether or not they are being used. On the other hand, batch files occupy memory only when you are executing them. Batch files reside on disk. Since batch files are saved to disk, there is no limit to the size of batch files. Macros are limited to one line with no more than 127 characters. You cannot call a macro from a macro, nor can you do branching or looping as you can with batch files.

As you know, DOS executes commands by first checking the internal table of commands, then .COM, .EXE, and .BAT in that order. Macros are executed prior to any other commands including internal commands, making macros very fast. The syntax is:

```
DOSKEY macroname=command
```

14.4 Activity: Creating Macros

Note: The A:\> is displayed and the path is set to C:\DOS. The DATA disk is in Drive A. DOSKEY is loaded.

Step 1   Key in the following: A:\>**DIR CLASS /ON** ⌷Enter⌷

```
 Volume in drive A is DATADISK
  Volume Serial Number is 2F26-1901
  Directory of A:\CLASS


      .            <DIR>         06-21-94   1:02a
      ..           <DIR>         06-21-94   1:02a
 APR       ABC            71 11-23-95  10:42a
```

```
APR        PAR             71 11-23-95   10:42a
APR        BUD             18 12-06-94   10:46a
FEB        ABC             74 11-23-95   10:41a
FEB        PAR             74 11-23-95   10:41a
JAN        ABC             72 11-23-95   10:41a
JAN        FIL             71 11-23-95   10:42a
JAN        PAR             72 11-23-95   10:41a
JAN        BUD             72 11-23-95   10:41a
MAR        ABC             70 11-23-95   10:42a
MAR        FIL             70 11-23-95   10:42a
MAR        PAR             70 11-23-95   10:42a
MAR        BUD             70 11-23-95   10:42a
           15 file(s)             875 bytes
                            647,168 bytes free

A:\>_
```

WHAT'S HAPPENING? You see an alphabetical display of the files in the CLASS subdirectory on the DATA disk. If you want DIR to display file names in alphabetical order in the CLASS directory every time, you can write a macro.

Step 2   Key in the following: **DOSKEY DIR=DIR A:\CLASS /ON** ⟨Enter⟩

```
A:\>DOSKEY DIR=DIR A:\CLASS /ON

A:\>_
```

WHAT'S HAPPENING? You have defined the DIR command so that every time you want a directory listing, it will display only the files in the CLASS subdirectory in alphabetical order by name.

Step 3   Key in the following: A:\> **DIR** ⟨Enter⟩

```
Volume in drive A is DATADISK
 Volume Serial Number is 2F26-1901
 Directory of A:\CLASS

 .              <DIR>           06-21-94    1:02a
 ..             <DIR>           06-21-94    1:02a
APR        ABC             71 11-23-95   10:42a
APR        PAR             71 11-23-95   10:42a
APR        BUD             18 12-06-94   10:46a
FEB        ABC             74 11-23-95   10:41a
FEB        PAR             74 11-23-95   10:41a
JAN        ABC             72 11-23-95   10:41a
JAN        FIL             71 11-23-95   10:42a
JAN        PAR             72 11-23-95   10:41a
JAN        BUD             72 11-23-95   10:41a
MAR        ABC             70 11-23-95   10:42a
```

```
    MAR       FIL           70 11-23-95  10:42a
    MAR       PAR           70 11-23-95  10:42a
    MAR       BUD           70 11-23-95  10:42a
            15 file(s)              875 bytes
                            647,168 bytes free


    A:\>_
```

WHAT'S HAPPENING? Now, every time you use the DIR command, the macro you wrote supersedes it. However, what if you want to use the DIR command and not the macro you created? You can always use the "real" command, but you must press the spacebar before executing the command.

Step 4   Key in the following: A:\>**DIR** *.99 Enter

Step 5   Key in the following: A:\>[Space Bar] **DIR** *.99 Enter

```
    FEB       ABC           74 11-23-95  10:41a
    FEB       PAR           74 11-23-95  10:41a
    JAN       ABC           72 11-23-95  10:41a
    JAN       FIL           71 11-23-95  10:42a
    JAN       PAR           72 11-23-95  10:41a
    JAN       BUD           72 11-23-95  10:41a
    MAR       ABC           70 11-23-95  10:42a
    MAR       FIL           70 11-23-95  10:42a
    MAR       PAR           70 11-23-95  10:42a
    MAR       BUD           70 11-23-95  10:42a
            15 file(s)              875 bytes
                            647,168 bytes free

    A:\> DIR *.99

     Volume in drive A is DATADISK
     Volume Serial Number is 2F26-1901
     Directory of A:\

    APR       99            71 08-14-94   9:18p
    JAN       99            72 11-23-95  10:41a
             2 file(s)              143 bytes
                            647,168 bytes free

    A:\>_
```

WHAT'S HAPPENING? When you keyed in DIR, you saw that the macro was executed. When you preceded the DIR with a space, you could run the normal DIR command. To cancel a macro, you key in the name of the macro equal to nothing.

Step 6   Key in the following: A:\>**DOSKEY DIR=** Enter

Step 7   Key in the following: A:\>**DIR *.99** [Enter]

```
A:\>DOSKEY DIR=

A:\>DIR *.99

 Volume in drive A is DATADISK
 Volume Serial Number is 2F26-1901
 Directory of A:\

APR       99              71 08-14-94   9:18p
JAN       99              72 11-23-95  10:41a
          2 file(s)            143 bytes
                          647,168 bytes free

A:\>_
```

WHAT'S HAPPENING? The DIR command is no longer a macro and has returned to its default value.

14.5 Replaceable Parameters in Macros

Just as you can use replaceable parameters in batch files, you can also use them in macros. However, instead of the symbols %0 through %9, you must use the dollar sign—$0 through $9. Macros are stored in the same buffer used to track command history. To use the redirection symbols, the pipe, or [Ctrl] + T to include more than one command on a line, you must use special macro symbols (see Table 14.3).

$T or $t	Command separator. Allows multiple commands in a macro.
$*	Replaced by everything following macro name on command line.
$G or $g	The redirection symbol >.
$L or $l	The redirection symbol <.
GG or gg	The append redirection symbol >>.
$B or $b	The pipe symbol ¦.

Table 14.3   **Special Macro Symbols**

14.6 Activity: Using Replaceable Parameters

Note: The A:\> will be displayed with the path set to C:\DOS. The DATA disk is in Drive A. DOSKEY will be loaded.

Step 1   Key in the following: A:\>**DOSKEY WHEREIS=DIR \$1 /S /P** [Enter]

```
A:\>DOSKEY WHEREIS=DIR \$1 /S /P

A:\>_
```

WHAT'S HAPPENING? You have created a macro that will locate any file in any directory.

Step 2   Key in the following: A:\>**WHEREIS *.TST** [Enter]

```
Volume in drive A is DATADISK
 Volume Serial Number is 2F26-1901

Directory of A:\

APR    .  TST           71 11-23-95  10:42a
         1 file(s)           71 bytes

Directory of A:\POLYSCI

FIRST     TST           72 11-23-95  10:41a
         1 file(s)           72 bytes

Directory of A:\POLYSCI\FRANCE

LAST      TST           72 11-23-95  10:41a
         1 file(s)           72 bytes

Total files listed:
         3 file(s)          215 bytes
                    647,168 bytes free

A:\>_
```

WHAT'S HAPPENING? You can now locate any file quickly. You can combine commands in macros, but remember that they must be on one line and that one line cannot exceed 127 characters. Furthermore, remember that the symbols are different from those you learned in batch files. To use the pipe, you must use $B.

Step 3   Key in the following:
A:\>**DOSKEY WHEREIS=DIR $1 /S $B FIND /V "Volume"** [Enter]

Step 4   Key in the following: A:\>**WHEREIS *.TST** [Enter]

```
A:\>DIR *.TST /S | FIND /V "Volume"

Directory of A:\
```

```
APR       TST                71 11-23-95  10:42a
          1 file(s)                 71 bytes

Directory of A:\POLYSCI

FIRST     TST                72 11-23-95  10:41a
          1 file(s)                 72 bytes

Directory of A:\POLYSCI\FRANCE

LAST      TST                72 11-23-95  10:41a
          1 file(s)                 72 bytes

Total files listed:
          3 file(s)                215 bytes
                           646,656 bytes free

A:\>_
```

WHAT'S HAPPENING? You can still locate any file quickly, but now you have excluded the Volume in drive A by filtering it out of your display.

Step 5   Key in the following:
          A:\>**DOSKEY RO=FOR %a IN ($*) DO ATTRIB +R %a [Enter]**

Step 6   Key in the following:
          A:\>**DOSKEY NRO=FOR %a IN ($*) DO ATTRIB -R %a [Enter]**

```
A:\>DOSKEY RO=FOR %a in ($*) DO ATTRIB +R %a

A:\>DOSKEY NRO=FOR %a IN ($*) DO ATTRIB -R %a

A:\>_
```

WHAT'S HAPPENING? You have created two macros that will allow you to make any group of files read-only. The $* is equivalent to %1 in a batch file.

Step 7   Key in the following: A:\>**RO *.99 *.AAA [Enter]**

Step 8   Key in the following: A:\>**DIR /AR**

```
A:\>ATTRIB +R APR.99

A:\>ATTRIB +R JAN.99

A:\>ATTRIB +R WILDTHR.AAA

A:\>DIR /AR
```

```
Volume in drive A is DATADISK
Volume Serial Number is 2F26-1901
Directory of A:\

APR        99             71 08-14-94    9:18p
JAN        99             72 11-23-95   10:41a
WILDTHR    AAA           180 05-07-93    9:03a
THIS       ONE            42 11-23-94    7:13a
HOMEBUD    TKR         8,064 02-28-94    6:19p
           5 file(s)          8,429 bytes
                           647,168 bytes free

A:\>_
```

WHAT'S HAPPENING? You have quickly made groups of files read-only.

Step 9   Key in the following: A:\> **NRO *.99 *.AAA** Enter

```
A:\>NRO *.99 *.AAA
A:\>FOR %a IN (*.99 *.AAA) DO ATTRIB -R %a

A:\>ATTRIB -R APR.99

A:\>ATTRIB -R JAN.99

A:\>ATTRIB -R WILDTHR.AAA

A:\>_
```

WHAT'S HAPPENING? You have just as easily made groups of files that are not read-only.

14.7 Saving Macros

If macros are available only in memory, then, whenever you reboot the system, you will lose whatever macros you have and/or the history of commands you have created. DOSKEY allows you to review what you have created and to save whatever macros you desire. You can save macros and commands in a batch file. The batch file can be included in your AUTOEXEC.BAT and loaded automatically when you boot the system, or you can simply store them in a batch file that you can execute at any time. The parameters are /HISTORY or /MACROS, which can be abbreviated to /H or /M. Since the output is displayed on the screen, it may be redirected to a batch file. In order for the batch file to execute, each command in the file must have a DOSKEY preceding it.

14.8 Activity: Saving Macros in Batch Files

Note: The A:\> will be displayed with the path set to C:\DOS. The DATA disk is in Drive A. DOSKEY will be loaded.

Step 1   Press [Alt] + [F7]

WHAT'S HAPPENING? You have cleared all the commands you keyed in.

Step 2   Press [Alt] + [F10]

WHAT'S HAPPENING? You have cleared any macros that you had created.

Step 3   Key in the following: A:\>**DIR *.CAP** [Enter]

Step 4   Key in the following: A:\>**VER** [Enter]

Step 5   Key in the following: A:\>**DOSKEY DIR=DIR /ON** [Enter]

Step 6   Key in the following: A:\>**DOSKEY HIDE=ATTRIB +H $1** [Enter]

Step 7   Key in the following: A:\>**DOSKEY /H** [Enter]

```
STATE     CAP           260 08-22-94  11:54p
SORTED    CAP           260 08-22-94  11:54p
          2 file(s)           520 bytes
                         647,168 bytes free


A:\>VER

MS-DOS Version 6.22


A:\>DOSKEY DIR=DIR /ON

A:\>DOSKEY HIDE=ATTRIB +H $1

A:\>DOSKEY /H
DIR *.CAP
VER
DOSKEY DIR=DIR /ON
DOSKEY HIDE=ATTRIB +H $1
DOSKEY /H

A:\>_
```

WHAT'S HAPPENING? The /H parameter showed you a history of all the commands you keyed in. The /M command used with DOSKEY will display only the macros.

Step 8   Key in the following: A:\>**DOSKEY /M** [Enter]

```
A:\>DOSKEY /M
DIR=DIR /ON
HIDE=ATTRIB +H $1

A:\>_
```

WHAT'S HAPPENING? Since the display wrote to the screen, the output from the DOSKEY /M command uses standard output. Therefore, you can redirect this to a file.

Step 9   Key in the following:
          A:\>**DOSKEY /M > BATCH\MACROS.BAT** Enter

Step 10   Key in the following: A:\>**TYPE BATCH\MACROS.BAT** Enter

```
A:\>DOSKEY /M > BATCH\MACROS.BAT

A:\>TYPE BATCH\MACROS.BAT
DIR=DIR /ON
HIDE=ATTRIB +H $1

A:\>_
```

WHAT'S HAPPENING? You have saved your macros to a batch file called MACROS.BAT in the BATCH subdirectory. This batch file will not work until you use EDIT and add DOSKEY.

Step 11   Use EDIT to edit and save BATCH\MACROS.BAT so it looks as follows:

        DOSKEY DIR=DIR /ON
        DOSKEY HIDE=ATTRIB +H $1

Step 12   Key in the following: A:\>**TYPE BATCH\MACROS.BAT** Enter

```
A:\>TYPE BATCH\MACROS.BAT
DOSKEY DIR=DIR /ON
DOSKEY HIDE=ATTRIB +H $1

A:\>_
```

WHAT'S HAPPENING? Now, you could either place MACROS.BAT in the AUTOEXEC.BAT to execute automatically every time you boot the system or just have it in your BATCH subdirectory to install when you choose, provided you have set your path to include the BATCH subdirectory. Obviously, DOSKEY would also have to be installed first.

Step 13   Press Alt + F7

Step 14 Press [Alt] + [F10]

WHAT'S HAPPENING? You have cleared all commands and the macros you created.

14.9 Introducing ANSI.SYS

ANSI.SYS is a DOS device driver that allows you to communicate with the keyboard and the monitor. ANSI stands for the American National Standards Institute. A device driver has special codes that lets a computer send and receive information from devices that are attached to it. Since you can already key in information and see it displayed on the screen, you may wonder why you need a special device driver to communicate. The answer is that ANSI.SYS is a driver that *extends* functions of this. Once installed, via the CONFIG.SYS file, it allows you to remap the keyboard, change colors on the screen, assign certain attributes to the cursor, and position the cursor. All ANSI.SYS does is allow you to activate these changes. To do so, you may use the PROMPT command, the TYPE command, or the ECHO command. Again, there are special codes you will need to use (see Table 14.4).

	Code	Description
	0	All attributes off—default values
	1	High-intensity text
	2*	Low-intensity text
	3*	Italic text
Screen Attributes	4	Underline
	5	Blink
	6*	Rapid-blinking text
	7	Reverse video
	8	Hidden characters
	30	Black
	31	Red
	32	Green
Foreground Colors	33	Yellow
	34	Blue
	35	Magenta
	36	Cyan
	37	White

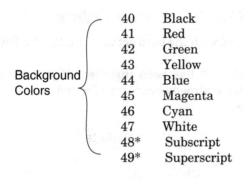

Background Colors	40	Black
	41	Red
	42	Green
	43	Yellow
	44	Blue
	45	Magenta
	46	Cyan
	47	White
	48*	Subscript
	49*	Superscript

*Not supported on VGA
Note: Not all values are supported in all versions of ANSI.SYS

Table 14.4   ***ANSI.SYS Codes***

You may note that your application programs display in color or remap keys without the installation of ANSI.SYS because most application programs communicate directly with the keyboard and the monitor and have special codes built-in to perform these functions. Remember, in order for ANSI.SYS to work, you must have a line in your CONFIG.SYS file that states DEVICE=C:\DOS\ANSI.SYS.

ANSI.SYS communicates with you. You give instructions to ANSI.SYS by sending special escape codes to the standard output device—the monitor. ANSI.SYS knows you want to do something because you send it a **signature**—a sequence of data that is used for identification. ANSI.SYS requires two signature characters: the escape character (ASCII value of 027) and the [(square left bracket with the ASCII value of 019). When you send these codes to ANSI.SYS, it knows it is supposed to do something. What it does depends on the codes that follow. For instance 44m sets the background color to blue. The 44 is the color blue and the m tells ANSI.SYS that you are working with the monitor. It must be a lowercase m because ANSI.SYS is case-sensitive. In the examples that follow, you must be sure to key in exactly what is shown in the steps—case and all.

Because the TYPE, ECHO, and PROMPT commands display characters on the screen, you can use any of these commands to send the escape sequences and instructions to ANSI.SYS. You cannot, however, merely press the **Esc** key to enter the escape sequence. If you press the **Esc** key, DOS will cancel the previously issued command. If you have DOSKEY installed, pressing the **Esc** key, returns you to the prompt. Again, you must use special techniques.

There can also be other problems. If you have programs that use certain escape sequences, you may not be able to use the ECHO or TYPE technique to alter colors. You will have to use PROMPT. Thus, ECHO or TYPE is shown, but if this does not work for you, the alternative PROMPT command is also shown. This seems to be true only in changing colors.

14.10 Activity: Using ANSI.SYS To Change Colors

Note 1: The A:\> will be displayed with the path set to C:\DOS. The DATA disk is in Drive A.

Note 2: It is assumed that ANSI.SYS has been installed. If you are in a lab environment, it should have already been done for you.

Note 3: Remember, case matters.

Step 1 Key in the following: A:\>**MEM /M ANSI** **Enter**

```
A:\>MEM /M ANSI

ANSI is using the following memory:

  Segment   Region        Total         Type
  -------   ------        ------        ------
   00278                  4192    (4K)  Installed Device=ANSI
                          ------
  Total Size:            4,192   (4K)

A:\>_
```

WHAT'S HAPPENING? You are verifying that ANSI.SYS is installed. If you get the message ANSI.SYS is not currently in memory, you know that it is not installed. If you are in a lab environment, check with your lab instructor. If you are working on your own computer, edit the CONFIG.SYS file and add the line DEVICE=C:\DOS\ANSI.SYS. After you save CONFIG.SYS, reboot the system.

Step 2 Key in the following: A:\>**PROMPT $e[44;31m$p$g** **Enter**

Step 3 Key in the following: A:\>**CLS** **Enter**

Step 4 Key in the following: A:\>**DIR *.99** **Enter**

```
A:\>DIR *.99

 Volume in drive A is DATADISK
 Volume Serial Number is 2F26-1901
 Directory of A:\

APR      99            71 08-14-94   9:18p
JAN      99            72 11-23-95  10:41a
        2 file(s)          143 bytes
                       646,656 bytes free

A:\>_
```

WHAT'S HAPPENING? Your display should be a blue background with red letters. The command you entered was PROMPT followed by $e and [. This sequence alerted ANSI.SYS that you were about to send it some characters. The 44 was the code for the blue background color. You then used a ; as a delimiter. The 31 was the code for a red foreground color. The m indicated it was for the monitor. You included the pg because if you did not, you would have no prompt displayed. Using CLS allowed the entire screen to reflect your color choice. Now you want to return to the default colors.

Step 5   Key in the following: A:\>**PROMPT $e[0m$p$g** [Enter]

Step 6   Key in the following: A:\>**CLS** [Enter]

```
A:\>_
```

WHAT'S HAPPENING? You have returned the colors to their default values. You may also use ECHO and TYPE. This is tricky because you cannot directly enter the [Esc] character. The secret is to use EDIT but disable the menu by pressing [Ctrl] + P. Then you can press [Esc]. When you see the notation [Ctrl] + P, it means to press the [Ctrl] + P keys.

Step 7   Use EDIT to create a file called BLUE.SCR. While in EDIT, do not press [Enter] unless indicated. When you are in EDIT, do the following:

Step 8   Press [Ctrl] + **P**

Step 9   Hold down the [Alt] key and press **2** then **7** on the numeric key pad. Release the [Alt] key.

Step 10   Key in the following: **[44;37m** [Enter]

WHAT'S HAPPENING? Pressing [Ctrl] + P disabled the EDIT menu. Pressing [Alt] activated the numeric key pad. The number 27 is the ASCII code for [Esc]. The ← represents the [Esc] character on the screen.

Step 11   Save the file.

Step 12   Key in the following: A:\>**TYPE BLUE.SCR** Enter

```
A:\>TYPE BLUE.SCR



A:\>_
```

WHAT'S HAPPENING? You should now have a blue background with white letters. If you do not see your screen change colors and/or you suddenly get erratic behavior with devices, such as a printer ejecting pages for no reason, it could be because you have other devices that have set ANSI.SYS values which conflict with using the BLUE.SCR file. This problem exists only with changing screen colors. If this is true, you can solve the problem by using the PROMPT command. The PROMPT command is not affected by any other programs or devices. You may key in PROMPT $e[44;37m$p$g at the command line and press Enter. Then key in CLS and press Enter, followed by CLS. If you wish to have a process that is automated, create a batch file called BLUE.BAT with the following commands in it:

> **@ECHO OFF**
> **PROMPT $e[44:37m$p$g**
> **CLS**

Step 13   Key in the following: A:\>**PROMPT $e[0m$p$g** Enter

Step 14   Key in the following: A:\>**CLS** Enter

```
A:\>_
```

WHAT'S HAPPENING? You have returned the colors to their default values. A third method involves using ECHO. It is also easy to place these commands in a batch file rather than writing a separate batch file for each color combination you wish.

Step 15   Key in the following: A:\>**CD BATCH** Enter

Step 16   Key in the following: A:\BATCH>**ADD A:\BATCH** Enter

Step 17   Key in the following: A:\BATCH>**CD ** Enter

```
A:\>CD BATCH

A:\BATCH>ADD A:\BATCH
```

```
A:\BATCH>IF  A:\BATCHnone==none GOTO END

A:\BATCH>PATH  > OLDPATH.BAT

A:\BATCH>PATH
C:\WINDOWS;C:\DOS;C:\PROG\MOUSE;C:\PROG\BATCH;H:\UTILS\ZIP;A:\BAT
CH

A:\BATCH>SHIFT

A:\BATCH>IF NOT \\==\\  GOTO  TOP

A:\BATCH>
A:\BATCH>
A:\BATCH>CD \

A:\>_
```

WHAT'S HAPPENING? You used the batch file ADD.BAT that you created in an earlier chapter. This allows you to add the A:\BATCH subdirectory to your path, which in turn allows you to place your new batch file in the BATCH subdirectory and to execute it.

Step 18   Using EDIT, create a batch file in the BATCH subdirectory called COLOR.BAT. In order to place the **Esc** sequence on the ECHO line in the batch file using EDIT, you must press **Ctrl** + P to disable the menu. Press the **Esc** key, then key in [%1m. Furthermore, if you experienced difficulty with BLUE.SCR, you cannot use the ECHO statement either. Instead, substitute the following for the ECHO line:

PROMPT $e[%1m$p$g

Otherwise, key in the following commands, remembering that when you see the ←, you must press **Ctrl** + P and then press the **Esc** key:

> **:TOP**
> **IF \%1\==\\ GOTO END**
> **ECHO ←[%1m**
> **SHIFT**
> **GOTO TOP**
> **:END**
> **CLS**

Step 19   Save the file.

Step 20   Key in the following: A:\>**COLOR 41 32** Enter

```
A:\>
A:\>_
```

WHAT'S HAPPENING? You have quickly changed the colors to a red background with a green foreground. If you wanted to make your batch file easier to use, you might want to include a list of colors from Table 14.4.

Step 21   Key in the following: A:\>**COLOR 7** Enter

```
A:\>
A:\>
```

WHAT'S HAPPENING? The attribute 7 is called reverse video and makes a light gray background with black letters.

Step 22   Key in the following: A:\>**COLOR 0** Enter

WHAT'S HAPPENING? The number 0 sets the colors to the default colors—a black background with a white foreground.

Step 23   Key in the following: A:\>**COLOR 5** Enter

```
A:\>
A:\>_
```

WHAT'S HAPPENING? Your screen should be blinking at you since 5 is the attribute for blink.

Step 24   Key in the following: A:\>**COLOR 0** Enter

WHAT'S HAPPENING? You have reset the attributes to the default, which is a non-blinking mode.

14.11 Remapping Keys

In Chapter 12, you used ERRORLEVEL to test for the value of the scan code for a key. You can also use `ANSI.SYS` to remap or reassign keys to whatever function you wish. For example. you used the `m` code in the **Esc** sequence to assign changes to the monitor. Rather then using the `m` code when you remap keys, you use the `p` code. Appendix F shows all the scan codes for all the keys including their values when used in conjunction with the **Shift**, **Alt**, and **Ctrl** keys. This remapping will not affect any application program, only the DOS command line. It is useful, but be careful in reassigning keys. If, for instance, you reassigned the letter `a` on the keyboard to the DIR command, you could not key in the letter `a`; every time you did, you would execute the DIR command. However, the **F10** key is not used at the DOS level, thus it would be a good key to reassign to the DIR command, so that every time you pressed the **F10** key, you would execute the DIR command. You can also swap key functions. For instance, when you need to change drives, you must hold down the **Shift** key to access the colon. If you press the colon key without **Shift**, you get the semi-colon. If you rarely use the semi-colon key, you might prefer to press the key without the **Shift** and get the colon. Remapping keys allows you this option. Again, it is easiest to place these commands in batch files.

14.12 Activity: Using ANSI.SYS To Remap Keys

Note 1: The `A:\>` will be displayed with the path set to `C:\DOS`. The DATA disk is in Drive A.

Note 2: It is assumed that `ANSI.SYS` has been installed. If you are in a lab environment, it should have already been done for you.

Step 1 Press **;** (semi-colon) **Enter**

Step 2 Press **Shift** **:** (colon) **Enter**

```
A:\>;
A:\>:
Bad command or file name

A:\>_
```

WHAT'S HAPPENING? Whenever you want to change drives, you must key in the drive letter, hold down the **Shift** key, and press the colon key. You are going to swap the semi-colon and colon keys so that when you want to change drives, all you need to do is key in the drive letter and the colon key, dispensing with the **Shift** key. The scan code for the semi-colon key is 59. The scan code for the colon key is 58 (**Shift** + semi-colon). You want to reverse these keys.

Step 3 Using EDIT, create a batch file called `SWAP.BAT` in the `BATCH` subdirectory.

Remember in EDIT to press the Ctrl + P to disable the menu. Then press the Esc key to get ←. SWAP.BAT will have the following commands:

ECHO ←[59;58p
ECHO ←[59;58p

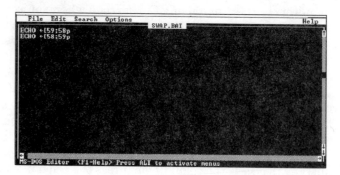

Step 4   Save the file.

Step 5   Be sure the path includes the A:\BATCH subdirectory. Key in the following: A:>**SWAP** Enter

Step 6   Key in the following (Remember, do *not* press the Shift key):
A:\>**C:** Enter

Step 7   Key in the following (Remember, do *not* press the Shift key):
C:\>**A:** Enter

```
A:\>SWAP

A:\>ECHO

A:\>ECHO

A:\>
A:\>
A:\>C:

C:\>A:

A:\>_
```

WHAT'S HAPPENING? You no longer need to hold down the Shift key to access the colon. To undo a key remap, you must reassignment the key to itself.

Step 8   Using EDIT, create a batch file called UNSWAP.BAT in the BATCH subdirectory. Remember in EDIT to press the **Ctrl** + P to disable the menu and the **Esc** key to get ←. UNSWAP.BAT will have the following commands:

ECHO ←[59;58p
ECHO ←[59;58p

Step 9   Save the file.

Step 10   Be sure the path includes the A:\BATCH subdirectory. Key in the following (Remember, you must press the **Shift** key):

A:>**UNSWAP** **Enter**

Step 11   Key in the following (Remember, you must press the **Shift** key):

A:\>**C:** **Enter**

Step 12   Key in the following (Remember, you must press the **Shift** key):

C:\>**A:** **Enter**

WHAT'S HAPPENING? Now, you must hold down the Shift key to access the colon. You can also assign functions to keys. The scan code for the F10 key is 0:68. Since Enter must be pressed after a command such as DIR, you want to automate that process also so that when you press F10, you will execute the DIR command, including pressing Enter. Using the code 13p is the same as pressing Enter.

Step 13   Using EDIT, create a batch file called F10.BAT in the BATCH subdirectory. F10.BAT will have the following commands:

ECHO ←[0;68;"DIR";13p

Step 14   Save the file.

Step 15   Using EDIT, create a batch file called UNF10.BAT in the BATCH subdirectory. UNF10.BAT will have the following commands:

ECHO ←[0;68p

Step 16   Save the file.

WHAT'S HAPPENING? You have created two batch files—one called F10.BAT that assigns the F10 key to the DIR command. The other, called UNF10.BAT, unassigns the F10 key.

Step 17   Be sure the path includes the A:\BATCH subdirectory.

Key in the following: A:>**F10** **Enter**

Step 18   Press **F10**

```
JOINED     SAM         104 06-21-94   10:36a
LAST       ONE          71 11-23-95   10:42a
FILE2      SWT          18 08-22-94   11:51p
FILE3      SWT          18 08-22-94   11:51p
TEST       TKR      16,516 06-21-94   10:37a
HOMEBUD    TKR       8,064 02-28-94    6:19p
APR        TST          71 11-23-95   10:42a
DRAMA      TV          198 11-23-94   10:19a
JANUARY    TXT         144 07-31-94   10:33p
PROG          <DIR>        06-25-94   11:58a
MEDIA         <DIR>        06-25-94   12:03p
FEBRUARY   TXT          74 11-23-95   10:41a
APRIL      TXT          71 11-23-95   10:42a
HELLO      TXT          52 11-23-95   10:44a
BYE        TXT          44 11-23-95   10:45a
AWARD      MOV          94 06-25-94   12:10p
BATCH         <DIR>        07-01-94    5:10p
OLDER         <DIR>        07-30-94   12:00p
STATE      CAP         260 08-22-94   11:54p
SORTED     CAP         260 08-22-94   11:54p
TEACHER    FIL         122 08-03-94   12:25p
        48 file(s)        44,762 bytes
                     643,072 bytes free

A:\>_
```

WHAT'S HAPPENING? Now when you press the **F10** key, you get a listing of the directory.

Step 19   Key in the following: A:\>**UNF10** **Enter**

Step 20   Press **F10**

```
A:\>UNF10

A:\>ECHO

A:\>_
```

WHAT'S HAPPENING? You have unassigned the **F10** key. When you press it, nothing happens.

14.13 *Controlling Devices*

In order to control peripheral devices, special software called device drivers is needed. Usually a **controller**, which is a piece of hardware, takes care of the hardware portion of communicating with a peripheral device. DOS groups physical devices into two basic categories: **character devices** and **block devices**. Character devices are those that handle data as individual characters, such as data from keyboards, the screen, serial ports, and parallel ports. Block devices handle data as "chunks" or blocks of data, such as data from disk drives.

Character devices are attached to the computer via a cable that is attached to a port on the system unit. A **port** is simply an input/output connection, like a plug, where you can connect devices to a computer. Devices include such things as the console, printers, a mouse, a light pen (a device to point draw on a special display screen), a fax board (a board that allows the transmission of facsimiles), or a modem (a device that allows computers to communicate over phone lines). DOS is not concerned with the actual device but with the method of interface. **Interface** means the hardware and/or software necessary to connect one system or device to another so they can transmit and receive information. DOS defines an interface as either **serial** or **parallel** and calls the plugs serial or parallel ports.

A serial or **asynchronous** port transfers data one bit at a time. It is called asynchronous because the transmission of data is not synchronized by a clock signal. The data is sent as bits one after another, with a start bit at the beginning and a stop bit at the end to mark the beginning and end of the data. For instance, the word "DOS" in binary is 01000100 (D) 01001111 (O) 01010011 (S). If you sent it serially, it would travel as in Figure 14.3.

Computer Cable Plug

Figure 14.3   Serial Communication

You can think of it as eight cars parading down the highway, one following the other, with a police car at the beginning and at the end of the parade.

A parallel port, on the other hand, transfers data one byte at a time (eight bits). The transfer of eight bits must be concurrent so that the byte (eight bits) looks the same on the receiving end as it does on the sending end. Thus, sending the word "DOS" in parallel fashion would look like Figure 14.4

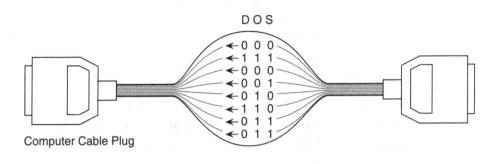

Figure 14.4 *Parallel Communication*

You can think of it as eight cars going down the highway side by side. Parallel communication is faster than serial communication.

Most computers have at least one parallel port and one serial port. You can upgrade the hardware to include more ports. You can have up to four serial ports and three parallel ports, and the number of both can vary depending on your computer system.

Ports are used to attach devices to the system unit. The devices most users are interested in are a printer, a modem, and a mouse or some other pointing device. Most printers are parallel printers, although there are serial printers. A parallel printer connects to a paral ave a length usually no more than 15 feet. In other words, parallel printers are limited to a radius of 15 feet from the system unit; any length beyond that can present data receiving problems for a parallel printer. Serial printers do not have this problem and can have cables more than 50 feet from the system unit.

A device such as a modem is a serial device and is "plugged" into a serial (communication) port. A serial mouse is plugged into a serial port. A mouse can be attached to the computer in a variety of ways. Today, most computer systems have a special mouse or track ball (pointing device) connection to free ports for other devices. If you add a mouse to an older system with no special mouse port, there are two ways to do it. If you have a bus mouse, you physically install an adapter card and attach your pointing device to the card. The second way is to purchase a serial mouse or serial pointing device. If you have only one serial port, you can have either a serial mouse or modem attached, not both. The operating system (DOS) has reserved names for each standard device. They are shown in Table 14.5.

Port Name	DOS Device Name	Alias	Meaning
Parallel port 1	LPT1:	PRN	Line Printer 1
Parallel port 2	LPT2:		Line Printer 2
Parallel port 3	LPT3:		Line Printer 3
Serial port 1	COM1:	AUX	Communications port 1—Auxiliary device
Serial port 2	COM2:		Communications port 2
Serial port 3	COM3:		Communications port 3
Serial port 4	COM4:		Communications port 4

Table 14.5   *Reserved Names for Standard Devices*

The MODE command in DOS performs several tasks that relate to controlling devices.

14.14 The MODE Command

The MODE command is actually several commands in one. It is used for configuring devices. You can use it to change the number of characters per inch and the number of lines per inch for IBM-compatible dot-matrix printers; to set the characteristics for a serial port; to display the status of one or more devices; to redirect output from a parallel port to a communications port; to prepare, select, and display code pages; and to set the number of rows and columns on a monitor. You can also use it to set the rate at which DOS repeats a character when you hold down a key on the keyboard (**typematic rate**). You will rarely use most of these options. For instance, the code page setting has to do with character sets for foreign countries. Unless you are working in a language other than English, you will never deal with this setting. You will use MODE for other configurations depending on what hardware you have. If, for instance, you have a serial printer or modem, you will have to set the characteristics of each to enable communication. You will find that most programs which deal with modems will set up your communications ports automatically.

Serial devices, such as a serial printer or modem, have to agree on the **communication protocol**. Communication protocol refers to the rules that the computer and device have to follow. Protocol determines how fast they will communicate and how many bits of information they will exchange at one time. These values include the baud rate, parity, data bits, stop bits, and retry value. **Baud rate** is a measure of how many times a signal can be changed in a second and is measured in cycles per second (cps). Bits per second (bps) is the actual amount of data bits that can be transmitted in one second. Often the baud rate (cps) and the bit rate (bps) are the same number.

Parity helps the computer and the device know when there is a bit error. An extra "parity" bit is often sent immediately following the data bits. When the device or computer receives the data, it counts the number of binary digits that had the value of 1. The results will be either an odd or an even number. A computer and device can agree on either even or odd parity. If the computer and the device have agreed on even parity, but the sum receive is odd, a transmission error has occurred. The default value is even parity. In order to tell when a transmission is complete, one or more **stop bits** are sent. Again, the communication protocol establishes this number.

Last, the **retry** parameter tells MODE what to do when it gets a "busy" signal from the device. In addition to setting the communication protocol, if you have a serial printer, you must redirect the output from the parallel port to the serial port. In other words, every time DOS sees output going to PRN, it will redirect it to COM1 or COM2.

Each one of these MODE command options has its own syntax and parameters. It is beyond the scope of this text to cover all of these details because MODE is so hardware-dependent. Modern software will automatically set up or "configure" the ports as needed. Also, when you do need to use MODE to configure a device, you can check the device's documentation for the appropriate values. Follow the instructions in the documentation to set up MODE with the proper values. Then place it in the AUTOEXEC.BAT file and do not worry about it again.

The MODE command is also a TSR external command. You will look at some of the options available to you using the MODE command. You will also change the way the display looks. You will then look at the status of your devices and manipulate the typematic rate.

14.15 Setting Printer Characteristics with MODE Command

With this command, you can customize your printing. MODE provides the opportunity to use one of three printers. The default printer settings are 80 characters per line (CPL) and 6 lines per inch (LPI). You can also print in a smaller or condensed mode where there are 132 characters per line and 8 lines per inch.

MODE is an external memory-resident command. When you set the MODE for the printer, it remains set at the parameters you specified until you change the mode, turn off the printer, or turn off the computer. The syntax is:

```
MODE  LPTn[:]  [COLS=c]  [LINES=l]  [RETRY=r]
```

```
LPTn          Specifies the parallel port the printer is attached
              to. Valid values for n are 1 through 3.
[COLS=c]      Specifies characters (columns) per line. The valid
              values are 80 or 132.
[LINES=l]     Specifies lines per inch. The valid values are 6 or 8.
[RETRY=r]     Specifies the retry action to take if the printer is
              busy.
```

Since MODE is an external command, DOS needs to access it initially to load it. Once the printing characteristics for the printer are set, they remain at this value until you either change them again with MODE or reboot the system. MODE does not work on laser or ink-jet printers. Furthermore, since today most dot-matrix printers offer far more printing choices than the MODE command, MODE is rarely used for this purpose.

14.16 Using MODE with the Monitor

You can specify with the MODE command how many characters you want displayed in a row and how many rows you want displayed on the monitor. The changes you can make depend on the type of monitor you have and the version of DOS you have. The syntax is:

```
MODE [display-adapter][,shift[,T]]
MODE [display-adapter][,n]
MODE CON[:] [COLS=c] [LINES=n]
```

display-adapter	Specifies a setting category. The following list shows the value(s) associated with each setting category for display-adapter:
40 or 80	Indicates the number of characters per line.
BW40 or BW80	Specifies a color graphics adapter (CGA) with color turned off, and specifies the number of characters per line.
CO40 or CO80	Specifies a color monitor with color enabled, and specifies the number of characters per line.
MONO	Specifies a monochrome display adapter with a constant width of 80 characters per line.
shift	Specifies whether to shift the CGA screen to the left or to the right. Valid values for shift are L (for left) and R (for right).
T	Enables you to align the screen by using a test pattern. MS-DOS prompts you to indicate whether the screen is aligned correctly.
CON[:]	Refers to the monitor.
COLS=c	Specifies the number of characters (columns) per line. Valid values are 40 and 80.
LINES=n	Specifies the number of lines that can be displayed on the screen. Valid values for n are 25, 43, and 50. Not all display adapters support all three settings. To set the number of lines, you must have installed the ANSI.SYS device driver by using a device command in your CONFIG.SYS file.

14.17 Activity: Using MODE to Change the Display

Note: The A:\> will be displayed with path set to C:\DOS. The DATA disk is
          in Drive A.

Step 1   Key in the following: A:\>**MODE 40** [Enter]

```
A:\>MODE 40

A:\>_
```

WHAT'S HAPPENING? You changed the display to show 40 characters instead of
80 characters per row. In essence, it makes the display twice as large. However, this
works only in DOS. Most application packages will not work if the MODE is set to
40.

Step 2   Key in the following: A:\>**MODE 80** [Enter]

```
A:\>MODE 80

A:\>_
```

WHAT'S HAPPENING? You returned the display to the default value.

14.18 Using MODE to Change Keyboard Response Rate

You can alter the keyboard typematic rate—the rate at which DOS repeats a
character when you press a key. You can increase the value, and DOS will increase
the speed of the typematic rate. Not all keyboards support this feature. There are
two parts to the syntax: the rate and time delay. The rate refers to the rate at which
the character is repeated on the screen when you hold down a key. Valid values
include 2 to 30 characters per second. The default value is 20 for IBM-AT style
keyboards and 21 for IBM PS/2 keyboards. If you set the rate, you must also set the
other component, the delay. The delay sets the amount of time that must elapse after
you press and hold down a key before DOS starts to repeat the characters. The valid
values include 1, 2, 3, and 4, which represent .25, .50, .75, and 1 seconds. The default
value is 2. If you set the delay, you must also set the rate. The syntax is:

```
MODE  CON[:]  [RATE=r  DELAY=d]
```

14.19 Activity: Setting the Quickest Typematic Rate

Note: The A:\> will be displayed with the path set to C:\DOS. The DATA disk
          is in Drive A.

Step 1   Hold down the letter x for a few seconds.

```
A:\>xxxxxxxxxxxxxxxxxxxxxx
```

WHAT'S HAPPENING? Note the speed at which the letter x repeats itself.

Step 2   Press **Esc**

Step 3   Key in the following: A:\>**MODE CON: RATE=32 DELAY=1** **Enter**

```
A:\>MODE CON: RATE=32 DELAY=1

A:\>_
```

WHAT'S HAPPENING? You set the rate to the fastest keyboard response. When you hold down a letter on the keyboard, it will repeat 32 times a second.

Step 4   Hold down the letter x for a few seconds.

```
A:\>xxxxxxxxxxxxxxxxxxxxxxxxxxxxx
```

WHAT'S HAPPENING? You should see the speed of the keyboard increase. If the keyboard seems to be too quick, try to adjust the delay value first so you have more time to release the key.

Step 5   Press **Esc**

Step 6   Key in the following: A:\>**MODE CON: RATE=21 DELAY=2** **Enter**

```
A:\>MODE CON: RATE=21 DELAY=2

A:\>_
```

WHAT'S HAPPENING? You returned the values to their defaults.

14.20 Checking the Status of Devices

You can check the status of different devices on your system. Using MODE with no parameters will display the status of all devices. If you use the /STATUS or /STA parameters with the MODE command, it will request the status of any redirected printer. If you specify a device name, it will display the status of the device. You can check either a specific device or all the devices. The syntax is:

```
MODE [device] [/STATUS]
```

14.21 Activity: Checking the Status of Devices With MODE

Note: The A:\> will be displayed with the path set to C:\DOS. The DATA disk
is in Drive A.

Step 1   Key in the following: A:\>**MODE CON /STATUS** [Enter]

```
A:\>MODE CON /STATUS

Status for device CON:
----------------------
Columns=80
Lines=25

Code page operation not supported on this device

A:\>_
```

WHAT'S HAPPENING? The /STATUS switch gives the information that this
monitor is set to 80 characters per column and 25 lines per screen.

Step 2   Key in the following: A:\>**MODE ¦ MORE** [Enter]

```
------------------
LPT1: not rerouted
Retry=NONE

Code page operation not supported on this device

Status for device LPT2:
------------------
LPT2: not rerouted

Status for device LPT3:
------------------
LPT3: not rerouted

Status for device CON:
------------------
Columns=80
Lines=25

Code page operation not supported on this device

Status for device COM1:
- More -
```

WHAT'S HAPPENING? As you can see, the MODE command is reporting the status of all the devices on this system. Your screen display can vary based on what peripherals are on your system. Also note that, since MODE writes to the screen—standard output—the output can be piped to the MORE command.

Step 3   Press **Enter** until you have returned to the system prompt.

WHAT'S HAPPENING? You have looked at some of the MODE options.

14.22 Checking for Computer Viruses

Computer viruses are computer programs which can replicate and spread among computers. Often, they exist without letting the user know that they are "infected." In order for a virus to infect your computer, you place an infected floppy disk in a drive which will then infect the hard disk. Viruses can also be aquired when you are downloading data and files from electronic bulletin boards. Viruses can range from one that is harmless, having no affect on your files and data, to one that is fatal and malicious, destroying programs and data on your hard disk. The symptoms can vary from virus to virus. Harmless viruses may produce messages or graphics at unexpected times, such as a peace symbol, or they may give you no notice and one day destroy the data on your hard disk.

The three most common ways viruses are transmitted include boot sector viruses, file infectors, and so-called Trojan horses. A **boot sector virus** will replace your disk's original boot sector with its own and then load the virus into memory. Once the virus is in memory, it can write to and infect other disks. A **file infector virus** adds programming instructions to files that run programs. The virus becomes activated whenever you run the program. Again, once the virus is activated, it can spread to other disks and files. Usually, the most deadly and dangerous virus is a **Trojan horse virus**. It is proffered as a legitimate program, and, when you run it, the Trojan horse begins a destructive process. Often a Trojan horse virus is fatal, and files that have been infected cannot be recovered. Even the so-called harmless viruses can be annoying, and no one should have the right to place files or items on your hard disk. In order to solve this problem, anti-virus programs have been developed that check your memory, floppy, and hard disks in a variety of ways to protect you from an invasion.

MS-DOS 6.0 and above includes such a program—MSAV. This program, a subset from PC Tools, allows you to scan your computer's memory for viruses (Detect) and also to remove viruses (Detect and Clean). Because new viruses are always appearing, Microsoft provides an Anti-Virus Update offer that will, for a fee, periodically send you new disks with the latest anti-virus software.

14.23 Activity: Using MSAV

The DATA disk should be in Drive A with the A:\> displayed.

Step 1   Key in the following: **MSAV** **Enter**

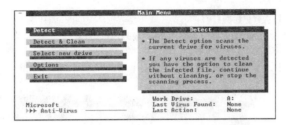

WHAT'S HAPPENING? You are presented with the Microsoft Anti-Virus screen. `Detect` is highlighted. If you are using a mouse, you can click your choice.

Step 2   Press **D**

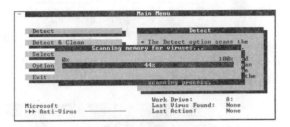

WHAT'S HAPPENING? On the screen, you see the progress of the memory search for viruses. When it is completed, the following screen appears.

WHAT'S HAPPENING? You see a report of the detected and cleaned viruses.

Step 3   Press ⌈Enter⌋

Step 4   Press the ⬇ until `Detect and Clean` is highlighted.

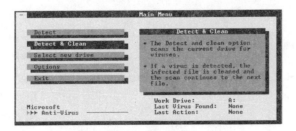

WHAT'S HAPPENING? Detect and Clean will detect all viruses for the current default drive, which in this case is Drive A.

Step 5   Press **Enter**

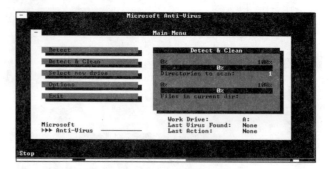

WHAT'S HAPPENING? Again, you see a progress report. When it is finished, you will see the following screen.

WHAT'S HAPPENING? There were no viruses.

Step 6   Press **Enter** Press **X**

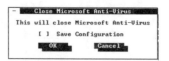

WHAT'S HAPPENING? You are presented with a dialog box that asks you if you want to close the Anti-Virus program.

Step 7   Press **Enter**

```
A:\>_
```

WHAT'S HAPPENING? You have returned to the system level.

14.24 VSAFE

In the previous activity, you specifically checked for viruses. You can also install a memory-resident program called VSAFE that will continuously monitor your computer for any viruses it might find while you are working on your computer. If it finds one, it will display a warning. VSAFE occupies about 22 K of memory. **Do not, under any circumstance, install VSAFE while Windows is running or when you are installing Windows**. The syntax is:

```
VSAFE [/option[+ ¦ -] ...]   [/NE] [/NX] [/Ax ¦ /Cx] [/N] [/D] [/U]

       option    One of the following:
         1        HD low level format warning
         2        Resident warning
         3        General write protect
         4        Check infected files
         5        Boot sector infection warning
         6        Protect hard disk BOOT area
         7        Protect floppy disk BOOT area
         8        Write Protect executable files

      /NE        Prevents VSafe from loading in expanded memory.
      /NX        Prevents VSafe from loading in extended memory.
      /Ax        Defines the VSafe hotkey to be Alt plus the key defined
                 by x.
      /Cx        Defines the VSafe hotkey to be Ctrl plus the key de-
                 fined by x.
      /N         Allows VSafe to monitor network drives for possible
                 viruses.
      /D         Disables checksum creation.
      /U         Unloads VSafe from memory.
```

If you wanted to install VSAFE, you would simply key in VSAFE at the prompt. Again, be sure you are not running or installing Windows. That is one of the reasons that there is the /U parameter that will remove VSAFE from memory.

14.25 Backing Up Data Using MSBACKUP

Backing up data is an important task that users should do regularly. There are many ways to back up data using the COPY command or the XCOPY command. In addition, earlier versions of DOS provided two separate commands, BACKUP and RESTORE, that were particularly useful for hard disk backup operations. DOS 6.0 and above has replaced both these commands with the program called MSBACKUP. This is a subset of Norton Utilities. When you install DOS 6.0 or above, you can choose or not choose to install this program for the DOS command line, for Windows, or for both DOS and Windows. If you install it for Windows, the install program creates a new group called Microsoft Tools that contains the anti-virus program, the backup program, and the undelete program.

When you run MSBACKUP from the DOS prompt, it looks very much like the Windows version. The first time you run it, the program will ask you to configure it. The configuration is a series of selecting the complexity level, configuring the screen and mouse, selecting the devices you are going to backup to, and testing those devices. There are essentially three kinds of backups: full, incremental, and differential. A **full backup** backs up all the files you selected. Although you could back up the entire hard disk, typically you would be backing up a specific subdirectory or specific kinds of files such as all the .TXT files. An **incremental backup** will back up only files that have changed since your last full or last incremental backup. A **differential backup** backs up only files that have changed since your last full backup.

Before you actually begin backing up, you must choose which files you wish to back up, where you want to back them up to, and other options such as file compression. Your choices are saved in what are called setup files. You may have up to 50 of them. If you do not make any specific choices, DOS uses the DEFAULT.SET, which are essentially the choices you made when you configured backup originally.

The backup program creates a **backup catalog** that contains the information about the files you backed up. These catalogs hold such information as the directory structure, the size of the backup, the date of the backup, and other such information. Also, every time you perform a full backup, a **master catalog** is created that is typically stored in the DOS directory. The master catalog tracks all the backup catalogs that were created during the backup cycle. A copy of the backup catalog is placed on the floppy disk you backed up to, as well as on the hard disk. Thus, if there is a problem, you have two places in which to rebuild your catalog and restore your data.

If you have never configured MSBACKUP, you will get different screens after configuring. If you are in lab environment, you will not be able to do the next activity. Lab environments will either have their own backup programs or, if they are using MSBACKUP, will have it configured it for the lab. Furthermore, information has to be saved to the hard disk, which you will not be able to do in a laboratory environment. If your own computer has been configured, you will not see these screens as they appear. Be sure that you have blank, formatted disks.

14.26 Configuring MSBACKUP

Since this process is completely different on every computer, these steps are merely one example of configuring MSBACKUP. You will only read about it. Should you choose, on your own, to complete Sections 14.26 and 14.28, be aware that your screens will look completely different from the screens shown in these sections. **Under no circumstances should you do sections 14.26 and 14.28 if you are on a network.**

Note: You should have several blank, formatted disks available.

A   Key in the following: A:\>**MSBACKUP** Enter

WHAT'S HAPPENING? This tells you that your system has not been configured for MSBACKUP.

B   Press [Enter]

WHAT'S HAPPENING? You see what hardware you have. Normally, you accept the default values.

C   Press [Enter]

WHAT'S HAPPENING? Tests are done as part of the configuration. Follow the prompts and remove any disks from all drives.

D   Press [Enter]

WHAT'S HAPPENING? It tells you what backup devices you have installed.

E   Press [Enter]

WHAT'S HAPPENING? Tests are being run.

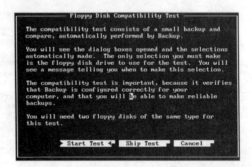

WHAT'S HAPPENING? MSBACKUP wants to test your floppy disk drive. If you do this test, you need two blanks disks. Although it is recommended, you can skip the test.

F   Press the `Tab` key until Skip Test is highlighted. Then press `Enter`

WHAT'S HAPPENING? Your devices have been configured, and your default set has been established.

WHAT'S HAPPENING? Now you can proceed to backup and restore files.

14.27 After Configuring MSBACKUP

Once the configuration is complete, you need not alter it unless you choose to do so. The following activity assumes that your system has been configured. Also if you are in a lab environment, please check with your instructor before doing this activity. You probably will not be able to do this activity if you are on a network or if the lab has its own backup procedures. Furthermore, the following example is based on a specific computer with a specific configuration. If you do this activity, your screens will vary depending on your catalog and your configuration. Your screens will not be exactly the same, only approximately the same. You can use the steps listed below, but substitute your own values where necessary.

14.28 Using MSBACKUP

A blank formatted disk should be in Drive A with the `A:\>` displayed.

Note: See comments under Section 14.26 before reading through these steps.

A   Key in the following: `A:\>`**MSBACKUP** `Enter`

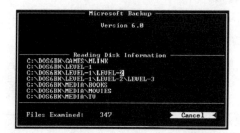

WHAT'S HAPPENING? As the BACKUP program loads, it reads the entire hard disk. When it has done so, it presents the next screen.

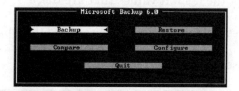

WHAT'S HAPPENING? As you can see from the choices on the menu, you back up and restore from the same command, MSBACKUP. `Compare` will allow you to verify that the original files and the backed up files are the same. `Configure` allows you to alter or test your configuration.

B   Press **B**

WHAT'S HAPPENING? This is a fairly typical default set backup. The `DEFAULT.SET` is of no particular description. The default drive to backup from is Drive C, and the backup will be backed up to floppy Drive A. You may select files and choose the `Backup Type`. Presently, the default selection is `Full`. You are going to back up some files in the `DOS6BK` directory to the disk in Drive A. You will need a blank disk of the proper media type. First, however, let us look at what options are selected on the system.

C   Press **O**

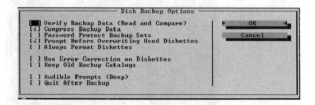

WHAT'S HAPPENING? Each item that has a check mark is enabled. Again, these are generally the default values. You can request to `Always Format Disks` or `Keep Old Backup Catalogs`, or whatever choices meet your needs. In this case, you will accept the default values that are there.

D   Press **Tab** until `Cancel` is selected (highlighted). Press **Enter**

E   Press **L** for `Select Files`

WHAT'S HAPPENING? After it quickly reads Drive C, you see the structure of your disk.

F   Press the ⬇ arrow key until you locate the DOS6BK directory.

WHAT'S HAPPENING? The left side of the screen displays the directory tree while the right side displays the files in that directory. The Include button allows you to select files using wildcards, and the Exclude button allows you to exclude files using wildcards. The Special button allows you to select files by a range of dates or to include or exclude read-only files, system files, and hidden files. The Display button allows you to display various combinations of file attributes and sorting choices. The files on the right side are automatically alphabetized.

G   Press the ⎡Tab⎤ key to move to the file side of the display. APR.99 should be highlighted. If it is not, press the arrow key until it is. Press the ⎡Space Bar⎤.

WHAT'S HAPPENING? By pressing the ⎡Space Bar⎤, you placed a check mark in front of APR.99 to select it to back up. To select files, you use the ⬆ and ⬇ arrow keys. When you find a file you wish to back up, you choose it by pressing the ⎡Space Bar⎤. If you have a mouse, you can instead choose a file by clicking the right mouse button when the pointer is on the file name.

H   Select APR.NEW, APR.TMP, APRIL.TXT, CAROLYN.FIL, and DANCES.TXT.

WHAT'S HAPPENING? You are now ready to back up these selected files to the disk in Drive A. Catalogs take much room on a disk, so you need a new blank disk. Since you did not select Always Format Disks, be sure you have a blank formatted disk of the correct media type in Drive A.

I   Press the Tab key to select the OK button. Press **Enter**

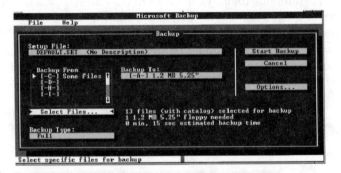

WHAT'S HAPPENING? Notice that the screen has changed. Now, the Backup From still states C but says Some Files. In addition, next to Select Files it tells you that you have selected 13 files, that you need a 1.2 MB 5¼-inch floppy disk, and that it will take approximately 15 seconds to backup these files.

J   Press **S**

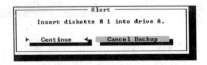

WHAT'S HAPPENING? After quickly reading the disk, the dialog box asks you to insert a disk into Drive A.

K   You should have a blank formatted disk in Drive A. Press **C**

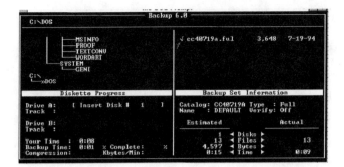

WHAT'S HAPPENING? The upper part of the screen tells you that it is storing the master catalog, `cc40719a.ful`, in the DOS directory. Each item in this file name means something. The first `c` is the first drive backed up. The second `c` is the last drive backed up in this set. The `4` is 1994. The `07` and the `19` are the month and day the set was created. The `a` is the position of this set in a sequence of backups. The extension `ful` tells that this was a full backup. The screen also gives you the time required. When the backup is complete, you see the following screen.

WHAT'S HAPPENING? The dialog box tells you how many files you backed up, that the backup was successful, and how much space they occupy.

L   Press **Enter**

WHAT'S HAPPENING? On the screen several dialog boxes flash by telling you that it is updating the master catalog. Then you are returned to the following screen.

M   Press **Q**

N   Key in the following: **DIR** **Enter**

```
A:\>DIR

Volume in drive A is DEFAULT FUL
Directory of A:\

CC40719A 001     1,213,952 07-19-94  11:36p
       1 file(s)         1,213,952 bytes
                         1,213,952 bytes free

A:\>_
```

WHAT'S HAPPENING? When you use MSBACKUP, you do not see the individual files, only the catalog.

O   Key in the following: A:\>**MSBACKUP** Enter

P   Press **R**

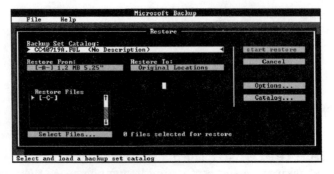

WHAT'S HAPPENING? The Restore menu lists the catalog you were working with. The catalog you just created is listed in the box under in the Backup Set Catalog: The default is to restore files from Drive A back to their original locations. The information should be correct in the Restore From and Restore To boxes.

Q   Press **L**. Use the ⬇ arrow key to move to the DOS6BK directory.

WHAT'S HAPPENING? You see the backed up files on the right side of the screen.

R   Press the [Space Bar]

WHAT'S HAPPENING? You have selected your files to restore. Each has a check mark.

S   Press [Enter]

WHAT'S HAPPENING? The Start Restore button is now available.

T   Press S

WHAT'S HAPPENING? The dialog box asks you to insert the correct disk. Since the disk you used is still in Drive A, you do not need to change disks.

U   Press C

WHAT'S HAPPENING? You see a status box telling you that your files were restored and are problem free.

V   Press **Enter**. Press **Q**

WHAT'S HAPPENING? You have backed up and restored files and have now returned to the DOS system level.

Chapter Summary

1. DOSKEY is an external memory-resident program that allows you to correct keystroke errors.
2. A memory-resident program is one that must be loaded from disk into memory. However, once loaded, it remains in memory and behaves like an internal command. A memory-resident program is also commonly called a TSR (Terminate and Stay Resident).
3. The arrow and function keys in DOSKEY allow you to do command line editing by recalling and listing the previously keyed in commands.
4. DOSKEY allows you to place more than one command on a line provided those commands are separated by the **Ctrl** + T.
5. DOSKEY allows you to create macros. A macro is like a batch file, but it resides in memory, not on disk. Furthermore, a DOSKEY macro is limited to 127 characters. DOSKEY macros run prior to internal commands.
6. You may use replaceable parameters in DOSKEY macros, but you must use the $ sign, not the % sign. You are limited to the range $0 to $9.
7. If you wish to use pipes or redirection symbols in your macro, you must use the special symbols.
8. Macros may be saved to a batch file using either the /M or /H parameter. Once in a batch file, each command must be preceded by DOSKEY.
9. One of the DOS-provided drivers is ANSI.SYS. Once installed in your CONFIG.SYS file via the statement DEVICE=C:\DOS\ANSI.SY, you will be able to change colors on the monitor or remap the keyboard.
10. To make changes using ANSI.SYS, you may use the PROMPT, TYPE, or ECHO commands.
11. In order to enter the codes you wish, you must precede them by **Esc** and a left bracket ([ ).

12. To verify that ANSI.SYS is loaded in memory, you may use the MEM /M ANSI command.
13. To insert the escape sequence with the PROMPT command, use $e.
14. To insert the escape sequence in EDIT, press **Ctrl** + P to disable the EDIT menu. Then press the **Esc** key. Alternately, you can use the numeric keypad and hold down the **Alt** key and press 27 for the escape character.
15. To remap keys using ANSI.SYS, you must know the scan codes for the key(s) of interest.
16. To control devices, you need special software called device drivers.
17. DOS groups devices into two categories: character and block devices.
18. Character devices are attached to the computer by a cable attached to a port.
19. A port is a connection for an I/O device.
20. A serial port transfers data one bit at a time.
21. A parallel port transfers data one byte (eight bits) at a time.
22. Nearly all computers have at least one parallel port and one serial port, although there can be more. You can have up to four serial ports and three parallel ports.
23. DOS has reserved names for devices.
24. The MODE command is used for configuring devices to the system, although today most software takes care of this when you install a device.
25. The MODE command can be used to alter the type style of a dot-matrix printer. It can be used to set the characteristics of a serial port (communications protocol). You can redirect the output of a parallel port to a serial port. You can change the characteristics of the monitor as well as the keyboard response rate (typematic). You may also get a status report on the devices on your system.
26. Computer viruses are programs that replicate and spread among computers and often cause serious damage to data. The three major types are boot sector viruses, file infector viruses, and Trojan Horse viruses.
27. DOS provides a virus-checking program called MSAV, which will check memory and disks for viruses.
28. DOS also provides a program called VSAFE, which is a memory-resident program that will constantly monitor your system by looking for viruses. If it finds one, it will alert you. Do not run VSAFE when using or installing Windows.
29. The separate BACKUP and RESTORE programs that were used to back up a hard disk have been replaced by MSBACKUP, a menu-driven program in DOS 6. It can be run in either Windows or DOS.
30. You may do a full, incremental, or differential backup using MSBACKUP. MSBACKUP creates catalogs that track what you have backed up.

Key Terms

Asynchronous	Block devices	Communication
Backup catalog	Boot sector virus	protocol
Baud rate	Character devices	Computer virus

Controller	Master catalog	Serial
Differential backup	Memory-resident	Signatures
File infector virus	commands	Stop bits
Full backup	Parallel	Trojan Horse virus
Incremental backup	Parity	TSRs
Interface	Port	Typematic rate
Macros	Retry	

Discussion Questions

1. Explain the purpose and function of the DOSKEY command.
2. What is a memory resident program and how does it work?
3. List and explain five of the DOSKEY editing keys that can be used to edit the command history.
4. Compare and contrast DOS batch files with DOSKEY macros.
5. Explain the purpose and function of DOSKEY macros.
6. What are some of the limitations of macros?
7. Explain how replaceable parameters are used in macros.
8. How can DOSKEY macros be saved?
9. When using the DOSKEY commands, what is the purpose of the /H parameter? The /M parameter?
10. What is the purpose and function of the ANSI.SYS driver?
11. What is the purpose and function of a signature?
12. Explain two signature characters that are used with ANSI.SYS.
13. Describe one way to change the color scheme on the monitor.
14. What does it mean to "remap a key"?
15. Why would you want to remap a key?
16. What is the function of a port?
17 What is the function and purpose of a serial or asynchronous port?
18. What is the function and purpose of a parallel port?
19. Compare and contrast serial and parallel ports.
20. Briefly explain "communication protocol."
21. List and explain three functions of the MODE command.
22. How can you check the status of all devices?
23. What are computer viruses? How are they transmitted?
24. What is the purpose and function of MSAV?
25. What is the purpose and function of VSAFE?
26. When do you not run VSAFE?
27. Identify at least two ways to back up files.
28. Describe the purpose and function of MSBACKUP.
29. Why can you typically not use MSBACKUP in a lab environment?
30. Compare and contrast full, incremental, and differential backups.

Chapter 15

Optimizing the System

After completing this chapter you will be able to:

1. Explain how to bypass `CONFIG.SYS`.
2. Explain the purpose and function of memory managers.
3. Explain how to use `EMM386.EXE` to convert extended memory to expanded memory.
4. Explain the difference between LOADHIGH and DEVICEHIGH.
5. Explain how STACKS and FCBS can be modified to save memory.
6. Explain the purpose and function of multiple configurations.
7. Explain how SMARTDRIVE can be used to allow caching.
8. Explain the difference between write caching and read caching.
9. Explain the purpose and function of FASTOPEN.
10. Explain the purpose and function of MemMaker.
11. Explain how DriveSpace can be used to optimize disk space.

1. Control the boot process by using the function keys to bypass `CONFIG.SYS` and `AUTOEXEC.BAT`.
2. Write and use a `CONFIG.SYS` file that prepares upper memory, loads DOS high, loads TSRs in upper memory, and determines how much memory is saved.
3. Create and use multiple configurations in `CONFIG.SYS`.

4. Install and use SmartDrive.
5. Describe the purpose and function of DriveSpace.

Chapter Overview

In the previous chapter you wrote and used a CONFIG.SYS file that included some basic configuration commands to set up your system. In this chapter you will explore more advanced concepts to optimize memory on your computer system.

15.1 Controlling the Boot Process

In Chapter 10, you learned that a feature introduced in DOS 6 allows you to bypass AUTOEXEC.BAT or CONFIG.SYS. To review, you enable this feature by pressing certain function keys when you see the following line displayed on your computer:

```
Starting MS-DOS ...
```

When you see that message, you can use certain function keys. When you use these keys the results are:

F5	If you press the **F5** key, you will bypass both the CONFIG.SYS and AUTOEXEC.BAT files.
F8	If you press the **F8** key, you will be prompted whether or not you want to process each line in the CONFIG.SYS and AUTOEXEC.BAT files.
Ctrl + **F5**	If you press the **Ctrl** + **F5** keys, you will bypass both the CONFIG.SYS and AUTOEXEC.BAT files and not install or load DoubleSpace or DriveSpace.
Ctrl + **F8**	If you press the **Ctrl** + **F8** keys, you will be prompted whether or not you want to process each line in the CONFIG.SYS and AUTOEXEC.BAT files. You will not load DoubleSpace or DriveSpace.

In the next activity, you will selectively install lines in the CONFIG.SYS file.

15.2 Activity: Bypassing CONFIG.SYS and AUTOEXEC.BAT

Note: Do not use the DATA disk. Use the Bootable DOS System Disk created in Chapter 13. The Bootable DOS System Disk is in Drive A. The A:\> is displayed.

Step 1 Reboot the system by pressing the **Ctrl** + **Alt** + **Delete** keys.

Step 2 When you see the prompt Starting MS-DOS..., press the **F5** key.

```
Phoenix 80486 ROM BIOS PLUS Version 1.10 A16
Copyright (C) 1985-1988 Phoenix Technologies Ltd.
Copyright (C) 1990-1993 Dell Computer Corporation
All Rights Reserved

Quadtel S3 86C801/805 Enhanced VGA BIOS, Version 2.13.06
Copyright 1987-1992 Phoenix Technologies Ltd.
Copyright 1992-1993 S3 Inc.
All Rights Reserved

Dell Embedded Diagnostics Version 1.11
Copyright 1992-1993 Dell Computer Corporation
All Rights Reserved

Dell System 466/M

640 K Base Memory, 15648K Extended

Starting MS-DOS...

MS-DOS is bypassing your CONFIG.SYS and AUTOEXEC.BAT files.

Microsoft (R) MS-DOS (R) Version 6.22
          (C) Copyright Microsoft Corp. 1981-1994.

A:\>_
```

WHAT'S HAPPENING? The directives in `CONFIG.SYS` and the commands in the `AUTOEXEC.BAT` file were not executed. You did not load DOS high, nor did you have your RAM disks installed. But, if you remember, you placed `COMMAND.COM` in the DOS subdirectory on the Bootable DOS System Disk and, using the SHELL command, instructed DOS to locate the command processor in that subdirectory. Since you never processed `CONFIG.SYS`, how did the system boot when there was no `COMMAND.COM` in the root directory of the booting disk? DOS 6.0 and above is smarter than earlier versions of DOS. When it could not find `COMMAND.COM` in the root, it looked further.

Step 3   Key in the following: `A:\>`**SET** **Enter**

```
PATH A:\DOS
PROPMT $P$G
COMSPEC=A:\DOS\COMMAND.COM
```

WHAT'S HAPPENING? Even though you bypassed both `AUTOEXEC.BAT` and `CONFIG.SYS`, a basic prompt and path statement were set. In addition, `COMMAND.COM` was located in the subdirectory `DOS` so that the COMPSPEC location could be set.

Step 4   Reboot the system by pressing the **Ctrl** + **Alt** + **Delete** keys.

Step 5   The minute you see the prompt Starting MS-DOS..., press the **F8** key.

```
Phoenix 80486 ROM BIOS PLUS Version 1.10 A16
Copyright (C) 1985-1988 Phoenix Technologies Ltd.
Copyright (C) 1990-1993 Dell Computer Corporation
All Rights Reserved

Quadtel S3 86C801/805 Enhanced VGA BIOS, Version 2.13.06
Copyright 1987-1992 Phoenix Technologies Ltd.
Copyright 1992-1993 S3 Inc.
All Rights Reserved

Dell Embedded Diagnostics Version 1.11
Copyright 1992-1993 Dell Computer Corporation
All Rights Reserved

Dell System 466/M

640 K Base Memory, 15648K Extended

Starting MS-DOS...

MS-DOS will prompt you to confirm each CONFIG.SYS command.
DOS=HIGH [Y,N]?_
```

WHAT'S HAPPENING? You will be asked to confirm each line in the CONFIG.SYS file. Then you will be asked to process all the lines in the AUTOEXEC.BAT file.

Step 6   Answer Yes (Y) to all the directives except the two RAMDRIVES. Answer No (N) so you do not install them. Answer Yes (Y) for all the AUTOEXEC.BAT commands.

```
DEVICE=HIGH [Y,N]?Y
DEVICE=A:\DOS\HIMEM.SYS [Y,N]?Y

HIMMEM is testing extended memory...done.
FILES=20 [Y,N]?Y
BUFFERS=30 [Y,N]?Y
DEVICE=A:\DOS\RAMDRIVE.SYS /E [Y,N]?N
DEVICE=A:\DOS\RAMDRIVE.SYS 360 512 112 /E [Y,N]?N
LASTDRIVE=H [Y,N]?Y
SHELL=A:\DOS\COMMAND.COM  A:\DOS /P /E:256 [Y,N]?Y
Process AUTOEXEC.BAT [Y,N]?Y
ECHO OFF [Y,N]?Y
PROMPT $p$g [Y,N]?Y
PATH A:\DOS [Y,N]?Y
A:\>_
```

WHAT'S HAPPENING? You processed all your commands and directives except those that installed the virtual drives.

15.3 Using EMM386.EXE to Emulate Expanded Memory

In order to use extended, expanded, or upper memory, you must first install a memory manager. A memory manager is a software program that controls and provides access to the kind of memory you have. MS-DOS 5.0 and above provides two memory managers—HIMEM.SYS and EMM386.EXE. You have already been introduced to HIMEM.SYS, used to manage extended memory.

If you have older programs that use expanded memory, you need an expanded memory manager. If you have an older computer system that has been upgraded with an expanded memory card (circuit board) that has physical expanded memory, you must include a device statement in CONFIG.SYS providing the proper information based on your hardware specifications. When you purchased expanded memory, it also had its own software—its expanded memory manager. This is a third-party installation, and each system and installation is different.

DOS enters the picture here because an expanded memory manager must be installed via CONFIG.SYS. As an example, if you had a third-party memory board called WONDER BOARD, it would have a disk with a file on it called WONDER.SYS, which would be the device driver for WONDER BOARD. The software installation program would typically create a subdirectory called WONDER with the WONDER.SYS file and any other supporting files it needs. Thus, the CONFIG.SYS file would look like the following:

```
DEVICE=C:\DOS\HIMEM.SYS
DEVICE=C:\WONDER\WONDER.SYS
```

The statement in CONFIG.SYS would manage your hardware and is unique to each piece of hardware. MS-DOS 5.0 and above provides *no* expanded memory managers. Each expanded memory board requires its own expanded memory manager. Thus, if you have an expanded memory board, you must install the expanded memory manager that was supplied with the board according to its specifications.

What then is EMM386.EXE, which is provided with DOS as one of the installable device drivers? It is an **expanded memory emulator**, which will work only if you have extended memory and a 386 or above computer system. The device driver, EMM386.EXE, takes extended memory and turns it into (emulates) expanded memory. In the early days of computing, expanded memory was the only kind of "extra" memory a user had for programs. Many programs, such as Lotus 1-2-3, could take advantage of expanded memory. As extended memory has become more prevalent, most newer versions of programs no longer use expanded memory, only extended memory. However, if your computer system has extended memory and you have programs that use only expanded memory, you can use EMM386.EXE to provide this memory management function. EMM386.EXE uses about 80 KB of extended memory. The partial syntax is:

```
DEVICE=[drive:][path]EMM386.EXE [ON ¦ OFF ¦ AUTO] [memory]
```

ON ¦ OFF ¦ AUTO   Activates or suspends EMM386.EXE device
                    driver, or places it in auto mode.
memory   Specifies the maximum amount of extended
                    memory in kilobytes that you want EMM386 to
                    provide.

The default value is ON, which keeps expanded memory support active. The OFF parameter loads EMM386.EXE but suspends it, letting a program enable the device support at a later time. The AUTO parameter tells the drive to provide expanded memory only when a program requests it. The *memory* parameter specifies the maximum amount of extended memory allotted to expanded memory. You allocate only as much expanded memory as your program requires. Refer to the program documentation to allocate the amount of expanded memory you need. If you are using Windows 3.0 or 3.1, use EMM386.EXE only if you have programs other than Windows that need expanded memory outside of Windows. There are numerous parameters that can be used. Generally, you do not need to use them unless you are having difficulty in running a specific program. Again, if you have problems, refer to the system and software documentation. Following is an example of a CONFIG.SYS file using EMM386.EXE to specify that no more than 4096 bytes be used from extended memory, and a guaranteed 256 bytes (the default) be allotted to expanded memory:

```
DEVICE=C:\DOS\HIMEM.SYS
DEVICE=C:\DOS\EMM386.EXE  4096
```

Order is important. HIMEM.SYS must come first, and EMM386.EXE must come *before* any other device drivers that use expanded memory. The question arises, if most computers today have extended memory and most programs today use only extended memory, why bother with EMM386.EXE? Read on.

15.4 Using EMM386.EXE to Prepare Upper Memory

You have learned that you can free up conventional memory by loading DOS into high memory (the first 64 KB of extended memory) with the DOS=HIGH command in CONFIG.SYS. The memory between 640 KB and 1 MB is reserved and was called the adapter area but is now called the Upper Memory Area. Beginning with DOS 5.0, you can use portions of this area for loading device drivers and TSRs (Terminate and Stay Resident programs). You do this by converting the unused areas into UMBs (Upper Memory Blocks) that DOS can use them for device drivers and TSRs. EMM386.EXE, on a 386 or newer, allows you to use the UMA (Upper Memory Area) by converting any unused portions to UMBs (Upper Memory Blocks). Using the upper memory area allows you to conserve conventional memory. You want to free as much conventional memory as possible because programs run in conventional memory. The more items you can move to upper memory, the more memory you will have to run programs. This process becomes critical if you begin to get **Out of memory** errors. If you are having no memory problems, you may wish to leave well enough alone.

Again, you must have a 386 or newer computer system. In order to use the UMBs after preparing them with EMM386.EXE, you must tell DOS to do so by entering the following line in the CONFIG.SYS:

```
DOS=UMB
```

If you also want DOS to load high, the line would read

```
DOS=HIGH,UMB
```

The DOS=UMB command does not use the reserved memory. It simply tells DOS that you plan to use it later for DEVICEHIGH or LOADHIGH commands. DEVICEHIGH is a statement placed in CONFIG.SYS that tells DOS to load device drivers in the available UMBs. The LOADHIGH command will load TSRs or memory-resident programs into UMBs. DEVICEHIGH is used in CONFIG.SYS. LOADHIGH is used in AUTOEXEC.BAT or on the command line.

Order, again, is very important because the process is quite complicated. You must first set up the UMBs, then use the MEM command to see what will fit into the UMBs. Although many DOS device drivers and DOS memory-resident programs such as DOSKEY will run successfully in upper memory, not all of them do. When you add "foreign" device drivers or TSRs, there is a danger that some will not work properly.

Unfortunately, the only way to tell whether a program or device driver will run successfully in upper memory is through trial and error. Move it there and see if it works. Remember to have a bootable floppy system disk and to use the [F5] and [F8] keys to bypass troublesome programs. When a device driver or TSR does not work, it can lock up your entire system, not allowing you to correct any errors unless you reboot and bypass those problem areas.

The goal is to make your system and programs work successfully. Set up your UMBs and use the MEM command to see what available space you have. Move the device drivers and/or memory-resident programs one at a time into upper memory. Make sure each is working. Then add the next device/program. Not only is it easier to add these one at a time, but it is also easier to diagnose problems. If a program does not work, it is easy to identify the culprit and remove it from CONFIG.SYS. Usually, you load the device drivers and TSRs in order of size—from the largest to the smallest. If your loading is unsuccessful, try different orders and different combinations to see what works most effectively on your system.

You have been introduced to RAMDRIVE.SYS and ANSI.SYS, both of which are device drivers that can be loaded into upper memory. In addition, you have been introduced to DOSKEY, which is a program that can be loaded high. You are going to install these into conventional memory first, and use the MEM command to see how much memory they take. Then you are going to prepare upper memory and move these items there to see how much memory you save. Because each computer configuration is different and each computer has different amounts of memory, devices drivers, and/or TSRs, each installation of a driver into the UMB will be different. Remember, your numbers will differ from the example. If you have no extended memory, you will not be able to do this activity.

15.5 Activity: Using EMM386.EXE

Note: The Bootable DOS System Disk is in Drive A. The `A:\>` is displayed.

Step 1 Used EDIT to edit your `CONFIG.SYS` file on the Bootable DOS System Disk so it looks as follows:

DEVICE=A:\DOS\HIMEM.SYS
DOS=HIGH
FILES=20
BUFFERS=30
NUMLOCK=OFF
DEVICE=A:\DOS\ANSI.SYS
DEVICE=A:\DOS\RAMDRIVE.SYS /E
DEVICE=A:\DOS\RAMDRIVE.SYS 360 512 112 /E
LASTDRIVE=H
SHELL=A:\DOS\COMMAND.COM A:\DOS /P /E:256

Step 2 Use EDIT to edit your `AUTOEXEC.BAT` file on the Bootable DOS System Disk so it looks as follows:

@ECHO OFF
PROMPT pg
PATH A:\DOS
DOSKEY /BUFSIZE=2048

Step 3 Reboot the system.

Step 4 Key in the following: `A:\>`**MEM /C /P**

Name	Total		=	Conventional		+	Upper Memory	
MSDOS	14,941	(15K)		14,941	(15K)		0	(0K)
HIMEM	1,104	(1K)		1,104	(1K)		0	(0K)
ANSI	4,208	(4K)		4,208	(4K)		0	(0K)
RAMDRIVE	2,400	(2K)		2,400	(2K)		0	(0K)
DRVSPACE	51,312	(50K)		51,312	(50K)		0	(0K)
COMMAND	2,928	(3K)		2,928	(3K)		0	(0K)
DOSKEY	5,680	(6K)		5,680	(6K)		0	(0K)
Free	571,744	(558K)		571,744	(558K)		0	(0K)

```
Memory Summary:

  Type of Memory        Total    =   Used    +    Free
  ---------------      --------      --------     --------
  Conventional          654,336       82,592      571,744
  Upper                       0            0            0
  Reserved               99,328       99,328            0
  Extended (XMS)      16,023,552      499,712   15,523,840
  ---------------      --------      --------     --------
  Total memory       16,777,216      681,632   16,095,584
Press any key to continue
```

WHAT'S HAPPENING? Remember, your numbers will vary depending on how much memory you have and what is installed on your system. The above example has DRVSPACE installed. This may not be true on your computer. However, you can see that **DOSKEY**, ANSI.SYS and RAMDRIVE.SYS are not using upper memory. If you have not loaded device drivers high, device drivers are located before COMMAND, whereas programs such as **DOSKEY** are after COMMAND. What does the rest of the report look like? (Note: if you have fewer items installed, you may be able to see the entire output on one screen).

Step 5   Press **Enter**

```
  Total under 1 MB     654,336        82,592       571,744

  Largest executable program size         571,648   (558K)
  Largest free upper memory block               0     (0K)
  MS-DOS is resident in the high memory area.

  A:\>_
```

WHAT'S HAPPENING? You have installed some device drivers and a TSR. On this computer, a lot of extended memory exists that is not available to DOS. The DOS-approved device drivers that can be loaded in upper memory include the following:

```
ANSI.SYS        DISPLAY.SYS       DRIVER.SYS      EGA.SYS
PRINT.SYS       RAMDRIVE.SYS      SETVER.EXE
```

Step 6   Use **EDIT** to edit the CONFIG.SYS file on the Bootable DOS System Disk so it looks as follows:

> **DEVICE=A:\DOS\HIMEM.SYS**
> **DEVICE=A:\DOS\EMM386.EXE NOEMS**
> **DOS=HIGH,UMB**
> **FILES=20**
> **BUFFERS=30**
> **NUMLOCK=OFF**

```
DEVICEHIGH=A:\DOS\ANSI.SYS
DEVICEHIGH=A:\DOS\RAMDRIVE.SYS /E
DEVICEHIGH=A:\DOS\RAMDRIVE.SYS 360 512 112 /E
LASTDRIVE=H
SHELL=A:\DOS\COMMAND.COM A:\DOS /P /E:256
```

WHAT'S HAPPENING? You are using a parameter with EMM386.EXE—NOEMS. This parameter means there are no programs that need expanded memory, but the system will want to access upper memory. The line DOS=HIGH, UMB means that the intention is to load device drivers high in Upper Memory Blocks. The DOS=HIGH, UMB directive does not use the reserved memory. It simply prepares DOS so that it can later be used with the DEVICEHIGH or LOADHIGH commands. DEVICEHIGH is a statement for the CONFIG.SYS file. LOADHIGH is for TSRs that can be loaded into the upper memory area and can either be placed in AUTOEXEC.BAT or loaded from the command line. DOS=HIGH refers to loading DOS high; the UMB directive allows the link between conventional memory and upper memory. If you have programs that need expanded memory and thus need to emulate extended memory as expanded memory, these lines could also be included:

```
C:\DOS\HIMEM.SYS
C:\DOS\EMM386.EXE 1024 RAM
DOS=HIGH,UMB
```

The RAM parameter following the EMM386.EXE 1024 command tells DOS to run EMM386 to manage both the upper memory area *and* emulate expanded memory. In this case, 1 MB was allotted. Use the NOEMS switch if you have no programs that require expanded memory. *Do not install* HIMEM.SYS *or* EMM386.EXE *in reserved or upper memory*. These two device drivers *must* be in conventional memory.

Step 7   Use EDIT to edit your AUTOEXEC.BAT file on the Bootable DOS System Disk so it looks as follows:

```
@ECHO OFF
PROMPT $p$g
PATH A:\DOS
LOADHIGH  DOSKEY /BUFSIZE=2048
```

WHAT'S HAPPENING? You are planning to place DOSKEY in an UMB. When you reboot the system, look carefully at the screen display to see a report as the different elements are loaded.

Step 8   Reboot the system.

Step 9   Key in the following: A:\>**MEM /C /P**

```
Name         Total      =   Conventional  +   Upper Memory
--------   ---------------    ----------------    ----------------
MSDOS       14,909   (15K)    14,909   (15K)         0    (0K)
HIMEM        1,104    (1K)     1,104    (1K)         0    (0K)
EMM386       4,144    (4K)     4,144    (4K)         0    (0K)
DRVSPACE    51,312   (50K)    51,312   (50K)         0    (0K)
COMMAND      2,928    (3K)     2,928    (3K)         0    (0K)
ANSI         4,208    (4K)         0    (0K)     4,208    (4K)
RAMDRIVE     2,464    (2K)         0    (0K)     2,464    (2K)
DOSKEY       5,680    (6K)         0    (0K)     5,680    (6K)
Free       727,152  (710K)   580,896  (567K)   146,256 (143K)

Memory Summary:

Type of Memory      Total     =   Used     +   Free
---------------   ----------    ----------    ----------
Conventional        655,360        74,464       580,896
Upper               158,608        12,352       146,256
Reserved             98,304        98,304             0
Extended (XMS)   15,864,944       676,976    15,187,968
---------------   ----------    ----------    ----------
Total memory     16,777,216       681,632    16,095,584
Press any key to continue
```

WHAT'S HAPPENING? Remember, your numbers will vary depending on how much memory you have and what is installed on your system. You can see that this report varies quite a bit from the first memory report. By using EMM386.EXE and DOS=HIGH,UMB, you arranged the upper memory area into upper memory blocks. You then moved ANSI.SYS, RAMDRIVE.SYS, and DOSKEY into upper memory via the DEVICEHIGH and LOADHIGH statements. Notice that their order in memory has also changed. However, device drivers are still listed first, followed by programs. What about available memory?

Step 10   Press ⌜Enter⌟

```
Total under 1 MB     813,968          86,816       727,152

  Largest executable program size       580,800   (567K)
  Largest free upper memory block       146,160   (143K)
   MS-DOS is resident in the high memory area.

A:\>_
```

WHAT'S HAPPENING? Instead of having only 558K of conventional memory to execute programs, you now have 567K of conventional memory, a gain of 9K. You have successfully freed up conventional memory. In addition, a free upper memory block of 143K is available to store other device drivers or TSRs. The safest way to do so would be to add each device driver one at a time to the CONFIG.SYS file with the DEVICEHIGH statement; if it were a TSR, you would use the LOADHIGH at the command line or in the AUTOEXEC.BAT file. LOADHIGH may also be used at the command line the first time you execute the program. It does not have to be in the AUTOEXEC.BAT file. The approved DOS-provided memory-resident programs that can be loaded high include:

```
APPEND.EXE        DOSKEY.COM        DOSSHELL.COM
GRAPHICS.COM      KEYB.COM          MODE.COM
NLSFUNC.EXE       PRINT.EXE         SHARE.EXE
```

Remember, placing device drivers or memory-resident programs in upper memory can be tricky. The DEVICEHIGH directive is smart enough to know when a device driver cannot fit into the UMB and will load it in conventional memory. Occassionally, some device drivers need more memory after they are loaded, in which case the computer system could hang. Once again, although many device drivers work in upper memory and DOS programs such as DOSKEY can be loaded high, this is not always true of other device drivers and/or TSRs. Unfortunately, the only way to ascertain what will work successfully is to move the driver or program to upper memory, reboot and see what happens. You typically move the device drivers and/or programs one at a time to ensure everything works before adding the next item. Remember, always have a bootable system disk that you can use if a program will not work correctly in upper memory and hangs the system, because sometimes even the [F5] and [F8] keys will not work in such situations.

15.6 STACKS and FCBS

There are two other directives that you can modify to save memory—the STACKS and FCBS directives. In Chapter 13, you learned about the FILES directive. The FILES directive determines how many files can be open a one time. DOS uses five files for itself, so you must increase the number of files open. DOS tracks the open files by using a "nickname," a two bit file handle. What then is the FCBS directive? The FCBS determines how many files can be open using another scheme called File Control Blocks. This is a leftover directive when DOS used FCBS instead of file handles to track open files. Very few programs today use the FCBS method. But, if you do not specify a value for the FCBS in your CONFIG.SYS file, DOS defaults to a value of 4. The syntax is:

```
FCBS=n
```

where *n* is a value that can range from 1 to 255. Since few programs use FCBS, you can save memory by lowering the value and not accepting the DOS default value of 4. Instead, in your CONFIG.SYS file, you can specify FCBS=1.

STACKS in some ways is self-descriptive. The "stacked" up "things" are **hardware interrupts**. Your peripherals are all competing for the CPU's attention. The signals they send to the CPU are called hardware interrupts because they interrupt what the CPU is doing and cause the CPU to direct its attention to the interruption. (Software also send interrupts to the CPU.) DOS essentially maintains a pool of stacks by stacking up the interrupts and retrieving them from the stack when it has finished the task and can return to the interrupt. You can vary how many stacks you have and how large each stack will be. The syntax is:

    STACKS=*n*,*s*

where *n* is the number of stacks and *s* is the size of each stack in bytes. The value for *n* can be 0 or numbers in the range of 8 through 64. The value for the size of the stacks (*s*) can also be 0. If not specified, size can range from 32 to 512. If you do not specify any values, DOS assigns 9 stacks of 128 bytes each. The stacks statement would then be STACKS=9,128.

If your CONFIG.SYS file has a directive of STACKS=9,128, DOS has allocated 9 stacks of 128 bytes each. With overhead, STACKS then occupies about 2K of conventional memory. Although you cannot place STACKS in upper or extended memory, you can disable it with no ill effects by setting STACKS=0,0. This again will preserve conventional memory. However, if you get the error message of Internal stack overflow or System halted before your computer crashes, you will need to reboot and alter the value of the STACKS directive until you get no error messages. It is a good idea to start small with a directive of STACKS=9,128. If you continue to get error messages, then up the number again to STACKS=9,256 and so on.

15.7 Multiple Configurations

New to DOS 6.0 is the ability to have multiple configuration files. You may need more than one configuration (CONFIG.SYS) depending on what programs you are planning to run. For instance, perhaps you do not always wish to load virtual drives. You have learned that you can press the **F8** key and choose not to install RAMDRIVE.SYS. One problem with this is that you may not remember which configurations are necessary to run particular programs. In addition, most users' CONFIG.SYS files are much more complex than the one you have been using. This is particularly true when you have more than one user for a specific computer. Some third-party software, such as Bootcon, helps you customize CONFIG.SYS, but now you can create configuration menus using newly introduced commands in DOS 6.0. These configuration menus can call alternate choices in your AUTOEXEC.BAT file. See Table 15.1.

Command	Description	Syntax
[MENU]	Identifies the beginning of a series of menu items and commands that describe the configuration menu.	
INCLUDE	Includes the commands of one configuration block within another.	INCLUDE=*blockname*
MENUCOLOR	Sets the text and background color for the startup menu.	MENUCOLOR=*x*[,*y*] where *x* is the menu text and *y* is the background color. Values are from 0 to 15.
MENUDEFAULT	Specifies the default menu item and sets a timeout value if desired.	MENUDEFAULT=*blockname*[,*timeout*]
MENUITEM	Defines an item on the startup menu. Limit is nine items per menu.	MENUITEM=*blockname*[,*menutext*]
SUBMENU	Defines an item on a startup menu that, when it is selected, displays another set of choices.	SUBMENU=*blockname*[,*menutext*]
NUMLOCK	Since the user needs arrow keys to make choices, especially important that it can be turned off.	NUMLOCK [on | off]
[BLOCKNAME]	Every block specified within the MENUITEM command must have a corresponding block defined. Similar to GOTO label.	

Table 15.1 **Start-up Configuration Menu Commands**

You can also add color to your menu choices. The color codes are listed in Table 15.2.

Code	Color	Code	Color
0	Black	8	Gray
1	Blue	9	Bright Blue
2	Green	10	Bright Green
3	Cyan	11	Bright Cyan
4	Red	12	Bright Red
5	Magenta	13	Bright Magenta
6	Brown	14	Yellow
7	White	15	Bright White

Note: On some monitors, color choices 8 through 15 will blink.

Table 15.2 **Menu Color Choices**

In the example you are about to create, you will have three choices. The first will be your normal or default configuration. The next will be a "clean" configuration file with a minimum number of choices, and the last will be the configuration file that will load your virtual disks.

15.8 *Activity: Creating Multiple Configuations*

Note: The Bootable DOS System Disk is in Drive A. The A:\> is displayed.

Step 1   Use EDIT to edit and save your CONFIG.SYS file on the Bootable DOS System Disk so it looks as follows:

```
[MENU]
MENUITEM=NORMAL
MENUITEM=CLEAN
MENUITEM=RAMDRIVE
NUMLOCK=OFF

[NORMAL]
DEVICE=A:\DOS\HIMEM.SYS
DEVICE=A:\DOS\EMM386.EXE  NOEMS
DOS=HIGH,UMB
FILES=20
BUFFERS=30
STACKS=0,0
FCBS=1
DEVICEHIGH=A:\DOS\ANSI.SYS
SHELL=A:\DOS\COMMAND.COM A:\DOS /P /E:256
LASTDRIVE=H

[CLEAN]
DEVICE=A:\DOS\HIMEM.SYS
DOS=HIGH
FILES=20
BUFFERS=30
SHELL=A:\DOS\COMMAND.COM A:\DOS /P /E:256

[RAMDRIVE]
DEVICE=A:\DOS\HIMEM.SYS
DEVICE=A:\DOS\EMM386.EXE  NOEMS
DOS=HIGH,UMB
FILES=20
BUFFERS=30
STACKS=0,0
FCBS=1
DEVICEHIGH=A:\DOS\ANSI.SYS
```

> **SHELL=A:\DOS\COMMAND.COM A:\DOS /P /E:256**
> **LASTDRIVE=H**
> **DEVICEHIGH=A:\DOS\RAMDRIVE.SYS /E**
> **DEVICEHIGH=A:\DOS\RAMDRIVE.SYS 360 512 112 /E**

Step 2   Save the file.

Step 3   Reboot the system.

```
MS-DOS 6.22  Startup Menu

   1.      NORMAL
   2.      CLEAN
   3.      RAMDRIVE

Enter a choice:  1




F5=Bypass startup filesF8=Confirm each line of CONFIG.SYS and AUTOEXEC.BAT [N]
```

WHAT'S HAPPENING? You have written a menu. After the [MENU] section, each item that was listed in [MENUITEM] is a menu choice. Number 1 (NORMAL) is shaded and is the default choice.

Step 4   Press 2 **Enter**

```
A:\>_
```

WHAT'S HAPPENING? You have executed the simplest configuration with a minimum number of drivers.

Step 5   Use EDIT to edit your CONFIG.SYS file on the Bootable DOS System Disk so it looks as follows:

> **[MENU]**
> **MENUCOLOR=4,2**
> **MENUDEFAULT=STANDARD,10**
> **MENUITEM=NORAMDRIVE Will not load the virtual disks.**
> **MENUITEM=CLEAN   Nothing except HIMEM.**
> **MENUITEM=RAMDRIVE   Will load all virtual disks.**
> **MENUITEM=STANDARD   Will not load ANSI.SYS.**
> **NUMLOCK=OFF**

```
[NORAMDRIVE]
DEVICE=A:\DOS\HIMEM.SYS
DEVICE=A:\DOS\EMM386.EXE  NOEMS
DOS=HIGH,UMB
FILES=20
BUFFERS=30
STACKS=0,0
FCBS=1
DEVICEHIGH=A:\DOS\ANSI.SYS
SHELL=A:\DOS\COMMAND.COM A:\DOS /P /E:256
LASTDRIVE=H

[CLEAN]
DEVICE=A:\DOS\HIMEM.SYS
DOS=HIGH
FILES=20
BUFFERS=30
SHELL=A:\DOS\COMMAND.COM A:\DOS /P /E:256

[RAMDRIVE]
DEVICE=A:\DOS\HIMEM.SYS
DEVICE=A:\DOS\EMM386.EXE  NOEMS
DOS=HIGH,UMB
FILES=20
BUFFERS=30
STACKS=0,0
FCBS=1
DEVICEHIGH=A:\DOS\ANSI.SYS
SHELL=A:\DOS\COMMAND.COM A:\DOS /P /E:256
LASTDRIVE=H
DEVICEHIGH=A:\DOS\RAMDRIVE.SYS /E
DEVICEHIGH=A:\DOS\RAMDRIVE.SYS  360 512  112  /E

[STANDARD]
DEVICE=A:\DOS\HIMEM.SYS
DEVICE=A:\DOS\EMM386.EXE  NOEMS
DOS=HIGH,UMB
FILES=20
BUFFERS=30
STACKS=0,0
FCBS=1
SHELL=A:\DOS\COMMAND.COM A:\DOS /P /E:256
LASTDRIVE=H
```

WHAT'S HAPPENING? You have added some items to the configuration menu.

Command	**Effect**
MENUCOLOR 4,2	This will give you a menu with red text on a green background. The colors will remain in effect for most DOS commands. However, if you key in CLS, the colors will return to the standard black and white. In addition, if you load ANSI.SYS, the colors will appear only on the menu.
MENUDEFAULT=STANDARD,10	This command will determine which configuration block you want the system to default to if no key is pressed. The 10 is the timeout period. In other words, if a key is not pressed in 10 seconds, your default STANDARD will be chosen.
MENUITEM=NORAMDRIVE	You changed NORMAL to NORAMDRIVE and added text to explain what this choice will do.
MENUITEM=CLEAN	You added text to explain what this choice will do.
MENUITEM=RAMDRIVE	You added text to explain what this choice will do.
MENUITEM=STANDARD	You added a new menu item called STANDARD, which will be your default if no key is pressed within 10 seconds.
[NORAMDRIVE]	You changed the block title from NORMAL to NORAMDRIVE to match your configuration block.
[CLEAN]	No changes.
[RAMDRIVE]	No changes.
[STANDARD]	A new section that is your default choice. It is identical to NORAMDRIVE except you removed the DEVICEHIGH=A:\DOS\ANSI.SYS

Step 6   Save the file.

Step 7   Reboot the system.

```
MS-DOS 6.22  Startup Menu

   1.    Will not load the virtual disks.
   2.    Nothing except HIMEM.
   3.    Will load all virtual disks.
   4.    Will not load ANSI.SYS

Enter a choice: 4            Time remaining: 05




F5=Bypass startup filesF8=Confirm each line of CONFIG.SYS and AUTOEXEC.BAT [N]
```

WHAT'S HAPPENING? You should have a green screen with red text. Choice 4 is highlighted because you made it the default. The clock is ticking. If you do not press any keys, you will be at the A:\>.

Step 8   Key in the following: A:\>**TYPE APR.99** **⌷Enter⌷**

```
A:\>TYPE APR.99
This is my April file.
It is my fourth dummy file.
This is file 4.

A:\>_
```

WHAT'S HAPPENING? Your screen should still be a green background with red text.

Step 9   Key in the following: A:\>**CLS** **⌷Enter⌷**

```
A:\>_
```

WHAT'S HAPPENING? Your colors are gone. Using CLS made the colors disappear and returned you to the default colors. You will have no colors if you select NORAMDRIVE or RAMDRIVE because each of those selections loads ANSI.SYS, which also disables the color feature. You may have noted that you did a lot of keying in when, in fact, each configuration section had many items in common. You can simplify your configuration file by using the INCLUDE statement.

Step 10   Use EDIT to edit your CONFIG.SYS file on the Bootable DOS System Disk so it looks as follows:

```
[MENU]
MENUCOLOR=4,2
MENUDEFAULT=STANDARD,10
MENUITEM=NORAMDRIVE   Will not load the virtual disks.
MENUITEM=CLEAN        Nothing except HIMEM.
MENUITEM=RAMDRIVE     Will load all virtual disks.
MENUITEM=STANDARD     Will not load ANSI.SYS.
NUMLOCK=OFF

[SHARED]
DEVICE=A:\DOS\HIMEM.SYS
DOS=HIGH
FILES=20
BUFFERS=30
SHELL=A:\DOS\COMMAND.COM A:\DOS /P /E:256

[NORAMDRIVE]
INCLUDE=SHARED
DEVICE=A:\DOS\EMM386.EXE  NOEMS
DOS= UMB
STACKS=0,0
FCBS=1
DEVICEHIGH=A:\DOS\ANSI.SYS
LASTDRIVE=H

[CLEAN]
INCLUDE=SHARED

[RAMDRIVE]
INCLUDE=SHARED
DEVICE=A:\DOS\EMM386.EXE  NOEMS
DOS=UMB
STACKS=0,0
FCBS=1
DEVICEHIGH=A:\DOS\ANSI.SYS
LASTDRIVE=H
DEVICEHIGH=A:\DOS\RAMDRIVE.SYS /E
DEVICEHIGH=A:\DOS\RAMDRIVE.SYS  360 512  112  /E

[STANDARD]
INCLUDE=SHARED
DEVICE=A:\DOS\EMM386.EXE  NOEMS
DOS=UMB
STACKS=0,0
FCBS=1
LASTDRIVE=H
```

WHAT'S HAPPENING? You have added some items to the configuration menu.

Command	Effect
[SHARED]	Includes the commands common to all configurations.
[NORAMDRIVE]	By adding INCLUDE=SHARED, this configuration will include all lines in the SHARED block. You removed any duplicate commands. You altered DOS=HIGH,UMB to DOS=UMB because DOS=HIGH is in the SHARED block
[CLEAN]	By adding INCLUDE=SHARED, this configuration will include all lines in the SHARED block. You removed any duplicate commands.
[RAMDRIVE]	By adding INCLUDE=SHARED, this configuration will include all lines in the SHARED block. You removed any duplicate commands. You altered DOS=HIGH,UMB to DOS=UMB because DOS=HIGH is in the SHARED block.
[STANDARD]	By adding INCLUDE=SHARED, this configuration will include all lines in the SHARED block. You removed any duplicate commands. You altered DOS=HIGH,UMB to DOS=UMB because DOS=HIGH is in the SHARED block.

Step 11 Save the file.

Step 12 Reboot the system.

```
MS-DOS 6.22  Startup Menu

   1.     Will not load the virtual disks.
   2.     Nothing except HIMEM.
   3.     Will load all virtual disks.
   4.     Will not load ANSI.SYS

Enter a choice: 4          Time remaining: 05




F5=Bypass startup filesF8=Confirm each line of CONFIG.SYS and AUTOEXEC.BAT [N]
```

Step 13 Press **2** Enter

```
A:\>_
```

WHAT'S HAPPENING? Your INCLUDE statement worked. You can also customize your AUTOEXEC.BAT file depending on what configuration you have chosen. When you use a multiconfiguration, DOS creates an environmental variable called %CONFIG% to indicate what choice the user made. You can use the environmental variable in your AUTOEXEC.BAT statement.

Step 14　Edit the `AUTOEXEC.BAT` file so it looks as follows:

```
@ECHO OFF
PROMPT $p$g
PATH A:\DOS
GOTO %CONFIG%
:CLEAN
GOTO END
:NORAMDRIVE
LOADHIGH DOSKEY /BUFSIZE=2048
:RAMDRIVE
LOADHIGH DOSKEY /BUFSIZE=2048
GOTO END
:STANDARD
LOADHIGH DOSKEY /BUFSIZE=2048
GOTO END
:END
```

Step 15　Save the file.

Step 16　Reboot the system.

```
MS-DOS 6.22  Startup Menu

    1.    Will not load the virtual disks.
    2.    Nothing except HIMEM.
    3.    Will load all virtual disks.
    4.    Will not load ANSI.SYS

Enter a choice:   4            Time remaining: 05




F5=Bypass startup files F8=Confirm each line of CONFIG.SYS and AUTOEXEC.BAT [N]
```

Step 17　Press 2 **Enter**

```
A:\>_
```

Step 18　Key in the following: A:\>**MEM /M DOSKEY** **Enter**

```
A:\>MEM /M DOSKEY
DOSKEY is not currently in memory.

A:\>_
```

WHAT'S HAPPENING? Because you chose 2, you did not load DOSKEY. You can make the `AUTOEXEC.BAT` file much simpler by using an IF statement.

Step 19   Key in the following: A:\>**SET** Enter

```
A:\>SET
CONFIG=CLEAN
COMSPEC=A:\DOS\COMMAND.COM
PROMPT=$p$g
PATH=A:\DOS
```

WHAT'S HAPPENING? Your environmental variable is CLEAN, your number 2 choice.

Step 20   Edit the `AUTOEXEC.BAT` file so it looks as follows:

> **@ECHO OFF**
> **PROMPT pg**
> **PATH A:\DOS**
> **IF "%CONFIG%"=="CLEAN" GOTO END**
> **LOADHIGH DOSKEY /BUFSIZE=2048**
> **:END**

Step 21   Save the file.

Step 22   Reboot the system.

```
MS-DOS 6.22  Startup Menu

   1.     Will not load the virtual disks.
   2.     Nothing except HIMEM.
   3.     Will load all virtual disks.
   4.     Will not load ANSI.SYS

Enter a choice: 4              Time remaining: 05




F5=Bypass startup files F8=Confirm each line of CONFIG.SYS and AUTOEXEC.BAT
[N]
```

Step 23   Press 1 Enter

```
A:\>_
```

Step 24   Key in the following: A:\>**MEM /M DOSKEY** Enter

```
A:\>MEM /M DOSKEY

DOSKEY is using the following memory:

    Segment   Region       Total        Type
    -------   ------   ---------------   --------
     0CA59      1        5,680    (6K)   Program
                                 ---------------
    Total Size:          5,680    (6K)

A:\>_
```

WHAT'S HAPPENING? Because you chose 1, you loaded DOSKEY.

Step 25   Key in the following: A:\>**SET** [Enter]

```
A:\>SET
CONFIG=NORAMDRIVE
COMSPEC=A:\DOS\COMMAND.COM
PROMPT=$p$g
PATH=A:\DOS
```

WHAT'S HAPPENING? Your environmental variable is NORAMDRIVE, your number 1 choice.

15.9 Caching with SMARTDRIVE

You have set buffers in CONFIG.SYS. Disk buffers occupy an area in memory that DOS looks to for necessary information before going to disk. DOS uses buffers because it is faster to go to memory than it is to read information from the disk. Disk buffers are really small caches. Caching programs improve the native DOS disk buffering and have two functions—read caches and write caches. A read cache intercepts, makes a copy, and places into memory whatever file you have read . When a program makes a request to DOS for data, the caching program intercepts the request and checks to see if it already has the requested information in memory. If it does, it passes the data to the program. If the cache does not have the requested information, it reads the disk, keeps a copy of the requested information in the cache, and passes the data onto the program. See Figure 15.1.

Caching programs are smart. They assume that if you read a sector of the disk, you will probably want to read the same sector again soon. They also assume that you will probably want the next sector of data even if you have not asked for it, so they will load that sector also. They try to set priorities by anticipating what you might need. As the cache gets filled, the caching program will discard the oldest or least-used data. If you have not previously asked for the data, the disk will have to be read.

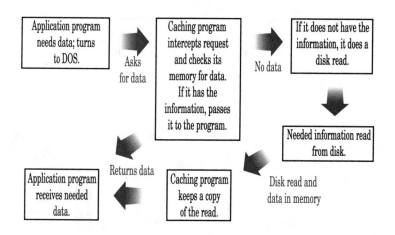

Figure 15.1   ***Read Caching***

When the caching program finds what it needs in memory, it is considered a "hit." You can think of a "hit" as an incident when the caching program had the data in memory and a disk read was avoided, therefore saving processing time. A "miss" would be the opposite—the data was not in memory and a disk read was mandatory, taking processing time. An 80% hit rate is not unusual. This improves processing speed because reading the cache is faster than going to the disk. Read caching is very safe. Since the data is actually on disk, even if you have a power failure while using a caching program, your data is safe.

Write caching is the opposite of read caching. When a program wants to write data to disk, the cache makes a copy of it and holds the data in the memory cache until a specified time period has elapsed or until the system is less busy, at which time the data is written to the disk with minimal impact on performance. Write-caching can be dangerous or even fatal to your data, since you may think that the data has been saved to disk when in fact it has not. However, anything that minimizes the amount of time a disk needs to be accessed and improves performance is a benefit. See Figure 15.2.

In summary, disk caching speeds performance because it works in RAM, which is always faster than going to disk for either a read or write option. Once again, you make a trade-off. You are trying to increase performance while taking some calculated risks with data.

You can purchase commercial third-party caching programs, but if you own DOS 5 or newer, you already have a disk-caching program called SmartDrive. The DOS 5 version is called `SMARTDRV.SYS`, and the DOS 6 version is called `SMARTDRV.EXE`. The two versions of SMARTDRV are very different. If you have the DOS 5 version, it is a read-only cache and caches hard-disk data only. You may set the size of the cache and decide whether you want to install it in extended or expanded memory. Because it is a driver, it can be installed only via a DEVICE or

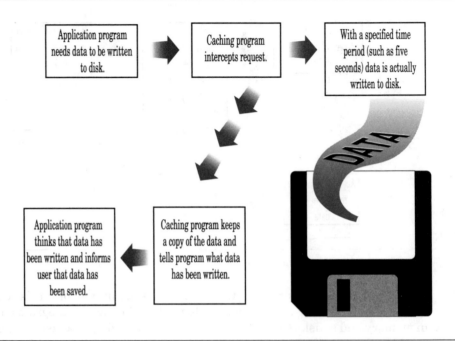

Figure 15.2 **Write Caching**

DEVICEHIGH statement in `CONFIG.SYS`. Windows 3.1 introduced `SMARTDRV.EXE`, the next generation of caching, which offers many more options. It is installed either from the command line or in `AUTOEXEC.BAT`.

DOS 6, which replaces `SMARTDRV.SYS` with `SMARTDRV.EXE`, further improves this utility program. It adds write caching and can cache floppy disks as well as CD-ROM disks. It will install only in extended memory. The early version of `SMARTDRV.EXE` installed write caching automatically with few provisions to turn it off. This caused much user concern, so the DOS 6 version of `SMARTDRV.EXE` installs with write caching off. In addition, it includes a switch (/X) that will disable write-caching. You should use the most current version of `SMARTDRV.EXE`. Versions could be located in either the WINDOWS or DOS directories. To identify the most current version, check the file creation date.

`SMARTDRV.EXE` has several advantages. First, since it resides in extended memory, it does not use conventional memory. Second, the cache can be very large, from a minimum of 256 KB up to 8 MB. It is specifically designed to improve performance and thus is very effective in shortening processing time. Since `SMARTDDRV.EXE` occupies extended memory, `HIMEM.SYS` must be installed in the `CONFIG.SYS` file. `SMARTDRV.EXE` will automatically install in extended memory. You do not have to load it high. It has many options and switches. The syntax is:

```
SMARTDRV [/X] [[drive[+|-]]...] [/U] [/C | /R] [/F | /N] [/L] [/V | /Q | /S]
     [InitCacheSize [WinCacheSize]] [/E:ElementSize] [/B:BufferSize]
```

/X	Disables write-behind caching for all drives.
drive	Sets caching options on specific drive(s). The specified drive(s) will have write-caching disabled unless you add +.
+	Enables write-behind caching for the specified drive.
-	Disables all caching for the specified drive.
/U	Do not load CD-ROM caching module.
/C	Writes all information currently in write-cache to hard disk.
/R	Clears the cache and restarts SmartDrive.
/F	Writes cached data before command prompt returns (default).
/N	Doesn't write cached data before command prompt returns.
/L	Prevents SmartDrive from loading itself into upper memory.
/V	Displays SmartDrive status messages when loading.
/Q	Does not display status information.
/S	Displays additional information about SmartDrive's status.
InitCacheSize	Specifies XMS memory (KB) for the cache.
WinCacheSize	Specifies XMS memory (KB) for the cache with Windows.
/E:ElementSize	Specifies how many bytes of information to move at one time.
/B:BufferSize	Specifies the size of the read-ahead buffer.

DOS typically places a line in your `AUTOEXEC.BAT` file that reads `C:\DOS\SMARTDRV.EXE`. In DOS 6.2, the line it installs is `C:\DOS\SMARTDRV.EXE /X`. The /X parameter disables write caching by default. If you had DOS 6.0 installed and upgraded to 6.2 or 6.22, the /X parameter *was not* added to the `C:\DOS\SMARTDRV.EXE`, so write caching is on.

What about the dangers of write caching? The good news is that, unless you specify, write caching is not enabled for floppy disks. The reason is that you could easily change floppy disks during a work session before caching can occur. In addition, if you press **Ctrl** + **Alt** + **Delete**, SMARTDRV intercepts those keys and writes any data in the cache to disk while presenting you with a message `Waiting for System Shutdown`. The bad news is, if you press a reset button, turn off your computer before the data in the cache has been written to disk, or have a power failure, you stand a good chance of losing data. This is particularly true if you have a large cache with many files. There are some ways to ensure not losing data. First, do not use the reset button. Second, use the command SMARTDRV /C. Keying in that command at the command line or with a batch file will flush the cache; i.e., write anything in the buffer to disk.

There is a more serious problem. A cache is dynamic; its contents are is always changing. The cache reads and writes to the FAT and the directory on the disk that is being cached. Thus, if you run a program such as CHKDSK /F, SCANDISK, or DEFRAG, each of which modifies the FAT and directory table, you have a prescription for disaster. Those programs will report bogus lost clusters or bad sectors. If you try to "repair" those bogus errors, you corrupt the FAT and directory, which makes data and programs unrecoverable. If you have disabled write caching, you are fairly safe, but the safest way is to do a clean boot so no caching program is running. Then, you may safely repair any "real" disk errors.

If write caching is so potentially dangerous, should you use it? The answer is yes if you want to maximize SmartDrive performance, and no if you want to be on the safe side. You can experiment with write caching enabled and disabled when you are using different programs, but be sure to pay attention to the previously mentioned warnings. If you see no improvement in performance, disable write caching. If you see a big improvement in performance, you may leave it enabled. You can monitor the "hit" rate by issuing the SMARTDRV /S command.

The next question is how big should you set the cache? When you install SMARTDRV, it uses the following default values:

Extended Memory	InitCacheSize	WinCacheSize
Up to 1 MB	All extended memory	Zero (no caching)
Up to 2 MB	1 MB	256K
Up to 4 MB	1 MB	512K
Up to 6 MB	2 MB	1 MB
6 MB or more	2 MB	2 MB

Again, if you have more extended memory, you can experiment with altering the size of the cache. Although many experts feel that the performance gain of a cache any larger than 2 MB is minimal, other experts feel differently. Some feel that if you have 8 MB or more of extended memory, you are not penalized for using the extended memory and it pays to install at least a 4MB cache. This assessment is particularly true if you are running both DOS and Windows programs. When you enter Windows SMARTDRV voluntarily downsizes the cache to let Windows use the extended memory. You can also set a minimum cache size. In addition, if you run Windows and set your command line to SMARTDRV 4095 2048, you will set the cache size to 4 MB when DOS is running and 2 MB when Windows is running. Do not use SMARTDRV after loading Windows.

SMARTDRV may also be installed as a device driver via CONFIG.SYS. You do this only if you need double-buffering. Double-buffering resolves various hardware conflicts that have to do with certain SCSI devices, some EDSI drives, and some other hard disk controllers. An explanation of this is beyond this text. However, you can easily tell whether or not you need double-buffering if you install SMARTDRV /DOUBLE_BUFFER in your CONFIG.SYS file and in AUTOEXEC.BAT. Be sure that you are using HIMEM.SYS and EMM386.EXE. When you key in SMARTDRV you will get a report that will help you determine whether or not you need double-buffering.

15.10 Activity: Using SMARTDRV

Note 1:   The Bootable DOS System Disk is in Drive A. The A:\> is displayed.

Note 2:   If you are on a network and do not have DOS on your local station, you will have to access the network to copy the files. Then you will have to log off the network to complete this activity.

Step 1   Key in the following:

   A:\>**COPY C:\DOS\SMARTDRV.EXE DOS** [Enter]

Step 2   Key in the following:

   A:\>**COPY C:\DOS\FASTOPEN.EXE DOS** [Enter]

Step 3   Key in the following:

   A:\>**COPY C:\DOS6BK\GAMES\MLSHUT*.*** [Enter]

```
A:\>COPY C:\DOS\SMARTDRV.EXE DOS
        1 file(s) copied

A:\>COPY C:\DOS\FASTOPEN.EXE DOS
        1 file(s) copied

A:\>COPY C:\DOS6BK\GAMES\MLSHUT*.*
C:\DOS6BK\GAMES\MLSHUT.DOC
C:\DOS6BK\GAMES\MLSHUT.EXE
        2 file(s) copied

A:\>_
```

WHAT'S HAPPENING? You have copied the necessary files for this activity and the next activity. You have also copied a program so you can see the results of using SMARTDRV.

Step 4   Key in the following: A:\>**COPY CONFIG.SYS CONFIG.MEN** [Enter]

Step 5   Key in the following:

   A:\>**COPY AUTOEXEC.BAT AUTOEXEC.MEN** [Enter]

```
A:\>COPY CONFIG.SYS CONFIG.MEN
       1 file(s) copied

A:\>COPY AUTOEXEC.BAT AUTOEXEC.MEN
       1 file(s) copied

A:\>_
```

WHAT'S HAPPENING? You want a much simpler CONFIG.SYS and AUTOEXEC.BAT.

Step 6   Edit and save CONFIG.SYS so it looks as follows:

> **DEVICE=A:\DOS\HIMEM.SYS**
> **DEVICE=A:\DOS\EMM386.EXE NOEMS**
> **DOS=HIGH,UMB**
> **FILES=20**
> **BUFFERS=10**
> **SHELL=A:\DOS\COMMAND.COM A:\DOS /P /E:256**
> **STACKS=0,0**
> **FCBS=1**
> **NUMLOCK=OFF**
> **LASTDRIVE=H**
> **DEVICE=A:\DOS\SMARTDRV.EXE /DOUBLE_BUFFER**

WHAT'S HAPPENING? You have installed SMARTDRV as a device with the double-buffering option. In addition, you reduced the number of buffers from 30 to 10. Since each buffer occupies about 512 bytes of conventional memory and since BUFFERS is a secondary cache, DOS still has to check the buffers. Thus, you can slow performance when you use SMARTDRV if you have a high number of BUFFERS set.

Step 7   Edit and save AUTOEXEC.BAT so it looks as follows:

> **@ECHO OFF**
> **PROMPT pg**
> **PATH A:\DOS**
> **LOADHIGH DOSKEY /BUFSIZE=2048**
> **SMARTDRV**

WHAT'S HAPPENING? You have a simpler AUTOEXEC.BAT file.

Note: If you had to log on to a network to copy files, you must log off the network prior to taking the next step.

Step 8   Reboot the system.

Step 9   Play the MLSHUT game.

Step 10   Create a file in **EDIT** called `TEST.FIL` with your impressions of MLSHUT. Save the file.

Step 11   Key in the following: `A:\>`**SMARTDRV** **/S** [Enter]

```
Copyright 1991,1993 Microsoft Corp.

Room for          256 elements of 8,192 bytes each
There have been    125 cache hits
   and           86 cache misses.

Cache size:     2,097,152 bytes
Cache size while running Windows:    2,097,152

           Disk Caching Status
  drive     read cache    write cache   buffering
  -------------------------------------------------
    A:         yes           no           no
    B:         yes           no           no
    C:         yes           yes          no
    H:*        yes           yes          no
    I:*        yes           yes          no

*Compressed drive cached via host drive.
Write behind caching data will be committed before command prompt
returns.

For help, type "Smartdrv /?".

A:\>_
```

WHAT'S HAPPENING? Your report will look different depending on how many drives you have, if they are compressed, how much memory you have, and how much work you did. Since the two programs you used are not very disk intensive, your "hit" rate using the cache is not very high. In this example, of the 211 times it went to the cache, it found ("hit") data 125 times. There were also 86 "misses," where the processor had to access the disk because the data was not in the cache. If you take the sum of the hits and misses (125 + 86 = 211) divide by the number of hits, and multiply by 100 (125 / 211 = .5924 * 100 = 59), you have a hit rate of 59 percent. In other words physical disk drive activity has been reduced by a factor of 59 percent. This is not too bad when you consider that you are not using any programs that are disk intensive. You can try this when you are using "real" programs to see what kind of performance you get. In addition, look at the Disk Caching Status. The buffering column reads `no` for every drive listed, which means that you have no need for double-buffering on this system. If you had a `yes` in a column, you would need to install double-buffering.

Step 12   Key in the following: A:\>**SMARTDRV /C** [Enter]

```
A:\>SMARTDRV   /C

A:\>
```

WHAT'S HAPPENING? Nothing appears to have happened, but in fact you have told SMARTDRV to write anything in cache to disk.

Step 13   Edit and save CONFIG.SYS so it looks as follows:

> **DEVICE=A:\DOS\HIMEM.SYS**
> **DEVICE=A:\DOS\EMM386.EXE NOEMS**
> **DOS=HIGH,UMB**
> **FILES=20**
> **BUFFERS=10**
> **SHELL=A:\DOS\COMMAND.COM A:\DOS /P /E:256**
> **STACKS=0,0**
> **FCBS=1**
> **NUMLOCK=OFF**
> **LASTDRIVE=H**

WHAT'S HAPPENING? You do not need double-buffering so you removed it.

Step 14   Edit and save AUTOEXEC.BAT so it looks as follows:

> **@ECHO OFF**
> **PROMPT pg**
> **PATH A:\DOS**
> **LOADHIGH DOSKEY /BUFSIZE=2048**
> **SMARTDRV /X**

WHAT'S HAPPENING? You have turned off write caching.

Step 15   Reboot the system.

Step 16   Play the MLSHUT game.

Step 17   Key in the folowing: A:\>**CLS** [Enter]

Step 18   Edit TEST.FIL with your impressions of SMARTDRV. Save the file.

Step 19   Key in the following: A:\>**DIR** [Enter]

Step 20   Key in the following: A:\>**DIR TEST.FIL** [Enter]

Step 21   Key in the following: A:\>**VER** [Enter]

Step 22   Edit TEST.FIL and add your further impressions of MLSHUT. Save the file.

Step 23   Key in the following: A:\>**SMARTDRV** /S [Enter]

```
Copyright 1991,1993 Microsoft Corp.

Room for         256 elements of 8,192 bytes each
There have been   38 cache hits
  and           55 cache misses.

Cache size:    2,097,152 bytes
Cache size while running Windows:   2,097,152

          Disk Caching Status
drive     read cache   write cache  buffering
--------------------------------------------------
  A:          yes          no           no
  B:          yes          no           no
  C:          yes          yes          no
  H:*         yes          yes          no
  I:*         yes          yes          no

*Compressed drive cached via host drive.
Write behind caching data will be committed before command prompt
returns.

For help, type "Smartdrv /?".

A:\>_
```

WHAT'S HAPPENING? Your report will look different depending on how many drives you have, if they are compressed, how much memory you have, and how much work you did. Since the programs you executed are not very disk intensive, your "hit" rate using the cache is not very high. In this example, of the 93 times it went to the cache, it required disk access 55 times. If you take the sum of the hits and misses (38 + 55 = 93), divide by the number of hits, and multiply by 100 (38 / 93 = .4086 * 100 = 40.86), you have a hit rate of 41 percent. In other words, physical disk drive activity has been reduced by a factor of 41 percent. You can see that by disabling write caching, you have decreased performance.

15.11 Optimizing System Performance with FASTOPEN

FASTOPEN, introduced in DOS 3.3, provides faster access to files that are constantly used. FASTOPEN keeps directory information in a memory buffer about the most recently accessed files. Remember, DOS must locate any file you want from the disk. Depending on your system, the amount of time that DOS spends looking for files can be considerable. The FASTOPEN command tells DOS to remember the starting location on the disk of the most recently used files. FASTOPEN places the file's name and starting location in a table in memory. When you open a file or execute an external command, DOS will first search the FASTOPEN table to see if it can find the file without having to search the directory on the disk. If the file is not in the table, DOS searches the disk and, when it finds the file, places it in the FASTOPEN table so it can be referenced again quickly. FASTOPEN works at the file level, whereas SMARTDRV works at the disk sector level. The syntax is:

```
FASTOPEN drive:[[=]n] [drive:[[=]n][ ...]] [/X]
```

     drive: Specifies the hard disk drive you want Fastopen to
                   work with.

      n   Specifies the maximum number of file locations
                   Fastopen retains in its filename cache.

     /X   Creates the filename cache in expanded memory.

If you wish to install FASTOPEN in CONFIG.SYS instead of at the command line, the syntax is:

```
INSTALL [drive:][path]FASTOPEN drive:[[=]n] [drive:[[=]n][ ...]] [/X]
```

    FASTOPEN works only on a hard disk and will not work on a network. Do not use DEFRAG, SCANDISK, or CHKDSK /F when you have installed FASTOPEN. Do not use FASTOPEN with Windows. FASTOPEN is most useful when you have large, deep directories, or you are using database programs, compilers, or programs like AutoCad that reopen the same file often. FASTOPEN uses about 5520 bytes for itself and about 48 bytes for every file it tracks. If you track too many files, DOS spends more time looking at FASTOPEN than it would have if it had gone directly to the disk.

    You can experiment with FASTOPEN. If you do not see any improvement in performance, you are not using files that can take advantage of FASTOPEN's capabilities. In that case, do not use it. Although FASTOPEN can track up to 999 files, it is inefficient to take up that much memory for files you probably will not access. As a rule of thumb, use 1 file for every MB of hard disk space you have. Thus, if you have a 60 MB hard disk, use the value 60. The command can be executed from the command lines or placed in AUTOEXEC.BAT as:

```
FASTOPEN C:=60
```

This command tells FASTOPEN to keep track of 60 files on Drive C. If you have more than one hard drive, you issue the command as

```
FASTOPEN C:=60 D:=30
```

This command tells FASTOPEN to keep track of 60 files on Drive C and 30 files on Drive D. If you want to use UMBs with FASTOPEN, you place the following line in your AUTOEXEC.BAT file:

```
LOADHIGH  C:\DOS\FASTOPEN.EXE  C:60  D:30
```

You can use SMARTDRV and FASTOPEN together. Remember, the extended and expanded memory managers must come *before* FASTOPEN in your CONFIG.SYS file.

15.12 MemMaker

You have been exploring different ways to alter your CONFIG.SYS and AUTOEXEC.BAT files to manage conventional, extended and high memory efficiently. The process has been very laborious. By trial and error you tried to get the maximum amount of memory. A command introduced in DOS 6.0 called MemMaker takes the labor out of the memory maze. You must have extended memory and a 386 or higher processor. You must also not be in Windows when you run this program. MemMaker automatically analyzes memory and reconfigures your CONFIG.SYS and AUTOEXEC.BAT files. Even after you run MemMaker, you can still edit CONFIG.SYS and/or AUTOEXEC.BAT and "tweak" it to gain more memory. However, for most people, it is much easier to run MemMaker and accept, at least initially, the default values.

To run MemMaker, you key in MemMaker at the DOS system level. MemMaker then analyzes your hardware and optimizes the computer's memory by moving device drivers and memory resident programs into upper memory. You will have to choose either Express Setup or Custom Setup. Unless you have memory problems, use Express Setup. Then, simply follow the prompts on the screen. You need to run MemMaker only one time. Once memory is optimized, there is nothing left to do. The only other time you would run MemMaker is if you added more memory or new devices to your system.

The following section will describe a system before and after running MemMaker. Obviously, each system will be different, depending on what is installed. The current CONFIG.SYS looks as follows:

```
DEVICE=C:\DOS\SETVER.EXE
DEVICE=C:\DOS\HIMEM.SYS
FILES=30
BUFFERS=30
SHELL=C:\DOS\COMMAND.COM C:\DOS\ /P
STACKS=9,256
DEVICE=C:\DOS\ANSI.SYS
```

The current AUTOEXEC.BAT looks as follows:

```
C:\WINDOWS\SMARTDRV.EXE
@ECHO OFF
PROMPT $p$g
set mouse=C:\MOUSE
C:\MOUSE\MOUSE.COM
PATH C:\DOS;C:\WINDOWS
DOSKEY
SET TEMP=C:\DOS
```

If you run **MEM**, it gives the following report:

Memory Type	Total	=	Used	+	Free
Conventional	639K		127K		512K
Upper	0K		0K		0K
Reserved	0K		0K		0K
Extended (XMS)	3,072K		1,088K		1,984K
Total memory	3,711K		1,215K		2,496K
Total under 1 MB	639K		127K		512K

```
Largest executable program size       512K (524,048 bytes)
Largest free upper memory block         0K      (0 bytes)
The high memory area is available.
```

WHAT'S HAPPENING? As you can see, there is much room for improvement. Although the process will be shown, this is not an activity for you to do.

A   You should always first backup your current `CONFIG.SYS` and `AUTOEXEC.BAT` to a floppy disk.

B   Key in the following: `C:\>`**MEMMAKER** [Enter]

```
Microsoft MemMaker

Welcome to MemMaker

MemMaker optimizes your system's memory by moving memory-resident
programs and device drivers into the upper memory area. This
frees conventional memory for use by applications.

After you run MemMaker, your computer's memory will remain
optimized until you add or remove memory-resident programs or
device drivers. For an optimum memory configuration, run MemMaker
again after making any such changes.
```

```
MemMaker displays options as highlighted text. (For example, you
can change the "Continue" option below.) To cycle through the
available options, press SPACEBAR. When MemMaker displays the
option you want, press ENTER.

For help while your are running MemMaker, press F1.


          Continue or Exit? Continue

ENTER=Accept Selection   SPACEBAR=Change Selection   F1=Help      F3=Exit
```

WHAT'S HAPPENING? MemMaker presents a welcoming screen that tells you its purpose and how to use it. To continue, which is the default value, you press **Enter**.

C Press **Enter**

```
Microsoft MemMaker
There are two ways to run MemMaker:

Express Setup Optimizes your computer's memory automatically.

Custom Setup gives you more control over the changes that
MemMaker makes to your system files. Choose Custom Setup
if you are an experienced user.

    Use Express or Custom Setup?  Express Setup

ENTER=Accept Selection   SPACEBAR=Change Selection   F1=Help   F3-Exit
```

WHAT'S HAPPENING? Again, since this is the first time you have used MemMaker, the easiest step is to accept the default values.

D Press **Enter**

```
Microsoft MemMaker

If you use any programs that require expanded memory (EMS), answer
Yes to the following question. Answering Yes makes expanded memory
available, but might not free as much conventional memory.

If none of your programs need expanded memory, answer No to the
following question. Answering No makes expanded memory unavailable,
but can free more conventional memory.

If you are not sure whether or not your programs require expanded memory,
answer No. If you later discover that a program needs expanded
memory, run MemMaker again and answer Yes to this question.
```

```
Do you use any programs that need expanded memory(EMS)?NO

ENTER=Accept Selection   SPACEBAR=Change Selection F1=Help        F3=Exit
```

WHAT'S HAPPENING? You are being asked if you want any expanded memory to be carved out of extended memory. MemMaker wants to know whether or not you need expanded memory. Essentially, you must know your application programs. If you have no programs that use Expanded Memory, you answer No, which is the default value. This is true with most new programs. If you had older programs that did use expanded memory, you would need to answer Yes. Basically, when you answer No, there will be a line in the CONFIG.SYS file that states EMM386.EXE NOEMS. If you do not use EMS, you gain memory.

E   Press **Enter**

WHAT'S HAPPENING? You next get a message that MemMaker is searching for Windows. This computer has Windows on it. You then see the next screen.

```
Microsoft MemMaker

MemMaker will now restart your computer.

If your computer doesn't start properly, just turn it off
and on again, and MemMaker will recover automatically.
If a program other than MemMaker starts after your computer
restarts, exit the program so MemMaker can continue.

   *Remove any disks from your floppy-disk drives and
    then press ENTER. Your computer will restart.

ENTER=Continue
```

WHAT'S HAPPENING? This screen states that MemMaker will restart your computer. Since it is analyzing your system, it is going to try things out while altering CONFIG.SYS. It must reboot to enable the new CONFIG.SYS.

F   Press **Enter**

WHAT'S HAPPENING? You will see some messages that tell you what changes it has made. The next screen appears.

```
Microsoft MemMaker

MemMaker will now restart your computer to test the new memory
configuration.
```

```
    While your computer is restarting, watch your screen carefully.
    Note any unusual messages or problems. If you computer doesn't
    start properly, just turn it off and on again, and MemMaker
    will recover automatically.

      *Remove any disks from your floppy-disk drives and
       then press ENTER. Your computer will restart.

ENTER=Continue
```

WHAT'S HAPPENING? Once again, it is asking you to press **Enter** to reboot.
MemMaker tells you to watch your screen carefully to note any problems (this is why
you first backed up CONFIG.SYS and AUTOEXEC.BAT). You see some screens flash
by telling you how many changes it made.

G   Press **Enter**

```
Microsoft MemMaker

Your computer has just restarted with its new memory configuration.
Some or all of your device drivers and memory-resident programs
are now running in upper memory.

If your system appears to be working properly, choose "Yes."
If you noticed any unusual messages when your computer started,
or if your system is not working properly, choose "No."

Does your system appear to be working properly: Yes


ENTER =Accept Selection  SPACEBAR-Change Selection  F1=Help  F3=Exit
```

WHAT'S HAPPENING? This screen tells you that MemMaker has restarted your
computer with the new configuration. It then asks you if your system is woking
properly. If you are happy, i.e., everything seems to work, you choose Yes, which
is the default. If not, you choose No and MemMaker removes the changes it made.

H   Press **Enter**

```
   Microsoft MemMaker
```

WHAT'S HAPPENING? Since you are happy with the changes, you press **Enter**.

I   Press **Enter**

J   Key in the following: C:\>**TYPE CONFIG.SYS** **Enter**

```
C:\>TYPE CONFIG.SYS
DEVICE=C:\DOS\HIMEM.SYS
DEVICE=C:\DOS\EMM386.EXE NOEMS
BUFFERS=30,0
FILES=30
DOS=UMB
LASTDRIVE=E
FCBS=4,0
DEVICEHIGH /L:2,12048 =C:\DOS\SETVER.EXE
SHELL=C:\DOS\COMMAND.COM C:\DOS\ /P
DEVICEHIGH /L:2,9072 =C:\DOS\ANSI.SYS
```

WHAT'S HAPPENING? As you can see, changes indeed were made to CONFIG.SYS. Device drivers were loaded high and EMM386.EXE NO EMS was added. MemMaker is not infallible. Notice that it did not load DOS=High. Also, you might want to "tweak" it more by adding STACKS=0,0.

K   Key in the following: C:\>**TYPE AUTOEXEC.BAT** [Enter]

```
C:\>TYPE AUTOEXEC.BAT
LH /L:0,1,45456 /S C:\WINDOWS\SMARTDRV.EXE
@ECHO OFF
PROMPT $p$g
PATH C:\DOS;C:;C:\WINDOWS
LH /L:1,56928 C:\MOUSE\MOUSE.COM
LH /L:2,6384 DOSKEY
SET TEMP=C:\DOS
```

WHAT'S HAPPENING? Again it made some changes. It took out the line set mouse=C:\MOUSE. Hopefully, that was the correct thing to do. It loaded everything it could high in specific memory locations.

L   Key in the following: C:\>**MEM** [Enter]

```
Memory Type        Total  =   Used   +   Free
---------------    -------    -------     -------
Conventional        640K        79K        561K
Upper               139K        53K         86K
Reserved            384K       384K          0K
Extended (XMS)    2,933K     1,241K      1,692K
---------------    -------    -------     -------
Total memory      4,096K     1,756K      2,340K

Total under 1 MB    779K       131K        548K


Largest executable program size        561K (574,832 bytes)
Largest free upper memory block         79K  (88,816 bytes)
The high memory area is available.
```

WHAT'S HAPPENING? You gained a lot of memory and are using upper memory. Again, you can improve on MemMaker by adding DOS=HIGH, UMB to CONFIG.SYS and setting the Buffers=10. Since you are using SMARTDRV.EXE. and setting the FCBS=1 you can further improve your memory usage.

M   Edit the CONFIG.SYS file to look as follows:

> **DEVICE=C:\DOS\HIMEM.SYS**
> **DEVICE=C:\DOS\EMM386.EXE NOEMS**
> **BUFFERS=10**
> **FILES=30**
> **DOS=HIGH,UMB**
> **LASTDRIVE=E**
> **FCBS=1**
> **STACKS=0,0**
> **DEVICEHIGH /L:2,12048 =C:\DOS\SETVER.EXE**
> **SHELL=C:\DOS\COMMAND.COM C:\DOS\ /P**
> **DEVICEHIGH /L:2,9072 =C:\DOS\ANSI.SYS**

N   Reboot the system.

O   Key in the following: C:\>**MEM** **Enter**

```
Memory Type        Total   =   Used   +   Free
---------------    -------    -------    -------
Conventional        640K        20K        620K
Upper               139K        53K         86K
Reserved            384K       384K          0K
Extended (XMS)    2,933K     1,241K      1,692K
---------------    -------    -------    -------
Total memory      4,096K     1,698K      2,398K

Total under 1 MB    779K        73K        706K

Largest executable program size      620K (634,688 bytes)
Largest free upper memory block       79K  (88,816 bytes)
MS-DOS is resident in the high memory.
```

WHAT'S HAPPENING? You can see these changes dramatically improved available conventional memory. You began with total memory under 1 MB, free memory of 512,K and a largest executable program size of 512K.

```
Total under 1 MB    639K       127K        512K

Largest executable program size      512K (524,048 bytes)
```

You ran MemMaker and increased total memory under 1 MB to 548 K and the largest executable program size to 561K.

```
Total under 1 MB       779K       131K       548K

Largest executable program size       561K (574,832 bytes)
```

You increased `CONFIG.SYS` total free memory to 706 and the largest executable program size to 620K. Quite an improvement.

```
Total under 1 MB       779K       73K       706K

Largest executable program size       620K (634,688 bytes)
```

You may also use Custom Setup. If you do, you will be led to a screen with the following choices:

```
Microsoft MemMaker

Advanced Options

Specify which drives and TSRs to include in optimization?      No
Scan the upper memory area aggressively?                              No
Optimize upper memory for use with Windows?              No
Use monochrome region (0000-B7FF) for running programs?  No
Keep current EMS386 memory inclusions and exclusions?          Yes
Move extended BIOS Data area from conventional to upper memory? Yes

To select a different option, press the UP ARROW or DOWN ARROW key.
To accept all the settings and continue, press ENTER.

ENTER =Accept All        SPACEBAR-Change Selection  F1=Help  F3=Exit
```

WHAT'S HAPPENING? If you use Windows exclusively, you may enter `Yes` for optimizing use with Windows. In addition, video memory in upper memory has a section reserved for both monochrome and color. If you use only a color system, you can answer `yes` and free up that area for UMBs. If you choose that option and you are a Windows user, MemMaker will add the line `DEVICE=MONOUMB2.386` to the [386enh] section in your `SYSTEM.INI` file. If this line is not in the `SYSTEM.INI` file, Windows will not run. If you choose `Yes` to scan the upper memory aggressively and `Yes` to optimize memory for Windows, again, you will claim memory. In this example, the computer is a notebook type with a monochrome monitor, so using the monochrome region is not viable. With those choices answered `Yes`, your `CONFIG.SYS` file looks as follows:

```
C:\>TYPE CONFIG.SYS
DEVICE=C:\DOS\HIMEM.SYS
DEVICE=C:\DOS\EMM386.EXE NOEMS HIGHSCAN WIN=ED00-EFFF WIN=DD08-DFFF
BUFFERS=10,0
```

```
FILES=30
DOS=UMB
LASTDRIVE=E
FCBS=1,0
DOS=HIGH
STACKS=0,0
DEVICEHIGH /L:1,12048 =C:\DOS\SETVER.EXE
SHELL=C:\DOS\COMMAND.COM C:\DOS\ /P
DEVICEHIGH /L:1,9072 =C:\DOS\ANSI.SYS
```

WHAT'S HAPPENING? Locations of programs in memory were altered. Your AUTOEXEC.BAT file looks as follows:

```
C:\>TYPE AUTOEXEC.BAT
LH /L:0,1,45456 /S C:\WINDOWS\SMARTDRV.EXE
@ECHO OFF
PROMPT $p$g
PATH C:\DOS;C:;C:\WINDOWS
LH /L:1,56928 C:\MOUSE\MOUSE.COM
LH /L:1,6384 DOSKEY
SET TEMP=C:\DOS
```

WHAT'S HAPPENING? Locations of programs in memory were altered. Your memory report looks as follows:

```
Memory Type          Total  =  Used  +  Free
----------------     ------    ------   ------
Conventional           640K      20K     620K
Upper                  115K      53K      62K
Reserved               384K     384K       0K
Extended (XMS)       2,957K   1,241K   1,716K
----------------     ------    ------   ------
Total memory         4,096K   1,698K   2,398K

Total under 1 MB       755K      73K     682K

Largest executable program size      620K (634,688 bytes)
Largest free upper memory block       58K  (59,456 bytes)
MS-DOS is resident in the high memory.
```

WHAT'S HAPPENING? You did not seem to gain as much memory this time so you would need to experiment with different combinations to arrive at the optimum memory usage. As you can see, although running MemMaker can automate your memory optimization, you can still manually edit using CUSTOM EDIT to increase base memory.

15.13 Optimizing Disk Space with DriveSpace

As program files and data files get larger, lack of disk space increasingly becomes a problem. Once a 60 MB hard drive was considered enormous. Today, most 486 computers will come with at least a 100 MB hard drive. Still, you can never have enough disk space. To solve this problem, disk compression utilities have come into vogue. Disk compression programs come in two types: **offline compression** and **real-time** or **on-the fly compression**.

Offline compression programs read in data from an uncompressed file and outputs to a new compressed file. Usually, offline compression can also **archive files**. Archiving combines several files into one large file, keeping each file separate within the combination. Both of these techniques help save disk space. Remember, DOS allocates disk space to files based on clusters (allocation units). The cluster is the smallest amount of space that DOS can read to and write from. Thus, a file that occupys 1 byte will actually occupy 512 bytes on a high-density disk (one sector equals a cluster) and 8192 bytes on a hard disk (16 sectors make up a cluster). This creates something called **cluster overhang**—a file occupying more space than it actually needs. Placing many files into one file will minimize cluster overhang and save space.

Offline disk compression programs can also save space within a file. Disk compression utility programs store repeated data in less space. For instance, in this paragraph, the word *the* appears many times. A disk compression program can analyze the data in a file, develop a binary shorthand notation for every occurrence of the word *the*, and create a **token** to represent it. When a file is compressed, the tokens represent repeated characters and the file occupies less space on a disk. When you uncompress or decompress the file, the tokens are read, and the original characters are restored.

The most popular compression program is a shareware program called PKZIP and its corresponding program PKUNZIP. These two programs are extremely useful because they help you control which files are compressed or uncompressed. You can manipulate compressed files the same as any other file; you can copy them or send them over a modem to another user. The disadvantage to PKZIP is that before you can use the zipped files, you must manually uncompress each with PKUNZIP. As you can imagine, this is time-consuming and unwieldy unless you are backing up files on a floppy or compressing a file to send over a modem. To remedy this, on-the-fly compression, or real-time compression, was developed.

On-the-fly compression will compress and uncompress data in the background. As you use the files, you are unaware of what is happening. That is, the process is **transparent to the user**. On-the-fly compression can work for a variety of reasons. The primary one is that files must be accessed by a disk drive. Disk drives (mechanical), are slower then memory (electronic), and although it may seem fast to you as DOS loads files from disk to memory or from memory to disk, there is plenty of time to compress and uncompress files on the fly since compressed files are smaller and take less time to read to or write from. In fact, on-the-fly compression can actually improve disk performance and be much faster because it takes longer to read and write files to disk than it does to compress and uncompress them. Read and write take place with physical devices, which are slow, whereas compressing and uncompressing takes place in memory, which is fast. Thus, if the files are smaller because they are compressed, they take less time to load and unpack than if they are not compressed. Tokens are also used to reduce redundant data.

Some popular third-party disk compression programs include Stacker and SuperStor. DOS 6.0 introduced an on-the-fly compression utility called DoubleSpace. Due to various legal problems with Stacker over the technology used to make DoubleSpace work, MS-DOS 6.2 was introduced without DoubleSpace. MS-DOS 6.22 introduced DriveSpace, the replacement for DoubleSpace. If you used DoubleSpace, you can convert any compressed drives to the new utility, DriveSpace, with the upgraded version of MS-DOS 6.22. You do not have to do this because DriveSpace recognizes DoubleSpace, although it is a good idea to do so because future versions of DOS or Windows will be compatible with DriveSpace.

DriveSpace, once installed, uses a file called `DRVSPACE.BIN`, which is the part of DriveSpace that provides access to the compressed disk. It is a hidden, read-only system file. If you delete this file, you lose access to your compressed disk. When you boot your system, `DRVSPACE.BIN` loads in conventional memory. DriveSpace creates a compressed drive called **Compressed Volume File** or **CVF**. When you install DriveSpace, it also creates a new disk drive and assigns a letter to it. For instance, if you have physical hard Drive C and floppy drives A and B, DriveSpace skips the next four letters and assigns logical Drive letter H to the new drive. DriveSpace "jumps" drive letters to avoid conflicts with RAM drives or any other logical drives the system may be using.

Of course, the compressed drive is not a physical drive. If you want to have more than one compressed drive, a CVF is created for each new compressed drive. Each CVF is located on an uncompressed drive, which is referred to as the host drive. A CVF is stored in the root directory of the host drive and has the file name `DRVSPACE.001`. Thus, if you install DriveSpace on the above system, Drive C is the compressed drive and Drive H is the host drive with `DRVSPACE.001` as the compressed Drive C. As an example, look at the following display:

```
C:\>DIR DRV*.* /AH

 Volume in drive C has no label
 Volume Serial Number is 1CD1-5E42
 Directory of C:\

DRVSPACE 002    209,720,832 09-09-94    9:55a
DRVSPACE INI            122 06-28-94    1:24a
DRVSPACE BIN         66,294 05-31-94    6:22a
DRVSPACE 001    129,744,896 09-09-94    9:55a
DRVSPACE MR1            512 05-31-94    6:22a
        5 file(s)    339,532,656 bytes
                      78,594,048 bytes free

C:\>_
```

This directory listing shows the various DriveSpace files. This system has two compressed drives, indicated by the DRVSPACE.001 and DRVSPACE.002. Notice how large they are—DRVSPACE.001 occupies 129,744,896 bytes while DRVSPACE.002 occupies 209,720,832 bytes. On this 500 MB drive, the CVF files take nearly 60 percent of the available disk space. The DRVSPACE.001 and DRVSPACE.002 files actually hold the data. If you deleted either of these files, you would no longer have any data or any programs!

DOS accesses the DriveSpace drives using the DRVSPACE.BIN file. It must be present in the root directory of the host drive. In this case the host is Drive C. DRVSPACE.INI is an initialization file that has information about how DriveSpace is configured and must also be present in the root directory of the host drive. DRVSPACE.MR1 is the utility that converts the DoubleSpace drives to DriveSpace drives. Once a DoubleSpace drive is converted to a DriveSpace drive, it is no longer is necessary to keep DoubleSpace in the root directory.

There is one more DriveSpace file—the device driver—called DRVSPACE.SYS. It does not provide access to the compressed drives. It merely tells the location of DRVSPACE.BIN in memory. When you install DriveSpace, it adds a line to your CONFIG.SYS, moving DRVSPACE.SYS into upper memory.

DriveSpace can compress data because it does not allocate whole clusters to a file. DriveSpace allocates sectors to a file one at a time. Although a DriveSpace drive emulates a "real" disk with a FAT and directory table, it does not require that every cluster have the same number of sectors like physical drives. Each cluster contains only the number of sectors it needs to store data. Thus, if you had a file that required only 5 sectors, DriveSpace would allocate exactly 5 sectors to it, not the 16 sectors that are required on a hard disk. This in itself saves an enormous amount of space.

In addition, as with offline compression programs, DriveSpace compresses data by using tokens to represent repeated data. The key to data compression is the ability of DriveSpace to search quickly for a string of bytes, identify them as repetitive, and replace the repetitive bytes with small tokens. A lot of duplication or repetitiveness of data has to occur before data compression is worthwhile. Since most files are large and contain large amounts of repeated information, this method is very effective in saving disk space. The usual ratio is two to one. In other words, you gain twice as much space using compression. One other important note: although data files usually compress at a 2:1 ratio, other files, such as sound files and some program files, do not benefit as much by compression and will often end up with a 1:1 ratio, which is little or no compression at all.

Although DriveSpace can uncompress a compressed drive, it is a difficult process, particularly if you have used up all your disk space. Installing DriveSpace is easy, but once you install DriveSpace, you cannot easily uninstall it, nor will you be able to go back to earlier versions of DOS without losing files on the compressed drive. Remember, if you delete a compressed drive, you will lose all the files on it.

Installing DriveSpace is quite simple. You must not be in Windows or DOS Shell. You key in DRVSPACE at the prompt. You then get a series of menus. Choosing EXPRESS SETUP is easiest way because most of the decisions are made for you. It will take about a minute for each megabyte (MB) of data. Thus, if you have an 80 MB hard drive, it will take about 80 minutes to compress. Once compressed, you will have a hard drive with approximately 160 MB. Again, this is transparent to the user. Once you have installed DriveSpace, you can use the DriveSpace menu to activate such changes as compressing floppy drives (a process called mounting and unmounting) or changing the size of the compressed drives.

Once DriveSpace is installed, you can compress floppy drives. The following is an example of how you would do this. This is not an activity for you to do.

A   Key in the following: C:\>**DIR B:** Enter

```
C:\>DIR B:

 Volume in drive B has no label
 Directory of B:\

DPWPCH13 COR         18,944 09-07-94    2:45p
GOODBYE  TXT             32 11-23-94    7:07a
DANCES   TXT             70 08-08-95    5:34p
JANUARY  TXT             72 11-23-95   10:41a
FEBRUARY TXT             74 11-23-95   10:41a
MARCH    TXT             70 11-23-95   10:42a
APRIL    TXT             71 11-23-95   10:42a
HELLO    TXT             52 11-23-95   10:44a
BYE      TXT             44 11-23-95   10:45a
TEST     TXT             64 03-14-93   11:07a
FILE_ID  DIZ            382 08-21-93    8:23a
FINANCE     <DIR>          09-09-94   11:46a
README   HPB         16,722 06-26-93    8:11a
HPB         <DIR>          09-09-94   11:45a
        14 file(s)        36,597 bytes
                         976,896 bytes free

C:\>_
```

WHAT'S HAPPENING? Drive B is a 1.44 MB disk with only 976,896 bytes free. This disk is about to be compressed.

B   Key in the following: C:\>**DRVSPACE** Enter

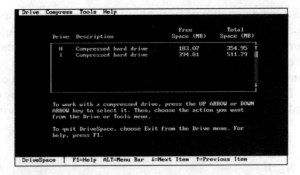

WHAT'S HAPPENING? DriveSpace is analyzing your system.

C Click C

WHAT'S HAPPENING? You have dropped down the Compress menu.

D Click Compress Existing Drive

WHAT'S HAPPENING? It is showing you that you can compress existing Drive B, which is highlighted.

E Press Enter

WHAT'S HAPPENING? It is warning you to back up your files first.

F   Click C

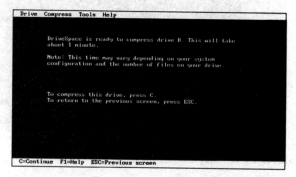

WHAT'S HAPPENING? It will take about one minute to compress the disk in Drive B.

G   Press C

WHAT'S HAPPENING? DriveSpace runs ScanDisk first to check the integrity of the disk. When it is finished, you see the following screen:

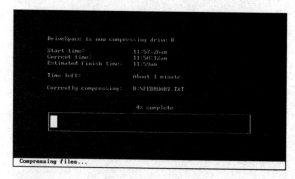

WHAT'S HAPPENING? It is compressing the disk in Drive B. When it is finished, you see the following screen.

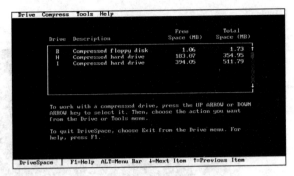

WHAT'S HAPPENING? Your disk is now compressed.

H   Click `Drive`

WHAT'S HAPPENING? You have dropped down the `Drive` menu.

I   Click `Exit`

J   Key in the following: `C:\>`**DIR B:** [Enter]

```
Volume in drive B has no label
Volume Serial Number is 1303-2953
Directory of B:\

DPWPCH13 COR        18,944 09-07-94    2:45p
GOODBYE  TXT            32 11-23-94    7:07a
DANCES   TXT            70 08-08-95    5:34p
JANUARY  TXT            72 11-23-95   10:41a
FEBRUARY TXT            74 11-23-95   10:41a
MARCH    TXT            70 11-23-95   10:42a
APRIL    TXT            71 11-23-95   10:42a
HELLO    TXT            52 11-23-95   10:44a
BYE      TXT            44 11-23-95   10:45a
TEST     TXT            64 03-14-93   11:07a
FILE_ID  DIZ           382 08-21-93    8:23a
FINANCE      <DIR>        09-09-94   11:46a
README   HPB        16,722 06-26-93    8:11a
HPB          <DIR>        09-09-94   11:45a
```

```
    14 file(s)          36,597 bytes
                     1,114,112 bytes free

C:\>
```

WHAT'S HAPPENING? As you can see, you have greatly increased your disk space. This disk can be read only by a computer on which DriveSpace is installed. DoubleSpace required you to mount and unmount floppy disks. DriveSpace takes care of that for you automatically. You have also created on this system a host Drive J for floppy Drive B. You can also uncompress the floppy by using the appropriate commands.

Chapter Summary

1. While booting, when you press the F5 key, you get a clean boot. When you press the F8 key, you get an interactive boot.
2. If you use an expanded memory board, you must install an expanded memory manager that is usually provided with the expanded memory.
3. The file EMM386.EXE provided with MS-DOS is an expanded memory emulator so you may run programs that use expanded memory. EMM386.EXE uses extended memory to emulate expanded memory.
4. The file EMM386.EXE also allows you to convert the upper memory area into upper memory blocks (UMB) where TSRs and device drivers can be loaded to preserve conventional memory.
5. The DOS=UMB statement in the CONFIG.SYS file informs DOS that you are going to be using upper memory.
6. DEVICEHIGH loads device drivers in upper memory and is placed in CONFIG.SYS.
7. LOADHIGH loads TSRs in upper memory and is usually placed in AUTOEXEC.BAT, although it can be issued from the command line.
8. By lowering the value of the FCBS, you can save space in conventional memory.
9. The STACKS directive in CONFIG.SYS allocates memory to the number and size of the specified STACKS. Stacks handle hardware interrupts.
10. You can create multiple configurations files by using the special configuation commands. These commands appear in Table 15.1.
11. You can alter your AUTOEXEC.BAT file to match your customized CONFIG.SYS file by using the environmental variable %CONFIG%. You must alter your labels to match your configuration blocks.
12. Cache programs have two basic functions. A read cache holds data in memory so that a program can access the cache rather than accessing the disk. A write cache holds data to be saved in memory until a time period has expired, until system activity is minimized, or until the system is rebooted.
13. Using caches improves performance. Read caches are safer than write caches.

14. SMARTDRV.EXE is the caching program included with DOS. SmartDrive uses extended memory and is automatically loaded high. The default for DOS 6.22 is that SmartDrive is installed with the /X parameter, which turns off write caching.

15. Do not use CHKDSK /F, SCANDISK or DEFRAG when you are using a cache program.

16. FASTOPEN provides faster access to files that are constantly used. It only works with a hard drive. It does not work on a networked system. FASTOPEN improves performance most with programs that constantly reopen the same files.

17. MEMMAKER automatically analyzes CONFIG.SYS and AUTOEXEC.BAT and reconfigures them to maximize memory. A combination of using MEMMAKER and "tweaking the system" will provide optimum results.

18. Off-line compression programs encode repeated data and can archive files. These programs work on a file by file basis.

19. On-the-fly compression programs, also called disk compression programs, compress and uncompress files in the background. They are effective because it is faster to compress and decompress files then it is to read a long file into memory from a disk.

20. DriveSpace is the disk compression program that was introduced in DOS 6.22. DoubleSpace was an earlier version.

21. DriveSpace allocates sectors to a file one sector at a time by using a host drive and a Compressed Volume File (CVF) to minimize cluster overhang.

22. DriveSpace also uses tokens to minimize repetitive data.

23. You must never delete DRVSPACE.BIN or any DRVSPACE.nnn file. If you delete DRVSPACE.BIN, you lose access to the compressed drive. If you delete any DRVSPACE.nnn file, you are deleting the programs and data that reside on that compressed drive.

24. Once installed, it is very difficult to uninstall a compressed drive.

25. You can compress floppy drives if DriveSpace is installed. Older versions of DOS required mounting and unmounting floppy drives. This is no longer true with DOS 6.0.

Key Terms

Archive files
Cluster overhang
Compressed Volume File (CVF)
Expanded memory emulator
Hardware interrupts

On-the-fly compression
Teal-time compression
Token
Transparent to the user
Tweaking the system

Discussion Questions

1. Explain what happens when you press the [F5] key when you see Starting MS-DOS ...
2. Explain what happens when you press the [F8] key when you see Starting MS-DOS ...
3. What is the purpose and function of memory managers? What memory manager does MS-DOS provide?
4. What is the purpose and function of EMM386.EXE?
5. What is the purpose of loading DOS into high memory?
6. Why would you use upper memory?
7. Why would you want to conserve as much conventional memory as possible?
8. What is the purpose and function of LOADHIGH?
9. Compare DEVICEHIGH and LOADHIGH.
10. How can you determine if a program or device driver will run successfully in upper memory?
11. Why is it a good idea to move device drivers and/or programs one at a time into upper memory?
12. What is the purpose and function of STACKS and FCBS?
13. What are hardware interrupts?
14. What is the purpose and function of multiple configuration files?
15. List and explain the function of two of the start-up configuration menu commands.
16. Explain the effect the following commands will have on your configuration menu:
    ```
    MENUCOLOR 4,2,
    MENUDEFAULT=STANDARD,10,
    MENUITEM= CLEAN.
    ```
17. Compare disk buffers to caching programs.
18. Compare and contrast read and write caching.
19. What are the advantages of disk caching?
20. What is the purpose and function of SMARTDRV.EXE?
21. What are the advantages of using SMARTDRV.EXE?
22. What are some of the dangers to write caching?
23. Why is it important to never run CHKDSK/F, SCANDISK, or DEFRAG with caching programs running?
24. What is the purpose and function of FASTOPEN?
25. When is FASTOPEN most useful?
26. What is the purpose and function of MEMMAKER?
27. Briefly explain how a disk compression program functions.
28. Compare and contrast off-line compression and real-time compression programs.
29. How can using on-the-fly compression improve performance?
30. Explain why and how DriveSpace can compress data.

Chapter 16

Windows

Learning Objectives

After completing this chapter, you will be able to:

1. Explain the purpose and function of Windows.
2. List and explain the hardware requirements for the different operating modes of Windows.
3. List and explain the elements of the Windows screen.
4. List and explain the pointing devices that can be used with Windows.
5. List and explain terms that describe actions that can be taken with pointer devices.
6. Explain the purpose and function of the foreground application.
7. Explain the purpose and function of online help.
8. Explain the purpose and function of File Manager.
9. List and explain items found in the Directory Tree window.
10. List and explain the icons that are used to distinguish file types.
11. Explain some of the ways that File Manager can be used to work with multiple files.

Student Outcomes

1. Load Windows and manipulate the appearance of different windows that are available to the user.
2. Load and use foreground and background programs.
3. Access and use online help.

4. Use File Manager to perform file management functions.
5. Use DOS commands in File Manager.
6. Use File Manager to work with multiple files.

Chapter Overview

In earlier chapters, you used COMMAND.COM as the command processor. To perform operating system tasks and to execute programs, you issued commands at the command line prompt. This process is known as a character-based user interface.

Windows is a graphical user interface that provides a more powerful operating environment. Windows allows multi-tasking, improves memory management, and, in general, uses the computer more fully. In addition, Windows comes with several application programs: clipboard, an easily accessible scratch pad; notepad, a simple text editor; and paintbrush, a drawing program.

Although Windows replaces the DOS command line, it does not replace DOS, but rather works hand-in-hand with DOS. All DOS-based application programs can run under Windows, but programs written specifically for Windows exploit the full power of Windows.

In this chapter you will be introduced to Windows, and will learn how to use some of the features of Windows.

16.1 What Is Windows?

You purchase a computer to use application packages that solve particular problems. If you must use DOS to run those application packages, how does Windows fit into the equation? Windows is a software program that is a **graphical user interface** or **GUI** (pronounced Gooey). It is not an operating system, but rather is an operating environment. To use it, you must first load DOS, then Windows, and then your application packages. Windows works hand-in-hand with DOS. It replaces the DOS command line but not DOS itself. See Figure 16.1

Figure 16.1 The Operating Environment

Windows changes how you communicate with your computer. Prior to Windows, there were user complaints with application packages running under DOS. First, DOS was perceived as being unfriendly. For example, you have to know what command to use when you boot the system and see the A:\> or C:\>. Second there were problems with different input and output devices. For instance, you might find if your printer would work with your word processing program, there would be no guarantee that the same printer would work with your tax package. Each hardware addition had its own set of problems. Another complaint was that each application package has an entirely different set of commands, making learning a new program a new learning experience. Running one program at a time under DOS complicated tasks, especially sharing data among applications.

Windows is a graphical environment that uses pictures and menus. Rather than the C:\> prompt, you are instead presented with pictures, called icons, that represent programs. To manipulate these programs, there are **drop-down menus** that work with the icons. Drop-down menus are exactly what they sound like. They are menus that "drop-down" so that, rather than having to learn commands, commands are presented as choices on menus. You can select items with the keyboard or with a pointing device such as a mouse or trackball.

Windows is an attempt to graphically represent the way people work. Windows operates on a "desktop" principle that allows you to place your work (programs) in "windows" that are set aside for particular tasks. A window can occupy the entire screen or part of the screen. You may have more than one window open and you are able to move among the windows as if you were shuffling pieces of paper on your desk. You can write a report with your word processor in one window while referencing the data for this report with your spreadsheet program in another window, with both windows on the screen at the same time. This multi-tasking environment allows you to perform more than one task at a time, and the multi-tasking opportunities are endless. You could, for example, print one document while working on another.

When you install Windows, you configure all your hardware to work in the Windows environment. Some special applications software such as Excel or Word for Windows are designed specifically to work with Windows, and the hardware configurations established by Windows. For instance, once you have installed your printer properly, it will work properly with every Windows application. Working with software packages designed for the Windows interface generates a new level of consistency and ease when going from one software package to another.

Windows has a standard interface for performing the same tasks in different software applications. These applications also use drop-down menus and icons, and they share a common set of commands. Once you learn how to open a file, for example, it will be the same process for every program designed to work in Windows. Skills learned in one application can easily be used in another application, making new applications quite simple to learn.

Windows also allows you to share data among programs by means of a feature called the Clipboard. Clipboard is an area in memory that Windows uses to store copied data temporarily. You can copy or move data or graphics from one application to another—from a spreadsheet directly into a word processor, for example. Again, once the technique is learned, it remains the same for all Windows applications.

Using Windows does not mean giving up your non-Windows applications. You can still run all the DOS-based applications in Windows. In fact, with the proper hardware you can even run DOS-based applications in a window.

Windows itself comes with some built-in applications, sometimes called "applets." These include the Clock, the Calculator, the Cardfile—an electronic Rolodex—and a Calendar for scheduling events. There is even an alarm in Calendar to remind you of meetings. It has Notepad, which is a text editor, as well as a true word processor (Write), a drawing program (Paintbrush), and a communication program (Terminal). It has a Character Map that allows you to insert special characters and symbols into applications. If you have the proper hardware, you can use the Media Player, which allows you to use multimedia files and control hardware devices to play audio compact disks or videodisks. In addition, there is a Sound Recorder to play, record, and edit sound files.

Windows version 3.1 has become extremely popular. Since its release, a new version has come out called Windows for Workgroups, 3.11. This version has networking capabilities, but it can be run as a stand-alone package and is considered the upgrade to Windows 3.1. Windows 3.1 and Windows for Workgroups, 3.11 are nearly identical in use and function. The biggest difference between the two versions is that, like all upgrades, Windows for Workgroups 3.11 has some enhancements, particularly in File Manager. The screens you will see in this chapter are based on Windows for Workgroups 3.11. However, if you are running Windows 3.1, nearly everything will work the same.

16.2 Hardware Requirements for Windows

Because Windows is such a powerful package, it needs powerful hardware and software to run successfully. There is some clarification necessary to understand what minimums are needed to run Windows. There are actually "two" minimum hardware requirements to run Windows: the absolute minimum and the recommended minimum. Microsoft has determined the absolute minimum hardware requirements to run Windows; without the absolute minimum, Windows will not work. However, at the absolute minimum, Windows runs slowly. Therefore, Microsoft has also determined the recommended minimum needed to capture all the features of Windows. In short, the more memory and disk space you have, the more features you can use.

Standard mode allows Windows to run on a microcomputer with a 80286 microprocessor or higher and 1 MB (2 MB is the recommend minimum) of memory. You must have a hard disk with 6 MB (9 MB is recommended) free for Windows programs. In standard mode, you can use memory above 640 KB. You can run Windows and non-Windows applications; however, non-Windows applications must use the full screen.

The **386 enhanced mode** allows Windows to run on a microcomputer that has an 80386SX, 80386, 80486, or Pentium microprocessor. You must have at least

2 MB (4 MB is the recommended minimum) of memory as well as a hard disk with 8 MB (10.5 MB is recommended) free. These are absolute minimums—to take full advantage of Windows you should have at least 6 MB or more of memory.

Enhanced mode is really the way that you want to run Windows. In enhanced mode, Windows can use **virtual memory**, which means that when you run out of RAM, Windows can write data to and from the hard disk temporarily, allowing almost limitless space to run application programs. In addition, you can not only run non-Windows applications as full screens in **foreground** or you can place these non-Windows applications in windows and continue to run them in **background**.

Windows runs best with a high-resolution color monitor and matching VGA or Super VGA card. Although you can run Windows with other types of monitors, they will not display high-resolution graphics and icons. In addition, the advantages of GUIs cannot be fully be exploited without a pointing device such as a mouse.

16.3 Elements of Windows

Windows has its own terms and concepts that are quite different from the DOS interface you have been using. Instead of seeing the `C:\>` or `A:\>` when you load Windows, either by keying in `WIN` or placing `WIN` in the `AUTOEXEC.BAT` file, you see the following screen:

This screen reflects the default installation. If you or someone else customized Windows, the screen will look different. Also, depending on what software you have, the icons at the bottom of the screen could be different. Furthermore, if your installation was an upgrade from Windows 3.0, it could look different from Windows 3.1 or Windows for Workgroups 3.11 installed on a new system. Regardless of any differences between this screen display and your own, there are common elements in all Windows screen displays. You will learn these common elements and how to manipulate them.

Study the labels and the explanations on the following screen :

Control-menu box

Application window
(Program Manager)

Minimize button
(sizing button)

Maximize button
(sizing button)

Menu bar

Program-
item icon

Title bar

Window
borders

Mouse
pointer

Work
area

Open document window
(Main group)

Closed document window
(Minimized document icon
or Group icons)

Desktop

Control-menu box

The **Control-menu box**, also called the **Control-menu icon** or the **System menu** is in the upper-left hand corner of every window. Clicking the mouse pointer on this box provides a drop-down menu that stays open until you make a choice or close it. The Control-menu allows you to resize, move, maximize, or minimize the current window. It also gives you the choice to switch to another window (task).

Title bar

The **title bar** displays the name of the application and/or the name of the document in the window. When you have more than one application open at one time, you can work on only one of them. This is called the "active" window. The **active window** is always differentiated by a title bar in a different color or of a different hue intensity.

Menu bar

The **menu bar** will drop down a menu which allows you access to most of the commands of a specific application. Often, drop-down menus will provide more detailed menus. The choices available on the drop-down menus will vary depending on what the application program does. Most Windows applications will have a File menu, an Edit menu and a Help menu.

Minimize button (sizing button)

The Minimize button, the downward pointing arrow, is designed to be used with a mouse. It allows you to shrink or minimize the window to an icon. When you minimize a window, you place it out of your way on the desktop, but the application remains open.

Maximize button (sizing button)

The Maximize button, the upward pointing arrow, is also designed to be used with a mouse. It allows you to maximize the window; that is, it makes the window fill the screen completely. If you want to devote all your attention to one application, you maximize the window. When you maximize the window, the upward pointing arrow becomes a two-headed arrow callled the Restore button, which returns the window to its previous size.

These buttons are referred to as sizing buttons. Sizing buttons can only minimize, maximize, or restore windows. They cannot change the size of the borders of a window.

Mouse pointer

If you have a mouse or other pointing device installed on your system, you see the arrow pointer on your screen. When you move the mouse on your desk, the position of the pointer changes on the screen. The shape of the pointer can change, depending on the task you are working on or the application software you are using.

Types of windows

Windows provides two types of windows—the application window and document window. The application window, as the name suggests, contains the application software program that is running. The name of the application software appears in the title bar with the application's menu bar directly beneath. **Program Manager** is an example of an application program that runs in an application window. There are many other applications you can run in Windows such as WordPerfect for Windows, Excel and Word for Windows. An application program opens its own application window.

You open an application program to edit or create a data file. In Windows, this data file appears in a framed work area called the document window which is a window within a window. The title of the document, as well as the title of the application, appears on the title bar. The document window uses the same menu bar as the application window, and you use the same menu commands to manipulate them.

Many applications in Windows allow you to have several document windows open at a time. Each data file is contained in its own document window inside the application window. Commonly, you have several data documents running under one application program, but only one data document can be active at a time, just as only one application can be active at a time.

As an application, Program Manager is unique in Windows because it is the interface between you and the computer system. Program Manager has document windows called group windows which contain the applications that can be run from Program Manager. The Main group is an open document window that contains the name of the available applications as well their associated icons. Since each of these items is a program, the Main group window does not have a menu bar of its own. Main is really a document window to Program Manager and uses the menu bar of Program Manager. Each application program, when loaded, runs in its own application window and has its own document windows. The icons in Main are called **program-item icons;** they represent applications you can start from Windows. All application programs are represented by unique program-item icons. There are cases, particularly with non-Windows applications, when the icons are identical. The only difference is the name under the icon.

The closed document window or minimized document icon or Group icons represent minimized document windows. These Group icons hold other applications, or they can contain document icons. These Group icons all look alike; only their titles indicate what might be in them. For instance, the Group icon named Games, created when Windows is installed, contains two game programs, three if you have Windows for Workgroups 3.11. You can also create group icons that contain similar items. For instance, if you had a Word Processing Program Group, it could contain the actual word processing application program as well as those data documents associated with the application.

Work area

The work area or workspace is inside the window. The work area for Program Manager shows you the open document window and the icons for the document windows that are not open.

Desktop

The **desktop** is the area outside the application window. All Windows activities take place on the desktop. It is called the desktop because it is analogous to working at a desk. You can move objects on the desk, bring new ones to it, or remove objects no longer needed. In this example, Program Manager is open and on your desktop.

Window borders

Window borders are the outside edges that define the window. You can make the window borders longer or shorter using the mouse.

16.4 Pointing Devices

Windows makes it easy to use other input devices. Although the keyboard is necessary when writing a letter, it is not so fast for choosing an item from a menu. A pointing device allows you to control the on-screen cursor to perform many tasks, such as selecting a menu item or cutting text from one location and pasting it to another. It is particularly useful in creating graphs or drawings. There are many pointing devices, such as a light pen or a joystick. The most common pointing device is the mouse, although a second popular choice is the trackball. There is a new intregrated pointing device which is a small stick-like object located on the keyboard. It has the functionality of a mouse or a trackball without forcing you to remove your hands from the keyboard. It was created originally by IBM and called the TrackPointII™. Many new computers, especially notebooks, have adopted this device and given it thier own name.

The mouse is a small hand-held device attached to the system unit, typically by a cable. It has a flat bottom and one or more buttons on the top. A ball protrudes from the bottom and functions as the electric signal detection device. As you move the mouse, it detects the movement and translates that signal into movement of the cursor (arrow) on the monitor.

A trackball is, in essence, an upside down mouse. It too has a ball and buttons, but the ball is on top. The only difference between a mouse and a trackball is how the ball is moved. When you use a mouse, you roll the entire unit over a surface. With a trackball, the unit is stationary and you move the ball with your hand, fingers, or thumb. The trackball which takes less space to use than a mouse is especially popular with laptop and notebook computers.

The integrated pointer allows you to move the pointer with your finger and has the same effect as rolling the ball in either the mouse or trackball. In this text, the instructions will refer to a mouse, but the same instructions can be used for a trackball or an integrated pointer. See Figure 16.2.

Figure 16.2 *A Mouse, a Pointer, an Integrated Pointing Stick, a Trackball*

A trackball and pointer usually have only two buttons. A mouse can have two or three buttons. You place your palm on the mouse and rest your index finger between the two buttons so you can press either the left or right button. In Windows, if you have a three-button mouse, the center button is not used. The mouse is usually located next to the keyboard. The mouse allows you control over the position of a "pointer"(arrow) on the screen. As you move the mouse, the pointer will move across the screen in the same direction you are moving the mouse. The mouse acts like an extension of the hand.

The pointer position lets you know where you are on the screen. In the Windows environment, it allows you to select and choose items. Selecting means marking with the selection cursor. Sometimes, selecting means highlighting an item of interest; other times it is simply placing an X in a check box. Selecting does not activate anything. Selecting is different than choosing. Once you select what you want to do, you then choose to carry out the requested action. When you click a button, you are selecting a task. When you double-click a button or press Enter, you are choosing it. Usually, double-clicking the left mouse button is equivalent to pressing Enter.

Windows can be used with either the keyboard or the mouse. Some tasks are easier with the mouse, others with the keyboard. As you work with Windows, you will find what best suits your needs. This textbook will emphasize mouse instructions with some keyboard instructions. These common terms describe actions you take with pointer devices:

Click	To press and release the button *quickly*. It is usually the left button and is pressed after you have pointed to an object on the screen.
Double-click	To press the button twice *quickly*. Again, this is usually the left button and is done after you have pointed to an object on the screen.
Drag	To hold down the specified button while you slide the mouse or roll the ball. The selected object is dragged across the screen.
Move	To move the mouse on the desktop or roll the ball in the trackball so that the pointer moves.
Point	To move the mouse or trackball so that the pointer is over some object on the screen. Usually, having the point of the pointer (arrow) just touching the object on the screen is sufficient. If you get results you do not expect, it is probably because the pointer is not sufficiently covering the item on the screen.

Most of the mouse and trackball actions—clicking, double-clicking and dragging—use only the left button, so you may assume that "button" refers to the left button, unless otherwise stated. Each mouse responds differently. You will have to experiment with your pointing device to get the right "feel" of moving the pointer, dragging, clicking, and double-clicking.

New mouse users have the most difficulty with double-clicking. You must press the left mouse button very, very quickly. It is almost a one-step process. Track ball users and pointer users will also need to experiment. You will have to practice rolling the ball or moving the pointer to see how far it moves the pointer on the screen. You will also need to practice clicking the buttons to get the right "feel" of moving the pointer, dragging, clicking, and double-clicking. Once you master these techniques, you will be ready to manipulate windows.

16.5 Activity: Loading Windows and Working with Windows

Note 1:   No disk needs to be in a drive at this time. The computer should be booted. You should be at the root directory of C so that C : \> is displayed.

Note 2:   On your computer, you may boot directly into Windows and begin with Step 2.

Note 3:   All screen displays in this chapter are based on the default Windows for Workgroups default installation.

Step 1   Key in the following: C : \>**WIN** [Enter]

WHAT'S HAPPENING? This screen represents the default installation of Windows.

Step 2   Click the upward pointing arrow (Maximize button) on the **Program Manager** title bar.

WHAT'S HAPPENING? You have maximized the window. It now fills the screen completely. If you look at the sizing buttons, you will see that you still have the downward pointing arrow, but instead of the upward pointing arrow, you now have a double-headed arrow. This arrow is known as the "Restore button," which restores the window to its previous size.

Step 3   Click the Restore button.

WHAT'S HAPPENING? You restored the window to the default size.

Step 4   Click the downward pointing arrow (Minimize button) on the **Program Manager** title bar.

WHAT'S HAPPENING? You minimized Program Manager, which appears in its icon form usually in the lower left part of the screen. Now called an application icon, it represents a program that is open and running. The program-item icon executes the program. Program Manager is still open and on the desktop, but it is out of the way. Each Windows application has a unique icon. Usually the program-item icon and application icon are the same. The difference is where it appears. A program-item icon appears in a group window, whereas an application icon appears on the desktop.

Step 5   Double-click the **Program Manager** application icon to restore the window.

WHAT'S HAPPENING? The Program Manager window is restored.

Step 6   Place the mouse pointer on the title bar labeled **Main**

Step 7   Hold down the left mouse button and move the mouse downward and rightward. The entire **Main** window should move down and to the right. When the screen display looks like the screen below, release the left mouse button.

WHAT'S HAPPENING? As you can see, you moved the Main window to a new location. You can move all windows using the same technique.

Step 8   Place the mouse pointer on the title bar labeled **Main** and return it to its original position. When it is in the correct position, release the left mouse button.

Step 9   Place the mouse pointer on the right **Program Manager** window border. The arrow should change to a double-headed arrow (⟨↔⟩)

Step 10   Press and hold the left mouse button, then move to the left. The border of **Program Manager** should contract or be pushed in to the left. When it looks like the screen below, release the left mouse button.

WHAT'S HAPPENING? You pushed in the left border of the **Program Manager** window, making it smaller. You can use the same technique to contract or expand the borders for any document or application window. Now you are going to return the border to the original position.

Step 11   Place the mouse pointer on the right border of **Program Manager** window border. The arrow should change to a double-headed arrow.

Step 12   Press and hold the left mouse button down, then move to the right. The border of **Program Manager** should expand to the right. When it looks like the original screen, release the left mouse button.

16.6 Using Windows

In the above activities, you manipulated different windows. In the next activities, you will learn how to start a program in Windows and also how to have more than one program running at a time. When you have only one application open, it is in the foreground. The foreground application is the one that Windows treats as the application you are working on. The foreground application is also known as the foreground window, the active window, or the current window. If you have more than one application open, only one application is in the foreground; the rest of the applications are in the background. The active window is always on the top of the desktop with its title bar highlighted.

16.7 Activity: Foreground and Background Programs

Note: You are in Windows. The Program Manager window is displayed with the Main window inside it. If Program Manager fills the entire screen, restore it to its default size by clicking the restore button on the title bar. If Program Manager is an icon, restore it by double-clicking the Program Manager icon. Do the same for Main.

Step 1   Click the word **Window** on the **Program Manager** menu bar.

WHAT'S HAPPENING? You opened Program Manager's Window menu. Main has a check mark by it because it is the active group window. The selection and order will differ on your computer, depending on what groups have been installed. This list is not necessarily a list of programs on your system, but only of the "group windows." It does not matter if the group is a window or an icon. It will still be listed on this menu. Anything on this list is a "document" to Program Manager. You usually have several choices from which to select. Each of these choices represents a group of programs that are in a group window. As you can see, each name on this list corresponds to one of the group icons or group windows. You are going to select Games. In this example, it is number 2. On your system, it probably will be a different number.

Step 2   Click **Games**

WHAT'S HAPPENING? You selected the Games group. Windows comes with two games: Solitaire and Minesweeper. Each game is represented by a program-item icon. If you had other games, you could add them to this program group. When using a mouse, you can bypass the menu and open a window directly by double-clicking the Games group icon.

Note: Exact sizing and placement of windows will vary with different computer systems.

Step 3   Double-click **Minesweeper**

WHAT'S HAPPENING? Minesweeper is now in the foreground and is the active application. The application program, in this case, is a game you can play. Program Manager is in the background. You can tell which application is active not only because Minesweeper is lying on top of Program Manager, but also because the title bar for Minesweeper is highlighted. You now have three open windows: Games, Program Manager and Minesweeper, but only two application windows open— Program Manager and Minesweeper. The Games window is an open document window (group window) that holds program-item icons but it is not an application. Between the open application windows, only Minesweeper is the current or active window. You can easily switch among the open applications. You can even open other applications.

Step 4   **Program Manager** should still be visible in the background. Click the **Program Manager** title bar, or anywhere in the **Program Manager** window. If you cannot see the **Program Manager** window, press the **Alt** + **Esc** keys.

WHAT'S HAPPENING? Program Manager is now the active window. You may still be able to see Minesweeper in the background, but its title bar will not be highlighted. Using the $\boxed{\text{Alt}}$ + $\boxed{\text{Esc}}$ keys and the $\boxed{\text{Alt}}$ + $\boxed{\text{Tab}}$ keys will cycle through all the open application windows.

Step 5   While holding down the $\boxed{\text{Alt}}$ key, tap the $\boxed{\text{Tab}}$ key once. Do not release the $\boxed{\text{Alt}}$ key.

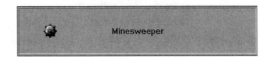

WHAT'S HAPPENING? When you use the $\boxed{\text{Alt}}$ + $\boxed{\text{Tab}}$ keys, you cycle through all the open applications. However, rather than seeing the applications, the $\boxed{\text{Alt}}$ + $\boxed{\text{Tab}}$ keys display the icon and the name of the open application. It does not display the window or the application. The $\boxed{\text{Alt}}$ + $\boxed{\text{Esc}}$ key combination shows not only the title bar and borders but also the window and its contents. Because graphics take so much time to redraw when you rotate through the open windows, the $\boxed{\text{Alt}}$ + $\boxed{\text{Tab}}$ key combination is much quicker than the $\boxed{\text{Alt}}$ + $\boxed{\text{Esc}}$ key combination.

Step 6   With **Minesweeper** displayed in the title box, release the $\boxed{\text{Alt}}$ key.

WHAT'S HAPPENING? Minesweeper is now the active application. When you released the $\boxed{\text{Alt}}$ key, you chose the Minesweeper program.

Step 7   Press the $\boxed{\text{Alt}}$ + $\boxed{\text{Esc}}$ keys to bring the **Program Manager** window to the foreground.

WHAT'S HAPPENING? Both the Program Manager and Games windows seem to be active, because both of their title bars are highlighted. How can this be if only one application can be active at one time? Only one application is active—Program Manager. Remember, Games is a document window (group window) inside the Program Manager window. Program Manager is the application window and Games is the document window. Games "belongs" to Program Manager and is subservient to it. Games is the active document window inside the active application window, Program Manager.

Step 8   Double-click the **Solitaire** program-item icon. (You may need to move the **Solitaire** window to be able to see the **Minesweeper** window in the background.)

WHAT'S HAPPENING? You now have three application windows open: Minesweeper, Program Manager, and Solitaire. Because Solitaire is on top, it is the active window. Its title bar is a different color or color intensity. As the foreground window, Solitaire takes the majority of the computer's processing time. Minesweeper and Program Manager are open but not active. They are in the background and therefore get a smaller share of the computer's processing time. You can always click the window you want to be active. If you cannot see the window you wish to use, you can use [Alt] + [Tab] or [Alt] +[Esc] to cycle through all the open application windows. Remember, if you hold down the [Alt] key and tap the [Tab] key, Windows will cycle through the open application windows showing only the title box. This is always faster because the [Alt] + [Esc] key combination shows the entire windows contents.

Step 9   Try the[Alt] +[Esc] and[Alt] + [Tab] key combinations a few times to see how they work differently. Be sure to end with **Solitaire** as the active window.

Step 10   Double-click the mouse anywhere on the desktop and outside of any window. If you cannot see the desktop, press [Ctrl] + [Esc].

WHAT'S HAPPENING? You opened the Task List window. In reality, this window is a dialog box. A **dialog box** is a window that appears temporarily to request or supply information. Many dialog boxes display available options you may select before you choose a command. But in "windowese," Task List is referred to as a window. In it is a list of all application programs presently open. This is different from choosing Window on the Program Manager title bar. Task List displays only the open application programs. The Window menu in program manager only displays all the group windows (document windows) that you have on your system.

Task List has command buttons at the bottom. A command button in a dialog box carries out or cancels a selected action. To activate a command, you click the button. The Task List command buttons are Switch To, End Task, Cancel, Cascade, Tile and Arrange Icons. Switch To allows you to switch to another open application program. End Task allows you to close an open application. The Cancel button allows you to take no action and leave the dialog box. **Cascade** and **Tile** change the arrangement of the open application windows. The Arrange Icons allows you to tidy up the placement of the icons. The first command button you will use is Switch To. You will use it to Switch To the application Minesweeper, making it the active window.

Step 11   Click **Minesweeper** in the **Task List**

Step 12   Click **Switch To**. You could have also double-clicked **Minesweeper** to make it active, combining this and the last step into one.

WHAT'S HAPPENING? You switched tasks and made Minesweeper the active program. Minesweeper is now the foreground window. Program Manager and Solitaire are still open, but they are not active and are therefore in the background. Their title bars are not highlighted. You are going to return to Task List and tile your applications.

Step 13   Double-click the mouse on the desktop or anywhere outside the windows. If you cannot see the desktop, press Ctrl + Esc

WHAT'S HAPPENING? You are now back at the Task List window.

Step 14   Click **Tile**

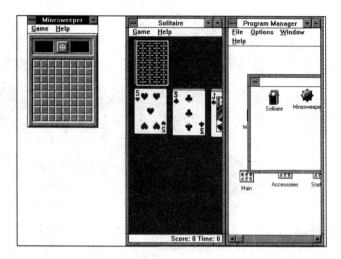

WHAT'S HAPPENING? Your open applications windows are divided equally on the desktop. Since you have only three open applications, the desktop was divided into three parts so that the applications are now displayed side by side. If you had two applications open, the desktop would be divided into two parts. If you had four applications, the desktop would be divided into quarters. That is what is meant by tiled. The title bar of the active window is highlighted. In this case, the title bar of Minesweeper is highlighted, making Minesweeper the active window or foreground application. Although you may think of foreground as being on top, in Windows, the term foreground is synonymous with active. You can work in any window once you make it active.

Step 15   Click the title bar of **Program Manager**. Then click **Solitaire**. Last, click **Minesweeper**

Step 16   To return to **Task List**, press Ctrl + Esc

WHAT'S HAPPENING? You returned to Task List.

Step 17   Click **Cascade**

Control-menu box ⎯⎯⎯

WHAT'S HAPPENING? Now the open windows are stacked on top of each other, a procedure called cascading. Once again, the active window title bar is highlighted. In this case, Minesweeper is active.

Step 18   Double-click the Control-menu box of **Minesweeper**. It is the box in the left corner of the **Minesweeper** title bar.

WHAT'S HAPPENING? You closed Minesweeper and are at the Solitaire window. You can also close an application by using Task List.

Step 19   Double-click on the desktop anywhere outside a window. If you cannot see the desktop, press Ctrl + Esc

WHAT'S HAPPENING? You returned to Task List.

Step 20   Click **Solitaire**. Click **End Task**

WHAT'S HAPPENING? You closed both Minesweeper and Solitaire. Next, you need to close Games.

Step 21   Double-click the **Control-menu** box on the **Games** title bar.

WHAT'S HAPPENING? You returned to the Program Manager window. The only button you did not use in the Task List dialog box was the Arrange Icons command button. This button neatly arranges the application icons you have minimized on the desktop. It does not arrange any icons in the group windows. Since you closed all the applications you had open and made the Games group window an icon, you can safely exit Windows. Although you could click File on the Program Manager title bar and then click Exit Windows, you are going to exit Windows the quickest way.

Step 22   Double-click the Control-menu box on the **Program Manager** title bar.

WHAT'S HAPPENING?Before you exit Windows, you are presented with another dialog box, giving you two options. If you click OK, it means you do want to exit Windows. If you click Cancel, it means you do not want to exit Windows.

Step 23   Click **OK**

```
C:\>_
```

WHAT'S HAPPENING? You returned to the DOS system level.

16.8 Working with Help

Windows provides online help. This means that, rather than looking in a manual for information about how Windows works, what different keystrokes combinations do, what the mouse does, or any other information, you can access help directly on the screen. Applications that are written for Windows will also have online help that will almost always look and work the same way. Remember, once you learn a task in one Windows application, it will be the same in other applications.

16.9 Activity: Using Help

Note: You should be at the C:\>.

Step 1   Key in the following: C:\>**WIN** [Enter]

WHAT'S HAPPENING? You have loaded Windows. The Program Manager window is displayed with the Main window inside.

Step 2   Click **Help** on the **Program Manager** menu bar.

WHAT'S HAPPENING? You selected the Help menu from the Program Manager menu bar, which gives you help with the Program Manager. You are going to choose an item from this menu.

Step 3   Click **About Program Manager**

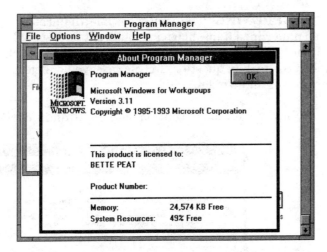

WHAT'S HAPPENING? Choosing About Program Manager identifies the mode of Windows you are running—standard or enhanced—and supplies other details about your hardware operating environment. In addition, it gives you copyright information and what version number you are working with.

Step 4   Click **OK**

WHAT'S HAPPENING? You returned to the Program Manager window.

Step 5   Press F1

WHAT'S HAPPENING? Pressing the F1 key takes you directly into Program Manager Help. In most Windows application programs, pressing F1 is the quickest way to get help.

Step 6   Place the mouse pointer under the word **Arrange**

WHAT'S HAPPENING? The pointer became a hand pointing at the word Arrange. This is an underlined item shown in a different color, usually green. Whenever you see an item solidly underlined, it means that it has further details on how to accomplish the task in question. In this case, you will get more information about arranging icons and windows.

Step 7   Click the left mouse button once on **Arrange Windows** and **Icons**

WHAT'S HAPPENING? You were taken to a screen with more specific help on arranging program icons and group windows.

Step 8   Click the **Back** command button under the menu bar.

WHAT'S HAPPENING? You returned to the Program Manager Help main screen.

Step 9   Click the **Glossary** command button under the menu bar.

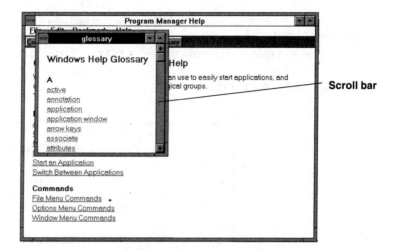

WHAT'S HAPPENING? The Glossary window is opened. Glossary is actually an executable program that displays a list of terms with dotted underlines. Clicking a term presents a definition of that term.

This window also introduces the scroll bar. A scroll bar appears when there are too many items to display in a window at any one time, either vertically or horizontally. A scroll bar can only be used with a mouse. Placing the mouse pointer on the up or down arrow at the top or bottom of the scroll bar. Each click will move you one line. There is a box in the scroll bar called the scroll box. If you click and drag the scroll box, it will allow you to move continuously. If you click above or below the scroll box, you will move in increments of one page. See Figure 16.3.

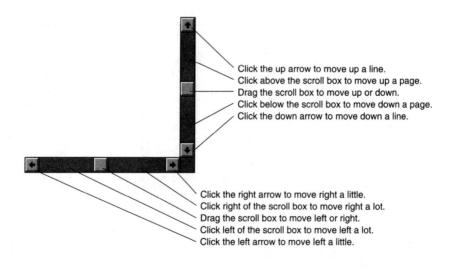

Figure 16.3

You can also navigate through this window using the keyboard. The PgUp and PgDn keys will move in one-screen increments. If you press Ctrl + Home or Ctrl + End you will move to the top or bottom of the document, respectively.

Step 10   Click on the term **arrow keys**

WHAT'S HAPPENING? You see a "pop-up" window containing a definition of the term arrow keys. You do not have to open Glossary to get definitions. The Glossary is like a dictionary for looking up definitions. However, any item with a dotted underline in any help screen will provide a definition of the term.

Step 11   Double-click the **Control-menu** box on the **Program Manager Help** title bar.

WHAT'S HAPPENING? You closed Program Manager Help. Glossary is still open. This is one way to tell that Glossary is an application window and not a document window. If it were a document window, dependent on Program Manager Help, it would have closed when you closed Program Manager Help. Since it did not, it is an application because it can stand on its own.

Step 12   Double-click the **Control-menu** box for **Glossary**

WHAT'S HAPPENING? You returned to Program Manager.

16.10 File Manager

File Manager allows you to accomplish many of the tasks you accomplished at the DOS command line prompt. You can copy files, delete files, create subdirectories, format floppy disks, and execute programs. In addition, File Manager also gives you options that were not available in DOS before version 6, such as the ability to rename a subdirectory or move a file.

16.11 Activity: Using File Manager

Note 1:   The DATA disk is in Drive A. You are in Windows. The Program Manager window should be displayed with the Main window inside.

Note 2:   Your display will vary depending on your hardware, software, subdirectories, files, and where Windows is installed. In the examples, Windows is installed on Drive D in a subdirectory called WINDOWS. If you are on a stand-alone computer, the WINDOWS subdirectory will probably be installed on Drive C. If you are on a network, the drives will vary and could be Drive F, Drive P, or whatever drive letter your administrator assigned.

Step 1   Double-click the **File Manager** icon.

WHAT'S HAPPENING? This is a directory window in two parts. On the left you see the structure of the directories on the hard drive—in this case Drive D. This structure is called the **directory tree** or **tree**. On the right, you see the current default directory—in this case WINDOWS—consisting of files and subdirectories that are in the WINDOWS subdirectory. The right portion of the screen is called the directory or contents. If you have Windows 3.1, you will see the following display:

Disk-drive icons   The disk drives on your computer system.

Up icon	An icon shaped like an arrow that will take you up one level in the directory tree.
Directory path	The default drive and directory. In this figure, it is C:\WINDOWS.
Scroll bar	If there are more directories or data than can be shown vertically on one screen, vertical scroll bar appears on the right side of the window. If there are more directories or data than can be shown horizontally in the window, a horizontal bar appears at the bottom of the window. The box in the scroll bar indicates your current position in the list of files, directories, or data. If the box appears in the middle of the bar, you are half way down the listing. You can move through the list by dragging the box up or down with the mouse. You can also move one item at a time by clicking on the arrows at either end of the bars, (up, down, right, or left). You can also "scroll" through the data by holding the left mouse button down on one of the arrows.
Tree	The left side of the directory window.
Directory icons	Represented by a file folder. Each of these represents a directory on the disk, in alphabetical order. In the directory tree window, each directory icon is connected by a vertical line to the directory level above it. On the contents side of the screen, directory icons indicate directories that are under the current directory.
Volume Label	A name that identifies the disk.
Network name	If you are on a network, the name assigned to your network drive connection will appear here. This is displayed instead of the volume label.
Current directory	The current or default directory is indicated by an open directory folder.
Split bar	This bar divides the window so you can see the structure of the disk on the left and the contents on the right. This bar can be manipulated.
File icons	Graphic representations of files.
Status bar	This bar supplies information about the current default directory.

The textbook examples will use the File Manager window that appears in Windows for Workgroups 3.11. Many items are the same, but there are enhancements. These include:

Drive List ——————— (pointing to drive list in image)

Tool Bar ——————— (pointing to tool bar in image)

Drive list	A drop-down list box that displays the current default and allows you to choose another drive.
Tool bar	The tool bar is a row of icons directly below the menu bar. By clicking on the icons, you make choices. The tool bar contains the following new items:

The first two icons allow you to choose how the files will be displayed:

 Displays only file names.

 Displays information about the file (date, time, size) with the file name.

Once you have decided how to display the files, the following four icons choose the sort order for the files:

 Sorts in order by file name.

 Sorts by file extension.

 Sorts by file size.

 Sorts by file date.

The next icons run different programs:

 Runs MS-Backup program for Windows.

 Runs Virus-protection program.

 Gives compression information for files on compressed drives.

 Runs MS Undelete for Windows program.

If you are on a Windows for Workgroups network, there are many more choices, including mail, sharing documents, directories, and printers, and other resources.

Step 2   Scroll up and click once on the DOS6BK folder.

WHAT'S HAPPENING? DOS6BK is now the current directory. The contents screen has changed. Now the files and directories within the DOS6BK directory are shown.

Step 3   Double-click the DOS6BK directory icon.

WHAT'S HAPPENING?   You expanded the DOS6BK directory listing in the directory window to show subdirectories inside the DOS6BK directory. The DOS6BK directory is the default. Remember, the left side (tree) displays the hierarchical structure of the directories. The right (contents) side shows files and directories in the default directory. If you look at the right side, you see that Windows uses four different file icons to distinquish file types:

The folder represents a directory.

The icon with lines on it simulating writing represents a document that has been associated with some program. Uses file extensions to associate files with programs. For instance, when you use Word for Windows, Word will assign a default file extension of .DOC to any document created with Word. Thus, if you create a file called MY, Word will assign the file extension to make the data file MY.DOC. Windows will then know that when you double-click the file icon MY.DOC, it is associated (belongs) to Word, and Windows will open Word and MY.DOC at the same time. You can also manipulate associations.

The icon with no simulated writing on it is a data file. It has no file extension that belongs to any specific program. Windows does not know what program to load with this file. You must know with which program you created this data file.

Any folder with a stripe or line across it is a program file. Windows recognizes a program by the file extension .COM, .EXE and .BAT. In addition, Windows recognizes the file extension .PIF (Program Information File) as a program.

Step 4   Click the DATA directory folder directly beneath the DOS6BK directory in the directory tree.

WHAT'S HAPPENING?   The contents on the right side has changed. It now displays the contents of the DATA directory.

Step 5   Double-click on the DOS6BK directory icon.

WHAT'S HAPPENING?   You have collapsed the directory tree display.

Step 6   Double-click on the DATA file folder in the contents window.

WHAT'S HAPPENING? You have once more expanded the directory tree, this time from the contents window. You can now see the files in the DATA directory.

Step 7   Double-click the file BONJOUR.TXT.

WHAT'S HAPPENING? Because BONJOUR.TXT has .TXT extension, Windows opened the program called Notepad (the Windows ASCII editor) and at the same time loaded the file called BONJOUR.TXT. You can edit this data file, add to it, delete from it, and save it in Notepad.

Step 8   Double-click the Control-menu box on the **Notepad** title bar.

WHAT'S HAPPENING? You have closed Notepad and are back in File Manager.

Step 9   Double-click the DOS6BK on the tree.

WHAT'S HAPPENING? You have collapsed the DOS6BK directory to its highest level. Notice the contents window still shows the files and directories in the DOS6BK directory, because it is still the default (highlighted) directory in the tree. One advantage of using File Manager to manage files is that you can see more than one directory at one time. This is one reason people prefer a graphical interface such as Windows over the character-based DOS.

Step 10   Press the ✱ (Asterisk) key on the numeric keypad.

WHAT'S HAPPENING?   You have expanded the entire structure of the DOS6BK directory. You are going to look at the MEDIA directory.

Step 11   Click MEDIA

WHAT'S HAPPENING?   MEDIA is a subdirectory under DOS6BK. The contents window now shows the files and directories in the MEDIA directory. MEDIA has only subdirectories, no files.

Step 12   Click **Window** on the **File Manager** menu bar.

Step 13   Click **New Window**

Step 14   Again click **Window** on the **File Manager** menu bar.

Step 15   Click **Tile Horizontally**

WHAT'S HAPPENING? You dropped down the Window menu for File Manager. You opened a new window that is an exact copy of the directory window already open. You then tiled the two windows horizontally. You may wonder why you would want a display of the same two directories. File Manager, rather then keeping open every directory you click, makes you consciously open more than one directory at a time. Since it does not know which directory window you want to open, it gives you an exact copy of the existing directory.

Step 16   Click **Window**

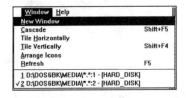

WHAT'S HAPPENING? The directory windows are considered document windows by File Manager. The Window menu shows you the two open windows, distinguished by numbers. You can move from one window to another by clicking on the window's title bar, or by pulling down the Window menu and clicking on the name of the document. In this case your choices are D:\DOS6BK\MEDIA*.*:1 or D:\DOS6BK\MEDIA*.*:2.

Step 17   Click outside the menu.

Step 18   Click on the title bar of the top window to make it the active window.

Step 19   Click **PHONE** (if you cannot see the directory icon, click the down arrow on the scroll bar).

WHAT'S HAPPENING? The window on the top now shows PHONE as the default directory, with the contents of PHONE in the contents window on the right. The window on the bottom still shows MEDIA as the default directory. You can manipulate these windows independently, enabling you to see separate directories at the same time.

Step 20   Click **Window**

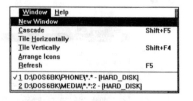

WHAT'S HAPPENING? You have two new document windows open (directory windows). Now your choices are D:\DOS6BK\MEDIA*.*:1 or D:\DOS6BK\PHONE*.*

Step 21   Click outside the menu.

Step 22   Double-click the Control-menu box on the title bar for the **PHONE** directory window.

WHAT'S HAPPENING? You closed PHONE.

Step 23   Double-click the **Control-menu** box on the title bar of **File Manager**

WHAT'S HAPPENING? You exited File Manager and returned to Program Manager.

16.12 DOS Commands in File Manager

File Manager is designed to help you manipulate your files. The commands you learned in DOS work the same way in File Manager. The difference is that in Windows you will get menus and prompts to assist you. There are some things you cannot do in Windows. Windows does not perform the pretender commands. You can not use APPEND, ASSIGN, JOIN, or SUBST while in Windows. CHKDSK /F can be harmful to your data if it is run from Windows. Do not run SCANDISK or DEFRAG while in Windows.

16.13 Activity: Using DOS Commands in File Manager

Note: You are in Windows. The Program Manager window should be displayed, with the Main group open.

Step 1   Insert the ACTIVITIES disk—Working Copy in Drive A.

Step 2   Double-click **File Manager**

Note: The root directory of the default drive should be the default directory. If it is not, scroll up and click it. If your directory window is too small, size it by dragging the borders to fill the screen.

WHAT'S HAPPENING? The directory window of the hard disk is displayed.

Step 3   Click the Drive A disk drive icon.

WHAT'S HAPPENING? You are looking at the directory window of Drive A. One important point is that when you change floppy disks during a File Manager session, File Manager may not update the directory information. You will see the directory of the old disk, not the new one you placed in the drive. To resolve this problem, you can use the Refresh command whenever you change disks.

Step 4   Place the DATA disk in Drive A.

Step 5   Click **Window** on the **File Manager** menu bar. Click **Refresh**

WHAT'S HAPPENING? When you click Refresh, you force File Manager to reread the disk. Now File Manager displays the contents of the DATA disk.

Step 6   Replace the DATA disk with the Activities disk.

Step 7   Click **Window** on the **File Manager** menu bar. Click **Refresh**

WHAT'S HAPPENING? You made File Manager reread the disk in Drive A. Now you are looking at the directory window for the ACTIVITIES disk, not the DATA disk.

Step 8   Double-click on the filename `APR.NEW` in the contents window.

WHAT'S HAPPENING? Since `APRIL.NEW` is not associated with a program, File Manager cannot execute it. This process is no different from keying `APR.NEW` at the command line prompt. `APR.NEW` is a data file, not a program. DOS and File Manager execute only program files. The rules do not change because you are using a graphical interface.

Step 9   Click **OK**

Step 10   Click **File**

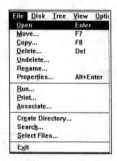

WHAT'S HAPPENING? You dropped down the File Manager File menu from the menu bar. You can see the same choices that you have been using at the DOS system level. There are some new commands, but most of them are familiar and indeed work the same way.

Step 11   Click **Copy**

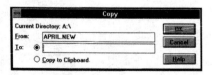

WHAT'S HAPPENING? File Manager presents you with a dialog box. Since you have already selected APR.NEW, it places that file in the From: text box. However, since it does not know where you want the file copied to, it places the cursor in the To: box.

Step 12   In the **To:** text box, key in the following: **APR.ONE** Enter

WHAT'S HAPPENING? You saw a quick message that the file was being copied, and you were returned to the File Manager screen. You can see APR.ONE listed near APR.NEW.

Step 13   Click APR.ONE

Step 14   Click **File.** Click **Move**

WHAT'S HAPPENING? APR.ONE has already been entered in the From: text box.

Step 15   In the **To:** text box, key in the following: **\TEST\APR.XYZ** Enter

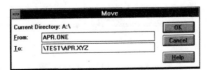

WHAT'S HAPPENING? You see a quick message that the file is being moved to the subdirectory TEST and has acquired a new name—APR.XYZ. You are then returned to the directory window.

Step 16   Double-click the TEST subdirectory.

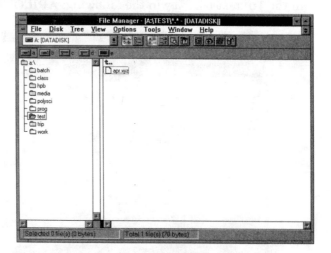

WHAT'S HAPPENING? The APR.ONE file from the root directory of the ACTIVI-TIES disk has been moved to the subdirectory TEST and has indeed acquired a new name—APR.XYZ. Furthermore, the APR.ONE file has been deleted from the root directory. As you can see, the Move command works the same way in File Manager as it does at the DOS command line.

Step 17   Click **Window.** Click **New Window.** Click **Cascade**

WHAT'S HAPPENING? You can see the directory window for the root of A behind the directory window for the A:\TEST directory.

Step 18   Click **Options**

WHAT'S HAPPENING? File Manager gives you options. In this case, you are interested in Confirmation. You can choose whether or not to be prompted when you take an action with a file, such as a move or a copy.

Step 19   Click **Confirmation**

WHAT'S HAPPENING? The Confirmation dialog box asks whether or not you wish to be queried on any of the actions listed in the dialog box. You can select such items as whether or not to be asked to confirm an action prior to deleting a file or subdirectory. If you want to be queried before a deletion, the appropriate check box must have an X in it. If there is no X in the check box, you will not be queried. You remove or add an X by clicking on the check box.

Step 20   Be sure the **Confirm on Delete** box is checked. Click **OK**

Step 21   Be sure APR.XYZ is highlighted. Click **File**. Click **Delete**

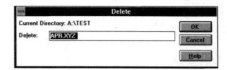

WHAT'S HAPPENING? The Delete dialog box on the screen displays the file name to be deleted and gives you a chance to cancel the deletion.

Step 22   Click **OK**

WHAT'S HAPPENING? Because you had the confirmation turned on, File Manager queried you prior to deleting the file.

Step 23   Click **Yes**

WHAT'S HAPPENING? You received a quick message that the file was deleted. You then returned to TEST.

Step 24   Double-click the Control-menu box on the File Manager title bar.

WHAT'S HAPPENING? You returned to Program Manager. As you can see, most DOS commands in Windows work the same way as they do at the command line.

16.14 Selecting Multiple Files

It is easy to work with multiple files in File Manager. You may select files one at a time, or as a group of files (files that are either next to one another or separated). Once you have selected a file or files, you may manipulate them any way you wish. You can copy them, move them, rename them, or use any of the other choices on the **File** menu. You may also use the mouse to drag the selected files to another drive or directory.

16.15 Activity: Selecting Multiple Files

Note 1:   Your data disk is in Drive A. You are in Windows. The Program Manager window is displayed, with the Main window inside the Program Manager window.

Note 2:   In the examples shown, the hard disk is Drive D. More typically the WINDOWS directory is located on Drive C.

Note 3:   The contents of your DATA disk may be different from the examples shown.

Step 1   Double-click **File Manager**

Step 2   The hard disk should be the selected drive.

Step 3   Click the DOS6BK directory.

WHAT'S HAPPENING? You have opened File Manager. You made the default directory \DOS6BK. The contents of that directory is shown in the window.

Step 4   Double-click the Drive A icon.

WHAT'S HAPPENING? When you double-click a drive icon, you open a new window, but do not close the directory window for the drive you were on. If you single-click a drive icon, you open the selected directory window and close the directory window you were in. You should be able to see title bar of the DOS6BK directory window. The Drive A directory window is the active window.

Step 5   Click **File**

Step 6   Click **Create Directory**

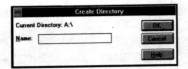

WHAT'S HAPPENING? You told File Manager you wanted to create a directory in the root of the disk in Drive A. The dialog box is requesting a name for this new directory.

Step 7   In the **Name:** text box, key in the following: **CHAP16** [Enter]

WHAT'S HAPPENING? File Manager has created the directory in the root of A. Notice the new directory, CHAP16, is shown in the directory tree window.

Step 8   Double-click the Control-menu box on the title bar of A:\[DATADISK] directory window.

WHAT'S HAPPENING? You have closed the Drive A directory window. The DOS6BK window is now the active window.

Step 9   Click APR.99 in the contents window.

Step 10   Hold down [Shift]

Step 11   While still holding [Shift], click APRIL.TMP. Release [Shift]

WHAT'S HAPPENING? You have selected all the files from APR.99 through APRIL.TMP. Using the [Shift] key will select all the files between the first file selected to the last file selected.

Step 12   Click **File**. Click **Copy**

WHAT'S HAPPENING? The COPY dialog box has filled in the From: text box with the names of the files you selected. It is waiting for you to key in where you want the files copied To:

Step 13   In the **To:** text box, key in the following: **A:\CHAP16** ⟨Enter⟩

WHAT'S HAPPENING? File Manager has copied the selected files to the CHAP16 directory on Drive A. The files are still highlighted in the DOS6BK directory window.

Step 14   Click the up-arrow icon at the top of the contents.

WHAT'S HAPPENING? By clicking on the up arrow icon, you unselected the files. The message on the status bar at the bottom of the window states: Selected 0 file(s) (0 bytes). (If the Status Bar is not visible, click Options. Then click Status Bar.)

Step 15   Double-click the Drive A drive icon.

Step 16   Click **Window**. Click **Tile Horizontally**

Step 17   Double-click the CHAP16 directory on the tree.

WHAT'S HAPPENING? You have changed the default directory to CHAP16 on Drive A. You have tiled the display so you may see both the A:\CHAP16 directory and the C:\DOS6BK directory at the same time.

Step 18   Double-click the Control-menu box for the DOS6BK directory window to close it.

Step 19   Click **Window**. Click **Cascade**

Step 20   Click CHAP16 on the tree to make it the default directory.

WHAT'S HAPPENING? You have made the Drive A directory window the active window and CHAP16 the default directory.

Step 21   On the contents side of the directory window, click APR.99. Hold down the
          Ctrl key. While holding the **Ctrl** key down, click APRIL.TMP.

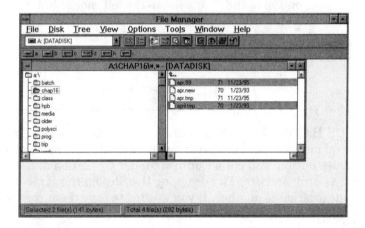

WHAT'S HAPPENING? You have selected two files that are *not* contiguous. The message on the Status Bar states: Selected 2 file(s) (141 bytes)

Step 22   Click **File**. Click **Copy**

Step 23   In the **To:** text box, key in the following: *.**FM** **Enter**

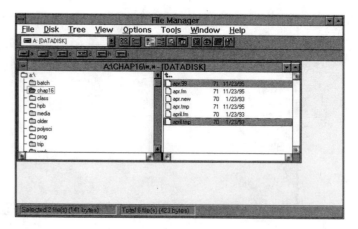

WHAT'S HAPPENING?   You have made copies of the two selected files, but changed the extension to . FM. The files should still be selected.

Step 24   Place the mouse pointer on one of the selected files. Holding down the mouse button, drag the files to the root of A : \ on the tree side. When they are on top of the A : \, release the left mouse button.

WHAT'S HAPPENING? When dragging the files, you should have seen the icon of several pieces of paper. When you dropped the files on the root of A and released the mouse button, you got a Confirm Mouse Operation dialog box. This process is known as *drag* and *drop*. By dragging the files on the same drive, you move them from one location to another. If you wanted to copy them, you could drag them, but hold down the **Ctrl** key when you drag.

Step 25   Click **No**

Step 26   Click APR . FM

Step 27   Press the **Ctrl** key and click APRIL . FM

Step 28   Click **File**. Click **Delete**

WHAT'S HAPPENING? You see the Delete confirmation dialog box. It asks if you want these two files deleted. If you clicked OK, you would see a Confirm File Delete dialog box for each file you wish to delete.

Step 29   Click **Cancel**

Step 30   Double-click the Control-menu box on the title bar of **File Manager**

Step 31   Double-click the Control-menu box on the title bar of **Program Manager**

WHAT'S HAPPENING? You have returned to Program Manager. You are exiting Windows.

Step 32   Click **OK**

```
D:\>
```

WHAT'S HAPPENING? You have exited Windows and returned to the DOS system level. Your introduction to Windows is complete.

Chapter Summary

1. Windows is a graphical user interface (GUI) that works with DOS. It is considered an operating environment.
2. Instead of the command line prompt that you see with DOS, you use icons and drop-down menus to maneuver in Windows.
3. Windows allows the user to perform more than one task at a time.
4. Program Manager is the Windows program execution shell.
5. Windows has a File Manager that allows you to perform operating system tasks.
6. In application software written expressly for Windows, consistency among the commands makes learning new applications easier.
7. Windows has a memory manager that makes efficient use of computer memory. In addition, programs written for Windows can break the memory barrier of 640 KB.
8. Windows runs in two modes—standard and enhanced. The mode depends on the microprocessor you have.
9. To take advantage of the power of Windows, it is best to run in enhanced mode, which requires a 386 or better processor. It is also advantageous to have at least 4 MB of memory, a mouse, and a color VGA monitor.
10. When running in enhanced mode, Windows uses virtual memory, which allows Windows to write information to and from the hard disk when it runs out of memory.
11. The Windows screen includes window borders, the title bar, the Control-menu icon, sizing buttons, the menu bar, program groups, the work area, and the desktop.
12. Minimizing and maximizing windows allow you to enlarge the window or to have a window reduced to an icon.
13. You can move and change the size of any window.
14. A foreground program is the one that is currently open and active. It can also be called the active window or the current window. The foreground program takes the majority of the processor's time.
15. Only one program can be active at a time, although many programs can be open. The active program lies on top of the other application programs. Its title bar is highlighted.
16. A background program is open but not active. It takes less of the processor's resources.
17. The [Alt] + [Tab] and [Alt] + [Esc] key combinations allow you to cycle through the open windows. The former does not draw the windows, whereas the latter does.
18. The [Ctrl] + [Esc] key combination opens Task List, which lists all the open programs. Task List, in addition to listing all the open programs, allows you to switch among the open applications, close applications, and tile and cascade windows.
19. Windows provides online help which can be accessed either by pressing the F1 key or by clicking the mouse on Help. The help facility includes an index, key

terms that provide capsule descriptions, and key words that call up major help screens.

20. File Manager allows you to accomplish operating system tasks.
21 When you activate File Manager, it provides a directory tree window that displays the structure of a disk (tree) and displays the contents of that directory.
22. In File Manager you can open and look at more than one directory window at a time.
23. Four types of icons are used to distinguish among file types. A plain folder is a directory window. A dog-eared paper with lines on it is a document associated with a program. A dog-eared paper with no lines on it is an unassociated file. A folder with a stripe on it is an executable program.
24. DOS commands can be used in File Manager.
25. DOS commands in File Manager are presented with menus and dialog boxes.
26. The rules of DOS do not change even though you are in File Manager.
27. Files must be selected to accomplish work such as moving or copying. You may select more than one file at a time, either in sequence or out of sequence.

Key Terms

Active windows	Drop-down menu	Sizing buttons
Background	Foreground	Standard mode
Cascade	Graphical user	Tile
Control-menu icon	interface (GUI)	Title bar
Dialog box	Menu bar	Virtual memory
Directory tree (tree)	Program Manager	Window borders
Desktop		

Discussion Questions

1. What is Windows?
2. What are some of the advantages of using Windows?
3. What is an icon?
4. What is a drop-down menu?
5. What are the two modes of operating in Windows?
6. What determines the mode Windows will run in?
7. What is virtual memory?
8. Why would you maximize or minimize a window?
9. What happens to an application program that is not active?
10. What is Task List?
11. How can you access online help?
12. What is the advantage of having online help capability?
13. What will be found in the Help facility?
14. What is File Manager?
15. How can File Manager be accessed?

16. What is the function of a scroll bar?
17. How can you expand a directory?
18. List the four types of icons that are used to distinguish among file types.
19. What command(s) should not be used when using Windows?
20. How can you make an application program active?
21. When using Help, what information will you receive for command terms that are underscored?
22. When you are using Help, what information will you receive for terms that are underscored with a dotted line?
23. How can you select files that are not contiguous? Contiguous?
24. How are DOS commands presented in File Manager?
25. What is the function of the Refresh command?

Appendix A

Installing the DOS6BK Directory and Shareware Registration

The disk that is supplied with the textbook provides programs and files for you use as you work through the textbook. The textbook assumes that DOS6BK directory has been installed on Drive C. You cannot merely copy the files to a directory you create because there are more files on the disk than get installed to the hard disk. If you wish to install the DOS6BK directory on a hard drive other than Drive C, you must substitute the correct drive letter in the instructions. If you are working on your own computer, you must not be in Windows or in DOS Shell. You must be at the root of C and the default drive and directory must be A:\.

If you are in a lab environment, the lab instructors should have installed the DOS6BK directory on the hard disk. The lab instructors, particularly if the lab is on a network, will have to give you instructions as to the location of the DOS6BK directory if it is not on Drive C. The instructor will inform you if you need to install the DOS6BK directory.

A.2 If You Boot Into DOS

Step 1   Have no disk in any drive. Turn on the monitor and computer.

```
C:\>_
```

WHAT'S HAPPENING? You are at the DOS system level. Your prompt may look different.

Step 2   Key in the following: **CD \ Enter**

> C:\>_

WHAT'S HAPPENING? You are now at the root level of Drive C.

Step 3   Place the ACTIVITIES disk that came with the textbook into Drive A.

Step 4   Key in the following: **A: Enter**

> A:\>_

WHAT'S HAPPENING? You have made the root of A the default drive and directory.

Step 5   Key in the following: **PUT C: Enter**

WHAT'S HAPPENING? The program will self-install and will let you know when it is finished. The DOS6BK directory is now installed on the hard disk. The textbook will instruct you when you need to access the DOS6BK directory.

IF IT DOESN'T WORK: If you get error messages such as File not found when trying to install the DOS6BK directory, be sure you are neither in Windows nor in DOS Shell. Be sure you are at the root of C and that the default drive and directory is A:\. Substitute PUTX for PUT in the instructions and try again.

A.3 If You Boot Into Windows

Step 1   Have no disk in any drive. Turn on the monitor and computer.

WHAT'S HAPPENING? If your screen looks similar to the one above, you are in Windows, not at the DOS system level. You must return to DOS. Do not double-click the MS-DOS icon.

Step 2   Click **File.** Click **Exit Windows**

WHAT'S HAPPENING? Windows is presenting you with a dialog box asking you if you really want to exit Windows.

Step 3   Click **OK**

```
C:\WINDOWS>
```

WHAT'S HAPPENING? You are at the DOS system level. Your prompt may look different.

Step 4   Key in the following: **CD \ Enter**

```
C:\>_
```

WHAT'S HAPPENING? You are now at the root level of Drive C.

Step 5   Place the ACTIVITIES disk that came with the textbook into Drive A.

Step 6   Key in the following: **A: Enter**

```
A:\>_
```

WHAT'S HAPPENING? You have made the root of A the default drive and directory.

Step 7   Key in the following: **PUT C: Enter**

WHAT'S HAPPENING? The program will self-install and will let you know when it is finished. The DOS6BK directory is now installed on the hard disk. The textbook will instruct you when you need to access the DOS6BK directory.

IF IT DOESN'T WORK: If you get error messages, such as File not found, when trying to install the DOS6BK directory, be sure you are neither in Windows nor in DOSSHELL. Be sure you are at the root of C and that the default drive and directory is A:\. Substitute PUTX for PUT in the instructions and try again.

A.4 If You Boot Into DOS Shell

Step 1: Have no disk in any drive. Turn on the monitor and computer.

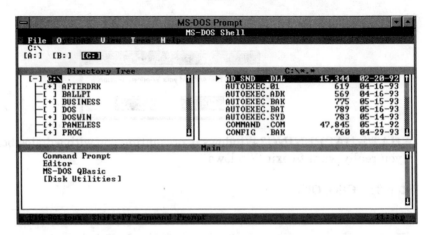

WHAT'S HAPPENING? If your screen looks similar to the above screen, you are in DOS Shell, not at the DOS system level. You must return to DOS.

Step 2   Press the **Alt** + **F4** keys.

```
C:\DOS>_
```

WHAT'S HAPPENING? You are at the DOS system level. Your prompt may look different.

Step 3   Key in the following: **CD ** **Enter**

```
C:\>_
```

WHAT'S HAPPENING? You are now at the root level of Drive C.

Step 4   Place the ACTIVITIES disk that came with the textbook into Drive A.

Step 5   Key in the following: **A:** **Enter**

```
A:\>_
```

WHAT'S HAPPENING? You have made the root of A the default drive and directory.

Step 6   Key in the following: **PUT C:** **Enter**

WHAT'S HAPPENING? The program will self-install and will let you know it is finished. The DOS6BK directory is now installed on the hard disk. The textbook will instruct you when you need to access the DOS6BK directory.

IF IT DOESN'T WORK: If you get error messages, such as File not found, when trying to install the DOS6BK directory, be sure you are neither in Windows nor in DOS Shell. Be sure you are at the root of C and that the default drive and directory is A:\. Substitute PUTX for PUT in the instructions and try again.

A.5   *Installing The DOS6BK Directory Manually*

Note: You may create the DOS6BK directory and copy the files to the DOS6BK directory. The following is the series of commands you must use. Be sure you are at the DOS system level. Punctuation and spacing are very important. You must key in the command exactly as listed.

Step 1   Have no disk in any drive. Turn on the monitor and computer.

```
C:\>_
```

WHAT'S HAPPENING? You are at the DOS system level. Your prompt may look different.

Step 2   Key in the following: **CD \ Enter**

```
C:\>_
```

WHAT'S HAPPENING? You are now at the root level of Drive C.

Step 3   Place the ACTIVITIES disk that came with the textbook into Drive A.

Step 4   Key in the following: **A:** Enter

```
A:\>_
```

WHAT'S HAPPENING? You have made the root of A the default drive and directory. The following are a series of commands. Each one must be keyed in individually followed by Enter before proceeding to the next command.

Step 5   Key in the following commands:

MD C:\DOS6BK Enter

COPY *.new C:\DOS6BK Enter

COPY personal.fil C:\DOS6BK Enter

```
DATE  < date1.nnn Enter
MD  C:\DOS6BK\MEDIA  Enter
MD  C:\DOS6BK\MEDIA\MOVIES  Enter
MD  C:\DOS6BK\MEDIA\TV  Enter
MD  C:\DOS6BK\MEDIA\BOOKS  Enter
COPY  MEDIA\MOVIES\*.*  C:\DOS6BK\MEDIA\MOVIES  Enter
COPY  MEDIA\TV\*.*  C:\DOS6BK\MEDIA\TV  Enter
COPY  MEDIA\BOOKS\*.*  C:\DOS6BK\MEDIA\BOOKS  Enter
COPY  y.fil  C:\DOS6BK  Enter
COPY  steven.fil  C:\DOS6BK  Enter
COPY  mark.fil  C:\DOS6BK  Enter
DATE  < date2.nnn  Enter
MD  C:\DOS6BK\SPORTS  Enter
COPY  SPORTS\*.*  C:\DOS6BK\SPORTS  Enter
COPY  exp94*.*  C:\DOS6BK  Enter
COPY  state.cap  C:\DOS6BK  Enter
DATE  < date3.nnn  Enter
MD  C:\DOS6BK\LEVEL-1  Enter
MD  C:\DOS6BK\LEVEL-1\LEVEL-2  Enter
MD  C:\DOS6BK\LEVEL-1\LEVEL-2\LEVEL-3  Enter
COPY  LEVEL-1\*.*  C:\DOS6BK\LEVEL-1  Enter
COPY  LEVEL-1\LEVEL-2\*.*  C:\DOS6BK\LEVEL-1\LEVEL-2  Enter
COPY  LEVEL-1\LEVEL-2\LEVEL-3\*.*  C:\DOS6BK\LEVEL-1\LEVEL-2\LEVEL-3
                                                                    Enter
COPY  goodbye.txt  C:\DOS6BK  Enter
COPY  grammy*.*  C:\DOS6BK  Enter
COPY  dances.txt  C:\DOS6BK  Enter
COPY  name.bat  C:\DOS6BK  Enter
COPY  go.bat  C:\DOS6BK  Enter
MD  C:\DOS6BK\FINANCE  Enter
```

COPY FINANCE\ORDER C:\DOS6BK\FINANCE `Enter`

COPY FINANCE*.BAT C:\DOS6BK\FINANCE `Enter`

COPY FINANCE\SHAREWAR.DOC C:\DOS6BK\FINANCE `Enter`

COPY FINANCE\THINK*.* C:\DOS6BK\FINANCE `Enter`

COPY FINANCE\TUTIL.EXE C:\DOS6BK\FINANCE `Enter`

COPY FINANCE*.* C:\DOS6BK\FINANCE `Enter`

COPY FINANCE*.TKR C:\DOS6BK\FINANCE `Enter`

COPY frank.fil C:\DOS6BK `Enter`

COPY carolyn.fil C:\DOS6BK `Enter`

COPY states.usa C:\DOS6BK `Enter`

DATE < date4.nnn `Enter`

MD C:\DOS6BK\PHONE `Enter`

COPY PHONE*.* C:\DOS6BK\PHONE `Enter`

MD C:\DOS6BK\GAMES `Enter`

MD C:\DOS6BK\GAMES\MLINK `Enter`

MD C:\DOS6BK\GAMES\CHEK `Enter`

COPY GAMES*.* C:\DOS6BK\GAMES `Enter`

COPY GAMES\MLINK*.* C:\DOS6BK\GAMES\MLINK `Enter`

COPY GAMES\CHEK*.* C:\DOS6BK\GAMES\CHEK `Enter`

COPY *.mak C:\DOS6BK `Enter`

COPY april.tmp C:\DOS6BK `Enter`

COPY bye.typ C:\DOS6BK `Enter`

COPY cases.fil C:\DOS6BK `Enter`

COPY second.fil C:\DOS6BK `Enter`

COPY goodbye.tmp C:\DOS6BK `Enter`

COPY bonjour.tmp C:\DOS6BK `Enter`

COPY january.tmp C:\DOS6BK `Enter`

COPY march.tmp C:\DOS6BK `Enter`

COPY february.tmm C:\DOS6BK `Enter`

COPY olive.oil C:\DOS6BK `Enter`

COPY   award.mov   C:\DOS6BK   Enter
COPY   exp93*.*   C:\DOS6BK   Enter
COPY   state2.cap   C:\DOS6BK   Enter
DATE   < date5.nnn   Enter
MD   C:\DOS6BK\TEST
COPY   TEST*.*   C:\DOS6BK\TEST   Enter
COPY   wild*.*   C:\DOS6BK   Enter
COPY   rns.exe   C:\DOS6BK   Enter
COPY   exp95*.*   C:\DOS6BK   Enter
COPY   *.jaz   C:\DOS6BK   Enter
COPY   *.99   C:\DOS6BK   Enter
COPY   january.txt   C:\DOS6BK   Enter
COPY   february.txt   C:\DOS6BK   Enter
COPY   march.txt   C:\DOS6BK   Enter
COPY   april.txt   C:\DOS6BK   Enter
COPY   hello.txt   C:\DOS6BK   Enter
COPY   bye.txt   C:\DOS6BK   Enter
COPY   file*.*   C:\DOS6BK   Enter
COPY   getyn.com   C:\DOS6BK   Enter
MD   C:\DOS6BK\DATA   Enter
COPY   DATA*.*   C:\DOS6BK\DATA   Enter
COPY   jan.tmp   C:\DOS6BK   Enter
COPY   feb.tmp   C:\DOS6BK   Enter
COPY   mar.tmp   C:\DOS6BK   Enter
COPY   apr.tmp   C:\DOS6BK   Enter
COPY   *.red   C:\DOS6BK   Enter
COPY   *.up   C:\DOS6BK   Enter
COPY   test.txt   C:\DOS6BK   Enter
COPY   emp*.*   C:\DOS6BK   Enter

WHAT'S HAPPENING? You have created all the necessary directories and copied the necessary files. You need to take one more step: enter the correct date. The date must be entered in the format of mm-dd-yy such as 2-5-94. You may not use any character data such as February. When you have entered the date, press the **Enter** key.

Step 6   Key in the following: **DATE** **Enter**

Step 7   Key in the current date.

```
A:\>_
```

WHAT'S HAPPENING? You have returned to the DOS system level.

A.6   Removing the DOS6BK Directory from the Hard Disk

Note: If you are working in a lab environment, do not take these steps. However, if you are working on your own computer, when you have completed the textbook, you will probably want to take DOS6BK and the files in the directory off your hard drive. You may, of course, use DELTREE to remove DOS6BK. However, the following program will also uninstall DOS6BK.

Step 1   Have no disk in any drive. Turn on the monitor and computer.

WHAT'S HAPPENING? Follow instructions that were given above so that you are at the C:\> prompt.

Step 2   Key in the following: **CD \ Enter**

```
C:\>_
```

WHAT'S HAPPENING? You are now at the root level of Drive C.

Step 3   Place the ACTIVITIES disk that came with the textbook into Drive A.

Step 4   Key in the following: **A: Enter**

```
A:\>_
```

WHAT'S HAPPENING? You have made the root of A the default drive and directory.

Step 5   Key in the following: **UNPUT C: Enter**

WHAT'S HAPPENING? The program will remove the DOS6BK directory and will let you know when it is finished.

A.7 Using DISKCOPY To Copy the ACTIVITIES Disk

Note: Use this technique if you want to copy the 5¼-inch ACTIVITIES disk to a 5¼-inch floppy disk or if you want to copy the 3½-inch ACTIVITIES disk to a 3½-inch floppy disk. The two disks must be the same media type.

Step 1   Have no disk in any drive. Turn on the monitor and computer. Follow the above instructions to be sure that you are at the DOS system level. You screen should look as follows:

```
C:\>_
```

WHAT'S HAPPENING? You should be at the root level of Drive C.

Step 2   Place the ACTIVITIES disk that came with the text book into Drive A.

Step 3   Key in the following: **DISKCOPY A: A: Enter**

```
Insert SOURCE diskette in drive A:
Press any key to continue. . . . . _
```

WHAT'S HAPPENING? The **ACTIVITIES** disk is already in Drive A.

Step 4   Press **Enter**

```
C:\DOS>DISKCOPY A: A:

Insert SOURCE diskette in drive A:

Press any key to continue . . .

Copying 80 tracks, 15 sectors per track, 2 side(s)

Reading from source diskette . . .

Insert TARGET diskette in drive A:
Press any key to continue . . . . . _
```

WHAT'S HAPPENING? DISKCOPY is waiting for a blank disk. The blank disk *must* be a high-density disk.

Step 5   Remove the ACTIVITIES disk from Drive A. Place a blank, high-density disk in Drive A:. Latch or shut the drive door. Press **Enter**

```
Writing to target diskette . . .

Do you wish to write another duplicate of this disk (Y/N)?
```

WHAT'S HAPPENING? In DOS 6.22, the enhancement to DISKCOPY feels that you might wish to make many copies of a floppy. It is giving you that opportunity.

Step 6   Press **N**

```
Volume Serial Number is 09FC-3951

Copy another diskette (Y/N)?_
```

WHAT'S HAPPENING? The prompt tells you that the program has finished executing and asks you a question. Do you want to execute this program again to make another copy of a disk? In this case, you do not wish to make another copy, so you key in the letter n for no.

Step 7   Press **N**

```
C:\>_
```

WHAT'S HAPPENING? You are returned to the system level. Your copy is complete.

A.8 Using PUTFLOP To Copy the ACTIVITIES Disk

Note: Use this technique if you want to copy the 5¼-inch ACTIVITIES disk to a 3½-inch floppy disk or if you want to copy the 3½-inch ACTIVITIES disk to a 5¼-inch floppy disk. The blank disk *must* be a formatted disk.

Step 1   Have no disk in any drive. Turn on the monitor and computer. Follow the preceding instructions to ensure that you are at the DOS system level. Your screen should look as follows:

```
C:\>_
```

WHAT'S HAPPENING? You are now at the root level of Drive C.

Step 2   Place the ACTIVITIES disk that came with the textbook into Drive A.

Step 3   Key in the following: **A:** **Enter**

```
A:\>_
```

WHAT'S HAPPENING? You have made the root of A the default drive and directory.

Step 4   Place a blank formatted high-density disk into Drive B.

Step 5   Key in the following: **PUTFLOP B:** [Enter]

WHAT'S HAPPENING? The program will self-install and will let you know when it is finished. It will take about thirty-five minutes. When the PUTFLOP program has copied all the files to the disk in Drive B, it will tell you. You will be returned to the A:\> prompt.

IF IT DOESN'T WORK: If you get error messages such as File not found when trying to install from one floppy disk to another, be sure you are not in Windows. Be sure you are at the root of C and that the default drive and directory is A:\. Substitute PUTFLOPX B: for PUTFLOP B: in the instructions and try again.

A.9 Shareware Programs Provided with the Textbook

Several programs on the ACTIVITIES disk that are installed to the DOS6BK directory are shareware programs. Shareware programs are for trial purposes only. If you find you like the programs and would like to keep them, you must register them and pay the registration fee.

Home Phone Book Shareware Program

Home Phone Book, Version 2.5

This shareware program is provided by:

> Thomas E. Bonitz
> 7903 Kona Circle
> Papillion, NE 68128

If you like Home Phone Book, please send $20.00 to Thomas E. Bonitz at the above address.

The Thinker Shareware Program

The Thinker, Version 3.0-0788

This shareware program is provided by:

> Alan C. Elliott
> TexaSoft
> P.O. Box 1169
> Cedar Hill, TX 75104

If you like The Thinker, please send $35.00 plus shipping and handling to Alan C. Elliott at the above address. Phone orders (214) 291-2115 or call 1-800-955-TEXAS or FAX: (214) 291-3400. You may also print a copy of the order form by keying in `PRINT \DOS6BK\FINANCE\ORDER`. The order form will allow you to specify your desired disk size.

Microlink Shareware Programs: Shut the Box, Yaht, Otra, Loyd, Push Your Luck, Crux

Shut the Box, Yaht, Otra, Loyd, Push Your Luck and Crux

These shareware programs are provided by:

Bob Lancaster
P. O. Box 5612
Hacienda Heights, CA 91745

If you like any of these games, please send $ 5.00 for each game to Bob Lancaster at the above address.

CHEKKERS Shareware Program

CHEKKERS, Version 4.1
This shareware program is provided by:

J & J Software
P.O. Box 254
Matamoras, PA 18336

If you like CHEKKERS, please send $ 15.00 to J & J Software at the above address.

ARGH Shareware Program

ARGH, Version 4.0

This shareware program is provided by:

David B. Howorth
1960 S.W. Palatine Hill Road
Portland, OR 97219

If you like ARGH, please send $ 10.00 to David B. Howorth at the above address.

Appendix B

EDIT—The Text Editor

B.1 *EDIT—The Text Editor*

EDIT, introduced in DOS 5.0, is the full-screen editor that allows you to create and edit any ASCII text document (unformatted text document) and uses menus to allow you to manipulate data easily. EDIT is *not* a word processor, so it has no ability to format data in the document. It *does not* provide such features as margins, word wrap, or any special fonts.

You may use either the keyboard or mouse to manipulate both text and the menus when in EDIT. In order to execute EDIT, EDIT must have access to QBASIC, usually located in the DOS subdirectory. The syntax is:

```
EDIT [[drive:][path]filename] [/B] [/G] [/H] [/NOHI]
```

[drive:][path]filename	Specifies the ASCII file to edit.
/B	Allows use of a monochrome monitor with a color graphics card.
/G	Provides the fastest update of a CGA screen.
/H	Displays the maximum number of lines possible for your hardware.
/NOHI	Allows the use of a monitor without high-intensity support.

B.2 Using EDIT

Note 1: A blank, formatted disk should be in Drive A. Do not use the ACTIVITIES disk, the DATA disk, or the APPLICATIONS disk.

Note 2: C:\> will be displayed with the path set to C:\DOS.

Step 1 Key in the following: C:\>**A:** [Enter]

Step 2 Key in the following: A:\>**EDIT** [Enter]

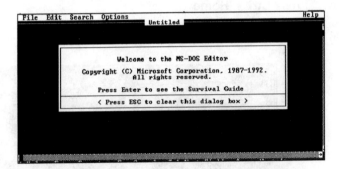

WHAT'S HAPPENING? This is the opening screen to EDIT.

Step 3 Press [Esc]

WHAT'S HAPPENING? You are presented with a blank screen. You may begin keying in data.

Step 4 Key in the following:**This is a test.** [Enter]
This is more data. [Enter]

WHAT'S HAPPENING? You have keyed in some data. If you did not press [Enter] and kept keying in data, you would move to character number 256. If you look at the bottom of the screen, you see that the status line tells you what line and what character position you are in.

WHAT'S HAPPENING? As you can see, you are on the third line, and the cursor is in the first position. You have two modes of operation, insert mode and overstrike mode. Insert mode is the default. You can tell you are in insert mode because the cursor is a blinking line. Insert mode means, as you key in data on an existing line, the other data on the line will not be replaced, just pushed along.

Step 5   Press **Ctrl** + **Home**

Step 6   Key in the following: **THIS IS MORE DATA.**

WHAT'S HAPPENING? The new data is there with the old data. Overstrike mode permits you to replace the characters that are there. You toggle between overstrike mode and insert mode by pressing the **Insert** key. You know that you are in overstrike mode because the cursor becomes a blinking block.

Step 7   Press the **Insert** key.

Step 8   Key in the following: **october**

WHAT'S HAPPENING? You replaced the characters that were there. Full-screen editing can be done using either keystrokes or a mouse. You position the mouse where you want it and click. Table B.1 lists the keyboard cursor movement keys.

Desired cursor movement	Key(s) to use	Keyboard Shortcuts
Character left	[←]	[Ctrl] + **S**
Character right	[→]	[Ctrl] + **D**
Word left	[Ctrl] + [←]	[Ctrl] + **A**
Word right	[Ctrl] + [→]	[Ctrl] + **F**
Line up	[↑]	[Ctrl] + **E**
Line down	[↓]	[Ctrl] + **X**
First indentation level of current line	[Home]	
Beginning of current line		[Ctrl] + **Q, S**
Beginning of next line	[Ctrl] + [Enter]	[Ctrl] + **J**
End of line	[End]	[Ctrl] + **Q, D**
Top of window		[Ctrl] + **Q, E**
Bottom of window		[Ctrl] + **Q, X**
Move to next window		[F6]
Increase size of current window		[Alt] + [+]
Decrease size of current window		[Alt] + [−]

Table B.1   *Cursor Movement Keys*

To select text to manipulate, when using a mouse, you hold down the left mouse button and drag the mouse pointer over the desired characters. Table B.2 lists the text selection keys.

Desired Text to Select	Keys to Use
Character left	[Shift] + [←]
Character right	[Shift] + [→]
Word left	[Shift] + [Ctrl] + [←]
Word right	[Shift] + [Ctrl] + [→]
Current line	[Shift] + [↓]
Line above	[Shift] + [↑]

Screen up	[Shift] + [PgUp]
Screen down	[Shift] + [PgDn]
To beginning of file	[Shift] + [Ctrl] + [Home]
To end of file	[Shift] + [Ctrl] + [End]

Table B.2   Text Selection Keys

B.3 EDIT Menus

EDIT has a series of menus located on what is called a menu bar at the top of the screen. Each menu has further choices. You must drop-down the menus to access the choices. You can drop-down the menus in one of three ways:

❑ Click the desired menu choice.

❑ Press the a key and the first letter of the desired menu.

❑ Press the [Alt] key, which will move the cursor to the menu bar at the top of the screen. Once there, you can move the left or right arrow keys to move among the choices. Once a choice is highlighted, press [Enter].

Once you have dropped down the menu, you choose a command from the menu. There are three ways to make a menu choice.

❑ Click the command name.

❑ Press the highlighted letter of the command you want.

❑ Press the [↑] or [↓] arrow keys to highlight your command. Then press [Enter].

You may change your mind at any time and cancel your choice in one of two ways:

❑ Click outside the menu.

❑ Press the [Esc] key.

The File Menu

New	Opens a new document.
Open	Opens an existing document.
Save	Saves the current document to disk.

Save As	Saves the current document under a new name, preserving the document that was loaded in its original form.
Print	Prints the document.
Exit	Exits EDIT.

The Edit Menu

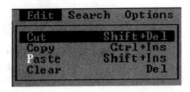

Cut	Selects text and cut it from the current location. Saves it in an area of memory (buffer) until you exit EDIT or copy or cut something else to the buffer.
Copy	Selects text and copies it to the buffer, leaving the original text in its location. Remains in the buffer until you exit EDIT or copy or cut something else to the buffer.
Paste	Pastes what is in the buffer to the selected location in the document.
Clear	Deletes current selection but does not place it in buffer.

The Search Menu

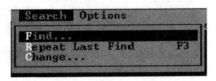

Find	Searches document for specified text.
Repeat Last Find	Continues searching for specified text.
Change	Searches for specified text and replaces it with specified text.

The Options Menu

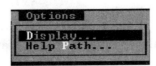

Display	Allows you to change the colors of the display.
Help Path	Allows you to change the location of the help file when it is located in other than the specified path.

The Help Menu

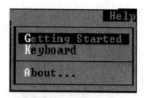

Getting Started	Gives instructions on how to use EDIT. Includes all menus.
Keyboard	Will display all the keyboard keys to manipulate text.
About	Displays what version of EDIT you are using.

B.4   Dialog Boxes in EDIT

Step 1   Press **Alt** + **F** + **S** or click File/Save.

WHAT'S HAPPENING? You have opened the Save dialog box. A dialog box either requests information from the user or needs information from the user. In this case, the Save dialog box is asking what you want to call the file. The current default drive is A:\ as is indicated in the Save dialog box. The cursor is positioned in the File Name: box. To move among the drives/directories and choices at the bottom of the dialog box (OK, Cancel, or Help>), you either click with the mouse or press the **Tab** key. To choose a different drive or directory, you either highlight your choice or double-click it with the mouse (double-click means to press the left mouse button twice rapidly.)

Step 2   Key in the following in the File Name box: **MYFILE.TXT** **Enter**

WHAT'S HAPPENING? The file has been saved to disk.

Step 3   Press **Alt** + **F** + **X** or click File/Exit

```
A:\>EDIT

A:\>_
```

WHAT'S HAPPENING? You have returned to the system level.

Step 4   Key in the following: EDIT **Enter**

Step 5   Press **Esc**

Step 6   Press **Alt** + **F** + **O** or click File/Open

WHAT'S HAPPENING? You have opened the Open dialog box. EDIT uses the
default extension of .TXT. It is showing that on this disk in the root directory, there
is one file with the .TXT extension. (*Note:* There could be more than one file listed,
depending on which disk you used.)

Step 7   Press the **Tab** key to move to the files area and press the **→** arrow key
          once or click MYFILE.TXT. (*Note:* If there is more than one file listed in the
          dialog box, press the **↑** or **↓** arrow key to select it.)

WHAT'S HAPPENING? Now that MYFILE.TXT is selected, you can open it by
pressing **Enter**. If you are using a mouse, you can open the file MYFILE.TXT by
double-clicking it.

Step 8   Press **Enter**

WHAT'S HAPPENING? You have opened an existing file.

Step 9   Press **Ctrl** + **End**. Press the **Backspace** key once.

Step 10   Key in the following: **This is some text that I am keying in** **Enter**
so that I can have different information. **Enter**

WHAT'S HAPPENING? By pressing **Ctrl** + **End**, you moved to the bottom of the file. You then added more data. You are going to save this file under a new name, preserving your original data.

Step 11   Press **Alt** + **F** + **A** or click File/Save As

WHAT'S HAPPENING? The file name MYFILE.TXT is already in the File Name: box. It is highlighted. There is a feature called typing that replaces selection which means that, rather than having to delete MYFILE.TXT in the text box, you can begin keying in data. Whatever you key in will replace what is there.

Step 12   Key in the following: **THAT.TXT** `Enter`

Step 13   Press `Alt` + **F** + **X** or click `File/Exit`

Step 14   Key in the following: A:\>**TYPE MYFILE.TXT** `Enter`

Step 15   Key in the following: A:\>**TYPE THAT.TXT** `Enter`

```
A:\>TYPE MYFILE.TXT
*THIS IS MORE DATA. october a test.
This is more data.


A:\>TYPE THAT.TXT
THIS IS MORE DATA. october a test.
This is more data.
This is some text that I am keying in
so that I can have different information.


A:\>_
```

WHAT'S HAPPENING? By using `Save As`, you saved your changes to a new file. If you know the name of the file you wish to open, you can open it from the command line.

Step 16   Key in the following: A:\>**EDIT THAT.TXT** `Enter`

WHAT'S HAPPENING? You opened THAT.TXT when you opened EDIT. The file name is displayed on the EDIT screen.

Step 17   Press `Alt` + **F** + **X** or click `File/Exit`

```
A:\>EDIT THAT.TXT

A:\>_
```

WHAT'S HAPPENING? You have returned to the DOS system level.

Appendix C

DOS Shell

Software developers are always looking for ways to make using computer software easier, not only to encourage novice computer users but also to let more sophisticated users take advantage of the power of the new hardware and software. This is especially true when it comes to operating systems. However, in the DOS world, there are new options that reach beyond the command line prompt to make using DOS easier. You can purchase innovative menu systems. You can write menu systems with batch files to make program access easier. In addition, commercial programs called **shells** provide a user interface different from the command line prompt. These programs are called shells because they surround DOS, covering its details. A shell is a program for using DOS. Shells differ from menus in that menus are just lists of options and suboptions. A shell is a complete operating system environment. A shell can contain menus, but menus alone do not make a shell. MS-DOS versions 4.0 through 6.0 come with a shell called DOS Shell (see Figure C.1).

Figure C.1   *Layers of Operating Environments*

Indeed, the direction in the computer industry is away from command-driven text-based programs like DOS to what is called a graphical user interface (**GUI**, pronounced "gooey"). GUIs let you use the keyboard, as well as a mouse. In addition to text, GUIs provide pictures called **icons** that represent program functions. GUIs are not limited to application programs; they can also be used with operating systems using icons for operating system functions. For instance, to access a file, a user would "point and shoot" with the mouse at an icon of a file cabinet. Generally, GUIs enhance DOS.

Windows 3.1, endorsed and written by Microsoft, is a shell with many more powerful features such as multitasking and memory managers. Thus, it is more an operating environment rather than a shell. However, Windows requires powerful hardware. In order to meet the needs of less powerful systems and to make DOS more "user friendly," Microsoft released a product called MS-DOS Shell, commonly referred to as DOS Shell, to utilize some of the features of a graphical environment for those without the hardware power that is needed to run Windows. However, Microsoft found that users who want a graphical user environment prefer Windows so the use of DOS Shell is nearly nil. Thus, beginning with DOS 6.2, DOS Shell was no longer included with DOS. If you desire it, you must order the supplemental disks. If you upgraded to DOS 6.2, you still have DOS Shell from previous versions of DOS in your DOS directory. The upgrade process did not delete DOS Shell.

C.2 MS-DOS Shell

MS-DOS Shell is a user interface that replaces the usual command line with a menulike system. MS-DOS Shell allows the user to select DOS commands from a list, instead of keying them in at the system prompt. However, the user still has access to the system prompt. Depending on the hardware, MS-DOS Shell is also somewhat graphical. For instance, a mouse can be used with MS-DOS Shell. You can also use the keyboard, in addition to or instead of the mouse.

MS-DOS Shell provides easy access to programs and DOS commands. You can install your own programs into the menu system. You can have password protection. You can use MS-DOS Shell to manage the files and use drop-down menus, a feature that DOS does not have at the command line. You can only use MS-DOS Shell with DOS 4.0 or above. MS-DOS Shell is a relatively small program and does not take up much memory. Therefore, you can run it on older computers.

In the next activities you are going to take a look at some of the functions of MS-DOS Shell and explore some of the different options. Once you see how it works, you will see that it is fairly easy to utilize. Since you are only sampling MS-DOS Shell, once you are comfortable with it, feel free to explore some of its other areas.

C.3 Activity: Installing MS-DOS Shell

Note 1:   A blank, formatted disk should be in Drive A. Do not use the ACTIVITIES disk, the DATA disk or the APPLICATIONS disk.

Note 2:   `C:\>` will be displayed with the path set to `C:\DOS`.

Step 1   Key in the following: `C:\>`**DOSSHELL** [Enter]

WHAT'S HAPPENING? You installed MS-DOS Shell. If you have a color monitor, the display will be in color. If you have a monitor that does not support graphics your display will differ. The nongraphics display is different because it does not show the icons, which are pictures that represent items. For instance, next to each file name is a picture (icon) of a file folder. The remainder of this chapter will use the graphics monitor display. Note: If this is not the display you see, take the following steps.

Step 2   Press **Alt** + **V**

Step 3   Press the **↓** key until Programs\Files List is highlighted.

Step 4   Press **Enter**

C.4   Explaining MS-DOS Shell

This screen display looks very different from the C:\> or A:\>. Although certainly not as cryptic as the system prompt you have been using, the display still needs some explanations. Figure C.2 outlines some of the major parts of the screen display.

The delineated portions of the screen are:

1.   The **title bar** of the screen you are in. In this case it is MS-DOS Shell.
2.   The **menu bar** which lists the choices of the available menus. When you choose an item from the menu, the menu bar will display a further list of commands you can use. In this case, your choices are File, Options, View, Tree, and Help.
3.   The default drive and directory. In this case, it is the root directory of Drive C.
4.   The drive icons and/or drive letters available on your specific computer system. In this example, there are Drives A, B, C, D, and E. When you select one of these drive letters, you make it the default drive.
5.   The Directory Tree area. MS-DOS Shell provides areas. The Directory Tree area displays the structure of the directories of the current disk drive. If you select another disk drive, then the Directory Tree would change to reflect the new disk drive structure.
6.   The file list area shows a list of the files in the default directory. The default directory is the one selected in the Directory Tree area.

4. Drive icons   12. Area Titles   1. Title bar   8. Scroll bars

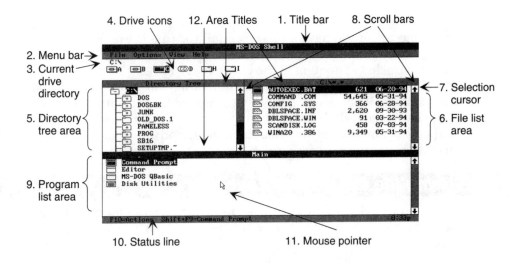

Figure C.2   The MS-DOS Shell Screen

7. The selection cursor. When an item is in a different color or the colors are inverted, it has been "highlighted" or selected. This tells you what selection you have chosen. In this case, C:\ is highlighted, which informs you that you are looking at the root directory of Drive C. In the file list area, AUTOEXEC.BAT is in inverse video or "highlighted" and is therefore the file selected.

8. If you have a mouse and a graphic monitor, you will see the vertical scroll bar. The scroll bar is an easy mechanism to "scroll" through the displayed information when it does not fit on one screen.

9. The program list area, considered the Main program list group, contains programs that you can execute directly from the shell. It includes two programs that you can start from this location, the Editor which is the full screen editor that comes with DOS and the programming language MS-DOS QBasic that comes with MS-DOS. If you select the Command Prompt, it allows you to leave MS-DOS Shell and go directly to the DOS command line prompt. The Disk Utilities contains several of the DOS programs to maintain disks such as FORMAT and DISKCOPY.

10. The status line displays the time and informs you of some function key options. **F10** allows you to take an action, and **Shift** + **F9** returns you to the DOS command prompt.

11. The mouse pointer—look closely for it because it is very mobile.

12.   The area titles tell you the name of the area you are in. When you select an area, it is indicated by a color change or inverse colors on the monitor. The area titles on this screen are Directory Tree, C:*.*, and Main.

You always work in an "area." However, before you can work in an area, you must select it. If you have a color monitor, the title bar of the area you select will change. If you have a monochrome monitor, the area you select will have a small arrow to the left of an item in the area you selected.

MS-DOS Shell allows you to select items from what are called drop-down menus. For example, if you select File, File then provides you with more choices via the drop-down menu. Here is where you perform such functions as copying or deleting a file. The drop-down menu remains on the screen until you either close it or select another menu item.

C.5   Using the Mouse and Keyboard

When using MS-DOS Shell, you can use either the keyboard or a pointing device such as a mouse or trackball or a combination of both. Obviously, if you do not have a mouse, you can only use the keyboard. It is useful to understand how you move within MS-DOS Shell using either the mouse or the keyboard. You also need to review some of the terminology.

If you have a mouse or trackball, it is attached to the system unit. It is called a mouse because it resembles a mouse with a tail. A trackball is a mouse turned upside down. The mouse has two or three buttons on it as does a trackball. The mouse pointer is the arrow-shaped icon on the screen that indicates where you are (see Figure C.3).

Figure C.3   Mouse and Trackball and Pointer

The arrow is the cursor. To move the cursor, you move the mouse around on a flat surface next to the computer, usually the table on which your keyboard is placed. That movement on the surface correspondingly moves the pointer on the screen. When you wish to select an item with the mouse, move the mouse pointer to the icon or text phrase that you wish to choose and click the mouse. Click means pressing the left mouse button once. To activate or run your selection, you double-click the mouse. Double-click means to press the left mouse button twice, quickly. To drag the mouse means to place the mouse pointer on an item, press and hold down the left mouse button, move the mouse pointer to the new location (i.e., drag the item), and then release the left mouse button. You will need to practice the necessary finger pressure to click, double-click, and drag the mouse. You will also find the pressure varies from mouse to mouse. In MS-DOS Shell, the right mouse button has no functions. A trackball works in principle the same way except that you roll the ball around and the trackball remains stationary.

If you do not have a mouse, you can still use MS-DOS Shell with keyboard commands. In general, when you use the keyboard instead of the mouse, you select an item by the use of the **Tab** key, the **Alt** key, the **F10** key, and the arrow keys. As you work with MS-DOS Shell, the keys used will be specified.

C.6 Activity: Using Help from the Command Prompt

Note 1: You are in MS-DOS Shell. If you are not in MS-DOS Shell, key in DOSSHELL at the C:\>. A blank, formatted disk should be in Drive A. Do not use the ACTIVITIES disk, the DATA disk, or the APPLICATIONS disk.

Note 2: **Highlighting** refers to differentiating choices. If you have a color monitor, highlighted choices will be displayed in colors. If you have a black and white monitor, the highlighted choices will be in reversed shades.

Step 1 Press the **Tab** key until Command Prompt is highlighted, or click Command Prompt.

WHAT'S HAPPENING? You highlighted the Command Prompt. The command prompt will take you to the DOS system level.

Step 2 Press **Enter**, or double-click the left mouse-button.

```
Microsoft(R) MS-DOS(R) Version 6.22
          (C)Copyright Microsoft Corp 1981-1994.

C:\>_
```

WHAT'S HAPPENING? As you can see, you returned temporarily to the C:\> prompt. However, MS-DOS Shell is still there waiting to be used. The C:\> prompt works as usual. You can execute any program or command you want. You can always return to MS-DOS Shell by keying in EXIT, which means that you are "exiting" the command line prompt and returning to MS-DOS Shell.

Step 3 Key in the following: C:\>**EXIT** **Enter**

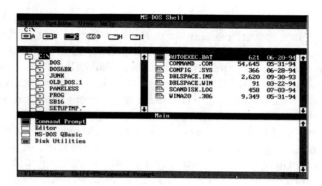

WHAT'S HAPPENING? You returned to MS-DOS Shell. MS-DOS Shell also provides online help. You access help by selecting Help from the menu bar.

Step 4   Press **Alt** + **H**, or click Help on the menu bar.

WHAT'S HAPPENING? The online Help menu dropped down to assist you. The choice Index is highlighted. If you prefer another selection such as Keyboard, you would either use the **↓** key to highlight it, or move the mouse pointer and click Keyboard to highlight it. Each choice will give you detailed instructions on how to use commands in DOS Shell.

Step 5   Press **Esc**, or click somewhere outside the menu.

WHAT'S HAPPENING? You returned to the beginning screen of MS-DOS Shell.

C.7 Returning to DOS

When you highlighted the Command Prompt and exited to the system level, you were merely suspending the use of MS-DOS Shell. It was still waiting to be used. This is why you could key in EXIT yet return to the shell. However, you also want to know how to quit the shell and not have it running in the background.

C.8 Activity: Quitting MS-DOS Shell

Note: You are in MS-DOS Shell.

Step 1   Press **F3**

```
C:\>_
```

WHAT'S HAPPENING? You returned to the system level. Now you have quit the shell. It is not in the background. You can prove this by attempting to use **EXIT**.

Step 2: Key in the following: C:\>**EXIT** Enter

```
C:\>EXIT

C:\>_
```

WHAT'S HAPPENING? Since there was no program running in the background, there was nothing to exit.

C.9 Managing Files and Directories with MS-DOS Shell

MS-DOS Shell allows you to manage your files and directories. It allows you to use many of the standard DOS commands you have already learned to accomplish such tasks as copying files, deleting files, and managing files.

C.10 Activity: Managing Directories

Note: You are at the C:\>. A disk is in Drive A.

Step 1 Key in the following: **DOSSHELL** Enter

Step 2 Press the Tab key until the Directory Tree title bar is highlighted, or click it.

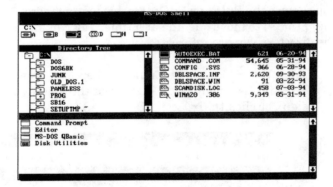

WHAT'S HAPPENING? When you loaded MS-DOS Shell, it read the information on the disk in Drive C. The display will vary based on what directories are on the hard disk. The default drive is C because the C icon is highlighted. You are looking at the root directory of C with its subdirectories. The subdirectories are in alphabetical order. It is important to recognize how you navigate the Directory Tree area.

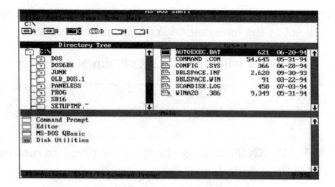

1. The drive icon identifies the default disk drive. If you have a nongraphic monitor, it will be displayed as [C:].

2. Because the Directory Tree area title bar is highlighted, it tells you that this is the active area.

3. The subdirectory icons are file folders. They have either a plus sign (+), a minus sign (-), or are blank. If a file folder has a plus sign in it, it means that it is expandable—that there are other subdirectories beneath it. If it has a minus sign, it means that it can be collapsed to a higher level so that you are only looking at the level you are interested in. If it has neither a plus sign nor a minus sign, there are no more levels. If you have a nongraphical display, instead of a picture of a file folder, you see [+], [-], or [ ] which serve the same functions.

4. To navigate the **Directory Tree**, you may use either the mouse or the keyboard. If you use the mouse, you use the scroll bar. If you use the keyboard, you can use the **PgUp** or **PgDn** key to move one screen at a time. You can use the ⬆ or ⬇ to move one line at a time. You can also key in the first letter of the directory you are interested in.

Step 3   Press the ⊟ key on the numeric key pad. (*Note:* If the file folder icon already has a minus sign in it, press the plus sign. Then press the minus sign), or click the ⊟ icon.

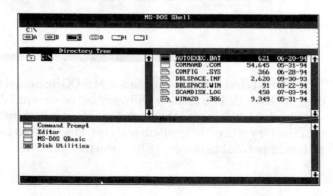

WHAT'S HAPPENING? You collapsed the root directory of C to its highest level. Because it now has a plus sign, you know that you can expand it.

Step 4   Press the ⊞ key on the numeric key pad, or click the ⊞ icon.

Step 5   Press the letter **D** and the arrow key until DOS6BK is highlighted. Click the DOS6BK subdirectory name, or click the scroll bar until you see the DOS6BK subdirectory name. Then click it.

WHAT'S HAPPENING? You selected (highlighted) the DOS6BK subdirectory. On the right side the displayed files are the files in the DOS6BK subdirectory. Because the DOS6BK subdirectory has a plus sign, you know it has lower level directories.

Step 6   Be sure DOS6BK is highlighted. Press the ⊞ key, or click once on the plus sign in the file folder icon.

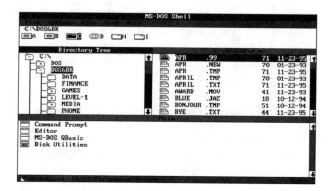

WHAT'S HAPPENING? The plus sign changed to a minus sign. The file list area shows all the files in the DOS6BK subdirectory. You may not be able to see all the subdirectories under DOS6BK.

Step 7   Press the ⬇ key until GAMES is selected. Press the ⊞ key, or scroll until you locate GAMES and click it.

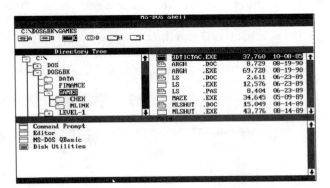

WHAT'S HAPPENING? You expanded the subdirectory called GAMES. It has two subdirectories called CHEK and MLINK. Look at the file list area. It shows you the files in the GAMES subdirectory. Because the DOS6BK icon has a minus sign and the GAMES icon has a minus sign in it, both can be collapsed.

Step 8   Move the ⬆ key until DOS6BK is highlighted. Then press the ⊟ key, or click the minus sign in the DOS6BK file folder icon.

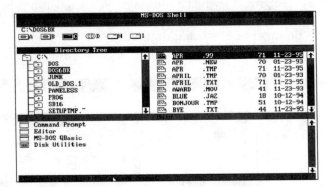

WHAT'S HAPPENING? You collapsed DOS6BK to its highest level so you do not see the subdirectories that are beneath DOS6BK. Be sure DOS6BK is highlighted. You can use the menu bar to accomplish the same tasks.

Step 9   Press **Alt** + T, or click Tree on the menu bar.

WHAT'S HAPPENING? You have dropped down the `Tree` menu. Listed on it are choices you can make. `Expand One Level` should be highlighted.

Step 10 Press **Enter** or click `Expand One Level`.

WHAT'S HAPPENING? By selecting `Expand One Level`, you expanded `DOS6BK` one level.

Step 11 Press **Alt** + T. Press the **↓** key until `Collapse Branch` is highlighted. Press **Enter**, or click `Tree` on the menu bar first and then click `Collapse Branch`.

WHAT'S HAPPENING? You collapsed the `DOS6BK` subdirectory to its highest level.

C.11 Managing Files

MS-DOS Shell also allows you to manage files on any disk. However, you must tell the DOS Shell which files you are interested in. You do this by selecting a file or a group of files. You have selected files when working from the system level by keying in a command, then typing in the file name. When you work in MS-DOS Shell, first you select a file, then you choose an action. You pick a file with the mouse by clicking the file name. When you use the keyboard, you use the **Tab** key to move to the file list area, then use the ⬆ and ⬇ keys to highlight the file you want. At the system level, you can use wildcards to select a group of similarly named files. In the Shell, you can also select groups of files. However, they do not need to have similar names. In the next activity, you will learn how to work with files in MS-DOS Shell.

Activity C.12 Using File Commands in MS-DOS Shell

Note: You are still in MS-DOS Shell. The `Directory Tree` area title is highlighted. The `DOS6BK` subdirectory in the `Directory Tree` area is highlighted. The disk is in Drive A.

Step 1   Press **Alt** + **F**, or click `File` on the menu bar.

WHAT'S HAPPENING? You dropped down the `File` menu. Listed are many of the DOS commands that you have used at the system prompt. Each command that has an **ellipsis** after it means that a dialog box will appear when the command is selected. If a command is dim, the command is not available at this time. If you are using a monochrome monitor, you will not see the commands that are not available. You must select a file in order to take action. Here you are going to cancel the menu.

Step 2   Press **Esc**, or click the mouse someplace outside of the menu.

WHAT'S HAPPENING? You canceled the `File` menu.

Step 3   Press the **Tab** key until the file list title bar is highlighted , or click the file list title bar.

WHAT'S HAPPENING? You selected the file list area of the DOS6BK subdirectory. If you look at the title bar above the file list, it states which subdirectory files you are looking at: C:\DOS6BK*.*. (If this is not what is on your screen, return to the Directory Tree area and highlight the DOS6BK icon.) As you can see, the files are listed alphabetically. Now that you have selected the file list area, you must then select a file to manipulate.

Step 4   Press **B**, or click **BLUE.JAZ**

WHAT'S HAPPENING? If you used the keyboard, you pressed the letter B to take you to files that began with the letter B. The **Home** key always takes you to the top of the file list, and the **End** key takes you to the last file in the list. If you are using a mouse, you used the scroll bar to move to the area you wanted. Then you clicked the file name to select it. Once you have selected a file, you can manipulate it with commands from the File menu. You are going to copy the file BLUE.JAZ from the DOS6BK directory on Drive C to the disk in Drive A.

Step 5   Press **Alt** + **F**, or click File on the menu bar.

WHAT'S HAPPENING? Now that you have selected a file, the File menu presents you with choices you did not have before. Either you can see commands like Copy or Rename or they are no longer dimmed. If you are using the keyboard, you can use the ⬆ and ⬇ keys to move down the file list. In addition, you can select the underlined letter in the command such as C in Copy or D in Delete. Some commands have key names next to them such as F8 which is a keyboard shortcut you can use to select the command. If you have a mouse, you only need to click the menu selection.

Step 6   Press **F8**, or click Copy

WHAT'S HAPPENING? You are presented with a dialog box. A dialog box requests more information from the user. The Copy dialog box is providing source information, the file name BLUE.JAZ in the From: box, but it wants you to provide the destination information. It assumed that you want to copy the file to the default drive and directory. That is why C:\DOS6BK is in the To: box. Since you want to copy it to Drive A, you must change the destination in the To: box.

Step 7   Press the **Backspace** key until C:\DOS6BK is erased. Key in A:\ **Enter**.

WHAT'S HAPPENING? You saw a brief message that one file was being copied. You were then returned to the file list area. How do you know that the file was copied? One way is to look at the disk in Drive A.

Step 8   Press **Ctrl** + A, or double-click the Drive A icon.

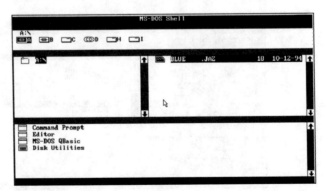

WHAT'S HAPPENING? By pressing **Ctrl** + A, or double-clicking the Drive A icon, you told MS-DOS Shell to read the disk in Drive A. The default is now Drive A. The file list title now says A:*.*. In this example, BLUE.JAZ is the only file on the disk

Step 9   Press the **Tab** key so that the file list area is highlighted and select
BLUE.JAZ or click BLUE.JAZ.

Step 10   Press **Alt** + **F**, or click File

Step 11   Press **N,** or click Rename

WHAT'S HAPPENING? You have opened the Rename dialog box. Since BLUE.JAZ
was selected, it is the file to be renamed.

Step 12   Key in the following: **REDDEST.FIL** **Enter**

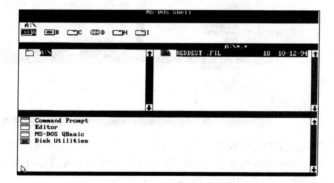

WHAT'S HAPPENING? The file BLUE.JAZ has been renamed to REDDEST.FIL
on the disk in Drive A. Each of the file commands works in the same way. First you
select the file you want to manipulate; then you choose the command you wish to use.

Step 13   Press **Ctrl** + **C**, or double-click the Drive C disk drive icon.

WHAT'S HAPPENING? You made Drive C the default drive. The DOS6BK
directory is still the default subdirectory.

C.13 Manipulating Many Files

When you are at the DOS system level and you wish to manipulate more than one
file, you can use wildcards if the files have part of their name in common. When using
MS-DOS Shell, you can also select files that have no commonality in names.

Nonetheless, remember that if a command cannot be used with more than one file—such as TYPE—it cannot be used with more than one file in MS-DOS Shell.

C.14 Activity: Selecting Files

Note: You are still in MS-DOS Shell. The file list area title bar is highlighted. The DOS6BK subdirectory in the Directory Tree area should be the selected subdirectory. The disk is in Drive A.

Step 1 Press the **Tab** key, or click the file list area to make it active.

Step 2 Press E

Step 3 Press the ⬇ key two times so you can see all three EMPLOYEE files, or use the scroll bar.

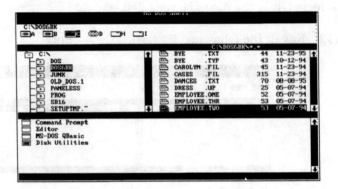

WHAT'S HAPPENING? You can see the EMPLOYEE.THR and EMPLOYEE.TWO files. You want to copy them to the disk in Drive A. The file called EMPLOYEE.TWO is highlighted if you used the keyboard.

Step 4 Hold down the **Shift** key and press the ⬆ key twice. If you are using a mouse, click EMPLOYEE.TWO. Hold down the **Shift** key and click EMPLOYEE.ONE

WHAT'S HAPPENING? You selected three adjacent files.

Step 5   Press [Alt] + **F**, or click `File` on the Menu bar.

Step 6   Press [F8], or click `Copy`

WHAT'S HAPPENING? You see the dialog box for the `Copy File`. Both the selected files are in the `From:` box.

Step 7   Change the `C:\DOS6BK` in the `To:` box to `A:\` [Enter]

WHAT'S HAPPENING? You see a message which tells you that the files are being copied one file at a time. Then you are returned to the file list area with the same three files highlighted. What if you wanted to perform some action on files that were not adjacent to each other?

Step 8   Press **C**

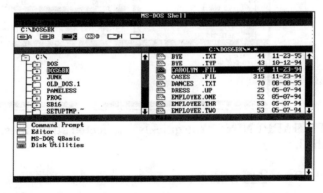

WHAT'S HAPPENING? You want to copy `CAROLYN.FIL` and `DRESS.UP` to the disk in Drive A, but they are not next to each other.

Step 9   Press [Shift] + [F8]. Press the [↓] key. When `DRESS.UP` is highlighted, press the [Space Bar]. If you are using a mouse, click `CAROLYN.FIL`. Hold down the [Ctrl] key and click `DRESS.UP`.

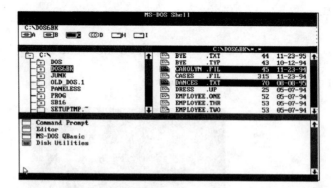

WHAT'S HAPPENING? If you were using the keyboard, you saw ADD appear on the status bar when you pressed **Shift** + **F8**. You selected two nonadjacent files. Now that you have selected them, you can manipulate them with the File menu. If you change your mind, you can "unselect" files.

Step 10   Press **Alt** + **F**, or click File on the menu bar.

Step 11   Press the letter L for Deselect All, or click Deselect All.

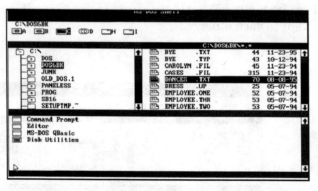

WHAT'S HAPPENING? You quickly unselected all the files. You can now exit MS-DOS Shell.

Step 12   Press **Alt** + **F4**

```
C:\DOS6BK>_
```

WHAT'S HAPPENING? Since you were last in the DOS6BK directory, that is where you were returned. You want to return to the root directory.

Step 13   Key in the following: C:\DOS6BK>**CD** \ **Enter**

```
C:\>_
```

WHAT'S HAPPENING? You have returned to the root directory of C.

Appendix D

Installing or Upgrading DOS

D.1 The Hard Disk

In order to use the hard disk, there are three things that must occur. The disk must be low-level formatted, partitioned, and then formatted, sometimes called high-level formatting. If you wish to boot off the hard disk, which most users do, you must install the DOS system files on the hard disk. Usually, when a person purchases a computer system, the low-level formatting, partitioning, formatting, and installation of DOS is done by the computer store or the computer manufacturer, but this is not always true. Sometimes, the hard disk will be partitioned, but DOS will not be installed. Sometimes, the hard disk is not partitioned, nor is DOS installed. In addition, prior to DOS 4.0, a hard disk could be no larger than 32 MB. Hence, if you had a hard disk larger than 32 MB, it was partitioned into two or more logical drives. If you are upgrading to DOS 6.22 and now wish to have only one logical drive, you will need to repartition the hard disk. If you have a very large hard drive, for instance in excess of 500 MB, you may want to partition the hard drive into smaller logical drives. No matter the circumstances, you will have to partition the hard disk and install DOS. If the disk is partitioned, you may need only to install DOS.

With DOS 3.3, 4.0, and 5.0, you are provided with a program that automates the process. As you become more sophisticated, you may choose to install DOS in a different location or by a different process. However, for beginners, it is best to stick with the installation program and let it do the work for you.

D.2 Low-level Formatting

A hard disk is comprised of many disks called drive platters. Each platter is divided into concentric rings (cylinders), and each cylinder is divided into sectors. On a floppy disk cylinders are referred to as tracks. The term *heads* refers to the number of heads on the drive itself, but, since there is a direct relationship between the drive heads and recording surfaces, heads usually refers to both the drive mechanism and the number of surfaces where data may be stored. On floppy disks heads are referred to as sides.

Low-level formatting tells where the cylinders and sectors lie on the disk. This process creates the sectors and cylinders by writing the ID numbers of the sectors to the disk surface so that each sector is located and numbered. This identification or address tells the hard-disk controller where the requested information is on the disk.

The numbering of each sector provides two primary benefits besides the obvious one of giving the controller a place to find the information on the disk. These include the sector interleave and marking the bad sectors on a disk. The sector interleave matches the rotation of the disk to the rate at which the disk controller can physically process data passing underneath the drive head. Thus, sectors may not be consecutively numbered on the disk. This occurs because not all computers can read a sector, write it to RAM, and get ready to read the next sector by the time the next consecutively numbered sector appears to the drive head. Rather than having to wait for an entire revolution of the disk for the next sector, the sectors are spaced so that when the head is ready to read the next sector, the next consecutively numbered sector is under the drive head. Thus, when the controller is ready to read the next consecutive sector, it is in the proper place. This procedure improves performance.

Newer computers, including most 386 computers can handle a 1:1 interleave factor where the sectors are consecutively numbered.

Low-level formatting also marks any bad sectors on the disk so that they will not be written to. This is usually done at the place of manufacture or by the Other Equipment Manufacturer (OEM) which receives a "defect" list supplied by the drive manufacturer.

Usually, a disk needs to be low-level formatted only once. If you wish to do this, you must have your own utility program. This low-level formatting is not a function of DOS. Some hard disks come with a low-level formatter; others have a low-level formatter than can be used with DEBUG. However, some hard disks can be formatted only at the factory. There are also commercially available utilities, such as SpinRite II from Gibson Research which allow you to low-level format a disk. In general, however, unless you are having problems, low-level formatting is unnecessary.

D.3 Partitioning a Hard Disk

A hard disk must be partitioned prior to installing DOS. Partitioning assigns parts of the disk to different operating systems. A partition defines what part of the hard disk belongs to which operating system. You may choose to have more than one operating system on the hard disk. For instance, you could have both DOS and UNIX on the hard disk. However, only one of these operating systems could be used at one time. You cannot run both at the same time.

DOS has three partition types: the primary DOS partition, the extended DOS partition, and the non-DOS partition. If you wish to use DOS on a hard disk, at least one partition is required and is called the primary DOS partition. The primary DOS partition must exist in order to boot from the hard disk. It is the first partition on the disk. In DOS 3.3, this partition size is limited to 32 MB. DOS 4.0 and above have no limitations.

The other type of partition is called an extended DOS partition. This partition can be any size within your hard disk size and can be subdivided into logical disk drives. Each logical disk drive is assigned a drive letter and acts like any other disk drive. The maximum number of partitions that DOS supports is four.

Whichever version of DOS you are using, you should back up your data before you partition your disk. If you are using DOS 6.0 or above you can use the MSAV option. You also should make a copy of DOS and place it on a floppy disk. You should always have a copy of DOS on floppies in case something happens to the original files. This is particularly true when using DOS 5.0 and above. The files on the DOS disk are compressed and must be extracted to be usable. You should carefully read the manual on how to install DOS and how to create the floppy disks.

Also remember that partitioning a disk removes/destroys all the data on the disk. Thus, if you are partitioning a disk that has data, first back up the data and programs prior to partitioning.

D.4 Formatting a Hard Disk

In order for a disk to be used, it must first be formatted. Formatting is the process of laying out the tracks and sectors DOS needs to keep track of files. If you wish to be able to boot off the hard disk, the DOS system files must be installed.

D.5 Identifying a Need for Partitioning and/or Installing DOS

If you do not know if your hard disk has been partitioned and/or formatted with DOS as the operating system, there is a simple way to find out.

1. Be sure there is no disk in any drive.
2. Turn on the computer and monitor.
3. If you see C>, the hard disk has been partitioned and formatted with DOS.
4. If you see a message, Non-system disk or disk error, replace and strike key when ready, the hard disk has been partitioned, but DOS has not been installed. You only need to install DOS.

5. If you see a message such as `Invalid partition table` or `Invalid drive` or `Drive  not  ready`, the hard disk has been neither partitioned nor formatted, and you must follow all the steps indicated.

D.6 Upgrading To DOS 6.22

If you have MS-DOS 6.2, you do not have to purchase the upgrade to 6.22. You may either download the files from Microsoft or CompuServe or you can purchase the Step-Up disks at any computer store at a nominal fee. The Step-Up kit from Microsoft does not have a bootable disk. You must have DOS already installed in order to upgrade to DOS 6.22. However, if you have the MS-DOS 6.22 upgrade kit, you do have a bootable floppy disk. The following instructions are assuming that you have the MS-DOS 6.22 upgrade kit. In addition, the steps for repartitioning your hard drive will be shown. Remember, you want to repartition your hard disk because the primary DOS partition is too small or too large. The size of the clusters or sectors are incompatible with DOS 6.22. There are more than four partitions. The primary DOS partition is inaccessible. A disk-partitioning program is not compatible with the setup program (see the README.TXT file on the Setup disk) if you have a hard disk larger than 32 MB and were forced in earlier versions of DOS to have logical disk drives. If any of the above statements are true, you must take the following steps:

1. Remove any memory-resident programs from the `AUTOEXEC.BAT` file.
2. Back up any critical files on your hard disk. You may use the DOS Backup program. Or, you may use any commercial program that does not come with DOS such as Fastback or PC Tools Backup.
3. Install DOS 6.22 to the hard disk. (Note: In some cases, you cannot install MS-DOS 6.22 unless you first repartition your hard disk. You will, instead, get an error message. In addition, if you used certain types of partitions such as SpeedStor or Disk Manager which replace the BIOS in interacting between DOS and the hard disk controller, DO NOT USE THE MS-DOS 6.22 FDISK program. You must use the same disk partitioning program you originally used. If you are not sure, you can look at your CONFIG.SYS file. They are recognizable because they will usually have a DEVICE= statement or the name of the disk partitioning files.)
4. Make a startup disk by using the SETUP /F parameter so you can boot from a floppy.
5. Remove the partitions from the hard disk using the program that created them. If you used MS-DOS FDISK to partition the hard disk originally, you may use the FDISK program on the MS-DOS 6.22 Setup disk.
6. Either place the Startup in Drive A or reboot the computer.
7. Use the FDISK command to remove the old partitions and logical drives.
8. Partition the hard disk.
9. Format the hard disk with the /S parameter.
10. Restore your files to the hard disk.

D.7 Activity: Upgrading To DOS 6.22 On The Hard Disk

Note: If you have critical data files, back them up now if you have not already. Installing DOS 6.22 on the hard disk should not impact the existing files. However, it is always wise to have backed up important data files to floppies.

Step 1   Remove any memory resident programs from AUTOEXEC.BAT.

Step 2   Reboot the system with the current version of DOS.

Step 3   Insert Disk 1—Setup from the MS-DOS 6.22 upgrade kit in Drive A.

Step 4   Key in the following: C:\>**A:SETUP** Enter

```
Microsoft MS-DOS 6.22 Setup

    Welcome to Setup

    The Setup program prepares MS-DOS 6.22 to run on your
    computer.

  .  To set up MS-DOS now, press ENTER.

  .  To learn more about Setup before continuing, press F1.

  .  To quit Setup without installing MS-DOS, press F3.

Note:  If you have not backed up your files recently, you
might want to do so before installing MS-DOS.  To back
up your files, press F3 to quit Setup now.  Then, back
up your files by using a backup program.

Before running Setup, you should check the README.TXT
file for information that pertains to your system
configuration. For more information, press F1.
must be used in Drive A.

  ENTER=Continue   F1=Help      F3=Exit     F5=Remove Color
```

WHAT'S HAPPENING? Setup is getting ready to install DOS. Be sure to have one or two floppy disks available.

Step 5   Press Enter

```
Microsoft MS-DOS 6.22 Setup

    During Setup you will need to provide and label one
    or two floppy disks. Each disk can be unformatted
    or newly formatted and must work in Drive A.  (If you
    use 360K disks, you may need two disks; otherwise,
    you need only one disk.

    Label the disks as follows.

            UNINSTALL #1
            UNINSTALL #2 (if needed)

    Setup saves some of your original DOS files on the
    UNINSTALL disk(s), and others on your hard disk in a
    directory named OLD-DOS.x. With these files, you can
    restore your original DOS if you need to.

    * When you finish labeling your UNINSTALL disk(s),
        press ENTER to continue Setup.

    ENTER=Continue   F1=Help      F3=Exit      F5=Remove Color
```

Step 6   Press Enter

```
Microsoft MS-DOS 6.22 Setup

    Setup will use the following system settings:

    DOS Type:           MS-DOS
    MS-DOS path:        C:\DOS
    Display Type:       VGA

    The settings are now correct.

    If all the settings are correct, press ENTER.

    To change a setting, press the UP ARROW or DOWN ARROW until
    the setting is selected.  Then press ENTER to see the alternatives.

ENTER=Continue      F1=Help        F3=Exit
```

WHAT'S HAPPENING? The default is highlighted. Since this is correct, you would press Enter

Step 7   Press Enter

```
Microsoft MS-DOS 6.22 Setup

    The following programs can be installed on your computer.

                            Program for          Bytes used
    Backup:                 Windows only         884,736
    Undelete:               Windows only         278,528
    Anti-Virus:             Windows only         786,432

    Microsoft MS-DOS 6.22 Setup

    The following programs can be installed on your computer.

                            Program for          Bytes used
    Backup:                 Windows only         884,736
    Undelete:               Windows only         278,528
    Anti-Virus:             Windows only         786,432

    Install the listed programs.

    Space required for MS-DOS and programs:
        6,849,696
    Space available on drive C:
       100,646,912

    To install the listed programs, press ENTER.  To see a list
    of available options, press the UP or DOWN ARROW key to
    highlight a program, then press ENTER..

    ENTER=Continue   F1=Help        F3=Exit
```

WHAT'S HAPPENING? In this case, you want only the DOS version of these programs. You can, at a later date, install them for Windows, particularly after you have compressed your hard disk.

Step 8   Use the ⬆ arrow key to highlight Backup and press **Enter**

```
Microsoft MS-DOS 6.22 Setup

    Backup for:

    Windows and MS-DOS
    Windows only
    MS-DOS only
    None
```

```
   If you want to install the highlighted program, press ENTER.
   To select a different option, press the UP or DOWN ARROW
   key to highlight the program you want, then press ENTER to
   choose it.


 ENTER=Continue    F1=Help         F3=Exit    ESC=Previous Screen
```

WHAT'S HAPPENING? In this case, you want only the MS-DOS version of Backup.

Step 9 Use the Down arrow key to highlight MS-DOS only and press Enter

```
 Microsoft MS-DOS 6.22 Setup

   The following programs can be installed on your computer.

                                Program for           Bytes
 used
    Backup:                     MS-DOS only           901,128
    Undelete:                   MS-DOS only           37,768
    Anti-Virus:                 MS-DOS only           360,448

   Install the listed programs.

   Space required for MS-DOS and programs:
        6,194,336
   Space available on drive C:
      100,646,912


   To install the listed programs, press ENTER.  To see a list
   of available options, press the UP or DOWN ARROW key to
   highlight a program, then press ENTER..

 ENTER=Continue   F1=Help        F3=Exit
```

WHAT'S HAPPENING? You are returned to the previous screen. Select MS-DOS only for each choice by repeating Steps 8 and 9 until your screen looks like:

```
 Microsoft MS-DOS 6.22 Setup

    Setup is ready to upgrade your system to MS-DOS 6.22.
    Do not interrupt Setup during the upgrade process.

 .  To install MS-DOS 6.22 files now, press Y.

 .  To exit Setup without installing MS-DOS, press F3.

 F3=Exit    Y=Install MS-DOS
```

Step 10 Press Enter

WHAT'S HAPPENING? As you can see, you have lots of chances to back out of the installation process.

Step 11   Press **Y**

```
Microsoft MS-DOS 6.22 Setup
Now is a great time to fill out your registration card. when
you send it Microsoft will:

·   Keep you up to date on the latest product improvements
·   Let you know about related Microsoft products.

2% Complete



ENTER=Continue   F3=Exit
```

WHAT'S HAPPENING? The installation process has begun. You will see a horizontal bar graph at the bottom of the screen as it completes each task.

```
Please label a floppy disk as follows

UNINSTALL #1
and insert it into drive A:

When ready to continue.
press ENTER.

Caution:: All existing files
on this disk will be deleted.
```

WHAT'S HAPPENING? You are to place the blank UNINSTALL disk in Drive A. A note of caution, the UNINSTALL disk will not restore your previous version of DOS if you repartition or reformat your hard drive, delete or move the hidden system files, delete the OLD_DOS.x directory, use DriveSpace, or any third party compression program.

Step 12   Remove the Disk 1—Setup from Drive A and place a blank disk in Drive A. Press **Enter**

WHAT'S HAPPENING? You will need to remove and reinsert the UNINSTALL disk. As Setup continues, it will prompt you when and which disk to insert into Drive A. Follow the instructions on the screen. You will see a horizontal bar graph at the bottom of the screen as it completes each task. When Setup is complete, you will see the following screen:

```
Microsoft MS-DOS 6.22 Setup

   Remove disks from all floppy drives,
   and then press ENTER
```

Step 13 Remove all disks. Press [**Enter**]

```
Microsoft MS-DOS 6.22 Setup

MS-DOS Setup Complete
   MS-DOS 6.22 is now installed on your computer.

        Your original AUTOEXEC.BAT and CONFIG.SYS files
        if any, were saved on the UNINSTALL disk(s) as
        AUTOEXEC.DAT and CONFIG.DAT.

   .            To restart your computer with MS-DOS 6.22,
        press ENTER.

   .            To learn more about new MS-DOS 6.22 features,
        type HELP WHATSNEW at the command prompt.

   ENTER=Continue
```

WHAT'S HAPPENING? You have upgraded to MS-DOS 6.22 to the hard disk.

Step 14 Remove all disks. Press [**Enter**]

D.8 The Startup Disk

A startup disk is simply a floppy disk that you can use to boot your computer. This is an emergency bootable floppy system disk. One way to create a bootable floppy is to format a blank floppy with the FORMAT /S parameter and then copy AUTOEXEC.BAT and CONFIG.SYS files to that floppy as well as any driver files that install devices on your system. However, you can also use the Setup disk to create a startup disk.

D.9 Activity: The Startup Disk

Step 1 Insert the Setup—Disk 1 into Drive A.

WHAT'S HAPPENING? Setup will create a minimal installation of MS-DOS 6.22 on a floppy disk.

Step 2 Label a blank disk as STARTUP. It is a good idea to include the current date on the disk.

Step 3 Key in the following: **SETUP /F** [**Enter**]

```
Microsoft MS-DOS .6.22 Setup for Floppy Disk

   Welcome to Setup

   You have chosen to perform a minimal installation of
   MS-DOS 6.22 on a floppy disk. You must provide a formatted
   or unformatted floppy disk that works in your computer's
   drive A.  Label the disk as follows

   STARTUP

   Setup copies the MS-DOS system files and a few important
   utilities to this disk.  You can use this disk to run
   MS-DOS 6.22

      .       For more information about Setup, press F1.

      .       To exit Setup without installing MS-DOS, press F3.

      .       To set up MS-DOS on a floppy disk, press ENTER.

   ENTER=Continue   F1=Help       F3=Exit        F5=Remove Color
```

WHAT'S HAPPENING? You are ready to begin.

Step 4   Press `Enter`

```
Microsoft MS-DOS .6.22 Setup for Floppy Disk

   Setup will use the following system settings:

   ****************************
   Install on Drive   : A
   Display Type : VGA

   The settings are correct.
   ****************************

   If all the settings are correct, press ENTER.

   To change a setting, press the UP ARROW or DOWN ARROW key until.
   the setting is selected.  Then press ENTER to see some alternatives.

ENTER=Continue    F1=Help     F3=Exit
```

WHAT'S HAPPENING? Again, if you have different hardware or want to make
other choices, you are instructed on how to do so.

Step 5   Press Enter

```
Microsoft MS-DOS .6.22 Setup for Floppy Disk

   Please wait while Setup copies files
```

WHAT'S HAPPENING? Files are being copied to the hard disk. As the Setup program works, it shows a bar graph filling as it completes each task. At the bottom of the screen, it tells you what file is reading into memory. When it is ready, it presents the following screen.

```
Please label a floppy disk as follows

STARTUP

and insert it into drive A:

When ready to continue.
press ENTER.

Caution::  All existing files
on this disk will be deleted.
```

WHAT'S HAPPENING? You are ready to create your STARTUP disk.

Step 6   Remove the Setup—Disk 1 from Drive A. Place a blank disk in Drive A. Press Enter

WHAT'S HAPPENING? As the Setup program is running, it shows a bar graph filling as it completes each task. At the bottom of the screen, it tells you what file is read into memory. The messages prompt you for each step. Continue following the steps on the screen. Remove and insert disks only when you are instructed to do so. Be sure you insert the correct disk. When the STARTUP disk is complete, you will receive the following message.

```
MS-DOS Setup Complete
Setup has finished creating an MS-DOS 6.22 startup
disk.
   ·   Press ENTER to exit MS-DOS 6.22 Setup.
```

Step 7   Press Enter

Step 8   Remove the STARTUP disk from Drive A and place in a safe place.

WHAT'S HAPPENING? You have a bootable floppy disk.

D.10 Repartitioning The Hard Disk

Now that you have backed up critical files, installed DOS 6.22 to the hard disk, created an emergency bootable floppy disk and backed up critical files, you are ready to repartition your hard disk. How you partition it is up to you. In the activity that follows, you will partition one hard drive into two logical drives. Again, remember that partitioning a disk is FATAL to the data. There is no going back once you begin this process, so be sure you do want to do this before you begin. Nearly all lab environments will not let you do the next activity but read through it and look at the steps you would take if you were not in a lab environment and wanted to partition your hard disk.

D.11 Activity: Repartitioning the Hard Disk

Note: You should have booted from the hard disk and the `C:\>` should be displayed.

Step 1 Key in the following: **FDISK** [Enter]

```
                     MS-DOS Version 6.00
                   Fixed Disk Setup Program
            (C)Copyright Microsoft Corp.1983-1993

                        FDISK Options

Current fixed disk drive: 1

Choose one of the following:

1. Create DOS partition or Logical DOS Drive
2. Set active partition
3. Delete partition or Logical DOS Drive
4. Display partition information

Enter choice: [1]

Press Esc to exit FDISK
```

WHAT'S HAPPENING? This is the partitioning utility. Before you can repartition the hard disk, you must delete the current partitions and/or any logical drives. It is also useful to see what you already have. You can choose (4) to display the partition information on your system. It is particularly useful because you will need to know the volume label, the partition number, and any other logical disk drives you have on your system.

Step 2 Press 4 [Enter]

```
Display Partition Information

Current fixed disk drive: 1

Partition   Status    Type      Volume Label   Mbytes   System Usage
C: 1          A      PRI DOS    HARDDISK         81     FAT16   100%

     Total disk space is   81 Mbytes (1 Mbyte = 1048576 bytes)

     Press Esc to return to FDISK Options
```

WHAT'S HAPPENING? This display shows no extended DOS partition. If you had one and you wanted to see it, you would press Y for Yes. The following two screens are examples of how the screens would look if you had an extended partition.

```
Display Partition Information

Current fixed disk drive: 1

Partition   Status    Type   Volume Label   Mbytes   System   Usage
C: 1          A      PRI DOS  HARD DISK        70     FAT16    64%
   2                 EXT DOS                   40              36%

    Total disk space is   110 Mbytes (1 Mbyte = 1048576 bytes)

The Extended DOS Partition contains Logical DOS Drives.
Do you want to display the logical drive information (Y/N)......?[Y]

    Press Esc to return to FDISK Options

Display Logical DOS Drive Information

Drv Volume Label   Mbytes   System      Usage
D:                            40       FAT16      100%

Total Extended DOS Partition size is 40 Mbytes (1 MByte = 1048576 bytes)

    Press Esc to continue
```

WHAT'S HAPPENING? This sample displayed the drive letter and size of the extended DOS partition.

Step 3   Press **Esc** once if you do not have extended partition. Otherwise press **Esc** twice to return to the FDISK main menu. Once you are there, you need to delete the partition.

Step 4   Press **3** to select Delete partition or Logical DOS Drive

```
Delete DOS Partition or Logical DOS Drive

Current fixed disk drive:     1

Choose one of the following:

1. Delete Primary DOS Partition
2. Delete Extended DOS Partition
3. Delete Logical DOS Drive(s) in the Extended Partition
4. Delete Non-DOS Partition

Enter choice:    [ ]

Press Esc to return to FDISK option.
```

WHAT'S HAPPENING? Your system information will be different depending on how the hard disk was partitioned. You must delete each logical drive, then the extended partition and last the primary DOS partition. You must delete in the following order: first (4), any non-DOS partitions—this was new in DOS 5.0. Then you delete (3) any logical DOS drives. It will ask you for the drive letter that you wish to delete. Then choose (2) delete the Extended DOS partition. Last, choose (1), Delete Primary DOS Partition. FDISK will ask you for the volume label prior to deleting the primary DOS partition. Be sure to make a note of your volume label if your hard disk has one. When you have deleted all the partitions, return to the main menu of FDISK.

Step 5   Press 1 **Enter**

```
Delete Primary DOS Partition

Current fixed disk drive: 1

Partition   Status    Type     Volume Label       Mbytes    System    Usage
C: 1          A       PRI DOS   HARDDISK           81        FAT16     100%

    Total disk space is   81 Mbytes (1 Mbyte = 1048576 bytes)

WARNING! Data in the deleted Primary DOS Partition will be lost
What primary partition do you want to delete..?   [1]

    Press Esc to return to FDISK Options
```

WHAT'S HAPPENING? The WARNING is flashing telling you how fatal this is to your data. In this case, since there is only one partition, 1 is in brackets.

Step 6   Press **Enter**

```
Delete Primary DOS Partition

Current fixed disk drive: 1

Partition  Status    Type     Volume Label    Mbytes   System   Usage
C: 1         A      PRI DOS   HARDDISK          81      FAT16    100%

    Total disk space is  81 Mbytes (1 Mbyte = 1048576 bytes)

WARNING! Data in the deleted Primary DOS Partition will be lost
What primary partition do you want to delete..?  [1]
Enter Volume Label..........................................?[   ]

    Press Esc to return to FDISK Options
```

WHAT'S HAPPENING? This hard disk does have a volume label, HARDDISK.

Step 7   Key in the following: **HARDDISK** [Enter]

```
Delete Primary DOS Partition

Current fixed disk drive: 1

Partition  Status    Type     Volume Label    Mbytes   System   Usage
C: 1         A      PRI DOS   HARDDISK          81      FAT16    100%

    Total disk space is  81 Mbytes (1 Mbyte = 1048576 bytes)

WARNING! Data in the deleted Primary DOS Partition will be lost
What primary partition do you want to delete..?  [1]
Enter Volume Label..........................................?[HARDDISK ]
Are you sure (Y/N)                                           ?[N]

    Press Esc to return to FDISK Options
```

WHAT'S HAPPENING? Again, because this is so fatal to the data, you have
another chance to back out. Notice that N for No is the default value for whether or
not you are sure.

Step 8   Key in the following: **Y** [Enter]

```
Delete Primary DOS Partition

Current fixed disk drive: 1

    Total disk space is  81 Mbytes (1 Mbyte = 1048576 bytes)
```

```
Primary DOS Partition deleted

    Press Esc to continue
```

WHAT'S HAPPENING? As you can see, the process is very fast and very, very fatal.

Step 9   Press **Esc**

```
                    FDISK Options

Current fixed disk drive: 1

Choose one of the following:

1. Create DOS partition or Logical DOS Drive
2. Set active partition
3. Delete partition or Logical DOS Drive
4. Display partition information

Enter choice: [1]

Press Esc to exit FDISK
```

WHAT'S HAPPENING? You have returned to the FDISK main menu. Now you are ready to create the DOS partition.

Step 10   Be sure 1 is in the Enter Choice box. If not, key in the following:
           1 **Enter**

```
Create DOS Partition or Logical DOS Drive

Current Fixed Disk Drive: 1

Choose one of the following:

    1. Create Primary DOS partition
    2. Create Extended DOS partition
    3. Create logical DOS Drive(s) in the Extended DOS Partition


Enter choice: [1]

Press Esc to return to FDISK Options
```

WHAT'S HAPPENING? You are ready to create the primary DOS partition. The [1] should be selected.

Step 11   Press Enter

```
Create Primary DOS Partition

Current Fixed Disk Drive : 1

Do you wish to use the maximum size for a DOS partition and make
the DOS partition active (Y/N).............? [Y]

Press Esc to return to FDISK Options
```

WHAT'S HAPPENING? Since you want to divide this disk into two logical drives, you want to answer N.

Step 12   Press N Enter

```
Create Primary DOS Partition

Current Fixed Disk Drive : 1

Total disk space is        81 MB (1 Mbyte =   1048576)
Maximum space available for partition is     81 MB (100%)

Enter partition size in Mbytes or percent of disk space (%) to
create a Primary DOS Partition                              [ 81]

No partitions defined.

Press ESC to return to FDISK Options
```

WHAT'S HAPPENING? It is telling you how much disk space you have. The easiest way to divide up the disk is by percentage.

Step 13   Key in the following: 30% Enter

```
Create Primary DOS Partition

Current fixed disk drive: 1

Partition  Status   Type    Volume Label  Mbytes   System       Usage
C: 1          A     PRI DOS                          24    UNKNOWN  30%

Primary DOS Partition created

    Press Esc to return to continue
```

WHAT'S HAPPENING? You have created the Primary DOS Partition.

Step 14   Press Esc

```
                          FDISK Options

     Current fixed disk drive: 1

     Choose one of the following:

     1. Create DOS partition or Logical DOS Drive
     2. Set active partition
     3. Delete partition or Logical DOS Drive
     4. Display partition information

     Enter choice: [1]

WARNING! No partitions are set active - disk 1 is not startable unless
a partition is set active.

     Press Esc to exit FDISK
```

WHAT'S HAPPENING? You have returned to the FDISK menu. In order to continue, you must first make the partition active.

Step 15   Press 2 [Enter]

```
Set Active Partition

Current fixed disk drive: 1

Partition  Status    Type     Volume Label  Mbytes   System           Usage
C: 1          A     PRI DOS                    24     UNKNOWN    30%

     Total disk space is  81 Mbytes (1 Mbyte = 1048576 bytes)

Enter the number of the partition you want to make ac-
tive...................[   ]

     Press Esc to return to FDISK Options
```

WHAT'S HAPPENING? Since you only have 1 partition, you will place 1 where the cursor is.

Step 16   Press 1 [Enter]

```
Set Active Partition

Current fixed disk drive: 1

Partition  Status    Type     Volume Label  Mbytes   System           Usage
C: 1          A     PRI DOS                    24     UNKNOWN    30%
```

```
    Total disk space is  81 Mbytes (1 Mbyte = 1048576 bytes)

Partition 1 made active

    Press Esc to continue
```

WHAT'S HAPPENING? You have made your primary partition active.

Step 17   Press **Esc**

```
                    FDISK Options

    Current fixed disk drive: 1

    Choose one of the following:

    1. Create DOS partition or Logical DOS Drive
    2. Set active partition
    3. Delete partition or Logical DOS Drive
    4. Display partition information

    Enter choice: [1]

    Press Esc to exit FDISK
```

WHAT'S HAPPENING? Once again you have returned to the FDISK menu. Now you want to deal with the other 70% of the hard disk.

Step 18   Press 1

```
    Create DOS Partition or Logical DOS Drive

    Current Fixed Disk Drive: 1

    Choose one of the following:

        1. Create Primary DOS partition
        2. Create Extended DOS partition
        3. Create logical DOS Drive(s) in the Extended DOS Partition


    Enter choice: [1]

    Press Esc to return to FDISK Options
```

WHAT'S HAPPENING? This time you want to create an extended DOS partition.

Step 19   Press 2

```
Create Extended  DOS Partition

Current Fixed Disk Drive : 1

Partition  Status    Type     Volume Label  Mbytes   System        Usage
C: 1          A      PRI DOS                 24       UNKNOWN   30%


Total disk space is     81 MB (1 Mbyte =  1048576)
Maximum space available for partition is   57 MB (70%)

Enter partition size in Mbytes or percent of disk space (%) to
create an Extended DOS Partition
[ 57]

Press Esc to return to FDISK Options
```

WHAT'S HAPPENING? If you wanted to have more than two partitions, you could
further divide the 70% into whatever proportions you desired. In this case, you are
going to have two partitions, so you will accept the value of the rest of the disk. You
are allowed a maximum of only four partitions on any hard drive.

Step 20   Press **Enter**

```
Create Extended DOS Partition

Current fixed disk drive: 1

Partition  Status   Type     Volume Label  Mbytes   System        Usage
C: 1          A     PRI DOS                 24       UNKNOWN   30%
   2                EXT DOS                 57       UNKNOWN   70%

Extended DOS Partition created

    Press Esc to continue
```

WHAT'S HAPPENING? You have divided this hard drive into two partitions, one
of 24 MB and the other of 57 MB.

Step 21   Press **Esc**

```
Create Logical DOS Drive(s) in the Extended DOS Partition

No logical drive defined

Total Extended DOS Partition size is 57 Mbytes (1 Mbyte - 104576 bytes)
Maximum space available for logical drive is    57 Mbytes (100%)
```

```
Enter logical drive size in Mbytes or percent of disk space  (%)        [57]

    Press Esc to return to FDISK Options
```

WHAT'S HAPPENING? Once again, you could further divide this partition into logical drives. In this case, you will accept the default value.

Step 22   Press **Enter**

```
Create Logical DOS Drive(s) in the Extended DOS Partition

Drv  Volume Label    Mbytes    System                     Usage
D:                       57            UNKNOWN       100%

All available space in the Extended DOS Partition
is assigned to logical drives.
    Press Esc to continue
```

WHAT'S HAPPENING? The next available drive letter, D, was assigned to this logical drive and all the space is occupied by this drive. You have partitioned your hard drive and created a logical drive in the extended DOS partition.

Step 23   Press **Esc** Press **Esc**

```
    System will now restart

    Insert DOS system diskette in drive A:
    Press any key when ready....
```

WHAT'S HAPPENING? You have left FDISK. You need to place your STARTUP disk in Drive A. When the system restarts, you will be presented with the date and time prompt. The hard disk has been partitioned. Prior to being able to use it, you still need to format the hard disk and install DOS on it. The STARTUP disk will be in Drive A. Remember, you want to format Drive C with the operating system on it that is the active, and hence bootable partition.

Step 24   Key in the following: A:\>**FORMAT C:/S** **Enter**

```
    WARNING, ALL DATA ON NON-REMOVABLE DISK
    DRIVE C: WILL BE LOST:
    PROCEED WITH FORMAT (Y/N)?_
```

Step 25   Press **Y** **Enter**

```
    Format complete
    System transferred
    Volume labeled (11 characters, ENTER for none)?
```

WHAT'S HAPPENING? The hard disk has been formatted. A volume label identifies the hard disk, an optional but non-required action.

Step 26   If you wish to have a volume label, enter it now, or just press [Enter]

```
   25,513,984 bytes total disk space
      200,704 bytes used by system
   25,313,288 bytes available on disk

        2,048 bytes in each allocation unit.
       12,360 allocations units available on disk.
```

WHAT'S HAPPENING? You have formatted Drive C and placed the operating system on it. Now you need to format logical drive D but without an operating system.

Step 27   Key in the following: A:\>**FORMAT D:** [Enter]

```
   WARNING, ALL DATA ON NON-REMOVABLE DISK
   DRIVE C: WILL BE LOST:
   PROCEED WITH FORMAT (Y/N)?_
```

Step 28   Press Y [Enter]

WHAT'S HAPPENING? You have now formatted both disks. In order to restore your files, you must reinstall DOS. Repeat Activity D.7. Be sure to install MSBACKUP for DOS. Once this is done, choose MSBACKUP. The first time you use MSBACKUP, it will need to configure itself, so follow the instructions on the screen.

Appendix E

ANSI.SYS Keyboard Scancode Values

E.1 ANSI.SYS Keyboard Scancode Value

Key	Standard	with **Shift**	with **Ctrl**	with **Alt**
A	97	65	1	0;30
B	98	66	2	0;48
C	99	67	3	0;46
D	100	68	4	0;32
E	101	69	5	0:18
F	102	70	6	0;33
G	103	71	7	0;34
H	104	72	8	0;35
I	105	73	9	0;23
J	106	74	10	0;36
K	107	75	11	0;37
L	108	76	12	0;38
M	109	77	13	0;50
N	110	78	14	0;49
O	111	79	15	0;24
P	112	80	16	0;25
Q	113	81	17	0;16
R	114	82	18	0;19

Key	Standard	with **Shift**	with **Ctrl**	with **Alt**
S	115	83	19	0;31
T	116	84	20	0;20
U	117	85	21	0;22
V	118	86	22	0;47
W	119	87	23	0;17
X	120	88	24	0;45
Y	121	89	25	0;21
Z	122	90	26	0;44
1	49	33	N/A	0;120
2	50	64	0	0;121
3	51	35	N/A	0;122
4	52	36	N/A	0;123
5	53	37	N/A	0;124
6	54	94	30	0;125
7	55	38	N/A	0;126
8	56	42	N/A	0;126
9	57	40	N/A	0;127
0	48	41	N/A	0;129
-	45	95	31	0;130
=	61	43	N/A	0;131
[	91	123	27	0;26
]	93	125	29	0;27
Space Bar	92	124	28	0;43
;	59	58	N/A	0;39
'	39	34	N/A	0;40
,	44	60	N/A	0;51
.	46	62	N/A	0;52
/	47	63	N/A	0;53
`	96	126	N/A	0;41
Enter (keypad)	13	N/A	10	0;166
/ (keypad)	47	47	0;142	0;74
* (keypad)	42	0;144	0;78	N/A
- (keypad)	45	45	0;149	0;164
+ (keypad)	43	43	0;150	0;55
5 (keypad)	0;76	53	0;143	N/A
F1	0;59	0;84	0;94	0;104

Key	Standard	with **Shift**	with **Ctrl**	with **Alt**
F2	0;60	0;85	0;95	0;105
F3	0;61	0;86	0;96	0;106
F4	0;62	0;87	0;97	0;107
F5	0;63	0;88	0;98	0;108
F6	0;64	0;89	0;99	0;109
F7	0;65	0;90	0;100	0;110
F8	0;66	0;91	0;101	0;111
F9	0;67	0;92	0;102	0;112
F10	0;68	0;93	0;103	0;113
F11	0;133	0;135	0;137	0;139
F12	0;134	0;136	0;138	0;140
Home	0;71	55	0;119	N/A
↑	0;72	56	0;141	N/A
PgUp	0;73	57	0;132	N/A
←	0;75	52	0;115	N/A
→	0;77	54	0;116	N/A
End	0;79	49	0;117	N/A
↓	0;80	50	0;145	N/A
PgDn	0;81	51	0;118	N/A
Insert	0;82	48	0;146	N/A
Delete	0;83	46	0;147	N/A
Print Screen	N/A	N/A	0;114	N/A
Pause	N/A	N/A	0;0	N/A
Backspace	8	8	127	0
Enter	13	N/A	10	0
Tab	9	0;5	0;148	0;165
Home (gray key)	224;71	224;71	224;119	224;151
↑ (gray key)	224;72	224;72	224;141	224;152
PgUp (gray key)	224;73	224;73	224;132	224;153
← (gray key)	224;75	224;75	224;115	224;155
→ (gray key)	224;77	224;77	224;116	224;157
End (gray key)	224;79	224;79	224;117	224;159
↓ (gray key)	224;80	224;80	224;145	224;154
PgDn (gray key)	224;81	224;81	224;118	224;161
Insert (gray key)	224;82	224;82	224;146	224;162
Delete (gray key)	224;83	224;83	224;147	224;163

Appendix F

Command Summary

* Internal command
# New to DOS 6.0
@ No longer included with DOS.

* <	*command < command*	Redirection symbol that tells DOS to get input from somewhere besides the standard input.
* >	*command > command*	Redirection symbol that tells DOS to redirect standard output of a command to a device or a file.
* >>	*command >> command*	Redirection symbol that also redirects standard output of a command to a device or a file but appends to the file instead of overwriting it.
*|	*command | command*	Pipe symbol that allows the standard output of one command to be the standard input of the next command.
* A:	A:	Switches the current drive to Drive A.

APPEND   APPEND [[*drive:*]*path*[;...] [/X:ON | /X:OFF] [/PATH:ON | /PATH:OFF] [/E]
              Accesses files in other directories as if they existed in the current directory.
           APPEND ;   Undo all appended paths.

ASSIGN   ASSIGN [*x*[:]=*y*[:][...]]   Assigns disk drive *x* to disk drive *y*.
           ASSIGN /STATUS   Displays all current assignments.
           ASSIGN   Undo all current assignments.

ATTRIB   ATTRIB [±A] [±H] [±R] [±S] [*drive:*][path]filename [/S]
              Displays or changes the attributes of a file. A plus sign (+) turns the attribute on. A minus sign (-) turns the attribute off.

		±A	Turns on/off the archive attribute.
		±H	Turns on/off the hidden file attribute.
		±R	Turns on/off the read-only attribute.
		±S	Turns on/off the system file attribute.
		/S	Processes all files in any subdirectory.

* B:	B:	Switches the current drive to Drive B.
* C:	C:	Switches the current drive to Drive C.

* CALL   CALL [*drive:*][*path*]*filename* [*batch-parameter*]
Calls one batch program from another without causing the first batch program to stop.

* CD   CD   Displays the current directory and path.
            CD [*path*]   Changes the current directory to path.

* CHDIR   CHDIR   Displays the current directory and path (same as CD).
               CHDIR [*path*]   Changes the current directory to *path*.

CHKDSK   CHKDSK [*drive:*] [[*path*]*filename*] [/F] [/V]
Examines and reports the status of the specified drive or file.
            CHKDSK /F   Fixes any errors found.
            CHKDSK /V   Displays filenames as disk is checked.

 # CHOICE   CHOICE [/C[:]*keys*] [/N] [/S] [/T][:]c,nn] [text]
Prompts the user to make a choice in a batch file.
            CHOICE *your*   Will display *your* on the screen waiting for user input.
            CHOICE /C:ync   User will see [Y,N,C]?
            CHOICE /N   Will not display the prompt.
            CHOICE /S   Will be case-sensative.
            CHOICE /T:n,5   If user has not pressed a key in 5 seconds, will choose n. If user presses key before 5 second, will accept what user keyed in.

* CLS   CLS   Clears the screen.

*COMMAND   COMMAND [[*drive:*]*path*] [*device*] [/E:*nnnnn*] [/P] [/C *string*] [/MSG]
Starts a new instance of COMMAND.COM.
            COMMAND A:\DOS /E:8192   Starts new COMMAND.COM from A:\DOS with an environment size of 8192 bytes.

@ COMP   COMP *file1 file2* [/D] [/A] [/L] [/N=*number*] [/C]
Compares the contents of two files byte by byte.
            /D   Displays differences in decimal format.
            /A   Displays differences as ASCII characters.

	/L	Displays the line numbers of any differences.
	/C	Ignores differences between upper and lowercase letters.
	/N=number	
		Compares only the first number lines.

* COPY	COPY *source destination*	Copy from the *source* file to the *destination* file.
	COPY [*d:*][*path*]*oldfile.ext* [*d:*][*path*]*newfile.ext*	
		Copy from the *oldfile* to the *newfile*.

* COPY CON	COPY CON *filename*	Copy all data entered into the keyboard to *filename* until a <Ctrl>+Z is entered.

* DATE	DATE [*mm-dd-yy*]	Changes the current date setting. DATE without parameters displays the current date.

@ DBLSPACE	DBLSPACE	Brings up a menu to allow you to compress a drive and otherwise manipulate the compressed drive.

# DEFRAG	DEFRAG [*drive:*] [/F] [/S[:]*order*] [/B] [/SKIPHIGH] [/H]	
		Reorganizes files on a disk to optimize disk performance.
	DEFRAG [*drive:*] [/U] [/B] [/SKIPHIGH] [/H]	
	/F	Defrags files and ensures no empty space between files.
	/U	Defrags files and leaves empty space between files if necessary.
	/S	Provides sort order.
		n by name (n- reverse order)
		e by file extension (n- reverse order)
		d by date/time earliest (d- reverse order)
		s by size, smallest (s- reverse order)
	/B	Restarts computer after files have been reorganzied.
	/SKIPHIGH	
		Loads DEFRAG in conventional memory. Default is upper memory.
	/H	Moves hidden files.

* DEL	DEL [*drive:*][*path*]*filename* [/P]	Deletes the specified file.
	/P	Prompts the user for confirmation before deleting the file.

# DELTREE	DELTREE [/Y] [*drive:*]*path* [[*drive:*]*path* [...]]	
		Deletes a directory and all the files and subdirectories that are in it.
	DELTREE *path* /Y	Will not prompt for confirmation prior to deletion.

* DIR	DIR [*drive:*][*path*][*filename*] [/P] [/W] [/A[[:]*attributes*]] [/O[[:]*sortorder*] [/S]	
	[/B] [/L] [/C]	Displays a list of a directory's files and subdirectories.
	/P	Pauses between screenfuls.
	/W	Displays filenames in a wide format.
	/A:H	Displays files ATTRIButed as hidden.
	/A:S	Displays system files.
	/A:D	Displays only names of directories.
	/A:A	Displays files ATTRIButed as archived.
	/A:R	Displays files ATTRIButed as read-only.
	/O:N	Displays alphabetically (A-Z) by filename
	/O:E	Displays alphabetically (A-Z) by extension.
	/O:D	Displays in date order, from oldest to newest.
	/O:S	Displays in size order, from smallest to largest.
	/O:G	Displays directories before files.
	/S	Searches through all subdirectories.
	/L	Displays in lowercase letters.
	/B	Displays only filenames and extension.
	/C	Displays compression ratio of compressed disks.

DISKCOMP	DISKCOMP [*drive1:* [*drive2:*]]	Compares the contents of two floppy disks.

DISKCOPY	DISKCOPY [*drive1:* [*drive2:*]]	Copies the contents of the floppy disk in *drive1* to the floppy disk in *drive2*.

DOSKEY	DOSKEY [/H] [/M]	Starts the DOSKEY program to recall commands, edit command lines, or create macros.
	/H	Displays list of all commands stored in memory.
	/M	Displays list of all DOSKEY macros. See Chapter 14 for use.

@ DOSSHELL	DOSSHELL [/T] [/B] [/G]	Starts DOSSHELL, the graphical interface to DOS.
	/T	Starts DOSSHELL in text mode
	/B	Starts DOSSHELL in black-and-white.
	/G	Starts DOSSHELL in graphics mode.

# DRVSPACE	DRVSPACE	Brings up a menu to allow you to compress a drive and otherwise manipulate the compressed drive. Key in HELP DRVSPACE for further details.

* ECHO	ECHO [ON | OFF]	Displays (on) or hides (off) text in batch files.
	ECHO [*message*]	Will display user message on screen.

EDIT	EDIT [[*drive:*][*path*]*filename*]	Starts MS-DOS Editor. See Appendix B for commands within EDIT.

@ EDLIN	EDLIN [[*drive:*][*path*]*filename*]	Starts EDLIN—a line editor.

| EMM386 | EMM386 [ON \| OFF \| AUTO] | Enables or disenables expanded-memory support on 386 or higher systems. EMM386 without parameters displays current status. |

| * ERASE | ERASE [*drive:*][*path*]*filename* [/P] | Erases the specified file. |

/P   Prompts the user for confirmation before erasing the file.

| * EXIT | EXIT | Quits the command processor and returns to the program that started the command processor. |

| EXPAND | EXPAND [*drive:*][*path*]*filename* [[*drive:*][*path*]*filename*[...]]*destination* | Expands a compressed file to retrieve files from Set-up disks. |

| # * FASTHELP | FASTHELP [*command*] | Displays a list of all DOS commands with a brief explanation. |

| FASTOPEN | FASTOPEN *drive*:[[=]*N*] [*drive*]:[[*N*][...]] [/X] | Improves performance on computers with large directories. Decrease amount of time DOS takes to open frequently sed files. Do not use with Windows. |

/N   Specifies number of files to track.

/X   Creates name cache in extended memory.

FC   FC [/A] [/C] [/L] [/LBn] [/N] [/T] [/W] [/nnnn] [*drive1:*][*path1*]*filename1* [*drive2:*][*path2*]*filename2*

Compares and displays differences between two ASCII files.

/C   Ignores upper vs. lowercase.

/L   Compares files in ASCII mode.

/W   Ignores white space in the files.

/N   Displays line numbers.

FC /B [*drive1:*][*path1*]*filename1* [*drive2:*][*path2*]*filename2*

Compares and displays differences between two binary files.

| FDISK | FDISK | Configures and/or partitions a hard disk for use with MS-DOS. |

FIND   FIND [/V] [/C] [/N] "*string*"[*filename*]

Searches for character strings within a file.

/V   Locates every occurence of the string except the one selected.

/C   Counts every occurence of the string.

/N   Locates and displays line numbers of each occurence of the string.

* FOR	FOR %%*variable* IN (*set*) DO *command* [*command-parameter*]
	Runs specified command for each file in set in batch file.
	FOR %*variable* IN (*set*) DO *command* [*command-parameter*]
	Runs specified command for each file in set on command line.

FORMAT   FORMAT *drive:* [/V[:*label*]] [/Q] [/U] [/F:*size*] [/B | /S][/C]
FORMAT *drive:* [/V[:*label*]] [/Q] [/U] [/T:*tracks* /N:*sectors*] [/B | /S]
FORMAT *drive:* [/V[:*label*]] [/Q] [/U] [/1] [/4] [/B | /S]
FORMAT *drive:* [/Q] [/U] [/1] [/4] [/8] [/B | /S]

          Prepares a floppy disk for use with DOS.

/V:*label*
        Specifies a volume label.

/Q   Deletes any previous file allocation table or root directory.

/U   Unconditional format.

/F:*size*
        Specifies the disk size.

/B   Reserves space for system files.

/S   Copies system files onto formatted disk.

/T:*tracks*
        Specifies number of tracks on the disk.

/N:*sectors*
        Specifies number of sectors on the disk.

/1   Formats on side of the disk only.

/4   Formats a 5¼-inch double-density disk on a high-density disk drive.

/8   Formats a 5¼-inch floppy disk to be compatible with MS-DOS version prior to 2.0.

/C   Test clusters that are curently marked bad.

* GOTO	GOTO *label*	Directs DOS to line in batch file marked by a user specified label.

GRAFTABL	GRAFTABL[*nnn*]	Displays extended characters for a specified graphics mode. Default is the U.S. character set.

* IF   IF [NOT] ERRORLEVEL *number command*

          Specifies true condition only if previous program run returned an exit code equal to or greater than *number*.

        IF [NOT] *string1=string2 command*

          Specifies true condition if strings match.

        IF [NOT] EXIST filename command

          Specified a true condition if *filename* exists.

        NOT Command should only be carried out if condition is false.

HELP	HELP [*command*]	Accesses online help about any MS-DOS command.
	command /?	
JOIN	JOIN [*drive1:* [*drive2:*]*path*]	Joins a disk drive to a directory on another disk drive. JOIN without parameters displays all JOINs in effect.
	JOIN *drive:* /D	Cancels the JOIN for this drive.
LABEL	LABEL [*drive:*] [*label*]	Updates the volume label of any disk.
LOADHIGH	LOADHIGH [*drive:*][*path*]*filename* [*parameters*]	
		Loads a program into the upper memory area.
	LH [*drive:*][*path*]*filename* [*parameters*]	
		Alternate shorthand.
* MD	MD [*drive:*]*path*	Creates a directory. Same as MKDIR.
MEM	MEM [/PROGRAM | /DEBUG | /CLASSIFY] [/FREE]	
		Displays current status of a system's used and free memory.
		/PROGRAM
		Displays status of currently loaded programs. May also use /P.
		/DEBUG
		Displays status of programs and drivers. May also use /D.
		/CLASSIFY
		Displays status of programs loaded into conventional and upper memory areas. May also use /C.
		/FREE
		Lists free areas of conventional and upper memory.
MEMMAKER	MEMMAKER	Starts memory optimization program. Key in HELP MEMMAKER for further details.
MIRROR	MIRROR [*drive:*[...]] [/1] [T*drive*]	
		Records information about one or more disks so that lost data may be recovered. Originally only available in PC Tools but now also available in DOS 5.0.
		/1 Records only the latest information.
		/T*drive*
		Loads a deletion-tracking program to be used by the UNDELETE command.
	MIRROR /U	Unloads deletion-tracking program.
	MIRROR /PARTN	Records hard disk partitioning information to be used by the UNFORMAT command.

* MKDIR	MKDIR [*drive:*]*path*	Creates a directory. Same as MD.
MODE	MODE [*device*] [/STATUS]	Displays the status of all or any devices.
	MODE [*display*] [*shift*[,T]]	Sets the monitor characteristics.Values for *display* are:

40	40 characters per row.
80	80 characters per row.
BW40	Black-and-white, 40 characters per row.
BW80	Black-and-white, 80 characters per row.
CO40	Color, 40 characters per row.
CO80	Color, 80 characters per row.
MONO	
	Monochrome, 80 characters per row.
shift	L or R shifts display left or right.
T	Aligns display with a test pattern.

MODE CON[:] [COL=*c*] [LINES=*n*]

Sets other characteristics for the monitor (CON).

COL=*c*

Number of columns.

LINES=*n*

Number of lines.

MODE LPT*n*[:] [COL=*c*] [LINES=*l*] [RETRY=*r*]

Sets characteristics for the printer (LPT*n*).

COL=*c*

Characters per line (80 or 132 only).

LINES=*l*

Lines per inch (6 or 8 only).

RETRY=*r*

Specifies retry action if printer is busy.

MODE CON[:] [RATE=*r* DELAY=*d*]

Sets the typematic rate for keyboards.

MORE	MORE < [*drive:*][*path*]*filename*	Displays one screenful of output at a time.
	command | MORE	

MOVE   MOVE [/Y | -/Y] [*drive:*][*path*]*filename*[,[*drive:*]*path*]*filename*[...] *destination*

Moves one or more files to specified location or renames directories.

/Y   Will not prompt user confirmation when replacing existing files.

-/Y   Will prompt for confirmation when replacing existing files. Default.

# MSAV	MSAV [*drive:*]	Scans disk for known viruses. Key in HELP MSAV for further details.
# MSBACKUP	MSBACKUP	Brings up a menu to allow you to back up or restore files on a disk. Key in HELP MSBACKUP for further details.

# MSD	MSD	Provides detailed technical information about your computer.
* PATH	PATH [[*drive:*][*path*[;...]]	Sets the path that DOS follows when searching for a file.
	PATH ;	Undoes all current paths.
	PATH	Displays all current paths.
* PAUSE	PAUSE	Suspends operation of a batch file until user presses a key.

PRINT   PRINT [/D:*device*] [/B:*size*] [/U:*ticks1*] [/M:*ticks2*] [/S:*ticks3*] [/Q:*qsize*] [/T]*filename*[...] [/C] [/P]

> /D:*device*
>> Specifies a print device.
>
> /B:*size*
>> Sets the internal buffer size in bytes.
>
> /U:*ticks1*
>> Specifies the maximum number of clock ticks to wait for the printer to be available.
>
> /M:*ticks2*
>> Specifies the maximum number of clock ticks it takes to print a character.
>
> /S:*ticks3*
>> Specifies the number of clock ticks to allocate to the scheduler for background printing.
>
> /Q:*qsize*
>> Specifies the maximum number of files allowed in the print queue.
>
> /T   Terminates all print jobs waiting in the print queue.
>
> /C   Cancels printing of the preceding *filename*.
>
> /P   Adds the preceding *filename* to the print queue.

PRINT   Displays the contents of the print queue.

* PROMPT   PROMPT [*text*]   Changes the current prompt display. Common values for *text* are:

> $p   Current drive and path.
>
> $v   Current version number.
>
> $t   Current time.
>
> $d   Current date.
>
> $g   > (greater-than sign).

QBASIC   QBASIC [/B] [/EDITOR] [/G] [/H] [[/RUN] [*drive:*][*path*]*filename*]

> Starts the QBasic programming environment.
>
> /B   Displays QBasic in black-and-white.
>
> /EDITOR

		Invokes the MS-DOS Editor.
	/G	Displays QBasic in graphics mode.
	/RUN	Runs program before displaying it.

* RD   RD [*drive:*]*path*   Removes a subdirectory. A subdirectory may not be removed if it is the root, the default, or if there are still files in it. Same as RMDIR.

* REM   REM   Allows use of comments in CONFIG.SYS or batch file. Useful for disabling commands. When REM is seen, DOS displays but does not execute what follows REM.

@ RECOVER   RECOVER [*drive:*][*path*] *filename*
     Recovers readable data from a defective disk.

* REN   REN [*drive:*][*path*] *oldname*[*.ext*] *newname*[*.ext*]
     Changes a file's name from *oldname.ext* to *newname.ext*. Same as RENAME.

* RENAME   RENAME [*drive:*][*path*] *oldname*[*.ext*] *newname*[*.ext*]
     See REN.

REPLACE   REPLACE [*drive1:*][*path1*]*filename* [*drive2:*][*path2*] [/A] [/P] [/R] [/S] [/U] [/W]
     Replaces files in the destination directory with identically named files in the source directory.

	/A	Adds new files to the destination directory. Cannot be used with /S or /U.
	/P	Prompts user for confirmation before each replace.
	/R	Replaces read-only files as well as unprotected files.
	/S	Replaces files in all subdirectories of the destination directory. Cannot be used with /A.
	/U	Updates (replaces) only files that are older than source files. Cannot be used with /A.
	/W	Waits for the user to insert a disk.

* RMDIR   RMDIR [*drive:*]*path*   See RD.

RNS   RNS [*drive:*][*path*]*oldname* [*drive:*][*path*]*newname*
     Not a DOS program. A utility program from Nick's DOS Utilities that renames subdirectories.

SCANDISK   SCANDISK [*drive:*[*drive...*] [/CHECKONLY]
     Starts disk analysis and repair tool that checks drive for errors and corrects any problems. Key in HELP SCANDISK for further details.

	/CHECKONLY	Check a drive for errors but does not repair any damage.
@ SELECT	SELECT	The installation program from DOS 4.0.
* SET	SET [*variable*=[*string*]]	Sets or updates variables in the DOS environment.
	SET	Displays current environment settings.
SETVER	SETVER [*drive:path*] *filename n.nn* [/D]	Sets the version number (*n.nn*) that DOS reports to *filename*. Used primarily for older applications that require a specific version of DOS to run correctly.
SHARE	SHARE [/F:*space*] [/L:*locks*]	Installs file-sharing and locking capabilities on a hard disk.
SHELL	SHELL=[*drive:*][*path*]*filename* [*parameters*]	Specifies which command interpreter to use.
* SHIFT	SHIFT	Changes position of replaceable parameters in batch files.
SMARTDRV	SMARTDRV /X	Starts or configures disk caching program. Do not use after Windows has started. For further details, key in HELP SMARTDRV
	/X	Disables write-behind caching. Should be used.
SORT	SORT [/R] [/+n] [<] *filename1* [> *filename2*]	Sorts the data in *filename1* in ASCII order, and optionally sends the output to *filename2*.
	[*command* |] SORT [/R] [/+n] [> *filename2*]	Sorts the output from *command* and sends it to *filename2*.
	/R	Reverses the sorting order.
	/+n	Sorts from the character in column *n*.
SUBST	SUBST [*drive1:* [*drive2:*]*path*]	Substitutes the single letter *drive1:* for [*drive2:*]*path*.
	SUBST *drive1:* /D	Undoes any substitutions for *drive1:*.
	SUBST	Displays all current substitutions.
SYS	SYS [*drive1:*][*path*] *drive2:*	Copies system files from *drive1:* to *drive2:*.
* TIME	TIME [*hh:mm:ss*]	Sets or displays the current time.

TREE	TREE [*drive:*][*path*] [/F] [/A]	Displays the tree structure of a disk.
	/F	Displays filenames as well.
	/A	Displays in text characters instead of graphics.

| * TRUENAME | TRUENAME | An undocumented command that displays the actual physical drive name of any assigned, substituted, or joined drives. |

| * TYPE | TYPE [*drive:*][*path*]*filename* | Displays the contents of *filename*. |

| UNDELETE | UNDELETE | Recovers one or more deleted files. Originally only available in PC Tools but now also available in DOS 5.0 and above. Key in HELP UNDELETE for further details. |

| UNFORMAT | UNFORMAT *drive:* | Restores a disk erased by FORMAT. Originally only available in PC Tools but now also available in DOS 5.0 or above. Key in HELP UNFORMAT for further details. |

| *VER | VER | Displays the current version of DOS. |

| VOL | VOL [*drive:*] | Displays the volume label of a disk. |

| WIN | WIN | Begins Windows, the graphical user interface that works with DOS. |

XCOPY	XCOPY *oldfile newfile* [/A	/M] [/D:*date*] [/P] [/S [/E]] [/V] [/W]	Copies files, subdirectories, and directories
	/A	Copies files ATTRIButed as archived without changing the archive attribute.
	/M	Copies files ATTRIButed as archived and turns off the archive attribute.
	/D:*date*	Copies files changed on or after the specified *date*.
	/P	Prompts you before creating each *newfile*.
	/S	Copies directories and subdirectories, except empty ones.
	/E	Copies directories and subdirectories, including empty ones.
	/V	Verifies each new file.
	/W	Prompts you to press a key before copying.

Glossary

Absolute path   The direct route from the root directory through the hierarchical structure of a directory tree to the subdirectory of interest.

Active window   Window currently in use when multiple windows are displayed in Windows.

Adapter cards   Printed circuit board that is installed in a computer to control some type of a device such as a printer.

Adapter segment   Area between the end of conventional memory and the beginning of extended memory. See also Upper memory area.

Allocation unit   See Cluster.

Alphanumeric keys   The keys on the keyboard that include letters (A to Z), the digits from 0 to 9, and other characters such as the punctuation characters.

ALU   Arithmetic logic unit is the circuitry that a computer uses for mathematical and logical functions and is an integral part of the microprocessor chip.

Application packages   See Application software.

Application program   See Application software.

Application software   Computer programs that are user-oriented, usually for a specific job such as word processing. Application software are also called packages, off-the-shelf, or canned software.

Archival Backup   Backup procedure in which all files on the hard disk are backed up by copying them to floppy disks or some other backup medium.

Archival data   Information that is stored in archive files

Archive attribute   See Archive bit.

Archive bit   A file attribute that gives the backup history of a file. which tells whether or not a file has been backed up. Archiving to "save" a file. Usually refers to long-term storage.

Archive files   Combine several files into one large file, keeping each file separate within the combination.

ASCII   Acronym for American Standard Code for Information Interchange. A coding scheme used for transmitting text data between computers and peripherals. Each character has its own numerical equivalent in ASCII.

ASCII sort sequence   The order in which data is sorted based on the assigned decimal number.

Associate   Method of saving time by "associating" a set of files that are generated by a specific program. A feature of MS-DOS Shell and Windows.

Asynchronous   Not synchronized or not happening at regular time intervals.

Asynchronous communication   Form of data transmission which comes into play when only two wires are used for communication between computers (generally used for communicating via modems). Data is transmitted by sending one character at a time with variable time intervals between characters with a start bit and a stop bit to mark the beginning and end of the data.

AUTOEXEC.BAT   A batch file (set of specific commands) that automatically executes every time the system is booted.

Background program   In Windows which has multitasking capabilities, background program refers to program that is being executed in the back at the same time that the user is working with another program in the foreground. For example, printing one document (background program) while at the same time editing another document (foreground program).

Background printing   Printing a document in the background while another program is being worked on in the foreground.

Backup   Process in which a user makes a copy of an original file or files for safekeeping.

Backup catalog A file that contains the information about files you backed up with MSBACKUP.

Bank switching Method of expanding an operating system's memory by switching rapidly between two banks of memory chips.

Batch files A text file of DOS commands. When its name is keyed in at the DOS system level, the commands in the batch file are executed sequentially.

Batch processing Manner of running programs without interruption. Programs to be executed are collected and placed into prioritized batches, and then the programs are processed one after another without user interaction or intervention.

Baud rate Measure of how fast a modem can transmit data. Named after the French telegrapher and engineer Jean-Maurice-Emile Baudot.

Beta-test Formal process of pretesting hardware and software that is still under development with selected "typical" users to see whether any operational or utilization errors (bugs) still exist in the program before the product is released to the general public.

BIOS Acronym for Basic Input/Output System. Program that controls Input/Output devices.

Bit Smallest unit of information that the computer can measure and is expressed in binary numbers, 0 or 1. Eight bits make a byte.

Block Group of data (words, characters, or digits) that are handled as a unit.

Block device Any device (such as a disk drive) that moves information from one part of the text to another as blocks rather than one character at a time.

Boot Starting up the computer by loading the operating system into memory.

Bootstrap The process a computer uses to get itself ready for user loading operating system into memory.

Boot record If the disk is a system disk this will contain the bootstrap routine used for loading. Otherwise, the disk will present a message to user that it is not a bootable disk.

Boot sector virus Replaces a disk's original boot sector with its own and then loads the virus into memory. Once in memory, it infects other disks.

Bootable disk Disk containing the operating system files.

Booting the system Process of "Powering On" the computer and loading the operating system into memory.

Buffer Temporary holding area for data in memory.

Bug Error(s) in software which cause programs to malfunction or to produce incorrect results.

Bus A set of hardware lines (wires) used for data transfer among the elements of a computer system.

Business Resumption Plan Disaster and recovery plan that includes the entire business spectrum in addition to data processing

Byte Unit of measure which represents one character (a letter, number, or punctuation symbol). A byte is comprised of eight bits. Computer memory and disk storage are measured in bytes.

Cache Place in memory where data can be stored for quick access.

Caching Process where DOS sets up a reserved area in RAM where it can read and write frequently used data quickly prior to reading or writing to the disk.

Cascade Windows layered one on top of another*. Used in Windows.

Case-sensitive A program that distinguishes between upper and lowercase characters.

CD-ROM Acronym for compact disc (disk) rea* MB).

Cells In a spreadsheet, the rectangle formed where a row and column intersect.

Central processing unit See CPU.

Chain(ing) Linking together two or more batch files.

Character device Computer device (i.e., keyboard or printer) that receives or sends information one character at a time.

Character strings   Set of letters, symbols and/or control characters that are treated as a unit.

Child directory   Analogous title given to offshoots (subdirectories) of any root or subdirectory.

Clean boot   In the booting process the CONFIG.SYS and AUTOEXEC.BAT files are bypassed.

Click   Pressing and releasing the mouse button once.

Cluster   Smallest unit of disk space that DOS can write to or read from. It is comprised of one or more sectors.

Cluster overhang   Since clusters are made up of one or more 512-byte sectors and DOS reads or writes only one cluster at a time, a file will occupy more space than it needs, causing cluster overhang.

Command   An instruction, which is a program, that the user keys in at the DOS prompt. This instruction then executes the selected program.

COMMAND.COM   That part of DOS that the user actually communicates and interacts with. It processes and interprets what has been keyed in. Also known as the command processor or command interpreter.

Command interpreter   See Command processor.

Command processor   That portion of an operating system that interprets what the user keys in.

Command specification (Comspec)   The location of COMMAND.COM so that DOS can reload the transient portion of COMMAND.COM. The default is the root directory of the booting disk unless altered by the user in CONFIG.SYS.

Command syntax   Proper order of command, parameters, and punctuation necessary to execute a command.

Communication protocol   Set of communication rules that enable computers to exchange information.

Compressed files   File written (utilizing a file compression utility) to a special disk format that minimizes the storage space needed.

Compressed Volume File (CVF)   A single file that contains all the compressed data for a drive compressed by DriveSpace or DoubleSpace.

Compressing a disk   See Optimizing the disk.

Computer virus   A computer program designed as a prank or as sabotage that can replicate itself by attaching to other programs and spread unwanted and often damaging operations. A virus can be spread to other computers by floppy disk and/or through electronic bulletin boards.

CON   Device name that is reserved by DOS for the keyboard and monitor.

Concatenate files   To combine the contents of two or more text files into a new file.

Conditional processing   A comparison of two items that yields a true or false value. Once the value is determined, a program can be directed to take some action based on the results of the test.

Contiguous (files)   Files that are written to adjacent clusters on a disk.

Control key   Key labeled Ctrl on the keyboard that, when held down with another key, causes that key to have another meaning.

Control-menu icon   In Windows, the icon that can be opened to provide a drop-down menu with additional commands. Also called the Control-menu box.

Controller   Board that goes into the computer and is needed to operate a peripheral device.

Conventional memory   First 640KB of memory where programs and data are located while the user is working.

Copy protected   Disks which cannot be "backed up" with regular DOS commands.

CPU   Acronym for Central Processing Unit. The CPU is the brains of the computer which carries out the instructions or commands given to it by a program.

Cross-linked files   Two files which claim the same sectors in the File Allocation Table (FAT).

CRT   Cathode Ray Tube. Another name for the monitor.

Current directory   The default directory.

Cursor   Location where the user can key in information.

Customized prompt   Modifying the prompt to suit the needs or preferences of the user.

Cylinder   The vertical measurement of two or more disk platters that have the tracks aligned. Used in referring to hard disks.

Daisy-wheel printer   Computer printer that uses a rotating plastic wheel as a printing element. The quality of print is comparable to that of a carbon-ribbon typewriter. Daisy wheel printers were considered high quality printers until laser printers became available.

Data   Information in the widest possible sense. Usually it refers to the numbers and text used by the computer to do the work wanted by the user.

Data bits   Group of bits used to represent a single character for transmission over a modem. A start bit and stop bit must be used in transmitting a group of data.

Data file   Usually composed of related data created by the user with an application program, organized in a specific manner, and which can be used only by this program.

Database   Collection of related information (data) stored on a computer, organized, and structured so that the information can be easily manipulated.

Database management programs   Application program that allows for manipulation of information in a data base.

Debug   To find and correct problems in a program. Also a program in DOS.

Default   What the computer system "falls back to" if no other specific instructions are given.

Default drive   Disk drive that DOS looks on to locate commands or files if no other instructions are given.

Default subdirectory   Subdirectory that the computer "falls back to" when no other specific instructions are given.

Delimiter   A special character that is used to separate information so that DOS can recognize where one part of the parameter ends and the next begins.

Designated drive   See Default drive.

Desktop   In Windows, an on-screen work area that simulates the top of a desk.

Destination file   Desired file location that data is to be sent.

Device   Piece of computer equipment that does one specific job, such as a disk drive or a printer.

Device drivers   Software necessary for the use of additional hardware devices. The program controls the specific peripheral devices.

Device name   Reserved name that DOS assigns to a device such as PRN for printer.

Dialog box   In a graphic user interface, a box that either conveys or requests information from the user. Used in MS-DOS Shell and Windows.

Differential backup   An MSBACKUP procedure that backs up only the files that have changed since the last full backup.

Direct read   When an application program reads the information directly from a disk bypassing DOS.

Direct write   When an application program writes the information directly to a disk bypassing DOS.

Directive   Used in the `CONFIG.SYS` file to refer to the available commands.

Directional keys   Keys used to move the cursor in various directions.

Directory   Index or list of files that DOS maintains on each disk. The DIR command displays this list.

Directory tree   The structure of the current disk drive.

Disaster and recovery plan   Backing up data files in case something happens to the original data.

Disk   Magnetically coated mylar disk that allows permanent storage of computer data.

Disk buffer   Acts as the go-between for the disk and RAM.

Disk drive   A device that rotates the disk so that the computer can read and write information to the disk.

Disk files Files that are stored on a disk.

Disk intensive Programs that are constantly reading and writing records to a disk.

Documentation Written instructions that inform a user how to use hardware and/or software.

Documented The process of writing the purpose and any instructions for a computer program.

DOS Acronym for Disk Operating System which refers to the most common operating system used on microcomputers.

Dot A subdirectory marker, a shorthand name, the . for the specific subdirectory name.

Dot-matrix printer Printer that produces text characters and graphs by creating them with a series of closely spaced dots.

Double-click Pressing and releasing the mouse button twice in rapid succession.

Double dot A subdirectory marker, a shorthand name, the . . for the parent directory of the current subdirectory.

Downward compatibility Software/hardware that can be used on older computer systems.

Drive letter Letter of the alphabet that identifies a specific disk drive.

Drag To move or manipulate objects on the screen by holding down the left mouse button.

Drop-down menus Menus that present choices which drop down from the menu bar when requested and remain open on the screen until the user chooses a menu item or closes the menu.

Dummy files Files without particular meaning usually created for test purposes.

Dummy parameters See Replaceable parameters.

Edit To alter the contents of a file. Also the editor that was introduced in DOS 5.0.

Electronic bulletin board Forum where people exchange ideas or solve computer problems. Usually accessed by a modem.

Enhancement To increase the capabilities of a computer by adding or updating hardware and/or software.

Environment Area in memory where DOS keeps a list of specifications that itself and other application programs can read.

EOF (end of file) Symbol that alerts DOS when the file has finished.

Executing a program Process where instructions are placed in memory and then followed by the computer.

Exit code A program that sets a code when it finishes executing, indicating some condition.

Expanded memory Additional hardware added to the computer that makes more memory available. Only programs that are designed to use expanded memory can take advantage of it.

Expanded memory emulator A memory manager that uses extended memory to emulate expanded memory.

Expanded memory manager (EMM) A software program that must be installed in order to use expanded memory.

Expansion slots Empty slots or spaces inside the main computer housing that can be used for adding new boards to expand the capabilities of the computer.

Extended memory Memory above 1 MB. Most programs do not know how to access extended memory.

Extended memory manager (XMS) A software program that must be installed in order to use extended memory. Must be installed prior to using extended memory.

Extension See File extension.

External commands Program that resides on a disk and must be read into RAM before it can be used.

External storage media A storage device that is outside the computer system. Floppy disks are the most common external storage media.

FAT Acronym for File Allocation Table. Map of the disk which keeps track of all of the spaces (tracks, sectors, and clusters) on the disk.

File Program or a collection of related information stored on a disk.

File Allocation Table See FAT.

File attributes Attributes are stored as part of the file's directory entry and describes and/or gives other information about the file.

File extension Up to three characters that can be added to a file name to extend the file name or to help identify a file. Usually file extensions describe the type of data in the file.

File handle Two-byte number DOS uses in referring to an open file or device.

File infector virus Adds programming instructions to files that run programs. The virus then becomes active when you run the program.

File name Label used to identify a file. Technically, it is the name of the file made up of no more than eight characters. However, when most users refer to the file name they are actually referring to the file specifications.

File specification Complete name of the file, including the file name and the file extension.

Filters Commands that redirect input through the process of reading information, changing the input and writing the results to the screen.

Firmware Software and hardware designed for a specific task that has been permanently stored in ROM (Read-Only Memory) rather than on a disk. Firmware cannot be modified by the user.

Fixed disk See Hard disk.

Fixed parameters Parameters where DOS supplies the value.

Flag A marker of some type used to process information. File attributes are commonly called flags because they indicate a particular condition of a file.

Floppy disk See Disk.

Floppy disk drive See Disk drive.

Flushing the buffer A process where DOS writes information to a disk after a buffer has been filled.

Foreground Application or window that the user is currently working on.

Form feed Operation that advances the hard copy on the printer to the next page.

Format / Formatting To prepare a disk so that it can be used by the computer.

Fragmented disks Disk that has many non-contiguous files on it.

Fragmented files See Noncontiguous files.

Full backup An MSBACKUP procedure that backs up all the files you selected.

Full screen editing To alter text by being able to move the cursor keys around the screen.

Function keys Programmable keys on a keyboard. F1 and F2 are examples of function keys. Function keys are program dependent.

Global file specifications See Wildcards.

Graphical User Interface Display format that allows the user to interact with the computer by using pictorial representations and menu choices to manage the computer resources and work with application programs.

Graphics Pictures and drawings that can be produced on the screen or printer.

GUI See Graphical User Interface.

Hard copy Refers to the printed paper copy of information created using the computer. Also referred to as printouts.

Hard disk Disk that is permanently installed in a computer and that has a larger capacity to store files and programs than a floppy disk. Its capacity is measured in megabytes.

Hard disk drive See Hard disk.

Hard sectored Relates to floppy disks that are marked with holes.

Hardware Physical components of a computer.

Hardware interrupts A request for service or a signal from peripherals to the CPU for attention so the device may be serviced.

Head slot Exposes the disk surface to the read/write heads via an opening in the jacket of a floppy disk.

Help Form of on-screen assistance provided by many computer programs that a user can turn to when a question arises or the user needs additional information on how the system or program works. Available in DOS 5.0 and above, MS-DOS Shell, and Windows.

Hexadecimal A numbering system that uses a base of 16 consisting of the digits 0-9 and the letters A-F.

Hidden attribute Prevents MS-DOS from displaying a file in a directory list.

Hidden files Files that are not displayed when the DIR command is used. In MS-DOS, the two hidden files are IO.SYS and MSDOS.SYS. In IBM PC-DOS, the two hidden files are IBMBIO.COM and IBMDOS.COM.

Hierarchical structure The logical grouping of files and programs based on pathways between root directories and their subsequent directories. Also called tree-structured directories.

High-capacity disks See High-density disks.

High-density disks Disks that can store up to 1.2 MB on a 5¼-inch floppy disk or 1.44MB on a 3½-inch floppy disk. Also called high-capacity disks.

High-level formatting Also known as logical formatting. It is the process DOS uses to structure a disk so files can be located.

High memory area (HMA) High memory is the first 64 KB of extended memory. DOS 5.0 and above can be installed in high memory.

Housekeeping tasks Any number of routines to keep the environment where programs run in good working order.

IBMBIO.COM One of the hidden system files that make-up the operating system of IBM PC-DOS. This file manages the input/output devices.

IBMDOS.COM Hidden system file that is one of the files that makes up the operating system of IBM PC-DOS. This file manages the disks.

Icon Symbol that represents a more simple access to a program file or task.

Impact printer Type of printer where the image is transferred onto paper through the process of a printing mechanism striking the paper ribbon and character simultaneously. Similar to the process of a typewriter.

Incremental backup An MSBACKUP procudure that backs up only the files that have changed since the last full or incremental backup.

Initializing The process of getting a medium (disks or files) ready for use.

Ink-jet printer Nonimpact printer that heats the ink before it deposits it on paper and sprays it through patterns to form letters or graphics.

Input Refers to data or information entered into the computer.

Input buffer Portion of computer memory that has been set aside to store keyed in data arriving for processing.

Input/Output The process of data and program instructions going into and out of the CPU (Central Processing Unit). Also referred to as I/O.

Insert mode Program mode used to enter data in which inserted text is entered at the cursor pushing all text that follows to the right and down.

Integrated circuit Electronic device that combines thousands of transistors on a small wafer of silicon (chip). Such devices are the building blocks of computers.

Interactive The ability to update data within the computer system instantaneously.

Interface Hardware and/or software needed to connect computer components. Also used as a synonym when the user interacts with the computer.

Internal commands A part of the third operating system file, COMMAND.COM, that includes commands that are loaded into memory when the operating system is booted and remain resident in memory until the computer is turned off.

I/O See Input/Output.

IO.SYS One of the hidden system files that make-up the operating system of MS-DOS. This file manages the input/output devices.

Keyboard Major device used for entering data into a computer consisting of typewriter-like collection of labeled keys.

Keyboard buffer See Input buffer.

Kilobyte (KB) One thousand and twenty-four bytes. Abbreviated as KB or K.

LAN Acronym for Local Area Network. Network of computer equipment located in one room or building and connected by a communication link that enables any device to interact with any other in the network, making it possible for users to exchange information, share peripherals, and draw on common resources.

Laser printer High resolution nonimpact printer that provides letter quality output of text and graphics. Based on advanced technology in which characters are formed by a laser and made visible by the same technology used by photocopy machines.

LIM EMS standard An acronym for Lotus Intel Microsoft Expanded Memory Specifications. Standards designed for adding memory to DOS based-systems. Called LIM EMS because it was developed by a Lotus/Intel/Microsoft Collaboration.

Light pen Pointing device (connected to the computer by a cable and resembling a pen) that is used to provide input to the computer by writing, sketching, or selecting commands on a special CRT screen which has been sensitized to respond to it.

Line editor Text editing program that numbers each line of text and then allows the user to edit the text only one line at a time. EDLIN is a line editor that was included with DOS.

Line feed Operation that advances the hard copy to the next line of text whether or not the line is full.

Loaded The process of placing information from storage into memory.

Logged drive See Default drive.

Logical devices Device named by the logic of a software system regardless of its physical relationship to the system.

Logical disk drives Drives named by the logic of the software (operating) system. "Imaginary drives" that act exactly like real disk drives.

Logical formatting See High-level formatting.

Look-ahead buffers A secondary buffer cache used to store contents of files that programs are using.

Loop A set of statements executed repeatedly within a program.

Lost clusters Sectors which have no directory entry and do not belong to any file that DOS knows about. They are debris resulting from incomplete data and should be cleaned up periodically as they waste space.

Low-level formatting Also known as physical formatting. Numbers sequentially the tracks and sectors of a disk so that they can be identified.

Macro Short key code command which stands for a sequence of saved instructions that when retrieved will execute the commands to accomplish a given task.

Master catalog   A file created by MSBACKUP that tracks all the backup catalogs that were created during the backup cycle.

Meg   Abbreviation for megabyte.

Megabyte   Unit of measure that is equal to roughly one million bytes. Abbreviated MB.

Megastring   Symbol used with the PROMPT command that returns a value for the symbol. For example, using the mega-string "d" will return the system date.

Memory   Temporary workspace of the computer where data and programs are kept while they are being worked on. Also referred to as RAM, (Random access memory). Information in RAM is lost when the computer is turned off.

Memory manager   Utility program that controls and allocates memory resources.

Memory-resident program   Program that remains in the computer memory after being loaded from disk. See also Terminate and Stay Resident (TSR).

Menu   List of choices/selections (within a program) that are displayed on the screen from which the user selects a course of action.

Menu bar   A rectangular bar (usually at the top of the screen) in a program in which the names of the available menus are shown. The user chooses one of the menus and by using the keyboard or mouse can cause the list of options in that menu to be displayed. Available in MS-DOS Shell and Windows.

Menu-driven program   Programs that make extensive use of menus to present choices of commands and available options.

Message   Text that appears on the screen and which provide information to assist the user in completing a task, suggesting an action, or informing the user of an error.

Microcomputer   Personal computer usually used by only one person.

Microfloppy disk   3½-inch disk encased in a hard protective shell.

Minicomputer   Midlevel computer larger than a microcomputer but smaller than a mainframe computer. Usually used to meet the needs of a small company or department.

Minifloppy disk   A 5¼-inch floppy disk.

Modem   Short for modulator-demodulator. Provides communication capabilities between computers utilizing telephone lines. Often used to access online information services.

Monitor   Device similar to a television screen that displays the input and output of the computer Also called display screen, screen, CRT (cathode-ray tube), or VDT (video display terminal).

Mouse   Small input device equipped with two or more control buttons that is housed in a palm sized case and is used to control cursor movement.

Mouse pointer   On-screen pointer that is controlled by the mouse.

MS-DOS   Abbreviation for Microsoft Disk Operating System which is an operating system for computers that use the 8086 (or above) microprocessor.

MSDOS.SYS   Hidden system file that is one of the files that makes up the operating system of MS-DOS. This file manages the disks.

Multi-tasking   Mode of operation in which the operating system of a computer allows the user to work on more than one task or application program at one time.

Network   A group of computers connected by a communication facility, most often called a server, that permits the sharing and transmission of data. Can include sharing of peripheral devices.

Non-bootable disk   Disk that does not contain the operating system files and the computer cannot boot from it.

Noncontiguous (files)   Files that are written to the disk in nonadjacent sectors.

Nonimpact printers   Type of printer where the image is transferred onto paper by means of ink-jet sprayers, melting ink, or through the use of lasers.

Norton Utilities Popular commercial utility program with programs that extend the capabilities of DOS.

Notepad Text editor available in Windows.

Null value A test for nothing (no data).

Numeric keypad Separate set of keys next to the main keyboard that contain the digits 0 through 9. Also includes alternate set of commands that can be toggled such as `PgUp` and the arrow keys. These functions are program dependent.

Online Indicates that the printer is not only attached to the computer but also activated and ready for operation.

Online help On-screen assistance consisting of advice or instructions on utilizing the program's features that can be accessed without interrupting the work in progress.

On-the-fly compression See Real-time compression.

Operating system Master control program (set of programs) that manages the operation of all the parts of a computer. Loaded into memory when the computer is booted and known as system software. Must be loaded prior to any application software.

Optimizing the disk Making files contiguous on the disk. Function of utility programs.

Optional parameter Parameters that may be used with a command but are not mandatory.

Overhead Information that provides support to a computing process but often adds processing time that cause performance of a program or peripheral to be slower than usual.

Overlay files Segments of a large program that get loaded into memory as the program needs it. This allows a large program to fit into a limited amount of memory.

Overwrite Process of erasing data by writing over it. Usually by copying over another file.

Overwrite mode Newly typed characters replace existing characters to the left of the cursor.

Page The section of expanded memory that can be swapped in and out of the page frame.

Page frame Physical address in conventional memory where a page of expanded memory may be stored.

Parallel In data transmission refers to sending one byte (eight bits) at one time.

Parameter A qualifier or modifier that can be added to a command that will specify the action to be taken.

Parent directory The subdirectory above the current subdirectory. The parent directory is always one step closer to the root than the child.

Parity Parity bit is a simple method used to check for transmission errors. An extra bit is added to be sure that there is always either an even or an odd number of bits.

Partitioning Process of physically dividing a section of the hard disk from the other sections of the disk and then having the operating system treat that section as if it were a separate unit.

Path Tells DOS where to look for the programs and files on a disk that has more than one directory.

Pause Temporarily stopping the execution of a program or a command by pressing the pause key on the keyboard. Also a batch file subcommand.

PC-DOS A disk operating system that manages the computer's resources and allows the user to manage the files and devices of a computer. Developed for IBM Personal Computer by Microsoft. Virtually identical to MS-DOS.

PC Tools Popular utility program that includes data recovery and protection programs.

Peripheral devices Any device connected to and controlled by the CPU such as a keyboard, monitor, printer, etc.

Physical formatting See Low-level formatting.

Pipes A method of stringing two or more programs together so that the output of one program becomes the input of another program.

Pixels Smallest element (a picture cell) on the display screen grid that can be stored or displayed and is used in creating and/or printing letters, numbers, or graphics. The more pixels there are, the higher the resolution.

Port A location or place on the CPU to connect other devices to a computer. It allows the computer to send information to and from the device.

Positional parameters See Replaceable parameters.

Pretender commands The commands SUBST, ASSIGN, and JOIN, which permit the manipulation of drives and drive letters.

Print buffer Section of memory where print output is sent for temporary storage until the printer is ready to print. Compensates for differences in rates of the flow of data by taking print output at high speed from the computer and passing it along at the much slower rate required by the printer thus freeing the computer for other tasks.

Print spooler Program that compensates for differences in rates of the flow of data by temporarily storing data in memory and then dolling it out to the printer at the proper speed.

Printer Computer peripheral that produces hard copies of text or graphics on paper.

Program A set of step-by-step instructions that tell the computer what to do.

Program files Files containing executable computer programs. See also Application program.

Program Manager The Windows program execution shell that enables user to view the applications as icons.

Programming language processors Tool for writing programs so that users can communicate with computers.

Prompt See System prompt.

Protected mode Operating mode in which different parts of memory are allocated to different programs so that when programs are running simultaneously they cannot invade each other's memory space and can access only their own memory space.

Queue A line up of items waiting for processing.

RAM (Random access memory) See Memory.

RAM drive Creates a disk drive in memory to emulate a disk drive.

Read-only attributes Prevents a file from being changed or deleted.

Real mode Program instructions can run under 1024 KB. A single-task working environment. DOS runs in real mode.

Real time Actual amount of time computer uses to complete an operation.

Real-time compression A background program that compresses and uncompresses data files as you use them.

Relative path The path from where you are to where you want to go in regards to the directory tree hierarchical structure.

Rebooting Reloading the operating system from the disk.

Redirection Process where DOS takes input or output from a nonstandard input or output device and sends it to a nonstandard input or output device.

Replaceable parameters Act as place holders for values. Allows user to write batch files that can be used with many different parameters.

Reserved memory A synonym for the adapter area or upper-memory area.

Resident commands See Internal commands.

Retry Tells MODE what to do when it gets a busy signal from a device.

ROM (read-only-memory) Acronym for read-only-memory. Memory that contains programs that are written on ROM chips and are retained when the computer is turned off. Often contain the start-up routines of the computer.

ROM-BIOS (read-only memory-basic input/output system) Chip built into the hardware of the systems unit. Its functions include running the self-diagnostics, loading the boot record, and handling low-level system tasks.

Root directory The directory that DOS creates on each disk when the disk is formatted. The backslash (\) is the symbol used to represent the root directory.

Scan code A code number transmitted when a key is pressed or released. Each key on the keyboard has a unique scan code.

Scanner Device that enables a computer to read a handwritten or printed page.

Screen dump Transferring the data on the monitor to a printer or another hard-copy device.

Script A series of instructions that tell a program what to do.

Script file A script that is saved as a file. In DOS a script file can be redirected into DEBUG to create a .COM program.

Scroll bar Used to move part of the list into view on the monitor when the entire list won't fit on the screen. Used in MS-DOS Shell and Windows.

Scrolling Vertical movement of text.

Search path The set search path for program files.

Secondary storage media Any data storage medium other than RAM. Typically a disk or tape.

Sector Data is stored on disks in concentric circles (tracks) that are divided into a sector. A sector is a portion of the track. Every sector is 512 bytes long.

Serial port The communications port to which a device, such as a modem or a serial printer can be attached. The data is transmitted and/or received one bit at a time.

Shareware Process where the software is initially free on a trial basis with the option to either purchase or return it.

Shell A program that surrounds DOS and presents menus or graphics for executing programs and managing files.

Sizing buttons Allow the user to minimize or maximize a window in Windows.

Soft-sectored A type of floppy disk whose sectors are marked with recorded data marks rather than punched holes.

Software Programs that tell the computer what to do.

Source file The file from which data is read in the transfer of data process.

Spreadsheet programs Programs that allow for budget management and financial projections.

Stand-alone programs Program run from the DOS prompt.

Standard error Where DOS writes error messages to the screen.

Standard input Where DOS expects to receive information—the keyboard. Keyboard from which DOS receives data.

Standard output Command that normally writes its output to the screen.

Startup disk A bootable DOS system disk.

Stop bit Indicates the end of asynchronous serial transmission.

Subdirectories A hierarchical filing system that allows the user to divide a disk into manageable portions. Subdirectories have names and are files.

Subdirectory markers Symbols used to move through the hierarchical structure easily. See also Dot and Double dot.

Substitute parameters See Replaceable parameters.

Switch An argument to control the execution of a command, typically the / is used. See also Parameter.

Syntax Proper order or sequence of the computer language and/or command.

Syntax diagram Graphic representation of a command and its syntax.

System configuration The components that make a specific computer system.

System attribute A special signal that DOS interprets to recognize a system file.

System board   Also known as a motherboard, it is the main circuit board controlling the major components of a computer system.

System date   The current date kept by the computer system.

System level   When the operating system has been loaded and you are not in any application program.

System prompt   A symbol on the screen that tells the user that the computer is ready for the next command. The prompt consists of the letter of the current drive followed by a greater than sign (A>, B>, C>).

System software   Set of programs that coordinate the operations of the hardware components.

System time   The current time kept by the computer.

System utilities   See Utility programs.

Terminate and stay resident (TSR) programs   Program that remains in memory after it has been initially loaded from disk. See also Memory-resident programs.

Text files   File that contains text as opposed to a program. It consists of data that can be read, such as letters and numbers, with the TYPE command. Text files do not contain any special symbols. Also referred to as unformatted text files.

Thermal printers   Nonimpact printer that prints by using heat to melt wire particles that contain ink and print on heat-sensitive paper.

Title bar   Contains the name of the program that the user is working on. Used in MS-DOS Shell and Windows.

Toggle switch   Turns function on and off.

Token   A binary shorthand for repetitive words or phrases. When a file is decompressed, the tokens are read and the original characters are restored.

Trackball   Device used to move cursor around on monitor. Usually consists of box with in which sits a ball. Cursor is moved by rotating ball.

Tracks   A concentric circle on the disk where data is stored. Each track is further divided into sectors. All tracts and sectors are numbered so that computer can quickly locate information.

Transient commands   See External commands.

Transparent to the user   A program or process that works so smoothly and easily that it is invisible to the user.

Trojan horse virus   A virus proffered as a legitimate program that, when run, begins a destructive process that unequivocally destroys data and programs on a disk.

Tree structure   The organizational properties of a tree that relates to the structure of a disk from the root directory down.

TSRs   Terminate and stay resident programs. See Memory-resident programs.

Tweak the system   To make final changes and to fine-tune a system to improve performance.

Typematic rate   Rate or speed at which MS-DOS repeats a character when the key for that character is held down on the keyboard.

Undocumented command   Command that exists but is not listed in the DOS manual.

Unformatting   The process of recovering lost data from a disk that was recently formatted.

Unfragmenting the disk   See Optimizing the disk.

Unformatted text files   See Text files.

Upper memory area   Area reserved for running system's hardware. Programs cannot store information in this area. Also called adapter area and reserved area.

Upper memory blocks (UMB)   Unused parts of upper memory area. Can be used for device drivers and TSR's if the computer is a 386 and you have DOS 5.0 or above.

Utility programs   Programs whose purpose is to carry out specific, vital functions that assist in the operation of a computer or software. DOS utility programs include such programs as FORMAT and CHKDSK. There are also commercial utility programs such as PC Tools and Norton Utilities. See also External commands.

Variable parameters   Value/information provided by the user.

Verbose   Parameter used in conjunction with CHKDSK that gives both the status report and lists every file on the disk, including hidden ones.

Verify   Command which "double-checks" a file or program and insures that sectors have been recorded correctly.

Version   The numbering scheme which indicates the progressive enhancements and improvement of software.

Virtual disk drive   See RAM drive.

Virtual memory   Method of extending size of computer memory by using a disk to simulate memory space.

Volume label   The electronic label for a disk that a user can assign at the time of formatting a disk.

Wildcards   The symbols, * and ?, also called global file specifications, used to represent a character (?) or a group of characters (*) in a file name.

Window borders   Edges that define the window in Windows.

Word processing programs   Software that allows the user to write, edit, and print any type of text and facilitates writing.

Write-protect notch   Cutout on the side of a 5¼-inch floppy disk that when covered keeps programs and data from being written to the disk. On a 3½-inch floppy disk, the write-protect is a slider.

Write-protected disk   Floppy disk that can only be read from, not written to.

Index

. (Dot), 160
>, 91, 493–495
<, 493, 495–497
>>, 494, 497–498
/ (Slash), 61
\ (Backslash), 32
  See *Subdirectories (root directory)*

A

Absolute paths, 163
Adapter segment, 615
Adapter cards, 7, 6
Allocation unit, 110
Alphanumeric keys, 40
Alt+F4, 34
ALU, 6
ANSI.SYS, 608, 656–662
  changing colors, 658–662
  remapping keys, 663–667
  signature, 657
APPEND, 409–413
  /PATH,411
  /E, 411
  /X, 411
Application packages, 30
Application program, 30
Application software, 17, 18
Archive bit, 304
Archive files, 736
Arithmetic Logic Unit (ALU), 6
ASCII file, 199, 208
ASSIGN, 406–407
  /STATUS, 407
  x, 407
  y, 407
Asynchronous, 668
ATTRIB, 304–318
  defined, 304

read only files, 305–311
using archive (A), 311–318
using hidden (H), 311–318
using R, 314
Attribute
  +, 305
  –, 305
  /S, 305
  A (archive), 304–305
  file, 304
  flags, 305
  H (hidden), 304–305
  R (read-only), 304–305
  S (system), 304–305
AUTOEXEC.BAT, 475–481, 598
  bypassing, 482–484, 694–696

B

Back-up, 230
  with COPY, 298–300
Backing up, 294–298
Backslash (\), 153
Backspace key
  correcting errors, 42
  defined, 41
Bank switching, 617
.BAT, 20, 188
Batch files,
  ::, 529–531
  AUTOEXEC.BAT, 475–481
  automating program loading, 485–488
  CALL, 436, 527, 578–586
  CHOICE, 436, 527, 559–562
  commands, 436–437
  creating menus, 460–475
  Ctrl+Z, 536
  CTTY, 528–531
  ECHO,436,439–443,527–528

EOF (end of file), 536
executing applications, 434–436
FOR, 436, 527
FOR..IN..DO, 571–578
GOTO, 436, 527, 531–533
how they work, 419–420
IF, 436, 527, 541–552
  ERRORLEVEL, 541, 552–554
  EXIST, 541, 548–552
  NOT, 541, 548–552
loading applications, 428–434
multiple replaceable parameters, 454–460
NUL, 528–531
PAUSE, 436, 527–528
positional parameters, 457
quitting, 445–447
REM, 437–439, 527–528
replaceable parameters, 447–454
saving keystrokes, 424–428
SHIFT, 437
using the PAUSE, 443–445
writing and executing, 421–424
Batch processing, 419
Bit, 10
Block devices, 668
Boot, 20
Boot record, 20, 110
Bootable disk, 110, 130
Booting the system, 32, 33
  bypassing AUTOEXEC.BAT, 694–696
  bypassing CONFIG.SYS, 694–696
Bootable DOS system disk, 598–602

Bootstraps, 20
Bugs, 29
BUFFERS, 592, 595–597, 602–605
Bus, 6
Bytes, 10

C

Cache memory, 7
Canceling a command, 44, 45
Capacity measurement, 10
Categories of computers, 2
CD, 39, 81, 155, 161, 174
CD-ROM, 13
Central Processing Unit (CPU), 3, 6
CGA, 8
Changing defaults, 78
Changing directories (CD), 39, 81–83
Changing the default drive, 78–80
Changing the name of files, 271
Changing the names of directories, 178
Changing the prompt, 171
Character devices, 668
CHDIR, 155, 161
Checking a disk and memory, 323
Child directory, 151
CHKDSK, 323–344
    checking a disk, 323
    checking contiguous files, 337–341
    information, 304
    using, 324–329
CHKSTATE.SYS, 608
CLS, 46, 470
Cluster, 15
    lost, 341
    repairing, 343–344
Color graphics adapter (CGA), 8
.COM, 20, 188
Combining text files with the COPY Command, 233–234
Command interpreter, 20

Command processor, 18, 20
Command syntax, 60, 61
COMMAND.COM, 20, 21, 32
Common cluster size, 111
Comparing files, 318–322
Compatibility
    VER Command, 45, 46
Components of a computer system, 3
Compressed file, 346
Compressed volume file, 737
Compressing a disk, 346
Computer components, 3–4
Computer configuration guide, 35
Computer memory sizes, 327
Computer types, 3
Computers, 2
CON, 424
Concepts of batch and interactive processing, 418–419
Configuration table, 36
CONFIG.SYS, 591–594, 598, 602–605
    See also Device drivers
    BUFFERS, 592, 595–597, 602–605
    bypassing, 694–696
    COUNTRY, 592
    DEVICE, 592, 609
    DEVICEHIGH, 592
    directives, 592
    DOS, 592, 627
    DRIVPARM, 592
    FCBS, 592
    FILES, 592–595, 602–605
    LASTDRIVE, 592, 623
    SHELL, 592, 629–631
    STACKS, 592
    SWITCHES, 592, 633–634
Contiguous files, 333, 335
Control key, 43
Control unit, 6
Controlling the boot process
    Ctrl+F5, 481
    Ctrl+F8, 481
    F5, 481
    F8, 481

Conventional memory, 615
COPY, 214–218
    backing up, 298–300
    combining files, 234–241
    combining text files, 233–234
    making copies, 201–205
    overwrite, 229
    overwriting files, 231–233
    review of file naming, 200
    using with TYPE, 211–214
    using wildcards, 205–206
    wildcards, 218–220
    with subdirectories, 220–227
COPY CON, 424
Copy protected, 294
COUNTRY, 592
CPU, 4, 6
Creating subdirectories, 155
CRT, 8
Ctrl, 43
Ctrl+Alt+Delete, 32
Ctrl+Break, 44
Ctrl+L, 96
Ctrl+NumLock, 44
Ctrl+S, 44
Current directory, 161
Cursor, 41
Cylinder, 13
Cylinders, 853

D

Daisy-wheel printer, 9
Data, 4
Data files, 30, 31, 139, 143
Data portion, 112
DATE, 46–48
DBLSPACE.SYS, 608
DEBUG, 555–556, 853
Default directory, 75, 170
Defaults
    changing, 78
    concept of, 71
    default drive, 71
    designated drive, 71
    logged drive, 71
    working with, 71–74
DEFRAG, 351–361
    parameters, 351

to optimize a disk, 304
using on DATA Disk,
   352–360
DEVICE, 592, 609
DEVICEHIGH, 592
Devices,
  controlling, 668–670
  block, 668
  character, 668
  interface, 668
Device drivers, 607–609
  ANSI.SYS, 608, 656–662
  CHKSTATE.SYS, 608
  DBLSPACE.SYS, 608
  DRVSPACE.SYS, 608
  DISPLAY.SYS, 608
  DRIVER.SYS, 608
  EGA.SYS, 608
  EMM386.EXE, 608, 697–704
  HIMEM.SYS, 608, 622
  INTERLNK.EXE, 608
  POWER.EXE, 608
  PRINTER.SYS, 608
  RAMDRIVE.SYS, 609–614
  SETVER.EXE, 609
  SMARTDRV.SYS, 609
  SMARTDRV.EXE, 609
  VDISK.SYS, 609
  XMAEM.SYS, 609
  XMA2EMS.SYS, 609
Directories
  renaming, 284–292
DEL, 253–265
  /P with DEL, 262–265
  eliminating files, 248
  management commands, 199
  using ERASE and DEL,
    248–253
  using wildcards, 259–261
  wildcards, 259
  with individual files, 253–258
Delete, 41
Deleting files, 248–261
Deleting subdirectories,
  186–188, 292–294
Delimiter, 63
DELTREE, 186–188, 292–294
  directory management, 155
  using with RD, 292–294

Designated drive, 71
Device, 6, 16
Device names, 16, 70
Devices
  CON, 424
  disk drive, 10, 15, 132
  LPT1, 94
  PRN, 94
DIR, 37, 45, 62, 141, 199
  /-, 158
  /A, 158
  /D, 158
  /H, 158
  /P, 62, 63, 65
  /R, 158
  /S, 158
  /W, 65
  locating a file, 141
  wildcards, 84–91
DIRCMD, 568–571
Directional keys, 41
Directories, 30–32
  changing names, 178
Directory, 19
Directory with subdirectory,
  163
Disk capacity, 11
Disk compression, 346
Disk drives, 10, 15, 132
  Drive A, 38
  hard disk, 10
  matching floppy drives to
    floppy disks, 116
  read/write head, 12
Disk files, 29
Disk
  formatting, 108, 114–118
  HD, 12
  logical structure, 108
  sectors, 109
  tracks, 109
DISKCOPY, 51–55, 188,
  295–298, 374–376
Disks, 10
  1.2 MB disks, 12
  1.44 MB disks, 12
  3 1/2 inch disks, 12
  5 1/4 inch disks, 12
  360 KB disks, 12

720 KB disks, 12
  bootable, 130
  cluster, 15
  cylinder, 13
  disk capacity, 11
  dividing the disk, 14
  double sided, double density,
    12
  double sided, high density, 12
  external storage media, 10
  floppy disks, 10
  formatting, 15
  hard disk, 14
  hard sectored, 12
  head slot, 11
  high capacity, 12
  high density, 12, 132
  inserting, 38
  matching floppy drives to
    floppy disks, 116
  mylar, 11
  nonbootable, 130
  secondary storage, 10
  sectors, 13
  soft sectored, 12
  tracks, 13
  valid disk sizes, 119
  Winchester disk, 13
  write protect notch, 11
Displaying files using the TYPE
  command, 207–210
DISPLAY.SYS, 608
Destination file, 200
Disk-intensive, 597
Documentation, 96
DOS, 19, 139
  bootable DOS disk, 598–602
  bugs, 29
  customizing, 590
  enhancements, 29
  external commands, 37
  installing DOS, 854
  loading high, 627–629
  managing data files, 149
  managing program files, 149
  path, 75
  resident commands, 37
  system disk, 11
  system utility files, 37

transient commands, 37
upgrade, 29
upgrading DOS, 854–862
versions, 29
DOSSHELL, 833
  explaining, 834
  file commands, 844–848
  graphic user interface (GUI),
    833
  help from command prompt,
    837–838
  installing, 833–834
  managing files, 839–844
  manipulating many files,
    848–851
  mouse and keyboard, 836–837
  MS-DOS Shell, 833
  quitting, 839
  shell screen, 835
  shells, 832–833
DOSKEY, 640–647
  /BUFSIZE=size, 642
  /HISTORY, 642
  /INSERT, 642
  /MACROS, 642
  /OVERSTRIKE, 642
  /REINSTALL, 642
  loading and using, 642–647
  macros, 647–650
    replaceable parameters,
      650–653
    saving, 653
Dot (.), 67
Dot-matrix printer, 9
Double dot (..), 160
Downward compatibility, 132
Drive A, 38
DRIVER.SYS, 608
Drives as device names, 70
DriveSpace, 736–743
  archive files, 736
  cluster overhang, 736
  offline compression, 736
  on-the-fly compression, 736
  optimizing, 736–743
  real-time compression, 736
DRIVPARM, 592
DRVSPACE.SYS, 608
Dummy files, 210

DX chip, 6

E

ECHO, 96, 242–243, 463
  OFF, 463, 470
EDIT, 420, 822–823
  cursor movement keys, 825
  dialog boxes, 828–831
  Edit menu, 827
  File menu, 826–827
  Help menu, 827
  menus, 826–827
  Options menu, 827
  Search menu, 827
  selection keys, 825–826
  using, 823–826
EDLIN, 420
EGA, 8
EGA.SYS, 608
Ellipsis (...), 366
EMM386.EXE, 608, 697–704
End, 41
Ending the work session, 55
Enhanced Graphics Adapter
  (EGA), 8
Enter key, 37
Environment, 562–568
ERASE, 248–262
  eliminating files, 248–253
  using, 259–261
  using wildcards, 259
Escape key, 42
Ethical considerations of
  copying disks, 51
Expanded Memory (EMM),
  617, 620
  bank switching, 617
  emulator, 697–698
  page, 617
  page frame, 617
  protected mode, 620
  real mode, 620
Expanded Memory
  Specification (EMS), 618
Expansion slots, 7
.EXE, 20, 188
Extended DOS partition, 854
Extended memory, 616, 620

protected mode, 619
real mode, 619
External commands, 19, 37
External storage media, 10

F

/F Parameter,
  with CHKDSK, 341–344
FASTHELP, 97, 100
FASTOPEN, 725–727
FAT, 110, 112
FC, 304, 319–322
  /A, 319
  /B, 319
  /C, 319
  /L, 319
  /LB*n*, 319
  /N, 319
  /*nnn*, 319
  /T, 319
  /W, 319
FCBS, 592, 704–705
FDISK, 863
File, 66
  ASCII, 199
  contiguous, 112
  destination, 200
  naming rules, 200
  noncontiguous, 112
  source, 199
  specification, 30
  storing, 113
  types, 30
  unformatted text, 208
File Allocation Table (FAT), 110
File area, 112
File attributes, 304
File extension, 30, 66
File name, 30, 66
  dot (.), 67
  as variable parameters,
    66–70
Files
  cross-linked, 323, 345
  deleting from
    other directories, 253–258
  deleting on other drives,
    253–258

and disks, 29
dummy, 210
loss clusters, 323
moving, 284–292
recovering deleted files,
    265–271
FILES, 592, 594–595, 602–605
Filters, 498
    and redirection, 502–505
    FIND, 499, 505–507
    MORE, 499, 509–514
    SORT, 499–505
FIND, 499, 505–507
    /C, 505
    /I, 505
    /N, 505
    /V, 505
Firmware, 7
Fixed disks, 13
Fixed parameters, 61
    with DIR, 62–66
Floppy disks, 10
FORMAT, 113–120
    /1, 118
    /4, 118
    /8, 118
    /B, 118
    /C, 118
    /F:size, 118
    /N:sectors, 118
    /Q, 118, 128–130, 156
    /S, 118
    /T:tracks, 118
    /U, 118, 128–130
    /V, 118, 120, 156
File Allocation Table (FAT),
    110
formatting a disk, 113,
    114–118
root directory, 111
structure of a disk, 108–109
Formatting
    a disk, 108, 113–119
    a disk with a volume label,
        118
    a hard drive, 543
    high level, 108
    initializing, 108
    logical, 108

low level, 108
physical, 108
process, 15
unformatting, 124
using /Q and /U, 128
volume label, 118
Fragmented disk, 336
Fragmented files, 335
Freezing the display, 44
Function keys, 40

G–H

Getting help, 96
Global file specifications, 84
Hard copy, 9
Hard disk, 10, 13–14
    cylinders, 852
    FDISK, 863
    fixed disk, 13
    formatted, 851
    heads, 852
    low-level formatting, 851–852
    organizing, 369–374
    partitioned, 851
    repartitioning, 863–873
    sector interleave, 852
    tracks, 852
Hardware, 4
Hardware interrupts, 705
Heads, 852
Head slot, 11
HELP, 97–103
    /?, 101
    /A, 101
    /B, 101
    /C[H], 101
    /L, 101
    /O, 101
    /ON, 101
    /S, 101
    getting, 96
Hierarchical
    filing system, 150
    structure, 152
    structure of a directory, 152
High-capacity disks, 12
High-density disks, 12
High-level formatting, 108

High memory area, 619
HIMEM.SYS, 608, 622–623
Home, 41

I–J

I/O, 8
IF, 436, 527, 541–552
    ERRORLEVEL, 541, 552–554
    EXIST, 541, 548–552
    NOT, 541, 548–552
Impact printer, 9
Initializing a disk, 108
Inkjet printer, 9
Input and output (I/O), 8
Input devices, 7
Insert, 41
INSTALL, 364, 592
Installing DOS, 853
Interactive booting, 476
Interactive processing, 419
INTERLNK.EXE, 608
Internal commands, 18
IO.SYS, 20
JOIN, 403, 408–409

K

KB, 10
Keyboard
    Backspace, 41
    Control (Ctrl), 43
    Delete, 41
    End, 41
    Escape (Esc), 42
    Home, 41
    input device, 7
    Insert, 41
    layout, 40, 41
    NumLock, 41
    Pause, 44
    PgUp, 41
    Print Screen (PrtSc), 43
    remapping, 653–668
    Shift, 42
Kilobyte (KB), 10

L

LABEL, 123
Laser printer, 9
LASTDRIVE, 592, 623
Light pen, 8
Lotus Intel Microsoft (LIM), 618
Loading a program
    automatically, 485–488
Logged drive, 71
Logical formatting, 108
Look-ahead buffers, 597
Lost clusters, 341
Low-level formatting, 108,
    852–853
LPT1, 94
LPT2, 94

M

Magnetic cards, 10
MB, 11
MD, 163, 176
Media types, 49
Meg, 11
Megabytes, 10, 11
MEM, 620–622
    /CLASSIFY, 620
    /DEBUG, 620
    /FREE, 620
    /MODULE, 620
    /PAGE, 621
MemMaker, 727–735
Memory, 6, 615–620
    adapter segment, 616
    conventional, 615
    extended, 616, 620
    expanded, 617, 620
    high memory area, 619
    reserved, 616
    UMA (upper memory area),
        616, 619
Metastrings, 170
Microcomputer hardware
    components, 4
Microcomputers, 4
Microfloppy disks, 12
Microsoft Diagnostics (MSD), 49
Minifloppy disks, 11

MIRROR, 265
MKDIR, 155, 163
MODE, 670–671
    baud rate, 670
    communication protocol, 670
    device status, 674–676
    monitor, 672–673
    parity, 671
    printer characteristics, 671
    retry, 671
    stop bits, 671
    typematic rate, 670, 673–674
Modems, 9
Monitor, 7–8
MORE, 499, 509–514
Mouse, 7
MOVE, 155, 178, 188, 366
    /Y, 285
    moving files and renaming
        directories, 284–285
    to rename a directory,
        179–180
    with RD and DELTREE,
        393–398
Moving files, 284–292
MSBACKUP, 679–690
    backup catalog, 680
    configuring, 680–683
    differential backup, 680
    full backup, 680
    incremental backup, 680
    master catalog, 680
MS-DOS, 19, 28
MS-DOS Shell Screen, 34
MSD, 49–50
MSAV, 676–678, 854
MSDOS.SYS, 20
Multiple configurations,
    705–716
    [BLOCKNAME], 706
    INCLUDE, 593, 706
    MENUCOLOR, 593, 706
    MENUDEFAULT, 593, 706
    MENUITEM, 593, 706
    NUMLOCK, 706
    SUBMENU, 593, 706
Multitasking, 615
Mylar, 11

N

Naming files, 67
Near letter quality, 9
Network, 22
Non-DOS partition, 854
Nonbootable disks, 130
Noncontiguous files, 335
Null values, 544–548
Numeric keys, 41
NumLock, 41
    turning off, 605–607

O

Offline compression, 736
Optimizing disk space, 736–743
On-the-fly compression, 736
Online help, 96
Operating system, 18
    fundamentals, 19
    boot record, 20
    boots, 20
    bootstraps, 20
    command interpreter, 20
    command processor, 20
    COMMAND.COM, 20, 21
    IO.SYS, 20
    MSDOS.SYS, 20
    prompt, 21
    ROM-BIOS, 19
Optimizing
    performance on disks,
        351–353
Optional parameters, 61
Organizing
    a disk, 368, 376–377
    a hard disk, 369–374
Output devices, 7
Overhead, 597
Overwriting files, 230
    with COPY, 229–231

P

Page, 617
Page frame, 617
Parallel communication,
    668–669

Parameter, 60
  delimiter, 63
  fixed, 61
  optional, 61
  switch, 61
  variable, 60
Parent directory, 151
Partition, 623, 851–853
Partitioning a hard disk, 853
  identifying a need, 853–854
Path, 75
PATH, 155, 188–193
PAUSE, 527–528
Pause key, 44
PC-DOS, 28
Peripheral devices, 7
Peripherals, 7–9
PgUp, 41
Physical formatting, 108
Pipes, 507–508
Pixels, 8
Pointer chain, 341
POWER.EXE, 608
Pretender commands, 401–403
Primary DOS partition, 854
PRINT, 241
Print Screen (PrtSc) key, 43
Printer, 9
  daisy-wheel printer, 9
  dot-matrix printer, 9
  impact printer, 9
  inkjet printers, 9
  laser printer, 9
  NLQ, 9
  nonimpact printers, 9
  thermal printers, 9
PRINTER.SYS, 608
Printing files, 241–244
PrintScreen, 44
PRN, 94, 96
Problems booting the system,
  481–484
Program, 4, 17
  files, 139, 30
Programming language
  processor, 18, 19
Prompt, 21, 32
PROMPT, 155, 170
  parameters, 171

pg, 171
  changing, 171

R

RAM, 4, 6, 10, 15, 19, 21
RAMdisk, 609–611
RAMDRIVE.SYS, 609–614
Random Access Memory
  see RAM
RD, 155, 183, 292–294
Read-only Memory
  see ROM
Read/write head, 12
Real-time compression, 736
Rebooting, 32
Recovering deleted files,
  265–271
Redirection, 91, 492–497
  >, 91, 493–495
  <, 493, 495–497
  >, 494, 497–498
  of output, 95
  of output to a file, 91–93
  of output to printer, 93–96
  of standard input, 492,
    495–497
  of standard output, 492–495
  standard error, 492
Relative paths, 163
REM, 463, 527–528, 593
Removing directories, 183
RENAME (REN), 199, 271–276
  on different drives, 279–284
  with directories, 279–284
  with wildcards, 276–279
Renaming
  directories, 284–292
  subdirectories, 398–401
Repartitioning a hard drive,
  864–874
  FDISK, 863
REPLACE, 386–393
  parameters, 387
Reserved memory, 615
Resident commands, 18, 37
RMDIR, 155, 183
RNS, 398–401
ROM, 4, 7

ROM-BIOS, 19
Root directory, 32, 75, 111
  file limits, 150

S

Save to disk, 10
Scan codes, 554, 874–876
SCANDISK, 304, 323
  commands, 344–351
Scanners, 8
Script file, 555–559
Scrolling, 40
Secondary storage, 10
Sector interleave, 852
Sectors, 13, 109
Serial communication, 668
SET, 563–566, 593
SETUP, 364
SETVER.EXE, 609
Shareware, 140
SHELL, 592, 629–631
SHIFT, 527, 533–540
Shift key, 42, 43
SmartDrive, 716–725
SMARTDRV.EXE, 609
SMARTDRV.SYS, 609
Software, 17, 4
SORT, 499–505
  /R, 499
  /+n, 499
  ASCII sort sequence, 501
Source files, 199
SpinRite II, 852
STACKS, 592, 704–705
Standard error, 492
Standard input, 492, 495–497
Standard output, 492–495
Startup disk, 598
Stdaux, 594
Stderr, 594
Stdin, 594
Stdout, 594
Stdprn, 594
Storing files, 113
Structure
  of a disk, 108
  of the Data disk, 177
Subdirectories, 32, 75, 153

a brief introduction, 75
COPY command, 220–227
creating, 155, 165–170
files, 154
markers, 160, 174
shortcuts, 228–229
SUBST, 403–406
Super VGA, 8
Super Video Graphics Array, 8
Switch, 61
SWITCHES, 592, 633–634
/F, 593, 634
/K, 593, 634
/N, 593, 634
/W, 593, 634
SX chip, 6
Syntax, 60
command, 61
diagrams, 61
SYS, 598–599
System
attribute, 304
board, 6
configuration, 4, 32
date, 46
level, 18
time, 46
utility, 18
utility files, 37
System software, 17, 18
command processor, 18
DOS, 19
internal commands, 18
MS-DOS, 19
resident commands, 18
system level, 18
System unit, 4, 5

T

Tape, 10
cartridges, 10
Terminate and Stay Resident
(TSR), 640–642
Thermal printer, 9
TIME, 46
Time-using command, 47, 48
Toggle switch, 41
Token, 736

Trackball, 8
Tracks, 13, 109
Transient commands, 19, 37
TREE, 180–183, 188, 190
Tree
structured directories, 150
structured filing system, 151
Trojan horse, 676
TYPE, 199, 206
displaying files, 207–210
dummy files, 210
using, 211–214

U

UNDELETE, 265–271
/ALL, 266
/DOS, 266
/DS, 266
/DT, 266
/LIST, 266
/S, 266
/STATUS, 266
/T, 266
/UNLOAD, 266
recovering deleted files,
265–266
UNFORMAT, 108, 265
/J, 125
/P, 125
/PARTN, 125
/Test, 125
/U, 125
using, 125–127
Unformatted text file, 208
Unformatting, 113
Unformatting a disk, 124–127
Upgrading DOS, 854–862
Upper Memory Area (UMA),
619
Upper memory blocks (UMB),
619

V

/V parameter,
using, 329–333
using DIR parameters,
331–333

Variable parameter, 60
VDISK.SYS, 609
VDT, 8
VER, 45, 46
Verbose parameter, 329
Versions of DOS, 29
VGA, 8
Video display adapter card, 8
Video Graphics Array (VGA), 8
Virtual disk, 609–611
Viruses, 676
boot sector, 676
checking for, 676
file infector, 676
MSAV, 676–678
Trojan horse, 676
VSAFE, 679
VOL, 120–122
Volume label, 118
VSAFE, 679

W–X

WAN (wide area network), 22
Wildcard, 84, 205–206, 218–220
*, 84, 85–90
?, 84
DEL, 259
RENAME, 276–279
Winchester disk, 13
Working with defaults, 71–74
Write protected, 11
Write to disk, 10
Write-protect notch, 11
XCOPY, 379–386
XMAEM.SYS, 609
XMA2EMS.SYS, 609